BRANN
THE ICONOCLAST

A COLLECTION

OF THE

WRITINGS OF W. C. BRANN

IN TWO VOLUMES

WITH BIOGRAPHY BY J. D. SHAW

VOLUME TWO

PHILLIPPS PUBLISHING CO.
ST. LOUIS,   MISSOURI

CONTENTS

	PAGE
A Couple of High-Toned Kids	396
A Crusade of Calumny	254
A Plague of Poets	233
A Message to Mary	164
An Infernal Fraud	112
Atheism and Orthodoxy	101
A Wail from the A. P. A.	58
A Brazen Humbug	50
A Friend of the Family	451
Bonds vs. Buncombe	189
Beecher and the Bible	176
Baron Hirsch	129
Behind the Smoke Stack	67
Barons vs. Barons	455
Bradley-Martin Bal Masque	299
Cyclones and Sanctification	5
Credit and Prices	441
Construction vs. Destruction	307
Christian England in India	179
Coronation of the Czar	135
Christ Comes to Texas	140
Catholic vs. Protestant "Cranks"	20
Church and Stage	243
Dutch, Deity and Devil	33
Dogmatism the Mother of Doubt	167
Evidences of Man's Immortality	329
Going Forwards Backwards	432
Garters and Amen Groans	97
Howell's New Horror	12
Hypnotic Power of Her	114
Jingoes vs. Jabberwocks	267
Judge Lynch and the Lawyers	375
Killing of Canovas	458
King Charles the Martyr	339
Life and Death	15
Les Enfants Terribles	229
Ladonia's Amazonian Guard	105
Looking Backward	249
Our Public Panders	110
Obscene Conversation	265
Professional Failures	124

CONTENTS

	PAGE
Price's Predicament	127
Prayers for the Pagan	461
Passing of the Stuffed Prophet	310
Panaceas for Poverty	184
Rainbow Chasers	198
Sherman and Cleveland	194
Sexual Sins of American Society	280
Some Millionaire Mendicants	242
Sexual Purity and Gunpowder	116
Slippery Bill McKinley	47
Some Kansas City Culture	93
The American Press	259
Thomas Carlyle	273
The Modern Sphinx	286
Those Blawsted Hawmerican Men	225
The Unwritten Law	427
The Courage of Womankind	448
The Science of Kissing	417
The Single Tax	351
The Meanest Man in America	367
The Rape Fiend Remedy	383
The Signs of the Times	389
The Henry George Hoodoo	400
The Last of Our Liberties	408
Trilby Parties and Piety	321
Thou Shalt Not	24
The Bike Bacillus	37
The Currency Craze	41
The Iconoclast and the Clergy	53
"Too Much World"	79
The Apostle's Rag Baby	86
The Sword and the Cross	90
The American Sovereign	119
The Transportation Problem	130
The Grecian Games	147
"There's One Comes After"	152
The Platonic Friendship Fake	155
The Seven Vials of Wrath	157
The Fisticphobia Folly	172
Victor Hugo's Immorality	411
Who is Mark Hanna	221
Wanted: One Word	420

CYCLONES AND SANCTIFICATION

Is Our Deity of Negro Descent?

The terrible cyclone which recently tore its way through St. Louis prompted a resident of the stricken city to complain to the Iconoclast, that a God of infinite justice and mercy would not indiscriminately destroy saint and sinner by flood and fire, and crush nursing babes beneath an avalanche of stone and brick. Like Jonah, he feels that he does well to be angry, for he declares that if the Deity really exists, he is a demon, and adds that "the God idea was born in the stupid brain of negroes on the upper Nile, and from thence o'erspread the planet like a foul pestilence."

As a Deity usually resembles his worshippers, both in physical appearance and mental and moral attributes—is, in fact, but an idealization of themselves—it follows as an inevitable sequence, if my correspondent be correct, that the Creator was originally a "coon." Dr. Seasholes, an autotheistic little Dallas dominie, recently declared in effect that the Deity was an Indian, who sometimes got off the reservation and raised merry hades among the early inhabitants—wore feathers in his hair and wielded a tomahawk; and now we are assured, by inference at least, that he is an Ethiopian. First thing we know Gran'ma Lease, of the Kansas gynecocracy, will be protesting that he is a Populist. I fear that the St. Louisan has brought his theological ducks to a bad market—he should have taken them to Talmage, who receives a princely salary for defending the Christian concept of the Creator. In my humble opinion, however, the Deity had naught to do with the St. Louis catastrophe. He may order matters mundane, but scarce follows every whirlwind, as a schoolboy does a top, governing its gyrations. He may note the fall of the sparrow, but certainly does nothing either to promote or prevent.

> "Remember man, the Universal Cause
> Acts not by partial, but by general laws."

These are the laws of nature, immutable, inexorable. The physical world knows naught of mercy; the mills of God make no distinction. A temple is liable as a bawdy-house to be struck by the levin brand, a saint as a sinner to be drowned at sea; tornado nor earthquake turns aside from the crowded city to spend its force in the unpopulated plain. By nature's laws we live, by nature's laws we die. 'Tis they which hold the stars in their eternal courses and send the planets rolling forever around the sun.

> "All this dread order break—for whom? for thee?
> Vile worm!—Oh, madness! pride! impiety!"

The fact that fearful catastrophes occur neither disproves the existence of a Deity nor brands him a demon. All things are but relative. If, in pursuing a journey whose object is the establishment of an empire, the founding of a religion, the extinction of a plague or the dethronement of a tyrant; you place your foot upon a populous ant hill, what then? Will not the survivors, as they gather up their dead and survey the ruins of their city, denounce you as a monster destitute of mercy, wanting wisdom? May not some argue that the catastrophe was not caused by the sentient act of a superior being, but by the blind force of nature? Imagine the foolish theorizing among the awe-stricken hymenoptera that must follow such a contretemps, then reflect upon thine own insignificance as compared with the Cosmic plans of the Creator!

Were this world perfect, what need of heaven? It is by unceasing struggle that the race rises to higher planes of existence. Had man remained in Eden he would have been a chump alway; but compelled to do battle for existence; to strive with the beasts of the field, with disease, with hunger, with the power of the elements, he grew in strength and wisdom—became in very truth a lord of creation. Because disasters occur, my correspondent, like a certain person mentioned by King David, "hath said in his heart, there is no God;" but I cannot see—in so far as cyclones and kindred calamities are concerned—that he has bettered himself. Whether the laws of nature, like Topsy, "jis' growed," or were framed by a Divine Legislator, their operations are the same. The difference between the atheist and the theist is that the latter is sustained in the hour of trial by faith that righteousness will not go unrewarded; that ultimately he will be reunited with the loved and lost in a land where there is neither suffering, sorrow nor sin. Dark and drear indeed must be life's pilgrimage to those who see in heaven no star of hope. Even tho' such faith were a pious fraud, I am barbarian enough to be thankful for it. If death ends all, we experience no disappointment, grasp no Apples of Sodom when we pass to ever dreamless sleep. If we waken never we cannot miss the sweet companionship of wife or child or friend—the world rolls on and we are as tho' we had not been. It is not in death we need the Deity, but rather while the heart beats high and warm and the tendrils thereof—softer than silk but stronger than hooks of steel—are weaving themselves about other lives, that we needs must have some faith that love and life defy the scythe of Death; that, breasting the stormy waves of Styx, they rise triumphant on the farther shore. To some the God-idea is a necessity absolute. Without the belief in immortality the dark shadow of impending doom would drive them mad. It is their sheet-anchor in storm and stress —the still, small voice that cries peace to their troubled souls. Only those of cold natures, of slow-pulsing blood, of weak affections can stand by the graves of their dead and deny the Deity. It is the stoicism of the stone, which feeling not, mocks the writhen bolt. In the hour of supreme agony, when all the heart holds near and dear is slipping into the sunless sea, the man of feeling calls, like Justinian's father, upon the name of God.

> "And this is the utter end of all our love,
> And shall we never meet and know each other
> Again, as we have known each other here?"
> "Then sobbing like a child the old man cried,
> Ask me not!—Pity me and ask no more,
> For lo, I seem as one whose house has fallen
> About his feet in ruins, and who stands
> Living, ghast, with ashes on his head,
> Clouded with horror, half awaked from sleep."

I cannot agree with my correspondent that the "God-idea was born in the stupid brain of negroes." I have encountered this remarkable statement hitherto only in Volney's curious theory that all religions sprang from the astronomical nomenclature of the early Ethiopians, who, he assumes, were the progenitors of the modern negroes. That the Ethiopians, whose capital was Thebes of the hundred gates, were a dark-skinned race is true; but we are in possession of no satisfactory evidence that they were ethnologically different from the inhabitants of lower Egypt, whose metropolis was Memphis. Diodorous says the Thebans considered themselves the inventors of divine worship, while Lucian states—upon what authority is in no wise clear—that "the Ethiopians invented the science of the stars." Unquestionably the earliest worship of which we have knowledge was solar and sidereal; but this theogony preceded any scientific information regarding the heavenly bodies. In fact, it was the science of astronomy that dethroned Apollo, Osiris and that innumerable host of deities born of the sun. The inhabitants of the upper Nile were not the only people who pretended to the origin of worship to supernatural powers. A similar claim was set up on the banks of the Ganges, the Euphrates and the Jordan. The inhabitants of lower Egypt have a tradition that the founder of their race, Mizriam, an Aryan, brought with him from Asia a religion similar to that which the Jews subsequently set up in Palestine, and that it was practiced by their priests and other learned men of their people, while a grosser faith was taught the illiterate rabble. The fact that Moses was educated by the Egyptian priesthood is worth considering in connection with the duly authenticated fact of the existence there of an exoteric and esoteric faith.

The origin of the religious idea is lost in the impenetrable night of antiquity. No matter how far back we explore a faith, we find internal evidence that it had predecessors. Zoroaster is supposed to have founded the ancient Persian religion, which had so marked a resemblance to modern Christianity; yet he seems to have been a compiler and apostle rather than an originator. The Vedas of Hindustan are but a compilation of the curious ideas of ancient cults. The oldest gods of Greece were borrowed. When Abram left Haran to view the land promised him by the Lord, Asia was filled with religious faiths. There are ideas which most cults have in common, such as the Trinity, Virgin Mother, Man-God, Resurrection, future rewards and punishments, etc., and from this fact has sprung the theory that they are but subdivisions of one original faith; but it must be borne in mind that these ideas are all old as Zoroaster, perhaps as the first civilization of Egypt, and might, during the unnumbered centuries that have elapsed, have become engrafted on many purely autochthonous religions, just as the doctrine of the immortality of the soul found its way into the old Hebrew faith during the diaspora. Religions react upon each other, just as do the political and commercial customs of various countries. Thus the religions of Egypt and Western Asia modified that of Greece; which in turn dominated that of Italy, while all nations seem to have collaborated in the formation of the Christian faith, which is really a religious ragout, in which we find strong traces of Parsee and Platonism, Fetich and Judaism, Greek polytheism and Phoenician idolatry.

It is probable that each people, as soon as it passed the purely savage pale, began to speculate upon its origin, and gradually developed a crude system of theology. They observed that the sun gave and nourished life, and it became the earliest object of their adoration. They gave to it a name expressive of its attributes—the light-bearer, the life-giver—and its apparent diurnal journey across the earth led them to believe it a sentient being, a God, who grew angry in summer and scorched them with heat, and withdrew in winter, leaving them to suffer with cold. Quite naturally, the moon became his consort, and the stars the children of this King and Queen of the sky, accredited with attributes significant of their seasons. Commerce, the vicissitudes of war and the respect which a weak and ignorant nation usually entertains for the customs and opinions of one more enlightened and powerful, resulted in the gradual engrafture upon most theologies of kindred ideas. At various times reformers like Moses and Zoroaster, Gautama and Jesus purified a faith of some of its most glaring absurdities, broadened and exalted man's conception of the Creator. We may safely assume that the religious idea is coeval with human intelligence—that so soon as man was capable of continuity of thought; so soon as he had framed intelligible speech; so soon as he began wondering what power moved the sun and moon in their orbits; so soon as he asked himself how came the first man and woman upon the earth, he began to pay homage to a supernatural power.

It occurs to me that this hypothesis—which subjects the religious idea to the law of evolution—better accords with the wisdom and dignity we attribute to the Deity than does the childish theory that he made a robber horde of semi-savages the custodians of all the knowledge which man was permitted to have of his Maker, knowing that they possessed no power to enlighten the teeming millions of far continents respecting his laws. It ground all religions upon a base truth, or at least upon a world-wide human instinct, instead of making someone of thousands—and who shall say which one?—the gate to heaven and all others highways to hell. It makes theology progressive, encourages us to pursue our inquiry as far back as possible into the wondrous secret of existence to seek for truth in every cult and creed instead of forever fixing our faith in the Serbonian bogs of barbarism, where so many ministers—following the bad example of Mahomet—would stay its march by shrieking "blasphemer" whenever an attempt is made to reconcile religion unto reason.

Regarding the evidence upon which we predicate belief in the existence of a sentient Architect of the Universe, much might be said—much has been said that was a foolish waste of words. Most religions profess a foundation of direct revelation by their Deity, and for proof thereof cite us to wondrous prodigies—the dead restored, mountains removed, storms allayed and children begotten—quite unnecessarily I think—without the assistance of an earthly father. In other words, we are asked to believe that God proved his prescience and power by reversing those very laws which he had framed for cosmic rule—just as my St. Louis friend would have him do by suppressing earthquakes and turning aside tornadoes. Unfortunately for this theory, the alleged revelations do not exhibit a conception of history, geography or astronomy superior to that of the people whom the Deity honored with his confidence. The God of the Jews, for instance, believed the world was flat and the o'erhanging firmament a solid concave filled with auger holes through which the rain leaked, and that he could precipitate a deluge by the simple expedient of pulling open a trap-door. The other Deities of the ancients were equally ignorant and imprudent, cranky and cruel. Their principal occupations were making war by proxy and committing fornication in *propria persona*. They would have just suited President Cleveland. Fortunately, however, the sacred mummery of miraculous births, angelic visitors and hasheesh visions do not constitute the real basis of any religion. These are but the futile attempts of finite man to express the inexpressible—the poor outward evidences of an inward grace. It is no proof of the existence of the Omnipotent to point to the wondrous universe; for, as the creator must be greater than the creature, it were more miraculous that the Supreme Artificer should be autogenous than that all the spheres that roll in unmeasured space should be self-created. The fact is, these ideas are a trifle too big for our heads. In ten thousand years man has been unable to settle the tariff question or decide what is the best material of which to make his circulating media; yet any fool preacher can tell us off-hand how the universe came into existence. Every religious cult has miracles in plenty and martyrs galore—the first all falsehood, the latter mostly fools. Calvin burned Servetus because they could not agree whether Christ was the eternal son of God, or the son of the eternal God—and he was neither. He was simply one of the thousands of Jews of his generation who had wandered from the faith of their fathers, and he met the fate common to many great reformers. A new religion would have developed on the shores of the Mediterranean, and on much the same lines, had he never been born, for the entire country, from Palmyra to the Pillars of Hercules, had become a theological chaos, and out of chaos new worlds must come.

The strongest evidence we can adduce that the world is governed by a sentient being is the absolute necessity for his existence. Of what avail is the mighty universe without him? Why should matter resolve itself into being, become blazing suns and symmetrical planets and roll thro' space forever? If it did so in conformity to a plan, the originator of that purpose, it is as ridiculous as an acephalous rooster running about in a circle. If there be no reason in the universe, how comes it that there is sentience in the ridiculous little mites that cling to the shell of one relatively insignificant planet—like microbes to a mammoth cheese? If we are generated by the laws of blind force, we have achieved the impossible—the creature has become greater than its creator! If the universe is but a soulless machine a—*mechanique celeste*—of what use are we to it? We can see no reason for the existence of the earth except the nourishment of life, and that presupposes a purpose; yet life that ends in everlasting death is a mistake—and the materialists tells us that nature never errs. What boots it to be born, if a few years of toil and travail, sorrow and suffering is to end it all? Why should women bring forth children in pain unspeakable only to glut the demon Death? Why should love burgeon and bloom only to be forever blasted? Why not adopt hedonism as the law of our lives instead of restraining the passions and sacrificing our ease, sometimes our fortunes and our lives for others' sake? "Result of social education" —generated how? "By the laws of nature." How came nature to have laws? Isn't it lucky, to say the least, that all matter consents to obey the law of gravitation—that the collision of two bodies generates heat instead of cold? Supposing that self-generated force operating on nothing created something—matter and mind: Is the greater of the two generations ephemeral and the lesser only eternal? "Pure reason" is the cry of the materialists—who then assume that the slightest speck of dust swimming in a sunbeam is eternal, while the mind that conceived the Novum Organum has perished utterly; that the intellects of Caesar and Socrates has been destroyed, but the parings of Ham's toenails are still here!

The religious idea is often perverted; yet so far back as we can trace the history of the human race, it has constituted the heart of civilization, the efficient cause of the social compact, the dynamo of the world. I do not mean that foolish fanaticism or blood-thirsty bigotry has been a blessing; they bear the same relation to the moral that cyclones and earthquakes do to the physical world. I allude to that feeling of moral responsibility which marks the first step of a people from subter-savagery, that concept of duty to what we call the Deity, which leads men to erect altars and supplicate the unseen power. This conscience or soul of man precedes civilization, makes progress possible. As it develops the race advances; as it becomes perverted the race returns to barbarism, carrying with it the adscititious curse of bigotry. God *has* revealed himself to man—not by laws graven on tables of stone, plates of silver or tablets of horn; not by feathered but non-oviparous angels seen in trance-vision by sanctified tramps who trotted about the country peddling hair-trigger curses and sacred hoodoes; but in human life itself. "You touch heaven," says Novalis, "when you lay your hand upon a human body." It is a temple in which dwells a portion of that divine intelligence which is God.

It really matters little how or when or where the God-idea originated. It is here—was here before the Tower of Babel reared its crest into the clouds, before the sphinx gazed out upon the desert waste, before Jason sailed in quest of the Golden Fleece or Agamemnon led forth his intrepid Hellenes to their ten years' war with Troy. The very name of that nation which first worshipped at the shrine of a supernal power has passed from earth; the altars and temples of countless ages have crumbled into dust and over their forgotten fanes great cities have reared their palaces of marble and porphyry, then perished utterly; but the God-idea still remains and grows with man's intellectual growth and strengthens with his social strength. The fact that it constitutes the very warp and woof of human history, that it is the one only idea in all the earth that has proven indestructible, argues its necessity, its accordance with the laws of the universe, howsoever and by what means it had its birth; and what is consentient with nature even the grossest materialist must recognize as worthy his respect.

HOWELLS' NEW HORROR.

William Dean Howells has made the momentous discovery that the tipping system is what is ruining the country, sucking the life-blood of Uncle Sam and poisoning our entire social system. It is not the gold-bugs, silver-bugs or straddle-bugs; not the tariff, treasury deficit or war fright that is pulling the linch-pin out of our political cosmos and preparing us for a resounding crash—it is the meretricious practice of paying six cents for a shine when the market price is five, of flipping a *garcon* a dime for bringing us black tea when we have ordered green. Here at last is a real live issue, upon which even McKinley may be persuaded to declare himself without waiting to consult a partisan platform—may have an opinion which he can claim as his own property. Tips or no tips; that's the question. Whether 'twere better to have a waiter call us "Colonel" and promptly serve us with pie on two plates, or dawdle for half an hour behind the kitchen screen, then empty a greasy bowl of noodle soup down the back of your neck. It appears that an association of New York coachmen, after carefully considering the tipping system, concluded that it was a good thing and advised its members to push it along. Mr. Howells immediately filed a caveat, and now comes into court to show reason why Dives should deal with Lazarus on a purely business basis, instead of conceding him an occasional crumb. He deposeth that a tip is the very antithesis of mercy—that it curseth him that giveth and him that receiveth, inflating the vanity of the one and debauching the manhood of the other. He wants to weed it out as a poisonous European exotic which is casting its upas-shadow upon our "uncrowned democracy" and breeding sturdy mendicants. The tip question, like the poor, we have always with us. Howells is not the first man to fear that Uncle Sam would die of enlargement of the heart. When a man recalcitrates against tip-giving I suspect him of apologizing for his own penuriousness. It is not the tip-givers who do the growling, but those whose meanness is made to serve as a sombre background for the sunny whole-souledness of their betters. Faith, Hope and Charity are the three cardinal virtues— "and the greatest of these is Charity." It does not hurt a well-to-do American to cross a servant's palm to secure a little extra service. Some people imagine that the Pullman company pays its porters to black their boots and brush their clothes, to take care of their tickets when they turn in and carry their grips to a cab when they leave the car. Because the porters expect pay for this supplemental service they are caricatured as parasites by the would-be funny papers, and denounced as presumptuous by travelers who carry their paltry souls within their purse. Tips are often given where no extra service is rendered—given from pure goodness of heart, the bestower suspecting that the servitor is poorly paid. It depends much upon the education of the recipient whether the largesse be calculated to lower his self-respect. A professional man would resent such gratuity as a gross insult, while a porter might regard it as a kindness. Those whose moral concept can be perverted by tips are seldom engaged in menial occupations. The native American will plow corn or punch cattle for $15 a month rather than don a suit of livery at $60. He has been educated to consider himself the peer of princes, and woe to the man who assumes the airs of superiority. He may work for wages, but is no man's minion. He deals with his employer as an equal, and wants never a copper beyond the letter of his contract. Our flunkeys, waiters, etc., upon whom tips are chiefly bestowed, are for the most part negroes and foreigners who have been bred to servile occupations, and who accept as an unalterable fact their social and economic inferiority. The tip sharply draws the social line, but does so without offense. It expands the heart of the giver and encourages the recipient to respectful and faithful service. The tipping system is not, as Mr. Howells supposes, a European transplantation; it develops naturally, inevitably in any country where one class of people wait upon and minister to the immediate wants of another. It is an evidence that the heart of man has not yet ossified—that our social system is still something more than a soulless commercial machine in which each gets all he can and keeps all he gets. But even in this so-called land of equality, servants, as the term is here understood, are not the only takers of tips. The minister who marries a couple and makes no charge for the service, yet accepts whatever honorarium the groom, in the first transports of hymenic deliration, may bestow—whether $5 or $500—differs in degree but not in kind from the coon who needlessly busies himself about a patron's plate in hopes of being "remembered." When the Vanderbilts bought the Duke of Marlborough, several distinguished dominies were invited to formally deliver the goods. Instead of presenting their bill for professional services—as a lawyer or doctor would have done—they waited to be tipped. Had the bride and groom been serving-maid and working-man they would have considered $5 ample for tying the nuptial knot; but the one being a multi-millionaire and the other a duke, they expected nothing less than $5,000 for a service which by implication at least, they had rendered as a social courtesy if not a sacred duty—for not even scorbutic dukes are exempted from the divine command to be fruitful and multiply. In other words, they expected money which they did not earn, just as a waiter hopes for a largesse to which he is not entitled by law. If the latter be a "sturdy beggar," as Mr. Howells says, the ministers are his brothers in presumptuous mendicancy. The Duke sailed away, however, without crossing the palms of the preachers, and they became so indignant that they told their troubles to the reporters. Then they complained to Mrs. Vanderbilt that her titled son-in-law had not settled a bill which they failed to present, and, disgusted with their "sturdy beggary," she flung them a few hundred dollars—about what they usually receive for performing fifty marriage ceremonies. But this was not what was expected, and they went away grumbling like a French garcon who has danced twice around an American millionaire, hoping for a dollar, only to be dismissed with a dime. Surely Mr. Howells should not criticise the New York coachmen for following the example so ostentationsly set by the ministers of that great ganglion of political morality— he might get hauled over the coals for heterodoxy. A doucer bestowed upon a chambermaid is a vulgar "tip;" but when the recipient is a minister it becomes an honorarium— a distinction without a difference. Should a gentleman whom Mr. Howells had courteously helped on with his overcoat, hand him a quarter, he would probably fling it in his face; but should a publisher send him a cheque for double the sum asked for an article upon The Evils of Tipping, he would feel highly flattered. Yet the publisher would be actuated by the identical motive which prompts some men to pay two-bits for a shave, and the largesse have the same effect upon the great literary Buzfuz that the additional dime has upon the man of lather—it would elevate rather than lower his self-respect, because a tangible acknowledgement of his efficiency. We are all willing to take tips when they come to us in a way that does no violence to our social prejudices. Few employes, even the highest in the service of government, have been known to refuse tips that came in the guise of a retroactive salary raise.

LIFE AND DEATH.

In a city beyond far seas there dwelt a Youth who claimed not land nor gold, yet wealthier was than sceptred sovereign, richer far than fancy ever feigned. The great round earth, the sun, the moon and all the stars that flame like fireflies in the silken web of night were his, because garnered in the salvatory of his soul. And the beaded dew upon the morning-glories, the crimson tints of dawn, Iris' bended bow and all the cloth-of-gold and robes of purple that mark the royal pathway of the descending sun; the perfume of all the flowers, the bulbul's sensuous song, and every flowing line that marks woman's perfect form he hoarded in his heart and gloated over as a miser does his gain. And the Youth was in love with Life and held her to his heart as God's most gracious gift. Ah, beautiful was she, with her trustful eyes of blue, and hair of tangled sunbeams blown about a brow of alabaster, arms of ivory and bust whose rounded loveliness were a pulsing pillow where ever dreamed Desire —beautiful beyond compare, and sweet as odors blown across the brine from the island-valley of Avalon, mad'ning as Lydian music, in which swoons the soul of youth while all the passion in the blood beats time in delirious ecstacy. And Youth and Life built fair castles in the air, with turrets of sapphire and gates of beaten gold, wherein they dreamed the days away on a bed of thornless roses, drained the chalice of the honey-suckle, ate the lotus-bud and thought of naught in all the world but love. Of this soft dalliance was born a son, and Life cried with falling tears, "Now I am shamed!" "Nay," said the Youth, "for I will hide our child within my heart and none shall know." And Life laughed and kissed the boy, and called him Ambition, and hid him in the secret recesses of her lover's heart, and gaily went and came as tho' her fair breasts had never burgeoned with a wealth of liquid pearl. But the child was restless within its prison house and beat against the walls, and grew day by day, and fought with teeth and nails, until the Youth cried out in agony. And Life said mockingly: "Hast not room enough within thy heart for one poor child to range—that heart which holds the earth, the sun and stars? Cast forth the foolish rubbish—the rainbow and the flowers, the incense and the summer sea. Make room, make room for thine and mine—tho' naught else doth remain." He cast them forth with fond regret, and Ambition grew and filled his heart and strove with all his strength. The Youth looked no more upon the fair field flowers, but thought only of the victor's wreath; he heard no melody but fame's shrill trumpet rising ever louder on the blast, and saw no beauty but in Minerva's laureled brow; the cool sylvan path became a blinding mountain trail, his hours of dalliance days of toil and nights of agony. The hidden son had become master of the sire, and all the host of heaven melted into a single star which poured its baleful fire into his face—the treacherous star of Hope.

And so he strove with augmenting strength, his goal the highest, his guerdon the immortelles. But oft he fell, and cursed his folly for having left the flowery vale to beat against the barren mountain rocks; but Life upbraided him, and with her soft breath fanned the paling star to brighter flame—the star behind which lay the throne. And Death followed them, shadowy, indistinct, like a spirit wrapt in mist. And Life mocked at Death, crying: "Behold the envious strumpet doth follow, to despoil me of mine own! Faugh! How uncanny and how cold! What lover would hang upon those ashen lips? Her bosom is marble, and in her stony heart there flames no fire. With her Ambition perishes and the Star of Hope forever fades. Her house is a ghastly tomb, her bed the granite rock, her lover childless, for her womb is barren." And the Youth, glancing with a shudder at the figure in the mist, drew close to Life and echoed her words with trembling lip, "How uncanny and how cold!" Thus fared he on thro' many a toilsome year, to where no shadow falls to East or West—to manhood's glorious noon. He looked at the towering heights before him with undaunted eye, measuring his strength against the walls of stone. He glanced back, and a chill swept over him, for he was standing far up on the mountain-side, he was in a barren desert whose level waste stretched back to the pathetic tomb where Love was left to starve and sweet Content lay festering in her shroud. "Fool," cried Life, "why looked ye back like wife of ancient Lot? Now are ye indeed undone!" The voice was harsh and shrill, and starting as from an uneasy dream, he looked on Life with wide-open eyes and soul that understood. He found her far less fair than in the heydey of his youth, when he reveled in her voluptuous charms and loved her well. Her face was hard and stern as that of some hag from hell; the sunlight had faded from her hair, the cestus of red roses become a poisonous serpent, her fragrant breath a consuming flame, her robe of glory, a sackcloth suit, begrimed with ashes, torn by thorns and stained with blood. "Thou hast changed, O Life!" he cried in horror. "Not so," she said; "the change is thine. In youth you saw me not, but only dreamed you saw. She you loved was a creature of your vain imaginings; I am Life, mother of that scurvy brat, Ambition." She pointed upward, saying: "Behold, thy star is gone, and the shining goal hangs pathless in the heavens. When the sun hath reached the zenith it must descend. Henceforth your path leads downward, for every hour will sap your lusty strength, and every step be weaker than the last, until you sink into senility. Come, my love, you do not know me yet; behold me as I am!" She cast aside her soiled and ragged robe and stood revealed in all her hideousness—a thing of horror. Her breasts distilled a poisonous dew, around her gaunt limbs aspics crawled, her eyes were fierce and hollow, and in one bony hand she held a scroll on which was writ the record of her frauds and follies, her sin and shame. "Come," she cried mockingly. "let us on together. You may caress me as in the days of old, and I will answer with a curse. Hold me to your heart and I will wither it with my breath of flame. Praise me, and I will requite you with dishonor and crown you with the gruesome chaplets of grief. Fool! Thou hast striven for a prismatic bubble bursting on the crest of a receding wave. Why scorned you gold and lands to grasp at castles in the air? Why dreamed of the Dimiurgus when desiring harlots beckoned thee? Why dealt with open hand and unsuspecting heart when thrown 'mid a world of thieves? Had'st thou been content and not aspired to rise above the grossness, the falsehood and the folly which is Life, I would have loved thee well and deceived thee with a painted beauty to the end—my foul breasts would have been to thee ever a fragrant bed of flowers. You have invaded Life's mysteries, the penalty whereof is pain. You have looked upon the past; behold the future!" He looked, and saw a tortuous path winding downward thro' bogs and poisonous fens and bitter pools. In the far distance an old man, tottering beneath his weight of years, stood leaning on a staff, reading a riddle propounded by a sullen sphinx, and striving with failing intellect to understand—*"Cui Bono?"* Near by was an open grave, beside which an angel of mercy stood and beckoned him. "Thou hast tarried long, my lover," she said in a low sweet voice that was the distant note of aeolian harp, or summer zephyr soughing thro' the pines. With a cry of gladness he cast himself into her cool arms; she touched his tired eyes with her soft white hands, she pressed a kiss upon his lips that drained his breath in an expiring gasp of pleasure all passionless, and, cradled upon her bosom like a weary child, he fell asleep. The burden and its bearer, hallowed by a pale glory as of St. Elmo's fire sank into the open grave, yet the sphinx sat stolidly holding the painted riddle in his stony hand—*"Cui Bono?"* But there was none to answer; the path faded like the phosphorescent track of a ship in midnight waters, and all was dark. He turned fiercely to Life, a question on his lip, but ere he could utter it she had answered, with a bitter shrug: "The angel with the pitying eyes; the beauteous one?" My rival,

Death—so uncanny and so cold! All who love me leave me for this sorceress, and she holds them 'neath the magic of her spell forevermore. But what care I? I do take the grain and give to her the husk; I drink the wine and leave the lees. Mine the bursting bud, hers the withered flower. Go to her and thou wilt. I have slain Ambition and blotted thy foolish *ignis fatuus* from the firmament. For thee the very sun henceforth is cold, the moon a monstrous wheel of blood, the stars but aged eyes winking back their tears as they look upon thy broken altars and ruined fanes, the grass grown green above the ashes of thy dead. Go; I want thee not, for thou hast seen me as I am. I am for the red wine and wild revel, where 'in Folly's cup still laughs the bubble Joy'—for the idle day-dream and the sensuous dance, the fond kiss of foolish Love and the velvet couch of Lust." Then Death came and stood near him, beautiful with a beauty all spirituelle, a world of pity in her eyes. But he shrank from her with a shudder, seeing which she said: "Am I indeed so cold—I, who warm the universe? Is the bosom of Mercy to be feared and the breath of peace despised? What is Life that she should mock me?—this hideous harlot whose kisses poison and whose words betray? Is she not the mother of all ills? Behold her demoniac brood: Hate and Horror, Discord and Disease, Pride and Pain! she is the creature of Time, the slave of Space. She is the bastard spawn of Heat and Moisture—was engendered 'mid the unclean ooze of miasmic swamps, in the womb of noisome fens. And I? I am empress of all that is, or was, or can ever be. Come dwell with me, and all the earth shall be thy home, thy period eternity. Would'st live again? Then will I make of thy clustering locks grasses to wave in the cool meadows green, of thine eyes fair daisies that nod in the dewy dawn, of thy heart a great blush rose worn between the breasts of beauty, of thy body an oak to defy the elements, of thy blood a wave breaking in slumbrous thunder upon a beach of gold, of thy breath the jasmine's perfume, of thy restless spirit the levin brand that crashes in thunder peal above the storm. Why press the cruel thorn into thy heart, the iron into thy soul? Thus do I clasp thee to a bosom ever true, and shield thee from the slings and arrows of the world. Thy hot heart beats faint and ever fainter 'gainst its pulseless pillow, until it ceases with a sigh, and thou art mine and eternal peace is thine."

CATHOLIC VS. PROTESTANT "CRANKS."

An unknown correspondent clips from the press a rather sensational account of the supposed appearance of the Holy Virgin to Louise Panniere at Tilly-sur-Seulles, together with the pilgrimings to the spot, and sends it to the Iconoclast with the following comment and query:

> About once a year the Catholics run off after some such crank, thereby bringing religion into contempt and creating Atheists by their religious mummery. Why don't you turn your iconoclastic batteries loose on this fol-de-rol? What is your opinion of people who countenance such idiocies?

The man who writes a letter reflecting upon the sanity or honesty of a numerous and patriotic body of American people, should have the moral courage to either sign his screed or burn it. An anonymous "roast" is a cowardly stab in the dark. Publishers do well to waste-basket such communications, as being the emanations of irresponsibles— of people who will say more in a minute than they will stand to in a month. However, as my correspondent has touched upon a subject of interest to many people, I will, in this instance, waive the rule applying to anonymity. Frankly, I think but little of miracles, ancient or modern, and regard supernatural appearances as but the idiosyncrasies of religious neuropathics. Mlle. Poliniere's vision of the Virgin was, in my opinion, but a day-dream, the fond imaginings of a maid with whom religion had become a monomania, her fervor an ecstacy bordering on delirium. Still, I realize that there may be more things in this world than I have dreamed of in my philosophy. In dealing with the supernatural, as with all things else, it is well to bear in mind the apothegm of Seneca, to the effect that "many persons would have attained to wisdom if they had not presumed that they already possessed it." If the age of the miraculous, of angelic visitations, ever began, we have no special reason for believing that it has come to an end. It is certainly no more remarkable that the Lord should reveal himself to St. Theresa, and the Virgin to the maid of Tilly-sur-Suelles, than that Jacob should wrestle with an angel and Jehovah speak to Moses from the burning bush. If there was ever a time in the world's history when something more than the written law becomes necessary to fix mankind's faltering faith, that time is even now. The man who scoffs at St. Theresa's vision, yet accepts unfalteringly the inerrancy of the Bible, strains at a diatom and swallows an entire drove of dromedaries. There are various reasons why the Iconoclast does not align its guns upon these so-called supernal visions. I am not aware that they are doing the world any serious damage, and the Iconoclast assails only those things which it believes to be really detrimental. Furthermore, to brand all such visionaries as "cranks," and those who countenance them as "idiots," were to vilipend the coryphei of the Reformation and deride the Protestant faith. If all who dream dreams and see visions; if all who profess to have seen the supernatural be written down as purveyors of ridiculous folde-rol, what is to become of our beloved Luther and his co-laborers? It was not the magic mirror which St. Theresa saw; not the Archangel Gabriel in the Rue de Paradis, nor the Virgin Mother standing beneath an elm in the canton of Calvados that Luther witnessed; such visitants were entirely too tame for that good man who denounced the Zwinglians as "damned fools and blasphemers," insulted the learned Erasmus, called the doctors of Louvain "beasts, pigs and pagans," incited the people to assassinate the Pope, and otherwise displayed that vigor and virulence which drew after him all the chronic kickers of Christendom. Luther's supernatural visitor was invariably the Devil, and these two worthies usually made it hot for each other. The Prince of Darkness appears to have gotten the best of the controversies, however, for Luther himself assures us that Satan, by his arguments, compelled him to make an important alteration in divine services; also that, on another occasion, his inframundane visitor worsted him in a debate and so terrified him by his voice that he was in danger of death. Zwinglius, the father of Protestantism in Switzerland, relates that when about to be turned down in a religious disputation, a black phantom appeared and helped him out of the hole. Whether this was the same party that amended Luther's creed we are not informed. Nor has this unhappy faculty of seeing the Devil yet been lost by Protestant divines. Entering a Protestant church some years ago at Tipton, Ia., I was surprised to see the pastor engaged in an *ex parte* dispute with an invisible person. He shook his fist and declared that he *"would* pray, despite all the powers of hell." And pray he did. After advising the Lord regarding a number of things of which he was supposed to have no knowledge, and telling him exactly how to manage the universe, he informed us that the Devil had come up to the pulpit and warned him not to call upon the name of the Lord. The name of this wonderful sight-seer was Crismus. At Ashton, Ill., a good old

Protestant lady assured me that, upon going into her cellar one day, she was confronted by Satan; that she fell upon her knees in prayer and he disappeared. As she was noted for her sauer-kraut, I have always suspected that the Prince of Darkness was on a foraging expedition. It were easy to cite hundreds of such visions, related by Protestants, since the days of Luther. There is, however, a marked difference between Protestants and Catholics in this respect: While the former usually see the Devil, the latter content themselves with visions of the Lord or Virgin. Why this is so, I know not; but as a good Protestant, the fact gives me ineffable pain. Some of those terrible Jesuits are liable to suggest that angels and demons, like men and women, usually visit those most in sympathy with themselves. Another remarkable fact which may well give us pause, is that, while the religious ecstacies of the Catholics are usually conducive to peace on earth and good will to men, those of their Protestant brethren are almost invariable trouble-breeders. It does no particular harm for a maid to get an idea into her head that she has seen the Virgin Mother; but John of Leyden proclaiming himself King of Sion, marrying seventeen wives and authorizing most brutal murders, is quite another matter. David George asserted that he was the Son of God; Hermann urged the massacre of all magistrates; Hackett declared himself to be Christ; Johanna Southcote issued passports to heaven, while scores of others indulged vagaries equally fantastic or dangerous. It must be remembered that these people were not only Protestants, but commanded considerable followings; that many of them demanded and received the worship of *latria,* which the most enthusiastic Catholics have ever withheld from their Popes and saints. True, Luther did not sanction the fierce fanaticism and egregious folly of the Anabaptists; but he was none the less responsible therefor. It was the natural sequence of his revolt against authority, of the doctrine—which is the basal principle of Protestantism—that each individual possesses an inalienable right to put such interpretation upon the Scriptures as he may please. Protestantism has, from its inception, been the unwilling wet-nurse of Infidelity.

Luther did more to propagate it than did the alleged moral laches of the worst of Popes, the sacred reliques that have been subjected to so much ridicule, the modern miracle, the doctrine of Papal Infallibility and so-called "Sale of Indulgences." The Catholic Church is based upon authority, whether real or assumed I shall not here pretend to say. It insists that it is the chosen salvatory and divinely ordained exegete of Christian dogma. We may decline to admit this claim; but we cannot deny that it was the sheet-anchor of Europe for a thousand years; the lone rock upon which Vandal and Visigoth beat in vain; the rallying-point for a society otherwise hopelessly wrecked. In politics, art, science, letters, there was chaos; but amid it the Roman Catholic Church stood immutable as a granite mountain. Suppose that it had faltered; had stopped to argue; had declared that it *believed* instead of that it knew; had implored instead of commanding: Every student of history knows what would have happened—the Christian religion would have perished utterly and Luther's revolt been against the Imaum of Islam. This authority once overturned throughout a large portion of Europe, the wildest excesses followed. Ignorant and violent men became the founders of sects whose ridiculous doctrines and unseemly orgies disgusted thinking men with the very name of religion. Atheism and Protestantism developed side by side, the scholar following the gonfalon of the first, the ignoramus trailing blindly in the wake of the last. A few learned men of well-balanced minds embraced Protestantism in its infancy; but almost without exception, they drifted into the camp of Doubt or returned to the Catholic Church. It is impossible to find, during the first century of the Reformation, one master mind which it caught and held. Even Melancthon, the beloved disciple of Luther, and by all odds the ablest of the early reformers, declared that he felt "like Daniel in the lion's den," and was "tempted to take flight." Nor is this all: While the Catholic Church has ever asserted its position and proclaimed its doctrines as those regarding whose truth there could be no doubt, the great Protestant divines have seldom been willing to accept the inevitable sequence of the dogmas they were employed to preach. Professing one thing, they have proclaimed another, or dodged the issue altogether. Beecher's lecture on Evolution is a case in point, being almost as materialistic as even Ingersoll could ask. But it is not alone in these decadent days that we find doubt among the Protestant divines. Luther himself declared that *he did not know whether he taught the truth or not;* and freely admitted that he *could not prevail upon himself to believe what he taught to others!* (The first of the foregoing statements we have on the authority of Luther himself; the latter on the testimony of his eulogist, John Matthei.) How is that for a *soi disant* reformer and founder of a new faith for one who separated from the Church of Rome because, as he assumes, it had connived at falsehood? It is somewhat remarkable that, while admitting his doubts, first to his *intimes*, then to the public, Luther should have declared: "It is certain that I received my dogmas from heaven. *I will not allow you to judge of my doctrine, neither you nor the angels in heaven.* Yet, as before stated, individual liberty of Biblical interpretation was the basic principle of Protestantism! Is it any wonder, in view of these inconsistencies—not to say absurdities—of the prime mover of the Reformation, that Protestantism should be today a mere jumble of contradictions, which repels men of analytical minds and leaves them to choose betwen Catholicity, Deism and Infidelity. Doubtless there were Atheists in the world before the Reformation, before the inauguration of the Christian era; but there were few in Europe until Luther began to preach toleration while persecuting, to demand abject submission to dogmas which he himself doubted. The Catholic Church had to deal with many schismatics before the Reformation, but it was reserved for Protestantism to wage a war of extermination on avowed Atheists—Cronus devouring his own children! The learned Gruet was the first "infidel serpent" to be strangled by the infant Hercules. His offense was greater even than that of Servetes—he not only disagreed with Calvin, that avatar of "toleration," but had the audacity to criticise him! Theodore Beza, contemporary of Luther and Calvin, and apostle of the Reformation in France, makes a declaration which proves that the Protestant leopard has not changed its spots during the past three centuries—that it was the same provocative of Infidelity at its birth that it is today: "On what point of religion (he plaintively asks) are the churches which have declared war against the Pope agreed? Examine all from beginning to end, and *you will hardly find one thing affirmed by the one which the other does not directly cry out against as impiety.*"

THOU SHALT NOT.

"Thou Shalt Not Press the Crown of Thorns to the Brow of Labor, and Thou Shalt Not Crucify the Best Interests of This Great Republic on a Cross of Gold."

The edict has gone forth—the era of privilege and proscription must pass. No more shall it be proclaimed in the high places of this nation that to him that hath shall be given, while from him that hath not shall be taken e'en that which he hath. The people must not be pauperized for the benefit of the plutocrat, nor will the many consent to want that the few may waste. The toiling millions refuse to longer suffer the oppressor's wrongs, the proud man's contumely. "Thou shalt not," says the dauntless young tribune of the people, and "Thou shalt not" comes ringing back in thunder tones from forest, and field and factory. 'Tis the Titan of Toil who speaks, and his voice is as of the voice of many waters. It is a proclamation that even he and no other is lord of this land, which the strength of his hands hath transformed from a wilderness and desert waste into fruitful garden—that no longer will he bow as low as Caesar's feet and ask in humble tones a tithe of that his brawn hath wrung from the earth's unwilling bosom, or his cunning fashioned at the forge. No more shall the high-priests and myrmidons of Mammon press the crown of thorns to his beaded brow, nor crucify him on an industrial Calvary—"thou shalt not."

It is a new declaration of Independence flung into tyrants' faces by men born for freedom. It is a second Emancipation Proclamation, a warning to the pitiless Pharoahs of the present, a hammer laid to the galling shackles of the slave. It is an indignant denial of the doctrine that the masses should toil for the enrichment of the classes. It is a declaration backed by tremendous power, that the rotten rule of political rings must pass and this become in very truth a government by the people. It is a proud assertion of American Sovereignty, before which the petty princelings who grind the faces of the poor, now stand appalled.

Bryan is the candidate of the people, not of the politicians. For over a century or more our presidential nominees have been compromises effected by warring political cabals. Booms have been laboriously worked up by systematic advertising, just as patent medicines are put upon the market. Had McKinley been a bogus remedy for bots, or proprietary cure for bleeding piles, Mark Hanna, as a business man, would have proceeded exactly as he did to "work up a demand." In many cases money has been freely used to purchase editorial influence and employ *claquers* to create a bogus furore and stampede the people—money contributed by men who were not in politics for their health, but expected these contributions to the corruption fund to yield a pecuniary profit—that it would enable them to fatten, directly or indirectly, at the expense of the public. Collectorships, cabinet portfolios, ambassadorships and other "spoils" have been partitioned out in advance of the convention to secure the influence of the prospective beneficiaries, powerful newspapers have been "seen" and an army of shrewd "workers" and wire-pullers turned loose upon the land. President-making has become of late years but little more than a well-laid conspiracy on the part of the plutocrats and politicians against the common people. The house of Have has regularly placed before us two puppets, one labeled Democratic and the other Republican; and, like two bad roads, to choose the one were to regret the other.

Bryan was not a candidate before the convention. Had he offered for that high honor all the political pie grafters and bunco steerers for New York and London boodlers would have declared him "unavailable." Why? Because he had been guilty of the heinous crime of presuming to think for himself. He had looked at public questions from the standpoint of a patriot rather than a politician—from that of a man who produces wealth in the sweat of his brow rather than of the impudent parasite who consumes it in idleness. He had sought to promote the welfare of the whole people rather than the selfish interests of a party. He had dared to offend those who fatten on their country's misfortunes, and who are expected to provide the "sinews of war" for political campaigns. He was regarded by the politicians with exactly the same suspicion that a nest of thieves contemplates a policeman. But the emissaries of Dives were not strong enough at Chicago to dominate the convention. Having tired of being hoodooed and humbugged by those who make politics a paying profession, the people had exercised more than usual caution in selecting their representatives. The result was a platform of principles containing no slippery-elm planks. Each declaration is clean cut and cannot be interpreted one way in the East, another in the West, one way by the people and another by the president. It says what it means and means what it says. It contains no "cowardly compromise." The man who stands upon the Chicago platform does not have to swear out a search-warrant to determine where he is "at." There is not an ambiguous phrase from preamble to conclusion, from Alpha to Omega —not the faintest suggestion of deception or double-dealing. Right or wrong, wise or unwise, the framers of that instrument dealt honestly by the people. It is the first time in five-and-twenty years that a national convention of either of the old political parties has neither trimmed nor tergiversated, begged a question nor dodged an issue, and its manly candor will sink like incense from God's own altar into the soul of every honest American Sovereign. With such a platform, Bryan of Nebraska was the logical candidate, for its sentiments echo his convictions and its honesty mirrors his manhood. He did not have to stultify himself—as did McKinley—to accept the platform upon which he was nominated. He took no foundlings to rear in becoming chief exponent of the principles enunciated at Chicago—they germinated in his own heart and were born of his own brain. McKinley takes the field with the sinister bastard-bar on his political bearings; but on the argent shield of Bryan there's but honorable blazonry.

"Under which flag, Benzonian?" Under that of a man who boldly utters his convictions and battles for the people, or that of one willing to accept *any* platform to reach the presidency. Is your chief in this struggle an American sovereign or a political slave?

Quite naturally, the nomination of Bryan caused a tremendous howl to go up from every man with an axe to grind at the expense of the government. The firm of Belmont, Morgan & Cleveland stands appalled. There is consternation among the big mortgage companies. There is weeping and wailing in Wall Street. The operators of the great trusts are in agony. The practical politicians have become prophets of evil, and papers that profit by the sale of editorial influence to professional plunderers are shrieking forth their displeasure. Bryan is being denounced as a red-flagger, a Jack Cade, a veritable Anarsharsis Cloots, or political Anabaptist by those whose private snaps at public expense his candidacy endangers; yet his most uncompromising enemies grudgingly admit that he is exceptionally able and incorruptibly honest. How in the name of all the gods at once can the best interests of this country be subverted by placing an able and honest man at the head of its affairs? What do these fellows so industriously doing the bay-steer act, really want? A president with neither honesty nor ability? Is that their ideal of a chief executive officer? Do they want another Cleveland, who entered the White House a poor man, and, in seven years of public service—on a $50,000 salary—accumulated several millions? Are they crying for a man like McKinley, who declined to have any monetary ideas until a professional booster inserted in his head the St. Louis bimetallic (?) platform in lieu of brains? "Able and honest." Is that why Bryan is so distasteful to the grain gamblers and railroad wreckers? Is that why the New York *Sun,* the Texas *Gal-Dal* and all the other journalistic trenchermen in the house of Dives are deluging him with their dirty intellectual dish-water? "He is a radical," they cry. Perchance that is the inevitable effect of which his admitted ability and honesty is the cause. Had he fewer brains or less integrity he might be as eminently "conservative" as McKinley himself. It is well to remember that those great men who established this government—despite the protest of the conservative Tories—were even more "radical and revolutionary" than even Bryan of Nebraska.

Somewhat more than a century ago the American people were being despoiled by a political tyranny. They plead for justice, and their supplications were mocked; they remonstrated and were unanswered with the musket. They grew restless beneath the brutal wrongs, and here and there the voice of an Adams, a Henry or a Paine was heard in fiery protest. The blessed "conservatives" wanted to execute such patriots as public enemies. Why? Because some of them held lucrative offices under the crown, others were profiting by the despoliation of the people, and gathered about these place-holders and commercial pirates was the same crew of crumb-grabbers, the same gang of God-forsaken lickspittles now pleading with the American people to endure a worse tyranny in patience. The same class of stall-fed cattle and the same yelping pack of intellectual yaller dogs insisted that we should remain the humble subjects of King George that now protest that we owe allegiance to King Carnegie, the industrial dukes and banker barons. Adams was denounced as an anarchist, Paine as a communist, and we may presume that Patrick Henry was the original "Pop." But the wail of the "conservatives" of '76 was vain as that now heard in Wall Street. The Conscript Fathers were not deterred by the frantic abuse heaped upon them by the Danas and Belos of their day. Finding that they could no more stem the rising tide than any other bad smell could stop a thunderbolt, some of the "loyal subjects of his most gracious majesty" attached themselves to the Continental army—in the capacity of sutlers—while others, caught trying to betray their neighbors to British vengeance, were given a short shrift and a hair halter. Those "conservatives" now crying "peace, peace," will find there can be no peace until the people are the rulers *de facto,* as they are *de jure,* of this mighty nation—that they did not cease to be British subjects only to become industrial serfs. They will find that they can no more check with their phrenetic calamity-clack this uprising against ring rule than could King Canute prevent the majestic ocean rolling in the wake of the silver moon. They will find that brazen robbery in the realm of industry is doomed—that a cabal of multi-millionaires will not much longer be permitted either to dictate national polity or fix the price of the farmers' products. The people propose to take a hand in these important matters, and they will begin by placing at the head of affairs, not the creature of an "industrial cannibal," not a sinister plotter with "nothing to say," but a man capable of swaying all hearts with the magnetism of his manly presence and the mystic power of his matchless genius—of compelling even the political condotteri to acknowledge his ability and testify to his integrity.

Bryan is neither anarchist nor communist. He is the friend of order, but not an admirer of a "Roman peace"—a peace enforced with sword and scourge and grinding slavery. The real anarchist is the man who attempts to perpetuate the present political and industrial conditions—who would ignore the protests of the people, would trample upon the rights of the toilers that Dives may double his fortune; who would reduce millions of American freemen to the condition of Russian peasants or Mexican peons and fill the land with bloated plutocrats and hungry paupers. He is the man who stands in the shadow of the red flag and builds bombs—is doing all in his power to precipitate a new and more terrible Reign of Terror. The true statesman tries to make all men equal before the law, to accord like opportunity in the field of industry and insure to each the full usufruct of his endeavor. The patriot puts the well-being of the whole people above the impudent claims of class and the selfish ambition of party. The astute politician imitates the example of Queen Elizabeth and graciously concedes what he could not long withhold. No man is fit to sit in a village council, much less to occupy the exalted position of chief magistrate, who does not recognize that the will of the people—whether it be wisdom or folly—is the fundamental law of free government, and any abridgement thereof an act of usurpation deserving of death. True, this is not the opinion of Mr. Cleveland and Ambassador Bayard; nor is it the opinion of those who would foist upon us a "new Napoleon;" but it is the irrevocable conviction of the common people. No man is fit to preside over the destiny of this republic who does not recognize, with Lincoln, that "the voice of the people is the voice of God."

Talleyrand never uttered a truer paradox than when he declared that "Everybody knows more than anybody." The cumulative wisdom of the country is greater, safer than the conclusions of a coterie, tho' it be composed of the Seven Sages, and this fact is the basic principle of the American

Republic. The people may make political mistakes; but it must be ever borne in mind that this is *their* country; that they made it what it is and have a perfect right to rule it as they deem best—to coin iron money if they want to, or abolish political currency altogether. The Belmonts and Morgans, the Vanderbilts and Astors hold a mortgage on the country; but, tho' it was obtained by fraud, there is no desire on the part of the people to cancel it by force. All they ask is conditions that make possible its payment and their emancipation from the pauperizing imposition; yet Dives, with his obliging law-builders and obsequious "able editors" of the Dana school, are doing all in their power, not only to perpetuate the present hard conditions, but to make the burden of the toilers too grievous to be borne—are day by day driving the masses nearer to revolt, adding fuel to the incipient flame.

This is not a battle of the East with the West, of the North with the South; it is a struggle between the patriots of every section with those who, in the pride of their wealth and power, have adopted the Vanderbiltian motto—"The people be damned." It is an attempt to decide an "irrepressible conflict" without the shedding of one drop of blood or the disturbance of any man's title to wealth which he has honestly earned—to adjust peaceably by virtue of the ballot what may otherwise result to the bullet. I have no debts to "repudiate." If the single gold standard makes for the benefit of the creditor, I might feel a slight interest in its perpetuation and join forces with those editors now striving to drown the Nebraska orator in a sea of acrid ink; but it does not. The man who, in times like these, considers only how he can make the "rascal counters" he may have at interest yield him a double increment; how he may play the contemptible pawnbroker and despoil a debtor of all his property; how he may squeeze a few more drops of lifeblood from the badly burdened people, is not only a rotten-hearted knave, but a purblind ass oblivious to his own best interests. America's multi-millionaires are standing on a powder mine and "monkeying" with lucifer matches. Labor is becoming desperate—savage as the antlered stag brought to bay. Beyond it lies starvation's dreadful abyss. Further it cannot, and it turns upon the bloodhounds with a fierce "Thou shalt not!"

Labor has been bamboozled by politicians and sandbagged by plutocrats until it is losing faith in everything but brute force. Already anarchy is rife in the great cities and communism is spreading in the country like a prairie fire. It has been but a little while since, in the very city where Bryan was nominated, workmen asked for bread and were given the bayonet. When Coxey's hungry horde went marching across the country the heart of the mass thrilled with the terrible fire that burst forth in the French Revolution. All the vast army of industry felt a keen sympathy for that pitiful regiment of ragamuffins. Had the aggregation of wretchedness been fired on at Washington by some "new Napoleon," it would have been regarded by millions as another Lexington, a challenge from the classes to the masses, and flames have roared and bullets hissed from Bedloe's Island to the Golden Gate. So strong was the sympathy even among the farmers for that mockery of militarism that governors dared not oppose the progress of "industrial armies," and state militia companies could not be depended on to protect corporate property. The cannon was silent. Coxey marched up the hill, marched down again, and the acute phase of the affair was past; but the danger still remains—will remain so long as men educated to believe themselves the equals of kings and the superiors of princes cannot obtain sufficient food for themselves and families. Another panic, another closing of factory or mine, another Homestead horror, another invasion of a state by federal troops to shoot down men who are striking blindly for self-preservation, may precipitate the explosion—then where will Dives find defenders?

Were it not wise to reduce the pressure somewhat, to loosen the thumbscrews a little? Were it not better to be satisfied with a reasonable increment than, by grasping for more, lose all? Were it not the part of wisdom to give to toil the full meed of its earnings lest it appropriate that of both labor and capital? Were it not better for the millionaire to concede a part while he may than all when he must? Were it not better to yield gracefully to an irresistible force than to stubbornly oppose it and be destroyed? "After us the deluge," cried the French aristocrats; but the cataclysm waited not their convenience—caught 'em without boats or umbrellas. The mechanic is rapidly concluding that a reign of anarchy could be no worse than an era of starvation; the farmer that the wildest "Populist vagary" were preferable to a scale of prices that will not meet the interest on his mortgage.

When matters become as bad as they can, any change whatsoever must be for the better. Having leaped from the frying-pan into the fire, resilience can scarce prove ruinous. Mr. Bryan's "radicalism" can be no worse for the country than Mr. Cleveland's "conservatism." A man possessing such "ability and honesty" as the goldbugs credit Mr. Bryan withal, would scarce add more than 262 millions to our bonded indebtedness in a time of peace, nor precipitate more than one panic during an era of plenty. Could he steer this nation to the very verge of a foolish war about anything of less consequence than the breeding place of moccasins and mosquitoes? Could he bring the mightiest of republics into more damning disgrace than by attempting the subversion of the Hawaiian republic while leaving struggling Cuba at the mercy of the modern Attila? Could even a radical of the radicals do worse for the country than fill it with hopeless farmers, idle mechanics and broken merchants? Would he dare, think you, having a reputation for ability and honesty to maintain—permit his plutocratic friends to elongate Uncle Sam's leg to the tune of more than eight million dollars in as many days? Were it not the part of wisdom to supplant with an able and honest man one whose stupidity has been frequently demonstrated and his integrity as often doubted?

We have been making presidents of scrub stock entirely too long. Not every man who can serve a subpoena and engineer a hanging, shoot ducks and play pinochle will make a capable chief magistrate of a mighty republic. The politicians have chosen for us, not the ablest men, but those "ablest to be chosen." Webster nor Clay, Benton nor Blaine could reach the presidency. The politicians would not have them; but at last the people have determined that ability and integrity shall be no bar to the highest office in the gift of the government; that if we have among us God's noblest—and rarest—work, an honest man; if there be a sure-enough genius at large in the land, Uncle Sam, rather than the courts of Nebraska, is entitled to his services.

The cry is raised that Bryan is too young. Fortunately, the defect is not constitutional—with the blessing of God he will get over it. I regret exceedingly that his complaint isn't contagious. What difference does it make, forsooth, how young he may be so long as his very opponents admit his great ability? The idea that wisdom comes only with age is the merest moonshine. Shakespeare wrote "Hamlet" at 36, and at that age Lord Byron laid down the burdens of life. At 30 Lord Clive was conquering India for the British crown, and at 33 Alexander the Great gave up the ghost. At 27 Napoleon took command of the Army of Italy, and at 32 Jefferson wrote the Declaration of Independence. At 31 Webster was holding his own with such intellectual Titans as Clay and Calhoun, and at that age the best essays of Macaulay had been written. Pitt was Chancellor of the Exchequer at 23, and at that age Fox resigned the office of Lord of the Admiralty. Whether in art or literature, in war or statecraft, in commerce or industry, the great bulk of the world's best work has been done by men for whom life's shadows were still falling towards the West. Youth boldly faces the unsolved enigma of the future; age turns its face regretfully to the past. The first seeks improvement; the latter looks to precedent. Youth stands for progress and age for petrifaction.

We have fallen into the bad habit of making the United States Senate an old folk's refuge or asylum for senility, sending to the lower house of Congress pettifogging attorneys who cannot pick up a livelihood by practice in the chicken courts, then accepting for President whatsoever chump is most satisfactory to the plutocrats. It is small wonder that, with such a captain and crew, the ship of state is drifting to the devil. It is small wonder that her precious cargo is appropriated by pirates—that Capitol and White House are permeated by Wall Street's subtle perfume. It is small wonder that trusts flourish, the national debt increases, confidence is shaken and our public servants save more than their salaries. It is small wonder that the farmer halfsoles his butternut breeches with cotton bagging while the mechanic goes hungry to bed. It is time we sent to Washington a man whose heart is with the toiling millions, and who can not be lulled by the golden sirens of Greed—one with courage to say to those who make the national temple a den of thieves, "Thou Shalt Not."

DUTCH, DEITY AND DEVIL.

God has been insulted again! Gabriel has gone into mourning, Michael wears his wings at half-mast and Ithuriel sits clothed in sackcloth and covered with ashes. The wounds on Calvary bleed afresh, the angels rend their white robes and there is weeping and wailing in the Holy City. The golden harp hath gone silent, hushed is the loud hosannah, the stertorous sob and spasmodic snuffle have supplanted the hallelujah. St. Peter hath double-barred the gate, and the Almighty leaves the universe to run haphazard while he forges punitive thunderbolts and lays up barbed arrows in his sagittary against the day of wrath.

The Dutch did it—and all heaven cries with one accord, "D——n the Dutch!"

On a recent Sunday "We Chermans" said to ourselves: The weather is hot. We will go into the woods and make us a picnic. So? We had music and beer and redbugs. We ran foot races, played ball and rode in the merry-go-round. We sang the Star Spangled Banner and the Watch on the Rhine. We danced with the pretty girls and swung them until the roses bloomed in their cheeks and their laughter echoed like music thro' the leafy aisles of the first temples of our Lord. We smoked our pipes beneath umbrageous boughs, discussed the latest news from the Fatherland, and watched our fat babies roll and tumble on God's carpeting of green embroidered with fragrant flowers. It was a day of pleasure, one of rest without weariness, and we came home feeling that life was well worth the living—was something for which to thank the giver of all good. But scarce had the last peal of laughter died away, scarce had the last note of music melted into the throbbing atmosphere ere the religious busybodies were upon us like a flock of unclean birds—defending an Omnipotent God from the deadly assaults of the Dutch! A Waco lodge of Good (for nothing) Templars lifted up its voice like discord at Peleus' nuptial *fete,* and declared that we had "desecrated the Sabbath." Where did this aggregation of atrabilarious bigots and irrepressible meddlers absorb its misinformation? Desecrated the Sabbath how? By being happy? By enjoying to the utmost our weekly respite from grinding toil? By playing ball instead of meeting together in solemn conclave to slander our betters? By dancing instead of consigning honest men and noble women to eternal damnation? By absorbing a glass of beer—when Christ made and blessed a more intoxicating tipple? Why, you small-brained, bilious-livered, acrid-hearted disciples of Cotton Mather, do you suppose for one moment that the Almighty can be injured by a toot on the trombone? And if it doesn't hurt him, why should you howl? Do you really suppose that the Creator of the Cosmos flies into a rage because Hans Brietman goes to church Sunday morning, then takes his best girl to the park in the afternoon and stuffs her corset full of hokey-pokey and peanuts? If he doesn't approve of Hans' method of passing the Sabbath can't he settle with him without your assistance? Has he commissioned you to see that Hans remembers the Sabbath day to keep it holy? Who are you that presume to interpret for us—quite unasked—the will of the Deity, and who would abrogate a fundamental law of this land, that of religious liberty? Are you in any wise responsible for our sins? Have you been commissioned as our religious guides? Do we interfere with your political privileges or religious prerogatives? And is it any of your d——d business what we do so long as your rights are sacredly respected? No? Then why in God's name do you persist in poking your meddlesome snouts into matters that in nowise concern you? Why don't you take something for the meddler's itch and respect that other law from the book which you are continually hurling at our heads, viz.: "Judge not lest ye be judged."

I have never a word to say in derogation of the Christian Sabbath; but I do insist that my observance or non-observance thereof is a matter solely between my conscience and my Creator; that I am free to determine for myself what I may and may not properly do on that day, and that every law upon the statute books of American states which prohibits me from doing on Sunday what I may lawfully do on Monday is an invasion of the natural rights of man, subversive of the teachings of Christ, and a flagrant violation of the Federal Constitution. We have millions of good citizens—the equals morally and the superiors mentally of Waco's Good Templars—who firmly believe that Christ was a fraud. We have tens of thousands of worthy people who regard Saturday as the true Sabbath. Because we chance to be in the majority shall we compel all these people to either stultify themselves or leave the country—this country of "religious liberty," where every man is supposed to be privileged to "worship God according to the dictates of his own conscience?" Certainly a man should not be allowed to fill his hide with mean whiskey and become personally offensive to those for whom Sunday possesses a sacrosanct character; but he should be compelled on all days to conduct himself with decency and decorum or suffer the consequences.

It is high time the old Yankee blue laws were relegated to oblivion. Christianity is optimism, not pessimism. It is a religion of joy instead of sorrow, of laughter rather than of tears, of light and life, not of gloom and death. Viewed from a purely economic standpoint, the Sunday holiday is to be commended; but it should be in very truth a holiday, not a day of penance—of the abject slavery of the whole people to the narrow theological views of those whom a different birth might have made high-priests of Mumbo Jumbo instead of western dogmatizers. It is doubtful if the workingman could create as much wealth without his regular Sunday rest as with it; but it is small gain to emancipate him from the slavery of the treadmill and deny him the right to recreate himself as he may choose. Sunday, to really benefit the workingman, to put fresh vigor in his veins and new courage in his heart—to remind him that he too is a man, and not a mere mechanic—should be as free from restraint as possible. Let him have a brass band and orderly beer garden if he likes; dancing platform and shooting gallery, concerts and clean theatrical performances, horse-racing and baseball. There is more true worship of God in a happy, joyful heart in a ten-pin alley than in a splenetic one repeating the catechism—and envying Solomon his 700 wives and 300 harlots. Avaunt, long-faced hypocrite, with thy Sunday law! Get thee into a corner with thy threnodies and be as miserable as thou mayst; but please to remember thou hast no warrant of God for making thy brother wretched; for shutting from him the sunshine; for robbing him of such happiness as he can find in this too unhappy world; for making him a canting pharisee like thyself—a thing despised by men and contemned by God.

Considered from a purely theological standpoint, there is absolutely no warrant for the Sunday laws in operation in most so-called Christian states and nations. The old Jewish Sabbath was a day of rest, of feasting and rejoicing—very different from that of the second temple, and the Puritanical Sunday which the laws in question seek to re-establish. Christ recognized the Jewish Sabbath, and the early Christians observed it and no other. Naturally the day upon which the Saviour was said to have risen from the dead possessed a sacrosanct character to those who accepted Him as the Son of God. As the new doctrine spread among the non-Semitic peoples, who knew not Moses, it was natural that they should observe "the Lord's day" to the neglect of the Hebrew Sabbath, and a clash between the Gentile and Jewish Christians occurred in the time of the Apostles. Hence we find Paul absolving his proselytes from observance of the Mosaic sacred day and magnifying "the Lord's day" into a new Sabbath—upon what authority is not clear, as the original Disciples and first converts maintained the continued obligation of the Mosaic Sabbath and the limitation of the promises to those who observed it. Not only did they insist upon the observance of the Mosaic Sabbath, but on the rite of circumcision. The fact is that the observance of Sunday as a sacred day is simply a custom, not a divine command. It does not date from Christ, but is a heritage bequeathed us by a very unchristian quarrel among his followers, and, true to its stormy origin, it has been breeding trouble ever since. Those who would suppress Sunday newspapers, bathrooms and barber-shops, and who have the willies over a Sunday picnic or ball game, inherit their Sabbatarian ideas, not from Christ, but from those hypocritical formalists he so bitterly denounced. The Mosaic Sabbath had been twisted from a day of rest and recreation into one of torture by the religious degenerates of Jerusalem. Christ took special pains to prove his utter contempt for those early blue laws; yet they are the models adopted by the ignorant fanatics of the present day, who pretend to follow in his footsteps.

That the American people have a legal right to enact such Sunday laws as they choose, there can be no question. There is nothing in the Federal Constitution prohibiting the people of any state establishing a church and supporting it by general taxation if they see fit to do so; but the legal right to do a thing does not prove either its justice or its wisdom. We must not forget, however, that secular is grounded upon moral law, and that in turn upon religion, or at least religiosity; that theology and jurisprudence are so interwoven that complete separation is practically impossible. But while all governments, whatsoever their name or profession, must, to some extent, be theocracies in which the theological views of the great body of people are shadowed forth, there can be no excuse for cramming non-essential religious formulas down the throats of dissenters with a policeman's bludgeon. Only Puritanical intolerance will compel those who reject the Christian religion, to observe its Sabbath; only bigotry, born of ignorance and nursed by insolence, will presume to dictate to an American citizen how he shall spend his Sundays.

THE BIKE BACILLUS.

The Women's Rescue League met recently at Washington and launched a double-shotted anathema at the female bike fiend. The Leaguers attribute to the bicycle craze "the alarming increase" in the number of courtesans, and call upon ministers and respectable women everywhere to denounce cycling by the sex as "vulgar and indecent." Nor do they stop there. The bike, in their opinion, is irremediably bad. While destroying the morals of the maid, it wrecks the prospective motherhood of the matron. It is provocative of diseases peculiar to women, and calculated to transform the sex into a grand army of invalids. These are a few of the reasons why the Women's Rescue League is scattering tacks in the pathway of the pneumatic tire. There are others.

Those whose specialty is the conservation of virtue should carefully study the causation of vice. In dealing with the redlight district, an ounce of prevention is worth a pound of cure. To remove the causes which produce courtesans were a nobler work than to drag debased womanhood out of the depths. Doubtless the Rescuers imagine they have made a new discovery of inestimable benefit to society—have laid the ax to the root of that evil of which the bawdy-house is the flower and hell the fruitage. After patient research in the science of sexual criminology, they have determined that the bicycle is naughty without being nice. It is perversity personified. It is the incarnation of cussedness, the avatar of evil. Turn it which way you will, it rolls into the primrose path of dalliance, whose objective point is the aceldama. No more do woman's feet "take hold on hell:" she goes scorching over the brink with her tootsies on the handle-bar. So say the ladies of the Rescue League.

What are we going to do about it? Clearly it were useless to denounce a "craze," sheer folly to argue against a "fad." We had better save our breath to cool our broth. The ministers cannot be depended on to lend their moral support to this new movement against the Magdalen maker —they have bought bikes and are chasing the girl in bloomers. One-half the great she-world's on wheels—the other wondering how it feels to ride clothespin fashion. Clearly the Women's Rescue League cannot stem the tide—not even with the help of the Iconoclast and Ex-Governor Hogg; it must either straddle a bike and join in the stampede, climb a fence or get run over. Hevings! is there no help for us—no halting-place this side of hetairism? Are we all pedaling at breakneck pace to the Grove of Daphne, where lust is law? Is the bike transforming this staid old world into one wild bacchic orgie or phallic revel? Have we toiled afoot thus far up the social mountain-side, only to go bowling down on a pneumatic tire—"as low as to the fiends?" Head us, somebody! Police!

Just why the bicycle affects woman so unfavorably, the leaguers do not inform us. We are left to surmise why tramping a bike should make her more reckless than treading a sewing-machine; why exercise in the open air should be more deleterious to health and morals than the round dance in a heated ball-room, or even the delightfully dangerous back-parlor hug; why segregation on the cycle should be more potent to evoke those passions which make for perdition than the narrow-seated buggy, with its surreptitious pressure of limb to limb and the moral euthanasia which the man of the world knows so well how to distill into the ear of womanhood. Why the bike should be more dangerous to morals than the French fiddle mentioned by Shakespeare appears to be a question solely within the province of the pathologist. As pantagruelism is proceeding almost exclusively on micrological lines, we may expect that, sooner or later, some "eminent physician" will startle the world by discovering the bicycle bacillus. All our ills appear to be caused by minute insects that get inside of us, demoralize our system of government and inaugurate a reign of anarchy. Everything, from mugwumpery to the meddler's itch, from corns to crime, is now traced to the pernicious activity of some microbian. Even our currency system is blasted by goldbugs, and Prohibition milk-sickness is being treated with vermifuge. A Kansas M. D. has succeeded in hiving the old-age microbe, and is now treating the ballet girls whom Weis & Greenwall and Rigsby & Walker will bring south next winter, while a New York empiric has discovered the insanity sect and is fumigating the brain of the Rev. Mr. Parkhurst. Thus does medical science go marching from conquest to conquest, reforming and rejuvenating this wicked and suffering world. Clearly the Rescue League should have cried for aid to the doctors of medicine instead of to the doctors of divinity. If the bicycle bacillus can be caught and killed, the redlight district will disappear and the Rescuers turn their wonderful energies in new directions. Once the existence of this nymphomania-micrococcus—as we philomaths would call it—is established, the rest will be dead easy. Whether patients will be treated externally or internally depends, of course, upon the habits of the infinitesimal vulture that is feeding on our social vitals. We do not know as yet whether it is a moral microbe or a physical phylloxera. If the former, the mind will have to be taken out, sand-papered, carefully rinsed in a strong aseptic solution and treated with soothing antaphrodisiacs after each meet of the bicycle brigade; if the latter, the evil can easily be obviated by providing the softer sex with medicated cycling suits, or half-soling their bloomers with asbestos. If the Rescuers really have the good of their frail sisters at heart they should co-operate with the physician—should provide themselves with compound microscopes and search assiduously for baccilli, instead of appealing to preachers who may themselves be veritable breeding grounds for the most destructive of all bacteria. It may be necessary, in order to compel success, for the Rescuers to sacrifice themselves upon the altar of science, to become martyrs to the cause. In striving to save others from the pestilence that walketh in darkness, they may be themselves destroyed; but the true reformer draws back from no danger. Let them take their lives in their hands, if need be, boldly seize the bicycle bacillus by the ears and bump his head.

The crisis is indeed acute; still we may rely on science to save us. It is possible that the first step in that direction has been already taken, for is not the insanity germ discovered by the New York doctor responsible for the "bicycle craze" as well as the reform frenzy? And if a "free-silver lunatic" or "goldbug crank" can be permanently cured by the simple expedient of boring a hole in his lumbar region and drawing off the cerebro-spinal fluid, and in it the microbes that build wheels in his head, is there not hope that the bicycle habit may be altogether abolished by the return of the "fiends" to mental normality? Now that Dr. Babcock has learned to cast out devils, will not the world be redeemed? Cert! Let the Women's Rescue League take courage, and bask in the sunny optimism of the Iconoclast. We'll soon have all the various brands of bacteria in the bouillon; then there'll be nobody to rescue, nothing to reform, and the Leaguers and the public can take a much needed rest.

In all seriousness, I opine that the bike is a harmless instrument when properly handled. The trouble is not so much with the evasive machine as with the woman who straddles it. It will carry its rider to church as rapidly as to the Reservation. Doubtless many women employ it to seek opportunities for evil—as a means of attracting the attention of libidinous men; but had the bike never been built, they would find some other way into the path of sin—would get there just the same. There were courtesans before it came; there will be *demimondaines* ages after its departure. Mary Magdalen either walked or rode a mule. Aspasia was a "scorcher," but she couldn't "coast." Helen of Troy never saw a pneumatic tire. Semiramis preferred a side-saddle. Cleopatra didn't attract Col. Antony's attention by mounting a machine in the market-place. The bike is no more an incentive to bawdry than is a wheelbarrow. It doesn't make a woman depraved; it only renders her ridiculous.

THE CURRENCY CRAZE.

Much Ado About Nothing.

I am inclined to suspect at times that watermelons would continue to grow and shoats to fatten, the bicycle girl persist in pawing the atmosphere with her shapely legs and the ice-cold schooner come sliding down the slippery bar should both the white and yellow metal saviors of the country contract paralysis of the jawbone. This currency agitation has developed into a veritable craze, reminds me of the one-legged man who insisted that physicians treat him for cramps in his missing foot. Uncle Sam's monetary troubles are purely imaginary, and even were he financially ill, it is beyond the power of the politicians to provide him with a panacea. Congress can no more increase or diminish the volume of our exchange media than it can increase or diminish the number of our quart cups or bushel baskets, and any attempt to do so were like a man in mid-ocean bailing water from one side of his boat to the other in the expectation of creating a hole and building a hill. Of course you can no more convince the perspiring goldites or conclamating silverites of this demonstrable fact than you can persuade a Digger Indian that the sun doesn't revolve around the earth. The men who believe that Congress can make or mar our exchange media, and thereby inaugurate a saturnian age or send us to the devil industrially, are cousins-german to those who believe the biblical miracles. Their financial convictions are purely a matter of faith, beyond the reach of reason, in nowise amenable to the laws of logic. Discussing monetary science with a confirmed goldite or silverite were equivalent to disputing anent forms of baptism with a Campbellite.

Those trailing in the wake of that political pariah, Bill McKinley, are sweating blood lest the free coinage of silver depreciate the purchasing power of the dollar and utterly destroy our commerce and industry. Their doleful jeremiads mount night and day, and the burden of their lamentations is the woes to be inflicted upon the working people by the "dishonest dollar." The seven vials of the seven angels of the Apocalypse were as benedictions by comparison with the plagues to be let loose on this unhappy land by the "repudiators." The Iconoclast has never advocated the free coinage of silver; but it will pay $100 in gold to the first man who sends to this office the name of any nation, ancient or modern, that has been pauperized by a depreciation in the purchasing power of its exchange media.

Patrick Henry having assured us that "we can only judge the future by the past," I am not a little anxious to learn from what historic predicate the McKinley boomers draw their hair-raising and blood-curdling conclusion. I would prefer that the "new Napoleon" send Mark Hanna around to claim the reward and add it to the campaign fund; but if that be inconvenient, any of the learned Thebans now discoursing so glibly of "free silver and industrial ruin" will be permitted to take a shy at the ducats. I want to secure a map of that country in which a depreciation in the purchasing power of the exchange media reduced the aggregate of wealth and drove the toilers hungry to bed. I want to hang it up with my collection of those wherein an appreciating currency pauperized the common people—enabled a few to despoil the many by lending a pup and compelling repayment of a pig. Don't be bashful, gentlemen; the latch-string hangs on the outside and the reward awaits you. Why waste your breath spouting on street corners, your energies writing labored essays for the press, when by carrying your wisdom to this office, you can exchange it for

"Gold, gold, bright and yellow, hard and cold."

Do not, I beseech you, waste your sweetness on the desert air, but make your ebullient learning butter your parsnips. Search the history of every people, from the day when old Abraham paid "current money with the merchant" for the cave and field of Machpelah, to Modern Mexico, answer this plain question and "put money in thy purse." If you can find no such instance; if you have absolutely nothing upon which to bottom your alarming predictions, then, in the name of common decency, take the mainspring out of your calamity clack and go bottle your wind.

I freely concede that a depreciating currency is a bad thing; but history amply demonstrates that an appreciating one is worse. The first robs the creditor; the latter despoils the debtor. The natural tendency of the first is toward an equal distribution of wealth; that of the latter toward its concentration, making the many helpless dependents of the few, crushing liberty and inaugurating insolent despotism. This fact is self-evident, and explains why the creditor East is for the gold standard, while the debtor West and South demand the unlimited coinage of silver. Selfishness is the basic principle of both policies. Each hopes to profit at the expense of the other—and both will be disappointed.

Peace for a moment, in heaven's name, and let us try to think that we're thinking. Let us quit rethreshing mouldy economic straw and size up the situation. How much governmental money have we?

About two billions.

What proportion of our exchanges are affected by it?

Approximately 5 per cent.

And that 5 per cent. is what we are worrying about, is it? Our trouble with one-twentieth of our trade is what is raising the very devil and Tom Walker and causing everybody, from Mrs. Lease down to Grover Cleveland to miss meals and lose sleep; With what is the other 95 per cent. of our exchanges effected?

With a commercial currency, manufactured from day to day, adapting itself automatically and infallibly to the exigencies of trade, and beyond the control of presidents and congresses. Money it is *not*, but an exchange medium it *is*. Clearly, whatsoever affects nineteen-twentieths of our volume of exchanges must be considered a very effective part of our volume of currency.

If it requires 2 billions of currency to do 5 per cent. of our money work, what is the actual volume of our efficient exchange media?

About 40 billions.

And yet half of the people are having one conniption fit after another lest a few silver dollars be added to this tremendous flood, while the other half declare that without such addition we are bound to the devil! No wonder the lunatic asylums of the land are filled to overflowing. How much silver do we produce in a year?

Enough to coin some 75 million dollars.

Suppose we coin it all for a period of 10 years, what have we added to the volume of our exchange media?

Less than a billion dollars.

If the expanding commerce of this country requires 40 billions now, what will it require 10 years hence?

Ask me something easy—perhaps 50 billions.

And the addition of less than 1 billion is what is giving you night sweats? Perhaps instead of a great financial idea you've got a tape worm.

But governmental money is the foundation upon which all this commercial currency rests—gold is the basis of the pyramid.

'Tis, eh? We have about half a billion gold coin in this country—and that upholds 39 1-2 billions of credit money! No wonder the "yellow boys" want to go abroad. Barnum's fat woman sitting in the lap of Tom Thumb were not a circumstance to it. Cheops turned upside down and balanced on a dinner plate! Great is Uncle Sam! He is doing a $40-business on a cash capital of 50 cents—all miracles hitherto heard of are out-miracled! Midas, we are told, had asses' ears, but his modern disciples go the whole head. No wonder there's a "lack of confidence"—40 billion of America's exchange media trying to balance on G. Cleveland's slippery gold reserve. Some day it may occur to a man here and there that our great volume of currency—political and commercial—is really bottomed on a very large and fruitful splotch of the North American continent.

Sometimes, in unguarded moments when forgetful of McKinley's newly discovered monetary wisdom, I imagine that if our pitiful half billion of gold would go abroad and forget to come back, England would still manage to trade her cutlery and cloth for our corn and cotton—just as she does at present. I noticed that when Confederate currency was being used for gun-wadding it required a good many ships of war to prevent our trading with the rest of the world about as actively as tho' we had been on a gold basis. Europe didn't want our money then, nor does she want it now. When a man begins to talk to you about "money good the world over," tell him that if he will procure a sample of such money and send it to this office he will receive therefor fifty times its face value. I'm something of a numismatist myself, but I never saw such money. All trade, whether domestic or foreign, is, when reduced to the last analysis, but an exchange of commodities. When that oft forgotten fact is well fixed in your mind you will be able to estimate at its true worth the inane prattle about "repudiation of our foreign debts by means of a debased currency." We pay our foreign debts with our products estimated in the currency of the country to which they are carried; hence we would neither save nor lose a red cent if our dollar should become so debased that it would purchase less than a dime does to-day.

It will be objected that the dollar has had a two-fold duty—that of effecting exchanges and of measuring values, the latter of equal importance with the first; that free coinage of silver will reduce the purchasing power of the dollar one-half—will saw our measure of value squarely thro' the middle. The purchasing power of the dollar—as of a day's labor or a pound of pork—can only be reduced one-half by doubling the supply relative to the demand, and to accomplish this by silver coinage is a physical impossibility. We are told that the first effect of opening the mints to the white metal will be to drive gold abroad. In that case it will require seven years to fill the void with cart-wheel dollars if we coin our entire annual product, then seven years to double the present volume of hard money and bring the dollar down to a 50-cent valuation—granting that in these fourteen years the demand for money does not increase. In so long a period commerce would quietly adjust itself to the changed conditions, and there could be no shock.

The dollar is our measure of value as the pound is of weight and the gallon of quantity. Suppose that commerce should agree to call 8 ounces a pound, 2 quarts a gallon and 50 cents' worth of metal a dollar. Would the earth come to an end, think you? Does it make any particular difference whether we express the value of a cayuse in Mexican or American money? Isn't he the same bundle of deviltry—exchangeable for so many bushels of beans or pounds of pork? Mexico, we are told, has to purchase gold wherewith to pay interest on her bonds, and give therefor 2 dollars for 1. What of it? When she gives two 50-centers for one 100-cent dollar is she any greater loser than when she gives two pints for a quart, two halves for a whole?

I said at the opening of this song-service that it is impossible for the politicians to either expand or contract our exchange media. It is one thing to make governmental money and quite another to compel its employment by the people. We already have more silver coin than can be kept in circulation. Commerce insists upon being the sole judge of its needs and selects its own trade tools. When it has sufficient exchange media with which to do its money-work, it will use no more; and when it needs more it makes it.

It must ever be borne in mind that a measure of value may be one thing and the circulating media quite another. We might effect all our exchanges with commercial currency without any change in our unit of value, which, after all, is purely hypothetical, a term by which we express the commercial relation of each commodity to all others. If we agree that 25.8 grains of gold of a certain fineness is intrinsically worth one dollar; if we nominate it our measure of value, what difference does it make whether it be coined or uncoined so long as we are content with its representatives—so long as these representatives will serve us even better—because more expeditiously and at less charge for transportation? Let gold skip, if it likes. If we need it, cannot we mine it, as we do iron and copper? or buy it abroad with our products, as we do silks and wines?

Clearly if commerce maintains the gold standard—as it is likely enough to do regardless of the character of our political money—it will use no more of the white metal than at present, no matter how much is coined. In a barbarous country, or one where the commercial exchange system is crude; in a country where the bulk of trade is effected by the actual passage of coin from hand to hand instead of by means of bank transfers, a cheap money metal would soon drive out the dear one—the high office of unit of value be quickly usurped by the less valuable coin; but in a country where comparatively little governmental money of any kind is employed, a sudden change in either the circulating media or the unit of value becomes a difficult matter—one which commerce will pass upon, quite irrespective of the acts of Congress.

The wisest thing the politicians can do is to cease meddling in matters monetary. It is a province in which they are powerful only for evil. The silverite agitators have convinced one-half the people that Congress can, by a simple "be-it-enacted," double the value of a day's labor and inaugurate a veritable Utopia; the goldite orators have succeeded in scaring the other half into convulsions by solemnly declaring that unless the impending silver tide be stayed, the country will go awhooping to hades in a hemlock coffin. Everybody has been wrought up to such a stage of feverish expectancy that if the ridiculous gold reserve should be exhausted to-morrow it were well nigh impossible to prevent a disastrous panic. It would have the same effect upon the people as the appearance of a bogus ghost has on a nigger camp meeting. The reserve is the tortoise which, in the mythology of the worshippers of the golden calf, upholds the world. If the mints should be opened to the unlimited coinage of silver to-day a cold chill would creep down the backs of millions, equal to that which the children of early Rome experienced when a comet appeared, "shaking war and pestilence from its horrid hair." And but for the mischievous prophesying of these unhung idiots, the gold reserve might be abolished altogether and not one man in ten thousand find it out; but for the gabble of these hydrocephalous apes, our governmental money might be contracted a billion or expanded two without ever raising a ripple on the great monetary sea.

All our exchange media, by whomsoever and of whatsoever made, rests upon and are representative of actual wealth. When A buys a horse for $100 on credit, the note he gives is a mortgage upon his property, actual and potential. When B secures a loan of $100 and invests it in tools he really borrows the tools. When C gives a check for $100, he simply instructs his banker to transfer that portion of his credit to another. When government issues a $100 greenback it draws a draft against every atom of property between the two oceans. Whatever enables us to expeditiously effect exchanges is as "good money" for all practical purposes as virgin gold—tho' coined of buffalo chips or stamped in Chinese characters on the hickory shirt-tails of Kansas Populists.

There is no reason why Congress should supply commerce with an exchange medium or that it should provide it with yardsticks, scales and other necessary tools. What the' 'ell do the politicians know about business, anyhow? Experience in office brokerage does not constitute a commercial education. Who sets a blacksmith to build a boat? Congress tinkering our exchange media were like a lot of tailors holding an autopsy—unable to distinguish between the lungs and the liver. Every man to his trade—and the trade of the average Congressman is keeping the public udder between his teeth—and this ridiculous, not to say damnable, currency craze is simply a portion of his political assets.

SLIPPERY BILL McKINLEY.

I have never voted other than for a Republican for President. How else could I have officiated for two years as editor of the San Antonio *Express?* I expected to vote the Republican ticket this year, not because I approve all the tenets of the party, but because the country has been generally prosperous under Republican rule—and "the proof of the pudding is in chewing the string." The party is usually consistent. As a rule, it knows where it is "at" and whyfore, and there is just Scotch enough in my composition to admire consistency—even tho' it be "the virtue of fools." The Scotch do not change with every phase of the moon—they are usually in the wrong, and proud of it. But this year my voice and my vote are for Bryan of Nebraska—not because he is a Democrat, for he isn't; not because he is a Populist, for he isn't; not because he is a free silverite; for I consider the hullabaloo anent the currency evidence of national paresis; but because he is an American sovereign possessing the courage of his convictions; because I must vote for Bryan or for Bill McKinley—for an intellectual Titan or for a moral vacuum and mental homunculus. The nominee of the Republican party should be relegated to the shades of private life. Because he is a political coward who dared not stand up in the majesty of American manhood and voice his honest convictions, but trimmed and tergiversated until a blatant congeries of monetary jackassi determined his political faith. Contrast McKinley's cowardice with the boldness of the Nebraskan who led his party instead of meekly trotting in the wake of the bandwagon. Contrast it with the political courage of Henry Clay, whose simple sentence, "I would rather be right than President," rings like sacred music in every true American soul! Look upon this picture, then upon that—the "Mill-boy of the Slashes" defiantly hurling down the gage to destiny, and the political policy playing of Ohio's Uriah Heep! Gods! 'Tis enough to make the uncrowned kings of this new Rome bow their faces to the very dust and weep bitter tears of shame to think that such a pitiful parody on American manhood stands even one chance in a million of reaching that high seat denied a Webster and a Clay, a Tilden and a Blaine. For months he stood waiting for delegates—chosen by Mark Hanna—to tell him whether it were good policy to apotheosize the free silver men or anathematize them as repudiators whose theories in practice would precipitate a frightful panic; to advise him whether he could secure more votes by denouncing Wall Street as a congeries of shameless vampires preying upon the lifeblood of the people, or by deifying it as the avatar of disinterested patriotism, the bulwark of our national honor and commercial credit. Henry Clay failed to reach the Presidency; but he lived and died an independent American sovereign. Few can recall even the names of all the Presidents; but that of Clay rushes to the lips and fills the heart like a song learned at our mother's knee. The politicians would not make him President, but Almighty God made him a prince among the people. He would not stoop to conquer, yet won the ever-fadeless bays. McKinley cast honor and manhood behind him and groveled like a Senegambian helot before the leaden whip of the Spartan—for what? The poor privilege of strutting for a brief day upon the public stage, of hiding the heart of an ass behind the lion's royal robe, then fading like a feculent odor into everlasting oblivion. Think of a man posing as a leader, a tribune of the people, who has "nothing to say" when the populace, uncertain of their path and doubting their own judgment, appeal to him for guidance in what they consider the greatest crisis of the nation's history! Why, if a man were to call my dog McKinley and the brute failed to resent to the death the damning insult, I'd drown it. Slug this impudent political adventurer at the ballot-box.

Because he has truckled to the A. P. Apes, alias the Aggregation of Pusillanimous Asses. His boomers now deny this, but the evidence against him—as outlined in the July Iconoclast—is too strong to be overthrown by the protestations of a coterie of professional pie grafters. No man is worthy to occupy the chair adorned by Washington and Jefferson and sanctified by Garfield and Lincoln, who is not in full accord with the American principle of religious liberty. Turn him down.

Because his nomination was not due to a spontaneous demand of the people or his party, but to the *finesse* of one Mark A. Hanna, whom Master Workman Sovereign aptly describes as follows: "He has ever been the vindictive foe of organized labor. He is an industrial cannibal. He has crushed union after union among his thousands of employes and taken delight in doing so. He is worse than Carnegie." Is it possible that this industrial tyrant should select a presidential candidate worthy the confidence of the working people? If Mark Hanna be our industrial enemy, shall we accept him as our political friend? Having done all in his power to beat down wages, hasn't the bullet-headed, ape-mugged egotist got his gall to ask us to believe that he is now engaged in a herculean attempt to raise them? Shall the lamb put confidence in the wolf and the fly accept the unctuous invitation of the spider to walk into his parlor? Nit! We prefer to judge the future by the past. We see the cloven hoof beneath the angelic robe of this suave hypocrite. The tens of thousands of toilers in mine and factory cannot be enticed to their ruin by the siren song of this industrial cannibal. They may fall into Charybdis, but they'll avoid Scylla. The American working people will mass against McKinley.

Because he is distinctively the candidate of the trusts, tariff barons, bond grabbers and others fattening at the expense of the people, and who have promised to raise $4,000,000—for what? To secure an honest government? To promote the general welfare? Nay, nay, Pauline; to perpetuate their private snaps! Can four millions of money, ostentatiously contributed by eastern boodlers, elect their cowardly creature, their pliant tool, president of this nation, despite the protests of the common people? Not on your life! The money will be consumed in the purchase of such venal papers as the Mobile *Register,* the Louisville *Courier-Journal* and the Santone *Distress*—the utterance of whose editors has no more influence on the public mind than has the baying of a mongrel on the phases of the moon. Bury McKinley Bill beneath an avalanche of adverse ballots.

Because the monetary system to which he stands committed is a brazen fake, and was denounced by him as such before he contracted the Presidential itch and required the assistance of those who could be depended upon to submit gracefully to the "fat-frying" process to protect their illegitimate profits—to enable such men as Mark Hanna to become industrial cannibals and devour the common people. Rebuke at the polls the presumption of this policy player.

Because in every 1,000 Americans can be found 900 better men, stronger mentally, nobler morally, worthier in every way for Presidential honors. Defeat him world without end,

Because this should be a government of, for and by the people, instead of a government of, for and by Mark Hanna and the gang of high-toned thieves and silk-stocking thugs for whom he is acting. Do not vote against him because he is a Republican; but because he is Bill McKinley, and if elected, must of necessity be the puppet of professional boodlers. The creature cannot rise superior to its creator, and McKinley as President would be the godless creation of corporate greed. He would be the hired man of the Carnegies and the Hannas, the Belmonts and the Morgans, and the workingman compelled to pay wages to a pitiful peon pledged to his despoliation.

A BRAZEN HUMBUG.

I am not much of a "free-silver fanatic," but I do dislike to see the people imposed upon by a set of editorial and oratorical frauds who brazenly juggle figures. Hundreds of papers, 'sputers and spouters are striving to create the impression that gold makes for high and silver for low wages; yet the biggest fool engaged in this disreputable sculduggery knows full well—if he knows anything—that he is perpetrating a brazen falsehood. If Cicero wondered that the Roman aruspices could look into each others' faces without hanging, what would he have thought of goldbug editors and orators who, after laboriously comparing the wage rate of England and the United States with that of China and Japan, solemnly advise the American workingman that if he doesn't want to toil for a dime a day— "in depreciated currency"—and live on rice and rats, he should give the glad hand to the "cross of gold." There isn't an editor on earth with sufficient sense to dodge "plate-matter" when wielding a pair of shears, who doesn't know that all such talk is the veriest tommyrot. There isn't an orator who employs it but does so for the express purpose of deceiving ignorant people. I here brand every man who indulges in such "argument" as a fool of the first water or a deliberate fraud. Certainly wages are higher in England and the United States than in China and Japan, and of right ought to be, for the productive power of the energetic Caucasian, with his improved machinery, is tenfold greater than that of the puttering Mongolian with his antediluvian devices. Every man versed in even the primary principles of economics, knows that the unit of value in vogue in a country has no more to do with its wage rate than with the number of wiggletails in its rainwater. We don't have to go to Ricardo, or Mill, or Montesquieu for this information—it is only necessary to turn to the latest published consular reports, which any man may obtain of his representative in Congress, free of cost. If the gold makes for high and the silver standard for low wages, how comes it that gasfitters receive $14.50 a week in Colombia and $18 in Venezuela, both silver standard countries, and but $4.08 in Germany and $3.40 in Italy, both on a gold basis? How comes it that cigar-makers receive $12.50 and tinsmiths $14 in silver-standard Venezuela, and $4.80 and $3, respectively, in gold-standard Spain? How comes it that distillers receive $12 per week in Mexico and but $3.90 in Denmark? How comes it that cabinet-makers receive $10 in Ecuador and but $4,25 in Germany, blacksmiths $12.83 in Venezuela and but $2.60 in Italy, telegraph operators $11.50 in Mexico and but $5.30 in Denmark, engravers $19.75 in Peru and but $3 in Spain? If the gold standard makes uniformly for high wages, why is there such a tremendous difference in the wage rate of gold-standard countries? The average weekly wages of bricklayers in the United States is $21.18, in Spain $3.80, in Canada $18 and in Italy $4.20, yet all are on a gold basis. Hod-carriers average $13.38 in the United States and but $1.70 in Italy; plumbers $13.50 in Canada and $3.25 in Spain, $19 in the United States and $7.90 in England, $13.35 in New South

Wales and $4.25 in Germany—all gold-standard countries. Coopers get $1.80 in China and $10 in Ecuador, masons $2.18 in Japan and $10.80 in Mexico, butchers $2.68 in Persia and $12.30 in Peru; cigar-makers $1.40 in China and $12.50 in Venezuela—all silver-standard countries. Yet the goldbugs ask the workingman to believe that upon the unit of value depends the scale of wages! Is it a wonder that when a man makes that kind of a talk to intelligent people he escapes being hooted—or hanged! In pointing out that wages are higher in gold-standard England and America than in silver-standard China and Japan, the McKinleyites leak just enough truth to give their assertion the full effect of a dangerous and damnable lie. Carnegie, Mark Hanna and McKinley are wonderfully interested in the welfare of the workingman—in a perfect agony lest he commit industrial hari-kari! Will they please inform us how the gold standard is to prevent American wages going to the English level? Will they kindly take a day off and explain how the adoption of the gold standard by China would raise her wage rate to a parity with that of New South Wales—while that of England, Germany, Denmark, Belgium, France, Italy, Spain and Switzerland remain so far below that of Mexico, Colombia, Peru, Ecuador and Venezuela? And when they have explained this matter to the satisfaction of the public, will they explain why gold-standard Spain is decaying, while silver-standard Mexico is going forward with giant strides? If silver is the *bete noire* of industry, why is it that Texas begs in vain for capital to develop the potential wealth of her fertile fields, virgin forests and fecund mines, while millions upon millions of eastern and European capital pours across her into Mexico? The people are tired of your infernal sophistry; now talk sense. If a depreciated currency be responsible for China's low wage rate, why didn't it have a like effect in America previous to the resumption of specie payments? Why did wheat go to $2.85 in 1867 and to .49 in 1895? In 1867 I was 10 years old, and received $2 a day for work in the harvest field; now 10-year-old boys can be employed at like labor for $2 a week. I am told that I was paid in a "depreciated currency." Cert! I could get only five sticks of candy for 5 cents; now the $2-a-week boy can obtain six! What a pity my birth wasn't delayed 30 years, so the blessed goldbugs could keep me from being sand-bagged by a depreciated currency! While handicapped with "the evils of a depreciated currency," my people raised and sold wheat and corn, cattle and hogs, purchased more land and built comfortable houses and mammoth barns; but under "the manifold blessings of a stable gold standard" they are selling the land because its produce will not yield a profit, and letting the buildings go to wreck because unable to repair them. Then the old gentleman was wont to put $1,000 bills in the family Bible and hide it under the bed; now when the tax-collector comes around he must go aborrowing. Then the farm, with its billowy wheat fields and golden corn, stretched out over an entire section and resembled a garden of the gods; now it is reduced to a pitiful 80 acres and looks like a desert of desolation. Seventy-five years of grinding toil has ended in "crucifixion upon a cross of gold."

THE ICONOCLAST AND THE CLERGY.

The Critics Criticized.

Quite a number of pulpiteers have taken the Iconoclast for text and preached therefrom sermons more or less interesting and instructive. Not to be outdone in courtesy, the Iconoclast will briefly discuss the dominies.

Strange as it may appear, the average pulpiteer does not approve of the Iconoclast; stranger still, those who have perorated about it most profusely admit that they have not read it, but condemn it altogether on hearsay evidence and insist that their parishioners shall do likewise. They have heard that it presumes to critize the methods of certain ministers, and, without pausing to inquire whether it be right or wrong, whether it is serving the Deity or the devil, they roll their sanctimonious eyes heavenward and exclaim that another of those "vicious atheistical sheets" which are striving to pull the linch-pin out of the Christian cultus and allow the whole majestic universe to go crashing back into the noisome realm of Chaos and old Night.

The average pulpiteer is a party who persistently stinks for attention. Like the skunk, he compels even nobility to notice him. While the wisest of this world are trying to trace here and there a line in the Heavenly hieroglyphs, "dark with excess of bright;" acknowledging that, strive as they may, they cannot think the thoughts of the Deity— can only grope toward His throne in fear and trembling— the pulpiteer poses as a modern Pallas, to whom the most recondite secrets of the Heavenly Hierarchy are as familiar as the face of the town clock—competent to glibly read every riddle in the vast apocalypse of nature; to interpret every blazing character traced by the unseen finger of God!

* * *

Of course, there are exceptions to this rule; there are to most rules. There is occasionally a minister of whom both his Maker and mankind may well be proud, as there are pedagogues who are somewhat more than parrots and politicians who are really patriots.

In its very first number the Iconoclast threw down the gage of battle to Frauds, Falsehoods and Fakes—and the pulpiteers promptly picked it up! Why? Why is it that at the cry of "stop thief" every purloiner of other people's property turns pale? Perhaps it is not so strange that the average pulpiteer should consider the Iconoclast's denunciation of Shams a personal affront—should feel called upon to assume the defensive!

Were the pulpiteers honestly striving for the salvation of souls, to eliminate evil, to weed falsehood out of the world, would they not welcome as an ally, instead of denouncing as an enemy a journal that tries to teach men to tell the Truth, lead pure lives, eschew vain shows and honor their Creator? Yet, in a world filled with foul wrong and brutal outrage; patrolled day and night by the Demon of Darkness; swept by the hot breath of Lust; reeking with wretchedness; millions of human creatures going down to destruction; society rotten to the core and faith in Almighty God slowly but surely fading from the earth, the pulpiteers pause in their alleged labors for the salvation of souls to drag through the dirt a journal that has the wellnigh unheard of audacity to assail Shams; to belittle and belie it; to pray their parishioners in God's great name to put all their pennies into the contribution plate; to refuse to patronize it—to starve it out.

* * *

The fact is, the pulpiteers want no allies in the work of regenerating the world. They consider that their special province—that they are entitled to all the perquisites it can be made to yield—and they look upon all extraneous aids as interlopers; regard them with the same feeling of commercial jealousy that one pack-peddler does another! That is the secret of the opposition of the pulpit-pounders to even clean Sunday newspapers, the stage and innocent forms of Sunday diversion. They detract from church attendance, lessen the amount of boodle corraled by the contribution boxes. They interfere with the business, with the bread-and-butter getting of the sacerdotal caste, which considers the Sabbath as its harvest time—of ha'-pennies! That is also the secret of the bitter war waged upon each other by the different denominations—they are *business rivals!* If a man go to heaven via the Catholic Route, the Protestant Through Line loses his fare; if he "get religion" at the "mourner's bench" of Methodism, the Episcopalian priesthood figures that it loses so much pew rent; if he fall in with the Campbellite flock the Presbyterian plate passers utter an audible groan!

The rivalry of these various Through Lines is very brisk, but so far there has been no cut in rates! On the contrary, the fiercer the rivalry the higher the fare. Salvation is now only "free" to paupers, and they must travel in fourth-class coaches, usually with a novice or superannuated track-walker pulling the bell cord.

* * *

While there are many men in the ministry who devote their lives unselfishly to the service of the Savior, the above is a true pen-picture of the average pulpiteer, of the minister who was manufactured by an orthodox theological college and stamped with its denominational trade-mark, much as muslin is made in Massachusetts cotton mills. These theological colleges are so many manufactories, warranted to turn out a particular brand of preacher, no matter what the raw material. Would you make an Episcopalian divine, Methodist exhorter or Presbyterian polemic of your young hopeful? There are the mills, all with signs plain to be seen. Throw him into the proper hopper, and take to thyself no trouble regarding the result. The Methodist mill could no more make any other kind of minister than a loom adjusted to weave jeans could turn out calico.

Such are the methods by which ministers are made. No independent inquiry; no search for Truth beyond the narrow confines of a particular creed! And yet these men, warped by education a certain way, unable to recognize a Truth unless stamped with the die of a certain dogma, set themselves up as teachers; presume to interpret the entire Plan of the Infinite; to tell mankind just what the Creator requires of them; are ever ready to measure men with their little one-foot rule—to howl "heretic" when one of their number dares carry his research beyond certain prescribed limits, or attack the Devil with weapons upon which their sect has not set its seal!

* * *

Time was when the ministry was venerated by all men; now it is a by-word and a reproach. It is not that it has become much worse, but that the world has grown wiser, refuses to be longer duped by its hollow pretenses to preternatural prescience or recognize its fiat as final in matters of religion and morals.

It is still an open question which has done most to retard the world's progress, the public pedagogue or the pretentious priest—false education, or arrant hypocrisy. Both have ever stood in the pathway of the car of progress and bade it stand like Joshua's moon in Ajalon; both have filled the world with doleful jeremiads because it would not await their good pleasure—and then toiled slowly, painfully along in its wake, disputing which furnished the power that pushed it forward. There has never been an advance made in theological science; never a death-blow dealt to debasing superstition; never a new Truth declared to the world; never an upward step taken from the weltering chaos of subter-brutishness that the rank and file of the professional pilots from Time to Eternity did not denounce as heterodox, blasphemous, calculated to send souls to Satan! Even to-day the progressive preachers of the various denominations are being denounced, vilified and misrepresented because they persist in learning something, refuse to sit on the dead limb of a decaying orthodoxy and hoot the hoots that awoke the echoes in the dreary days of the English Court of High Commission and the Spanish Inquisition; because they believe that all the truth is of God, and worthy reverence wherever found; will not consent to turn their faces from the Future to the Past, to bob up and down like so many manikins whenever the conference or synod pulls the string.

* * *

One-half the ministers of America continue to desecrate the grave of Paine; to heap calumny upon the dead; to denounce him as an "atheist," as a man who denied the existence of God, when he only called in question some of the cherished traditions of professional dogmatizers—pulled aside the stage scenery of the sacerdotal caste, exposing to the gaze of their dupes the thunder-boxes, lightning machines and bogus terrors. Let it be said of a man that he is an infidel—that he does not swallow, unquestioned, every draught prepared by preachers; does not accept as literally true everything found between the lids of the Bible, and the ministry, instead of attempting by kindly arguments to convince him that he is in error, begins a bitter war of denunciation and misrepresentation; opens the sluice-gates of its vindictive hatred, deluges him with a torrent of "Christian" calumny! He may be honest, brave, charitable; he may put more money in the pockets of the deserving poor than any devout deacon of double his worldly wealth; may clothe the naked and feed the hungry, defend the weak, and make of this weary work-a-day world a pleasant Paradise for wife and children—it matters not! He has called in question the legitimacy of the business by which the preachers thrive, and may expect no mercy—not even simple justice at their hands. If he aspires to office they shriek "anti-Christ" and "infidel;" if he embarks in business they make a bushwhacking boycott upon him; if he prints a book or paper the public is warned not to read it—lest it learn something!

* * *

In olden times preachers were presumed to be "holy men" —men from whose natures worldly dross had been purged by penance and prayer. They were regarded not only as teachers, but exemplars—better, purer, truer, more God-like than common mortals. Does any, even the most ignorant, suppose them to be so now? Is there a man so simple that he would put his young daughter in the power of the average preacher more readily than that of other men? Is there a banker who would discount the unsecured note of a preacher more readily than of an infidel? Is it not true that the penitentiaries contain as large a proportion of preachers as of other professional classes, and that many a one now occupying a prominent pulpit would, if justice were done, be wearing stripes? Have they shown superior learning, purity, generosity, forbearance? Is it not true, and so recognized by the world, that the *odium theologicum* is even more virulent than the *odium medicum?* Then, how comes it that they arrogate to themselves the position of exemplars, and resent even kindly and well-meant criticism as presumptuous.

* * *

By what right do they pronounce the Iconoclast "a publication inspired by Satan?" By whom and when were they made infallible? Does not the Book which they pretend to reverence, say, "Judge not lest ye be judged?" How comes it that the ministry has never turned its attention to purifying the daily press, but feels flattered to find its sermons sandwiched in among swindling and unclean advertisements? Why is it that when the press is seized with one of its periodical attacks of moral hysteria, and commences a crusade on prostitutes, it appeals to the pulpit in vain for aid? Is it not true that the clergy are restrained by the consideration that many of their best paying parishioners, of their most liberal patrons are the landlords, the silent partners of prostitutes, and divide their gains with them—giving a portion thereof to the support of popular preachers?

Is it not true that in the manufacture of homilies the clergy consider more what will make their ministry popular, the contributions large, the pew rent prolific, than what will snatch brands from the burning, save souls from the clutches of Satan? Is it not true that the greater proportion of the preachers now toiling more or less assiduously in the Lord's vineyard were tempted thither by hope of earthly reward or the attractions of a lazy life? Is it not true that many of them are narrow-brained bigots or hypocritical frauds and fakirs, and consequently legitimate game for a journal devoted to the destruction of Shams? Is it not true that each and every one belonging to the above named classes will now rail at the Iconoclast louder and longer than ever, while the true and faithful servants of the Saviour will go quietly on with their labors, never suspecting that this article is intended to cast any discredit upon them or the cause of their Master? Is it not the galled jade that winces?

A WAIL FROM THE A. P. A.

CRITICISING THE ICONOCLAST.

Editor Iconoclast: Having for several years been a reader of the Iconoclast, I am constrained at this late day to take issue with you respecting an article appearing in the July number of your magazine, under the caption: "Catholic vs. Protestant Cranks." I take issue with you, not because I am a Protestant, but rather despite the fact that I am not. I am of neither persuasion, but believe in giving the devil his due. That you should espouse the cause of "Romanism" is a thing not only to be discredited, but likewise to be marveled at. And yet from the tenor of the article in question one can only conclude that such is the fact. I shall not speak disparagingly of anything good or commendable that the Catholic church may have accomplished in this world. A good deed will always outlive a bad creed. I am addressing myself to the foundation of Romanism. It claims to be the only true interpretation of Christ's teachings or Christianity and regards all other sects as being unbelievers and traitors to the cause of Christianity. From the fact that the columns of your magazine are not open to contributors, I harbor the inference that you do not invite criticism. Be this as it may, journalistic courtesy should prompt you to give even a dissenter, whether religious or political, a fair hearing through the columns of the Iconoclast, and I trust you will do as much for me. But to return to the issue. From the article in reference I glean enough to convince me that you are either an avowed champion or an apologist in the cause of Romanism. Whether you are this from personal convictions or for personal and pecuniary gain, is no affair of mine. Your abuse and denunciation of certain advocates and leaders of the well known A. P. A. were, I opine, quite amiss. In doing this you are waging a warfare upon persons, not principles. Abuse is no argument and to indulge in disparaging personalities were not elegant. It is certainly evident to you that the Catholic church in this country openly violates the constitution by demanding a portion of the free school fund for the support of their parochial schools. Will you please explain why Catholics persistently attempt to have nuns placed in our public schools as teachers, whereas it is a notorious fact that Catholics regard the public schools as institutions of ignominy and hot beds of infidelity? And, furthermore, why is it requested that they (the nuns) be permitted to wear their convent garb? Please tell us this rather than dilate upon the alleged colloquy between Luther and the Prince of Darkness! If perchance you should be harassed with doubt as to the veracity of these statements, I can adduce sufficient evidence to verify the same. And facts that may or can be established by strong and sufficient evidence should not be discredited. It is, furthermore, a notable fact that all nuns and communicants of the Catholic church are bound by allegiance to an infallible (?) Pope. Any one subject to the authority of any foreign potentate or power can not, in my opinion, at the same time, be a loyal and patriotic citizen of this great commonwealth, unless he be traitor to his religious convictions. It is incumbent upon you as an advocate and champion of the rights and liberties of the American people, and as an outspoken enemy of all that encroach upon our Constitution, to raise the lance in warfare against them. You have as much as asserted that it is your lifework to fight frauds, humbugs and their kindred. In doing this you should not allow sectarian preferences to influence you. A Catholic fraud is as bad as a Protestant humbug, and vice versa. In your reply to the anonymous screed which appeared in the July number of the Iconoclast, I note the following: "I am not aware that they (speaking of supernal visions) are doing the world any serious damage; and the Iconoclast assails only those things which it believes to be really detrimental." Now, since this is your honest purpose and intention, why do you not assail an institution which is trying to undermine the public school system of our country? You should evince enough fairness to swallow the Catholic whale if you persist in straining at an insignificant Protestant little gnat. Once you pose as a disciple of John the Baptist, and in the next breath you denounce the sect that received its name from this distinguished scriptual personage.

"*Tempora mutantur, et nos mutamur cum illis.*

GEO. C. KNOLL.

Wiemar, Texas, *en route,* July 20, 1896.

Having read the Iconoclast so long, has my correspondent yet to learn that with the dogmatical dispute between Protestantism and Catholicism it has nothing to do? "Romanism" may claim what it likes in matters theological, and "Lutherism" deny it until the crack o' doom for aught I care. I concern myself only with their deeds, leaving to others the disputation anent the respective merits of their *creeds*. Pope expresses my sentiments exactly when he says:

> "For modes of faith let graceless zealots fight;
> His can't be wrong whose life is in the right."

I care never a copper whether people regard the Pope as the Vicar of Christ or anti-Christ, so long as their theology, does not prompt them to interfere with my religious privileges or political prerogatives. A man sufficiently learned to successfully assume the role of critic, should know that an editor who—"whether from personal convictions or for pecuniary gain"—becomes "an avowed champion or apologist in the cause of Romanism," would scarce give his journal a name so distasteful to the Catholic Church. I am, sir, an "avowed champion" of *every* religion that has pierced Life's dark shadows with one ray of sunshine. I am an "avowed champion" of every American citizen whose civic rights are invaded because of his religious convictions. Should the Catholic conspire to exclude from the honors and emoluments of office either Protestants, Jews, or Agnostics, because of their supposed theological heresy, I would never cease denouncing them until either I or the damnable conspiracy were dead. In the dozen years of my editorial ministry I have assailed no religious faith, howsoever much I may have criticised its professors. A man's theology is his own affair, his political acts are the concern of every citizen. It was only with the *political* phase of this organized warfare upon Catholicism that I concern myself. Nor do I pretend to unselfish patriotism. If the civic rights of Catholics are circumscribed, may not Jews and Agnostics next fall under the ban? May not I wake up some morning and find myself ineligible for office, because I am a disciple of John the Baptist, instead of John Calvin? Once this proscription begins, where will it end? "Eternal vigilance is the price of liberty." In assisting the Catholics to preserve their rights, I strike a blow in defense of my own freedom.

I was not hitherto aware that the A. P. A.'s considered "abuse and denunciation" as cardinal sins. If it be a grievous error into which I have fallen, it is the fault of their own bad example. The A. P. A.'s are the Thersitæ of the century. The advocates of no other cause depend so much on denunciation and so little on logic. They cannot speak of the Catholic church without coupling it with a curse, nor mention the Pope without a malediction. And do members of this order, which has filled the land with the fumes of sulphuric acid, complain that I have proven too apt a pupil—that my vocabulary of invective is abnormal? Disparaging personalities are not to be commended—but who began the thing? I was combatting the principles of the order well within the pale of polemical courtesy when these modern Chesterfields proceeded to serve me much as the Yahoos did the unfortunate Gulliver. Nor did they stop at "abuse and denunciation." They were not content with outcursing Caliban and overdoing Termagant, but resorted to the scurrilous methods of the pot-house politician, "answered" my courteously worded objections to their order much as Sid Williams did the criticisms of Ingersoll—by the deliberate concoction of stupid calumnies. And must I retort with the soft answer that turneth away wrath, while spewed upon by such featherless buzzards, such moral hyenas as Slattery and Hicks? I could never make a success in the role of other-cheek Christian. Like Sancho Panza, I object to having my face handled by hoodlums. That's why I have unearthed the records of some of the arch-angels of this great "American order." It might be well for the A. P. A.'s to get the bridge beams out of their own eyes before reaching for the diatoms in the optics of others.

I may presume that a man who "gives the devil his due" would not deliberately create a false impression regarding even the Catholics. Now will Mr. Knoll kindly turn to his copy of the Federal Constitution and inform us what article and section these dangerous Romanists "openly violate by demanding a portion of the free school fund for the support of their parochial schools?" I am unalterably opposed to such diversion of the free school fund—even in a community where the Catholics pay nine-tenths of the taxes; but before shelling the Vatican and assassinating the papal legate, I want to know wherein such "demand" is subversive of the fundamental law of the land. Because I disapprove a thing it does not follow, as a matter of course, that it's either *malum in se* or unconstitutional. What in the name of Lindley Murray has the Federal Government to do with the school system of a sovereign state? It doesn't even prohibit Texas setting up a religious establishment and supporting it by general taxation. The public school fund of Texas is the property of the people, to do with as seemeth unto them best. The Catholics, as a portion of the people, have a right to be heard in the matter, but must bow to the will of the majority. So long as they do the latter they are patriotic Americans, true to the principles of democracy. They have as much right to ask that nuns be employed as teachers and that they be permitted to wear their convent garb as I have to ask the appointment of Baylor graduates and that they be compelled to wear bloomers. It must be remembered that the American citizen—of whatsoever creed or no creed—is a sovereign to the extent of his vote and influence. He has perfect right to urge the enactment of such laws as he may like, whether state or national, and the amendment of all charters and constitutions that may do violence to his opinions. If the Catholics regard the public schools as "hot beds of infidelity" can they be blamed for urging the employment of teachers "sound in the faith?" Does my correspondent consider it a crime for Catholics to combat infidelity here at home while we Protestants spend millions of dollars in our fruitless tussle with it abroad?

And why, pray, am not I privileged to dilate upon the *historical* "colloquy between Luther and the Prince of Darkness," when worthy A. P. A.'s complain to me of the celestial visions seen by Catholic virgins? Have I no right to comfort the souls of Protestants by citing the history of our great prototype as evidence that it is no sin to dream dreams and see visions? Suppose that Satan should suddenly appear to my correspondent. Would he not be pleased to know that his visitor was eligible for A. P. A. membership—having induced Luther to counsel the assassination of the Pope? Nay, sir; you shall not thus summarily deprive me of my occupation as counsellor and consoler to the Protestant clergy. But please tell us something more about the Constitution "rather than dilate upon the alleged" endeavor of the Catholics to stamp infidelity out of the public schools. State, I prithee, for the benefit of a benighted editor—who has failed to worship at the sacred shrine of Whiskey Bill Traynor and absorb his patriotism from unfrocked Irish priests who apostrophize the British flag—to what kind of "foreign potentate or power all communicants of the Catholic church owe allegiance." Is he some Cæsar or Alexander with vast armies and navies at his command? or is he a frail old man, having kings and princes for his subjects in matters spiritual, yet bowing to the authority of the humblest magistrate in matters temporal? What have the religious convictions of a Catholic to do with his political allegiance? Cannot I recognize the sovereignty of Christ Jesus without getting up in the middle of the night and pulling the tail feathers out of the American eagle? Catholics regard the Pope simply as the representative on earth of One who said, "Render unto Cæsar the things that are Cæsar's and unto God the things that are God's." If the Pope be eager for temporal power, and all Catholics owe him paramount allegiance in matters political as well as spiritual, why doesn't he grab Italy, France, Mexico and all the nations of South America and set up a new and greater Roman Empire? Why doesn't he take his 235,000,000 subservient janizaries and conquer the earth? If the A. P. A.'s be telling the truth, the Pope could blot Protestantism out of existence, subdue all political opposition and rule the world with a rod of iron! Excuse me! I don't mind tackling a bucking broncho, but I'm tampering with no earthquakes! As "a champion of the rights and liberties of the American people" I do not propose to raise the "lance of warfare" against the Pope unless he crowds me.

And why should I, as a Protestant, war on Catholicism any more than a homeopathic doctor would take a fall out of Hippocrates? It may be antiquated, but it is respectable. It constituted our only hope of salvation for long ages before we succeeded in evolving the holiness fad, the campmeeting jerks, or even the blessed doctrine of the Anabaptists, just as the old-school practitioners were our refuge in measles and mumps ere the dawn of Christian Science, the coming of Schrader or the invention of the microbe mitrailleuse.

It is well to sometimes remember that but for these selfsame Catholics we might have no beloved constitution to worry about. When they wrung the Magna Charta from King John they became the grandsires of the American Government. True, we are not altogether indebted to them for the development of our institutions; but the part played by them in our great national drama has been very important. They decreed religious liberty in the new world—whether before or after the Roger Williams' rescript is of no particular moment. They were among the first—if not indeed the first—to move for the independence of the American colonies. They sanctioned—and signed—the Declaration. They poured their treasure into the coffers of the new-born nation and their blood upon its battlefields with an enthusiasm that called forth a letter of thanks from even the phlegmatic Washington. Many prominent

Catholics, like Baron de Kalb and Marquis de Lafayette, crossed the sea to fight for American liberty. When all seemed lost, Catholic France sent her chivalric sons to draw about the cradle of liberty a lethal circle with the sword. In our own day American Catholics have ever been ready to set foot as far as who goes farthest in defense of the old flag. I don't give a d—n what may be their creeds about "allegiance to a foreign potentate or power;" there's the *record* of my Catholic countrymen—seamed with fire and sealed with blood! With that before me, it will require something more than prattle about nuns, frocks and "hotbeds of infidelity" to silence the guns I have aligned upon the Guy Fawkes' conspiracy engineered by the A. P. A.

And can I not be a devout disciple of John the Baptist without approving all the practices of a people who have adopted his agnomen—perhaps to signify that they have no head? John was something of an iconoclast himself, and—like his Lord—somewhat addicted to "denunciation." I can but wonder that his allusion to the eminently respectable Pharisees and Sadducees as a "generation of vipers" has not called forth a withering rebuke from honey-tongued A. P. A. orator. Albeit he was somewhat addicted to "abuse," I heartily approve his creed and cheerfully commend it to those whom religious intolerance has led to depart from time-honored American principles. "Repent ye—every tree which bringeth not forth good fruit is hewn down and cast into the fire." That's all there is to it—and it's enough.

I have fought the A. P. A. from its inception; not that I approve the Catholic creed, but because I approve that clause in the constitution which declares that no religious test shall ever be required as a qualification to any office or public trust under the United States; not that I accept either Papal Infallibility or the Apostolic Succession; but because it were a violation of the principle of liberty, equality and fraternity—our political trinity—to circumscribe the rights of the humblest citizen because of his religious opinions. The privilege of defending my own prerogatives obligates me to sacredly respect the rights of others.

If I have exhibited aught of "sectarian preference" it was not altogether my fault. As a citizen, I place our political constitution above all religious creeds—the rights of life above the hopes of death. I have judged Protestantism and Catholicism—as political forces—not so much by reading their professions as by observing their practice. For ten years the Protestant clergy have waged unrelenting warfare upon me for presuming to exercise the American prerogative of free speech—for disagreeing with them have denounced me with far more vigor than they brought to bear on the devil. They have demanded my discharge from editorial positions and advocated boycotts on newsdealers who handled papers on which I was employed. Yet I never spoke disparagingly of their religion or denied their Deity— I simply criticised people who confess themselves "the chiefs of sinners" and "poor miserable worms of the dust." I have dissented from Catholicism also, but its priesthood have ever treated my rights as a citizen with the utmost respect. Doubtless the Pope would place many of my articles in the *Index Expurgatorius;* but no Catholic priest or prelate has ever tried to deprive me of employment or to injure my business by means of that most cowardly of all un-American weapons, the contemptible boycott. Reasoning by induction, how could I avoid the conclusion that Catholicism is far more friendly than is Protestantism to intellectual liberty—to "freedom of speech and freedom of the press?" When I find prominent in the councils of the A. P. A., men who, for years past, have striven to suppress my pen and seal my lips for questioning their theological infallibility, am I likely to look to that order for the preservation of my American prerogatives, and turn, like a wolfish hound upon those who never planned me harm? Believing—with such cogent reason—that the A. P. A. is a conspiracy against liberty of conscience, is it not my duty to war upon it to the death—to denounce its every advocate as a potential Benedict Arnold, a political Judas Iscariot? And must I be careful not to wound the sensibilities of these teachers of high treason, these political heretics? Should I regale them with oil of Smyrna and honey of Hymettus? No; I prefer to imitate the example of our Lord, and scourge with a whip of cords those who would make the temple of my fathers a den of thieves.

I put it to you, sir, and to every member of your order: could a devout Catholic, even tho' his ancestors were at Runnymede and penned Maryland's first proclamation of religious toleration; even tho' his gran'sire signed the Declaration and helped frame the Federal Constitution; even tho' he had sacrificed his fortune and risked his life in defense of our liberties—could such a Catholic, I say be elected president of this country? You know he could not. You know that a Catholic wife would be an almost insurmountable handicap to even a lineal descendant of Cromwell or Calvin. And why? Protestant prejudice. Yet in those cities, counties and districts—both in Europe and America—where Catholics predominate, Protestants are frequently advanced to the post of honor. Could "Pagan Bob" Ingersoll be elected president? He could not. Why? Protestant prejudice—the admixture of religion and politics by those clamoring for "complete separation of church and state." We know that Ingersoll is a man of superior intellect. His patriotism is above suspicion. The Constitution is his Bible, the Declaration his Confession of Faith. While Cleveland was saving the country by proxy and wiping away the tears of buxom widows, Ingersoll, at the head of 800 Illinois troopers was cutting his way thro' Forest's redoubtable cavalry corps numbering more than 8,000 men. Were he nominated for chief magistrate, Jews, Agnostics and Catholics would promptly divide on political lines. They would not ask his opinion of the Immaculate Conception, but rather his position on the tariff and currency, and act accordingly, but the Protestants would mass against him almost to a man, regardless of political predilections. Three-fourths of their preachers would thunder at him from the pulpit, while the Epworth Leaguers and Christian Endeavorers, the Y. M. C. A. and B. Y. P. U. would all sweat their boots full of blood. The Pastors' Association of Dallas would stand appalled; Sam Jones would predict the Day of Judgment and Doc Talmage fall into the opening of his own face; while all the sectarian advertising grafts, like Hayden's *Holy Fake* and Cranfill's *Weekly Slumgullion* bristled with double-leaded diatribes against the damning disgrace of making an Agnostic chief magistrate of a "Christian country." Don't you know they would? Don't you know that J. D. Shaw—as stainless a man as God ever made, couldn't be elected Governor of Texas tho' he possessed the combined statecraft of Washington and Webster, Clay and Calhoun—simply because he doesn't know so much about God as does Sin-Killer Griffin? Don't you know that the A. P. A. would vote almost solidly against him—while belly-aching about religious liberty and damning the Catholics for objecting to casting their children into "hot-beds of infidelity?" Don't you know that if the Protestant priesthood could have its way, it would transform this nation into an intolerant theocracy and disfranchise every Jew and Catholic, every Atheist and Agnostic—"for the glory of God?" If you do not, you have read the signs of the times as inattentively as you have the Constitution. *Auf wiedersehen.*

BEHIND THE SMOKESTACK.

A Talk With Trainmen.

For some time past railway employees have been forwarding to this office specimens of politico-financial literature distributed among them, and requesting that it be subjected to impartial analysis. From the tenor of the letters received, I infer that the million of American railway employees are, to a considerable extent, undecided what would make to their best interests in matters monetary, and honestly desire an expression of opinion by a strictly non-partisan journal. I cannot presume to speak authoritatively on any question regarding which so many men of acknowledged ability and integrity disagree; but I can examine the literature submitted and state whether it conforms to conceded economic facts. For many years I have made a careful study of the science of money; not with a view to bolstering up any pre-conceived theory, but in the humble hope that my conclusions might be absolutely correct. I have invariably found that the men most rabid for or against any proposed monetary system, are those who received their education in such matters from heated political orations and the special pleadings of a partisan press. Graduates of such a school are usually impudently intolerant of dissenting opinion. They know exactly what should be done—another illustration of the axiom that "a little learning is a dangerous thing;" but the man who, for long years has sweat blood over the standard works of political economy and the industrial history of nations, isn't so cock-sure. He is willing to admit that there are two sides to every shield. Savants disagree so radically on almost every proposition, the experience of various countries has been so divergent, that he stands, like another Hamlet, lost in his own irresolution.

Many of the specimens of monetary literature sent me by trainmen bear the imprint of the *Railway Age,* and are evidently intended to grossly deceive those whose arduous duties leave them insufficient time for an exhaustive study of the currency question. The *Age* is trying to convince railway employes that free silver means their industrial destruction—striving desperately to drive them, like a flock of frightened sheep, into the McKinley shambles. The *Age* has a perfect right to plead for the gold standard if it deems best, but is not privileged to resort to the persuasive methods of the Malayan pirate, or to reinforce its argument with falsehood. Of course—like Desdemona—it "may be honest;" but it is certainly not supplying Mark Hanna with so many tons of literature at its own cost. If it has entered into a compact to exert its very considerable influence as a class journal to deliver the railway vote to McKinley; if it is grinding out campaign literature for a consideration, then it is simply a disreputable decoy, whose every statement should be regarded with profound distrust. The methods adopted by the *Age* are not calculated to inspire confidence that it is incorruptible. I cull the following excerpt from a card bearing its imprint, and which I am creditably informed the employes of various railways have been notified by the general managers to "either sign or decline to do so." This simply means, if not the merest baby-play—to which railway managers are not much addicted—that men who refuse to sign this card may look for an early "lay-off," without time limit. This is certainly a much more satisfactory way of "bringing the men to their senses" than undisguised coercion of American citizens, which might result in a very disagreeable revolt.

Notice: This is a statement of my personal reasons for being opposed to the Free Coinage of Silver:

1. Because my present pay won't quite enable me to buy everything on earth, and I have no desire to have that pay cut in two.
2. Because I prefer to have what few dollars I earn worth 100 cents apiece, not 53 cents.
3. Because I do not see why I should be any better off if the price of everything I had to buy was doubled.
4. Because I have no idea it would profit me if the whole country went bankrupt.
5. Because, though the ratio may now be 16 men out of work to 1 who has a job, I do not desire to swell the ratio by turning tramp myself.
6. Because, though I do not happen to be general manager of this road, I am still no blooming fool.

I freely concede that a railway employe might attach his signature to the foregoing symposium of financial folly without being a "blooming fool." Having a family to support, and feeling morally certain that the slightest exhibition of political independence would cause the loss of his situation, he might sacrifice his manhood rather than see his loved ones suffer. True, only weaklings could thus cower before the grim spectre of Want; the man with iron in his blood would make answer that 'twere better that children should die in the faith that they were sired by sovereigns, than live in the knowledge that they were spawned by slaves. One may sell his political birthright for a mess of pottage without being a "blooming fool;" but I cheerfully undertake to demonstrate that the author of the card is a blooming burgeoning, ebullient ass, who can easily fan himself with his ears. The idea floating about in his majestic mind is that free-coinage of silver would, by doubling the price of all products, bankrupt the country and leave devil a thing for the railway man to do. This idea is the pivot around which all gold-bug arguments revolve. I sometimes think the McKinley magpies have rehearsed this ridiculous romance until they believe it appears somewhere in the Bible. To see them all weeping and wailing around Mark Hanna—protective tariff baron and professional wrecker of labor unions—because of the enhanced price of everything the workman has to buy, were enough to wring the briny from a terra-cotta bust of Sitting Bull.

Doubling the price of the products of farm, and mine and factory, would, as the veriest tyro in political economy knows, powerfully stimulate production. Millions of acres of land that have long lain fallow would come under cultivation, the flocks and herds increase, new mines vomit forth their hidden wealth, the roar of long-silent furnaces and the hum of new factories be heard in the land. Every transportation line would be taxed to its utmost limit. All the antiquated engines capable of turning a wheel would be pressed into service, every old "flat-footed" box refurbished and sent pounding down the long lines of shimmering steel. There would be a tremendous demand for labor—employers would bid against each other until the wage rate in every calling reached the highest point the business would bear. Who said so? Every standard authority on political economy for 200 years—excepting only the editor of the *Age*. It is a lesson taught in the school of experience—that academy where even "blooming fools" are supposed to be educated. The *Age* editor takes issue with all the experience of the past and all the wisdom of the present in declaring that free silver would double prices, and, at the same time, send us industrially to the devil. According to his theory, carried to its legitimate conclusion, all we need to become wonderfully prosperous is one-cent cotton and five-cent corn. That is the genuine gold-bug idea, to benefit the poor by decreasing the cost of everything they have to purchase—by electing Protective Tariff McKinley president! The *Age* editor wants a high tariff to push the price of American products up, and a gold standard to push it down—all for the benefit of the poor brakeman. But he is only playing on the currency string at present. When the country comes to one-cent cotton and five-cent corn, the railway employe will be right "in the push." 'Cause why? He can feed and clothe himself at so little cost—his salary will enable him to "buy everything on earth." And being on a gold basis, of course there won't be the slightest danger of its being "cut in two." If an engineer receives $4 a day when corn is 50 cents a bushel, he'll get no more if it goes to a dollar, no less if it slumps to a dime. While on a gold basis, everything has a tendency to decline in price except the labor of the railway employe! A man with such ideas as that ought to consult an alienist.

This remarkable mental homunculus who lays down economic law for the poor benighted railway employe, will doubtless attempt to crawfish out of his awkward predicament by saying he meant that free-silver would increase prices nominally, but not actually. Reference to paragraphs 2 and 3 of his card will demonstrate that he meant nothing of the kind; that the idea he meant to convey, and he did convey, was that free-silver would both reduce the purchasing power of the dollar to 53 cents in gold, while doubling the price, as measured by the yellow metal, of all that the railway employe must purchase. To interpret the two propositions in any other manner were to reduce them to the merest drivel. I am charitable enough to concede that —despite the abnormal length of his ears—he would not file a kick with both hind feet because, under free coinage, workmen would give two pieces of metal worth 50 cents each, for what they now give one worth 100 cents each— because it would still require two pints to make a quart, two halves to make a whole. He is on record either as urging that free-silver would double the price of all American products, and at the same time create universal bankruptcy and turn railway employes into tramps, else as making a foolish roar because a man, having a piece of metallic property, could not exchange it for that worth twice as much. He may take either horn of the dilemma he likes.

But let us give him an opportunity to "saw-by," to "take the slack" and get over the grade. In railroading, the "boys" are very careful of new beginners, and the same rule should obtain in economics. We will concede that he is really trying to say that the silver would have only about one-half the purchasing power of the present gold dollar —that it would require two of the former to obtain what can now be had for one of the latter; in other words, that prices of products would remain really as now, but would be nominally doubled when measured by the white metal. So free-silver is not to affect actual prices—they will remain even as they are now; and while they so remain how can there be any marked change in industrial conditions? From whence is to arise that forbidding cloud which will envelop us in universal bankruptcy? An era of panic and general bankruptcy, synchronous with stationary prices, were a miracle never yet witnessed by mortal man. It were an effect without a cause. I have often wished I could think the thoughts of Infinity—and here am I, trying to analyze the amorphous ideas of an ass.

He lays it down as financial law and economic gospel that, under the new dispensation, you would receive exactly the same number of "50-cent" silver dollars for labor that you now get "100-cent" gold dollars; ergo, your wages—or their purchasing power, which is the same thing—would be greatly reduced. In other words, railway labor is to be the one lone, lorn sufferer by free-silver. The farmer who now gets 40 cents gold for his corn, will receive its equivalent, or 80 cents silver, and cannot kick. The planter, instead of 7 cents gold will get 14 cents silver for his cotton, and go bury his sorrow. The carpenter, who will now build your house for two gold-basis dollars per day, will receive four blonde jinglers and go on his way rejoicing. You will pay 30 cents for a shave, because the gold basis has been knocked from under the pale metal, and it stands on its own bottom. Your cook lady will demand a double salary as measured in silver, and your wash-lady wants two-bits for starching the tail of your Sunday shirt. The railway sandwich will cost you 20 cents and the cannon-ball doughnuts scoff at your dime. The milk man will raise the price of the product of his pump, your butcher, baker and candlestick maker just double their bills. But in this general equalization of prices, this doubling up of "50-cent dollars" to secure to all others their present purchasing power, nobody will care for the down-trodden conductor, the autocrat of the locomotive will be left out in the cold. Whether out of this wreck and wraith the Pullman porter will rise triumphant, like an ebony phoenix from the ashes, deponent saith not. Just why the trainman is to be side-tracked at a flag-station with a dead engine, I was unable to understand until I had waded through the more pretentious economic efforts sent out by the *Age* for the world's enlightment. From its "Sound Money Talks to Railway Men—No. 1," I learn that, "within six months after the enactment of a free-coinage law, every railway company in this country will be unable to meet its interest payments, and go into bankruptcy." I give him a chance to make you shiver.

"The gold wherewith to meet charges will not be obtainable in this country and will only be obtainable in Europe by paying for it in silver at the ruling market rate for bullion—not our 16 to 1 ratio, but the ratio of the London bullion market. Every American railway would have to pay every cent of its gold obligations (about) twice over. I say "about," because there is no knowing where the bullion price of silver would go to. And there is no railway in the country which could do that. In the struggle to do it there would be such a cutting of wages and forces as we have never yet dreamed of."

So it appears that railway companies, as well as their employes, will go thro' the financial trestle, weakened by the free-silver flood. Why? Because they will have to carry great ship-loads of our silver to Europe and with it buy gold to meet the interest on their bonds—will have to pay every cent of their obligations "about twice over." The *Age* editor quotes—in a yaller-back pamphlet accompanying his "Talks"—President Ashley of the Wabash as saying that the American railways are mortgaged for 5 billion dollars, principal and interest—the latter aggregating 250 millions per annum—payable in gold. Now boys, line up alongside o' this box-car and let us test the wisdom of our new Solomon.

The proposition is that we will have to send abroad every year enough silver bullion to purchase 250 millions of gold, with which to meet interest charges on railway mortgages. We now have 500 million of silver coin. At bullion rates that would secure the necessary gold for one year. Once abroad it would not come back because worth no more here under free coinage—so say the gold-bugs—than anywhere else. We produce less than 100 millions of silver a year, coin value; less than 50 million bullion value. Of this we use one-tenth in the arts. Now where in God's name are we going to get silver the second year with which to buy in Europe 250 millions of gold? And if we send abroad all the silver we can rake and scrape, to buy gold to pay interest on our railway bonds, from whence is to come that awful avalanche of 53-cent dollars which is to wreck our industries? But suppose that we can produce the requisite amount of silver with which to purchase 250 millions of gold every year and turn it loose in the land: In 10 years we'll have a gold currency of $2,500,000,000. Hully gee! The free silverites seem to be the only sure-enough gold standard men after all. While Cleveland has been worrying about the "reserve," and haunted by the free-silver bogey, Teller, Peffer, et al have concocted a scheme whereby all the troublesome white metal will be unloaded on Europe, while Uncle Sam runs a corner on the gold of the world! "But hold," says somebody in the crowd; "big blocks of that 5 billion o' bonds are held in Europe. These will drain us of both gold and silver." Don't open your throttle till you get the signal! This nation is mortgaged for some 15 billions—gold. The real estate and railway mortgages amount to nearly 12 billions, to say nothing of the federal, state and municipal funded debts. About two-thirds of these securities are held here at home; hence, if our gold goes abroad, and we buy it with our silver to meet interest charges, we will have to bring two-thirds of our purchase to America, or some 500 millions annually—the exact amount we now have in circulation! But let us find another car and tackle the problem from a different point. "Figures won't lie"—but there's lot o' romance in them. We now have the blessed gold standard, and are expected to believe that the annual interest charge on some 15 billions of mortgages are paid in the yellow metal. About 5 billions of these securities being held abroad, it follows that we send to Europe 250 millions of gold annually. Now we produce an average of about 35 millions of gold per year, of which we use 8 millions in the arts. Yet, while steadily exporting 9 times our annual product available as an exchange medium, we have managed to accumulate 556 millions! Talk about the miracle of the loaves and fishes! Why it wasn't in it a little bit with the financial thaumaturgy of Uncle Sam! Mark you, I am simply working out the prize "examples" which I find in the monetary arithmetic used by the *Age* editor and President Ashley. I think it might be a good idea for these distinguished economists to "verify their running orders." They're liable to telescope their logical sequence.

I only proposed to prove the *Age* editor a "blooming ass;" but as he's a fine large animal, I'll ride him a little further. A vast amount of American securities are held in foreign countries; but the annual interest charge thereon is not paid in either our gold or silver coin, but in cattle and hogs, cotton and corn. In 1896 we sent to Great Britain goods to the value of nearly 400 millions and received from that country merchandise valued at less than 160 millions. Did 240 millions of British gold come to this country to settle the balance? Have you seen any of it? From all the nations of the earth combined we imported but 35 millions of gold that year, exported to all combined but 66 millions — and these trifling imports and exports of the precious metal were chiefly for speculative purposes. That

240 millions, which England apparently owed us at the end of the year, was largely applied to the payment of interest on our foreign indebtedness. Europe doesn't want our gold; it wants our goods, and when it buys our securities that is what it expects to get—knows it to be the only thing it can get. When England "lends us money," does she give us gold? Nit!—she lends us her credit.

If the free coinage of silver should really drive gold abroad, and we needed it to meet interest on mortgages, what then? The *Age* says we can get it by selling silver at the market price in London. Then why worry? If we obtain the market price for our bullion, how are we robbed? And if we can obtain gold by selling silver bullion, can we not get it by selling beef? And when we sell our products for their full value in the world's markets and apply the proceeds to the discharge of our gold obligations, how in the name of Socrates do you figure it out that we "pay every cent of our obligations twice over?" Will the editor of the *Age* explain how we get gold now, either here or in Europe, except by selling something? Some obtain it by selling peanuts to the people, some by selling their labor to railway corporations, and some by selling their souls to Mark Hanna. We are solemnly assured that "gold is the basis of our currency system, the mainstay of our credit." Why, all the gold we've got would not pay the expenses of government, federal, state and municipal, so long as it took the *Age* editor to write himself down an economic idiot. There are ten men in this country who could corner all we've got. Suppose they should decide it to their interest to do so, and should bury it and forget to mark the spot: Wouldn't this nation be in a hell of a fix? Is it really possible for a street-car load of men to everlastingly wreck this, the wealthiest, most progressive and powerful nation in the world, by gathering up all its pound weights? Yet our dollar measure of value is really of no more importance than our pound measure of quantity—we are no whit more dependent upon it for our prosperity. Were they both taken we would quickly devise other trade tools. "Our gold will go abroad!" Not unless somebody wants it worse than we do—and will give more for it. Why does any American product go abroad? Isn't it because it makes to our profit to assist its departure?

All this prattle about free silver giving us a depreciated dollar and wrecking our industries, is the merest moonshine. Who says so? Every gold-bug orator and editor in this country solemnly declares it. Cleveland, McKinley and Col. Dan Malvin all frankly admit it. There are one million railroaders in this country. Suppose that half of them should go to Europe and forget to come back; that it would require 15 years to fill their places, the railways increasing both their mileage and their tonnage all the time: What would be the effect on the railway wage rate? Would it go up or down? You know it would jump like a jack-rabbit that had inadvertently gone to roost on a red ant hill. Very well: Now it is an axiom of economists that the purchasing power of money is affected like the wage-rate—by the supply relative to the demand. Money must do the exchange work of this country just as you do its railway work. When there are more men than jobs the tendency of the wage rate is downward; when there are more jobs than men the tendency is upward. When there is more money than business its purchasing power decreases, because it all presses for employment; when there is more business than money its purchasing power increases. We will say that we have 556 millions of gold and 500 millions of silver coin: That, according to the gold-bugs, is all the real money we've got, our paper dollars being simply checks issued against it. What do Messrs. Cleveland, McKinley and Malvin say would be the immediate effect of opening our mints to silver? The banishment of gold—the contraction of our volume of real money more than one-half. They further assert that it would require from 15 to 20 years to accumulate enough silver coin to fill the hiatus caused by the expatriation of the "yellow-boys"—and our population and volume of commerce constantly increasing. In other words, 1-2 billion of money would have to do the money work now performed by a billion, just as 1-2 million railroaders would have to do the railway work of this country if the other half went away. The inference is dead easy: If coin be in fact the basis of our currency—as they claim—reducing its volume one-half would double the present purchasing power of the dollar. It has been time and again conceded by the wisest economists of the world; it has been time and again demonstrated by actual experience that, no matter of what the exchange media be made, its purchasing power will be enhanced by a reduction of its volume relative to the exchange work to be done. Twisting a brake is one way of making money out of a railway; there are others. It is sometimes more profitable to bring about conditions that enable the "railway magnates" to freeze out the small stockholder—of whom we are hearing so much at present

—than to increase the tonnage of a road and swell the ranks of the industrial army. Pawnbrokers thrive best when the people are "broke"—and the great capitalists and mortgage companies are simply *doing a pawnbroking* business.

I am privileged to speak plainly to the railway men of America, for I have served a term "behind the smokestack." I did not get my railway experience in the political department. I was never wound up by professional railway "wreckers" and sent forth to tell the man in the grimy jacket how to vote if he desires to retain his situation. I may not know so much about the currency question as do those supplying "industrial cannibals" with campaign literature; still I feel like warning my old companions in cab and caboose of the slick artists now trying to play them for rank suckers. You are told that free silver will cause railway construction to cease and throw existing companies into the hands of receivers. That were much like flagging a train already in the ditch.

Railway construction practically ceased sometime ago, and the receiver is numerously in evidence. The wage rate tends steadily downward and thousands of experienced railroaders are living on hope deferred. And the "honest money" of the McKinleyites is "in our midst!" Our great period of industrial development was between the close of the war and 1879—when gold had gone into hiding and you were "suffering the manifold ills of cheap money." Those were the days when railway men wore diamonds. Not only railway construction, but all industrial development is at a stand-still here—the capitalists preferring to plant their good money in free silver Mexico, the home of "repudiation." What they put out here is in pursuit of their pawnbroking business—in taking advantage of the people's necessities; what they send to Mexico goes to develop new industries and augment the legions of labor. Despite the enterprise and industry of its Celt and Saxons, America is really retrograding; despite the native worthlessness of her people, Mexico feels the magic thrill of progress.

In his blood-curdling yaller-back the *Age* editor quotes from President Hill of the Great Northern, who has much to say about "the 25-cent wage rate of Mexico, paid in depreciated dollars." They all do, and strive to create the impression that free-silver would inevitably place the American laborer on a parity with the Mexican. I exposed this falsehood in the August Iconoclast, but as the supply of papers was not equal to the demand, it may be well to put the gaffles into it again. How can men receive much for their labor when it produces but little? Furthermore, this "25-cent Mexican wage-rate" is an impudent falsehood. The man who peddles it is either a liar by profession, else he ought to be castrated to prevent him getting fools. I quote the Mexican wage scale for 1895 from U. S. consular reports—compiled by a gold-standard department of state: Bricklayers $10 per week, masons $10.80, bakers $7.60, brass-founders and cabinet-makers $10 each, stevedores $9, tailors $7.14, telegraph operators $11.50 and other skilled labor in proportion. Unskilled labor is paid an average of $2.90 per week, or nearly 50 cents per day—a Mexican dollar purchasing fully as much of the comforts of life in that country as will a gold-standard dollar in this state. If President Hill is looking for a "25-cent wage" he can find it in gold-standard Italy, where drivers are paid 25 and hod-carriers 28 cents per day. The general wage-rate of silver-standard Mexico, Colombia, Ecuador, Peru and Venezuela is higher than that of gold-standard England, Scotland, Ireland, Belgium, Germany, Italy, Spain and France. The measure of value has no more effect on the wage-rate than has a pair of scales on the price of putty.

"Then why," you may well ask, "should capitalists really care to preserve the gold standard?" They have made of gold a fetich and are robbing and enslaving the people by playing upon their economic ignorance. They have builded a golden Joss and, by the assistance of such evangelists as the editor of the *Age*, persuaded the people to pay it almost divine honors; to offer upon its foolish altar the first fruits and fat of the land—all of which is promptly referred to the larders of its chief priests and Levites. By means of this financial hoodoo they have induced the Titan of Toil to add to his already grievous burden 262 millions of interest-bearing bonds in a time of abundant crops and profound peace. Why? That a coterie of capitalists might pick up 10 million dollars in as many days on the ridiculous pretext of "protecting the credit" of a 2-billion dollar currency, with 100 millions of gold! The *Age* explains that if you draw $1,000 worth of orders against $100 due you by the company, they will be worth only 10 cents on the dollar; yet our $1,660,000,000 of paper and silver money is supposed to be drawn against the $100,000,000 gold reserve of Uncle Sam! There's 16 to 1 for you with a vengeance! Of course government can get more gold—by selling bonds —to redeem its promises to pay; just as you can get more money—by selling labor—to keep your orders at par. The great capitalists have employed gold to create panics that have closed factories, bankrupted merchants, augmented the army of tramps and precipitated bread riots that ended in blood, simply to enhance the gains of a pitiless system of pawnbrokerage. Gold, by itself considered, has given them no more power than tho' they possessed an equal value of other forms of property; but they succeeded in convincing the people that the auriferous Joss was their industrial Palladium, just as the sacred thieves of ancient Ilium did the superstitious Trojans that, upon the preservation of a block of stone and the payment of tribute to its priests, depended the safety of their city.

I have no "free-silver wheels." The currency question, stripped of the bogy feature given by capitalists to gold, is simply a political pipe dream, an issue to get office. Considered from a purely economic standpoint, it is of no more consequence whether we open the mints to silver than whether you feed your face with a spoon or a fork. But I have treated of this phase of the question in previous issues of this paper. After careful study of the monetary rate-sheet, the economic time-card, I have concluded that should we ditch both the gold-bug string o' Pullmans and the free-silver freight, Uncle Sam as general manager of the system, would require no explanation of the disaster. They are both political excursions running wild on the regular time of the hog-train. They should be pitched into the woods and the commerce of the road given the right-o'way. The heads of these currency agitators are so many hot-boxes that are filling the atmosphere with the malodor of frying dope and setting the culverts afire. Commerce will fix the measure of value and provide the necessary exchange media if these political tramps will but avoid a tail-end collision with their own brains and refrain from putting soap in the boiler. Our present hard times are almost entirely due to political agitation. The blessed saviors of the country won't let it be saved. They are forever reporting imaginary landslides and paranoic wash-outs up the line, and impeding the commerce of the country by tinkering around their d—d old work-train.

As a business man, I cannot see that free-silver would help or hurt me, whether it remained at par and circulated side by side with gold, or drove the latter out and slumped to 53 cents. A change in our measures of value might be inconvenient, but not necessarily disastrous. Commerce would quietly adapt itself to the changed conditions. Our bull would still gender, our cow still calve; the earth would continue to yield its increase and food-fish be caught in the sea. The manufacturer and the farmer would persist in exchanging their products though the Chinese yen or German mark became our exchange medium. I do not expect that free-silver will fill the Mississippi with honey and the Missouri with milk; but gold has been made a ridiculous idol, and I'm in the idol-breaking business. Like Mahomet, I say to men who bow down to this foolish fetich, "Behold! Your god has flies on it." When I was a little Sunday school boy, a school teacher named Decker tried to frighten me out of all my faults. Assuming a hideous disguise, he entered my bedroom and informed me that he was Satan himself. As I had been told that the Devil would get me for swearing, I was not much surprised. I said: "You're a hell of a looking devil, but I believe you're lying; I'll just call you with this iron boot-jack." Satan didn't "get behind me," but he got. I'm all aweary of this bugaboo set up by the gold-bugs. It has thrown Columbia into commercial spasms and industrial convulsions. If she will but muster up sufficient courage to call it with a double-barreled bootjack, she'll find it another harmless old Decker in disguise.

"TOO MUCH WORLD."

Famine the Handmaid of Fortune.

"There's too much world. There are not enough consumers. Too many fields have been opened by science. The world has not yet adjusted itself to limiting production to consumption."

What's that? It is the Republican explanation of the present industrial depression.

The words quoted are copied from an interview had by the London *Telegraph* with "a prominent Anglo-American banker, whose opinions are those of an expert." His name is withheld by the *Telegraph* "for business reasons;" but he speaks as an avowed champion of McKinley, and his utterances have been reproduced and approved by all the leading gold-bug papers on both sides of the ocean. We are thus asked by "the party of progress and prosperity" to believe that the masses are poor because they have created too much wealth. According to the latest economic theorem of the McKinleyites, half the world is hungry because there is too much hog and hominy, butter and beef; it is naked because we grow too much wool and cotton and weave too much cloth; it is inhabiting unhealthy huts because we have too much lumber, building stone and brick; it has no spot of earth hallowed by the name of home, because "there's too much world."

Excuse my Latin—but it's a damned lie!

Unless the Anglo-American banker aforesaid and his industrious claquers be talking the veriest tommyrot, the way to become prosperous is to close every factory and let our fertile fields lie fallow until the surplus is consumed. We could compel the return of "good times" by burning up half our breadstuffs, cloth and building material, or slinging it into the bottom of the sea. According to this theory, much wealth is the equivalent of poverty, a part is greater than the whole. If the McKinleyites be correct, the anarchists who destroy property are patriots, those who persist in creating it in times like these are public enemies. The opponents of the "Boy Orator" have practically told us that the torch of progress and the brand of the firebug are synonymous if not exactly the same. When the people cry to these economic savants that the auric standard hath filled their cities with silent factories and bankrupt merchants, their country lanes with penniless tramps and disputatious Populists, they calmly reply: "Nay, good friends; what ails you is too much wealth." When the giant of Labor, his hands fastened with golden fetters and watching the gaunt wolf of Want creep ever nigher those he loves, cries out in agony, "Unhand me, that I may shield my home from hunger and rags and wretchedness," this Anglo-American McKinley booster softly smooths his red brawn with lily fingers and makes reply: "Nay, my good man; those hands of thine have been busy to the country's hurt. Because of thy pernicious activity, there's a glut of products, which moulder in the market place. In thy too fecund brain were born those accursed wealth-creating devices which, like the monster of Frankenstein, torment their maker. Patience, kind sir, until the surplus is exhausted, when—like another Satan—you may be loosed for a little season."

If this be all that "expert opinion" can do for us, then is our condition desperate indeed. If, with a million idle men, we produce too much, how many must stand outside the industrial pale, in the limbo of beggary, ere the McKinley system of economics can save the country? "Peace," says the poet, "hath its triumphs no less than war;" must it have its victims too? I am no "expert" in matters industrial, and am loth to take issue with the eminent authority paraded by the McKinleyites; but if our present ills be indeed due to overproduction, then are we entering upon an age of agony, of suffering and of sin such as the world has never seen. If the Republican theorem be correct, then here is an application of the law of the survival of the fittest which dooms half mankind to the hell of famine. The poor man has naught to exchange for life's necessaries but his labor, and if that becomes at times a public curse, what is left him but to steal or starve? Americans are notoriously an impatient and headstrong people. They have not been bred like the bloodless Bengalese to meekly bear the oppressor's wrong, the proud man's contumely, and perish without a murmur in a land of plenty. They are firmly convinced—whether right or wrong—that their hard condition is due to deliberate despoliation. With tireless industry and rigid economy the masses cannot get out of the morass of poverty; yet on every side they see those who neither toil nor spin, arrayed like unto Solomon in all his glory. A bitter hatred has found place in their hearts for those who waste while they must want—a hatred that may yet flame forth in desperate deeds.

"Slowly comes a hungry people, as a lion drawing nigher,
Glares at one that nods and winks behind a slowly dying fire."

For five years past the famished lion of Labor has been creeping closer and ever closer to the silken tent of Croesus; for five years past the patriot has been stroking its mane with trembling fingers and preaching patience; for five years past every political party has been promising that its wisdom would soon transform the dark night of industrial depression into glorious day. If by such means we could scarce keep the "blatant beast" under control; if our prayers and tears and flattering promises—flanked here and there with a double-shotted battery or forest of bristling bayonets—could scarce prevent it fleshing its murderous fangs in Croesus' throat, what will the monster do when it gathers from "expert opinion" that the night is perpetual, that for it the long-cherished hope of dawn was but an idle dream!

If the idea that he must be sacrificed to "save the country"—that he occupies no important place in the scheme of things, and will be turned out to starve that decreased production may enhance price—once finds secure lodgment in the head of Labor, the world will soon witness a new and more terrible Reign of Terror. Yet that is the idea promulgated by this economic "expert" and loudly applauded by the Republican and Mugwump press. "There is too much world," say they—while millions depend on charity for six feet of earth in which to lay their marrowless bones. "Too many fields have been opened by science"—and this blessed night a million Americans will go supperless to bed. "The world has not yet adjusted itself to limiting production to consumption"—which means that an universal trust, higher prices, another million tramps pressing for employment and forcing down wages, is the economic idea of the Republican party. For three-quarters of a century political economy was tainted with the black pessimism of Malthus, who insisted that population had a tendency to increase faster than its means of subsistence could be made to do; that unless mankind placed a prudential check on its procreative passion, millions would finally perish for lack of food; but what is the bogy of Malthusianism to that of McKinleyism? The former would wreck us in some far-off time; the latter declares damnation even now at our door. The first would consign us to Famine's clutches; the last would make us butt our own brains out on bursting smokehouses and bloated wheat bins!

And this is the kind of unadulterated damn nonsense sanctioned by the McKinleyites as a part of the curriculum in their wonderful "campaign of education!"

There never was, and there never can be, in this world such a thing as over-production. A man's gray matter must be full o' maggots before he can entertain for a moment such a crazy economic idea. Under normal conditions—where each receives that proportion of the world's wealth which he actually earns—as the productive power of labor increases the standard of living advances. When there is enough of necessaries the surplus energy of the nation turns to the production of luxuries, which in turn become necessaries—mankind ever rising higher above the habits and condition of the brute. If my banker friend thinks there is "too much world," let him attend the next opening to settlement of an Indian reservation. If he thinks there is overproduction, let him consider how many of us would decline to live on the elegant plan of the Astors were we able.

The trouble is not overproduction, but enforced underconsumption. The wealth annually produced congests at a comparatively few points instead of flowing into the coffers of its creators. If every workman were regularly employed, and the productive power of each enhanced an hundredfold, it were impossible to create more wealth than the world wants. If distributed in accord with the earning power of each, the result would not be glutted markets and falling prices, but better food, clothing, houses, more of the comforts and conveniences of life for the toiling millions. The "dignity of labor," anent which the politicians prattle—about election time—would become something more than an iridescent dream. The workingman would have more leisure in which to do battle with the demon of Ignorance and the foul gorgon of Superstition. Soup-houses and penitentiaries would practically disappear, and where now stands the wretched hovel would rise the cultured home. Where Famine grimly stalks Plenty would show her smiling face, Despair yield place to Hope, and upon the strong shoulders of sweet Content the Republic sit secure.

This is no fancy sketch. Despite the fact that we are on the threshold of the age of invention—the mighty era of intellect; that we have obtained as yet but slight mastery over the power of the elements; that vast armies stand idle, producing nothing—despite the fact that Labor, that wonder-worker, is cribbed, cabined and confined by unnatural conditions—we create enough wealth every year to comfortably clothe, feed and house every human being who stands within the shadow of our flag. Take off the accursed interdict, give place in the industrial ranks to every man able to wield the hammer or swing the steel, strengthen his heart and nerve his arm with the knowledge that whatsoever of wealth is created by his work that he shall surely have, and the most extravagant dream of the optimist were to the reality but

"As moonlight unto sunlight, and as water unto wine."

Products remain unsold in the market place and the tendency of prices is downward because those who produce are not permitted to consume—because the producers of wealth are not its possessors. If the usufruct of my farm be taken to pay my taxes, interest and insurance, what have I to exchange for the product of labor in other lines? And if these, too, be similarly confiscated, what have my brother toilers to exchange for the fruits of my farm? Nothing. Exchange between us cannot be effected, simply because neither has aught to give, and some wild-eyed yap posing as an economic "expert"—lifts up his voice and protests that our troubles are due to overproduction! If the farmer and artisan have nothing left to exchange when they produce much, how will their purchasing power be enhanced if they produce little?

"There are not enough consumers" (and that's no lie), cries the gentleman who is peddling "expert opinions," with the approval of the McKinley campaign committee. But how does he propose to increase the number? By limiting production and raising prices, by decreasing the number of people employed, by depriving another million or so of all purchasing power! Dr. Sandrago has long been laughed at for attempting to cure a man of the gout by drawing off all his blood and filling his stomach with warm water; yet here is a scheme to relieve an acute case of industrial prostration by hitting the patient in the head with a hatchet. It must be patent to every man whose brain has not become ossified by allowing a steady stream of Markhanna literature to trickle through it that so long as a vast number of people depend for existence upon their immediate earnings we cannot reduce production without reducing consumption; that so long as we have a great army of destitute people unemployed, it is impossible to increase production without increasing consumption.

It is a trifle strange that the apostles of Republicanism should, in one breath, demand protection as a means of developing American industries, and in the next complain that we do not limit production to consumption—that they should approve a protective tariff, which is intended to raise prices, and damn free-silver, which they say will do exactly the same thing. They assure us that gold makes for high and silver for low wages. Labor can only be paid out of the price received for its product; yet it is a part of the Republican profession of faith that gold, while raising wages, makes the cost of living less, and that silver, while lowering wages, makes the cost of living more. I confess, with a feeling akin to shame, that Republican economics is beyond the range of my comprehension. Its parabolical paradoxes and supernatural syllogisms remind me of those amorphous monsters which a high priest of Bacchus can sometimes see with his eyes shut. The man who enters the labyrinthine maze of McKinley argument needs a ball of twine, a piece of chalk and an inextinguishable torch if he hopes to ever find his way back to the sunshine of common sense. Solomon admitted that there were three things too wonderful for him—yet David's wisest son died before Markhanna began turning loose his campaign literature.

What we want and needs must have is not a national trust to limit production and add to the idle legions of labor, but conditions that will enable every man to produce to his fullest capacity and enjoy the usufruct of his endeavor to the uttermost farthing. That's the ideal industrial system to the attainment of which we must bend all our energies, instead of sitting supinely down in the Serbonian bogs dug by this Anglo-American banker, and wailing that "there's too much world." We cannot afford to tie fast to any party in whose heaven there blazes no star of hope—which calls a halt to the workingman just as he has seized the genie's wand for the multiplication of wealth. We have here a land capable of sustaining five times its present population, so rich is it in natural resources; yet millions struggle from the cradle to the grave for a bare subsistence, while tens of thousands beg in vain for this poor privilege. How to break the accursed spell—to make it possible for this people to utilize to the utmost the good gifts of a gracious God—is the problem of problems, the riddle which the American Œdipus must read or be destroyed; yet McKinleyism makes answer that the Almighty has ruined us with his munificence! Better that we should align ourselves with the wildest dreamers and strive ever so blindly to remove the blight, than to cast in our lot with those blessed "conservatives" who have naught to offer but bread boluses already proven abortive, and who denounce all who would lead the masses to a higher plane as alarmists and demagogues! Were not John the Baptist and Jesus Christ alarmists in the view of the eminently conservative Sadducees? Did not George III and all his "most loyal and dutiful subjects" denounce Washington as a Jack Cade, Adams and Jefferson as demagogues? Courage, faint heart! Remember that, since the dawn of human history, every man who became dissatisfied with existing conditions, howsoever bad; every man who dared cry out against prescriptive right entrenched in brutal wrong, has been denounced and denied, belittled and belied by the blessed "conservatives" of his day. Surely it was not intended that any man of woman born should sit with folded hands and starve while all about him the potential wealth of nature beckons. There is in heaven a star, the radiant star of Hope.

"Not in vain the distant beacons; forward, forward let us range;
Let the great world spin forever down the ringing grooves of change."

I do not believe that any possible tinkering with the

currency can bring about ideal industrial conditions; but the abolition of the single gold standard will be a step in the right direction. It will be a second Declaration of Independence, a timely warning to all the world that Uncle Sam has outgrown his financial leading-strings and assumed the management of his own affairs. It will be an impressive notice to the little knot of millionaires who have so long been taking exorbitant toll in so many different ways of American labor that the masses are h—l bent on industrial emancipation. Having demonstrated their ability to secure what they want, despite the organized opposition of monopolies and trusts, the people will be encouraged to undertake other and more important reforms. We know that there is something radically wrong, and that if the gold standard did not cause our ills it has done nothing to cure them. We have learned by sad experience that it is no commercial palladium or industrial deity. It is an idol whose impuissance for good has been amply proven, its capacity for evil strongly suspected. We know that at its shrine worship those who fatten on the fruits of others' toil; that its chief priests and Levites are the great money lords, the protective tariff beneficiaries, the wreckers of railways, the sworn enemies of labor unions, the managers of trusts and monopolies, the dardanari who gamble in life's necessaries, and the newspapers which pander to the plutocracy, fake up coats-of-arms for parvenues and prove their un-Americanism by bowing down with a noisy adoration that endangers their diapers before every two-by-four princeling and chancerous dukeling. If we may judge idols, as men, by the company they keep, then indeed are we justified in laying the iconoclastic hammer to the golden calf. Perchance its fall will serve as a warning to the house of Have that Labor, which hewed this nation out of the wilderness, is still lord and ready to enforce its rights, humbugged and driven with contumely from a table which groans beneath viands wrung from the earth's bosom in the sweat of his brow.

THE APOSTLE'S RAG BABY.

In the year of our Lord, 1891, I became pregnant with an idea. Being at the time chief editorial writer on the Houston *Post*. I felt dreadfully mortified, as nothing of the kind had ever before occurred in that eminently moral establishment. Feeling that I was forever disqualified for the place by this untoward incident, I resigned and took sanctuary in the village of Austin. As swaddling clothes for the expected infant, I established the Iconoclast, which naturally gravitated to Waco, the political ganglion and religious storm centre of the state. When the youngster made his appearance in this troublesome vale of financial buncombe and economic idiocy, it was given the ponderous title of "Inter-convertible Bond-currency Plan." It's a wonder the name didn't kill it; but, turned out to grass, it thrived and grew in grace. The infant was generally supposed to be an unholy cross between incipient insanity and a well developed case of confluent Populism; but when the bankers of Germany, assembled at Berlin, approved the little waif, the suspicion passed. Hon. Tom Johnson became the Congressional champion of some features of the plan, which now finds earnest advocates among all political parties. I have an abiding faith that, in a couple of million years or so, it will be generally accepted as the proper solution of the much vexed currency problem; but it may be that my exuberant optimism misleads me. If the plan possesses genuine merit, that is no indication that it will ever become popular; if it be the wildest nightmare that ever kicked a vagrom-minded man, that will not prevent the public accepting it as another Pegasus, and politicians riding it into power. At the request of many patrons of the Iconoclast—and with apologies to those who have already gone with me over the ground—I submit a brief compendium of the plan and the propositions upon which it is based, promising that I do not recommend it as the *ne plus ultra* of financial wisdom, but suggest it as an improvement on our present unsatisfactory currency system.

I shall not weary the reader with a long dissertation on economic science, but assume, as praecognita already proven, that our national exchange media has absolutely nothing to do with our foreign trade; that nations do not swap money, but exchange commodities; that our gold and silver coin is valued as bullion when carried abroad, and would have as great purchasing power in foreign markets if never minted, consequently we need consult only our domestic convenience in establishing an exchange media. Further, that the word "dollar" is an abstract term by which we express, not so many grains of gold or silver, but the commercial relation of each commodity to all other commodities; that whatsoever enables us to expeditiously effect exchanges is "good money," no matter of what made;

that an irredeemable paper currency will not depreciate in purchasing power so long as it is not, and cannot be, issued in excess of the necessary money-work to be done. I also assume that we can never have a currency both safe and flexible grounded on one or two comparatively unimportant products, of fluctuating value, and that the exchange media should be removed entirely from the province of partisan politics and subjected to the direct and absolute control of commerce.

Some of the foregoing propositions are in conflict with monetary theories bearing the sanction of centuries; but this fact no more establishes their falsity than the *ipse dixit* of the college of cardinals disproved Galileo's cosmogony. Economic writers were loud in their denunciation five years ago; but are gradually accepting these propositions, a fact which prompted a witty but incorrigible "gold-bug" to send me the following lines from Pope:

> "Vice is a monster of so frightful mien,
> As, to be hated, needs but to be seen;
> Yet seen too oft, familiar with her face,
> We first endure, then pity, then embrace."

To this sally I retorted with an excerpt from the same author:

> "Old politicians chew on wisdom past,
> And totter on in bus'ness to the last,
> As weak, as earnest, and as gravely out
> As sober Lanesb'rough dancing with the gout."

A governmental money that will automatically and infallibly adapt itself to the varying needs of commerce, preserve the equilibrium between the money-work to be done and the money available to do it, and thereby obviate all danger of either appreciation or depreciation of the purchasing power of the dollar, is universally conceded to be the great desideratum. To attain this I propose:

(1) That the government keep constantly on sale at all postoffices of the presidential class low interest-bearing bonds in denominations of $100 to $1,000, redeemable at the option of the holder in full legal tender currency.

(2) That this new currency be added to the general revenue fund, and paid out the same as other money, until currency bonds to the amount of $250,000,000 be taken— the proceeds constituting a redemption fund—when such additions to the general revenue fund shall cease and not

be resumed until, through bond redemption, the fund set aside for that purpose falls below the foregoing figure.

That's all there is to the Inter-convertible Bond-Currency Plan. When there is too little money, the government will supply more; when too much, the government will absorb the surplus, and the equilibrium at all times be maintained. There could be no "money famines" and consequent enhancement of the purchasing power of the dollar; there could be no depreciation, caused by the pressure of a redundant currency for employment. The redemption fund would be an infallible indication of the monetary needs of the country. The volume of currency would be controlled by the natural laws of commerce—Congress could neither add to nor take from it a single farthing. The administration would be powerless to mint a single coin or print a dollar bill until notified by the nation, through the medium of the redemption fund, that it needed more money. Silver might become plentiful as in the days of Solomon and cheap as scrap-iron; gold might advance in value another 100 per cent., and only the fine arts be affected—the American currency would maintain the even tenor of its way, the dollar be "the same yesterday, today and forever." The unit of value could no more be affected by the varying fecundity of the mines, good or bad crops, legislative ineptitude, war or pestilence, than could the length of the yard or weight of the pound. The dollar would be tripped to the commodity feature, which makes it mutable. The supply relative to the demand would ever be the same. It would measure each by all instead of itself, and, therefore, be a true and unchangeable denominator of value.

Perhaps I have fixed the normal redemption fund at too high a figure; 100 millions were sufficient but for the danger that those interested in preventing proper currency expansion might buy and hold sufficient bonds to make automatic operation of such a system impossible. The redemption fund must be too large for even Wall street manipulation. There would be little danger of any coterie of conspirators tying up 250 million in government bonds, bearing merely a nominal rate of interest, while commerce was bidding for more ready money. With so large a redemption fund, and bonds bearing even so high an interest rate as 1 1-2 per cent., our exchange media would cost us but $3,750,000 a year, or less than one-tenth the annual commercial interest on the wealth we have invested in a metal tool of trade.

It will be exclaimed that this is "fiatism." It is the fiatism of which Dr. Adam Smith fondly dreamed and which his successors have unqualifiedly approved. It is the fiatism of Thomas Jefferson and Henry Clay. It is the same fiatism by means of which 95 per cent. of our exchanges are now effected; for, as I have frequently pointed out, our "commercial money," approximating 40 billions, is not grounded on a pitiful 1-2 billion of gold. Back of it is all the wealth and credit of its makers; behind the bond currency, which I propose, would be all the wealth and credit of the richest nation in the world, the earning power of 70 million people. "But it would be irredeemable," cries one. Not so long as it remained a legal tender and was accepted at its nominal value in trade. In what do you want a paper dollar redeemed? If you exchange it for a gold or silver coin you have got but another governmental order for goods, which you must present for redemption to the people. When you have exchanged your dollar for corn or cotton, pork or pig-iron it has been redeemed—not till then have you received final payment. So long as the people will redeem a paper dollar at its nominal value, isn't it as good an exchange medium as gold? Even that incorrigible economic ass known as Edward Atkinson will answer in the affirmative. If we can discover Dr. Adam Smith's "wagon-way thro' the air," why incur the expense of building turnpikes? If we can make an effective trade-tool at so little cost, why keep more than a billion of wealth tied up in gold and silver coin? Why imitate the Chinese and burn a house to roast a pig, when the porker may be done brown with a billet? Holding such views, why does the Iconoclast advocate the free coinage of silver? The goldites would base our exchange media on one, the silverites on two, the Iconoclast on all forms of national wealth. In my humble opinion the question at issue between the two political parties is of precious little importance; but, while the silverites manifest a slight inclination to get into the right, the goldites exhibit a stubborn resolution to remain in the wrong.

THE SWORD AND THE CROSS.

A correspondent asks "whether the great nations owe most to the sword or the cross." That were much like asking whether the usefulness of a watch be due most to the case or the works. Religion has ever been the heart of the body social, the dynamics of civilization. A great nation of Atheists is a practical impossibility, because the basic principle of such a society must needs be selfishness, and from such a foundation no mighty superstructure can ever rise. "Ye cannot gather grapes of thorns nor figs of thistles." War is but an incident in the history of a nation, while religion is its very life. In the latter it moves and breathes and has its being. From the standpoint of a statesman it makes little difference what the religion of a people may be so long as most of them believe it. History abundantly demonstrates that when a nation begins to doubt its gods, it begins to lose its glory. Without religion the contract social is simply a rope of sand. "No union of church and state" is simply a protest against the union of body and soul. The greatest rulers of ancient and modern times regarded religion as the palladium of national power. True it is that religion has time and again strengthened the hands of the tyrant and stoned the prophets of progress; but every good gift bequeathed to man has been at times abused. The sword has been wielded by the assassin; it has been employed to enslave and despoil the people; yet we dare not break the blade. Men of narrow minds, seeing many warring cults, imagine them to be disturbing factors in the human brotherhood—that if they could be eliminated, the body politic would have peace. They cannot understand that the discords of the finite make the harmony of the infinite. They fail to see that these warring creeds are but the necessary differentiations of a common faith. Lay the winds, still the tides, and old ocean, that perennial fount of health, becomes a stagnant pool of putrefaction—a malodorous "mother of dead dogs." Force presupposes friction. Let the sectaries fight, each doing valiant battle for his own dogma, for when they all agree religion will be dead and progress at an end. It is not necessary that you and I should stand close enough to be stifled with the dust of conflict, to taste all the bitterness of sectarian controversy—we may mount above it all and watch it beat like the convolutions of a mighty brain. We may take refuge in the philosophy of religion and say that all are right in conception and wrong in expression; we may call it blind superstition if we will; but if we mount high enough to obtain a clear vision we must confess that religion has ever been the dominant factor in the forging of mighty peoples. Were I required to give a reason for this fact I would say it is because man is not altogether a machine—because he is not content to eat and sleep and propagate his kind like the lower animals. Despite his thick veneer of selfishness, man is at heart a creature of sentiment, and religion is the poetry of the common people. Crude it may be, but its tendency is toward the stars, while all else in man is animalistic and of the earth. Strike the religion, the poetry, out of a people, and you reduce them to the level of educated animals. Annul the power that draws them upward and they must sink back to primordial savagery. The individual may accept logic as a substitute for sentiment, but a nation cannot do so. The masses are not swayed through the head, but through the heart. Sentiment is the divine perfume of the soul. Of sentiment was born the dream of immortality. It is the efficient cause of every sacrifice which man makes for his fellow man. It is the parent duty, and duty presupposes the Divine. Could the materialists inaugurate their belauded age of reason, sentiment would perish utterly in that pitiless atmosphere, and the world be reduced to a basis of brute selfishness. The word duty would disappear, for why should man die for man in a world whose one sole god was the dollar. Why should a Damien sacrifice himself if selfish ease be the only divinity? If there be no Fatherhood of God there can be no Brotherhood of Man— we are but accidents, spawn of the sun and slime, each an Ishmael considering only himself. Atheism means universal anarchy. It means a kingdom without a king, laws without a legislator, a machine without a master. An Atheist is a public enemy. He would not only destroy the state but wreck society. He would render life not worth the living. He would rob us of our garden roses and fill our hands with artificial flowers. And why? Because, forsooth, he finds that some articles of religious faith are impossible fables. He sits down with a microscope to examine the tables of the law for tracks of the finger of him whose sentences are astral fire. He finds a foolish contradiction in some so-called sacred book and imagines that he has proven either that man's a fool or God's a fraud. "By geometric scale he takes the measure of pots of ale." He calls himself a "liberal," while fanatically intolerant of the honest opinions of others. He is forever mistaking shadow for substance, the accidental for the essential. He "disproves" religion without in the least comprehending it. He hammers away at the Immaculate Conception and the miracles with a vigor that amuses those who realize that cults and creeds are but ephemera, while faith in the Almighty endures forever. And of all the Atheists and Agnostics Bob Ingersoll is the most insupportable. He is but a mouthful of sweetened wind, a painted echo, an oratorical hurdy-gurdy that plays the music of others. He's as innocent of original ideas as a Mexican fice of feathers. He gets down on the muddy pave and wrangles with the "locus" preachers. He's a theological shyster lawyer who takes advantage of technicalities. He is not a philosopher—he's emphatically "a critic fly." He examines the Christian cult inch by inch, just as Gulliver did the cuticle of the Brobdingnagian maid who sat him astride her nipple. He never contemplates the *tout ensemble*. He learns absolutely nothing from the cumulative wisdom of the world. He doesn't even appreciate the fact that the dominant religions of the world today are couched in the language of oriental poetry. He wastes his nervo-muscular energy demolishing the miracles. When he gets through with the Bible I presume that he'll take a fall out of Æsop's Fables. He doesn't understand that the soul of man has never learned a language—that all sacred books are but an outward evidence of an inward grace. He doesn't know that religion, like love, cannot be analyzed. Because the orient pearls are imbedded in ocean slime he denies their existence. Ingersoll and the "plenary inspiration" people are welcome to fight it out—it's none of my funeral. Religion proper is not at all concerned with the result. You may prove Zoroaster a myth, Moses a mountebank, Gautama a priestly grafter and Christ the prototype of Francis Schlatter and other half-witted frauds; but adoration of a superior power will remain a living, pulsing thing in the hearts of the people. It is this poetry, this sentiment, this sense of duty, which transcends the dollar that constitutes the adhesive principle of society and makes civilization possible.

SOME KANSAS CITY CULTURE.

I chanced some time ago to spend a couple o' days in Kansas City, a bustling little place situated at the mouth of the Kaw, and somewhat celebrated at headquarters for the jug trade of Kansas. It is also distinguished for the size of its pork-packeries and the garish splendor of its parvenues. The arms of Kansas City are a gallon jug rampant, a fat porker regardant, a blood pudding couchant, and the motto, "There's nothing like licker and lard." The place has grown somewhat since trains began stopping there a dozen or so years ago, but is a city as yet in nothing but name, inartistic piles of brick and pitiful contrasts of wealth and poverty. It is an overgrown country town in which one is reminded of Jayville at every turn. There's a bucolic air about its people, its pulpit, and especially its press, which is really refreshing after a sojourn in St. Joseph or Sedalia. I am told that its swagger set still attend its social functions *sans* coats and collars, feed themselves with knives and for napkins use the corners of the table-cloth. My informant further stated that Mr. W. S. Halliwell, the Beau Brummel of K. C., recently spent some days in St. Joseph and there caught on to the finger-bowl fad and has been trying ever since to transplant it to that select circle of which he is the Hermes Trismegistus, or iridescent glory, but without much success—the Kansascityans still persist in absorbing the lavatory and "cussing out" the waiters for not putting ice in their drinking water. Kansas City is to St. Joseph what Chicago is to St. Louis: a big, blustering, uncouth and uncultured "yap" town, doing business on borrowed capital—a place where the individual is measured by the size of his bank account instead of that of his cerebrum. Its wealthy people are for the most part pork-packers, soap-boilers, political corruptionists, and the immediate descendants of those who ran variety dives in the early days of "squat" on land worth two-bits an acre and hung to it like death to a defunct Senegambian until enriched by the labor of others. The professional grafters, dive-keepers and squatters who founded most of Kansas City's big fortunes, took an annual bath in the Big Muddy, wiped on the narrative of their hickory shirts and felt refreshed. One by one they dropped off, leaving behind them a lot of anaemic dudes and splay-footed dudines who now constitute Kansas City's *creme de la creme*. This it was that barred a working girl from a public pageant lest she brush gowns with those whose mammies caught and skinned catfish and cooked them on driftwod fires. The elite of Kansas City run very little to art and literature. Their pantheon is a pork-packery and Phil. D. Armour their Olympian Jove. Their salons are ornamented with chromos representing the slaughter of fat kine and swine. Their hero is the man who can stick the most pigs in a given number of minutes, and their popular melodies are a variation of the death squeal of that homely but useful animal. The Jesse James dime novel and the New York "yaller" newspapers suffice to satisfy Kansas City's rather moderate longing for literature, while the circus and the negro minstrel show are her favorite amusement. Of course there are cultured people in Kansas City—those who feed with a fork, carry pocket handkerchiefs and use tooth-brushes—but they are few and far between. The great bulk of the population are devout worshippers at the shrine of Mammon and find far more satisfaction in gazing at a pool of porcine gore than in contemplating the masterpieces of a Raphael or a Phidias. As might be expected, the press of Kansas City is a true reflex of its life—stupid, ignorant and obstinate as the hog upon which the commercial greatness of the place is grounded. The *Times,* most pretentious of the morning papers, was really a first-class journal under the management of Dr. Morrison Munford; but when he retired its name became Ichabod—or more properly, Mud. From a circulation of 25,000 or almost one-fourth that of the Iconoclast—it slumped to 5000 or less, and most of this output was purchased not for reading purposes but to underlay carpets or paper pantries. It took up the gold-bug yoop in the hope of retrieving its fallen fortunes, but the experiment miserably failed, and it became a veritable journalistic Lazarus which even the political dogs refused to lick. It soon saw that something desperate had to be done or the old bawd would go bump, so it switched again—returned to the advocacy of silver coinage and supported Billy Bryan. As a man is usually judged by the company he keeps, it is small wonder that the Nebraskan lost the race, handicapped as he was with this old journalistic harlot. The change in the *Times'* policy was so plainly the result of business expediency that it only provoked contemptuous pity. Since Munford's retirement the *Times* has been acephalous—every employe apparently doing as he pleases and doing it as badly as possible. The *Times* now has about as much circulation as an oyster, as little influence with the general public as the bray of an asthmatic burro. If you see it in the *Times* it's a pretty safe bet that it isn't so. The *Journal* is another has-been newspaper that has turned its intellectual toes to the daisies, and now appears to be living, as Carlyle would say, "to save salt." If I remember aright it was founded some 45 years ago by Col. R. T. Van Horn, a very able newspaper man, who gave it a national reputation for honor, decency and intellect. Col. Van Horn sold his interest in the paper and retired disgusted—jumped the dirty game—and when it became a toad-eating tip-taking organ-grinder for the gold-buggers. Col. Van Horn took all the brains and honor of the *Journal* with him when he went, the paper lost all its prestige and most of its patronage, and is now living on a very attenuated variety of wind-pudding. It pays its leading editorial writer the enormous sum of $27.50 a week for "moulding public opinion"—and he does it with one hand. Other salaries on the paper range from $20 downwards, the art, dramatic and lecture critic receiving $8 a week and feeding on the tailings of a brass foundry. The *Star* is the name of "Baron Bill" Nelson's "twilight twinkler," which shines softly luminous as a dyspeptic fire-fly or a tin-lantern at 2 o'clock, g. m., in the fogs of Lunnon town. "Baron Bill" lives out on Brush Creek in what is known as Nelson's Baronial Castle, but whether because of its turreted splendor or simply as a "josh," deponent saith not. Bill did not make his money by his brains. I am told that his first "hist," as the Kansas City grammar sharps would learnedly call it, was born of a good stiff borrow made of the National Waterworks Co., which had a water monopoly hen on and needed Bill to help turn the trick. He then found a widow with more money than taste and succeeded in marrying her, got his hands into the deep pockets of his Hymenic predecessor, and—the beggar suddenly found himself on horseback and is industriously riding to the devil. Bill's holy trinity is G. Cleveland, Queen Vic and the almighty dollar. Since he got hold of enough long green to enable him to dodge the 15-cent restaurants and avoid the graybacks of 10-cent lodging houses, he has become hawfully Henglish y' knaw. This blawsted country hisn't 'alf culchawed enough for such a bloomin' swell as Windy Bill— the joint creation of a corrupt waterworks corporation and a foolish widow. All of his servants are English and wear side-wheel whiskers; he docks the tails of his horses to make them resemble English cobs; he turns up his twousahs —paid for by the widow and waterworks—whenever it's raining in Lunnon. Aw! weally. He keeps a bottle of Atlantic ocean water to anoint himself with morning and evening because the Prince of Wales once fell into that goosepond when dead drunk. Bill employs as his newspaper assistant—public educators and all that—those mental malinformation which the *Times* doesn't want, the *Journal* can't pay and the devil wouldn't have. I saw one or two specimens of Bill's peons and mistook them for hotel bell boys—I now apologize to every hotel menial I meet—One called at my room who looked like an emasculated puppy that was being brought up by hand and had been neglected by his nurse. He had the head of an ape, the mouth of a "tenor singer" and the beady eyes of a canton-flannel elephant. And the poor thing wanted t' knaw ye knaw, why the deuce y' knaw, I was publishing the Hiconoclast, doncher knaw.

I tried to explain to him in words of one syllable; but all he could understand was the word "damn," which I inadvertently let slip when the miserable mental miscarriage had made me so infernally tired that forbearance ceased to be a virtue. Baron Bill sends $6-a-week grafters to teach reformers their duty, give advice to governors, write essays on art, report philosophic lectures and other little things like that, and instructs them to praise whatever or whoever lick the boots of John Bull, to puke upon whatsoever or whosoever dares intimate that America could exist a single hour should the queen become costive and be rendered thereby unable to dispense God's blessings. Meantime Baron Bill is riding around behind his Henglish coachman and bob-tailed cobs—by the grace of the foolish widow and corrupt waterworks company aforesaid. It is said that more hogs are slaughtered in Kansas City than in Chicago—but it seems that a few swine are saved from the shambles to supply vacancies on local dailies occasioned by old employes starving to death. It was at Kansas City that prisoners were so cruelly mistreated by an official bigot-brute named Chiles for refusing to listen to the foolish yawp of a lot of itinerant gospel sharps. Chiles has not yet been removed from office or imprisoned for his cowardly crime against the intelligence of the age, which fact serves to show that pious spleen is a concomitance of a new and crass civilization. Kansas City will come out all right in time— there are enough people of brains and culture there to eventually leaven the whole lump. In time the ambitious little town at the mouth of the Kaw will find other gods than the millionaires, will adopt nobler ideals than the almighty dollar—will run more to high art and less to hogs.

GARTERS AND AMEN GROANS.

On one page of the Houston *Post* for Sunday, Dec. 12, I find several columns devoted to "Our Boys and Girls," on the next the following advertisement prominently displayed by a Houston haberdasher:

"Our Ladies' Garter Department: We can give you an All Silk Garter for 50c. with nice buckles with such reading on them as 'Private Grounds,' 'Stop, Mama is Coming,' 'Look Quick,' 'Good Night, Call Again,' 'I Am a Warm Baby,' 'Take Off Your Things,' etc."

The paper contains the usual Sunday morning quota of

church notices, religious news and editorial moralizing—
constituting a delectable olla-podrida calculated to turn
the stomach of a self-respectable yaller dog. Doubtless
many purveyors of garters keep in stock those peculiarly
adapted to the trade of the "tenderloin;" but this is the
first time that I have seen such truck advertised in any
paper permitted to pass through the mails or enter the
homes of respectable people. Imagine a Houston parson
rising from family prayers on Sunday morning and placing
in the hands of his young daughter a "great moral daily"
which sets forth in display type that, for the small sum of
50 cents, she can secure a pair of silken garters that warn
the great he-world that she's "a warm baby," and bid it
"look quick" at her shapely legs! Think of a modest old
mother in Israel watching the face of her youthful son as
he learns for the first time of garters that invite him to
"take off your things!" Fine Sabbath morning reading
that for the so-called Christian people of Harris county!
Such an "ad." would forever damn even the Nashville *Banner*, or show in the feculent columns of the Kansas City
Star like a splotch of soot on the marble face of Raphael's
Madonna. The *Police Gazette* and *Sunday Sun* are debarred from the mails, yet neither ever contained aught
one-half so horrible. We keep the "Decameron" and Daudet's eroticisms under lock and key; yet they are only
"suggestive," while this is frankly feculent, a brazen bid for
bawdry. Should the Iconoclast publish such a thing it
would be promptly denounced from ten thousand pulpits
as a pander to pruriency; yet against the iniquity of the
Daily Chippie Chaser, alias the Houston *Post,* not one
preacher has raised his voice in protest! Why? Because
the dirty rag does not attack their religious dogma—does
not strike at their bread and butter! The shortest route
to the heart of the average parson is through his pocket—
hit him there and you raise a howl that startles high heaven,
Print his church notices, report his foolish little sermons,
kneel with him in prayer, slander agnostics and atheists,
serve the Iconoclast as the foul yahoos did Gulliver, flip a
plugged nickel into the contribution box, and you may
safely flaunt the patois of the *nymph du pave* in the fair
face of every honest girl between Cape Cod and the Golden
Gate. And as it is with the average preacher so it is with
the bulk of his parishioners. The *Post* introduces the language of the prostitute into the parlors of its patrons. It
boasts a boys' and girls' club—"The Happyhammers"—
of more than 600 members, and to these children it carries

the first knowledge of sexual perversity, gives them their initial lesson in social sin. Were this the paper's first offense we might attribute it to the carelessness or stupidity of a clerk in its counting-room and the incompetence of its business manager; but it is an old, a shameless, a persistent sinner against all life's decencies and proprieties. Its "personal column" was for years the most revolting thing known to yaller journalism. Its counting-room was an assignation postoffice. The paper was the recognized organ of "Happy Hollow," the Hell's Half Acre of Houston. It was a pander to all the worst passions that run riot in the "tenderloin," a procurer of young girls to glut the lust of godless libertines. Its sign was the ligniyoni, its ideal the almighty dollar. Through its feculent columns Muckle-mouthed Meg and Doll Tearsheet made assignations with forks-of-the-creeks fools, while blear-eyed bummers and rotten-livered rounders requested respectable women to meet them at unfrequented places and wear campmeeting lingerie. The Iconoclast compelled its unrespected contemporary to purify its "personal column"—and this service to society has never been forgiven by the bench-legged hydrocephalous grand panjandrum of that paper. The *Post* next proceeded to publish a directory of Houston's redlight district, giving names and addresses of the "madames," the number of their "boarders" and the condition of the merchandise thrown upon the market. All that was necessary to make the Post's Bawdy-house Guide complete was the addition of rate-cards. On that little bit of journalistic "enterprise" the Icon. put a kibosh also, much to the satisfaction of every decent family in Harris county. Now the fecular sheet has found a new road to infamy—is advertising garters fit only to adorn the crummy underpinning of negro prostitutes. It does seem that the *Post* will do anything for a dollar—except be decent. Owing to the mental perversity of its management, respectability is for it impossible. It is a social leper, a journalistic pariah. It is devoid of political principle as a thieving tomcat of conscience. It has no more stability than a bad smell in a simoon. It has deified and damned every statesman by turn. It has been on every possible side of every public question, and wept bitter tears of regret because further change of policy were impossible. It is a perfect maelstrom of misinformation, the avatar of impudence, the incarnation of infamy—a social cesspool whose malodor spreads contagion like the rank breath of the gila-monster or the shade of a upas tree. Yet its editor, I am told, aspires to the lieutenant governorship of Texas. Verily, he's "got his gall." He will indeed be "a warm baby" if elevated to that inconsiderable office and permitted to monkey with the sceptre while the guv. is doing the elegant elsewhere. Texas may certainly consider herself fortunate if he does not pawn the fasces of power and blow in the proceeds of the erstwhile John Bell's variety joint. Should he do so, he will probably be permitted to "take off his things." The *Post* "ad." is worse than that of Holy John Wanamaker, who once announced in the Philadelphia papers that "Parisian thoughts are sewn in our underwear." With such lingeries I should imagine that "call again" garters would be the proper caper. Such a combination would suggest the patent medicine certificate of the happy husband who joyfully testified that "My wife was so nervous that I could not sleep with her, but after taking two bottles of your remarkable, etc., she has so far recovered that anybody can sleep with her." Just what effect the "Parisian thought" underwear of Holy John Wanamaker had upon the pre-eminently respectable people of Philadelphia I shall not assume to say, but I should consider such goods contraband of war when found on a Sunday school bargain counter. Imagine the result of introducing "Parisian thoughts" into the unbleached muslin lingerie of a lot of single-standard-of-morals old maids! There's really no telling for what Harrison's professional Sunday school superintendent is responsible. He's a rank conspirator against the Seventh Commandment. The *Post* should be abated as an incorrigible nuisance—it is a standing menace to the morality of the community. It has never been a legitimate journal. Its chief sources of revenue have been fake voting contests and unclean "ads." that range in sphacelation from abortion pills to garters for prostitutes. What this country seems to need is a press censorship. The second rate newspapers are mistaking liberty for license. The dogma that public opinion can be depended upon to correct the evil is an "iridescent dream" —the public will stand almost anything so long as its religious theses and political confessions of faith are let alone. Men claiming to be quasi-decent, if not altogether respectable, will carry home day after day and suffer to be read by their young daughters such a paper as the Houston *Post*—with its "w. y. o. d.," and "take off your things" advertisements, its puffs of abortion pills and syphilitic panaceas—who would have a conniption fit and fall in it should a copy of Bob Ingersoll's eloquent lecture on Abraham

Lincoln creep into their library. The stench of such a paper creeps abroad like the malodor of a cloaca, beslimes the senses like the noxious exhalations of an open sewer. How in God's name men can be found so debased as to work on such a sheet is beyond my comprehension. I once undertook to hold down its editorial page; but soon "got sore at myself," cursed everything connected therewith, from the pink-haired president of the company to the peewee business manager, got out, purified myself— and have been sick at the stomach ever since. Should a man lay a copy of the foul sheet on my parlor table, I'd blow his head off with a shotgun. All that I now see of the paper is the clippings sent me by disgusted Houstonians, and I take those out behind the barn to read— then bury them lest they poison the hogs. I regard my temporary connection with the sheet much as Jean Valjean must his tramp through the Parisian sewers. It is a ten-legged nightmare, an infamy that I can never outlive. I strove manfully to make the foul thing respectable, but the Augean stables proved too much for my pitchfork. I managed to occasionally inject into the sphacelated sheet a quasi-intelligent idea, to disguise its feculence with a breath of sentiment that by contrast seemed an air from Araby the blest; but the stupid ignorance and dollar-worshipping of the management soon dragged it back into the noisome depths of hopeless nescience and subter-brutish degradation. Poor old Houston! A morning newspaper should be a city's crown of glory, an intellectual Aurora ushering in the new-born day; but in Houston's case her chief newspaper is a sorrow's crown of sorrow, her inexpungable badge of shame.

ATHEISM AND ORTHODOXY.

This is rapidly becoming a government of the church, for the church and by the church. The Deist, the Atheist and the Agnostic have no political rights which the religionists feel bound to respect. Though Robert G. Ingersoll possessed the wisdom of Solomon, the patriotism of Washington and the justice of Aristides, he could not be elected governor of any state in the American Union—the pulpit and religious press would strike his trail, remorseless as death, persistent as taxes. Not only is the unbeliever boycotted politically, but the taboo not unfrequently extends to business. An acknowledgment of the orthodox God has become a *sine qua non* for success in every walk of life; hence we see men like Taber and Hitchcock professing Christianity during their lifetime, even posing as church officials of exemplary piety, and promulgating their real sentiments after death has deprived vindictive bigotry of power to help or harm. Yet this is supposed to be a land where every individual enjoys the broadest religious liberty! Only those enjoy it who care to pay the price—and that price is persistent calumny and political ostracism. "No union of church and state" is the nation's shibboleth; yet the union exists both *de facto* and *de jure*, and is growing stronger every day. Not only does the political boycott extend to unbelievers, but includes Catholics, Jews, and all others who dissent from the loose-jointed Protestant dogma which has this nation under its heel. It were as impossible to elect a Catholic or a Jew to the presidency as to elevate an avowed Atheist to that high office. And yet this is really a nation of "Liberals," if not of Agnostics. Of our 70,000,000 people less than 25,000,000 are church communicants, and at least 70 per cent. of these are women and children. A great majority of American voters regard the church with indifference if not with aversion, yet the religious tail continues to wag the political dog. This is because the dissenters from religious dogma, as a rule, are not aggressive, while its devotees are engaged in a perpetual crusade. The church people are active while the dissenters are passive. The latter, unorganized, and ignorant of their numerical strength, follow in the wake of the religious bandwagon to avoid the inevitable boycott. The result is that the church dominates the nation and compels even those who despise it to contribute to its support. Millions are donated annually as a matter of expediency—a sop to the ever-hungry Cerberus—by men like Taber, who regard it as a millstone slung about the neck of the giant of civilization. Its vast properties are exempted from taxation, thereby placing a heavier burden upon those who consider it the nursing mother of ignorance and superstition. Atheists and Agnostics, Jews and Catholics are taxed to provide fat salaries for army and navy, legislative and prison chaplains of the Protestant persuasion, while every state has a law making it a crime to do on Sunday what is considered praiseworthy on Monday. Those whose religion requires them to respect the seventh day of the week as the Sabbath are compelled by law to observe another. Such is the condition today of a nation that was christened by a Deist, whose greatest president was an Agnostic, whose wisest philosopher was an Atheist, and to establish which men of all faiths fought and suffered and died side by side! Such is the condition of a nation so secular in its incipiency that Almighty God is not mentioned in its constitution! From the brain of Thomas Paine, Columbia sprang, full-panoplied, like Minerva from the brow of Olympian Jove. When the colonists stood hesitating, uncertain whether to endure present ills or fly to others they knew not of, he threw the gage of battle full and fair in Britain's haughty face. It is universally conceded that his "Crisis" precipitated the conflict. When defeat followed defeat; when the new-born nation was bankrupt and her soldiers starving at Valley Forge, it was Paine's burning words that revived their faltering faith. His pamphlets were read to the ragged Continentals drawn up in battle array, and again and again they set their breasts against the bayonet until even the British lion recoiled and the star of empire rose in the western world. Yet were Paine alive today he couldn't be elected dog-catcher of this blessed county of McLennan. Were Benjamin Franklin publishing a newspaper in Waco the Baptists would boycott it. Were Thomas Jefferson a resident of this city the pruriently pious would accuse him of reading the Iconoclast. I am neither Atheist, Catholic nor Jew, but I protest against the present status of affairs as a rank injustice. Every man should be privileged to exercise his brains without being placed under a ban, to speak forth his honest thought without paying a penalty, for only where there is freedom of expression is progress possible. Those who regard revealed religion as a rank superstition should not be taxed, directly or indirectly, for its support. Frankly, I regard Atheism as rank folly, the God of the Jews a savage and the claims of the Pope as preposterous; but I have no more quarrel with a man for differing with me in religon than for fancying a blonde type of beauty while I prefer the brunette. I would take God out of politics—would ask only of the candidate for office, Is he a patriot with a reasonable stock of honesty and intellect? I would base all secular laws on human necessity. I would accord to all the fullest religious liberty. Not only would this be justice to the dissenter, but it would redound to the benefit of the church. It would win for it the respect of those who now regard it with distrust, and render them more inclined to receive its doctrines. It is not the Ingersolls but the religious intolerants who make Atheists. It is attempted coercion that breeds rebellion. Whenever I see a sanctified yap who is short on brains and long on gall standing up in the Texas legislature and unwinding a two-minute perfunctory prayer for a $5 bill which I must help to pay I feel less kindly to his creed and all his class. When I am denied a bath, a shave or a glass of beer on Sunday because my enjoyment thereof would give a joblot of whining pietists a pain, I conclude that if God interests himself in such bigots he's in precious small business. When I hear it urged against a candidate for office that he's a Catholic or Atheist, I instinctively reach for a stuffed club. And I presume that such things provoke in like manner all men whose minds are not affected with the mildew of prevalent orthodoxy. It provokes an anti-church prejudice. "Thou shalt" and "Thou shalt not" are scorpion whips that goad the sons of men to mutiny. The church has never gained aught by persecution. It may compel lip-service, but cannot drive love and respect into the hearts of men with a maul. A just and humane policy on the part of the church; more charity and less dogmatism; a recognition of the right of every sentient creature to its own opinion; a confession of the fact that the wisest theologian is but groping toward the light and may misinterpret God's message; the absolute elimination of religion from secular affairs; less thunderous pulpiteering and more example of the true Christian kind, would eliminate Atheism from this land, for the spirit of Christ when made manifest in men appeals to all humanity with irresistible power. But just so long as the church appeals to the law to enforce its edicts; so long as it makes it a crime to do that which works no injustice to others; so long as it compels an unwilling support; so long as it boycotts those who dissent from its ever-shifting dogma, it will breed hypocrites and multiply humbugs. The day inevitably comes when men weary of a presumptuous and cruel master and rise in revolt. And the stronger the repression the fiercer the explosion. It was not altogether the fault of the French people that they once humiliated the priesthood to the very dust and crowned a courtesan Goddess of Reason in Notre Dame. When all the pent-up antagonism to American Protestantism explodes, we may find the church declared a nuisance, and not only taxed, but compelled to pay a special license like the saloon and other supposed pests of the body social. If it be true that "Pride goeth before a fall," then is American Protestantism preparing to hit the ground and hit it almighty hard. I have no objection to Protestantism nor to any other religious ism, but I do object to the engrafting of sectarian dogmas upon the laws of this land. Protestant presumption is dividing the people of this country into two great classes, one of which it is driving toward Atheism, the other toward Catholicism. It would be difficult to convince the average camp-meeting spouter and baptismal 'sputer that this is true; but it is a fact nevertheless, and quite familiar to all careful students of cause and effect. Meantime there is a third class, small but gradually expanding, composed of those who study the philosophy of religion, and who are gradually rising above the meshes of sectarianism and the mistakes of dogmatism into that pure light where all religions are found to be fundamentally the same, all equally true, each being God's message as he has delivered it to men of varying minds. These regard both the Atheist and the Dogmatist with toleration and—pity. These read God's word in the Koran as well as in the Bible, and find in Gautama a Son of God as well as in the Man of Galilee. These require no celestial laws graved on tables of stone, no revelation by prophet or seer: for the Universe is their Sacred Book, and as they scan its mystic pages they forget the foolish visions and idle dreams of little men. These require no petty "miracles" to confirm their faith, for in all that is they find a natural supernaturalism, an everlasting testimony. These can worship equally well in Protestant church or Catholic cathedral, in Mohammedan mosque or Buddhist temple—wheresoever God is adored, by whatsoever name, they reverently bend the knee. High above the clash of creeds and the war of cults, these men look down with painful surprise at an Ingersoll charging full tilt at mythical miracles, and Talmage exploiting his "scriptural evidence," gleaned from the mummified cats of ancient Egypt and the hoary rubbish of Palestine; then they turn their faces once again to God's perpetual revelation and forget those who seek him in the printed page and drink in with greedy ears the sing-song dissonance of the pulpiteer.

LADONIA'S AMAZONIAN GUARD.

Pope declares that "the worst of madmen is a saint run mad;" but Pope never saw a female Prohibitionist with her war-paint on, blood in her eye, a cow-hide in her lily-white hand—chasing John Barleycorn around a stump, hitting him a lick at every jump. The mania of a saint run mad were as nothing to the fury of a female who devotes her physical energies to the cause of temperance "reform." There appears to be something in Prohibition that excites a kind of moral *mania a potu*. As a craze producer it lays over the gold-cure and rivals the Georgia evangelist. The effects of Prohibition on its devotees are worthy the profoundest study by neurologists and insanity experts. It seems to be a kind of black magic or mental thaumaturgics that transposes the sexes—converts men into long-haired, hysterical Miss Nancys, women into dangerous cranks. Manhood degenerates beneath its blight into a chronic itch for petty meddling, the modest virtues of womanhood are supplanted by a feverish craving for mob violence. There are exceptions, 'tis true; but they only prove the rule. There are male Prohibs who are not canting Pharisees, and female victims of the cold water craze who are not vicious-minded fanatics—just as there are three-legged calves and red-headed "coons." A recent occurrence at Ladonia, Texas, aptly illustrates the evil inherent in the Prohibition idiocy—the awful effects of that anti-Christian and un-American folly. A dispatch to the Fort Worth *Mail-Telegram* says:

For about ten days a number of women at Ladonia, Fannin county, have been carrying on a crusade against the liquor traffic at that place. They began by visiting cold storage houses and other places where whiskey and beer was supposed to be sold, and conducting prayer meetings. On Tuesday they called on Dr. J. M. Hancock, who had recently moved here from Bonham, and requested him to attend church regularly. He replied that he would consult his own feelings about it, and they then tried to get him to agree to attend prayer meetings for ten consecutive nights, but he would not promise, and later in the week they gave him a peremptory order to leave town. This evening he packed his grip and went to the depot to take the train. While in the waiting room fifteen women marched in armed with cowhides and proceeded to apply the lashes to him with all their might. His face, hands and neck were terribly lacerated, and the blood poured from the gashes in streams, and after whipping him the women went to their homes, and a great crowd gathered around and intense excitement prevailed. Dr. Hancock insisted on leaving, but his friends interposed and would not let him go, declaring they would kill the first man or woman who attempted to lay violent hands on him again. He did not leave. Ladonia is a local option town, and the doctor's offense consisted of writing prescriptions for whiskey. The women who did the whipping are prominent church workers. It is feared that the affair will lead to serious trouble. The act is condemned by a majority of the best people.

A dispatch to the Dallas *News* declares that the party was "composed of twenty highly respected ladies;" that they gave the doctor 500 lashes because he was suspected of having written whiskey prescriptions for those afflicted only with abnormal alcoholic appetites, and that he immediately left town. Had not publicans, sinners and others not powerful in prayer, gone to his rescue, these "prominent church workers" might have wound up the seance by hanging the doctor or beating his brains out with a crowbar! But why this discrimination between the man of medicine and the proprietors of "places where whiskey and beer are supposed to be sold?" Was it because he would not go to church regularly, or attend prayer-meeting ten nights at a stretch? Were the former favorites with the "ladies," while the latter had no one to love him? Or was the doctor a little man, and the beer-jerkers big fellows —liable to lay obstreperous visitors across the bar and beat their patent health-bustles off with a bung-starter? Does this interesting band of female reformers pray only for those they can't lick, and put the bud to the balance? Prayers and tearful pleadings one day, cowhides the next, all in the name of Christ—who could make his own wine and was independent of both Prohibitionists and medicinal prescriptions! The crowd that did up the doctor was composed of "ladies" undoubtedly. Bulwer says that every woman is a lady, still there are many incapable of giving such remarkable outward evidence of an inward grace. They may have been "highly respected;" but if so it was an honor they evidently did not deserve. If the doctor had violated the law, there were courts provided for his punishment. If he had committed a heinous crime, really deserving of heroic treatment, we may safely conclude that the men of the community would have attended to his case. It seems that he was only suspected of a venial fault, yet an indignity was visited upon him that will curse him as long as he lives. Should he go to the antipodes and by his talents and industry, win wealth and honors, sooner or later some kind Christian soul would whisper it about that he was licked and run out of Ladonia by the "ladies," and men would shun him as tho' he had committed some cowardly crime. Those Ladonia "ladies" would have dealt much kindlier by the doctor and done far more honor to themselves had they taken a club and killed him. I suppose that he quietly took the medicine measured out to him by those good Christian ladies who prayed so fervently for the other fellows; there was really nothing else for him to do, for a gentleman is not expected to raise a hand in his own defense when brutally assaulted by the "softer sex"—those dear creatures "created but little lower than the angels." If attacked by all the old "cats" that ever howled their obscene curses thro' "Hell's Halfacre"—and that's the kind who are most expert with the cowhide—he must "grin and bear it," however undeserved his disgrace. The Iconoclast has ever been a devout worshipper at the shrine of the gentler sex. The person of a true woman is sacred as the body of Christ. To strike such a one were to commit the chief of crimes; but when "ladies," however "highly respected," deliberately unsex themselves, and, without grievous provocation, set upon a man like a gang of brutal sand-baggers, he should be privileged to treat them as tho' they wore pants instead of petticoats. Had Dr. Hancock waltzed into those "highly respected ladies" and trimmed them up to the queen's taste with their own cowhides, his breach of the laws of chivalry would have been generally condoned. It would have afforded a salutary lesson to alleged ladies elsewhere, who seek notoriety by brandishing a whip about some unresisting man's head. I can sympathize with a woman who puts a knife into her paramour in a fit of jealous passion, or shoots the liver out of some scurvy dog who has defamed her; but when a mob of females go chasing around with bull-whips in the name of morality, they deserve an heroic dose of their own medicine. Those twenty Ladonia "ladies" have disgraced Dr. Hancock in the eyes of the unreasoning rabble—who tie a man's hands, then damn him for suffering an indignity; but to do so they put themselves on a parity with the African king's amazons, and branded their husbands as moral bankrupts and intellectual miscarriages. I would rather be Dr. Hancock and suffer all the penalties of his disgrace, than husband to a female who had thus publicly proclaimed me incapable of keeping my seldom brains above my belly-band—that it devolved upon her, as head of the household, to remove temptation from my path by fair means or by foul. The husbands, brothers and sons of those twenty "ladies" must indeed be proud of the brawny Amazonian Guard that is standing so valiantly between them and the destructive "rum demon!" How sweet and soul-satisfying must be their sense of safety! While we do daily battle with the world, the flesh and the devil, they sit secure beneath their vine and fig tree with none to molest them or make them afraid—the Ladies' Cowhide Legion hath driven the cholera-morbus prescription and snake-bite antidote far from the sacred roost of the featherless goslings! With what lofty disdain they must curl their lips as they contemplate the doctor, wandering, an outcast on the earth, the brand of the cowhide on his brow—driven forth in disgrace by the dauntless Jezebels for not knowing whether their dear hubbies were lying or not when they claimed to really need red licker. And what a picnic the "cold storage" and "soft-cider" men must be having since the drug-store competition is cut off—and the ladies "never teched 'em!" It is a noteworthy fact that the class of "ladies" who lead crusades on saloons, smash bottles and spill beer; who pray for liquor dealers and cowhide doctors, are usually the very ones who become hysterical over noted criminals and fill the cells of condemned murderers with cut flowers. Texas has been "damned to everlasting fame" by the outbreak of the Ladonia females. It will do the State more harm than anything that has hitherto happened. It will kill the town of Ladonia—make its very name a by-word and a reproach among the nations. Everybody will think of Ladonia as an excellent place to stay away from; and so it is, if the cowhiders are a fair sample of its female inhabitants. It is not only an irreparable injury to the good name of the State, but a blot on womanhood throughout the world. After learning that such excesses are possible by "highly respected ladies," it is difficult indeed to regain the old idea of womanhood so dear to the masculine heart. We have been accustomed to think of woman as "with us, but not of us;" and the revelation that she too is but a gilded savage comes in the nature of a shock. Those chiefly concerned may not thank me overmuch for this plain sermon; but it is honestly intended for their good. Apparent cruelty is sometimes the greatest kindness. Our best friends are those who frankly tell us of our faults. "Faith, Hope and Charity" is the Pauline credo—"and the greatest of these is Charity." This may be news to the "prominent church workers" of Ladonia, but it is none the less true. If the cowhiders would prove that they are both true women and consistent Christians, let them apologize to Dr. Hancock for their brutal outbreak, give the church in which they learned such barbarities the marble heart, go back to their babes, where they properly belong, and leave the management of municipal affairs to men. That may not be the religion taught by Dr. Leatherhead; but it's the creed of Christ and the Iconoclast.

OUR PUBLIC PANDERS.

Had I lived in the land of the Pharoahs when it was overrun with lice I should have fought the vermin, not with any hope of exterminating the disgusting parasites, but because such protest would have afforded me some slight satisfaction and kept a few square inches of space free from them. I war on the corrupt American press for the selfsame reason that I would have expended my best energies crushing lice in Egypt—and with about as little hope of exterminating the nauseous plague. Battling with vermin were an appetizing occupation compared to warring upon a press reeking with moral rottenness, flooded with the foulest filth and destitute of the faintest shadow of shame; still it is some poor comfort to strike at it—to call the attention of the American people to the fact that while prating of God and morality, honor and virtue, they are fostering and feeding a coterie of inhuman harpies who, for a few pence, are day by day flaunting in the faces of the children of their benefactors flaming advertisements calculated to familiarize them with every species of crime, with the foulest phases of human degradation, the deepest damnation ever touched by any creature created in the divine image of God.

Take up almost any newspaper published in this country, daily or weekly, large or small, and you will find staring you in the face display advertisements of nostrums for the cure of criminal complaints, charlatans, promising to restore the worn out roue's power for evil, abortion recipes, gambling devices, love philters, quack doctor's books filled with suggestive pictures—especially designed for the young—and probably, to crown the crime, a "personal column," wherein the lawless libertine sets his snares for foolish school girls; the whole making a symposium of reeking rottenness that might cause the gorge of the very prince of Hell to rise.

As I might, had I lived in Egypt during the plagues, have killed a few lice, so have I, since beginning this crusade upon the press, compelled a few papers to purify or altogether abandon their assignation column; but I am not aware that a single one has acquired sufficient shame to decline an advertisement of a disgusting quack nostrum if the payment was guaranteed. The crime of printing such ads. is a two-fold one. Not only does it familiarize the very school children with the lowest forms of vice, robbing youth of its purity and sweetness, but it fosters crime. A medicine guaranteed to produce abortion has been advertised for years past in nearly every American newspaper, great and small. Such extensive advertising costs many thousands of dollars. The investment pays or the advertisement would be discontinued. Do you understand what that means? It means that the printing of that one advertisement has caused thousands of crimes to be committed or attempted, probably hundreds of lives to be sacrificed. Yet newspapers making great pretense to respectability are printing it; papers are printing it that have the polite and elegant gall to denounce the Iconoclast as an "unclean sheet"—to go into moral hysterics because it presumed to criticise the hippodroming methods of Sam Jones! People subscribe for such papers and carry them home for their daughters to read, who think it simply dreadful that the Iconoclast does not cross itself every time a priest sneezes, or cry God bless you, whenever a preacher says amen! It is strange what a small gnat will gag some people who have just gulped down a very large and mangy camel! A man who will allow the average newspaper, bearing its cargo of disgraceful and disgusting advertisements to come into his house, cannot be really shocked by anything short of an electric bolt or the kick of a mule. If his stomach will stand syphilitic literature it will stand anything. A postmaster-general who admits to the mails publications containing such ads. and bars out anything whatsoever that the brain of a demon could devise and the hand of a human being pen, is a rank hypocrite, a sanctimonious fraud.

If I had to choose between robbing graves and printing such advertisements for hire as can be found in nine-tenths of the American newspapers, I would not hesitate a moment, but proceed to tumble the dead out of their coffins and strip their cold, clammy fingers of their trifling ornaments. I could not harm the dead by thus despoiling their bodies, but by printing such ads. I could and would corrupt the souls of the living. The cutpurse and the burglar, the bunco-steerer and sheep thief are honorable men, are gentlemen, aye, demi-gods by comparison with the publishers who will accept the class of advertisements I am here discussing. The latter only find their level among rape fiends, panders, scandal-mongers, paid assassins and perjurers. This is plain talk, but so obviously true that the offenders will not dare quarrel with it. They will swallow it to a man, with the stolid indifference of a Digger Indian absorbing a gourdful of grasshopper soup—and continue to sell their space to the foulest of all Hell's foul hierarchy, while posing as public educators and ranting about morality! The average American editor posing as a public pedagogue were like the devil rebuking sin—or a skunk lecturing on sweet incense!

AN INFERNAL FRAUD.

The most colossal fraud ever perpetrated on a free people is the federal pension fake. It smells to heaven. It is infamy incarnate. It is the apotheosis of impudence. That the American people will tamely submit to such a brazen imposition is circumstantial evidence that there's something wrong with their heads, or that they are "white-livered and lack gall." They certainly lack something, or they would have made a "roar" long ere this that would have appalled the shameless robbers. It is popularly supposed that the Republican party is chiefly responsible for this wholesale despoliation of the people; but that's a josh. The Democrats have bid the public money for the "old soldier vote" fully as freely as have the Republicans. In the seven years they have had a whack at the treasury since the war, they have got away with more than 724 millions of money coddling "the saviors of the country." The first year of Cleveland's first term the annual expenditure for pensions was raised nearly 8½ millions, and during the first year of his second term it touched high water mark by a saltation of more than 17 millions. The Democrats had been accused of being "Southern sympathizers," "copperheads" and "enemies of the old soldier," and they were determined to rout their critics or bankrupt the country. When a man has suffered serious injury in his country's service and is unable to properly provide for himself and those dependent upon him, he should be given a pension, and no niggardly one either; but that the generosity and patriotism of the American people have been shamefully abused in this pension business, a glance at the statistics will prove. We may reasonably infer that by the year 1870 every man disabled in the war had discovered that fact and called the attention of Congress to his case. The men who overthrew the Confederacy were in control of the government, and looked carefully to the interests of their old comrades. Every applicant having a reasonable claim on the public bounty was promptly pensioned; yet in 1870 there were less than 200,000 names on the roll, and the annual expenditure was under 28 millions. In 1893 there were more than 966,000 names on the roll and the annual expenditure exceeded 158 millions. The total number of pension claims allowed from 1861 to 1895 inclusive, was 1,436,191—a larger number than the Federal Government ever had soldiers south of the Ohio! Men are drawing pensions who received fat bounties for enlisting, yet were never provided with arms. The government is paying out millions annually on account of diseases contracted and injuries received fifteen years after the last gun was fired. It is providing liberal pensions, because of "disabilities," men who are making journeymen's wages at blacksmithing and other trades requiring more than the average physical strength. It is taxing people who are poor as poverty to pension men whose fortunes reach seven figures. If the people must have a political issue in order to be happy, here's one that's a howling jimhun. From 1861 to 1895 inclusive we paid out nearly two billion dollars in pensions, or double the amount of the national debt. It has already cost more to save the "old soldier" than it did to preserve the government, and we are still touched to the tune of 40 millions every twelvemonth, or about $2 per capita, including infants and idiots, penitentiary inmates and preachers. It was supposed that we had reached the high-water mark in 1893, and that thenceforth the decline would be rapid; but the expenditure in '95 was greater than in '94, and we know not what the future will bring forth. If the annual expenditure decreases during the next 25 years, in the same ratio that it increased, during the last 25 years, we may get out of this for something in excess of the value of all property in the insurgent states at the close of the war; but God only knows where it will end. We are still paying pensions on account of the Revolution, which ended 113 years ago. Some of the conscript fathers took young wives to comfort their old age, and left their support as a legacy to posterity. As many of the veterans of the late unpleasantness are following the example of their illustrious predecessors, we are liable to have "civil war widows" on our hands a century hence—some of whom have not yet been born! Sentiment is all right; but it should be tempered with reason. Grant declared the pension expenditure should not exceed 50 millions per annum a quarter of a century after the close of the war, and should then rapidly decline, but Grant was a soldier rather than a "statesman," a patriot instead of a politician. It never occurred to him to give the "old soldier" the country in part payment for saving it, and let the people to work out the remainder. Make it an issue in this campaign that no man able to earn journeyman's wages, no person of either sex possessing health and strength, or an income of $500 per annum, shall be quartered on the people—that the pension expenditure be cut to the figure given as the maximum by General Grant.

HYPNOTIC POWER OF HER.

I have received a letter from Tyler, Texas, propounding the following fateful conundrum: "Can Woman Hypnotize Man?" My correspondent adds that "by answering, the Iconoclast will confer a favor on the people of Tyler, decide a bet and settle a vexatious question."

The affirmative scoops the stakes—wins dead easy, and world without end. The man who puts his doubloons on the negative either never saw a woman until after she was dead, or didn't know what ailed him when under her hypnotic influence. Perhaps he imagined that he had a chronic case of yellow jaundice, was threatened with paresis or had been inadvertently struck by lightning. Perhaps he's under the mystic spell of some "wily Vivien" even now, and laying foolish wagers in his mesmeric sleep. "Can woman hypnotize man?" Well, I should snigger. She can hypnotize anything that wears pants, from the prince at his gilded poker game, to the peasant scattering worm poison in the lowly cotton patch and revolving in his think tank the tenets of Populism; and I'm not sure but the clothing-store dummies and their brother dudes are simply the physical wrecks and mental ruins of her hypnotic medicine. She hypnotizes because she can't help it. She's built that way. The Tyler savants are 'way behind the times. They are plunging into the shoreless realm of psychology in search of information that was trite in antediluvian times. They are trying to determine whether man is a free moral agent in matters matrimonial, when the sire of Solomon had made answer, and Lillian Russell's multitudinous husbands settled the "vexatious question" forever and for aye. But perhaps Tyler has been too busy raising politicians to keep pace with the psychological procession. Eve hypnotized Adam and made him cast away the empire of the earth for a scrubby apple, and ever since her fair daughters have been making men imitate their remote forefather's folly.

Woman does not "operate" as do the professional he-hypnotists. Instead of giving you a bright button or brand-new dime to look at, she puts her dimples in evidence —maelstroms of love in a sea of beauty. She dazzles you for a moment with the dreamy splendor of her eyes, then studies the toe of a boot that would raise a Kansas corn-crop for Trilby or supply Cinderella with bunions. She looks down to blush and she looks up to sigh—catches you "a-comin' an' goin' "—and you're gone! You realize that the linchpin is slipping out of your logic, but you let 'er slip. You suspect that your judgment has taken unto itself wings, and that you couldn't tell whether you're a red licker Democrat or a hard-cider Prohibitionist; but you don't care. You simply bid farewell to every fear and give the "operator" your undivided attention. She plays with a skilled hand on all your senses, until the last one of them "passes in music out of sight" and leaves you a mental bankrupt. She makes you drunken with the music of her voice and maddens you with the low, sweet melody of her skirts. She permits you, quite accidentally, of course, to catch a glimpse of an ankle turned for an angel, and, as she bends forward to chastise you with her fan, your vagrant gaze rests for a fleeting moment on alabaster hemispheres rising in a billowy sea of lace, like Aphrodite cradled in old ocean's foam. You are now far advanced in the hypnotic trance, and very fond of it as far as you've got. Her every posture is a living picture, her slightest movement a sensuous symphony, her breath upon your cheek a perfumed air to waft you to the dreamy but dangerous land of the lotus-eaters. You drift nearer, and ever nearer, like a moth revolving in narrowing circles around an incandescent light, until you find yourself alone with her in some cosy nook, the world forgetting if not by your creditors forgot. Being naturally industrious, you seek employment, and she gives you her hand to hold. Of course, she could hold it herself, but the occupation pleases you, and she doesn't mind. Besides, you make more rapid progress into the realm of irresponsibility by taking care of it for her occasionally. You conceive that what is worth doing at all is worth doing well, and freeze to that little fragment of pulsing snow like a farmer to his Waterbury in a camp-meeting crowd She rewards your devotion to duty by a gentle pressure, and a magnetic thrill starts at your finger tips and goes through your system like an applejack toddy, until it makes your toes tingle, then starts on its return trip, gathering volume as it travels, until it becomes a tidal wave that envelops all your world. You are now uncertain whether you have hit the lottery for the capital prize or been nominated for justice of the peace. You have lost your identity, and should you chance to meet yourself in the middle of the road would need an introduction. The larger the supply of brains you sat into the game with, the less you have left. You begin to talk incoherently, and lay the premise for a breach of promise case. You sip the hand-made nectar from the rosy slot in her face, harrow the Parisian peach bloom on her cheek with your scrubbing-brush mustache, reduce the circumference of her health-corset with your manly arm, and your hypnotism is complete. Right there the last faint adumbration of responsibility ends and complete mental aberration begins. You sigh like a furnace and write sonnets to your mistress' eyebrow—you cut fantastic capers before high heaven for the divertisement of those who don't yet know how it is themselves. The "operator" may break the spell by marrying you, in which case you will return by easy stages to the normal and again become a sane man and useful member of society; but if she lets you down with the "sister" racket, your nervous system is pretty apt to sour. When a woman loses her hypnotic power she either straddles a bike, becomes a religious crank or seeks surcease for her sorrow among the female suffragists.

SEXUAL PURITY AND GUNPOWDER.

The Iconoclast can scarce be accused of being an "organ" of Governor Chappie Anserine Culberson. It certainly doesn't smell like it. It would gladly forego its regular Wednesday evening prayer-meeting to attend his political funeral in full regalia; but it halts the procession to remark that he has of late been subjected to considerable unjust criticism for declining to pardon a man who had been sentenced to the pen by a jury of his peers for slaying the supposed seducer of his daughter. Quite naturally, public sympathy is with the aged father who attempted to wash out in blood the dark blot upon the honor of his family; but Governor Culberson should be commended for referring the matter to the board of pardons for careful consideration. If the girl was under the age at which a female becomes the legal guardian of her virtue; if she was of weak mind, or her debauchment was accomplished by means of force or drugs, her destroyer deserved to die, and the father should be given not only a pardon but a pension for ridding the world of a cowardly and lustful cur; but a governor sworn to uphold the law should make haste slowly to set the seal of his approval to a homicide. I presume, from the esteem in which the Haskell County prisoner is held, that his act was justifiable; but if so, it is an exception to the rule. Entirely too many people kill the wrong party to a case of crim con. The modern young lady of marriageable age is amply able to protect her virtue if she really values it. It were difficult indeed to find a female who has reached her eighteenth birthday who does not understand full well that illicit intercourse is a sin against herself and society. If any such there be, their parents or guardians should be severely punished for dereliction in a most important duty. Every maid should, upon arriving at the age of puberty, be taught the relation of the sexes and the full meaning of the Seventh Commandment. She should be taught also that while all men should be chaste as Joseph, they are not so—that Dr. Cranfill and the editor of the Iconoclast are the only living illustrations of that exalted ideal. The immortal Washington could neither tell a lie nor resist the winsomeness of a pretty woman. Grover Cleveland, proclaimed by the golden harpers as "the grandest man of the century," once succeeded in "telling the truth," and we learned thereby that he had a well developed weakness for widows. Tom Ochiltree's kind of men stood together, however, and were numerous enough to make him chief magistrate. I do not defend the male debauchee; but I do say that every girl should be early taught that it depends entirely upon herself whether she becomes a noble and virtuous woman or a miserable wanton—that the shotgun is powerless to preserve her purity, that maidenly modesty is her only Palladium. Parents are too often responsible for the degradation of their daughters. Mothers neglect to properly instruct them regarding the duties they owe to society and the dangers inseparable from male companionship. They learn the sacred mysteries of reproduction from "flip" girls who are "on the mash" and rather glory in being considered a trifle rapid, and are too often led upon the reefs before they realize that sexual purity is the noblest jewel of perfect womanhood—that when it is lost she is already dead and damned. They are permitted, when the demon of passion is first stirring in their blood, to "keep company" with gay young men beyond the maternal eye, to dance and flirt, and the logical sequence of such license is a coroner's inquest on one of their boasted "conquests," a military marriage or another addition to the demi-mondaines. If young girls left so unguarded do not go to perdition, no credit is due to their parents. Even if they pass the ordeal without debauchment of body, they are so debased in mind as to be forever unfitted for noble wifehood, for no man possessed of refinement equal to that of a scurvy ape, will marry a maid who has been pawed over by Tom, Dick and the Devil. She's "damaged goods" the very moment she submits to the kisses and caresses of a man who does not make her the empress of his heart and home. All the perfume of the rose has disappeared—she has become entirely too promiscuous, too experienced. When a man learns that his wife delivered to him as a dowry a job-lot of reechy kisses, collected of male acquaintances much as she might accumulate picture cards or cancelled postage stamps, he should be privileged to sear her slobber-trap with a redhot iron and turn her loose to wander like a she-Cain thro' the world. Her sin differs in degree but not in kind from that of the common courtesan, and to a man of real refinement the degree is not so broad that it must be measured with an astronomer's instrument. The French manage young people much better than do we Americans. They afford them no opportunity to become unduly intimate. They do not commit snips of girls 15 or 16 years of age to the tender mercies of accomplished libertines, then proceed to "vindicate the family honor" by making a killing. They defer the dark parlor spooning, the paddling of perspiring palms, the "sitting down waltz" and single chair funny business, until the law hath given them Hymenic liberties. True it is that virtue which must be ever guarded is not worth the sentinel; but the proverb applies to adults, not to young girls enjoying their first attack of the giggles. The French maid goes to her husband with mind unpolluted by sexual sins, imagined if not committed with other men. A better plan than either the French, which takes it for granted that an unmarried woman only awaits a good opportunity to go astray; or the American, which assumes that all men are wingless angels, would be for the state to hold parents responsible for the purity of their daughters until the latter have reached the legal age of consent, and erase the word "seduction" from the criminal code. A woman rightly reared and carefully guarded until she is of marriageable age will never be "led astray" unless she furnishes the string. The wildest rake that ever went unhung will attempt no criminal familiarity with any woman unless she extends to him encouragement. No married woman possessed of sufficient intellectuality to successfully evade the lunatic asylum was ever "seduced." When a wife goes wrong she should come in for at least one barrel of the shotgun if the wronged husband decides that a dirty drab is worth the price of an ounce of powder.

THE AMERICAN SOVEREIGN.

An Egotistical Ignoramus.

The "able editor" and "prominent politician" are indulging a defenseless reading public with jejune speculations anent the salvation of the political feline next November. Predicting what the "American sovereign" will do with his vote half a year hence were much like standing in the vortex of chaos and betting on the phenomena—or forecasting the result of turning a lot of lunatics loose on a country pregnant with opportunities for self-slaughter.

We are wont to boast of our superior intelligence of the American sovereign, so-called, yet the fact must be patent to every man who hath eyes to see and a headpiece to understand the simplest social phenomena, that more than a moiety of the votes cast in this so-called enlightened land are but random shots into the darkness. It is safe to say that three out of five men who cast ballots at state and national elections, and thus, to a great extent, determine national polity and State policy, have no more idea of what they are doing than the automatons at a Punch and Judy show. Not one-half, not one-fourth of those good souls who are industriously huzzahing for Democracy or Republicanism, could, to save their supposed immortal souls, give a lucid explanation of the real difference existing between those "parties." Not one American sovereign in ten can explain wherein the so-called McKinley bill differs from the erstwhile Wilson bill. Yet he parades himself in foolish torchlight processions, fractures his lungs huzzahing for "Jeffersonian Democracy," of the "Grand Old Party;" drinks to the success of "principles" of which he knows no more than does the "yaller" dog following at his heels; quarrels with his neighbor about the tariff or silver coinage, vigorously curses the "free trade Democrats" or the "trade exclusion Republicans;" imagines that he is full to the neck with political prescience when he is but charged to the bursting point with prejudice and ridiculous egotism.

As a rule, the so-called American sovereign knows less of the science of political economy than of chemistry; can forecast with more intelligence the effect upon our solar system of the elimination of the planet Venus than the effect upon American trade and industry of the adoption of free trade or the unlimited coinage of silver.

And this politico-economic nescience, this partisan prejudice doing duty for political prescience, is not confined to the unlettered laborer, but permeates all classes. We boast ourselves a liberal and progressive people, yet there is no land beneath the sun where pure reason has a harder battle with stupid ignorance. One-half the American people inherit political and theological prejudices—are born with a mental strabismus which it were as idle to attempt to cure as to metamorphose a wooden Indian into a marble Madonna. The other half is led about by the nose by blind and blundering leaders or mendacious mountebanks, falling into every foul ditch which busy Superstition or brazen Charlatanism can dig for their foolish feet.

The shibboleth of the first class is, "Baptist, Baptist I was born and Baptist I will die." If one of this class be born a Democrat or Republican he can be depended upon to vote the ticket "straight" all his days, if the devil be the nominee or the "principles" of the two parties are violently transposed every four years. He will swallow any bitter bolus that his party in state or national convention assembled prepares for him. He calls himself a freeman, yet he is the most abject and pitiful slave that ever bowed his neck to a yoke or cowered beneath the lash; he does not possess the moral courage, the intellectual independence of the mangiest "yaller dawg" that ever trotted at the heels of a negro chicken-thief. He is not an intellectual entity, but an unimportant portion of a machine—and proud of it. He boasts that he always voted his party ticket "straight;" that he has been a life-long Democrat or Republican—is as proud of his fealty as niggers of ante-bellum days were of the fact that they never ran away—never attempted to be other than obedient slaves, diligently performing the tasks set for them by others! I would rather be a flea-bitten dog and bay at the moon than such an "American sovereign."

"But we must have political parties," I will be told. I do not see why. The very existence of various political parties is confirmation strong as proofs of holy writ that in the realm of statecraft the so-called American sovereign is but an intellectual infant in leading strings. Is not government what the press and politicians so delight to proclaim it, a vast stock company in which all are shareholders? Should it not be conducted, as they so often assert, "on strict business principles?" Now if all the stockholders of a company are wise business men will they not work together in harmony and thus promote the best interests of the concern? True, differences will arise, but they will be temporary and each division will be on different lines. Those who vote together on one proposition may vote against each other on the next. The stockholders will not split into permanent parties unless many of them be either ignorant of true business principles or dishonest—unless a portion of them are intent upon sacrificing the interests of the company to subserve their private ends. The honesty and intelligence of the personnel of the company can be correctly gauged by the extent, virulence and permanence of its factions.

The science of government is scarce more complex than the science of business. No man of average intelligence who makes an honest effort to understand it need fail, and the permanent division of the governmental stockholders into several warring factions argues inexcusable ignorance or widespread turpitude. To say that the average American voter is both dishonest and ignorant were indeed a terrible indictment and thousands would characterize it as libelous to a scandalous degree; but let us see whether such a statement would be so very wide of the mark:

It is a fact too patent to permit of debate that the public treasury is looted of tens of millions annually for the benefit of ex-federal soldiers who were never under fire, received no injury in the war and who were better paid for their services, better clothed and fed than ever theretofore; yet both great parties, eager for the "soldier vote," smile approval on the shameless robbery. We have a little starveling sugar industry in the South that has been languishing along for half a century or so—one of those "infants" that never take the trouble to cut teeth so long as they can feed on public pap. This lean and hungry nonentity of an "industry" had its greedy fingers in every poor man's pantry in the American Union—was being protected at a shameless cost to the entire people; yet when it was proposed to put sugar on the free list, the whole South—"tariff reform" Democracy and all— protested bitterly and refused to be pacified even when another public teat was slipped into the mouth of the small-armed but big-bellied infant.

"The old flag and an appropriation" is the shibboleth of the American sovereign. He cares not how much public treasure be squandered if it be wasted in his bailiwick. No matter how rank a "tariff reformer" or free-trader he be, he is ever willing that the industry in which he is interested should be protected with a tariff wall that towers into the very skies. He may pose as the avatar of Honesty, yet he looks, if not with favor, yet without protest, on shameless partisan trickery and deceit that enables his party to triumph at the polls. Of course, there are exceptions to the above indictment, but they are so rare as to be regarded as "cranks."

Every political party has an executive committee, whose duty is to achieve success by any possible means. An executive committee without a long purse and an able liar, without a man who understands how to place money where it will do the most good; without one capable of trading and trafficking principles for success, making unholy compromises with the devil, springing effective campaign falsehoods at the proper moment, making black appear white, and white black, glossing over or brazenly lying down the shortcomings of his own party and misrepresenting the motives and plans of the opposition—would be regarded as a dam in a desert, about as useful as a wooden watch. Political campaigns have come to be regarded by the public at large as wars of conquest wherein the spoils belong to the victors—in which all is fair, however flagrantly false.

The American people may be honest commercially, but their political conscience is irremediably "rotten."

Were the American sovereign one-half so intelligent as he thinks himself, so smart as a sycophantic press and the public birds of prey assure him is the case, he would realize that there is not to-day an "issue" worthy of the name squarely before the people. The tariff is the chief bone of contention, yet despite their noisy clamor, the two great parties are practically as one; they are both high tariff parties, only disagreeing about the architecture of the wall—or pretending to disagree, for if an "issue" does not exist one must be made, or politicians go out of business and the "able editor" drag his seldom brains for subjects. One party insists on a tariff for protection, the other a tariff for a revenue—a distinction without a difference so long as both parties regard the public treasury as their oyster. If a surplus accumulates under the administration of one party the other feels in duty bound to get rid of it; if one party creates a deficit, the other must mark its antithesis by piling up a surplus—for an "issue" is the very life of American politics! The Democracy is tempted to make "free and unlimited coinage of silver" an issue, but hesitates because the Eastern Shylocks would not furnish the sinews for such a war.

There is no political issue before the American people, and the war now being waged is one of men, not of measures; for plunder, not principles. The tug of war will be between Republicanism and Democracy, so-called—one great amorphous party divided into two factions, engaged in what we may call an internecine civil war for office. Yet seven-eighths of the so-called "intelligent American sovereigns" who are industriously wearing out their lungs, imagine there is as great a difference between these alleged "parties" as between white and black, between the Colorado coyote and a Numidian lion; that the salvation of the country depends upon the elevation of this or the other coterie of politicians to the public offices.

It is not to be wondered at that the great bulk of the American people are politically dishonest and ignorant. Where in God's name can they learn? From what fount imbibe political morality? They must depend chiefly on the press and politicians for information, and how can that which is corrupt inculcate honesty? how can that which possesses no wisdom give valuable instruction? Do not our national lawmakers spend long weary weeks in striving for party advantage? Is it not one of the articles of the confession of faith of each party in Congress to oppose whatsoever the other party approves, be it good or bad? Are not the political speeches made throughout the country in every campaign, state or national, but special pleas for party? Are not a vast majority of the newspapers but party organs, whose business it is to beatify one coterie of politicians and blacken the others? Can any mortal man form a correct conception of President Cleveland's administration by reading the Republican or Democratic newspapers, or both? by listening to a thousand political speeches by any or all brands of politicians? Has not the Republican press persistently painted him as an intellectual infant playing at Julius Cæsar? Have not the Pops and free-silverites branded him as the tool of Wall Street while the cuckoos were exercising their sweet voices in his praise? Really, the more newspapers a man reads, the less apt is he to form a just opinion of public men and measures; the fewer political speeches he listens to the more likely is he to bring to the discharge of public duties an honest, upright mind.

We must have schools to teach theology and medicine—even book-keeping and penmanship, dancing and boxing; but the uncrowned kings of America are expected to pick up the science of government "on the run;" to learn from "able editors," who reached the sanctum through the composing room instead of the library, what will subserve the best interests of 70,000,000 people, engaged in a thousand diverse industries and spread out from ocean to ocean, from Manitoba to the Mexican Gulf! The wonder is not that the

American sovereign knows so little of the science of government, but that he knows anything about it at all; not that he so often follows the bell of a political mountebank with the pathetic trust of a blind jackass plodding in the wake of a hay-wagon, but that he is not led to commit economic follies that would plunge both government and people into irremediable ruin.

PROFESSIONAL FAILURES.

I am always getting into trouble. Either my star is evil or my liver is out of its orbit. Scarce had I succeeded in soothing Dr. Riddle, the pretty man of Waxahachie, and jollying up Jehovah Boanerges Cranfill until his face shone like a new milk pan or a full moon beaming on a summer sea, ere a Sedalia, Mo., woman took her pen in hand to jab large rectangular orifices in my long-suffering soul. She is what editors are wont to refer to as "a widow lady," in contradistinction, I suppose, to a widow gentleman, and hath a son who is the apple of her eye. She explained to me by mail that the young man is a three-ply, all-wool and yard-wide genius who is destined to enact the role of Phaeton and set the world on fire if he does not slip his trolley wire in the selection of a profession, and besought my advice. I am always ready to advise the ladies—that's why they all come to me with their troubles—so I responded promptly and at my own expense that were the boy mine—which, of course, is not the case—I would advise him to give up all thoughts of a profession and become a farmer; not such an agriculturist as Col. Wilyum Shaw, but one of those people who can manipulate the turgid udder of the muley cow, harvest the esculent roasting ear and make the industrious potato bug wish he had been born a Populist. Hence these tears, this new addition to my increasing burden of agony. The young man was created for better things than pulling the bell-cord over a roan mule in the cotton patch and trailing blithely in the wake of a double-shovel plow—so his fond mother says. She thanks me for my advice in a tone of voice that leads me to doubt the genuineness of her gratitude; yet it was really the best I had in the shop. I mapped out for her genius-stricken olive-branch the one only "career" in which industry and frugality are reasonably certain to be rewarded with health, happiness and manly independence. Entirely too many youngsters are rushing into the professions instead of the corn field. Lawyers and preachers, doctors and dentists are being ground out by the thousands—and two-thirds of those already at large in the land have nothing in their pockets but an elegant assortment of holes. The woods are full of barristers without briefs, preachers without pulpits and physicians without patients. True it is that "there's always room at the top;" but it's a long, hard climb, and the road is thick strewn with wrecks. Furthermore, the most exalted merit, united with tireless industry, does not always reap its proper reward. In professional, as in commercial life, tact outstrips talent. We have abler preachers than Talmage toiling along year after year, in obscure villages at paltry recompense. Men have reached the supreme bench who possessed less legal ability than some of their brethren who wear out their lives in the chicken-courts. Hoyt made bushels of money out of such insufferable nonsense as "A Hole in the Ground," while really meritorious dramas had to be withdrawn from the stage. A Yvette Guilbert revels in riches while a Mrs. Bowers goes broke. A Du Maurier becomes rich and celebrated while William Marion Reedy—the greatest writer of his generation—is "a youth to fortune and to fame unknown." Not ten people in the city of Waco ever heard of him; yet Carlyle in his prime and Macaulay in his glory were not his peers. The "intellectual American public" will starve him to death—then build him a monument. A professional man, like a mantua-maker or milliner, must be "in vogue" or he'll have a deuced hard sledding, whatever may be his merits. If a physician can get a few ultra-fashionables to "call him in," his fortune is assured, tho' he couldn't distinguish between phrenics and physics, the pharmacopœia and Poor Richard's almanac. Without such an introduction he may be wise as Hippocrates and confined to a pauper practice. Lord Chief Justice Russell of England declares that the young lawyer "may consider himself fairly lucky if, after three or four years at the bar, he is making enough to keep soul and body together." True enough; but the chief justice makes a sad mistake when he advises the youthful wearer of the forensic toga to subsist meantime by newspaper work—"by reporting or leader writing." Journalism has become even a harder master than the law, and a briefless young barrister gets no opportunity to replenish his larder by "leader writing." He may consider himself in great luck if the editor gives him an opportunity to chase fire engines, or do a little police court reporting at $7 or $8 a week. English journals may furnish a hold-up for impecunious young men of other professions for aught I know; but just imagine a smart young preacher, lawyer or doctor applying for an important position on a great American daily! He'd be lucky if he escaped being locked up as a lunatic. The young professional men in this country who are doing the Micawber act usually patch out their scant incomes with cheap clerkships, and when once settled in such positions are apt to forget their early ambition and cling to their bread and butter. But granting that the professional man is always rewarded according to his merit, the youngster plunges in the dark, for his capabilities cannot be known even to himself until he has been tried on the world's battlefield. Too many mistake ambition for ability—a longing for the bays for inherent power to win them. Parents and preceptors are too prone to think that if a boy be apt in his studies he is a nascent genius and advise him to "aim high"—forgetful of the fact that exceptionally precocious youngsters seldom amount to much. The early unfolding of talent is evidence that it is of a low order. As a rule, girls are more apt than boys of the same age, and I am told that during a limited number of years negro children learn more readily than do those of Caucasian birth. Many of the world's greatest men graduated near the foot of their class; more did not obtain diplomas at all. Agriculture has ever been considered a noble occupation. The farmer is still a freeman. Many an intellectual Titan came with regret from the farm to the forum and returned to the peace of the country with pleasure. The city is a maelstrom, the mad whirlpool of life. Its bitter struggles and petty triumphs; the mad ambition of each inept goose to get its head above those of other foolish geese; the swirl and rush and jostle in the pell mell race for preferment—what does it all amount to? Who will know what politician was chief magistrate of Texas in this year of grace when our granite capitol has crumbled 'neath its burden of age? What of learned jurist, distinguished physician, pompous millionaire a thousand years hence—one tick of the mighty clock of Time! Why should we not live while we do live, beneath heaven's blue vault, amid the fragrant fields, by the rippling brook and watch the cool mists creep around the purple hills and God's banners flung like cloth of gold across the sunset sky? Only in the country can man feel that he's really free—elsewhere the proudest are but slaves. Why don't I experiment on myself, as does the doctor who will take his own draught! Perhaps I'm the original of Will Carleton's "Jim," whose judgment was too slim for a farmer, so his father concluded to be "makin' a editor outen o' him." I hope to spend my declining days in the country—"the world forgetting and by the world forgot." I will not even follow the example of Horace and bestride my mule for an occasional pilgrimage to Rome. Maecenas can have his costly suppers all by himself—"give me the bowl of samp and milk by homespun beauty poured." When I once get my lares and penates established where I can listen to the hum of the honey bee amid the clover blooms and the mocking bird trilling to its mate; where I can wander amid the spreading oaks and commune with "the spirits of the hills with all their dewy hair blown back like flame," I'll send just one message to the city, and it will read, "The public be damned."

PRICE'S PREDICAMENT.

Warren E. Price, editor of the *A. P. A. Magazine,* of San Francisco, the leading journal of the politico-religious darklantern conspirators, has just been sentenced to eighteen months penal servitude and to pay a fine of $500 for sending obscene matter through the mails. Price appears to be a thrifty-minded kuss, for in addition to editing the great organ of the Apes—the sewer through which most of the bigotry and bile of those fanatics and fools pours out upon the public—he conducted a bookstore which served as a "fence" for contraband art and libidinous literature. One would suppose that such merchandise would be kept sub-rosa and displayed only to the aphrodisiacal dames and habitues of the Chinese opium dens; but it developed at the trial that Price had actually sent circulars to school children, calling attention to his unequalled stock of moral corruption. And Price, be it remembered, is one of the high muck-a-mucks of those tearful patriots and pious parrots who are "rallying around the little red school-house" to protect it from the corruptive influence of the Papists! "Angels and ministers of grace defend us!" Set the wolf to guard the lamb, the jackal to keep watch and ward among our sacred dead, and the Apes to protect our innocents! Not does the attempt of Price to corrupt the school children measure the deep damnation of this moral pervert. It was proven that he had betrayed to the police other dealers in like literature that he might monopolize the sale of such filth in San Francisco. There may be truth among pirates and honor among thieves, but we look in vain for either among those legitimate descendants of Gulliver's unclean yahoos, the professional

Apes. While corrupting the children Price vented his rheum upon the garments of the brides of God. Page after page of his paper was devoted to the most bestial abuse of the Roman Catholic sisterhood—to branding the inmates of convents as but little better than bawds. I am not surprised that he broke into prison. A man capable of such calumnies as he emitted month after month is equal to any crime requiring no physical courage. Instead of being incarcerated in a well-regulated penitentiary, he should have been hanged in a hair halter and his foul carcass left to fatten kites. Doubtless some honest and earnest people identify themselves with the A. P. A.—ignorance is easily misled by designing demagogues; but I have yet to learn of an Ape leader in whom a cathode ray would discover a good moral character. Warren E. Price and Ex-Priest Slattery are fair samples of the fellows who make A. P. Apeism a profession and fatten at the expense of fools. Price is in a federal prison for an offense worse than murder, that of corrupting the very babes for boodle—an infamy that would crimson with shame the brazen brow of Pandarus and add new obloquy to the detested name of Tarquin. Slattery has gone, whither God only knows, and even the Devil doesn't care. He seems to have crawled off the earth after his Texas itinerary, in company with the alleged ex-nun whom he was carting around the country to pander to the prurient appetites of off-color dames by relating naughty tales of desiring nuns and accommodating priests. Slattery didn't get into the penitentiary; but he got out of Waco p. d. q.—and he'll never come back. He came as the avowed exponent of "muscular Christianity," and promised a congregation—composed chiefly of women—that he'd do something awfully dreadful to any editor who "dared assail his moral character." Then he undertook to make the same kind of play at a stag party, but didn't succeed. "His coward lips did from their color fly." He meekly took the fighting lie and canine epithet, then folded his tent like the Arab and made an inglorious sneak. The Apes must indeed be proud of their spokesman. An "American Protective Association" with Price bearing aloft its gonfalon and Slattery enunciating its principles! Think of men, born in Old Glory's sacred shadow, trailing in the wake of a brace of he-bawds who peddle obscene literature to babes and seek to corral the dirty dollar by defaming "The Angels of Buena Vista," those heroic women who are ever ready to do battle to the death with "the pestilence that walketh in darkness." Nor are these bipedal brutes, these professional panders to the prurient, these assassins of reputation, these high-binders in the world of morals, the exception to the rule—the black sheep of the A. P. A. hierarchy. Every professional exponent of A. P. Apeism is either a shameless political adventurer or graceless mountebank who's in the unclean business for boodle. Pick up any paper published in the interest of the catacombers and you'll find the same base innuendoes aimed at the sacerdotal order that has been glorified by a Pere Marquette and hallowed by a Father Damien—the same cowardly and unclean flings at consecrated women who would go to Price himself, and minister to him with more than motherly tenderness, were he stricken with the black death and deserted by those to his heart most dear. "By their fruits ye shall know them." The fruits of A. P. Apeism are hate and discord that may yet flame forth in civil strife and desolate the land. The fruits of the Catholic orders are love and charity to all, regardless of race or creed, glory or shame. Even a Slattery cannot fall so low that the Sisters of Charity would decline to succor him in his hour of distress. I am no sectarian; I care naught for the Catholic creed. Nor am I fighting the battles of the priesthood—its members are usually able to give a good account of themselves; but when men professing to be countrymen of mine —guardians of the flag of my fathers—assail with vindictive calumny women whose mission is one of mercy, I long for the power to transform the English tongue into the writhen bolts of Jove and hurl the cowardly and unclean curs to the profoundest depths of hell.

BARON HIRSCH.

I would like to gather all the Jew-baiters in this world about the bier of Baron Hirsch and preach that great philanthropist's funeral sermon. I believe the God of Israel would give me power to call a blush of shame even to the brazen front of that beery bum, Doktor Ahlwardt—to make all the professional persecutors of the race of Judah repent them in sorrow and in shame. The life of Baron Hirsch was sufficient answer to all the detractors of God's chosen people, fitting rebuke to those sceptred bigots whose thrones were stained with Israel's consecrated blood. No son of Rome, when the Imperial City "sat upon her seven hills and from her throne of beauty ruled the world," was prouder of his lineage; but there was room in his great warm heart for all the sons of men of whatsoever creed or clime. He paused not to inquire whether the recipients of his bounty were Jews or Gentiles. Year by year his charities grew—millions following fast upon millions, until it seemed his benefactions must exhaust the treasures of the world; yet he asked only that the golden tide, enriched by an all-embracing love, be used to soften the pangs of pain, to exorcise the demon of Ignorance and ennoble the human race.

> "His life was gentle, and the elements
> So mix'd in him that Nature might stand up
> Before all the world and say, *This was a man.*"

THE TRANSPORTATION PROBLEM.

Is Government Ownership the Proper Solution?

Despite the herculean efforts of the "decentralizationists" to head it off, the current of popular opinion is setting ever stronger toward government ownership and control of railroads.

It is not worth while to enter into a discussion whether "non-government" in the economic sphere is the normal order of things. As J. K. Ingram has well said: "Social exigencies will force the hands of statesmen, whatever their attachment be to abstract formulas; and politicians have practically turned their backs on *laissez faire.*" The question revolves itself to this: Can the government furnish better transportation at present prices? Were it wise to improve the service even at some cost to the treasury?

It will be conceded by the veriest tyro in statecraft that the transportation facilities of the United States constitute an important factor in our industrial, political and social well-being. If money is the life-blood of commerce, the transportation facilities are the veins and arteries through which it pulses. Without rapid transit the American nation as at present constituted could not be kept intact a decade. Before the development of our great railway system, the wisest of American statesmen scouted the idea that the Trans-Missouri country and the Atlantic seaboard could long be held in political unity. Wipe out the railways and the nation would quickly split up into several petty principalities, and America, like Europe, resound with the tramp of armed squadrons. The homogeneity of the people could not be preserved.

While we do not trust the delivery of mail matter to private enterprise; while we insist that it is the business of the government to improve rivers and harbors, maintain highways and coin money, we leave to private enterprise a still more important, an infinitely more complex function—that of transportation.

Private enterprise affords us a service infinitely better than none; but that it could be greatly improved without material increase in cost is rapidly becoming a settled conviction in the public mind. Whether this conviction be correct or otherwise is the most important question involved in this controversy—one of the most important with which the American economists have now to deal.

* * *

Transportation charges constitute a mighty tax upon American production. It does not fall upon the farmer alone, but upon all producers, upon all consumers; sometimes with crushing weight, ofttimes unequally. Clearly it were wisdom on the part of the government, it were in line with its duty of "promoting the public welfare" to reduce this tax if possible, at least to equalize it.

Adam Smith declared that "servants of the most negligent master are better superintended than the servants of the most vigilant sovereign." Prof. F. A. Walker, one of the ablest as well as one of the most perspicacious and impartial of modern economists, says that "the state as a capitalist is at no small disadvantage; as *entrepreneur* (employer of capital), that disadvantage is greatly aggravated." Yet the latter writer admits that the "rule of failure * * * is not unbroken," and cites as the instance which goes farthest to contradict the theory of the hopeless incapacity of the state to conduct industrial enterprises, the railways of Germany. Prof. Walker intimates elsewhere that Adam Smith's views of governmental incapacity to manage property may require some modification in the case of a country like Germany, with its admirable civil service and systematic administration of public trusts, but adds that "no one would think of questioning the full literal truth of Adam Smith's declaration if applied to our own country with its civil service based on rotation in office."

Not very encouraging truly; especially when we remember that most reputable writers on finance and industry have expressed practically the same views regarding government supervision of properties and business, or how the public domain has been frittered away, how the government has almost invariably "got the worst of it" whenever it has meddled in matters of business. Certainly it were the acme of folly to turn the American railways with their enormous revenues over to a coterie of political jobbers to be used for their own emolument, to promote their own ambitious ends. When we remember that the amount of money collected yearly by the railways, vastly exceeds all taxes paid in the United States, federal, state and municipal, including tariff and internal revenue collections; that the amount paid into the coffers of the railways yearly is more than four-fold the value of the annual product of all metals in the United States; that it vastly exceeds in value the annual output of all American manufactures; that it exceeds the value of the annual export of American agricultural products, including live stock and fibres, we may well hesitate to turn them over to the management of "patriots for revenue only."

* * *

Still it were well to remember the evils we suffer under the present system; well not to forget that the postal service (at least so far as letter mail is concerned) has been, on the whole, very successfully, very satisfactorily managed by the government; much more so indeed than has the transportation service by private enterprise. It has been urged that Uncle Sam has succeeded with the postal business by virtue of the monopoly he enjoys. Then might he not also make a success of the carrying trade if allowed to monopolize it? Private enterprise does not appear able to deal with it satisfactorily even when liberally aided by government, federal, state or municipal, or all these combined.

Government ownership and control could at least prevent discriminations and obviate disastrous strikes and forced estoppages of general business. Private ownership and management of the railways has identically the same effect on production and exchange that the old free banking system had. It keeps trade ever in a feverish state of unrest, ever fearful of the future. Few careful students of finance will fully approve the National banking system, yet none would advise a return to the old method. The former establishes confidence—the prime requisite of trade—which the latter failed to do. Government control of railways would have the same effect on trade that the National banking system has.

I am loth to believe, despite the solemn asseverations of high authorities, that the railways would be worse managed by the government than they are at present. Despite the apprehensions of the decentralizationists, I doubt much if their potency for evil in the world of politics would be much enhanced; still I would suggest that every possible precaution be taken against such contingencies. There has been great progress made in the public service since the days of Adam Smith; considerably even since Prof. Walker penned his scathing criticism of American methods. The theorem that "a public office is a public trust" has been promulgated, not without effect. Plundering of the public by officials was long regarded as a matter of course, something to be expected. Really the public felt something like contempt for the man who had the opportunity to plunder it and neglected to do so—vaguely wondered whether he were deficient in thrift or overstocked with self-righteousness. Happily public sentiment became inoculated with Cleveland's doctrine, is undergoing a rapid metamorphosis, and the acts of public men are being subjected to a rigid scrutiny—ofttimes a hyper-critical one. When we contrast the spirit of tolerance with which official shortcomings were once viewed, with the jealous scrutiny to which their every act is now subjected, surely we may flatter ourselves that we have made some progress—may ere long be able to manage public business without wasting or stealing the invested capital.

* * *

Mr. Collis P. Huntington, president of the Southern Pacific, made a strong plea in the *North American Review* some years ago for railway consolidation. He showed wherein our present system is weak and wasteful, and urged that the service would be much more economical and satisfactory if all our American railways were owned and controlled by one great company. Mr. Huntington must know that if railway consolidation is ever carried to the lengths which he urges—and defends by unanswerable logic—the government and not a vast private corporation will be owner and manager. Every argument that he advances in support of consolidation in the hands of private owners will apply with equal or greater force to consolidation in the hands of the government. Even his plea that such consolidation would furnish a safe investment for surplus American capital, cannot but suggest that such investment would be safer, less liable to sudden depreciation, if invested in government bonds than in the stock of a vast private corporation. Should the government decide to purchase and operate the railways, it could issue fifty or hundred year bonds, bearing a low interest rate, which would readily exchange for railway stock at a fair valuation. Thus could the transfer of the roads from private to government ownership be effected without any great financial jar, and the consolidation which Mr. Huntington pleads for be realized. Of course, he saw all this when he penned his article for the *Review,* knew that he was strengthening the lines of "State socialism" on the one hand, and provoking the "anti-monopoly" element to renewed activity on the other.

If such men as C. P. Huntington hoped to consolidate all American railways in one vast corporation, they would not be talking about it in the public prints. The fact is, they read the signs of the times aright; now that government ownership sooner or later is inevitable, and, worn out with battling the anti-railway sentiment, are preparing to yield gracefully—and make what they can by the change.

* * *

The two chief objections urged to government ownership and control are that the purchase would entail a heavy financial burden upon the people, and that the railway service would degenerate into a vast political machine and be used by the dominant party to perpetuate its power. Whether the railways are owned by private corporations or the public, the people must support them. It is simply a question whether it is cheaper to purchase or rent. Can Uncle Sam successfully do the business on money borrowed at 3 and 4 per cent. that private corporations do on money borrowed at 6 to 8 per cent.? Many thousand people are employed in the postal service and they have not yet degenerated into political peons. The political party that would attempt to use them as its property and vote them like cattle would quickly be swept out of power. But should the railway service show signs of degenerating into a political machine, employes, from general manager to switch-tenders and track men, might be disqualified for voting during their term of service. A strict civil service rule should be adopted and rigidly adhered to. Men should be enlisted for a fixed period and required under pains and penalties to perform the service agreed upon; then "tie ups" of the business of vast sections of the country because some brakeman or switchman had a "grievance" would become an impossibility, or be speedily untied by the strong fingers of the federal government.

Under some such arrangements as the foregoing it might be possible for the government to operate the railways more satisfactorily than at present; to greatly reduce transportation charges—all of which would go into the pockets of the people—and at the same time secure that much discussed desideratum, the elimination of the railways from the sphere of politics, where they have long been so potent for evil.

CORONATION OF THE CZAR.

AMERICAN TOADYISM ON TAP.

With more barbaric mummery, flummery and vulgar waste of wealth than characterized even the late Marlborough-Vanderbilt wedding, Nicholas Two-Eyes was crowned Emperor of the rag-tag and bob-tail of creation, officially known as "all the Russias." Nick has a nice easy job at a salary considerably in excess of ye average country editor, and he gets it all in gold roubles instead of post-oak cordwood and green water-melons, albeit his felicity is slightly marred by an ever-present fear that he may inadvertently swallow a few ounces of arsenic or sit down on an infernal machine.

Nick is emphatically an emperor who emps. He isn't bothered with do-nothing congresses or Populist politicians who want him impeached. When he saith to a man "come," he cometh p. d. q.; to another "go" he getteth a hustle on him that would shame a pneumatic tire. Nick is the greatest monarch "what they is." He is the divinely ordained Chief Gyasticutus of that motley aggregation of tallow-munchers and unwashed ignorami whose very existence is a menace to modern civilization. The Goths and Visigoths were models of cleanliness and avatars of intelligence compared with a majority of the seventy different breeds of bipedal brutes who acknowledge the rule of the Romanoffs. A Russian peasant smells like the Chicago River on a summer's day, or Tolstoi's Kreutzer Sonata. He's more disagreeable to the olfactories than old John Jacob Astor's hide house, from whose effluvia sprung the master spirits of Gotham's Four Hundred. He will eat what would send a coyote howling out of the country. To him a jug of train-oil were as angel-food, a keg of stale soap-grease a ferial feast. During his entire life he enjoys but two baths—one when he's born, the other when he's buried. A religious fanatic, he obeys but one scriptural injunction—"Be fruitful and multiply." Even the Russian ladies wash only to suit the dresses they wear—high-necked or decollete. The average Slav is as stupidly ignorant as an agency Indian. He respects no law but that of blind force. His Magna Charta is the dynamite bomb. He is courageous with the bravery of the brute, which has no conception of life's sacredness. Doubtless the rule of the bayonet is the only government possible for such a barbarous people—and the Romanoffs have not allowed it to rust.

The Czar is the immediate ruler of nearly 130,000,000 semi-savages, his lightest word their supreme law, while the chiefs of the robber hordes of Central Asia acknowledge him their official head. Such tremendous power in the hands of a weak-minded, vacillating monarch like Nicholas II—descended from Catherine the Courtesan, and having in his veins the blood of cranks—may well cause western Europe to lie awake. Bonaparte declared that in a hundred years the continent would be all Russian or all Republican— by which he meant that unless this nation of savages *in esse* and Vandals *in posse* were stamped out it would imitate the example of Alaric and Attila and precipitate such another intellectual night as that known as the Dark Ages. In western Europe Republicanism is making but slight progress, while in the east the power of the Great White Khan is rapidly increasing. In a struggle between the semi-savagery of the East and the civilization of the West, China and Turkey would be the natural and inevitable allies of the Czar. Small wonder that the Great First Consul trudged home from Moscow with a heavy heart!

Some faint idea of the savage ignorance of Russia may be had from the history of the Siberian exiles and the fiendish persecutions of the Jewish people. Siberia is the Ice Hell of the old Norse mythologists, into which men, women and children have been indiscriminately cast on the bare suspicion of desiring to better the wretched condition of the Russian people. Its horrors, which have long been a hideous nightmare to civilized men, need no description here. The very name of Siberia causes humanity to shudder—it casts a shadow on the sun! The experience of the Jews in Russia was akin to that of the early settlers in America, who were exposed to the unbridled ferocity of the Aborigines; yet the so-called Christian nations dared do no more than petition the Czar that these savage atrocities should cease— futile prayers to the hog-headed god of the Ammonites!

The young man who has just been crowned at Moscow at an expense of some millions, and whose emblem of authority is ornamented with rubies as large as eggs and ablaze with 2,564 costly diamonds—while half his people are feeding on fetid offal—is a weak-faced pigmy who would probably be peddling Russia's favorite drunk promoter over a pine bar had he not chanced to be born in the purple. Having been spawned in a royal bed—perchance the same in which his great gran'dame Catherine was wont to receive her paramours—he becomes the most powerful of princes—haloed with "that divinity which doth behedge a king"—and all the earth rejoices to do him honor.

For months past wealthy Americans have been hastening to Moscow to enjoy the barbaric fete and perchance pick up a greasy count or scorbutic duke for their daughters. They were not permitted to witness the coronation, but they could look at the Kremlin, stand in the street and watch the Czar and his wooden-faced wife sail by in their chariot of gold, and perhaps get cuffed out of the way by a court chamberlain Surely that were felicity enough for fools! Our boasted Republican government, whose shibboleth has ever been the equality of all men—that the harvester of the lowly hooppole stands on a parity with a prince swinging a gilded sceptre and robbing a poverty-stricken people—considered that its paid representatives in Russia would be unequal to the task of spilling sufficient slobber over the chief representative of "divine right," the great arch-enemy of human liberty and sent special envoys to assist at the ceremony. These haughty American Sovereigns were not permitted, however, to enter the sacred presence of the Czar attired in their regal robes—the dress of American gentlemen; but were required to dike out like English flunkeys at a fancy feed. "Evening coat with plain metal buttons, white vest, knee-breeches, black silk stockings, no ornaments"—such was the ukase issued to the envoys of Uncle Sam by the royal seneschal. They "obeyed with alacrity." Of course they did. Had they been ordered to appear in their shirttails, one flap dyed green and the other yellow, their legs painted like barber-poles and wearing asses' ears, they would have "obeyed with alacrity"—without ever a thought of advising the seneschal to go to Siberia. The rear admiral in command of the Mediterranean fleet was ordered to Kronstadt with his flagship; sent to attend the coronation "as the naval envoy of the United States"—a journey of some thousands of miles at a minimum expense of $1,000 a day, to watch a young dude stick a million-dollar dog muzzle on his own foolish pate, while his female running mate cavorted around with a dozen dudines supporting her tail-feathers! And "Jones he pays the freight"—puts up for this egregious folly. It has cost the American tax-payers a quarter of a million dollars to have their misrepresentatives prancing around the Kremlin in short-stop pants and silk stockings, bowing and scraping like a Pullman porter who has just received a dollar tip from some reckless Texan.

We have nothing in common with Russia. One government is the antithesis of the other. They are "on friendly terms" because they have practically no intercourse. Russia has no American possessions upon which we can pull the foolish manifesto of the erstwhile Monroe. There's no trade between the two countries—hasn't been since Russia unloaded her Alaskan glaciers upon us at a fancy price. It would have been eminently proper had Minister Breckinridge presented himself—togged out in his best Arkansas jeans instead of being attired like a troubadour—to wish Nick exemption from the Nihilists and express the hope that the occasion wouldn't swell his head; but there was absolutely no excuse for sending warships on an expensive cruise, and special envoys 5,000 miles to make unmitigated asses of themselves.

The unpalatable fact is that we are a nation of toadeaters. President Cleveland is, in this respect at least, eminently representative of the American people. The axiom that "like takes to like" accounts for his popularity. It was that which enabled him to beat Jim Blaine. When the Grand Duke Alexis was in this country, upper-tendom slopped over him so persistently and offensively that the young man incontinently fled. The adulation he received from American belles made him such a misogynist that he never got married. The girl who got an introduction to the Duke was pointed out for years thereafter as an especial favorite of fortune. The obituary of a Louisville lady who died a short time ago contained the startling announcement that she had actually danced with the Duke. Every Chappie who was permitted to pay for a mint julep absorbed by this subject of a crack-brained Czar secured a certificate to that effect and had it framed.

In 1892, when more than the usual number of Russians were going hungry to bed, America undertook to abrogate the law of the survival of the fittest by sending the starving wretches a ship-load of provisions. Dr. T. DeWitt Talmage, Dr. Louis Klopsch and other prominent Americans were sent over as commissioners to give out the grub. While in Russia they were permitted, as a special concession, to speak to the Caesarovitch, who afterwards succeeded to the crown. Of course these American Sovereigns were "overcome with such condescension," could "hardly get their breath"—even in short pants. They all wrote it up for the American press, and now Dr. Klopsch is rehearsing every detail of that important event—the crowning felicity of his life. He tells us how the commissioners "received full instructions as to dress;" what a "bountiful repast" they enjoyed with the crown prince's servants—while millions were starving to death; how they cooled their heels in the hall for an hour or two while their invisible host finished his cigar; how their "hearts fluttered" when the seneschal gave them their final instructions in court etiquette—not to expectorate on the carpet or scratch the furniture—then trotted them in; how the crown prince graciously permitted them to stand with uncovered heads for a few moments in his august presence, and then managed to get rid of them without actually kicking them down stairs! He "shook hands" with the party as a signal for them to pull their freight. And to this good day Drs. Talmage and Klopsch will not use toilet paper with the hand that has been pressed by royalty! But the charity commissioners wreaked a terrible revenge on the crown prince—whose starving people they were feeding—for thus insulting American manhood; they sent him a handsomely bound copy of Talmage's book! The fact that he has not broken off diplomatic relations with the United States may be accepted, however, as *prima facie* evidence that he has not yet read it. Perhaps he added insult to injury by sending it to the Siberian exiles. The Czaritza, or Empress, is a grand-daughter of Queen Victoria. She is rather handsome, but her face, like that of all those born to the house of Hanover, is expressionless as a clothing-store dummy, hard as a blue-steel hatchet. Princess Alice, as she was known in England, was a very devout Protestant; but she promptly abjured her religion in which she was raised and changed her name to Alexandra Theodorovna for the blessed privilege of sharing an emperor's bed and board. Thrift is a characteristic of Queen Victoria's kids, and their religious scruples count for naught when weighed against a crown.

CHRIST COMES TO TEXAS

And Calls on the Iconoclast.

The editor was reading a report of the regular meeting of the Dallas Pastors' Association, at which the Second Coming of Christ was learnedly considered. Dr. Seasholes declared that all good people will rise into the air, like so many larks, to meet the Lord and conduct him to earth—with flying banners and a brass-band, I suppose—where he will reign a thousand years. At the conclusion of this felicitous period Satan is to be loosed for a little season, and after he has pawed up the gravel with his long toe-nails and given us a preliminary touch of Purgatory, we are to have the genuine pyrotechnics. Some of the divines did not agree with the spectacular ceremonies arranged by Dr. Seasholes for the Second Coming; but he seems determined to carry out his program or enjoin the procession. The editor was musing on this remarkable controversy and wondering, in a vague, tired way, why the fool-killer did not take a pot-shot at the Dallas Pastors' Association, when there came a gentle rap at his door and a strange figure stood before him. It was that of a man of perhaps three-and-thirty years, barefoot, bareheaded and clothed only in a single garment, much worn and sadly soiled.

"Peace to this house," he said, in a voice soft and sweet as that of a well-bred woman. "A cup of cold water, I pray you."

"Water? Cert. Steer yourself against the cooler over there. You look above the Weary Willie business. Sit down until I find a jumping-off place in this article on The Monetary Situation, and perhaps I can fish up a stray quarter that's dodged the foreign mission fund."

He bowed his thanks and sank wearily into the proffered seat. In five minutes he was sleeping softly, and the editor made a careful study of his face. It was of the Jewish type, strong but tender. The beard was glistening black and had evidently never been to the barber's, while a shock of unkempt hair, burned by the sun, hung around his shoulders like the mane of a lion.

"Hello," said the business manager, as he helped himself to the editor's plug tobacco; "another of your Bohemian friends? Some fellow who's tramping around the world on a wager of 'steen million dollars? Good face, but a bath wouldn't hurt him."

The stranger roused himself and the b. m. continued: "Neighbor, we were just about to crack a bottle of beer. Have you any conscientious scruples about joining us?" He winked at the book-keeper, and the stranger bowed his thanks, accepted the amber fluid, scrutinized it curiously and drank it off with evident relish.

"That is very refreshing," he commented as he wiped the foam from his black beard with his sleeve. "Will it intoxicate?"

He was informed that if taken on the allopathic plan it would make one drunk some, but not the wild-eyed, murderous mania peculiar to Prohibition booze. He declined a second glass, saying gently, "We should not abuse the good things of life." The book-keeper was so startled that he missed his face with a pint cup, and the mailing clerk did up a package of hymn-books for a dealer who wanted "Potiphar's Wife." But the stranger was evidently unconscious that he had forever queered himself with the Bohemian Club. He took a dry crust from a leathern wallet, and, blessing it, offered a portion to the editor.

"Jesus Christ! You don't eat that, do you?"

The visitor rose, a startled look on his face.

"You know me, then? Yes, it is I—Jesus of Nazareth. I have walked the earth an entire year, clad as I was eighteen centuries ago, living as I did then, mingling with those called by my name, conversing with those who profess to teach my doctrine, and none knew me. Nay more: They sometimes spurned me from their doors, and even delivered me to the minions of Caesar as a vagabond. You look incredulous. Behold the nail-prints in my hands and feet, the spear wound in my side, the scars made by the crown of thorns upon my brow."

"But I thought your second-coming would be in power and glory, and all the righteous would rise up into the atmosphere to meet you and show you a soft spot to 'light. Dr. Seasholes says so, and if he doesn't know, who does?"

"I attended the discussion by the Dallas Pastors' Association," he said wearily. "They permitted me to sweep out the room and stand down in the hall. It may appear incredible; but there are just a few things that the Dallas Pastors' Association doesn't know. Of course you couldn't make those gentlemen believe it; but it is a lamentable fact. The world is young; it must run its course. Our Heavenly Father did not create it as the Chinese make crackers—just to hear it pop. Not until its power to produce and nourish life is exhausted will the end be. Your poet, Campbell, was a true prophet. The sun itself must die, and not until that mighty source of light and heat becomes a flickering lamp, will those fateful words be spoken. 'Time was, but times shall be no more.' I am not come as yet to judge the world, but to mingle once again with the sons of men, and observe how they keep my laws."

An expression of unutterable sadness stole into his face and he sat a long time silent.

"I have suffered and sacrificed much for this people," he said at length, as tho' speaking to himself, "and it has borne so little fruit. The world misunderstood me. The church planted by toil and nurtured with my blood has split up into hundreds of warring factions, despite my warning that a house divided against itself cannot stand. Nor has it stood —the Temple of Zion is a ruin, the habitation of sanctified owls and theological bats. The army of Israel is striving in its camp, tribe against tribe, or wandering desolate in the desert while the legions of Lucifer overrun the land. Here and there, among the simple poor, I find traces of the truths I taught—here and there a heart that is a holy temple in which abide Faith, Hope and Charity; but the shepherds do not keep my sheep."

He leaned his head upon his hands and wept, while the editor shifted uneasily in his chair and strove in vain to think of something appropriate to say. During his reportorial career he had interviewed Satan and the arch-angel Gabriel. He had even inserted the journalistic pump into Gov. Culberson and Dr. Cranfill without being overwhelmed by their transcendent greatness; but this was different. The city hall clock chimed 10, the hour when the saloons set out the mock-turtle soup and potato salad, the bull-beef and sour beans as *lagniappe* to the heavy-laden schooner. The editor remembered that Christ first came eating and drinking, sat with publicans and sinners and was denounced therefor as a wine-bibber and a glutton by the Prohibitionists and other Miss Nancys of Palestine. Still he hesitated. He wanted to do the elegant, but was afraid of making a bad impression. A glance at the dry and mouldy crust determined him. He tapped the visitor on the shoulder and said:

"Let's go and get some grub."

"I wouldn't worry about the world if I were you," I continued, as he led the way to the elevator. "It is really not worth while. If the devil wants it, I'd let him have it. I can think of no greater punishment you could inflict upon him than to make him a present of it. It were equivalent to England giving Canada to the United States for meddling in the Venezuelan matter. Perhaps you know your business best, but I have lived the longest. I used to think that perhaps the world would pay the salvage for saving it; but that was before I moved to Waco. I tell you frankly that if I had your job in the New Jerusalem I'd nurse it and let Bob Ingersoll, Doc Talmage and the rest of the noisy blatherskites scrap it out here to suit themselves."

He did not reply, and the editor, remembering that his advice had not been asked, changed the subject.

"I'm not going to steer you against a first-class hotel. Jim I. Moore wouldn't let you into his dining-room with your shoes off, even tho' you brought a letter of credit from the Creator. Jim loves you dearly, but business is business. There's a place down here, however, run by a man who doesn't trot with the sanctified set, where you can waltz up to the feed trough in the same suit you wore when you preached the Sermon on the Mount, and that without giving the ultra-fashionables a case of the fantods."

"Ah, there we will doubtless meet with many of the good brethren who do not observe empty forms and foolish ceremonies."

"Rather. But perhaps I should tell you that the church does not approve of the place where we are going. They —er—sell wine there you know; also that amber liquid with the —er—froth on it."

"And why not wine?"

"Damfino—I mean—Oh, you'll have to ask Bro. Cranfill. I s'pose because old Noah jagged up on it."

"Noah who?"

"Why just Noah; that old stiff—I mean that good man who was saved for seed, when the overflow came, and who's the great gran'daddy of all the niggers."

"Is it possible that the church is retailing that wretched old myth which my Hebrew fathers borrowed of the barbarians. Noah? There was no such man. By the shifting of the earth's axis about 16,000 years ago a portion of the Asiatic continent was overflowed."

"But the Noah story is in the Bible."

"So is the story of Adam and Eve, and many other absurdities which really intelligent people would purge it of. O will men be mental children ever!"

He ate sparingly, but scanned the visitors closely. At the next table a quartette of Texas colonels were absorbing mint juleps through rye straws. The Nazarene nudged the editor and inquired what the beverage consisted of. The latter explained the mystery, and would have placed one before his guest, but the latter insisted that a little wine for the stomach's sake would suffice. Several entered into conversation with him and would have given him money, but he gently declined to accept it, saying that the good Father would provide—that he was seeking to do good, not to lay up treasures.

"Are these people sinners?"

He was informed that, according to the theology of the Prohibs, they would occupy the hottest corner of Perdition.

"But they give to the poor, speak kindly to the stranger, even tho' he be clothed in rags. I am sure they would not lie or steal or kill."

"But they will blaspheme a little sometimes. Just listen to those colonels. Didn't you hear them say 'damn' and 'Hell's fire' and 'Devil'? O, according to our theology there's no hope for 'em. A man may defraud a widow or swindle an orphan and make a landing; but when he talks about the Devil and Hell he's sure to be damned."

"Is Satan a sacred person, or Hell a place to be mentioned reverently? Blasphemy is speaking evil of God. The priesthood of every religious cult has manifested a propensity to magnify venial faults into cardinal sins and thereby bring worship into contempt by trifling. To Hell with those who make religion a trade and thrive thereby!"

We were on the street and it chanced that a well-fed silk-hatted dominie, sporting a diamond stud, was dawdling by as the man of Galilee uttered this emphatic protest against gain-grabbing preachers. His face flushed with anger, and turning upon the ill-clad stranger, he said:

"Do you mean to insult me, fellow?"

The Nazarene faced his heated interlocutor and replied with quiet dignity: "Assuredly not. I did not suspect you of being a minister. You are not clad like one of the Apostles. Surely you are not one of those disputatious sectaries who wear purple and fine linen and fare sumptuously every day while countless thousands cry to their Father in Heaven, 'Give us to eat and to drink lest we die?'"

"I want no lectures from you, sir: I know my business," exclaimed the man of God, with rising color.

"Ah, I fear that 'business' is to coin the blood of Jesus of Nazareth into golden guineas."

The infinite pity in the speaker's voice cowed the pugnacious preacher, and he was about to pass on; but a brown, toil-stained hand—the hand of a carpenter—was laid upon his shoulder. "Wait, my brother. Let not the sun go down upon thy wrath. Him ye serve was even as I am—poor and friendless. He spake as I speak, the truth that welled up in his heart. Cruel things were said of him, but he resented it not. He was beaten with many stripes, and mocked, and crucified; but he freely forgave. Be thou humble as he was humble; be thou forgiving even as he forgave. Love God and thy fellow men. That is the whole law given by him ye serve. Words are but as sounding brass and a tinkling cymbal, but a good example endureth forever."

"Lord! Lord!" exclaimed the editor, "Why didn't you reveal yourself to him?"

"He would not have believed me. No; tho' I performed before him miracles more wonderful than those accredited to me in Palestine. I have resumed my earthly raiment and adopted my old mode of life as the best possible disguise. Believing me a vagabond, those pretending to worship with all their heart and all their soul, show unto me what they really are. Now as ever do men polish the outside of the cup while within is all uncleanliness."

"Have you interviewed many of the big preachers?"

"Many, almost all. I attended Sam Jones' recent services at Austin. He is simply a product of the evil times upon which the church has fallen. In religion, as in art and letters, decadence is marked by sensationalism. The trouble with Sam is that he mistakes himself for me—thinks he has been called to judge the world. I was pained to hear him consign about fifteen different classes of people to Perdition without sifting them to see if, perchance, there might not be one in the lot worthy of salvation. I presented him with a copy of my Sermon on the Mount. He took a fresh chew of tobacco and remarked that he was inclined to think he had read it before somewhere. Then he took up a collection. Sam represents the rebound from the old religious belly-ache. For years preachers had an idea that there was nothing of gladness in the worship of God—that it consisted simply of a chronic case of the snuffles. Jones has simply gone to the opposite extreme and transformed the Temple of the Deity into a variety dive. Nero fiddled while Rome burned; but Jones indulges in the levity of the buffoon while consigning millions of human beings to Hell. Alas, that so few preachers understand the pity which permeates all true religions."

"All true religions?"

"Even so. All are true and of God that make people better, nobler, more pitiful. The Father is all-wise. He tempers the wind to the shorn lamb. He gives to each people a religion commensurate with its mentality. I had hoped that the church established nearly nineteen centuries ago would suffice until the end of the world; that the simple theology I taught would grow with the world's mental growth and strengthen with its intellectual strength. It was a religion of Love. I bound its devotees to no specific forms and ceremonies—these were after-growths. I expected them. The child must have something to lean upon until it can walk; the barbaric worshipper must have symbols and ceremonies to aid his comprehension. These should have passed ere this in Europe and America. A religious rite appropriate to semi-savages becomes, when injected into an age of civilization, that good custom which doth corrupt the world. The people, seeing these savage non-essentials insisted upon by the priesthood as something sacred and necessary unto Salvation, turn skeptic and reject religion altogether because it is encumbered by ridiculous rubbish. O, when will men understand that the whole world is a temple and all right living is worship!"

The editor was becoming really alarmed. He was fearful that his visitor was frightfully heterodox, hence he broke in with, "If you're not careful, Doc. Talmage will denounce you as an infidel!"

"Brother Talmage is like unto the west wind—he bloweth whithersoever he listeth, and no man knoweth whence his blow cometh or whither it goeth. I tried to have a talk with him while in Washington, but he was too busy writing a syndicate sermon on the political situation, demonstrating that Dives had already done too much for Lazarus, and peddling hallelujahs at two dollars apiece. I had heard much of him and expected to find him toiling early and late among the poor and wretched, the suffering of the Capital city. When I called at his residence the servant told me that his master could not be disturbed—said there had been a dozen tramps there that morning. I asked him what salary his master received in a city filled with homeless vagabonds for preaching Christ and him crucified, but he vouchsafed me no answer. I went to hear the great man preach, but the usher told me there was a mission church around the corner where my spiritual wants would be attended to. If I failed to find a seat there I could stand on the street-corner and hear the Salvation Army beat the bass drum and sing 'Come to Jesus.' I lingered in the vestibule, however, and heard his sermon. I asked for bread and he gave me wind-pudding. I was sorry that I didn't attend the Salvation Army exercises. I prefer the bass drum to the doctor. It may be equally noisy, but hardly so empty. I saw men attired in fine cloth and women ablaze with jewels kneel on velvet cushions and pray to me. Then the choir sang,

'Oh how I love Jesus, for Jesus died for me.'

"And Dr. Talmage exclaimed, 'Come dear Lord, O come!' I came. I walked down the center aisle, expecting that a mighty shout of joy would shake the vaulted roof of heaven and be echoed back by the angels. I supposed that Dr. Talmage would advance and embrace me. But no; the men stared their disapproval; the women drew back their perfumed skirts of glistening silk, and Dr. Talmage thundered, 'Sirrah! who are you?' I raised my hand and exclaimed in a loud voice:

"Jesus Christ!"

The editor started up from his siesta and rubbed his eyes —the foreman of the *Baptist Standard* had "pied a form."

THE GRECIAN GAMES.

A Lesson for the Lah-de-Dahs.

The revival of the Olympian games of Greece will suggest to the careful student of human history that a progressive people invariably takes a keen delight in contests of personal skill or prowess. Boxing and diskos-throwing, running and wrestling, have ever been the sports of world-compellers, never the divertisement of anaemic dudes. Men who are really masculine—men possessing strength and courage and do dare—are not those who play Presbyterian billiards with a bevy of old maids, lisp in their speech and waddle in their walk. Tell me the favorite pastime of a people and I'll tell you whether they are facing the darkness or the dawn—whether they are climbing the rugged mount of Knowledge, or descending into the noisome vale of Ignorance, where Slavery and Superstition sit enthroned. The Olympian Games were the nurse of Grecian glory. They fostered that love of athletic exercises, that spirit of manly self-reliance, that proud contempt for danger that made possible the Field of Marathon and the Pass of Thermopylae.

The origin of the games was attributed to Hercules— "the strong man"—probably the original of the Hebrew Sampson; but the first formal festival, from which the Hellenes marked time, was celebrated 776 years before the birth of our Savior. These quadrennial games rapidly grew in favor until they became the chief national fete and were participated in by representatives from the Grecian settlements in Africa, Asia Minor and Italy. After more than eleven centuries of continuous popularity, the Olympic festival was prohibited by edict of the Christian Emperor Theodosius, and from that time Greece gradually degenerated until she became "the vassal of a slave," a land of cowardly beggars and importunate bawds. Doubtless many things contributed to the debasement of a people for so many centuries the models for all mankind.

> "'Twere long to tell and sad to trace
> Each step from glory to disgrace;"

but there can be no doubt that the decree of Theodosius did more than the brand of the Roman legionary to promote that physical debasement and mental decay which led Byron to exclaim, as he looked upon the broken altars and ruined fanes of a mighty past—immortal marbles in whose shadows slunk the patient slave, unworthy descendant of Homer's heroes:

> "Shrine of the mighty! Can it be
> That this is all remains of thee?"

When Greece was at the zenith of her glory, when her people were the recognized models of physical perfection; when her orators and statesmen, her sculptors and generals, her poets and philosophers were making her name immortal; when her civilization was superior to anything attained by other nations before or since; when the "City of the Violet Crown" was undisputed mistress in the world of mind, the sports of the Olympic arena were such as would have appalled that congeries of blatant jack-asses yclept the American Congress, and given the various Pastors' Associations of Texas a virulent attack of the piles. We, whose ancestors were gibbering cave-dwellers but a few short centuries ago; we, who have so recently discovered that people are not created for the especial pleasure and profit of scorbutic princes or clabber-brained kings; we, who turn for inspiration to Grecian art and oratory, happy if we can but comprehend the deep philosophies of that early age, or catch the subtle perfume of its poetry, know so much better what sports are calculated to make men manly than did those who "socked with old Socrates and rippled with old Euripides!" Verily we should employ our gall to transform the seas into ink with which to chronicle our own greatness.

The sports of the ancient Greeks were the sports of men

strong of hand and heart; of men who didn't spill hysterical tears like a ruptured pickle-barrel, and protest that the civilization of the world were gone to hell, if some brawny athlete got a black eye. There was no feather pillow funny-business for "points" in their boxing-matches, no ennui-breeding hippodroming in their wrestling-bouts. The people did not put up $10 apiece to witness a "conversazione." Yet these sports were approved by and participated in by men whom the wisest of moderns are proud to acknowledge as masters. Even Sam Jones would probably concede that Socrates knew enough to remove his "chaw of plug terbacker" before taking a "bowl"—albeit he regarded preachers with such suspicion that the super-sanctified concluded the only way to convert him was to kill him.

America and Great Britain give more attention to athletics than do other nations, and they represent the highest reach of modern civilization; but even in these countries really masculine sports are left largely to professionals, the people enjoying them by proxy. We pay our money to be entertained by professional pugilists and expert ball-players. We have even become too indolent to manage our own horses at the races, but employ jockeys for that purpose while we consult the "bookies" or dawdle in the grand-stand with sporty girls. The men who "hang up purses" to be striven for, and those who strive, have nothing in common with the patrons of or participants in the Olympian Games. When Xerxes the Great invaded Greece he asked what was the prize at these celebrated contests He was informed that it was but a wreath of wild olive, upon which a Persian grandee exclaimed to his commander, "Good heaven, Mardonius! what manner of men are these you have brought us to fight against—men who do not contend for money, but for honor?"

Special privileges were accorded by the state to the winners in these historic games; but our highly civilized and eminently aesthetic Solons consider a skilled athlete a dangerous criminal. The Greeks regarded those who won the olive wreath as special favorites of the gods; Rev. Dr. Seasholes fears that their presence would pollute a town in which he has the street and number of 800 *nymphs du pave!* The sentiment against really virile sports—those that require not only manly strength and skill, but courage and contempt for pain—is already strong in this country and apparently increasing. Pugilism has degenerated into a soft-glove farce for the long green; horse-racing has become a little better than a cut-throat gambling device; college football is decried because it retains a little manly vigor, and even our so-called national game is regarded with aversion by some effeminate pseudo-moralists who believe it sufficient physical exercise to swallow the miracles and endure the fatigue of prosy sermons. We cannot even dance and escape damnation, nor pitch pennies at a crack without becoming objects of suspicion. About all the professionally godly elect to leave us is the privilege of riding our bikes to Wednesday evening prayers. The development of our calves by the latter simian-shaping exercise may be useful in case of a renaissance of common sense that will permit us to kick the bearded babes out of the country.

And as the sentiment against manly exercise rises our superiority as a people declines. Jack will work pretty much as he plays. Give him a cat, a croquet mallet and tell him to be careful of his complexion, and he'll become a cad with a predilection for decadent art and Parisian literature. Give him a pair of boxing gloves and a bull pup for companions and he'll force his way to the front.

America has too evidently reached the zenith of her physical and intellectual glory and entered upon that stage of milksopishness and sybaritism which eventually extinguished the glory that was Greece and the grandeur that was Rome. The United States Senate, once justly regarded as the foremost deliberative body of the world, has become but little more than a congress of small-bore politicians whose inane gabble distresses the very geese. Our Supreme Court, once the acme of judicial wisdom, the very avatar of Justice, maunders and mumbles like a drunken casuist pleading in defense of his own folly. Our great orators and editors, statesmen and jurists are all of the past. Should a Webster or Clay, a Jefferson or Jackson develop among us, we'd "peep about his huge legs" like Roman bondmen contemplating the greatness of Julius Caesar. America shines only by the light of other days—reflected from her lucre. The deterioration of our literature, religion and morals is strongly marked. We have not one living author whose fame will long outlast his life. The turgid Talmage has succeeded the solid Beecher, and the mantle of old Peter Cartwright fallen upon the unworthy shoulders of a Georgia blatherskite. We must have in the pulpit a sentimental sentence-turner to lull us with rhetorical trifles, or a brazen blackguard to shock us with his unforgivable *gaucheries,* else will we remain at home to read novels, all whose heroines are harlots, then rinse our minds with the feculent dish-water dished up by the Sunday dailies. The morals of the nation sink ever lower and lower as the red tide in its veins is diluted with the whey of dudeism—as we drift farther and farther from the solid literature and rugged sports that rejoiced our ancestors. We admire as "sharp practice" successful villainy which our fathers would have denounced as d—d rascality, and welcome to our homes wealthy wantons whom our mothers would have driven from their doors with scalding water and an omnivorous dog. I can think of but one plan to check the moral, mental and physical decay, and that is to castrate the dudes, suppress all anaemic preachers who forget that "the glory of the young man is his strength," and commission Dan Stuart to establish a permanent physical culture college in every county.

While America was enjoying a moral spasm over the Corbett-Fitzsimmons fluke and Fitz-Maher fiasco, Greece was reviving the old Olympian Games. It is an apt illustration of my theory that civilization travels in a circle— from savagery to sybaritism, then back to barbarism to get more iron in its blood. Greece has completed one great cycle and started on the second. The revival of learning is keeping step with the revival of athletics. Those who till the field of Marathon are again becoming manly. The bow of Ulysses may again be bent. Another Demosthenes may launch his verbal thunderbolts to resound through two-and-twenty centuries. The Isles of Greece may echo the song of a second Sappho. The muses may once more haunt the Castilian Spring and the gods return to High Olympus. Greece is awakening from her lethargy, after all these centuries of intellectual savagery and political shame. The star of intelligence is sinking in the West only to illume the East. While Macaulay's New Zealander is musing on the broken arch of London Bridge, an Athenian philosopher may read the record of our departed glory in our ruined monuments, and exclaim:

"Yes! self-abasement paved the way
To villain-bonds and despot-sway."

"THERE'S ONE COMES AFTER."

A Sketch.

None so poor but they may build fairy castles in the air; none so wretched but they may fondly gaze upon the fickle star of Hope, flaming ever in that heaven we see by Faith.

A man, worn with suffering and sorrow and sin, was toiling homeward in the night from a far hunter's camp, whither he had been banished by a doctor's edict, "Rest from labor lest ye die." "That indeed is a misfortune," he had said, and redoubled his vigils at the desk. Then they brought his little son, the last gem in the sacred circle of the home whose breaking up broke his heart, and placed the child upon his knee. He looked at its fair face and said, "I will go." A man for whom the shadows should still be falling toward the west, but old before his time, deep scarred by angry storms, battered and bruised like some presumptuous mortal who had seized his puny spear and plunged into such wars as the Titans were wont to wage upon the Grecian Gods. The jaded steed stumbled along the dark and dangerous way, while its rider dreamed with wide open eyes and sometimes muttered to himself in that dreary solitude.

"There's one comes after—in dying I do not die, in losing I simply pass the sword from sire to son. I may but fill a ditch for a better to mount upon and win the mural crown. What, then, if that other be——"

The owl hooted as he passed, and from the thicket came the angry snarl of wolves. "How human!" he bitterly exclaimed. "Hoots and hungry howls, all along life's path—a weird pilgrimage in the dark."

He nodded, his head bowing almost to the saddle-bow, then awoke humming, he knew not why,

> "As long as the heart knows passion.
> As long as life, as long."

His dog, a powerful mastiff, bristled and uttered an angry growl as a great grey wolf slunk along in the dry grass but a few yards distant. "The brutes follow the wounded," he muttered, "and I am stricken deep." He unslung his heavy fowling piece and fired. The eyes of the brute glowed like green globes of phosphorence in the light of the gun, then sank down with a howl that drew its comrades about it, not to succor and to save, but to tear and rend. He watched them a moment, muttering again, "How human!" and turning to an aged oak that spread its branches wide, built a fire of brush and bivouacked. But he could not sleep—the blue devils were playing at hide-and-seek within his heart, and phantoms that once were flesh came trooping from out the gloom and hovered round him. He put out his hands to them, he cried to them to speak to him, but they receded into the darkness from whence they came—the grave had given up its dead only to mock him, to emphasize his utter desolation. He embraced the sturdy oak as though he would draw strength from its stubborn heart which had defied the storms of a thousand years, then sank prostrate at its base and, with only dumb animals to note his weakness, wept as only strong men weep when shivered by the bolts of Destiny.

"One left—but one of those I loved; my strength is broken, my labors are in vain—I can but die; yet must I live, lest the one in whom is centred all my hopes, doth fall in evil ways and also come to naught."

He dreamed of the days that were dead, and of those rushing upon him from the mystic future, "each bearing its burden of sorrow." He trod again life's thorny path, from the cradle to manhood's sombre noon, a path strewn with wreck and wraith and wet with blood and tears. Again the well-known forms came from beyond the fire-light and, winding their shadowy arms about his neck, wept for his loneliness. He tried to embrace them, to gather them to his heart as in the old days when they welcomed his home-coming with glad acclaim, but clutched only air—his kisses fell on vacancy. As they receded into the gloom he followed crying, "Stay! Stay!" and wandered here and there through bogs and briars and over the rough rocks, calling them each by name with many an endearing term, until he fell exhausted, and, putting forth his hand to break his fall, encircled the neck of his faithful dog and lay there bruised and bleeding. Then other phantoms came, two women, one old, one young, bearing a ghastly burden, around which little children wailed. They laid it down at his feet, a horrid thing with wide-staring eyes and gaping wounds all wet with gore. And the elder bowed herself upon it and kissed the rigid hands, the lips and hair and moaned that she was left childless in her age, but the younger stood erect, imperious, the frightened children clinging to her skirts and, calling him by a name that froze his blood, bade him look upon her widowhood.

"It was self-defense," he doggedly replied, as he met the glance of her scornful eyes.

"O egotist!" she cried; "must a man die that a dog may live? Must a mother's grey hairs be brought in sorrow to the grave; must the heart of a wife be crushed within a bloody hand and children never know a father's loving care, that such a thing as thou may'st yet encumber this fair earth? Precious indeed must be that life, purchased at such a price!"

But again the forms that had fled returned, and one, a frail, sweet-faced woman with a world of pity in her eyes, stood between him and his accuser. She took the scornful woman's hand and gently said: "Sister, 'twas thee or me, 'twas thine or mine;" and in the music of her voice the ghastly object vanished.

The hoot of the owl and the howl of the wolf grew faint and far away; he fell into an uneasy slumber and saw himself, aged and grey, trying to keep pace with a fair youth, who mounted with free and graceful step a mountain whose summit was crowned with the light of everlasting day. Steeper and steeper grew the path, yet he strove with failing strength. The youth reached out a strong hand to him and said, "Lean on me;" but he put it back, crying fiercely: "No! no! climb thou alone—farther I cannot go. On! On to the summit, where breaks the great white light, and there is no death!"

The youth struggled with the steeps and overcame them one by one, and mounted higher and ever higher, until he stood where never man had stood, the glory of the gods upon his face, the immortelles upon his brow. And people wondered and said to him, "Who is it that stands upon the mountain top where only tread the gods?" And he answered, "It is I—it is my other self." And they said, "The poor old man is mad; let be, let be."

The dog crept closer to its master and laid its head upon his breast. The vision changed, and he sat by a seacoal fire in chambers that once had echoed the glad voices of those whose graves were 'mid the soughing pines. He held his one treasure to his heart and sang to it the old ditties that its mother was wont to sing when soothing her babe to slumber, until the golden head drooped low upon his breast. He wove about it fond dreams of what should be in the years to come, when, grown to manhood, it entered the arena of the world. A bony hand stole over his shoulder and seized the child, and looking up he beheld Death standing by his chair. He clasped his treasure close and struggled with the grisly spectre, but it only mocked him, and tearing the child from him, fled into the outer void. He struggled to his feet and from his parched lips there burst a cry that echoed and re-echoed through the dark woods and was hurled back from the distant hills.

At dawn the rustics found him, lying cold as his rocky bed, the beaded dew upon his grizzled beard, his horse with head low hanging over him, his dog keeping watch and ward.

THE PLATONIC FRIENDSHIP FAKE.

A charming little lady, the front elevation of whose name is Stella, takes pen in hand and gives the Icon. a red-hot "roast" for having intimated that Platonic Love, so-called, is a pretty good thing for respectable women to let alone. Judged by the amount of caloric she generates, Stella must be a star of the first magnitude, or even an entire constellation. She "believes in the pure, passionless love described by Plato as sometimes existing between the sexes—the affinities of mind as distinguished from the carnal lusts of matter," and opines that the Apostle "must be gross indeed not to comprehend this philosophic and highly satisfactory companionship."

> "Twinkle, twinkle little star,
> How I wonder what you are,
> Up above the world so high,
> Like a diamond in the sky."

I plead guilty and cast myself upon the mercy of the court. I sorrowfully admit that my aestheticism is not 18 karats fine, but mixed with considerable slag. When I should have been acquiring the higher culture, I was either playing hookey or planting hogs. Instead of being fed on the transcendental philosophy of Plato, I was stuffed with mealy Irish spuds and home-grown "punkin" pie. When I should have been learning to relish *pate de foie gras* and love my neighbor's wife in a purely passionless way, I was following one of McCormick's patents around a forty-acre field or arguing a point of ethics with a contumacious mule. That I am unable to appreciate that Platonic yearning of soul to soul, that deep calling unto deep on which Stella dotes, is my misfortune rather than my fault. It appears to me too much like voting the Prohibition ticket or playing poker with Confederate currency. When I love a woman I love her up one side and down t'other. I may be an uncultured and barbaric noodle, but

I want to get hold of her and bite her neck. I want to
cuddle her sunny curls on my heaving shirt-front when I
talk to her about affinities. I believe with Tennyson in the
spirits rushing together at the touching of the lips, and I
just let 'em rush. Men may esteem women and enjoy their
society with never a thought of sex. I have many female
friends, some white-haired gran'dames, some mere girls in
short dresses. But for their kindly interest and encouragement I would have cast aside the faber and fled to the
desert long ago. The friendship of a noble woman is life's
holiest perfume; but that is not the affinity of souls, the
supernatural spooning, the Platonic yum-yum for which
fair Stella pleads. Love, as I understand the term, is to
friendship's non-consuming flame what the fierce glare of
the noon-day sun is to the mild radiance of the harvest
moon. It is something which makes two people of opposite sexes absolutely necessary to each other. It is a glory
in which the soul is bathed, an almost savage melody that
beats within the blood. It is—O dammit; it's that which
transforms a snub-nosed dairy-maid into a Grecian goddess, a bench-legged farmer-boy into a living Apollo
Belvedere. "Love is love forevermore"—differing in degree, but never in kind. The Uranian is but the nobler
nature of the Pandemian Venus, not another entity. Love
is not altogether of the earth earthy. It is born of the
spirit as well as of the flesh, of the perfume as of the beauty
of the great red rose. Few of those women who have led
captive the souls of the intellectual Titans of the world
could boast of wondrous beauty. The moment man passes
the pale of savagery he demands something more than
mere physical perfection in a companion. Purity, Gentle-
ness, Dignity—such are the three graces of womanhood
that ofttimes make Cupid forgive a shapeless bosom and
adore a homely face. The love of a parent for a child is
the purest affection of which we can conceive; yet is the
child the fruition of a love that lies not ever in the clouds.
Platonic affection, so-called, is but confluent smallpox masquerading as measles. Those who have it may not know
what ails 'em; but they've got a simple case of "spoons"
all the same. If Stella were "my dear heart's better part,"
and tried to convince me that she felt a purely Platonic
affection for some other fellow, I'd apply for a writ of injunction or lay for my transcendental rival with a lignum-
vitae club loaded to scatter. Nobody could convince me
that the country was secure. The Platonic racket is being
sadly overworked in swell society. Like charity, it covers

a multitude of sins. Married women go scouting around at all hours and in all kinds of places with Platonic lovers, until the "old man" feeds a few slugs into a muzzle-loading gun and lets the Platonism leak through artificial holes in the hide of some gay gallant. When madame must have her beaux, and maids receive attention from married men, there's something decayed in the moral Denmarks. Mrs. Tilton thought she felt a Platonic affection for Henry Ward Beecher—was simply worshipping at the shrine of his genius; but she made as bad a mess of it as though she had called her complaint concupiscence. Even here in Texas, where we do preserve a faint adumbration of the simplicity and virtue of ye olden time, it is no uncommon thing to see a chipper married female, who moves in the "best society," flitting about with some fellow who's recognized, as the servants say, as her "steady company." But as we have improved on the Pompeiian "house of joy," so have we added to the French fashion of married flirtation a new and interesting feature. The French allow maids but little liberty so far as male companionship is concerned; but we remove the bridle altogether, and while the matron flirts with the bachelor, the maid appropriates the lonesome benedict. All the old social laws have been laid on the shelf and life rendered a veritable go-as-you-please. In real life there is no "pure Platonic affection," whatever may betide in fiction. No man waits upon another's wife, provides her with carriages and cut flowers, opera tickets and wine suppers with never a suspicion of sex, and no maid who values her virtue will receive marked attentions from a married man. When a virgin finds an "affinity" she should steer it against a marriage contract at the earliest possible moment; when a wife discovers one to whom she is not wedded she should employ a bread and water diet to subdue her "natural super-naturalism" and reinforce her religion with a season of penitence and prayer

THE SEVEN VIALS OF WRATH.

A World-Wide War.

Unless all signs fail, the world is on the eve of a war such as was never known in all the mighty cycles of human history. Lucky indeed will it be if the Twentieth Century is not born amid the shock of universal battle.

Is our boasted civilization breaking down beneath its own ponderous weight—the rotting props and pillars unable to sustain the gilded roof? Are the prophecies of Scripture about to be fulfilled—the world rushing headlong to the final catastrophe?

A murderous mania hath everywhere seized upon the minds of men. The pulse of the race is beating the reveille; the soul of the world is sounding "boots and saddles." Savagery is re-asserting itself—the Christian nations are further than ever before from that age of gold,

> "When the war-drum throbs no longer,
> And the battle-flags are furled
> In the parliament of man,
> The federation of the world."

Peace? "There is no peace—war is inevitable." The ostrich may avoid seeing the approach of the fierce simoon by hiding his head in the sand, but cannot stay its onward march. The craze for slaughter, the lust for blood, is abroad in the land. The stars are evil, and Ate, ranging hot from hell, plants her burning feet on every brow.

For years the brute passions of man have had no outlet—a prolonged peace hath become that good custom which doth corrupt the world. A new generation hath arisen in Europe and America which knows naught of the horrors of war, but is intoxicated by its glory. Its superfluous energy must find expression, its pent-up passions are ready for explosion. It is all aweary of these piping times of peace—wildly eager for the glorious pomp and circumstance of war—the bullet's mad hiss and the crash of steel. Civilized man is but an educated savage—sooner or later his natural ferocity will demand its pound of flesh.

*   *   *   *   *   *

I know not whether Deity or Devil be the author of war. All human advancement is born of strife. Only warlike nations march in the van of the world's progress—prolonged peace has ever meant putrefaction. The civilizations of Greece and Rome were brightest when their blades were keenest. When the sword was sheathed there followed social degradation and intellectual decay. When all Europe trembled at the haughty tread of her matchless infantry, Spain was empress in the realm of mind. The Elizabethan age in England was shaped by the sword. America's intellectual pre-eminence followed the long agony of the Revolution, and blazed like a banner of glory in the wake of the Civil War. The Reign of Terror gave forth flashes of true Promethean fire—the crash of steel in the Napoleonic war studded the heavens with stars. It required an eruption of warlike barbarians to awaken Italy from her lethargy, while Celt and Saxon struck sacred fire from the shields of the intrepid Caesars. The Israelites were humble and civilized slaves in Egypt, cowering beneath the lash and finding a sweet savor in the fleshpots of the Pharaohs. Thrust forth into the wilderness, they became the fiercest of all barbarians before giving us the Psalms of David and the Song of Solomon. They had to become conquering warriors—had to be heroized—before they could breed inspired poets.

The age of "blood offering" has not yet passed. Is it possible that these awful rites are necessary to foster that spirit of self-sacrifice which marks the highest reach of humanity? To feed the golden lamp of love? To inculcate the virtue of valor? Can heroes be forged only with the hammer of Thor? Is genius the child of blood and tears? Are wars the tidal waves in the mighty social sea, ordained by the Deity to prevent putrefaction? Was the Phoenix of the ancients but an old civilization, enervated by luxury and corrupted by peace, that could only be purified of its foul dross and infused with new energy by fire? Was that poet inspired who declared that, "Whatever is, is right?" I do not know.

* * * * * *

The trend of events points to a war that will involve the world—will align the Old against the New. I will be told the idea that Europe will combine against America is sheer madness. Is it even so? Has the time arrived when young men dream idle dreams and old men see lying visions? Scan the European press for six months past, and you will find such an event foreshadowed by the ablest editors and most distinguished diplomats. The probable necessity of such a coalition has been seriously discussed by various European cabinets.

Great Britain is the pariah of nations, feared by most, detested by all. Continental Europe would gladly see her humbled in the very dust. Had war resulted from the Venezuelan complication, England would, in all probability, have been left without allies, albeit the president's ultimatum was not relished by other transatlantic powers. Realizing his inability to cope with the Giant of the Occident, the world's bully stopped blustering and began sniffling about his beloved cousin across the sea and the beatitude of arbitration. The American Congress passed resolutions of sympathy with the Cuban insurgents, and from so slight a spark the Spanish people took fire. Instead of acting as peace-makers, the official organs of most European governments proceeded to fan the flames—encouraged Spain to resent the fancied affront by assuring her that she would not lack powerful allies. There was no recognition by this government of Cuban independence; no recommendation that we wrest the island from the moribund nation that has so long misgoverned it; but a semi-official expression of concern for men striving to achieve their liberty afforded Europe a pretext to "get together" and work off on a distant people that war spirit, so long suppressed at home, lest it disturb the balance of power. The British journals, which had warbled so sweetly anent their American cousins and "the indissoluble bond of Anglo-Saxon brotherhood," when there was a fair prospect that John Bull would have to toe the scratch alone, at once forgot the blessed ties of consanguinity and assured the bombastic Spaniard that he would have "plenty of help should he decide to humble American impudence." The press of France and Germany discoursed in much the same manner, while the diplomats of those countries agreed that "Europe would yet find it necessary to materially modify the Monroe Doctrine." But the Spaniard, believing discretion to be the better part of valor, had apologized for the acts of his undiapered babes and the excesses of his hungry beggars before his neighbors could stiffen his backbone with their ostentatious insolence.

The Monroe Doctrine, literally interpreted, is simply a warning to transatlantic powers to keep off the American grass—an official notice that they will not be permitted to overrun and parcel out this continent regardless of human rights as they have done in Asia and are doing in Africa. The "Doctrine" is ridiculous, in that it establishes a quasi-protectorate over a number of petty powers that have no valid excuse for existing; still it works no injury to any European government not bent on international buccaneering. Uncle Sam's promulgation of the Monroe Doctrine proves him a fool; Europe's frantic objection to it demonstrates that she is a knave.

The Spanish incident served to show that the war spirit is rife throughout Europe, and that her mighty armaments cannot much longer be kept inactive. It proved conclusively that Europe is feverishly eager to set limits to the growing power of this government while such limitation is yet possible—that she cannot view with composure the slightest inclination on the part of America to take a hand in the world's politics. With wealth aggregating seventy-five billions, and as many millions of warlike Americans back of it, the Monroe Doctrine becomes something more than an iridescent dream. When such a nation decides upon "a vigorous foreign policy," the balance of power problem cannot be long confined to the European continent—a fact which explains the pernicious activity of transatlantic governments during our late unpleasantness.

But all the danger of an international complication does not come from across the sea. The war-spirit is well nigh as rife in this country as at Barcelona and Cadiz. The great mass of the American people would welcome a controversy with any country, with or without good cause. "The glory of the young man is in his strength," and Uncle Sam is young and strong. He longs to grapple with his contemporaries, to demonstrate his physical superiority. He has a cypress shingle on either shoulder and is trailing his star spangled cutaway down the plank turnpike. While a few mugwumps, like Josef Phewlitzer and Apollyon Halicarnassus Below, and tearful Miss Nancys of the Anglomaniacal school, are protesting that this country wants peace, Congress, that faithful mirror of public opinion, if not always the repository of wisdom, proves that it is eager for war. And just so sure as the Cleveland interpretation of the Monroe Doctrine is insisted upon, we are going to get it, and that before babes now nursing wear beards. And the "Doctrine," as applied by the administration, will not only be insisted upon, but public opinion will force the hands of our public servants and compel them to push it further. The fact that it is distasteful to our transatlantic brethren makes it ridiculously popular with a people determined to burn gunpowder. Aside from the epidemic of murder which seems to have girdled the globe, the spirit of petty jealousy and assumed superiority with which Americans are treated in many European countries, has imbued this people with the idea that the quickest way to win the respect of their supercilious neighbors is to slaughter them. Uncle Sam is in an ugly humor and will suffer no legitimate *casus belli* to be side-tracked by arbitration. He is "dead tired" of having the European ants get on him —of being harried by petty powers whom he knows full well he could wipe from the map of the world. He is just a little inclined to do the Roman Empire act—to take charge of this planet and run it in accordance with his own good pleasure. Some of these days he's going to drive his box-teed boot under John Bull's coat-tails so far that the impudent old tub of tallow can taste leather all the rest of his life.

We may deplore this spirit of contention, but to deny its existence were to write one's self down an irremediable ass. It is in evidence everywhere, from the American senate to the country clown. To argue against the war-spirit were like whistling in the teeth of a north wind. You cannot alter a psychological condition with a made-to-order editorial. It is urged that we should sing small, as we are "not prepared for war." We are always prepared. Hercules did not need a Krupp cannon—he was capable of doing terrible execution with a club. Samson did not wait to forge a Toledo blade—he waltzed into his enemies with an old bone and scattered their shields of iron and helmets of brass to the four winds of heaven. The mighty armaments of Europe are costly trifles; whenever America has been called to fight she has revolutionized the science of destruction. It hath been said, "In time of peace prepare for war." Europe bankrupts herself to build steel cruisers and maintain gigantic standing armies; America prepares by strengthening her bank account and developing her natural resources. When the crisis comes she has "the sinews of war," and brains and industry quickly do the rest. It was not necessary for Gulliver to sleep in the land of the Lilliputs with a gun at his side.

Vast armies and costly fleets of battleships in time of peace are indication of conscious weakness. The Western Giant goes unarmed; but let the embattled world tread upon his coat-tails if it dares! The American does not have to be educated to soldiership—he's to the manner born. Those who can build are competent to destroy. Our civil war was fought by volunteers; yet before nor since in all the struggles of mankind were such terrible engines of destruction launched upon land or sea. Never did so many bullets find their billets. Never did men set their breasts against the bayonet with such reckless abandon. Never were the seas incarnadined with such stubborn blood. The "Charge of the Six Hundred" was repeated a thousand times. The Pass of Thermopylae was emulated by ploughboys. The Macedonian Phalanx was as nothing to the Rock of Chickamauga. The Bridge of Lodi was duplicated at every stream. The spirit of the Old Guard animated raw recruits. The Retreat of the Ten Thousand became but a holiday excursion. Sailors fought their guns below the water line and went down with flying colors and ringing cheers.

We have been more than once dangerously near a rupture with European powers because of the ridiculous Monroe Doctrine, which assumes for Uncle Sam a quasi-protectorate over a horde of Latin-American oligarchies masquerading as Republics. We have now been fairly warned that should such a catastrophe occur, we would have to contend with more than one European power. We must either recede from the position we have assumed or prepare to do battle for the very existence of this government. Such a war would draw all the nations of the earth into the bloody vortex. If Russia held aloof from the Anti-American coalition, she would seize the opportunity to push her fortunes in the Orient, making a collision with the Moslem inevitable. At such a time the latter would be intent upon the extension of territory. Occupy Western European with an American war, and the Mohammedan would rise against their oppressors. Unfurl the sacred banner of the Prophet, and millions of murderous fanatics would erase the raids of Goth and Visigoth from the memory of mankind. Turkey, jeered at even by Spain, flouted even by Italy, yet potentially the most powerful nation for evil upon the earth, would spread as by magic over Roumania and Austro-Hungary, and pour through the Alpine passes like a torrent of fire upon Germany and France. Back of the much contemned "Sick Man of the East"—whom combined Christendom has failed to frighten—are nearly two hundred million people, scattered from the Pillars of Hercules to the Yellow Sea, all eager to conquer the earth for Islam. They are warriors to a man; their only fear is that they will not find death while battling with "the infidel dog" and be transplanted bodily to the realm of bliss. Within the memory of living men Christian nations have turned their eyes with fear and trembling to the Bosphorus. Islam is the political Vesuvius of Europe, and is once again casting its lurid light athwart the troubled sky. For years the Moslem has been robbed without mercy and persecuted without remorse. The bayonet has been held at his throat while strangers reviled his religion. It is no part of his creed to love his enemies and pray for those who despitefully use him. The Koran does not adjure him to turn the other cheek to the smiter. He has nursed his wrath to keep it warm, and prayed for an opportunity to wreak barbaric vengeance upon his oppressors. When Christian Europe marches forth to do battle with

America, she will need to wear armor upon her back as well as upon her breast, for while terror stalks before hell will lurk behind.

A MESSAGE TO MARY.

I have received a dainty epistle from Temple, Tex., signed "Mary," and propounding the following important conundrum:

> Should woman be given the ballot?

Cert.—if she asks for it. I insist that lovely woman be given everything she may happen to want, from a ducal coronet to a pug dog, from a bicycle to the ballot. I wouldn't deny her anything if I could, and couldn't if I would, because I'm not built that way. If my fair correspondent will 'fess up to one-and-twenty golden summers, I am conscious of no reason why she shouldn't don a pair of bloomers, a stiff hat and a starched shirt, participate in political powwows and yoop with her mouth open for "our party"—if the performance will afford her any real pleasure. If she wants to deposit in the urn of political destiny an embroidered ballot, printed with sympathetic ink on lavender silk, with a postscript at the bottom, and smelling of attar of roses and unadulterated democracy—then go around in a day or two and insist on changing it—I shall never file an objection. But, to the best of my knowledge and belief, the average woman would rather have one baby than forty ballots. The fact that she doesn't vote—"early and often"—is prima facie evidence that she doesn't want to; for

> "When a woman will she will,
> You may depend on't,
> And when she won't she won't,
> And there's an end on't."

There has been a great deal of talk during the past three decades anent female enfranchisment; but I have yet to see one really representative American woman clamoring for the blessed privilege of saving the country via the thorny path of politics. After having interviewed, as a working journalist, most of the leading lights of the "reform" movement, I am inclined to suspect every woman who wants to vote of having failed in an earnest attempt to get married, or of having been so unfortunate as to miss her "affinity" and get tied to some other fellow. Generally speaking, it is the matrimonial failures, the hen-pecked husbands and women with voices like a cat-fight and faces that would frighten a trolley car who compose the female suffrage contingent. The exceptions only prove the rule. Instead of being a thing of beauty and a joy forever, the "strong-minded woman" is almost invariably a faded wallflower. Man doesn't know any too much himself; but he aspires to be the head of his own household. That is why he dodges women who want to take him to educate. He has no ambition to play the tender and clinging vine to some sturdy female oak. Theoretically, "taxation without representation" is all wrong, whether the object of the mulct wear breeches or bloomers; but that woman who cannot find a worthy husband or rear a valiant son to "represent" her in the forum and the field should acknowledge herself a failure. The right kind of a woman may be pressed and repressed, but never oppressed or suppressed by "tyrant man." I have yet to see a maid in love, with a fair prospect of making a landing; I have yet to see a beautiful woman, after whom men gazed as though they longed to steal her; I have yet to see a woman with a kindly, sympathetic face and a low, sweet voice that thrills the hearts of men with a fiercer joy than trumpet's blow for war, clamoring for female enfranchisement. The woman who looms up in a calico gown like a Grecian goddess on dress-parade; who can, with a glance of her eyes, set every man's soul on fire and bring him to her feet; who can transform an humble cottage into a happy home gilded with God's own glory; who can make a husband play the lover through a long lifetime, and rear a crop of boy babies fit to wear the crown of American sovereignty, never suspects that the world will go to hades awhooping if she doesn't hustle down to the polls and express her political preferences. She knows that every law that does her wrong is written upon the sand; that every government that fails to guard her as its chief glory is doomed to nameless death. Served by the world's wisdom and circled by its chivalry, she stands secure—an Empress by Right Divine. When a man is good for nothing else, he goes to preaching or starts a "reform" newspaper. When a woman either fails to catch a man or in a fit of desperation marries some whiskered Miss Nancy without sufficient moral courage to manage her, she concludes that the times are out of joint and that she has been raised up to put them right. The woman who is the crown jewel of a good home keeps off the hustings; but the one who commands neither love at home nor admiration abroad feels that she is being robbed of her "rights." Give a woman youth and beauty and she asks not—needs not—political power; but when, still a maid, her mirror tells her she could not pass for five-and-forty in the moonlight; when her bracelet slips over her elbows and a thumb-ring would make her a garter; when she becomes either a perambulating tub of unwholesome lard or has to pad her diaphragm to cast a shadow, she is apt to be morbidly sensitive to

> "The oppressor's wrong, the proud man's contumely,
> The pangs of despised love, the law's delay."

declines to endure the ills she has, but flies to others she knows not of. Attend any female suffrage convention, and you will find more wrinkles than roses. It is a startling aggregation of brawny fists and big feet, or scrawny necks and bosoms either flat or formless—a nightmare for the artist, the despair of a poet. One can scarce blame such a crowd for pleading the right of self-protection. They certainly need it. In states where full or partial female suffrage now prevails, the home-woman ofttimes goes to the polls; as well as her "progressive" sister; but she does so simply because those she loves are pulling for the success of party, and have called upon her to offset the female vote of the opposition. The home-woman—the woman we love, and whose slightest wish is our law—cares never a copper who is president or poundmaster so long as the lord of her life is well content. The very fact that it has taken forty years to bring woman such a little way on the road to "emancipation" proves that politics is foreign to the law of her being. She doesn't have to embark in bitter crusades to wring concessions from those who live only to serve her; to whom wealth and power are as bitter ashes and the mural wreath a crown of thorns unless illumined by her love. The true woman—the woman who is really a helpmeet unto man; the woman who is "first at the cradle and last at the grave;" the woman who meekly obeys us while ruling us with a golden rod; the woman who laughs at us but loves us; the woman who asks our forgiveness when we are the offender; the woman who doesn't believe one-half we tell her, yet would make any sacrifice to serve us, simply asks for what she wants, and if it is not promptly forthcoming makes a quiet sneak on our inside pockets while we sleep for circumstantial evidence that will force a verdict in her favor. It is usually the woman who is not welcome anywhere, who has no one to love her, whose very presence makes a man feel like reaching for a fence picket, who wants to be a torchlight procession.

DOGMATISM THE MOTHER OF DOUBT.

A Worship for the World.

"Church Unification" has long been the dream of many earnest souls, who regret to see the various denominations wasting energy warring upon each other that should be brought to bear on the legions of Lucifer; but even the most sanguine must admit there is little prospect of their dreams becoming more tangible—at least for some ages yet. The bloody chasm which Luther and his co-laborers opened will not be bridged during the lifetime of the present generation, and human wisdom is not competent to formulate a "creed," to devise a "doctrine," upon which the Protestant world will consent to unite. The present tendency is not toward church unification, but greater and more sharply defined division. Instead of dogmatic controversy dying away it is becoming more general; "heterodoxy" is being hunted with a keener zest than for years, and doctrinal disputation has become well nigh as virulent as the polemics of partisan politics.

In the meantime a majority of mankind in highly civilized countries remain away from church—take no thought of the future or seek truth in science rather than revelation. Dogmatism is the fruitful mother of Doubt. By assuming to know too much of God's great plan; by demanding too abject obedience to his fiats; by attempting to stifle honest inquiry and seal the lips of living scholars with the dicta of dead scholastics, by standing ever ready to brand as blasphemers all who presume to question or dare to differ, the church has driven millions of God-fearing men into passive indifference or overt opposition, and the number is rapidly increasing. The church does not realize how stupendous this army really is. Not every man who regards the church as but a pretender proclaims that fact on the house tops. It is not "good policy," and policy is the distinguishing characteristic of this day and age. Church people are very sensitive to criticism of their creed (perhaps the mother of a malformed or vicious child could tell why), and most men have loved ones or patrons who are trying to find a little comfort among the husks of an iron-bound orthodoxy. If any devout dogmatizer really desires to learn how general is this attitude of non-receptivity of the orthodox religion, let him assume the role of a scoffer; then he will hear the truth from men's lips; for while the doubter may yield passive assent to the prevalent orthodoxy, the earnest believer is not apt to enact the role of Peter without compulsion. Instead of conquering the world, the church is rapidly losing what it has hitherto gained. True, it still retains a semblance of vigor and prosperity; but, like many a great political structure, its brilliancy is born of decay. It is no longer the dominating factor in social life, the heart and soul of civilization, but an annex—increasing in magnificence as wealth increases and mankind can afford to expend more for ostentation and fashionable diversion.

It is noticeable that the less attention the minister pays to creeds, the less dogmatism he indulges in, the more popular he becomes with the people, the more eagerly they flock to hear him. The world does not care to listen to prosy lectures on foreordination and the terrors of Tartarus, because its reason rejects such cruel creeds; it takes little interest in the question whether Christ was dipped or sprinkled by the gentleman in the camel's-hair cutaway, because it cannot, for the life of it, see that it makes any difference; it does not want to be worried with jejune speculations anent the Trinity, because it considers one God quite sufficient if it can but find him; does not want to hear much about the miracles, because it considers it a matter of absolute indifference whether they are true or not. But just the same, the great world is heart-hungry for real knowledge of the All-Father, eager to embrace any faith that does no violence to its reason, to grasp at any tangible thread of hope of a happy life with loved ones beyond the tomb's dark portals.

Prof. James T. Bixby, in a powerful plea for truth-seekers, quoted approvingly the words of an eminent ecclesiastic of the church of England who characterized the present age as "pre-eminently the age of doubt." Another writer says that Europe is turning in despair toward Nirvana. The almost unprecedented success of Hartman's "Philosophy of the Unconscious"—which is little more or less than Buddhism—gives a strong color of truth to the startling assertion. While Europe is sending missionaries to the Ganges, India is planting the black pessimism of Gautama on the Rhine and the Seine! Nineteen centuries of dogmatizing, to end in an "age of doubt" and a cry for the oblivion of Nirvana! Clearly there is something wrong, for doubt and a desire for annihilation is not the normal condition of the human mind. A belief in God, that the universe is the result of design, is inherent in man. It is not a belief that must be implanted and tenderly nursed; it is one that manifests itself in the lowest form of savage life of which we have cognizance—one that is well-nigh impossible to crush out—and complementing this belief, in most instances, is the hope of immortality. No cataclysm of crime into which man can plunge is able to eradicate his belief that he is the creature of a supernatural power and intelligence. The tendency of scientific research is to strengthen it by making more manifest the wondrous works of God. It is doubtful if the belief in man's divine origin was ever entirely obliterated from any human mind—if there ever was or will be an "atheist." Many men believe themselves such; but if they will carefully examine their position, they will usually find that they have been carried to this extreme by a powerful revulsion from incredible dogmatism, and that they can only maintain it by a continual and unnatural effort—by a persistent outrage upon that very intelligence of which they boast. The moment they cease to act on the defensive they begin to drift back under the divine spell; to pay homage, conscious or unconscious, to the All-Father.

Those who deny the inspiration of the Bible are, for the most part, but doubting Thomases who ask to see the nail-prints in the hands of their risen Lord; who are disposed to question him, not because they are irreligious, but because they want the Truth, and they know for a verity that it is the truth.

It is not possible to found a church in which may be gathered the millions who cannot swallow the miracles, the incarnation, the plenary inspiration of the Bible, and other non-essential husks that enshroud the Christian cultus; where that religion which exists, conscious or unconscious, in their nature, may find room for expansion; where honest inquiry may be persecuted, doubts freely and fairly discussed and perhaps dispelled; where all Truth, whether found in the Bible or the Koran, the Law of Mana or the Zandavesta, science or philosophy, may be eagerly seized and carefully treasured? If it were possible to thus bring together and utilize the vast amount of religious energy which lies without the pale of all present churches, unrecognized by the most, warred upon by the many; if it were possible to gather all believers in God together where they may strengthen their faith by communion and worship; extend their knowledge by research in every field, spiritual and material, secular and religious, what a mighty recruit would thus be added to those powers that are working for the world's salvation!

Let me briefly sketch such a church as I would like to be a member of—such as I imagine millions of others who are not, will never be members of existent communions, would worship in with pleasure. Its chief "essential" should be belief in God—not the God of the Jews, Mohammedans or Christians, but the God of everything, animate and inanimate in the whole broad universe; the God of Justice and Wisdom, Truth and Love; the God seen in the face of every noble woman and honest man, heard in every truth, felt in every holy aspiration. Everyone believing in the existence of such a God—and I doubt if any do not—should be eligible for membership, no matter what their theories regarding his personality, plans and powers. Truth should be sought assiduously, and welcomed wherever found. We should not attempt to make it fit a preconceived theory, but to make the theory conform to it. Science should be the handmaid of the church, philosophy its helpful brother; but its ecumenical council, its court of last resort, should be the religious instinct inherent in man—that perception so fine, so subtle, that all attempts to weave it into words to clothe it so that the eye may perceive and the reason handle it, have signally failed; which logic has hammered at with all her ballistae and battering-rams for thirty centuries or more in vain; which, above all things else, binds the human race in one great brotherhood, has supplied the missing links in every cult, bridged its laches, surmounted its incongruities, comprised its inexpugnable fortress upon which the high flood-tide of worldly wisdom beats in vain.

Its body doctrine should be Love of God, Charity for man, Truth, Honor, Purity. In these are comprised "the whole Hebrew Decalogue, with Solon's and Lycurgus' Constitutions, Justinian's Pandects, the Code Napoleon and all codes, catechisms, divinities, moralities whatsoever, that man has hitherto devised (and enforced with altar-fire and gallows-ropes) for his social guidance." They embrace all that is blessed and beautiful, gracious and great in every sect, science and philosophy known to man. These are "points of doctrine" upon which there can be no dissension; Buddhist and Mohammedan, Jew and Gentile, Catholic and Calvinist, philosopher and "free-thinker," will all approve.

Regarding what provision the Lord will make for us hereafter, the plenary or partial inspiration of the Bible, the evidential value of the miracles, the divinity of Christ, and kindred subjects, every communicant may properly be left free to exercise his individual judgment. To formulate a cast-iron article of faith upon any or all these questions would be to enter the realm of dogmatics, to add one more voice to the ecclesiastical wrangle that is filling the earth and heaven and hades with its unprofitable din—to found a sect instead of a world-embracing church devoted to the simple worship of God and the inculcation of morals. To many a religion without a future-life annex may appear as unfinished as a building without a roof; as ephemeral, as unstable as one put together without nails or mortar; but such forget that future reward and punishment was no part of the early Hebrew cult—that the doctrine of man's immortality is but a late and apparently a Gentile graft; that the Buddhist religion, which has held the souls of countless millions in thrall, teaches complete extinction of the ego as the greatest good. Man does not embrace religion "for what there is in it;" does not worship because God possesses the power to reward and punish, any more than he stands entranced by the glory of the sunrise because the rays of the Day-god will ripen his cotton and corn. He pays involuntary homage to the Higher Power, as he does to men of genius who benefit him but indirectly, to women of great beauty whom he never hopes to possess.

We may safely trust our future to the same great Power to whom we owe the present. It is of far more importance that we make the most possible of this life than that we have fixed convictions anent the next. It is safe to assume that had the great God intended we should know for a surety what awaits us beyond Death's dark river, he would have made it so manifest that diversity of opinion would be impossible; that had he intended we should each and all accept Christ as a divinity, he would have driven stronger pegs upon which the doubting Thomases of this late day could hang their faith; that had he intended the Bible should stand for all time as his infallible word, it would not have been intrusted for so many centuries to the care of fallible men; that had he intended we should each and all believe the miracles, he would have made better provision for their authentication—or built our heads on a different plan. Belief in immortality is a very comforting doctrine—for such as hope to dodge hell-pains—and is so general, so prone to manifest itself, where the mind of man has not been persistently trained in an opposite direction, that we may almost call it a religious instinct, which is but a vulgarism for a divine and direct revelation of God; therefore, it should not be discouraged in our new world-church, but given every opportunity for expansion. No one should be excluded, however, if he fail to find evidence, within or without, to sustain the theory.

Such a church would embrace all others as the ocean-stream of the ancients encompassed and fed every sea. It would be the tie that would bind all in unity. It should welcome to its pulpit all ministers of whatsoever denomination who desire to treat the worship of God from a non-sectarian standpoint or read a homily calculated to strengthen the morals of mankind. Its hymns should be songs of praise to that God who made us the greatest in his visible creation; its prayers should be thanks for past mercies and petitions that he will make our brightest dreams of life eternal beyond the skies a blessed reality—that having brought us so near his bright effulgence increate for Time, he will gather us to his loving bosom for all Eternity.

Such is the church in which I hope one day to see the whole world gathered—a church whose paeans of praise to the great God would drown dogmatic dialectics as the swelling notes of an organ drown the fretful complaining of a child.

THE FISTICPHOBIA FOLLY.

The Fool-killer is dead. He took one look at the *fin de siecle* crop he was expected to harvest, softly murmured,

> "The burthen laid upon me
> Is greater than I can bear."

and gave up the ghost. With a two-edged scythe, operated by electricity, he could not scoop in even the preachers and politicians demanding his attention in this day of decadents and demagogues. Doubtless many of them are more knave than fool; but when a man deliberately signs a certificate of his own irremediable idiocy, I am inclined to let it go at that. The terms may be interchangeable, the doctors having decided that rascality is a disease.

I am no apologist for pugilism. If I thought a son of mine would enter the squared-circle to do battle for boodle and the distinction of being known as chief of brutes, I'd hang him with his own diapers. I'd rather see him a preacher than a pugilist. He might outgrow the one, but he could never live down the odium of the other. But—

to drop from the classic to the vulgar—it "makes me tired" to see a lot of plotting politicians and half-baked preachers tearing around like a hen on a hot griddle, or a skye-terrier with a clothes-pin anchored to his tail, simply because a couple of professional pugs want to pound each other with feather pillows for a fat purse. I cannot see, to save me, where their kick comes in. Suppose the pugilists do maim each other: Who will mourn? Not the ministers; for, to judge by their utterances, they would gladly see the whole gang under the grass. If they kill each other, who will weep? Not the politicians—they have troubles of their own. "But the public will be corrupted," I am told. The public appears amply able to take care of itself—it has put more than a thousand preachers in the penitentiary. The modern politicians "guarding public morals" were like setting the wolf to watch the lamb—or placing Sextus Tarquinius in charge of a female seminary. There's Culberson, for instance—"our heroic young Christian governor"—what? Imagine Son Charles guarding anything—except Dan Stuart or a stack of poker chips! Think of the erstwhile paramour of Widow Halpin—who saved more than a million out of a salary aggregating less than $350,000—keeping watch and ward lest the pugilists "corrupt the country!" Think of a crap-shooting, chippy-chasing legislature—with its pockets full of complimentary passes—shielding Texas from pugilistic contamination; of a Congress addicted to closed carriages and French *bal masques,* rushing in hot haste to the rescue of the cacti and cayuses of New Mexico—guarding the morals of the greasers!

I am assured by the ministers that "only the *canaille* witness pugilistic controversies"—that "none but the roughs and rowdies gather at the ring side." How can a prizefight, however brutal, "corrupt" cattle of that kind? How can you spoil a rotten egg, or debase those already debauched? If El Paso is willing to be made the rendezvous of all the roughs and rowdies, should not all the rest of Christendom rejoice over the "good riddance of bad rubbish?"

Every day men beat each other to a pulp with brassknuckles, bowie-knife their brethren or shoot respectable citizens. Every day we hang or electrocute or lynch somebody—and civilization goes marching on; yet we are expected to believe that if one skilled athlete keeps another on the floor for ten consecutive seconds, our Car of Progress will stick in the mud and the Christian world be relegated back to barbarism! To prevent this awful catastrophe Culberson called a special session of the legislature and massed the rangers on the Rio Grande. To prevent it Cleveland deprived himself of a duck hunt and remained reasonably sober an entire day. No wonder the chief magistrate of New Mexico sweat blood at this awful crisis, while the world resounded with the grandiloquence of the head greaser of a Mexican province known to the world only because of the brutality of its bullfights and its peculiar breed of fices. And Congress—praise heaven!—rose equal to the emergency. After having tried—without the shadow of an excuse—to hurry this nation into a war that would have cost a million lives and filled the land with widows' moans and orphans' tears, it dropped the currency question, leaving the business interests of the world to wait, and spent days patching up a law, making it a penal offense for one pug to smack another with a wind-blown bladder in any of the territories of these United States!

But the Fool-killer is dead.

Public sentiment favored a war with England, with or without valid excuse; ergo, the politicians were for it. Public sentiment is supposed to be "agin" prize-fights; ergo, the politicians oppose it. They are trying to ride the popular wave—that's what they are here for; but the first thing they know some of 'em will hit the beach with the bust of their panties with the solid impact of a ton of lead toying with a stone wall. "You can't sometimes most always tell" about this thing we call public sentiment. If Corbett and Fitzsimmons were to fight in Dallas to-day—without admission fee—Waco, the religious hub of the world, would be depopulated. Half the preachers of Texas would go early to secure front seats.

As evidence that the politicians and preachers don't care a coffer-dam about the public further than it can be "worked" for their personal profit, I would call attention to the fact that cock-fighting—the most brutal and debasing of all so-called sports—is still permitted in Texas, is liberally patronized by legislators who have made prize-fighting a felony, and seldom calls forth a protest from the preachers. These "guardians of the public morals" are too cussed good to permit trained pugilists to box each other with soft gloves until one wears out his "wind;" yet in proximity to our schools and churches innocent birds are armed with steel gaffles and incited to butcher each other to make a hoodlum holiday, while half-grown boys elbow old "sports" for a better view of the pit and gamble their nickels on the result. "Interstate cocking mains" are reported at length by canting newspapers in the self-same issues with fierce denunciations of prize-fighting—ofttimes in the same column with the reports of revival meetings or pretentious sermons. The man who swallows the cock-pit and gags on "physical culture contests" is a large piebald ass, with ears so long that he needs no tail to keep the gad-flies off his heels.

The idea of Mexico "beefing" about "the brutality of the prize-ring," while torturing bulls and disemboweling hack-horses in the name of "sport"—going mad with joy when, by God's favor, Taurus gets a matador on his horns or tramples him beneath his hoofs! Mexico turning up her yaller snout at games that have been immortalized by the harp of Homer; that served to mark time for Greece when in the hey-dey of that intellectual glory to which we bend the knee as to the immortal gods; that were the pride of Rome when the Imperial City "sat upon her seven hills and from her throne of beauty ruled the world!" Mexico is afraid that a brace of pugilists would put a crimp in her "civilization!" Mexico is simply an aggregation of those tribes of Indians who were too cowardly to fight and too lazy to run away. When one of them learns that the occasional use of a fine-tooth comb will save him the labor of scratching, he is considered civilized. Mexico, like Texas, is a great cock-fighting country—is addicted to the torture of beasts and birds in the name of "sport," but entirely too "civilized" to tolerate the squared circle!

For shame! When I have to see blood spilled in order to corral an appetite, I want it to be the blood of men who do battle of their own accord, not that of innocent beasts and birds that have no option but to work the will of their subter-brutish masters.

Scientific pugilism is no more brutal than many sports having the sanction of society. It is of precious little importance whether it be encouraged or repressed. In some way man will continue to exhibit his personal prowess, for now, as in the days of David, "The glory of the young man is in his strength." Did this blatant opposition to prize-fighting bear the imprint of honest idiocy I could respect it; but it is too evidently policy playing seasoned with canting hypocrisy. Corbett and Fitzsimmons were to fight at Hot Springs; but Gov. Clark made a roar that rocked the state of Arkansaw to its foundation stone, and the project had to be abandoned. Yet in less than two months a fight far more brutal than the big "mill" was likely to be, was pulled off at Hot Springs in a public hall, and "well attended." The explanation is easy. The eyes of the world were on the "big 'uns," while the "little 'uns" were almost entirely overlooked. By interfering with the first, Gov. Clark was able to attract public attention; meddling with the second would have awakened no enthusiasm among the professionally godly, but would have "queered" him politically with Arkansaw's sporting element. Neither the sporty governor of Texas nor the immaculate ass who officiates as chief magistrate of New Mexico, ever thought of interfering with prize-fighting until a match was made between two men of international reputation, and the politicians thereby accorded an opportunity to make a grandstand demonstration. Prize-fights can be pulled off to-day in perfect safety in either Arkansaw or Texas, and with never a "cheep" from the politicians and preachers, if the contestants be not sufficiently prominent in the world of pugilism to attract general attention. Cock-fighting may be all right so long as the roosters do not acquire too much reputation. But should Great Britain produce a fifteen-pound cock that could whip a wildcat, and America one that could see the foreign bird and go him one better; and should it be proposed to bring them together in Dallas, Hot Springs or El Paso for a large purse; should steel gaffles be barred, their natural spurs sawed off and capped with medicated cotton, Dr. Seasholes would rear up on his hind legs and bray like a two-year-old. Ministerial associations would whereas and resolute; politicians would perorate and legislate; Governors would call special sessions and mobilize the militia, and we'd have the same ridiculous to do about nothing that for six months past has made me well-nigh ashamed that I was born an American sovereign.

BEECHER AND THE BIBLE.

A gentleman writing from Hot Springs, Ark., deposeth as follows:

A number of gentlemen were discussing the "Apostle's" religious views in the lobby of a hotel. One declared you an Atheist, another insisted that you were a Catholic, while a third felt sure that you were a Baptist. Kindly take us into your confidence. Do you believe the Bible to be an inspired book? P. S. There is something up on the decision, the winner to forward you a cask of pure spring water if a Baptist, a basket of champagne if an Atheist and a demijohn of old Mountain Dew if a Catholic.

I am not surprised that such a discussion should occur in Hot Springs, the great theological ganglion of Arkansaw.

The very visitors who seek its thermal waters carry with them the "odor of sanctity." It is the Mecca of those poor penitents of whom it was said that "the spirit is willing but the flesh is weak." For the benefit of my correspondent, and others unable to determine by taste the trade-mark of the spiritual pabulum ladled out by the Iconoclast, I will state that I cannot claim either the cask of pure spring water, the basket of blue label or the demijohn of old Mountain Dew. I say this with fond regret; but I cannot win on such a combination. I belong to no particular cult or creed; but I do know, beyond the peradventure of a doubt, that this mighty universe is not without a Master. His origin and attributes are beyond my comprehension. I cannot understand the creature; how, then, shall I comprehend the Creator?

"Know thyself; presume not God to scan;
The proper study of mankind is man."

I know nothing of the Future; I spend no time speculating upon it—I am overwhelmed by the Past and at death-grips with the Present. At the grave God draws the line between the two eternities. Never has living man lifted the sombre veil of Death and looked beyond. "Revealed Religion" was not born of Reason or nursed by Knowledge; it is the child of Love and Pain, and lives between the rosy breasts of Hope.

There is a Deity. I have felt his presence, I have heard his voice, I have been cradled in his imperial robe. All that is, or was, or can be, is but "the visible garment of God." I ask no written covenant with God, for he is my Father. I will trust Him without requiring priests or prophets to endorse His note. As I write my little son awakes, alarmed by some unusual noise, and comes groping thro' darkness to my door. He sees the light shining thro' the transom, returns to his trundle-bed and lies down to peaceful dreams. He knows that beyond that gleam his father keeps watch and ward, and he asks no more. Thro' a thousand celestial transoms streams the light of God. Why should I fear the sleep of Death, the unknown terrors of that starless night, the waves of the river Styx? Why should I seek assurance from the lips of men that the wisdom, love and power of my heavenly Father will not fail?

I came very near being a Baptist, having been bred a Campbellite, but reneged when an attempt was made to baptize me in cracked ice on a winter's day. Perhaps I made a mistake. Some of my ancestors were Presbyterians.

If given so good a chance Jack Frost might have killed the germs of original sin, which formed the distinctive feature of my patrimony.

My view of the Bible was set forth very succinctly by Rev. Henry Ward Beecher in his great lecture on "Evolution." Now that sectarian bitterness is again becoming rife, and heresy-hunting a popular sport with non-progressive preachers, it may be well to consider the judgment passed upon the Good Book by the ablest divine within the memory of living men. He said in part:

> The Bible is itself one of the most remarkable illustrations and examples of Evolution. There are some people who think that God sent down for a dozen or fifteen reporters and told them to come up because he wanted to tell them something, and so they sat down at a table and wrote what he had to say, and out come Genesis and Exodus; and then they went through Leviticus, and Deuteronomy, and Numbers, and God kept talking and they kept writing. He had it all fixed for them, and all they had to do was to write it down. That is what is called the verbal theory—the theory that the Bible was given word for word and sentence for sentence from the lips of God.
>
> *I call in this age the verbal theory the devil's broad way to infidelity. The man that holds that theory in this age of the world ought to be ashamed of himself, and he is not fit either to call himself a teacher, or to be even a teacher of babes.*
>
> What is the anatomy of the Bible? I believe it to be simply the history of an inspiration of the human race. * * * * I believe there is a universal and imminent constant influence flowing directly from the bosom of God and that is the inspiration of the human race. * * * * The Bible is the history of the progress of this inspiration; and there was no inspiration of this prophet or of that prophet, or of this singer or of that singer, so that he should not make any mistakes, but it is the inspiration of the human race, of men raised up who gave a record for it. * * * * To undertake to tell me that the book is directly inspired by God, so that everything that is said in it is a fact, is to indicate that you have not the first twilight dream or dawn of what the book really is * * * * They (religious ignorami) are afraid it (the theory of Evolution) will sweep away the foundation of their faith—an unworthy fear. A faith that trembles and totters every time that God speaks, is not a faith that should sustain any body of men; but that old practice of firing a Bible at every new thing ought at least to come to an end. They fired it at the sun and astronomy, and it came back on their heads, and astronomy marched on. They fired it at geology, and geology triumphed, and men had to find new constructions for their Bible. They are firing it now at the Origin of Man, and they will take it back with new constructions again. For I hold that then was not the first time that God wrote on tablets of stone, that he wrote his thoughts on the vaster strata of stone that run around the globe and mark the great epochs of time.

Heterodoxy? Perhaps; but jump onto Beecher first—he's the biggest.

CHRISTIAN ENGLAND IN INDIA.

Her Tears Anent Turkish Atrocities.

"Christian England" is agonizing over the pitiful condition of the Armenians under Moslem rule, but has nothing to say anent her own awful record in India. It were well for John Bull to get the beam out of his own eye before making frantic swipes at the mote in the optic of the Moslem. The oppression of the children of Israel by the Egyptian Pharoahs, the Babylonian king and Roman emperors were as nothing compared to that suffered by the patient Bengalese at the hands of Great Britain. The history of every barbarous prince of the Orient, in those dark days when might made right and plunder was the recognized prerogative of royalty; the annals of every potentate who has reigned by the grace of Allah and kneeled to kiss the robe of the prophet, may be searched in vain for a parallel in unbounded rapacity and calculating atrocity. England's despoilment of India constitutes the supreme crime of all the ages, the acknowledged acme of infamy. Europe never dreaded Alaric the Visigoth, nor hated Attila the Scourge of God, as India dreads and detests John Bull, "the white beast from over the black water." He has not persecuted because of difference of religious dogma, as have the Mohammedan Sultans and the Christian Czars. That kind of enterprise doesn't pay, and John Bull never wastes on theological sentiment one ounce of energy that can be coined into cash.

A British trading company had leased land at Madras and Calcutta, for which it paid rent to the native powers. For the protection of its warehouses it was permitted to build forts and keep a few armed police, but was in no sense independent. Its position in India was analogous to that of British capitalists in America who are operating a mine or factory and have been authorized to police their property. The mighty house of Tamerlane had become a political nonentity, the empire of the Great Mogul was divided among nominal viceroys who were really independent sovereigns, gorgeous but indolent. The teeming millions of India were, for the most part, as unfitted by nature and occupation for the fatigues of war, as were the countless host which Xerxes led into Greece, or Darius hurled upon the steel-crested phalanxes of that bloody prototype of John Bull, Alexander the Macedonian marauder.

The governments of India were showy rather than strong, and a condition of semi-anarchy had been engendered by the frequent incursions of fierce tribes of robbers, the jealousies and ambitions of rival nabobs and the mischievous schemes of a French adventurer named Dupleix. The company continued to augment its forces until strong enough not only to protect its own property, but to over-awe the native governments. Then, on one dishonest pretext or another, it began the work of transforming India into a British province. Robert Clive succeeded in accomplishing in Asia what Dr. Jamieson attempted with far better excuse in South Africa. Rival powers applied to the company for assistance, and it mattered not with which it allied itself, both were in the end destroyed or enslaved, compelled to pour their wealth into the coffers of the British corporations. No crime was too horrible, no breach of faith too brazen if it promised to further the ambition and increase the gains of the company. Its policy was to unite with a weak government to plunder a strong one, then, by subjugating its ally, to make itself master of both. By treasons and stratagems, by forged treaties and briberies, by infamies planned in cold blood and executed with more than Kurdish barbarity, the garden spot of the earth, with its teeming millions and inestimable wealth, was made to pay tribute to British greed. Macaulay, the eulogist of both Lord Clive and Warren Hastings, thus describes India when Great Britain, without a shadow of excuse, laid her marauding paw upon it in the same manner and for the self-same purpose that Cortez invaded the halls of the Montezumas:

"The people of India when we subdued them, were ten times as numerous as the vanquished Americans (the Indian subjects of Montezuma), and were at the same time quite as highly civilized as the victorious Spaniards. They had reared cities larger and fairer than Saragossa or Toledo, and buildings more beautiful and costly than the cathedrals of Seville. They could show bankers richer than the richest firms of Barcelona or Cadiz, Viceroys whose splendors far surpassed that of Ferdinand the Catholic, myriads of cavalry and long trains of artillery which would have astonished the Great Captain. It might have been expected that every Englishman who takes any interest in any part of history would be curious to know how a handful of their countrymen, separated from their home by an immense ocean, subjugated, in the course of a few years, one of the greatest empires of the world. Yet, unless we greatly err, this subject is, to most readers, not only insipid, but positively distasteful."

Good God! Is it any wonder that British readers should find the conquest of India "positively distasteful?" Is it not quite natural that Englishmen had rather read of Turkish atrocities in Armenia than of British atrocities in India? Lord Macaulay rehearses all the treacheries and cruelties and double-dealings by which "a handful of his countrymen subjugated one of the greatest empires of the world," then complains that British readers find such a catalogue of horrors positively distasteful! Did he expect even Englishmen to become enthusiastic over the hiring of British troops to the infamous Surajah Dowlah for the massacre of the brave Rohillas? Did he expect them to peruse with pleasurable pride the robbery of the Princesses of Oude, the brutal execution of Nuncomar, or the forged treaty by which Ormichund was entrapped? Having painted the atrocities and craven cowardice of Chief Justice Impey, could he reasonably expect them to be proud of this representative Englishman in India? Having told us that Lord Clive was a freebooter in his boyhood and a butcher in his prime, did he anticipate that even Englishmen would be proud of this countryman of theirs who founded the British Empire in India? Lord Macaulay gives us the following description of conditions in Bengal under British domination, then wonders that his countrymen find its perusal "positively distasteful."

"They (the servants of the East India company) covered with their protection a set of native dependents, who ranged thro the provinces, spreading desolation and terror wherever they appeared. Every servant of a British factor was armed with all the power of his master. And his master was armed with all the power of the company. Enormous fortunes were thus accumulated at Calcutta, while thirty millions of human beings were reduced to the last extremity of wretchedness. They had been accustomed to live under tyranny, but never tyranny like this. They found the little finger of the company thicker than the loins of the Surajah Dowlah. It resembled the government of evil genii rather than the government of human tyrants."

The people of India, it must be remembered, had experienced the tyranny of the Brahman and Buddhist, of Moslem and even the terrible Mahratta; they had groaned beneath the exactions of the Great Moguls, plundering viceroys and robber chiefs; they had paid tribute to Aurungzebe and to Hyder Ali, but here we are told they never experienced such tyranny and pitiless despoliation as under the rule of Christian England, and this upon the testimony of an Englishman! Now that British preachers and pamphleteers are agonizing over Mohammedan atrocities in Armenia, let us see what the latter thought of Christian domination in India. "If," says the Mussulman historian of those unhappy times, "if to so many military qualifications, they

(English) knew how to join the art of government—if they exerted as much ingenuity and solicitude in relieving the people of God, as they do in whatever concerns their military affairs, no nation in the world would be preferable to them, or worthier of command; but the people under their dominion groan everywhere, and are reduced to poverty and distress. Oh God! come to the assistance of thine afflicted servants, and deliver them from the oppressions they suffer."

Lord Clive, having acquired an immense fortune, concluded to round out his political career by inaugurating a reform that would in some manner atone for his past excesses, and did succeed in giving India more than a Roman peace and abating some of the worst abuses; but the reform was ephemeral. In his essay on Warren Hastings, Lord Macaulay—who wonders that the conquest of India is "distasteful" reading to Englishmen—gives us the following pen-picture of conditions under the administration of his ideal:

"The delay and the expense, grievous as they are, form the smallest part of the evil which English law, imported without modification into India, could not fail to produce. The strongest feelings of our nation, honor, religion, female modesty, rose up against the innovation. Arrest on mense process was the first step in most civil proceedings; and to a native of rank arrest was not merely a restraint, but a foul personal indignity. That the apartments of a woman of quality should be entered by strange men, or that her face should be seen by them, are in the East intolerable outrages—outrages which are more dreaded than death, and which can be expiated only by the shedding of blood. To these outrages the most distinguished families of Bengal, Bahar and Orissa were now exposed. A reign of terror began—a reign of terror heightened by mystery. No man knew what was next to be expected from this strange tribunal. It had collected round itself an army of the worst part of the native population—informers, and false witnesses, and common barrators, and agents of chicane; and above all, a banditti of bailiffs' followers compared with whom the retainers of the worst English spunging-houses, in the worst times, might be considered as upright and tender-hearted. There were instances in which men of the most venerable dignity, persecuted without cause by extortioners, died of rage and shame in the grip of the vile alguazils of Impey. The harems of noble Mohammedans—sanctuaries respected in the East by governments that respected nothing else—were burst open by gangs of bailiffs. The Mussulmans, braver and less accustomed to submission than the Hindoos, sometimes stood on their defense and shed their blood in the doorway, while defending, sword in hand, the sacred apartments of their women. No Mahratta invasion had ever spread through the province such dismay as this inroad of English lawyers. All the injustice of former oppressions, Asiatic and European, appeared as a blessing when compared with the justice of the Supreme Court."

No wonder that "Christian England" is horrified by the atrocities of the Moslems in Armenia! She cannot understand persecution for the sake of religious opinion—having done her dirty work for the sake of the almighty dollar. It is true, that a Hastings, with his forged treaties and despoilment of ancient "bee-gums," is no longer governor-general of India; it is true that an Impey no longer deals out "Justice" in that unhappy land; but the industrial condition of the toiling millions is worse to-day than when they were being despoiled to erect the Peacock throne at Delhi, adorned with its "Mountain of Light." Sir David Wedderbun—who will be accepted as authority even by our Anglomaniacs—says: "Our civil courts are regarded as institutions for enabling the rich to grind the faces of the poor, and many are fain to seek a refuge from their jurisdiction in native territory." "We do not care for the people of India," writes Florence Nightingale; "the saddest sight to be seen in India—nay, probably in the world—is the peasant of our Eastern Empire." Miss Nightingale declares that the Indian famines, which every few years cost millions of lives, are due to British taxation, which deprives the ryots of the means of cultivation and reduces them to a condition far worse than the worst phases of American slavery. Mr. H. M. Hyndman, an English writer of repute, declares that in India men and women cannot get food, because they cannot save money to buy it, so terrible are the burdens laid by Christian England on that unhappy people. Just as Ireland exported food to England during her most devasting "famines," so does India send food to the "Mother country" in the discharge of governmental burdens, while her own people are starving by millions. Henry George, who has never been suspected of anti-English tendencies, says: "The millions of India have bowed their necks beneath the yokes of many conquerors, but worst of all is the steady grinding weight of English domination—a weight which is literally crushing millions out of existence, and, as shown by English writers, is inevitably tending to a most frightful and wide-spread catastrophe."

"Christian England" wouldn't murder a Moslem because of his religion—she's too good for that; but she starves millions to death to fill her purse, then tries to square herself with God and man by singing psalms and pointing the finger of scorn at the barbarities of Islam.

PANACEAS FOR POVERTY.

Dives and Lazarus.

How to secure "a more equal distribution of wealth" is a problem that has perplexed publicists since the dawn of civilization, the genesis of government. A thousand solutions have been proffered, all panaceas for poverty; but despite the fecundity of social therapeutics the evil grows ever greater; Fortune and Famine, Waste and Want continue to divide the world between them—the walls that separate their territories to reach higher and higher. Year by year the hoard of Dives is increased and the poverty of Lazarus made more poignant; ever does the dismal howl of the gaunt wolf draw nearer the cottage of Labor, retreat further from the mansion of the Capitalist; ever is it true that to him that hath shall be given and from him that hath not shall be taken even that which he hath.

Civilization, the introduction of machinery, the more minute division of labor, the concentration of capital, while multiplying the world's wealth-producing power, but serves to accentuate the division between Rich and Poor; to enable the former to demand a larger, to compel the latter to accept a lesser share of the joint product of Capital and Labor. It is an open question whether our "progress of civilization," taken collectively, is a blessing or a curse. That Progress is the order established by the Infinite, natural and necessary, must be conceded. That it brings a curse rather than a blessing to the majority of men; that only the favored few reap its rich rewards, while the last state of the mass of mankind is worse than the first, must be due to individual greed and general ignorance rather than to evil inherent in the principle of Progress; that its car rolls over the heads of the millions instead of under their feet, crushing into hell those it should bear into heaven, setting the world ablaze instead of warming it into perennial summer, must be due to the fact that it is driven by a presumptuous Phaeton who cannot or will not properly manage it.

* * *

Many methods, almost as arbitrary and unnatural as that of Lycurgus, are still seriously proposed for securing financial equality, serving sometimes as artificial wings upon which aspiring politicians mount skyward until an iconoclastic sun precipitates them into Icarian seas. Of these catholicons, the communistic—under various brands and trademarks—is the most common. It proposes to purge away "the primal eldest curse," to re-imparadise man, to inaugurate the millennium by fiat of the state.

Then there are more or less "conservative" plans for putting more pie in the dinner-pail of the poor man. One would save for him some two or three cents per diem by pulling the top rows of brick off the tariff wall; another would add as much to his daily stipend by building the wall some inches higher—and there you have a political issue; worthy labored disquisition by "able editors," statistical harangues by "prominent politicians"—the whole nation groaning in an agony of excitement; parading itself in torch-light processions; electing representatives pledged to pry off or plaster on; constables and county commissioners who cannot get at the blessed tariff with either trowel or pick, but whose moral support this or the other tariff wall toiler can rely upon. Another plan for pulling a few feathers from the Gessler-cap of a presumptuous Plutocracy and inserting them in the hat-band of the man with the hoe, is to get up more steam at the mints, to grind out more money—it being argued that the more coin there is in the country, the better chance the toiler will have to clutch some of it. Of course it is "money" the shivering wretches need—but would not filling the stores and shops with cook-books and fashion-plates answer as well? Let the political issue-makers consider this. It is a Pegasus that if properly bridled and saddled may carry a skillful rider afar—perhaps to the White House and the distinction of having a nation bawling under his windows while his babies are being born!

The "radical reformer" is not satisfied with saving less than the whole world; he would drag in a visual and tactual millennium broad enough to enfold the earth. The "conservative" is satisfied if he can save the particular portion of it in which he resides—and where a vote will avail him; proclaims more or less articulately that he cares not if the rest of it miss salvation and get quite the reverse—even rejoices that, bad off as his little dog-kennel of a country may be, other countries are in infinitely worse condition, fuller far of woe and wail. Between the enthusiastic radical, with his impracticable Utopias, the cold-blooded conservative, with his impotent bread boluses, you can take your choice—and dodge regret as best you may.

* * *

The fact is, Society is sick unto death; to such dire extremity have the doctors in their disagreements and experiments reduced their patient. If the radicals ever get an opportunity to give it one full dose of their horse-medicine even prayer cannot pull it through; the treatment of the conservatives is about as potent as rattling beans in a dried bladder to stop an eclipse of the sun—about as satisfactory as a drop of water to Dives after Death has transported him to the torrid regions of the damned.

Clearly something must be done, and that quickly—but what? It were as idle to attempt the complete extirpation of Poverty as to banish Sin from the world. "The poor ye have always with you;" there will ever be improvidents and unfortunates. But while we cannot relegate Poverty altogether to the Past, and, with perfumed airs, waft every human sail to happy havens in Fortunate Isles, it is certainly possible to circumscribe it somewhat; to reclaim a portion of that arid, monster-bearing desert in which wander so many millions with infinite woe and wail, without God and bereft of hope, fiercer than famished wolves, desperate as demons who tread the deepest depths of the Divine displeasure and fear no further fall, do what they may.

We need not pause to mourn over the fact that some men have more wealth than they need; it is that other all too palpable fact that many have less than their necessities require that concerns us here. We need not care how excessive some fortunes are if all be sufficient. Surely with our improved methods of producing wealth—and in a country whose government is of, for and by the people—a man of average muscle, intelligence and thrift should be able to support a family comfortably, tide over ordinary mishaps, educate his children, sustain his old age in dignity, meet the expenses of a decent funeral and prove to the satisfaction of St. Peter that he does not come as an "assisted immigrant." To accomplish this he should not be compelled to make a self-denying slave of himself during the greater part of a long life, but have time for that social enjoyment which makes life worth the living, for that mental culture supposed to be necessary to the "American sovereign." But, unfortunately, such is not the case. From youth to old age, from the cradle to the grave, the average mortal is at very death-grips with destiny, feels that he is fortunate if he can retain some shadow of manhood, if he sink into nothing worse than quasi-pauperism or industrial peonage. Why is this? In a new country, where every man is his own farmer and dairyman, his own butcher and bootmaker, homely Plenty abounds; but when population increases, government is set up and labor made a hundred-fold more productive by means of division and the introduction of machinery, the great mass of mankind find the battle of life more bitter and bootless. Ever are people leaving the thickly populated countries, where the wealth-producing power of labor is great, for the thinly populated sections where it is small—being taught by observation or experience that our boasted Progress bears in its bosom no blessings for Labor—that the further they get beyond the confines of "our great industrial system," the less they are affected by our "government for the people," the less their danger of dying of starvation.

* * *

Clearly it is not a high or low tariff on imported goods; not the lack of a few more in-God-we-trust dollars in the channels of trade that drives men from the great industrial centers of the east, from the fertile, half-tilled prairies of Illinois to seek a livelihood in the wild west, where each man must be his own manufacturer and carrier—expending more time and labor to make for himself one pair of moccasins or a few shingles for his cabin than it would require for his Eastern brother to shoe a regiment or get out lumber for a palace. There must be a linch-pin loose in our much-vaunted Car of Progress, when the further the simple laborer gets from it the better his condition. Evidently the putting on or taking off of a few leaves of gilding—by means of "tariff reform," free silver, reciprocity, etc.—will have little appreciable effect. Some more radical remedy must be resorted to or we might as well give the patient up to Death and Destruction.

There are two forces that are grinding labor down into the dust—Government and Monopoly. The first robs it of wellnigh half its scanty earnings, the latter takes most of the remainder. First or last, directly or indirectly, Labor pays every dollar of taxes—tariff, excise, State, county and municipal—and the grand total is simply appalling. In 1879 the amount of taxes paid in this country amounted to nearly $600,000,000. Every dollar of that was drawn, directly or indirectly, from the pockets of Labor. In that year there were less than ten million families within the United States, so that the average cost per family for the sustenance of government was more than $60. Subtract the families of our vast army of "public servants," the wealthy non-producers, paupers, criminals, preachers, actors, saloonists, able editors, etc., and it will be found that our blessed government, in its various ramifications, does not cost the wealth-creating laborer much if any less than $100 per annum! That is what he pays for protection; for the inestimable privilege of suing and being sued; for being prohibited the pleasure of drinking a mug of beer on Sunday, paying too much interest or putting a mortgage on his homestead—if he chance to have one! American Labor staggering along under a $600,000,000 government must make Atlas feel that his lot is by no means the worst.

Of course, we need and must have a government; but we are overdoing this thing sadly—are buying more "protection" than we can readily pay for. Perhaps if we would buy more bread and less buncombe; raise more pork and fewer politicians, we would not need a bluecoat on every block, a constable at every corner grocery to prevent our pulling each other to pieces.

* * *

Seven-eighths of the laws now in existence are worse than worthless; seven-eighths of our "public servants" are but so many flunkeys, kept for show, and who eat out our substance. Let us reduce the weight of government of some hundreds of millions and we will find ourselves in better condition to deal with that other and even more adroit robber, Monopoly. When a business man finds that he is "running behind" he at once concludes that he must reduce expenses. Every employe that can be spared has to go; every expense not imperatively necessary is shut off. It is the true commercial instinct; let us follow it. Let us go through the various departments of our great governmental shop and see if we cannot manufacture an article of justice in every way as serviceable as the present one for considerably less than two million dollars a day! Economy is not the only road to wealth, but it is the safest and surest.

When the great body of the American people can be made to understand that every penny collected by whatever method, by any department of government, comes out of the scant purse of Labor—the only source of wealth—we may confidently hope to hear of "political issues" that really mean something. When American Labor acquires enough business acumen to put the Goddess of Liberty in a calico gown until richer raiment can be afforded—until her devotees can provide themselves with pants—then may it take up that more difficult task, the readjustment of our industrial system; then may it gird on its armor for the battle with the monster Monopoly, and hope to escape being hoodooed and cajoled thereby, made to turn its broadsword into its own bowels.

BONDS VS. BUNCOMBE.

Cleveland and the Currency.

Day by day my conviction strengthens that the American press is "a great public educator." Hour by hour my faith in its infallibility burgeons and blooms. Since the announcement of still another bond issue to bolster up the moribund gold reserve, I have examined several hundred papers, great and small, and carefully considered their opinions anent this important public measure. I was pleased to note that in every instance they spoke "as one having authority and not as the scribes." At least, not as the old Jewish scribes, who, being only learned doctors of the law, could seldom feel cock-sure. The great dailies have monetary wisdom corded up like patent medicine electrotypes, while the Archimedii of the Washington hand-press utilize it for paper weights. Some philosopher has said that there's nothing so cheap in this land as intellect, and his conclusion is eminently correct. Brains are cheaper than liver at the very butcher-shops. I am a trifle confused, however, by the fact that, while one-half of these public educators proclaim, in effect, that the government planted by the sword of Washington and watered by the blood of Lincoln, would have gone to hades in a hand-basket had not Providence, in a burst of generosity, sent Cleveland to tide us over the awful crisis, the remainder are equally sure it cannot much longer survive his costly mistakes. You pays your subscription and takes your choice.

I much fear that editors, like politicians, regard public measures thro' partisan rather than patriotic glasses, and bless or curse according to the party trade-mark adopted by the business office—that, in attempting to ride the popular wave in his own little frog-pond to the sunny haven of pecuniary profit, the editor too often forgets his role of "public educator." The Iconoclast, while strictly orthodox in religion, is a political maverick. There's where it has the advantage of Barney Gibbs, who wears the Democratic brand and the Populist bell, and of the "Little Giant," whose partisan trade-marks are only circumscribed by the extent of his cuticle.

I am the only man in America who doesn't understand the financial problem from A to Izzard. That is my misfortune rather than my fault, for I have wrestled with it, as did Jacob with the angel, for a quarter of a century. I have even remained away from prayer-meeting to pore over ponderous tomes of political economy, and fractured the Fourth Commandment in a futile effort to master the intricacies of national finance. I have burned the midnight tallow dip over the monetary acumen of every authority from Lycurgus to Mrs. Lease, without taking a vacation to run for office, and now frankly admit that I do not even know what effect the free and unlimited coinage of silver would have upon the commerce and industries of this country. Several thousand learned Thebans have taken pity upon my stupid nescience and explained it to me; but I could discover never a Daniel to explain the explanations. They are more exasperating than the prophecies of the Pythoness. And even if I could work the silver problem thro' my seldom hair and be able to predict with certitude whether, in the end, we would be better off by defrauding our crediors with cheap money, or permitting them to squeeze the immortal ichor out of us with dear money, I would stall irremediably at the gold reserve. Of course its maintenance is necessary to preserve the public credit, for Morgan and Belmont, Cleveland and Carlisle have said so, and "that do settle it." Faith is our only salvation. If without faith in J. Christ and his apostles we go whooping to hell, how without confidence in G. Cleveland and his paladins and peers can we hope to reach the financial heaven? Of course, I have unbounded faith in the orthodox plan of salvation; but I would like to understand it so that, while whittling a pine box in front of my favorite grocery store, I could explain it to Governor Culberson and his brother Populists. How can I hope to convert these financial heathens while unable to give a valid reason for the faith that is filling my heart with the rhapsodies of heaven? I want to be able to explain how $100,000,000 of the "real" money can "guarantee" more than $1,600,000,000 of "token" money; why the great capitalists of the country, who must lose by any depreciation in the purchasing power of our currency, are continually assailing the base upon which its credit rests; why, if they desire to commit financial hari-kari, the great debtor class should tax itself to prevent their destruction; what nation ever issued money that was "good the world over;" what has our circulating media to do with our foreign trade so long as nations do not swap money but exchange commodities; but the orator is silent. The preachers assure us that there are some things which the Lord did not intend that we should understand; that he

"Moves in a mysterious way his wonders to perform."

And is not Cleveland a kind of political Christ? The higher mathematics of our financial Providence is beyond my comprehension. During the few days I attended school—between "corn-shuckin' and corn-plantin' "—I studied Ray's arithmetic. If I remember correctly, he proceeded on the hypothesis that a part can never be greater than the whole. New discoveries are ever exploding old dogmas—Ray laid down his premises and drew his conclusions in utter ignorance of the hole in the treasury. He made his arithmetic to conform to idle theories; Cleveland figured with an eye single to conditions. One of the "examples" in the new Cleveland arithmetic reads substantially as follows:

If Sam owes to his playmates 16 pennies, payable on demand, how many pennies must be in his possession to inspire the boys with perfect confidence in his ability to promptly discharge his obligations?—*Ans.* One!

Copernicus revolutionized the science of astronomy and Napoleon the art of war; but it remained for our own and only Cleveland to induct the world into the higher mathematics. The American exchange media consists of $556,100,818 in gold and $1,659,342,832 other forms of currency, "bottomed on the precious metal;" which means, if it means anything, that it is merely "token" money for which gold must be given on demand to prevent its depreciation in purchasing power. Of this "token" money less than $500,000,000 is in silver, and more than $1,159,000,000 in paper, worth intrinsically nothing; yet, according to Cleveland, the presence in the treasury of a few pounds of gold is what makes this vast amount of cheap silver and worthless paper "money current with the merchant!" That may be mathematics, but it looks to me more like thaumaturgy. Cleveland has evidently discovered the philosopher's stone. As a miracle worker, Schlatter is not in it. Were Cleveland a farmer, obligated to supply half-a-dozen full-grown hogs, he'd simply hang a pig's tail up in the smokehouse as hoodoo and have swine to sell. The egg is made to stand on end by our new and greater Colombo, the financial pyramid to safely balance on its apex! The $100,000,000 reserve is the Atlas warranted to uphold our monetary world! It must be kept intact at any cost. What were a few more hundred millions, or even billions, of bonded indebtedness—principal and interest to be paid in gold by the working people—compared with the unutterable evils that would ensue should the linchpin be pulled out of our financial cosmos, our currency be discredited!

Of course there be Doubting Thomases who declare that

the "bulwark of our currency's credit" is not composed of a few paltry bags of

"Gold, gold, bright and yellow, hard and cold,"

and which may be spirited away any moment by a handful of wealthy men; but of commercial confidence that United States money, of whatsoever made, will answer the purposes for which it was created, that of effecting the exchange of commodities. These financial heretics even declare that, by persistent calamity-clacking and pernicious activity in the matter of bond issues, the president has practically destroyed this real fortress and brought us to the verge of ruin.

The people have been led to believe that unless the gold reserve be kept running over the top of the tank, the silver dollar will depreciate fully 50 per cent., and its paper companion not be worth a tinker's dam. And to this idiotic jeremiad, which mounts heavenward night and day like the feculent odor of a dead fice, is ever added the information that, under present conditions, the preservation of the reserve is a practical impossibility. No wonder the people become panic-stricken and strive to unload their silver and paper—"withdraw gold for hoarding." No wonder the gold purchased at fancy prices of the Morgan Syndicate and poured into the treasury went thro' it like a dose of salts thro' a tin horn!

The Cleveland administration reminds me of an old darkey I once heard discoursing to a badly frightened small boy: "Chile, if dat wolf cotch y' he gwine t' eat y'; an' chile, dat wolf shuah done gwine t' cotch y'!"

That is the administration's method of "restoring confidence." Cleveland was probably sent in response to prayer, for up in Illinois an old Methodist exhorter was wont to fervently pray that "this yere weeked and parvarse gineration be hair-hung and wind-shaken over the orful abyss o' hell, for Christ's sake, amen." Cleveland certainly has us hair-hung and wind-shaken over something unutterably awful.

Our circulating media is unquestionably a ridiculous moon-calf. It represents various compromises effected between warring political factions and adverse interests. It should be reformed on common-sense lines; but the task should not be undertaken during a period of incipient panic. That were to invite disaster. Let us wait to swap equines until well out of the water. What we need just now is, not so much a new currency as a revival of confidence; and this can easily be attained if the calamity clackers of the Cleveland type will arrange to consume their own sound, and the politicians maintain a masterly inactivity. If the gold reserve is exhausted, a disastrous panic will probably ensue, simply and solely because Mr. Cleveland and his coterie of cuckoos and bond-clippers have educated the people to expect it. Under normal conditions—which would exist but for Cleveland and his kind—the national treasury might become as guiltless of gold as Hamlet of gall, without doing the slightest damage. Those who needed gold in considerable quantities for export—as they might need corn, cotton, or any other commodity—would have to look elsewhere for it and pay the commercial instead of the governmental price. Gold coin might go to a slight premium until it could again be had of the government; but the country would never suspect that it was passing thro' a "crisis"—the cart-wheel and paper dollar would continue to do their duty. The idea that any sane man holding for silver or paper bearing the sign-manual of Uncle Sam, would have a financial jeminy fit because the government did not maintain a supply warehouse where exporters could, at all times, secure any commodity they choose to call for, is the veriest moonshine. Something of the kind might happen during a disastrous war, when the perpetuity of the government was seriously menaced, when its ability to ever meet its obligations was in doubt; but to say that such a thing were probable in an era of profound peace—that commerce would contemptuously reject the I. O. U.'s of the wealthiest country in the world because it could not convert them into yellow coin at a moment's notice—were to concede that the American people have precious little confidence in the wisdom and honesty of those they have placed in charge of federal affairs.

Cleveland has increased the interest-bearing debt of the nation $262,000,000 in conformity with his peculiar ideas of finance, and now frankly confesses that his plan of salvation leads deeper into the Slough of Despond instead of to the Delectable Mountains; but announces a determination to persevere in his folly regardless of cost unless Congress will consent to become responsible for additional public burdens in time of peace, retire the greenbacks and rely upon the patriotism of national bankers to provide an antidote for this arbitrary contraction of the currency and the consequent decline in the price of commodities—the enhancement of all debts. Of course the bankers will cheerfully come to the relief of their suffering country—that's what they are here for! By making it possible for them to absolutely control the volume of currency, we place an Archimedean lever under every debtor and hoist him out of the hole! Having permitted the Morgan-Belmont syndicate to pull Uncle Sam's leg in a former bond deal to the extent of $8,418,757, the administration decided to make the last a "popular loan." It was urged in the former instance that the government was in dire straits and absolutely at the mercy of the bankers—those patriots who propose to see that we do not suffer because of a withdrawal of the greenbacks—and the president pompously avowed his responsibility for the shameful hold-up of the tax-paying public. The treasury is in worse condition now than then; yet Mr. Morgan has been given his *conge* and a successful appeal made to the people. There may be nothing rotten in Denmark; but when a public official saves more than a million out of a salary aggregating less than $350,000, it is pretty safe to use disinfectants.

SHERMAN AND CLEVELAND.

For more than a third of a century John Sherman has been regarded by politicians of all parties as authority *par excellence* on matters monetary. His motives have often been called in question, but his ability never impugned. He is regarded by the "gold-bugs" as a god, by the "cheap money" men as a veritable Mephistopheles. He was the heavy villain of "the crime of '73," and brought about the resumption of specie payments in '79. He is largely responsible for the redemption of the greenback bonds in gold. He has never been suspected by Wall street of being "tainted with financial heresy." Sherman and Cleveland belong to the same monetary school, occupying the respective positions of preceptor and pupil. They have ever worked for the attainment of the same end—the appreciation of the purchasing power of the dollar for the special behoof of the creditor class; but the latter has evidently not thoroughly mastered the lessons laid out for him with such care by "Sly Old John." Or, perhaps, it were more correct to say that the pupil has become ambitious, aspires to out-Herod Herod in the slaughter of the debtor innocents. Sherman has never forgotten that he has at stake the reputation of a financier. He has served his masters with a strong sideglance at self. Cleveland has all to gain and nothing to lose by becoming the humble servant of the great capitalists, and he has gone to lengths which Sherman solemnly warned him were suicidal. To please the bond-clippers he has run Uncle Sam's nose in the sand to the tune of $262,000,000 on the shallow pretense of attempting what his master protested was impossible. The following excerpt from a speech delivered by Mr. Sherman in the U. S. Senate Jan. 16, 1874, is at this time particularly significant, and well worth perusal by those good people who insist that the exhaustion of the gold reserve for a single day would bring the nation down with a violent crash to "a 50-cent silver basis;" who have sharply criticised the assertion of the Iconoclast that a temporary suspension of specie payments would—but for the wild yodel of the Cleveland-Carlisle cuckoos and calamity clackers—produce scarce a ripple on the great monetary sea. The utterances of Mr. Sherman anent the maintenance of specie payments accord so closely with those of the Iconoclast that it would doubtless be difficult to convince him that I had not read his '74 speech until this good day. Whether I have plagiarized from Sherman, or *vice versa,* is of no consequence to the public. I reproduce his words to prove that, in the view of America's leading financier, the temporary suspension of specie payments—which would necessarily follow the exhaustion of the gold reserve—would not, *per se,* produce those evils predicted by Cleveland, and that increasing the bonded debt to prevent such a contingency is the rankest financial nonsense. Mr. Sherman said:

"I entirely object to conferring upon the secretary of the treasury the power of issuing $100,000,000 or any less sum of bonds with a view of buying gold to hoard in the treasury to maintain resumption. I believe that it is impossible, in the very nature of things, to maintain the resumption of specie payments at all times and under all circumstances; and if anything has been established by modern experience, it is that all a nation that issues paper money can do is to maintain it at a specie standard in ordinary times; but in times of panic, such as by periodical revulsions come over every country, specie payments cannot be maintained. They can scarcely be maintained in England, and are not now maintained in France, tho' they are approached. Therefore, every plan for specie payments ought to have some provision for the temporary suspension of such payments, or to provide some means by which, in times of great panic and financial distress, there may be a temporary departure from specie payments."

Let the gold-bugs "learn of the wise and perpend." Had Peffer or Pap Reagan given utterance to such sentiments the gold-bugs would have hastened to brand him as "a ass;" what are they going to do with Sherman—the very god of their idolatry. If Waco's Bob-tailed Warwick can secure his consent to a column type-written "interview," to be run next to pure patent medicine ads. in the *Dal.-Gal.*, I would like to see him take a fall out of Old John anent the imperative necessity of maintaining specie payments at any cost to the people. But, perhaps, he does not consider Old John a foeman worthy of his steel!

What did Cleveland do "in times of panic, when specie payments cannot be maintained," according to the *ipse dixit* of the Dalai Lama of the honest money cult? Did he provide a method for a "temporary departure from the specie standard," as suggested by an authority so eminent? Did he forestall alarm, as did Sherman, by calling attention to the fact that in France more than $531,000,000 of paper was "practically maintained at par with gold" despite a suspension of specie payments? Did he bid the people allay their fears by turning to "the history of almost all the commercial nations of Europe?" Not exactly. Like the boy who hollered "Wolf! Wolf!" to alarm the neighbors, he began to prophesy that the bottom would fall out of our industrial cosmos if there was ever so slight a lull in specie payments, and to further frighten the people by the reckless issue of bonds to bolster up our tottering gold reserve! As tho' this were not sufficient to scare commerce into convulsions, he assumed that the credit of the country was at so low an ebb that it was necessary to appeal to a syndicate of bankers to hasten to its rescue, and reward their patriotism by allowing them to purchase the bonds at their own price! Sherman insisted upon resumption of specie payments at a time of general prosperity, when the government was paying a heavy premium on its unmatured bonds and canceling them to reduce its treasury surplus; Cleveland insisted on maintaining them "in times of panic," when the former declared it folly to attempt it. Sherman was the father of resumption; yet in the most solemn manner he pointed out the fallacy—yea, the danger—of either purchasing gold or cancelling the greenbacks to maintain it even in a time of exceptional prosperity. Cleveland would do both in a time of general depression bordering upon panic! Yet there are men—I call them men because they are featherless bipeds— who damn Sherman as a contractionist and tool of Wall Street, and deify Cleveland as the people's friend!

I defy any mortal son of Adam's misery to demonstrate that the gold reserve—for the maintenance of which the Cleveland administration has saddled $262,000,000 of indebtedness upon this people—is of one whit more value than would be a boil on the rear elevation of Pickwick's Fat

Boy. Not only is it worthless, but Wall Street knows as well as did John Sherman, that it is worse than worthless —an expensive nuisance. It is simply a tool in the hands of bankers who desire more bonds. Did the credit of our currency depend upon its maintenance, not one interest-bearing obligation would be necessary to keep it at the maximum—the capitalists would attend to its preservation as a measure of self-defense, instead of continually raiding it. The costly attempt of the Cleveland administration to maintain the useless gold reserve will be classed by the future historian as on an intellectual parity with the sacrifices to Moloch, the burning of witches and the pounding of tin pans by the Celestials to prevent an eclipse of the sun. If I have not made this fact plain in previous issues of the Iconoclast to the dullest dunderheads, further effort would be but love's labor lost. It may not be amiss, however, to add that opposition to the gold reserve folly does not necessarily imply a leaning to either "greenbackism" or the full and unlimited coinage of silver. My contention is that, like Ben Franklin, we are paying too dear for our whistle; that, under existing currency conditions, the segregation of gold at enormous cost is calculated to produce that very lack of confidence which it is expected to cure. On another important point the great "honest money" advocate endorsed the views frequently promulgated by the Iconoclast, while squarely joining issue, not only with the radical protectionists of his own party, but with Cleveland, Carlisle and many others of his democratic disciples, who insist that we must maintain a gold currency to promptly meet our foreign obligations when "the balance of trade" chances to be against us. In the address from which I have already quoted, Mr. Sherman said:

"This fallacy of 'the balance of trade' ought not to enter into the calculations of prudent men. * * * * It is not a question of a 'balance of trade,' but a question of prudence and judgment in the trade itself. Only a year ago I had a controversy with a senator about this 'balance of trade.' He insisted that when the 'balance of trade' was against any nation it was an evidence of decay. I said this was a fallacy. He replied that no country could be prosperous unless the 'balance of trade' was in its favor. I asked him if he thought Great Britain was a prosperous country, and he said he thought it was a very prosperous country, and that the 'balance of trade' was always in favor of Great Britain. We made a friendly bet on the subject, and it turned out that the 'balance of trade' was against Great Britain to the tune of over $300,000,000 per annum, and had been for twenty years. By the fallacious theory of the 'balance of trade' Great Britain was on the high road to ruin Yet the whole of this balance of imports was in commodities sent to pay interest on English investments in foreign countries—profits of trade, and so forth. The profits of trade were all in favor of Great Britain, which imported raw articles and exported high-priced productions, while the 'balance of trade' only represented increased and increasing wealth, instead of ruin and poverty; so that all this talk about the 'balance of trade' is the sheerest nonsense."

Yet it is nonsense which Cleveland and his cuckoos are continually indulging in. Mr. Sherman adds that "the 'balance of trade' (between nations) is precisely like the 'balance of trade' between the merchant and the farmer. If the farmer buys less than he sells, he is surely on a safe footing; if he buys more than he sells, the result will depend entirely upon what he buys, whether luxuries consumed in the using, or materials for actual productive improvement on his farm. If the latter, he is prosperous and happy, tho' the 'balance of trade' may be against him. It is not a question of 'balance of trade,' but a question of prudence and judgment in the trade itself?"

Do the "balance of trade" cranks begin to see a glimmer of daylight? Do they "cotton" to the fact that America has become a mighty manufacturing nation—which imports vast quantities of raw materials and exports high-priced manufactured articles? Are they capable of understanding that it is sometimes possible for a man to grow rich prosecuting industrial enterprises on borrowed capital? Can they comprehend that a nation may borrow largely abroad and satisfy the interest charge with her products and at the same time increase in wealth? Can they work it thro' their hair that foreign capital invested here takes out of the country no more than its earnings after paying American wages and American taxes? Balance of trade the devil! If I buy more than I sell haven't I the surplus goods representing the coin paid? And if they are not worth to me as much or more than the wealth surrendered, do I not need a guardian?

RAINBOW CHASERS.

This is the lecture that Mr. Brann delivered and was to continue on his lecture tour, which was cut short by his death.

Ladies and Gentlemen: There are many things which I very cordially dislike; but my pet aversion is what is known as a "set" lecture—one of those stereotyped affairs that are ground out with studied inflection and practiced gesture and suggest the grinding of Old Hundred on a hurdy-gurdy; hence I shall ask permission to talk to you to-night as informally and as freely as though we were seated in friendly converse around the soda fount of a Kansas drug store; and I want you to feel as free to talk back as though we had gotten into this difficulty by accident instead of design. Ask me all the questions you want to, and if I'm unable to answer offhand I'll look the matter up later and telegraph you—at your expense. With such unbounded liberty there's really no telling whither we will drift, what subjects we may touch upon; but should I inadvertently trample upon any of your social idols or political gods, I trust that you will take no offense—will remember that we may honestly differ, that none of us are altogether infallible. Lest any of you should mistake me for an oratorical clearing-sale or elocutionary bargain-counter, expect a Demosthenic display and be disappointed, I hasten to say that I am no orator as Brutus was, but simply a plain, blunt man, like Mark Antony, who spoke right on and said what he did know, or thought he knew, which was just as satisfactory to himself. He's dead now, poor fellow! Woman in the case, of course. Shakespeare assures us that "men have died from time to time and worms have eaten them, but not for love." However that may be, Antony's just as dead as though he had died for love—or become a gold-bug "Democrat." Yes, Mark Antony's gone, but we still have Mark Hanna. One threw the world away for Cleopatra's smile, the other threw Columbia's smile away for a seat in the Senate, and so it goes. Of the two Marks, I think Antony was the easiest.

* * *

But let us take a look at our text. The rainbow is a sign, I believe, that the Prohibitionists once carried the country and would have made a complete success of the cold water cure had not the Rum Demon engineered the Ark. Still it does not necessarily follow that a rainbow chaser is a fellow on the hot trail of a blind tiger. He may be one who hopes to raise the wage rate by means of a tariff wall, or expects John Bull to assist Uncle Sam in the remonetization of silver. A rainbow-chaser, in the common acceptance of the term, is a fellow who mistakes shadow for substance and wanders off the plank turnpike into bogs and briar patches. Satan appears to have been the first victim of the rainbow-chasing fad—to have bolted the Chicago convention and run for president on the reform ticket. At a very early age I began to doubt the existence of a personal devil, whereupon my parent on my father's side proceeded to argue the matter in the good old orthodox way, but failed to get more than half the hussy out of my hide. But we will not quarrel about the existence or non-existence of a party who Milton assures us slipped on a political orange peel. We know that frauds and fakes exist, that hypocrites and humbugs abound. Whether this be due to the pernicious activity of a horned monster or to evil inherent in the human heart, I will not assume to say. We may call that power the devil which is forever at war with truth, is the father of falsehood, whether it be an active personality or only a vicious principle.

* * *

Under the direction of this devil, real or abstract, the world has gone rainbow chasing and fallen deep into the Slough of Despond. Conditions have become so desperate that it were well for you and I, who are in the world and of it, to abate somewhat our partisan rancor, our sectarian bitterness, and take serious counsel together. Desperate, I say, meaning thereby not only that it becomes ever more difficult for the workman to win his modicum of bread and butter, to provide his own hemlock coffin in which to go to hades—or elsewhere; but that honor, patriotism, reverence—all things which our fathers esteemed as more precious than pure gold—have well nigh departed, that the social heart is dead as a salt herring; that all is becoming brummagem and pinch-beck, leather and prunella; that a curse hath fallen upon the womb of the world, and it no longer produces heaven-inspired men but only some pitiful simulacra thereof, some worthless succedona for such, who strive not to do their god-given duty though the world reward them with a gibbet, but to win wages of gold and grub, to obtain idle praise by empty plausibility. They aspire to ride the topmost wave, not of a tempestuous ocean which tries the heart of oak and the hand of iron, but of some pitiful sectarian mud-puddle or political goose pond. Under the guidance of these shallow self-seekers we have abandoned the Ark of the Covenant with its Brotherhood of Man, its solemn duties and sacred responsibilities, and are striving to manage matters mundane on a basis of brute selfishness, with a conscience or a creed of following the foolish rainbow of a fatuous utilitaria and getting even deeper into the bogs.

* * *

I have frequently been called a "chronic kicker," but do not object to the epithet. There's need of good lusty kickers, those whose No. 10 tootsie-wootsies are copper-toed, for the world is full of devilish things that deserve to die. Lest any should accuse me of the awful sin of using slang, and thereby break my heart, I hasten to say that the Bible twice employs the word "kick" in the same sense that I used it here. In fact, a goodly proportion of our so-called slang is drawn from the same high source, being vinegar to the teeth of pietistical purists, but quite good enough for God. Some complain that I should build instead of tearing down, should preserve and not destroy. The complaint is well founded if it be wrong to attack falsehood, to exterminate the industrial wolves and social rottenness, to destroy the tares sown by the devil and give dollar wheat a chance to arise and hump itself. In determining what should be preserved and what destroyed, we may honestly disagree; but I think all will concede that what is notoriously untrue should be attacked, that we should wage uncompromising war on whatsoever maketh or loveth a lie. I think all will agree that this is pre-eminently an age of artificiality—that there is little genuine left in the land but the complexion of the ladies. Even that has been called in question by certain unchivalrous old bachelors, those unfortunates whom the ladies of Boston propose to expel from politics for dereliction of duty. Somehow an old bachelor always reminds me of a rainbow; not because he looks like one in the least, but rather because he's so utterly useless for all practical purposes. He also reminds me of a rainbow-chaser, because what he is compelled to admire is beyond his reach. When hope deferred hath made him heart-sick he begins to growl at the girls—and for the same reason that a mastiff barks at the moon. You will notice that a mastiff seldom barks much at anything he can get hold of and bite.

* * *

We are solemnly assured that the world is steadily growing better; and I suppose that's so, for in days of old they crucified men head downwards for telling the truth, while now they only hammer them over the head with six-shooters and drag 'em around a Baptist college campus with a rope. All that a reformer now needs is a hard head and a rubber neck. The cheerful idiot, *alias* the optimist, is forever prating of the world's progress. Progress is a desirable thing only when we make it in the right direction. It may be sure and swift down a soaped plank into wild ocean depths; or it may be with painful steps and slow toward the eternal mountain tops where breaks the great white light of God, and there's no more of darkness and of death. Progress industrial, the productive power of labor multiplied by two, by ten; and with such improved weapons for waging war upon the grisly gorgon of Want, nearly nine millions of the industrial army in India alone died upon their shields. Hosannahs mounting in costly churches here, the starving babe tagging at the empty breast of the dead mother there!—and we send to the famine-sufferers many bibles and hymn books, little bacon and beans. Bibles and hymn-books are excellent things in their way, but do not possess an absorbing interest for the man with an aching void concealed about his system. Starving people ask a Christian world for grub, and it gives them forty'leven different brands of saving grace—each warranted the only genuine—most of these elixirs of life ladled out by hired missionaries who serve God for the long green, and who are often so deplorably ignorant that they couldn't tell a religious thesis from an ichthyosaurian.

Progress in religion until there's no longer a divine message from on high, no God in Israel; only a fashionable pulpiteering to minister to languid minds, the cultivation of foolish fads and the flaunting of fine feathers—the church becoming a mere Vanity Fair or social clearing-house, a kind of esthetic forecourt to hades instead of the gate to heaven. At the opposite extreme we find blatant blackguardism by so-called evangelists, who were educated in a mule-pen and dismissed without a diploma, yet who set up as instructors of the masses in the profound mysteries of the Almighty. Men who would get shipwrecked in the poetry of Shakespeare, or lost in the philosophy of one of his fools, pretend to interpret the plans of Him who writes his words in flaming worlds on the papyri of immensity, whose sentences are astral fire.

* * *

Progress in science until we learn that the rainbow was not built to allay the fears of the roachin family, but is old as the sun and the sea; that bourbon whisky drills the stomach full o' blow-holes and that the purest spring water is full o' bacteria and we must boil it or switch to beer; that Havana cigars give us tobacco heart, pastry is the handmaid of dyspepsia, while even the empurpled grape is but a John the Baptist for appendicitis; that a rich thief has kleptomania and should be treated at a fashionable hospital instead of a plebeian penitentiary, while even the rosebud of beauty is aswarm with bacilli, warning the sons of men to keep their distance on pain of death. If all the doctors discovered be true then life isn't half worth living—is stale, flat and unprofitable as a Republican nomination in Texas. When the poet declared that men do not die for love, the doctors had not yet learned that a cornfed kiss that cracks like a dynamite gun may be equally dangerous. I think the bolus-builders are chasing rainbows—that if I wait for death until I'm killed with kisses old Methuselah won't be a marker.

Our car of progress, of which we hear so much, has carried us from the Vates' vision of Milton and Dante to Alfred Austin's yaller doggerel—to the raucous twitterings of grown men who aspire to play Persian bulbul instead of planting post-holes, who mistake some spavined mule for Bellerophon's Mount and go chasing metrical rainbows when they should be drawing a fat bacon rind adown the shining blade of a bucksaw; from the flame sighs of Sappho, that breed mutiny in the blood, to the green-sick maunderings of atrabilarious maids who are best qualified to build soft-soap or take a fall out of the corrugated bosom of a washboard. We now have poetry, so-called, everywhere—in books and magazines innumerable, even sandwiched in between reports of camp-meetings, political pow-wows and newspaper ads. for patent liver pills. O, that the featherless jaybirds now trying to twitter in long-primer type would apply the soft pedal unto themselves, would add no more to life's dissonance and despair! Most of our modern poets are bowed down with more than Werterean woe. Their sweethearts are cruel or fate unkind; they've got cirrhosis of the liver or palpitation of the heart, and needs must spill their scalding tears over all humanity. It seems never to have occurred to the average verse architect that not a line of true poetry was ever written by mortal man; that even the song of Solomon and the odes of Anacreon are but as the jingling of sweet bells out of tone, a dissonance in the divine harmony; that you can no more write poetry than you can paint the music of childhood's laughter, or hear the dew-beaded jasmine bud breathing its sensuous perfume to the morning sun. The true poets are those whose hearts are harps of a thousand strings, ever swept by unseen hands—those whose lips are mute because the soul of man hath never learned a language. Those we call master-poets and crown with immortelles but caught and fixed some far off echo of deep calling unto deep —the lines of Byron or a Burns, a Tasso or a Tennyson are but the half-articulate cries of a soul stifling with the splendor of its own imaginings.

* * *

But we were speaking of progress when diverted by the discordant clamor of featherless crows. I am no pecterist with my face ever to the past. I realize that there has been no era without its burden of sorrow, no time without its fathomless lake of tears; that the past seems more glorious than the present because the heart casts a glamour over days that are dead. From the dust and glare of the noon of life we cast regretful glances back to the dewy morn, and as eve creeps on the shadows reach ever further back until they link the cradle and the grave and all is dark. I would not blot from heaven the star of hope, nor mock one earnest effort of mankind; but I would warn this world that its ideals are all wrong, that it's going forward backwards, is chasing foolish rainbows that lead to barbarism. Palaces and gold, fame and power—these be thy gods, O! Israel—mere fly-specked eidolons worthy no man's worship.

* * *

When we have adopted higher ideals; when success is no longer a synonym for vain show; when the man of millions who toils and wails for more is considered mad; when we realize that all the world's wealth cannot equal the splendor of the sunset sky 'neath which the poorest trudge, the astral fire that flames at night's high noon above the meanest hut; that only God's omnipotence can recall one wasted hour, restore the bloom of youth, or bid the loved and lost return to glad our desolate hearts with the lambent light of eyes that haunt all our waking dreams, the music of laughter that has become a wailing cry in memory's desolate halls; when we cease chasing lying rainbows in the empty realm of Make-Believe and learn for a verity that the kendal green of the workman may be more worthy of honor than the purple of the prince—why then the world will have no further need of iconoclasts to frankly rehearse its faults, and my words of censure will be transformed into paeans of praise,

> "Sweet as the smile when fond lovers meet
> And soft as their parting tear."

We have "progressed" from the manly independence and fierce patriotism of our forbears to a namby-pamby foreign policy that compels our citizens abroad to seek protection of the consuls of other countries from the spirit that made our flag respected in every land and honored on every sea, to the anserine cackle of "jingoism" whenever an American manifests a love of country or professes a national pride. What is "jingoism?" It is a word coined by enemies of this country and used by toad-eaters. It is a term which, under various titles, has been applied to every American patriot since our gran'sires held the British lion up by the caudal appendage and beat the sawdust out of the impudent brute— since they appealed from a crack-brained king to the justice of heaven and wrote the charter of our liberties with the bayonet on the back of Cornwallis' buccaneers. Its synonym was applied to Thomas Paine, the arch-angel of the Revolution, whose pen of fire made independence imperative—who thro' seven long years of blood and tears fanned Liberty's flickering flames with his deathless faith that the Omnipotent arm of God would uphold the banner of the free. From the brain of that much-maligned and long-suffering man Columbia sprang full-panoplied, like Minerva from the brow of Olympian Jove. And what has been his reward? In life he was bitterly belied by the foes of freedom and the slaves of superstition; in death a mighty wave of calumny rolls above his grave. Greater men have lived and died and been forgotten, but a nobler heart ne'er beat and broke—grander soul ne'er struggled toward the light or bowed before the ever-living God. When the colonists stood debating whether to bear their present ills or fly to others they knew not of, he seized the gage of battle and flung it full and fair in Britain's haughty face. When defeat followed defeat, when the new-born nation was bankrupt and its soldiers starving in the field; when coward lips did from their color fly and men brave as Roman tribunes wept tears of grim despair, his voice rang out again and again like that of some ancient prophet of Israel cheering on the fainting legions of the Lord, and again, and again, and yet again the ragged barefoot Continentals set their breasts against the bayonet, until from the very ashes of defeat dear Liberty arose Phœnix-like, a goddess in her beauty, a titan in her strength.

* * *

The term "jingoist," or its equivalent, was applied to Washington and Henry, to Jefferson and Jackson. It was applied to James G. Blaine, the typical American of his time—a man from beneath whose very toe-nails enough intellect might be scraped to make an hundred Clevelands or McKinleys. All were jingoes in their day and generation, because all preferred the title of sovereign to that of subject; because all believed that Columbia should be mistress of her own fate, the architect of her own fortune, instead of an appendage of England, or political orphan under a European protectorate, because all believed that she should protect her humblest citizen from wrong and outrage wheresoever he may be, tho' it cost every dollar of the nation's treasure and every drop of the nation's blood—and if that be jingoism then I, too, am a jingo from alpha to omega, from beginning to end.

* * *

Who are those who recalcitrate about jingoism? They are people who have never forgiven Almighty God for suffering them to be born American sovereigns instead of British subjects. They are those whose ideal man is some stupid, forked radish "stuck o'er with titles, hung 'round with strings," and anxious to board with a wealthy American wife to avoid honest work. They are the people whose god is the dollar, their country the stock exchange, and who suspect that a foreign policy with as much backbone as a scared rabbit would knock some of the wind and water out of their bogus "securities." It is those who would sell their citizenship for a copper cent and throw in their risen Lord as *lagniappe,* who are forever prating of "jingoism" and pleading for peace at any price. And these unclean harpies of greed and gall have been too long permitted to dominate this government. The result is that the greatest nation known to human history—the sum and crown of things—is an object of general insult. If it be rumored that we contemplate protecting American citizens in Cuba, every European government emits a growl—there's talk of rebuking Uncle Sam's "presumption," of standing him in a corner to cool. If it be suggested that we annex an island—at the earnest request of all its inhabitants worth the hanging—there's more minatory caterwauling by the European courts, while even the Mikado of Japan gets his little Ebenezer up, and the Ahkound of Swat, the Nizan of Nowhere and the grand gyasticutus of Jimplecute intimate that they may send a yaller-legged policeman across the Pacific in a soap-box to pull the tailfeathers out of the bird o' freedom if it doesn't crawl humbly back upon its perch. If a fourth-class power insults our flag we accept a flippant apology. If our citizens are wrongfully imprisoned we wait until they are starved, shot, or perish of blank despair in dungeons so foul that a hog would die therein of a broken heart; then humbly ask permission to investigate, report that they are dead, and feel that we have discharged our duty. Why? Because this nation is dominated by the dollar—is in the hands of those who have no idea of honor unless it will yield somewhat to eat, no use for patriotism unless it can be made to pay. When we concluded to protect our citizens from Weylerian savagery, instead of sending a warship to Havana to read the riot act if need be in villainous saltpetre we had our ambassador crawling about the European courts humbly begging permission of the powers, and as we got no permission we did no protecting. When the church people elect me president of this Republic I'll have ante-mortem investigations when American citizens are held prisoners by foreign powers, and those entitled to Old Glory's protection will get it in one time and two motions if Uncle Sam has to shuck his seer-sucker and fight all Europe to a finish. I shall certainly ask no foreign prince, potentate or power for permission to protect American citizens in the western world. There'll be one plank in my platform as broad as a boulevard and as long as a turnpike, and it will be to the effect that the nation which wrongs an American citizen must either apologize with its nose in the sand or reach for its six-shooter. I'd rather see my country made a desolation forever and a day, its flag torn from the heavens, its name erased from the map of the world and its people sleeping in heroes' sepulchres, than to see it a mark for scorn, an object of contempt.

In continually crying "Peace! Peace!" Uncle Sam is chasing a rainbow that has a dynamite bomb under either end. If history be philosophy teaching by example what is the lesson we have to learn? In little more than a century we've had four wars, and only by the skin of our teeth have we escaped as many more, yet we not only refuse to judge the future by the past, but ignore the solemn admonitions of Washington and Jefferson and stand naked before our enemies. We have no merchant marine to develop those hardy sailors who once made our flag the glory of the sea. We have a little navy, commanded chiefly by political pets who couldn't sail a catboat into New York harbor without getting aground or falling overboard. We have an army, about the size of a comic opera company, officered largely by society swells who cannot even play good poker, are powerful only on dress parade. We have a few militia companies, scattered from Sunrise to Last Chance, composed chiefly of boys and commanded by home-made colonels, who couldn't hit a flock o' barns with a howitzer loaded to scatter; who show up at state encampments attired in gaudy uniforms that would make Solomon ashamed, and armed with so-called swords that wouldn't cut hot butter or perforate a rubber boot. And that's our immediate fighting force. Uncle Sam is a Philadelphia tenderfoot flourishing a toy pistol at a Mexican fandango. When I succeed Mr. McKinley I'll weed every dude and dancing master out of the army and navy and put on guard old war dogs who can tell the song of a ten-inch shell from the boom-de-aye of a sham battle. I'll call the attention of my Hardshell Baptist Congress to Washington's advice that while avoiding overgrown military establishments, we should be careful to keep this country on a respectable defensive posture, and that if that advice is not heeded, I'll distribute the last slice of federal pie among the female Prohibitionists of Kansas. If this is to be a government of, for and by a lot of nice old ladies, I'll see to it that none of my official grannies grow a beard or wear their bronchos clothespin fashion. And I'll warrant you that were this nation ruled by sure-enough women instead of by a lot of anaemic he-peons of the money-power, Columbia would not be caught unprepared when "the spider's web woven across the cannon's throat shakes its threaded tears in the wind no more."

* * *

To the American patriot familiar with the rapid development of this country it seems that the hour must assuredly come when its lightest wish will be the world's law

—when foreign potentates will pay homage to the sovereigns of a new and greater Rome; but let us not be too sanguine, for nations, like individuals, have their youth, their lusty manhood and their decay; and despite the rapid increase in men and money there are startling indications that Uncle Sam has already passed the zenith of his power.

"First freedom, then glory, when that fails,
Wealth, vice, corruption—barbarism at last."

Freedom we have won, and glory, yet both have failed—we have become, not the subjects of native Caesars, but the serfs of foreign Shylocks. Wealth we now have, and Oriental vice, and corruption that reaches even from the senate chamber thro' every stratum of society. That we are approaching barbarism may be inferred from the magnificence of the plutocrat and the poverty of the working people. The first reaps where he has not sown and gathers where he has not strewn, while if the latter protest against this grievous injustice they are branded as noisy Bryanites or lampooned as lippy Populists. To the superficial observer, a nation seems to be forging forward long after it has really begun to retrograde. There's an era of splendor, of Lucullus feasts, of Bradley-Martin balls and Seeley dinners; there's grand parade of soldiery and ships, miles of costly palaces, and wealth poured out like water in foolish pageantry; there's refinement of manners into affectation, dilettanteism, epicureanism—but 'tis "the gilded halo hovering 'round decay." The heart of that nation is dead, its soul hath departed, and no antiseptic known to science will prevent putrefaction. How is it with us? Forty thousand people own one-half the wealth between two oceans, while 250,000 own more than 80 per cent. of all the values created by the people. What is the result? Money is omnipotent. Power is concentrated in the hands of a little coterie of plutocrats—the people are sovereigns *de jure* and slaves *de facto*. A mongrel Anglomaniaism is spreading among our wealthy, like mange in a pack o' lobo wolves. Our plutocrats have become ashamed of their country—probably because it permits them to practice a brutal predacity—and now cultivate foreign customs, ape foreign fashions, and purchase as husbands for their daughters the upper-servants of European potentates—people who earned their titles of nobility by chronic bootlicking or sacrificing their female relatives to the god of infamy. Year after year these titled paupers—these shameless parodies on God's masterpiece—paddle across the pond to barter their tawdy dishonor for boodle, to sell their shame-crested coronets to porcine-souled American parvenues, who if spawned by slaves and born in hell would disgrace their parentage and dishonor their country. Our toadies and title-worshippers now have a society called the "Order of the Crown," composed of puppies who fondly imagine that they have within their royal hides a taint of the impure blood that once coursed thro' the veins of corrupt or barbarous kings. Perchance these dudelets and dudines will yet discover that they are descended in a direct line from King Adam the First and are heirs to the throne of Eden. Our country is scarce half developed, yet it is already rank with decadence and smells of decay. Our literature is "yellow," our pulpit is jaundiced, our society is rotten to the core and our politics shamefully corrupt—yet people say there's no need of iconoclasts! Perhaps there isn't. The iconoclasts used hammers, while those who purify our social atmosphere and make this once again a government of, for and by the people may have to empty gatling guns and load them with carbolic acid.

National decay and racial retrogression may be inferred from the fact that alleged respectable white women have been married to black men by eastern ministers who insist on solving the race problem for God and the South by giving to the typical American of the future the complexion of a new saddle and the perfume of a Republican powwow. When those ethnological experts tire of life, they should—come to Texas. When white people lose their racial pride they've nothing left that justifies the appointment of a receiver. We hear a great deal about "race prejudice," and I want to say right here that there's just enough of it in my composition to inspire an abiding faith that the white man should be, must be, will be, lord paramount of this planet. I promise you that when you elect me to the presidency, nothing that's black, yaller or tan gets an office under my administration. I shall certainly not follow Mark Hanna's understudy and fill the departments at Washington with big, fat, saucy blacks, to employ white women as stenographers and white men as messenger boys. There's lots of good in the Senegambian—lots of it; but not in a thousand years will he be fit for American sovereignty. Half the white people are not fit for it, else instead of a wooden-headed hiccius doctius we'd have Billy Bryan in the presidential chair today. Whenever I look at McKinley, I think of Daniel Webster—not because Bill resembles old Dan, but because he doesn't. I like the negro in his place and his place is in the cotton patch, instead of in politics, despite the opinion of those who have studied him only thro' the rose-tinted lorgnette of "Uncle Tom's Cabin." I also like the Anglomaniac in his place, and that is the geographical center of old England, with John Bull's trade-mark seared with a hot iron on the western elevation of his architecture as he faces the rising sun to lace his shoes. As between the nigger and the Anglomaniac, I much prefer the former. The full-blooded nigger is a fool positive, but the Anglomaniac is an ass superlative. The first is faithful to those who feed him; the latter is a sneaking enemy to the country that has conferred upon him every benefit.

Despite the optimistic cackle anent the march of science, industrial progress, and all that sort o' thing, it appears to be the general consensus of opinion that there's something radically wrong. There's no lack of remedies—the political drug store is full of panaceas, each with the trade-mark of some peculiar school of therapeutics blown in the bottle. Strange that all these catholicons for earthly ills propose to inaugurate the millennium by improving the pecuniary condition of the people—as tho' the want of money in this or the other pocket were the only evil. Certainly a better distribution of wealth were desirable, but a general dissemination of God's grace were far preferable. Given that, all worthy reforms will follow; without it we will continue to chase foolish rainbows to our fall, Dives becoming more insolent, Lazarus left more and more to the care of the dogs. I do not mean that by acquiring a case of the camp-meeting jerks we will solve the riddle which the Sphinx of Time is propounding to this republic—that we will find the solution of all life's problems in the amen-corner. Not exactly. The average church is about the last place to which we need look for relief. It's too often a lying rainbow painted on the dark mist of ignorance by the devil's own artist. It promises more and performs less than a Republican candidate for Congress. I've noticed that shouting hosannahs has little tendency to make one more truthful—that when a man professes himself the chief of sinners, he may feel obligated to substantiate his statement. I've never known a man to borrow any money of the bank on the unctuosity of his amen, but

I have known people who could double-discount Satan himself at dodging an honest debt, to weep real water because I declined to come into their sectarian penfold and be measured for a suit of angelic pin-feathers. There are many church people who will slander you unmercifully for dissenting from their religious dogma, then seize the first opportunity to stick you with a plugged dime or steal your dog. There are worshippers who do not consider in outward rites and specious forms religion satisfied; but these never accumulate vast fortunes. The path to heaven is too steep to be scaled by a man weighted down with seven million dollars. He may be long on hope and faith, but he's short on charity, and without charity religion is as big a fraud as McKinley's international bimetallism. Charity is a word that is awfully misunderstood. If a man's income be $5,000 a year and he gives half of it to the less fortunate, he's a pretty decent fellow, but if he reserves for himself half of a $100,000 income while people are going hungry to bed, he's simply a brute. With a world full of woe and of want, what right has any professed follower of Jesus to shove $50,000 a year down his jeans? The true test of a man's charity is the sum which he reserves for himself; hence when Jno. D. Rockefeller—my good Baptist brother who's building collegiate monuments to his own memory with other people's money—reserves tens o' millions in excess of his needs and imagines himself full to the muzzle with the grace of God, he's simply chasing a rainbow that may land him in Malebolge with the dull sudden plunk of a Republican campaign promise hitting the tidal wave of prosperity. Imagine Christ Jesus with John D.'s money —loaning it at 5 per cent. a month! Why if he'd had half so much cash he'd never have been crucified. Those who clamored for his death would have run him for mayor of Jerusalem on the reform ticket and tried to work him for his last dollar.

* * *

If all who call themselves Christians were Christlike, then indeed might there be hope for humanity; but what is there to inspire belief that the church will ever win the world from a foolish quest of rainbows? What hope in Talmage, with his nightmare visions and stertorous dreams, his pilgrimings to Palestine and rummaging among the mummified cats and has-been kings of ancient Egypt for "Scriptural evidence?" What hope for a people so mentally emasculate that they can patiently listen to his jejune wind-jamming, can read and relish his irremediable tommyrot? What hope in Sam Jones and other noisy ignorami of that ilk, with their wild war on dancing and the euchre deck, the drama and decollete? Be these the strongholds of Abriman in his ceaseless war on Oromasdes? Does the Prince of Darkness, who once did fill the wondering cosmos with the clangor of celestial steel, now front the hosts of Heaven armed with a euchre-deck? Is Tara Boom-deaye the battle-hymn and the theatre hat the blazing gonfalon of him who strove with Omnipotence for universal empire? Does Lucifer expect to become lord paramount of all the gleaming worlds that hang like jewels pendant in heaven's imperial concave by persuading some miserable son of Adam to work his toes on Sunday, dance with the girls on Monday or play seven-up for the cigars? O Jonesy, Jonesy! would to heaven that thou and all thy brother blabsters and bubblyjocks would go hang yourselves, for you know naught of the war that rages ever like a sulphurous siroc in the human soul. Ye are but insects that infest great Igdrasyl, the ash tree that upholds the universe. One atheistical Stephen Girard playing Good Samaritan in a plague-swept city while the preachers hit the turnpike; one deistical Tom Paine, braving the guillotine for the rights of man; one Father Damien, freely laying down his life for the miserable lepers of Molokai; one sweet-faced sister of charity bravely battling with the reeking slums of a great city, striving to drag souls from that seething maelstrom of sin, were worth legions of those sanctified lollypops who prate of sacrificing all for the Savior, yet never risk life or gold in the service of their God.

* * *

"Work is worship," said those old monks who carried the cross into the Western wilds despite all hardships, in defiance of all dangers—men for whom life was no Momus-masque, but a battle and a march, men who sacrificed all for other's sake, accepting without a sigh disease and death as worldly reward. Those monks were real men, and real men are ever the world's heroes and its hope. The soul of a real man is never hidden behind the cowardly superficies of policy or expediency—his heart is an open book which he who runs may read. Deceive he cannot, for the lie blooms only on the lips of cowards. Public opinion he may treat with kingly contempt, but self-respect is dearer to him than life, tho' dowered with a monarch's sceptre and all the wealth of Ormus and of Ind. There's something in the words of a woman, spoken during the civil war, which indicates that despite all artificiality and folly, beneath the cheap gilding and showy lacquer of life, the heart of the race still beats steady and strong; that above the infinitude of goose-speech and the trumpeting of tin-horns on the housetops may still be heard "the ever-pealing tones of old Eternity." From out the mad hell of the fight a wounded hero was borne to the hospital. Neither pain nor approaching death could break the courage of that heart of oak, but a prurient little preacher, one of those busy smooth-bore bigots whose mission seems to be to cast a shadow on the very sun, convinced the stricken man that he was an awful sinner, whereupon he began crying out that he was doomed to be damned. The nurse, a muscular woman who believed with the old monks that "work is worship," took the parson by the pendulous 8x10 ear, led him aside and sweetly said: "Mr. Goody Two-Shoes, if I catch you in this ward again I'll throw you out of the window." The brimstone peddler felt that he had an urgent "call" to other fields. He stood not upon the order of his going, but hit the dim and shadowy distance like Nancy Hanks. He couldn't even wait to pray for his persecutor to take up a collection. In vain the nurse strove to soothe her patient by telling him that the man who gave his life for his native land cannot miss heaven's mercy—he but wailed the louder that he was lost. "You came to me a hero," she cried, "and you shall not leave me a coward. If you must go to hell, go like a man." If Romans nursed by a she-wolf became demigods, what might not Americans be when sprung from the loins of such a lioness! Milton has almost made Satan respectable by endowing him with an infernal heroism, by making him altogether and irremediably bad, instead of a moral mugwump—by giving him a heart for any fate instead of picturing him as willing to wound and yet afraid to strike.

* * *

By God's grace, I mean not the kind you catch at campmeeting with sand-fleas, wood-ticks and other gifts of the Holy Ghost; but rather an end everlasting to brummagem and make-believe, a return to the Ark of the Covenant, a recognition of the fact that the soul is not the stomach—that a man owes debts to his fellows which cannot be cast up at the end of the month and discharged with a given number of dollars. Man was not made for himself alone, but all were made for each and each for all. The doctrine which now prevails of "every man for himself," is the dogma of the devil. It means universal war, shameful wrong and brutal outrage—the strong become intolerable tyrants, the weak go to the wall. It transforms this beautiful world into a basket of adders, each biting, hissing, striving to get its foolish head above its fellows. If the Christian religion contained naught else of worth, its doctrine of self-sacrifice should earn for it the respect of every Atheist in the universe. Through the fogs of ignorance and the clouds of superstition that enshrouded the Biblical ages that touch of the divine shines like a pilot star.

* * *

That Persian poet who prated of "the sorry scheme of things" would deserve pity were he not beneath contempt. He imagined that there was a screw loose in the universe because his quest of pleasure slipped its trolley-pole and could not make the bubble Joy to dance in Folly's cup.

Millions make continual moan that they are not happy when they ought to be thankful that they are not hanged. They shake their puny hands at heaven because not provided with a terrestrial Paradise, when they ought to be giving thanks that I'm not the party who holds the sea in the hollow of his hand. I'd make good Baptists of the whole caboodle—would hold them under water long enough to soak out the original sin. A man complains because Fortune doesn't empty her cornucopia into the pockets of his pantalettes while he whittles a pine box and talks municipal politics instead of humping himself behind an enterprising mule in the cotton-patch. If his sweetheart jilts him, he's in despair, and if she marries him he wishes he were dead. He has the mulligrubs because he cannot plant himself on a Congressional cushion, or because he finds his wife awake and nursing a curtain lecture to keep it warm when he falls thro' the front fence at 5 o'clock in the morning. It seems never to have occurred to these Werterian wailers that the happiest existence is that of the lower animals—that the human being of fine brain and keen sensibilities cannot possibly be content. It is this very unrest, this heart-hunger that drives man on to noble deeds—that lifts him out of the gutter where wallow the dull, dumb beasts and places him among the gods. Of suffering and sorrow were born all life's beauty. The kiss of Pyramus and Thisbe is an ecstasy of pain. The hope of immortality sprang from breaking hearts. Nations rise through a mist of tears. Every great life-work is an agony. Behind every song there lurks a sigh. There's an element of sadness in humor itself. The Virgin Mother is known as Our Lady of Pain. The cult of Christ is hallowed by the blood of self-sacrifice and known as the Religion of Sorrow. The first breath of life and the last gasp are drawn in suffering; and between the cradle and the grave there lies a monster-haunted Sahara. Yet men choose that *ignis-fatuus* called Happiness, and mourn that they cannot cover it with a No. 6 hat. They should pray the gods to transform them into contented goats and turn them out to grass. People who cannot find happiness here begin to look for it in heaven. Eternal beatitude is another ridiculous rainbow. Nirvana is nonsense. If there be a life beyond the grave, it means continued endeavor, and there can be no endeavor unless there's dissatisfaction. The creature cannot rise superior to its creator—and the universe is the result of God's unrest. Had he been perfectly content he would not have made me.

Carlyle—not Mugwump Carlisle of Kentucky, but Thos. Carlyle of Great Britain—the lord of modern literature—says the hell most dreaded by the English is the hell of not making money. We have imported this English Gehenna, duty free, despite Mr. Dingley, and now the man who doesn't succeed in accumulating dollars is socially damned. How many of this generation can understand the remark of Agassiz that he had no time to make money?—can realize that such occupation is not the sole end of man?—that time expended in the accumulation of wealth beyond the satisfaction of simple wants is worse than wasted? It is so because from our numbered days we have stolen years that should have been devoted to soul-development, filled with the sweets of knowledge; hallowed by the perfume of love, made gracious by noble deeds—because we have blasted life's fair fruitage with the primeval eldest curse. Omar strikes one true chord when he doth sing:

> "A book of verses, underneath the bough,
> A jug of wine, a loaf of bread, and thou
> Singing beside me in the wilderness—
> O wilderness where Paradise enow!"

* * *

Diogenes was content with a tub while Alexander sat him

down by the ever-moaning sea and wept his red bandana full of brine because he didn't know that the empire of Czar Reed yet remained unconquered. And now both Diogenes and Alexander have "gone glimmering thro' the dream of things that were," and little it matters to them or to us whether they fed on honey of Hymettus and wine of Falernus or ate boarding house hash off a pewter plate and guzzled Prohibition busthead out of a gourd. The cynic who housed in a tub and clothed himself with a second-hand carpet is rich to-day as he that reveled in the spoil of Persia's conquered king and kicked the bucket while enjoying a case of katzenjammer. King and cynic, tub and palace, lantern and sceptre—all have perished; and he that butchered thousands to glut his greed for what fools call glory, shines less brightly thro' the murky shadows of the century than he that made a nobler conquest of himself. The haughty empires one did rear have long since crumbled into dust; the wild goat browses in their deserted capitals, the lizard sleeps upon their broken thrones, and the owl hoots from their forgotten altars and ruined fanes; but the philosophy of the other lives on from age to age, to point the folly of such mad rainbow-chasing as that of him who thought to make the world his monument.

* * *

Know ye not that the poorest beggar is an earth-passenger also, that thy brother, traveling his millions of miles per day?—where, think you? Among the stars. For him as for thee does Aurora gild the morning and Apollo hang the evening sky with banners of burnished gold; for him as for thee doth Selene draw the limpid waters behind her silver car around the rolling world and Bootes lead his hunting dogs afield in their leash of celestial fire. Ten centuries hence the dust of the millionaire will have mingled with that of the mendicant, both long forgotten of men; ten centuries hence the descendants of those now peddling hot wienerwurst may proudly wear the purple, while the posterity of present monarchs creep thro' life as paupers. A thousand years are but as one tick of the mighty horologe of time—and the allotted life of man but three score years and ten! And this brief period we expend, not in living, but in providing the means of life; not as creation's lords, but as slaves to our own avarice, the most pitiful passion that ever cursed mankind. If there be a God, be thou his messenger unto men; if there be no God, then have thy unfortunate fellows the more need of thee. Wait not until a man is driven to crime by the iron law of necessity, a woman to dishonor, a child to beggary, then organize some fake relief society for thine own glory, but put forth a helping hand in time to avert the sin and shame. The most pitiful failure in all God's universe is the man who succeeds only in making money. A thieving fox will grow fat by predacity while an honest dog starves in the path of duty. And we have too many sleek Reynards prowling 'round the sheep-pens and dove-cotes of this people, too few faithful Gelerts doing stubborn battle with predaceous beasts.

There's one class of people whom we cannot brand as arrant knaves and put in the pillory, yet who are a curse to any country. These are your Laodiceans in religion and politics, your luke-warms, your namby-pamby milk-and-cider set who are neither cold nor hot. These are your eminently proper people, your stereotyped respectables. They accept the Gospel as true, not that they can comprehend it, but rather because they lack sufficient mental vigor to deny it. They join the church and align themselves with that political party to which the local nabobs belong. "What will people say?" is to them the all-important problem. They have followed some old bell-wether or lead-gander into the wiregrass pasture of Respectabilia. They observe all the proprieties—at least in outward appearance. These are the animals whose *vis inertia* perpetuates all the abuses of wealth and power—whatsoever has the approval of two or more generations of infamous rascals is so eminently respectable. These are the people who are so profoundly shocked by the alleged slang of Hugo and vulgarities of Goethe, while compelling their daughters to read the Canticles. They have a conniption fit and fall in it because some shapely danseuse kicks up her rhythmic heels on the vaudeville stage, then organize Trilby auctions, kissing bees and garter raffles for the glory of God. Their ideal is expediency and their moral law the Eleventh Commandment—Don't get caught. These are the people who stone the prophets of progress. They are to the social organism what a pound of putty would be to the stomach of a dyspeptic. They are a mill-stone slung about the neck of the giant of civilization. "What will people say?" Well, if you tell them a new truth, they will say that you are a demagogue or a blasphemer, an anarchist or a Populist; but when your new truth has been transformed by Time's great alembic into an old falsehood, they will have absorbed it—it will have become respectable—and you couldn't purge it from their soggy brains with Theodorus' Anticyrian hellebore. They said of Galileo, "Imprison him!" because he denied the old falsehood that the world is flat; of Servetus, "Burn him!" because he dissented from the *ipse dixit* of another heretic; of Socrates, "Poison him!" because he laughed at the too amorous gods of Greece; of Robert Emmett, "Hang him!" because he wasn't a Cleveland-Bayard Anglomaniac; and they said of Christ Jesus, "Crucify him!" because he intimated the fashionable preachers of his time were a set of splenetic-hearted hypocrites. That's what people say; but occasionally there's one to answer that 'tis not in the power of all Xerxes' hosts to bend one thought of his proud heart—"they may destroy the case of Anaxarchus, himself they cannot reach." It is not what foolish sound is shaped by a deal of stinking breath and blown adown the wind to be forgotten like the bray of an asthmatic burro, to perish like the snows of yesteryear, that should be our concern—not what the idle gabble of Mrs. Grundy proclaims us, but what we actually are. Public opinion is an ever-shifting rainbow. The "heretics" of one age are the saints of the next: the "cranks" of our own time may be the philosophers of the future; the despised rebels of a century ago are the men whose graves we bedeck with our garlands. Soon or late, those who court the many-headed monster, who "flatter its rank breath and bow to its idolatries a patient knee," are trampled beneath its iron heel; but those who take duty for guiding star and are strong enough to withstand the gibes of malice and the jeers of ignorance will find that the years are seldom unjust. It has been well said that one eternity waited for us to be born, that another waits to see what we will do now that we are here. Do what thou canst and do it with all thy might, remembering that every fice that doth bark at thee this day, every goose that stretches forth its rubber neck to express its disapproval, will be dead in hell a hundred years hence, its foolish yawp gone silent forevermore, but that thy honest act affects in greater or less degree all God's universe.

I am neither a Jeremiah with a lung full o' lamentations, nor a Jonah rushing round like a middle of the roader and proclaiming, "Yet forty days and the woods will be on fire." I do not believe that we can pick ourselves up by our own embroidered boot-straps and hop blithely astride a millennium built to order by McKinley, Bryan, or any other man; but I do believe that the human race is slowly but surely working the subsoil out of its system, is becoming ever less the beast and more the god. Nations grown corrupt with wealth and age may fall, but others strong in youth and innocence will arise. Old faiths may be forgotten, but from other and purer altars will ascend the smoke of sacrifice. Freedom may be wounded grievously in her very temple by Anglomaniacs who needs must have a royal master, yet her banner, torn but flying, will stream triumphant over the grave of tyranny. The black night of barbarous ignorance may often engulf the world, but "Thou, Eternal Providence, wilt cause the day to dawn." The Star of Bethlehem cannot go down in everlasting darkness—the bow of promise gleams softly luminous behind the thunderbolt. I care not whether the Noahian tale be true that never again will the shifting axis of the earth pour the sea upon the plain—the rainbow is nature's emblem of peace, her cestus of love, and in its splendor I read a promise that never again will this fair earth of ours be swept with sword and fire, deluged with blood and tears. Not to the past, but to the future, do I look for the Saturnian age, when the demons of need and greed will be exorcised, when love will be the universal law, the fatherhood of God the only faith. Such, my friends, is the rainbow to which I have turned my feet. It lies afar, across dismal swamps, in which noisome reptiles creep, beyond mountain ranges o'er whose icy summits only the condor's shadow sweeps—across arctics vast and desert isles beyond tempestous oceans rank with dead men's bones and the rotting hulls of ships. I shall not attain it, nor shall you; but he that strives, tho' vanquished, still is victor. A dreamer, say you? Ah yes, but all life is but a dream, mystic, wonderful, and we know not when we sleep nor when we wake. I love to dream so when the storm beats upon the great oaks, hoary with their hundred years, and they put forth their gnarled arms and grapple with the blast, when the lightning cleaves the inky sky with forked flame and the earth rocks neath the thunder's angry roar. When the dark clouds roll muttering unto the East and the evening sun hangs every leaf and twig and blade of grass with jewels brighter than e'er gleamed in Golconda's mines; when the mock-birds renew their melody and every flower seems drunken with its own incense, I look upon the irisate glory that seems to belt the world with beauty and my heart beats high with hope that in years to be the storm-clouds that o'ershadow the souls of men will recede also—that time shall come when the human race will be one universal brotherhood, containing neither a millionaire nor a mendicant, neither a master nor a slave.

WHO IS MARK HANNA?

HE IS THE VAMPIRE OF POVERTY, THE ATTILA OF INDUSTRY, THE AVATAR OF GREED, THE SCOURGE OF GOD.

If the bones of all the women and children he has starved to death, and those of all the workmen he has slain to increase his heaps of gold, were gathered together, a triumphal arch could be built therewith thro' which McKinley might ride to his inaugural.

If all the suffering, and heartache, if all the crime born of Need and all the despair begotten of his insatiable Greed were used to form another Hell, the Prince of Darkness would stand appalled.

If all the blood and tears he has caused to flow to fertilize his fortune could be collected in one pool, his navy might ride at anchor there, while his half-starved seamen manned the yards and fired salutes in honor of that blessed era of "Progress and Prosperity" which he is contriving for the sons of toil.

Who is Mark Hanna? He is the man denounced by Master Workman Sovereign as an "Industrial Cannibal— worse even than Carnegie." Why was he thus denounced? Because he has entrapped hundreds—perhaps thousands— of confiding workmen into signing contracts which enabled him to withhold one-half their wage and add it to his hoard. Because he has for years owed thousands of dollars to empaupered ship-builders, which he confesses was honestly earned, yet declines to pay, pleading that under the contract he is not liable "until the ships are sold;" yet these same ships are sailing the lakes in his service. Because he has deliberately swindled thousands of poor working people out of the little homes which their toil had paid for, and driven them forth to perish Because he has ruthlessly trampled the life out of a dozen labor unions, and today—both on land and on sea—pays the lowest wages of any American employer. Because he organized and managed the infamous coal pool of 1893, which threw thousands of miners out of employment in the dead of winter, while netting the conspirators millions of dollars—wrung from the American people during the hardest period in their history. Because across the door of his every shop and above the mouth of every mine is written in letters of nether fire, "Abandon hope all ye who enter here!"

Every dollar of Mark Hanna's millions has been coined from the life-blood of labor. Do any doubt it? Then let them turn to the hell-born horrors of Spring Valley and read there an epitome of Hanna's history. There he and his Republican associates builded cheap cottages, which were sold to their mine operatives on the installment plan at exorbitant prices. When these homes were more than paid for at an honest valuation, Hanna reduced wages to the starvation point, making complete payment impossible. The wretched dupes of the damnable plot appealed for simple justice, and were given the "horse-laugh" by Hanna. They went out on a strike, defaulted in their payments, and the state was appealed to by this modern Shylock, hungry for his pound of flesh, to drive them from their homes. The grand old state of Illinois was compelled to do the dirty work of this brute-beast, because it was "in the bond"—to evict the poor bilked home-buyers with the bayonet! In all the history of English landlordism in Ireland there is naught so hellish. A crime so damnable could have originated only with the Hellene Harpies—or Mark Hanna. McKinley's master next scoured all southern Europe for cheap labor, and soon congregated at Spring Valley the most grotesquely wretched aggregation of ignorant helots ever seen on American soil. The homes of evicted American miners were resold to these foreign mendicants—from whose competition the McKinley tariff was supposed to afford protection! Driven to despair, Hanna's ex-employes attacked his imported peons, troops were called out to protect them, and Spring Valley's gutters were reddened with gore. Hanna triumphed, as a matter of course—then cut down the pauper wages of his new employes! But even the ignorant Huns and lousy Lazzaroni could not stand the pitiless oppression of this "Industrial Cannibal." Another strike, more troops, bayonets and blood—and the twice paid for huts returned to the possession of Mark Hanna! Finding that white men, howsoever debased, would not submit to his merciless exactions, he brought negroes from the South to supplant his wretched Huns, and again Spring Valley became a seething Hell—more workmen, driven to desperation, left their bones upon its sanguinary battlefields.

That is but an episode, and by no means the darkest one, in the history of Mark Hanna. Such is the man who is posing as the friend and benefactor of the tinbucket brigade; who "views with alarm" the prospect of having to pay his beloved employes with "depreciated dollars"—who would build a Chinese wall about this blessed land of Christ to "protect American labor from European competition." Such is the man now tearfully appealing to the people to "preserve the honor of our common country!"

What I have here written is but as the shadow of gossamer upon a summer sea to Gibraltar's massy rock, compared to that I am prepared to prove. "Industrial Cannibal." The term is tame. It were like calling Medusa dreadful, Caliban uncomely or the devil displeasing. It would require a Mirabeau to express in a single phrase the character of a man so graceless in his greed, so insensate to all the nobler promptings of the soul. I doubt if a taskmaster has been so abhorred by the toiling millions since Pharaoh oppressed God's chosen people—if in all the mighty tide of time the premeditated infamies of this human octopus can be paralleled. To understand the methods by which he has mounted; to look behind the gilded veil of this modern Mokanna and know what it really is that his dupes are following to their destruction, were to crave the power to weave sentences with warp of flames and woof of aspic's fangs to lash the rascal naked thro' the world.

If McKinley is elected president, Mark Hanna will be the power behind the throne. Why? Because he owns McKinley more completely than he did the Spring Valley miners when master of their employment and holding mortgages on their homes. He holds McKinley's notes for $118,000, representing that indebtedness which he assures us was wiped out "by the spontaneous offerings of a grateful people." The grateful people aforesaid consisted of a syndicate of high-tariff beneficiaries with Mark Hanna at its head—men not in the habit of helping debtors out of a hole unless they can use them in furtherance of their own ends. These notes are relics of the McKinley-Walker collapse. It is now known that the former was partner to the latter and expected to share his profits

—that the "sweet friendship's sake endorsement" story was an arrant fake perpetrated by Mark Hanna to strengthen the credit of his creature with the people. The inside history of that failure has never been made public; but Mark Hanna has the interesting secret safe-locked in his nice fat head. McKinley was saved for a purpose— was regarded by Hanna and his associates as a good investment; but to make sure of his slavery—to prevent him going on strike—neither his notes nor the carefully guarded papers pertaining to his commercial collapse, have been destroyed. They repose in the safety vaults of Hanna—with the deeds to those Spring Valley homes— and there they will remain until McKinley has purchased his freedom by serving the purposes of the syndicate at the expense of the people.

"Gratitude?" Mark Hanna and the coterie with which he consorts—who were allied with him in the coal pool and the Spring Valley installment plan—pay $118,000 for a "dead horse?" Seek gratitude in the wolf, altruism in the ape, charity in the hawk, but none of these human attributes in the stony heart and crafty brain of McKinley's master. When was he ever known to give up a nickel unless there was six cents in sight? Go ask the widows and orphans of those he slew upon the thresholds of their hard-earned homes! Go ask the starving ship-builders who have tried in vain to sell him his own musty paper at 10 cents on the dollar! Go ask the men and women in the insane asylums of Ohio and Illinois, whom his double-dealing has driven mad, then write the answer in letters of fire across the firmament that every workman may hail him as a friend and benefactor. It is possible that, having deprived the miners of those squalid huts for which they had paid him more than an honest price, he would put his hand so deep in his purse only to protect McKinley's home? Can the leopard change his spots? Has the life-long foe of labor become at last its guide, philosopher and friend? Will this crass animal, who is utterly incapable of appreciating those luxuries and refinements which great wealth affords, and who grasps for gold only because it gives him power, forbear to use his "pull" should McKinley be elected president? Nit.

THOSE BLAWSTED HAWMERICAN MEN.

Mrs. Gertrude Atherton recently made a startling bid for notoriety and achieved it. You can get anything you want in this world if only able and willing to pay the price; and Mrs. Atherton has deliberately put herself up as a mark for the shafts of ridicule, evidently preferring to be laughed at rather than altogether ignored. She has fired the Ephesian Dome to secure for herself a celebrity which her intellect could not earn—has compelled the satirists to afford her standing-room among those "damned to everlasting fame." Writing to the London News, she attempts to explain the supposed "affinity between American women and Englishmen," by assuming that they are, respectively, superior to American men and English women. She pictures the Englishman as God's most glorious work, and declares that "the vast majority of American men are composed of two elements only—money-greed and sensuality." The English women, according to Gertie's diagnosis, are veritable chumps, while American women—"one of whom she is which"— are the most irresistibly captivating creatures this side of the Celestial City. As the Iconoclast has a world-wide beauty contest pending (page 279) it would ill become me to either deny or indorse this latter proposition. I will say, however, that the woman does not live who is catholic enough in her views to make her comparisons of different nationalities of any particular importance. What pleases even the most liberal minded of the gentler sex is "charming," and what she takes a notion—with or without reason—to dislike, is simply "horrid," and there you are! No woman should turn herself loose in the well-nigh boundless realm of comparative ethnology—she is sure to get lost. Still, the Iconoclast, as official organ of the American ladies, accepts for them Gertie's little gob of taffy with the profoundest gratitude. I am inclined to suspect that it is well deserved; for "a good tree bringeth forth good fruit," and the American woman is but a reflection of her father. If there be in all the world a land where the ladies are more lovely, I have failed to find it. Perhaps it is just as well, for I'd sure get into trouble by trying to monopolize the whole lot.

Here in America I have to work with my back to the window. Whenever I face the street I do nothing but look at the girls go by and scribble anacreontics, when I should be writing sermons or engaged in silent prayer. I fancy myself Siddartha sitting beneath the sacred Bodhi-tree and surrounded by

"Bands of bright shapes with heavenly eyes and lips,"

until the wild yoop of some political orator saving the country reminds me that life is real, life is earnest and things not what they seem. I do not much blame Gertie for driving her hair-pin dagger clear thro' the quivering diaphragm of the typical American and hanging a six-pound sad-iron on either end. Having found no one to love her in this land of the free and home of the Bryan boom, she may easily be forgiven for asserting that a most dutiful British subject is preferable to an American sovereign. "Hell hath no fury like a woman scorned." Gertie has a kick coming and must, perforce, give vent to her "felinks" by pounding her pink tootsie-wootsies against a brick wall, and turning up her nosie-wosie at the unappreciative sons of Uncle Sam. I am sorry that she is compelled to waste her loveliness in a foreign land; but 'tis not my fault. When she exported her ebullient beauty I was not old enough to make a bid. Of course we are dreadfully naughty; but I cannot, for the life of me, imagine how Gertie discovered it. I am dreadfully sorry that we should have given her cause for complaint. If she will send the names of the designing villains to the Iconoclast, it will print them as a warning to other women. Still I suspect that her ethnological conclusions will not stand analysis. It has become an axiom with sociologists that boys usually inherit their dominant traits from the mother and girls from the father; hence it follows, as an illative consequence, that if English women are wooden, English men are stupid; that if American women are bright, brainy and spirituelle, their sons inherit these characteristics. I cannot now recall a single great man who attributed his success in life to the old man; almost invariably they refer the credit for their achievements to the mother; hence the o'er hasty *ipse dixit* of this female Anglomaniac, stands discredited. The typical American is a mighty money-maker, the typical Englishman a grasping money-hoarder. John Bull puts his wife on "allowance;" Uncle Sam lays his purse in her lap. The American will spend a dollar like a prince while his British cousin is haggling over ha'pence. Throughout the world the American is worshipped by menials, while the Englishman is abhorred. The latter inquires what is the customary "tip" and gives it grudgingly; the former pays what largesse he likes, and it is given with kindly courtesy. The Englishman is a chronic kicker; the American "takes things as they come." The first vaunts his superiority by snubbing servants; the latter can afford to be gracious, because he's a sovereign. The American works hard to make money that he may enjoy spending it, and he lets it go easily because of his supreme confidence in his own ability to make more; while the Briton seems to think his only salvation an inheritance or a wealthy wife. "Save the pence and the pounds will take care of themselves," is the axiom of England. The "tight little isle" animadverting on the "money-greed" of Americans were almost as laughable as the pictures in *Punch*. American women are better dressed and better educated than those of England, simply because they possess the sesame to the purses of men who make the most money and care the least for it. The grievous charge of sensuality cannot lie against Columbia's sons without including her daughters, for they are "bone of the same bone and flesh of the same flesh." The ewe lamb and the lion's whelp cannot spring from the same loins. We men don't mind; but Gertie should ask the American women's forgiveness. She assures us that the wonderful Briton "loves sport better than women." Then indeed must he be a model companion—creation's masterpiece! It would appear from this that Tennyson's "Cousin Amy" didn't make such a bad match after all, for he assures her that

"He will hold thee, when his passion shall have spent its novel force,
Something better than his dog, a little dearer than his horse."

The typical English husband would have preferred his fox-hounds, so Gertie says, and she speaks from experience. The American loves women better than aught else in this world—and his preference has my hearty approbation. Uncle Sam is pre-eminently a Squire of Dames. The American's heart beats faster, his blood is warmer, he is more susceptible to female beauty than is the Briton. Beneath bright skies the sun-god pours his consuming flame into mortal flesh, while those reared in clammy fogs become half fish. But despite this, the American is not so carnal as his trans-Atlantic cousin. To him a woman must be more than a mere female. He loves his mistress, idealizes her, shares his purse with her—will fight for her if need be. The Englishman buys illicit indulgences with the same *sang-froid* that he might purchase a plum-pudding—or a pup. Harlotry flourishes in England and starves in America. There men of social prominence frequent houses of ill-fame with as much unconcern as they visit the cafes; here no man of respectability goes to such places except by stealth, or when in his cups. Wine and women may be an American weakness; that of England—in view of recent interesting disclosures—seems to be brandy and boys. The Englishman is a gourmand, a slave to his belly; the American is not. The first lives to eat; the latter eats to live. The first spends an hour or more at table, gorging himself like my Lord Archbishop at Talleyrand's *diner diplomatique*, hoists in a gallon or two of drunk-promoter and drowses off content—feeds and lies dormant like a boa-constrictor; the latter snatches a frugal meal in fifteen minutes, and is then ready to build a railroad, run for Congress, discuss the latest scientific discovery, or—murder will out—flirt with his neighbor's wife. The "sensuality" of the Englishman is that of the old Vikings; the "sensuality" of the American is that of the ancient Greeks. The first is grossly materialistic. Give him a full paunch and a brace of painted sepulchres from the slums, and melud is in the halls of Valhalla; but it requires beauty, love, and the spice of danger attending stolen sweets to carry the American in Elysian fields. This may explain why Gertie imagines the first a Joseph, the last a Lovelace. The difference in the twain is simply this: A pretty woman has to drop a brick down on the thick head of John Bull to make him take a hint, while a rose leaf is sufficient to bring your Uncle Samuel to her side. If there really exists an "affinity between American women and Englishmen," I can account for it on no other hypothesis than the British one, that every woman needs and must have a master. We do not "boss" our wives to any great extent; we haven't time. We do not consider them our slaves. When we want a household drudge we hire a coon or an Englishman who has been bred for the coach or the kitchen. Perchance we are treating our wives too well. They may long for representatives of what Gertie calls "the most highly developed race of men the world has ever known;" men who will

"lam" them occasionally—in conformity with English law!
If such be the case it were an easy matter to break up
this trans-Atlantic "affinity" business and keep our heiresses at home. There was no necessity for Lil. Hammersley or Nellie Grant to go abroad to get licked. We
can all take a day off, secure baseball bats and "w'ale
bloody 'ell" out of 'em. Then they will understand that
we are "masterful;" will realize that we are quite superior
creatures—almost equal to Englishmen! Or we can
give Bill Sykes, or even the late Duke of Marlborough
pointers on household management if we have a mind to.
After this exhibition of our manly "forcefulness" we ought
to create that "domestic peerage" of which Gertie prattles.
Surely we will have "ennobled" ourselves, and ought to
establish forthwith an Order of the Garter and wear, as
insignia of our exalted rank, the stocking support a tough
old "cat," as do those "healthy-minded men" whom Gertie
so much admires, and in whom she assures us "there
is no taint of morbidity"—Oscar Wilde to the contrary
notwithstanding, howsoever, but!

LES ENFANTS TERRIBLES.

I much fear that before this confounded election is over
I'll have a whole wheel-factory in my head. As a sacred
duty owed to myself, I read the argument on all sides of
every issue, for I hold with Byron that "he that will not
reason is a bigot, and he who dares not is a slave." But
I'll not be able to continue this labor of love much longer.
The logic employed by the McKinleyites is tying my brain
up in a double bow-knot. To save me, I cannot catch onto
its combination, for its predicates look one way, its conclusions another, while its syllogisms fail to syllogize; its
argumentum ad ingorantiam seems to be sadly overworked,
and its *judicium* suffering from the jim-jams. Perhaps
it's all too deep for a mere lad of six-and-thirty who had
the misfortune to be named "Willie," and may, for aught
I know, have willieisms, or even something worse. I am
evidently too recent to fully comprehend the deep workings of McKinley's master mind when it is dealing with
money. I may grow to it—may catch some fleeting glimpse
of what the McKinleyites really mean by the time I am old
enough to be available as the candidate of the gold-bug

"Democrats." Just as I think I've got their esoteric science of money mastered it rears up on its subsequent legs and walks on me till it dislocates my liver. It is evasive and uncertain as a cake of soap in a cistern. I would give four bits for instantaneous photographs of it in its various attitudes. It is the Proteus of politics. Just as you have sized it up it becomes something else. It is the only thing in existence that can be on all sides of a subject at one and the same time, swallow itself and then turn a double somersault. I don't so much mind the brain-fag necessary to keep tab on its saltations, but its pernicious activity makes my eyes ache. "The Silver Trust Circular," which the McKinley organs are all printing in screamer type under scare-heads, is the latest agony inflicted up. n me. All the gold-bug orators have copies of it in their inside pockets, pull it on every occasion and cry Ha! ha! but damfino where the laugh comes in. I am naturally a frolicsome fellow, and can outlaugh Teufelsdrockh when there's any provocation; but somehow this circular looks more like McKinley's wake than his wedding, and I can not cachinnate in the presence of a corpse. It gives the lie point-blank to the charge of "repudiation." It knocks the "50-cent dollar" theory higher than Gilderoy's kite. I presume that everybody has read the circular, for the McKinleyites have sown it broadcast—why I know not, unless as an official certificate of their own insanity. It is an address by one Thos. G. Merrill to the silver mine managers, and sets forth that they should contribute to the Bryan campaign fund, as free coinage would greatly benefit 90 per cent. of the American people and cause "the immediate return of silver to its former price of $1.29 per ounce." Do the McKinleyites deny that free coinage would thus affect the market value of silver? Not at all; they admit it, and proceed to thunder against "this infamous scheme of the mining barons to add $35,000,000 to the value of their annual product at the expense of the entire people." Yet in the self-same breath they declare that "free coinage means a 50-cent dollar," and tearfully protest against "repudiation." In other words, they assert that free coinage would send the selling price of silver to $1.29 per ounce—just as Bryan and the mining barons predict—which means that, at a ratio of 16 to 1, the white would possess equal intrinsic value with the yellow dollar and be as acceptable in any part of the world; and then, without so much as a change of countenance, declare that free coinage means a debased curency! This may all be true. Mark

Hanna and McKinley, Edward Atkinson and Bob Ingersoll, Cleveland and his cuckoos and Cuney and his coons all say so; but alack! I'm too young to understand it! The "Boy Orator" can't make it out. The only "Little Willie" who has mastered it is the editor of the St. Louis *Mirror*. The auriferous economists assert that "it is impossible to create value by law;" and before this *ipse dixit* can soak into us, they point out that Congress can, by a simple "be it enacted," add $35,000,000 per annum to the value of a single American product! That looks like a flat contradiction to ye youngsters; but it requires age and experience to deal with these stunning paradoxes. I have no desire to pose as an *enfant terrible;* still I opine that grown people should not permit we kids to perish in our ignorance. It is barely possible that the philosophers of the McKinley school have discarded prosy logic for poetic license. The Republicans pose as "the real bimetallists, the true friends of silver"— declare that all they want is "an honest dollar, one worth its face the world over." Then why wait for that "international agreement" which ever recedes like the pot of rupees at the rainbow's base, when, by simply opening our mints, we can make 412 1-2 grains of coin silver equal to 25.8 grains of coin gold anywhere, and add $35,000,000 per annum to the value of American products? I know that it is impertinent for thoughtless kids to harass a New Napoleon with vexatious questions when he wants to talk about the tariff; but juvenile curiosity cannot be easily overcome. We are told that "this tremendous profit of the mine-owners would come out of the pockets of the working people." What profit, if the silver dollar "will sink at once to its bullion value?" But I forget; it will sink, and still it won't sink. It is to go up and down and stand still simultaneously. Silver is to double in selling price without affecting the intrinsic value of the dollar! I seem to be catching on. How beautiful it all is, when you once get really into it! Poor Willie Bryan! I wish I had him here to explain it to him. He might resign in favor of McKinley and thus end the agony. But how are the mine-owners to get this tremendous profit—which they will make and at the same time won't make—out of the people's purse? I'm stuck again! Will some Republican Oedipus rede me this riddle? I don't like to make trouble; still, if McKinley or any of his lieutenants will explain it satisfactorily, I'll contribute something handsome to Mark Hanna's slush fund. I respectfully refer it to Dana of the New York *Sun,* and McCullagh of the *Globe-Democrat*. "If anybody kin they kin." But they can't. The only effect which the advancement of silver to $1.29 an ounce could have on the workingman would be to make the white dollar in his possession intrinsically worth 100 cents and relieve him of further taxation to pay interest on bonds sold to bolster up the gold reserve. Suppose I carry silver bullion to the mint and have it coined into "dollars worth 100 cents the world over," and employ labor therewith: What then? Suppose that I had carried gold bullion to the mint and employed my money in like manner. Does the workman have to give more for a white than for a yellow dollar "of equal purchasing power, the world over?" True, the mining companies will make money—may, after so many years of disaster, be able to declare a dividend, much to the satisfaction of some millions of small shareholders who have known only assessments; but how will they make it? By taking from the pockets of the people the coin already there, a la the tariff beneficiaries, and hoarding it up in their coffers until Cleveland gets ready to sell another block of bonds at private bids? They will make it by adding to the volume of our exchange media, thereby causing a revival of business, the advancement of the wage-rate and the employment of the idle legions of labor. And the people will also be in on the "rake-off." The silver coin they would own will be enhanced in value more than $250,000,000! Doubtless that would be a great evil, else it would not be so vigorously condemned by the McKinley-ites. Now "youze kids," understand the situation—"git on" to the *fin de siecle* monetary science as expounded to us by McKinley and other of our elders whose superior wisdom it is our duty to honor: The free coinage of silver will double the value of the raw material and cut the value of everything of which it is made, square thro' the middle. See! We'll have a deluge of white dollars, each worth 100 cents if you melt it down in New York, or Amsterdam or Timbuctoo; but so long as it's got Uncle Sam's spread eagle on it it's worth only 50 cents. You've got to believe that or you're an anarchist, a repudiationist, a popocrat and full o' prunes. You've got to swallow it or you've got wheels in your head and an attack o' the willies. If you ask any questions you're "a lippy kid" and a rainbow chaser. That's what. But that's only part of the new monetary science. These 100-cent silver dollars are going to drive all the 100-cent gold dollars out of circulation, reduce our volume of "final payment money" 50 per cent., and at the same time cause a tremendous depreciation in the purchasing power of every remaining dollar. You see the goldites have repealed both Gresham's law and the law of supply and demand. They're going to tackle the law of gravitation next—in fact its elimination is necessary to the success of their monetary system, for while it's in effect things can't go up while they're coming down without considerable difficulty. They have amended the law of interest, and now all those old economists who held that the purchasing power of money has absolutely nothing to do with fixing the interest rate, are dead wrong. They have "proved" in all their big papers and from every stump and the head of every beer barrel that the value of gold has fallen one-half during the past few years, because where the government formerly paid a rental of 6 per cent. for its use it now gets it for 3! This is a glorious thing and entitles them to our eternal gratitude. But don't examine it too closely—never look a gift-horse in the mouth. Just take the good the gods provide and hold your peace. Should a man ask you if a farmer pays 6 bushels per acre rent when wheat is worth a dollar, and but 3 bushels per acre when it is 50 cents, shoot him on the spot; he's a red-flagger, an enemy of vested rights and a dangerous crank. Ten-to-one he's got a dynamite bomb in one coat-tail pocket and a copy of the Iconoclast in the other. Don't read anything but gold-bug literature, don't think, don't disagree with the powers that be. Just see what happened to Jesus for questioning the supernal wisdom of the money-changers of Jerusalem!

A PLAGUE OF POETS.

Machine-Made Melody.

In days of old it was supposed that poets were born, not made, and bright indeed was that century considered which could boast of more than one true son of song; but in this progressive age we easily circumvent niggard nature. When chemists can manufacture eggs, and even hatch 'em without the aid of hens, can we wonder that bards are as thick as birds? Surely it were as easy to produce a poet as a pullet —easier, perhaps, since Pindars and Petrarchs wear no plumes. Plato defines man as a two-legged animal *sans* feathers; hence we may infer that our modern crop of warblers are the 'prentice work of science—the product of the incubator ere curious ornithologists discovered what to add to the artificial ovum to bring forth the full-pinioned bird.

Silas Wegg's unlucky habit of "dropping into poetry" threatens to become a pandemic disease. Every frog-pond is now a Pierian spring; the woods are literally aflame with the divine afflatus; the Muses Nine have multiplied as did Jacob's fecund seed in ancient Mizriam, while every sand-dune hath become a Parnassus, every mole-hill a Helicon. The cities swarm with Meistersingers, the towns are overrun with Troubadours, each hamlet boasts its jay Jongleur, while from Texas ranch and Yankee hedge-row the "poet lariat" or Della-Cruscan rhymster blithely carols his roundelay. Every biped, with feathers or without, is doing the bulbul act—piercing its panting brisket in the Gardens of Gul and weeping melodious tears. No modern magazine is considered complete without a hand-me-down "poem" or two about nothing in particular; Jenny Wrens twitter in the cross-roads press; true hearts bleed in an endless procession of books, while half-fledged Homers pour their divine harmony in gushing torrents adown the column rules of the great diurnals. Poetry, poetry everywhere! Youth's shrill treble and manhood's lusty roar mingling with the cracked bassoon of age—the "sweet girl graduate" and shriveled gran'dame, the rough plow-boy and sleek sybarite all twanging the Apollonic harp, tuning the Pandean pipes and pouring forth their quivering souls in song! Not a withered leaf can be blown adown the wynd or porker squeal aneath the garden gate; not a measly brat can creep into the world or old rooter make his exit, but some poet half consumed with Promethean fire bursts his tether and takes a rhythmic dog-fall out of his mother tongue! I think the *Poetische Trichter*—or Poetical Funnel—manufactured at Nurnberg some two centuries since, and "professing within six hours to pour in the whole essence of this difficult art into the most unfurnished head," must have been perfected and brought into common use in this country:

> "Hence bards, like Proteus, long in vain tied down,
> Escape in monsters and amaze the town."

Poets? We've got 'em; got 'em in flocks, swarms, droves and shoals—got 'em to burn, perhaps. The population of America is 73 million people—72 million poets, the rest Populists. The Homeric era and Elizabethan age have become mere grease spots on the robe of the gods. Then man toiled and prayed thro' long years to bring some single poem to perfection; and when he had wrought his life into it—a master-mind its warp, an all-embracing heart its woof—he cast it forth into the mighty sea of Time and died unknown; but in succeeding ages the flickering torch which he had nourished thro' the laborious night that was his day, kindled from altar to altar until a radiance as of heaven beat upon the world—a celestial search-light seeking out the nameless grave of a god! Now poems are manufactured to order while you wait. Drop a nickel in the slot and get a tune—sonnet, ode or elegy. Great is science! Of all labor-saving inventions the Poetical Funnel is certainly *facile princeps*. Yet there be pessimists who insist that we are making no progress! No progress indeed! Why, we have donned seven-league boots and are pounding up the plank turnpike like the devil beating tanbark. See with what difficulty Alfred Austin squeezes his titanic form into the overcoat once occupied by Alfred Tennyson. Observe how Algernon Charles Swinburne improves upon the awkward scrawl of Pope. Note how the Rileys and Stantons are making Horace tired, while the Wilcoxes and Chanlers, with their animalistic oestruation, knock "burning Sappho" off her perch. And there's the Emely Evans Hendricks and Bessie Campbell Galbraiths, the James Clarence Harveys and Sydney Thompson Dobells, and a hundred others striving to gild three-story names with immortal glory. And there's Dobson, the greatest of the decadents—Austin Dobson! No wonder the muses have deserted their ancient haunts and learned that medley of antilogies known as the English tongue. With apologies to Byron:

> Oh Austin Dobson!—Phoebus! what a name
> To fill the speaking trump of future fame!

Still the horrid thought will intrude itself that all living twangers of the lyre would be much better employed manipulating the humble but useful washboard, or trailing the meek-eyed mule thro' the lowly cotton-patch. I am no complaining preterist; I do not hold, as do some, that the age of true poesy is forever past—that science is a pitiless Car of Jaganath beneath which the poetic muse must perish. Promethean fire should burn brighter in the brain of Wisdom than in the breast of Barbarism. True, the Delphic Oracle hath long gone silent and Dodona's Oaks ceased whispering strange secrets to credulous souls. Chaste Dian's lips will never more touch those of sleeping Endymion, nor

Aurora's blushing charms grace aged Tithonus' bed. Gone are all the Gods from High Olympus,

> "the Spirits of the Hills
> With all their dewy hair blown back like flame,"

appeal no more to the wondering minds of men. These were but crude conceits of the world's infancy, the coat of many colors with which it clothed its ignorance. Science, "creeping on from point to point," displays even greater wonders than the naiads and nereids, the gorgons gray and chimeras dire that recede before her lamp; and until Wonder, Reverence and Ambition forsake the human heart and Love and Beauty perish from the earth, true poesy cannot pass. The more exalted the singer, the purer his song. If it be objected that never in modern days has the poetic muse mounted with so strong a wing as in those far years when Rome indeed was crowned with grandeur and Greece with glory, yet science lay wrapt in swaddling clothes, we answer that Prose, too, suffers by comparison with the days that are dead, while Art blushes for her own decadence and Eloquence stands dumb. Despite our boasts that we are heirs "of all the ages and foremost in the files of time," no modern nation has reached those intellectual heights trod by the Hellenes when the noblest poesy, since the hymning of the morning stars, came virgin from the harp. Modern is no superior to ancient civilization—it has simply developed differently. In the province of Utilitaria we stand the acknowledged superiors of all preceding ages; but in all that pertains to the spiritual life of man we turn instinctively to the crumbling tombs that mark the grandeur that was Rome and the glory that was Greece. Aristotle and Plato, Phidias and Praxiteles, Homer and Demosthenes—our masters have been dust and ashes so long that their very graves are forgotten; yet we assume that the weight of our superior wisdom will break the muse's wing!

It simply happens, as indeed it has happened so often before—for in five thousand years less than a score of true bards have been born—that the poets are all dead. In such interregnums the petty versifiers tune their paltry pipes. When the sun has set the stars peep forth; but when the day-god resumes his throne these flickering points "pale their ineffectual fires." When the lion is dead in his lair indifferent beasts do range abroad. When genius departs from earth Mediocrity and Stupidity hold high carnival.

The mawkish sentimentalists are weeping "tears, idle

tears" and know not what they mean—and little the great world cares. People really suffering for pills imagine themselves pregnant with poems—mistake a torpid liver for the divine afflatus. Those who couldn't beat time on a bass drum to a bull-frog duet, bestride a cock-horse or old gray goose as Pegasus and soar at the sun, only to be pitched headlong into Icarian seas. If this old world has one real live poet concealed about her person, he must be some "mute inglorious Milton." To paraphrase Epictetus, Show him to me; by the gods! fain would I see a poet!

> "Behold! in various throngs the scribbling crew,
> For notice eager, pass in long review;
> Sonnets on sonnets crowd, and ode on ode,
> And tales or terror jostle on the road."

Thus wrote Bryon of the poetasters of his time. When it is remembered that in the "scribbling crew" he placed Tom Moore, Walter Scott and Southey, can I be blamed for protesting against the doggerel of the Dobsons and Dobells of our day? Pope was not so exacting. He spared the faintest gleam of genius, the smallest floweret that lifted its face to greet the sun, but "damned to everlasting fame" the devotees of Dullness:

> "Some strain in rhyme; the muses, on their racks,
> Scream like the winding of ten thousand jacks;
> Some, free from rhyme or reason, rule or check,
> Break Priscian's head and Pegasus's neck."

Still, not all the verses ground out in this twilight of poesy are to be condemned. I have no desire to remove Marsyas' pelt because he does not play as sweetly as Apollo. Here and there is heard a note, not of the strongest or purest, yet not altogether unpleasing. James Whitcomb Riley gives forth an occasional gleam, as of fox-fire or a valetudinarian glow-worm, casting a faint radiance into the general gloom. His muse never carries him high, which is fortunate, as she has an unhappy trick of dropping him, and he falls quite as frequently into Serbonian bogs as upon odorous banks where the wild thyme grows. When President Harrison's wife died, Riley spilled a few soul-sobs over the dear departed which transformed the general gloom into hilarious gladness. Even the stricken husband was so pleased that the loved and lost was insensible to the splayfooted nenina of the Hoosier numbskull that he well-nigh forgot to weep. He realized that the Lord tempers the wind to the shorn lamb, and in a few months was striving manfully to found another family. Father Ryan, the poet-priest, has somewhat of the sweetness of Tom Moore, greatest of Irish bards, the truest singer but scarce the noblest poet of his time. One indispensable pre-requisite of the poet Father Ryan had—the love which never dies. Despite his sturdy Americanism, the Emerald Isle was never forgotten.

> "Yes, give me the land where the ruins are spread,
> And the living tread light o'er the hearts of the dead."

Thus sang Father Ryan. Like Elaine, sweetly could he make and sing. We would not care to spare all the poetic fragments left us by Eugene Field. They are fragile flowerets, 'tis true, the corolla mere flakes of foam; but oft the ovary is a drop of blood which every heart feels that it has furnished. There is a dash of genius in the work of Paul Verlaine, who so lately followed Field into the shadows, behind the mystic veil, leaving the muse of *la belle France* widowed like those of England and America when Tennyson and Longfellow laid down the cross to take up the crown. Verlaine was a glorious vagabond, a celestial tramp, a wild son of Bohemia—sometimes an angel of light, too often a goblin damned; but however crass or criminal his surroundings, he sang from the heart, often wisely, always well! and when amid grime and grisettes, among debaucheries terminating behind prison-bars his voice was hushed by the grim Destroyer, Dullness extended her drowsy sceptre over a weary world. Of those left to us, on either side of old ocean, none have any message to the sons of men. They are poetasters and pretenders all, who are striving to steal Promethean fire, not to illumine a world, but to boil a pot. They grind out profitless rhyme as a mill does meal, their finical manner harmonizing well with their worthless matter. They want the art to conceal their art. The public hears the creaking pulleys, as with monster derrick-crane they hoist unconsidered trifles out of the great inane, the labored breathing of their asthmatic muse as she hammers the diotomic raw material into Hudibrastic verse, where

> "Maggots half-formed in rhyme exactly meet
> And learn to crawl upon poetic feet."

What is poetry? Ask me rather to define Love's soft desire, Ambition's mad'ning flame, or the fierce ecstasy that beats in manhood's heart of oak when trumpets are blown for war. The veriest tyro can tell you what poetry is not; the world's wisest may well stammer when asked to say what it is. Despite the critics, there are no rules by which it can be measured, any more than there be rules by which the charm of woman may be defined. Some say that poetry is truth. Perhaps; but all truth is not poetry, else were the law of gravitation the grandest of epics. Who are, or say rather, who were the poets? Not every man who versifies, else were a rhyming dictionary and plodding patience sufficient to transform a Dempster into a Pope. A Pope say you? Was Pope then a poet? Nay, 'tis not my province to settle a controversy that has raged for near two centuries among the critics. Philosopher he certainly was, and his rhyme as smooth as oil upon a summer sea. Strange as it may appear, when the controversy regarding his right to the bays was raging most bitterly, classical scholars were vigorously debating whether in his translation of the Iliad, he had improved on Homer! I submit that a man who was strongly suspected of bettering the verse of Chios' immortal bard, may well pass for a poet in a land where Alfred Austin tunes the laureate lyre. Still, many a time I've wished that Pope had eschewed all petty tricks of the versifier and delivered his message in rugged prose. His ideas are hewn and hacked to fit a procrustean bed of rhyme, when they should have been given us, like those of crabbed old Carlyle, in all their massy strength. No man should write poetry who is capable of expressing himself in prose. The latter is the towering oak, the former but the ornamental vine, and beautiful indeed must it be to have a valid excuse for existence. Still, where prose ends and poetry begins is a disputed point. There is more true poetry in Ingersoll's oration at his brother's grave than in Pope's "Essay on Man," Longfellow's "Evangeline" and Byron's "Childe Harold" all combined. It sweeps with one master stroke every heart-string, stirs to its profoundest depths that lake of tears which is the true heart's Acheron and the trifler's Lethe. There is no garish tinsel, no labored rhyme to clothe the simple scene with dramatic gauds. There lies the corpse, a tragedy in itself as grandly pitiful as Aeschylus ever pictured; here stands the dead man's alter ego, battling like a giant with his despair, biting back the sobs that fain would burst the bonds of his stern philosophy—grasping despite himself at a forlorn perhaps—at what

Reason, that god of his idolatry, has branded as the shadow of a shade. In this, his hour of supreme agony, he seeks with straining eyes to discern that Star of Hope which he has denied, and listens for the fl tter of that Wing he has denounced as folly. A few t ken words, the dead is consigned to its mother dust, the living is led away, and the grandest elegy ever said or sung has passed into the treasure-house of history, a poetic gem that will shine ever on and on,

> "As long as the heart knows passion,
> As long as life has woes."

Poe declared forty years ago that Alfred Tennyson, then but upon the threshold of his fame, was the greatest poet of all the ages. But was Poe a competent critic? I think not—else he would have burned four-fifths of his own effusions. The public is accustomed to regard this madcap as an incantation of Orpheus or Apollo. There is a wild charm about some of his work—a kind of mania a potu fury; but at the risk of being called an Ishmaelite by the faddists and cast into the outer darkness of Philistia, I do protest that Edgar Allen Poe earned for himself no place even among the minor poets. "The Raven," his best production, might have been written by almost any reporter, if comfortably full of wienerwurst and dollar-a-bottle wine. Tennyson, like Moore and Burns, was a genuine bard. The shadow of his muse's wings falls not on Parnassus' lofty brow; but some of his songs, like Longfellow's "Bridge," sink into the soul as softly as aromatic dews into the parched plain. We cannot imagine Tennyson, Moore or Burns writing prose. They "lisped in numbers and the numbers came." They appear to have thought in verse, hence they spoke as those "to the manner born." They constitute the poetic trinity of the English-speaking world. People read them, while they only talk of Byron and Milton, Dante and Homer. The first are welcome guests at the fireside; the latter hang sombre in the heavens like dark portents of Fate. But I'm glad Dante and Milton wrote—they gave artists a chance to cultivate their morbidity and at the same time earn a meal. Tennyson is the Sir Galahad of poets. His song, while seldom cold, is ever chaste as ice. To turn from Byron to Tennyson is like passing from a drunken revel with *nymphs du pave* into the society of vestal virgins. There is neither "the lilies and languors of virtue" nor "the roses and raptures of vice;" but a wholesome human nature, the fragrance of the dew-washed fields, the music of falling waters—a rolling world circled by "the star-domed city of God." Moore is a Troubadour of ye olden time, who sweeps with a free hand

"The harp that once through Tara's halls,"

or touches with equal felicity the gay guitar beneath the windows of "Gades' soft desiring train." Tennyson sometimes becomes didactic, but Moore is content to ravish us with his melody. Wine, Woman and Song is his poetic triune, and he leaves it to the dull plodder of prose to appeal to the understanding, while he plays at will on all the passions.

P. S.—Since the above was put in type I have discovered that "Mr." Paul Lawrence Dunbar, whose verse is commended by William Dean Howells and "has found frequent admission into leading American magazines," is a young coon, black as the hinges of Hades, and, "until recently, elevator boy at Dayton, O." I, therefore, desire to retract all the naughty things I have said about the magazine poets of the present day. They may all be nigger elevator boys or colored cooks, and, if so, deserving of kindly encouragement rather than adverse criticism. Carlyle tells us that it is not wonderful that a dog walks but indifferently on its hind legs, the wonder being that it can be taught to so walk at all. It is not wonderful that pickaninnies cannot write poetry—the wonder being that they can make rhymes which even the patrons of Harper's will read. I trust that the busy versifiers will forgive me for having inadvertently mistaken them for po' white trash. A British sovereign once advised a gentleman of his court to "leave the making of verses to little Mr. Pope;" but it had not occurred to me that poetry might become a side-line for colored servants. I presume that bootblacks will soon be writing blank verse for Mr. Howells, barbers mixing lyrics with their lather, and old "aunties" cease repining for the good times "befo' d' wah" and turn an honest penny by penciling poems of passion on cold pancakes. Verily, "the world do move." It simply has to—William Dean Howells is behind it.

SOME MILLIONAIRE MENDICANTS.

"Poor and content is rich, and rich enough:"

And wealth without content were poverty indeed. "The boast of heraldry, the pomp of power," cannot make that man a prince whom nature intended for a peon, nor all the gold of Ophir and of Ind revoke the fiat of the Fates that he shall tread life's path in poverty and pain.

Poverty? I have seen millionaires whose poverty beggars might pity, and men without a dollar in the world whose wealth an emperor might envy.

Wealth? What is it but content? but absence of sorrow, of suffering? Is that man wealthy who has heaps of gold but lacks health? Who possesses princely estates but whose life is one long agony? In whose ears that sorrowfullest of threnodies, "nevermore," is ever sounding like a funeral knell? Whose soul is sick with a sorrow no sweet psychiatry can cure? Gold?

"Can gold calm passion, or make reason thine?
Can we dig peace or wisdom from the mine?"

Gold make wealthy those whose hearts have been torn by the dread bolts of destiny? Can a man be wealthy upon whose life there ever rests the shadow of a crime? Rich, and his dearest treasure but a pitiful handful of dust; his every breath a stifled sob, his every heart-beat a dull, dead agony—the very perfume gone from the flowers, the sunrise robbed of its glory, music of its melody and life of its object. Gold? Riches? Dead sea fruit!

Wealth? Who is wealthy? Was it Maecenas in his marble banquet hall, drunk with flattery and Falernian wine; or Horace, drinking from the rippling spring on his little farm and flinging priceless jewels in a shower over generations yet to be?

Riches? The simple cottager who this day divides his crust with his little family; who has never tried with faltering lips and bursting heart to repeat, "The Lord gave, and the Lord hath taken away, blessed be the name of the Lord;" who has health and strength and can look the whole world in the face without a blush; who is not racked with the fever fangs of fell ambition, but content with his lot, "is rich and rich enough." Many whose signatures are a power among the money changers would give all their possessions to purchase a tithe of his peace; many whose names are blazoned in the world's intellectual hierarchy would gladly barter the laurel wreath to buy his content; many a proud potentate repines that God did not so ordain his lot!

Gold! What will it purchase but food and raiment, more or less fine, lip-service and vain show? It cannot buy health or happiness; it cannot put brains in the head of the fool or assure length of days; it cannot purchase the love of woman or the friendship of man; it cannot bring back the loved and lost; it has no purchasing power at the Throne of Grace. Far other coin is current there.

The poor? A man poor because as he passes swiftly through life—"like a bird flying through a lighted room, between the night and the night"—he does not fill both hands with yellow dross and hold it for a moment? Why a man clothed in rags, eating rude fare and sleeping on the cold bosom of our common mother, may be richer far than Peru's primeval kings!

Poorest are they who suffer most; richest those who in this brief life find most of sunshine, least of shadow. Joy and love, honor and sweet content are riches, more precious than pearls, greater than fine gold; without these were poverty indeed. Yes, "God pity the poor!"

CHURCH AND STAGE.

The phenomenal success of Wilson Barrett's religio-libidinous drama, "The Sign of the Cross," seems destined to have a far-reaching effect. It may even result in a complete transposition of the church and stage, assigning to the first the amusement of the worldly, consecrating the latter to divine worship. Since this now famous play inoculated London with the camp-meeting jerks, quite a number of Biblical dramas have been announced; and, as might have been expected, they revolve around the most disreputable female characters to be found in Holy Writ. Blasphemy masquerading as religion is made the excuse for suggestions of bawdry that might put even the *fin de siecle* French school to shame. Sarah Bernhardt is to appear in the title-role of "Mary Magdalene," while Mrs. Potter, the soiled society dove who is "elevating the stage" with her sexual neurasthenia, has purchased "Joseph of Canaan," and will play Potiphar's wife to the immaculate he-virgin of Kyrle Bellew! One would expect this announcement to put addled eggs, last year's cabbages and has-been cats at a premium— that these mimetic back-number bawds, who have dragged upon the stage all the putrescence of dramatic degenerates and now propose to make the Bible a stalking horse for even more flagrant harlotry, would be driven from the boards in disgust; but if present indications count for anything, they will be welcomed by the ultra religious element with open arms. Thus far all the protests against this prostitution of the Book of Books to advertise the inherent animalism of the faded beauties of the foot-lights and fill the box-office with boodle—this sugar-coating with pseudo-sanctification of illicit oestruation—have come from so-called sinners.

If the remarkable craze of church communicants over "The Sign of the Cross" be an earnest of the manner in which "Mary Magdalen" and "Joseph of Canaan" will be received, then indeed is the stage to be revolutionized—if not "reformed!" We have a large contingent of semi-conscious hypocrites who damn the stage with all the virulence of a jealous man denouncing another's amours, yet who want but the shadow of an excuse to become conspicuous at the play. The Biblical drama, so-called, affords them a pretext—enables them to urge that the theatre has, for the nonce, become a kind of post-graduate Sunday-school, which it is their sacred duty as professing Christians to attend; and thus far they have fairly fallen over each other in availing themselves of the coveted oportunity to revel in moral rottenness exploited in the name of religion! These are the people who call Voltaire a vulgarian, while wallowing in Sam Jones' open-sewer sermons and Parkhurst's tenderloin escapades. Their stomachs will stand anything if it but have a religious trade-mark blown in the bottle, while "vulgar" and "blasphemous" constitute their idea of argument and serve to conceal their ignorance.

Measles, la grippe, nor even lice in a nigger school propagate so fast as a "fad;" hence by the end of the century we may expect to see the churches deserted by their present habitues and the temples of Thespis solemnly dedicated to the worship of the Deity, with the Bellews, Rices and Corbetts as high-priests, the Bernhardts, Potters and Russells in the role of the Vestal virgins! It need not surprise us if Miriam yet does the skirt-dance to the sound of timbrels in a free-and-easy, and the gibbous Lillian introduces the Song of Solomon in "An American Beauty." If anybody can sing the Canticles so that 'twill not only "catch the crowd," but wear down the rugged edges of religion and fill its paths with green-room plaisance, that songstress is the multitudinously married and ebulliently beautiful queen of opera-bouffe. Having begun to explore the Bible for startling plots that will permit of all kinds of "specialties," where will the enterprising playwrights pause? Are we foredoomed to have "The Creation" in six acts, with Kyrle Bellew speaking the Cosmos into existence, making man of mud and evolving Mrs. Potter from a spare-rib of our Edenic ancestor? Will Ed. Rice favor us with a realistic presentation of "The Judgment Day"—with epilogue by Ingersoll? Just think what a howling "hit" the tank-show manager could make with "The Deluge"—the dead in *puris naturalibus,* a la Gustave Dore! "Adam and Eve" would afford living picture possibilities not yet dreamed of by the most progressive managers; "David and Bath-Sheba," with Fanny Davenport in the bath-tub act, would doubtless do much to popularize Biblical research; while "Judah and Tamar" contains dramatic climaxes calculated to convince even an agnostic that religion is a good thing and induce him to push it along.

As the melodramatic style of worship spreads, the occupation of those conservative ministers who neglect to adapt themselves to the new conditions, but insist on preaching Christ and Him crucified, will pass; but the sensation monger, like the famous Vicar of Bray, will not be easily ousted. If they lose their old congregations, they can be depended upon to make frantic bids for new ones—may even occupy the field abandoned by the stage and do a song-and-dance in the pulpit, or organize their choirs into burlesque ballets and regale us with "Black Crook," "The Devil's Auction" and "An Adamless Eden." Bishop Newman as a melodramatic star and Kiralfy making the sun stand still for the edification of a Sunday-School, Thos. Dixon as Iago and Jim Corbett swiping out the Philistines with his own jaw-bone, were not so great a transposition as many ill-informed people might suppose. The stage has long been weaving a small amount of religion into its performances as a sop to the moral Cerberus, while many church choirs and pulpiteers manifest a decided penchant for opera-bouffe. Dramatic companies "on their uppers" have yet considerable to learn from impecunious churches in the matter of raising of money, known in the parlance of the "profesh" as angling for angels. While the "shifty" manager of a party of barn-stormers struggles in vain to get his "props" out of a dollar-a-day hotel, the country preacher pulls a bankrupt church from the subsequent end of a forty-foot hole without putting his hand in his purse. From the *Arkansas Methodist* I learn that during the present year American churches resorted to the following novel expedients to corral the long-green "for the Glory of God": "Black-faced minstrel performances by young ladies; kissing matches (a la Olga Nethersole, I presume); pretty feet exhibitions; pantomime of 'Cupid in the Kitchen;' trapeze performances and fencing by young ladies in very abbreviated costume." Our contemporary overlooked the old maids' auction at Lampasas, Tex., and the sale of feminine legs to the highest bidder so successfully conducted by the Epworth Leaguers at Suffern, N. Y. Clearly the church hasn't far to go to fill the hiatus threatened in the amusement world by the sanctification of the stage. Quite a number of fashionable choirs could, at a moment's notice, furnish women who have attained sufficient unsavory notoriety to make them available as Cleopatras and Camilles.

I have not been favored with an acting copy of "Mary Magdalen," but hope the "divine Sarah" has sufficient conception of the eternal fitness of things to place the finale of the play previous to the poor woman's repentance. Sarah in the role of a devout penitent would bankrupt the imagination of an average audience. It is rumored, however, that the drama will be carried to its historical conclusion —that this Parisian *fille de joie* will actually anoint the feet of an imitation Jesus with the alabaster box of ointment, bathe them with stage tears and give them massage treatment with her own fair hands and boughten hair! I trust that this is a mistake; or if it be not, that she will reserve the sacrilegious scene for her own beloved Paree, instead of bringing it hither to wreck what little reverence yet remains in this, the home of Smart Alecism, the Gibraltar of Infidelity. Religion in this utilitarian land is at best a spider's web o'erhanging a black abyss, a flimsy gossamer beneath which yawns the noisome depths of Unbelief. The shock of seeing a woman notoriously immoral, even at an age when the hey-dey in the blood is tame and waits upon the judgment, slobbering over some half-baked guy personating the Man of Galilee, and in accents wild beseeching his forgiveness—for a box-office guarantee—might prove more disastrous than the melodious sophistry of a thousand Ingersolls.

I am curious to note the effect when "Joseph of Canaan" is first presented to an American audience—with Kyrle Bellew playing sweet innocence to Potsie's desiring Egyptian dame. The sensual appeal will be in perfect keeping with her character; but when Kyrle turns a deaf ear to the siren's song and tears his clothes in a frantic effort to escape the female rape-fiend, to thwart her "hellish design," will the audience be, as we preachers say, "particularly edified?" Will the scene have the same effect on the congregation as an old-time camp-meeting sermon? Will it cause the sisters to shout and the brethren to confess their sins? Will the finale of the play be an appropriate time to hold an "experience meeting?" Will even a fat policeman astride the neck of each individual gallery god be able to hold 'em down?

My bump of reverence is not so large as to wear out the crown of my hat; still I would be pleased to see such cattle as Bernhardt and Potter let the Bible severely alone—at least refrain from making it an excuse for flaunting their own foulness in the public's face under the specious pretext of making religion popular. Christianity needs no aid from Magdalens who have not reformed and Dame Potiphars who have not been deified. There is a valid excuse for the appearance in Holy Writ of Joseph's temptation and " a woman of the city who was a sinner;" but none for dragging upon the stage the long forgotten and forgiven *liaisons* of Mary Magdalen, or making a peep-show of Madam Potiphar's nymphomania. I have hitherto held that the story of Joseph's continence was a priestly fiction like those of Adonis and Siddartha, intended to portray that ideal purity toward which the passion-cursed sons of men should ever strive with such strength as they can, such success as they may; but it had not occurred to me that a bag of superannuated bones and penciled eye-brows, ghastly enameled shoulders and pendulous udders might be the prototype of Cleopatra. If the lady in the case resembled Potsie, the self-restraint of the young man was in nowise remarkable. We can only be certain that he was somewhat better than Kyrle Bellew. Under such distressing circumstances Joseph was justified in crying for his mommer, or even in demanding police protection. The only part of the story that staggers belief is that he stopped running before clear out of the country.

The phenomenal success of books and plays having a religious warp and a sensual woof goes far to confirm the theory advanced by some psychologists, that excessive religious excitement and abnormal sexualism are co-natural—that where we find the one we may reasonably expect the other. I am no more responsible for this fact, if fact it be, than for thorns upon the rose-bush or disease bacilli on the lips of beauty. Nor do I cite it here to cast discredit upon any religious creed or cult, but rather to emphasize a theory I have oft advanced—that what frequently passes for religious fervor is but a disturbance of the mental equipoise, or derangement of the nervous system, produced by too "powerful" preaching—that partisan politics and religious "revivals" may cause the same complaint. "The Sign of the Cross," "Joseph of Canaan" and "Mary Magdalen" constitute the natural sequence of sensational sermons. The latter may be compared to a stimulant, of which the more one drinks, the more he desires. Sacrilegious dramas and novels "spiked" with religion to disguise a sea of erotic slush, follow the slumming sermon and whoopla evangelist as naturally as straight corn-juice takes the place of the milder alcoholic tipple. A depraved appetite, whether mental or physical, seeks ever a stronger excitant. Holy zeal, so-called, becomes so ardent that the devotees are content with lurid descriptions of a suffering Savior, but long to see him and feast their eyes upon his agony; hence the "Passion Play."

Worship of the Celestial Powers is human love directed to the unseen, and human love at best is but a refinement of brute passion; hence lust and religion spring from the same source as surely as the fragrant jasmine bud and noxious jimson bloom are products of the same soil. To deny this were to quarrel with the law of evolution; so complain not of me, but of the philomaths and philosophers. Human love in all its ramifications, from lowest to highest, lives in imagination. When the mind is rendered morbid by religion, it is simply a degeneration of the master passion—love has a tendency to revert to first principles; and thus we not infrequently find united in the same person the religious fanatic and moral pervert. On this hypothesis only can we account for the tens of thousands of praying prostitutes—women who morn and night petition the Throne of Grace with no desire to be other than as they are. It may explain why so many women in the respectable walks of life are at once deeply religious and morally corrupt—will take grievous offense at a kindly criticism of their faith while keeping an assignation. It may account for the remarkable fact that a greater proportion of preachers than of any other professional class are in prison for sexual sins, as well as the equally surprising truth that the church regards the honest and upright heretic with more horror than it does the professed Christian who has tripped on the Seventh Commandment. Of course those afflicted with what we may call incurable religiosity will assume that this article is intended to cast discredit upon the "Cloth" and insult the Church of Christ. Far otherwise; it is simply a red light hung out to enable the church to see whither it is drifting upon the broad tide of a mind-wrecking, morality-perverting, nerve and soul destroying sensationalism. *Voila tout.*

LOOKING BACKWARD.

When it comes to "Looking Backward," Bellamy isn't in it a little bit with Prof. Herman V. Hilprecht. The retrospective glance of the latter covers a period of at least 11,000 years; and what is of infinitely more importance, it is that of a learned paleologist instead of a sensation-mongering empiric. The Professor has succeeded in lifting a corner of that black veil which hangs between the prehistoric and the present, in affording us a fleeting glimpse of our fellow man as he appeared long ages before the birth of Abraham. He has demonstrated that man has been a civilized animal much longer than is popularly supposed—that at least 5,000 years before the supposed advent of Adam he not only lived sociably in cities and had gods and kings, but was able to read and write! For eight years past the Professor and his co-laborers, under the patronage of the University of Pennsylvania, have been carrying on their explorations. The site of Nippur, the ancient capital of Kengi, later known as Babylonia, is the scene of their labors. Hitherto Nippur has been supposed to have been the world's oldest city; but the excavations made not only prove that it rose upon the ruins of others, but affords some knowledge of a long line of kings who lived so long ago that their very names were forgotten before the flight of the Israelites from Egypt, or even the building of the Tower of Babel.

> "What is the story of this buried past?
> Were all its doors flung wide,
>   For us to search its rooms?
> And we to see the race, from first to last,
> And how they lived and died."

Sargon is the most ancient Chaldean monarch mentioned in the Bible, and hitherto archaeologists have agreed that he was a fiction; but the Professor has not only proven that he had a habitation as well as a name, but has catalogued some thirty of his predecessors. Science has amply demonstrated the existence of man upon the earth long before the psychozoic era of the Biblical cosmogony; but Prof. Hilprecht is the first to demonstrate the high antiquity of his civilization. To the average man this will appear neither more interesting nor profitable than a two-headed calf or petrified corpse; but to the philosophic mind it affords much food for reflection. We have presumed that we could trace the history of man back to the time when he began to practice the art of writing, as distinguished from the transference of thought by crude pictorials—that our prehistoric progenitor was simply a savage. It now appears that people may build indestructible temples, and kings and priests write intelligently on imperishable material, and the nation be as utterly forgotten as tho' it had never existed. With these facts in mind, it were curious to speculate on what the world 11,000 years hence will know of our now famous men—such, for instance, as Cleveland and McKinley! What will the historian of that far-away time have to say of Mark Hanna? Printing has been called "the art preservative;" but is it? Suppose the priests of Bel—that deity who antedates by so many centuries the Jewish Jehovah—had committed the history of their temples to "cold type" instead of graving it upon sacred vases: Would Prof. Hilprecht and other Assyriologists be deciphering it to-day? Printing has substituted flimsy paper for parchment just as the pen substituted parchment for waxen tablets, as the stylus substituted the latter for the far more enduring leaflet of torrified clay. Imagine the effect of 11,000 years upon a modern library! Where will the archaeologists of the year 12,896 turn for the history of our time—where search for those "few immortal names that were not born to die?" Oral transmission of historic data, such as prevails among savages, such as prevailed among the Hellenes in the age of Homer, has been supplanted by the press. Long before Macaulay's New Zealander stands on a broken arch of London bridge to sketch the ruins of St. Paul's, every book now extant will have perished. Will they be continuously reproduced, and thus, like the human race itself, run ever on? *Quien sabe?* Eras of barbarism have overtaken civilizations as pretentious as our own—intellectual nights in which the patiently acquired learning of ages was lost. Petrifaction as in China, retrogression begotten of luxury as in Athens, submersion beneath an avalanche of human debris as in Rome, ignorance-breeding despoliation as in Ireland—these be the lions in the path of civilization. No race or nation of which we have any record has avoided a recrudescence of barbarism for an hundred generations. A few centuries of our wasting climate obliterates inscriptions on brass and wrecks the proudest monuments of marble. The recently imported Egyptian obelisk, which stood for ages on Nilus' plain, is already falling into ruins. We can scarce decipher the deep-cut epitaphs of the Pilgrim Fathers. The mansion of the sire is uninhabitable for the son. The history of McKinley's promised era of "Progress and Prosperity" will be written by the press reporter, that busy litterateur who has neither yesterday nor tomorrow. Some subsidized biographer may bind McKinley up in calf, and chance preserve a stray copy for some centuries—then good-bye to all his greatness! The mighty Washington has not been dead a hundred years, yet has already become—as R. G. Ingersoll informs us—"merely a steel engraving." Adams and Hancock and Franklin are paling stars, despite our printing-presses, have become little more than idle words in the school-boy's lexicon. Our proud Republic, our boasted civilization will pass, for change is the order of the universe. What records will they leave behind? What is to prevent them being as utterly forgotten as were Sargon's predecessors? Here and there the delver of far years will find the fragment of a wall, perchance an inscription carved in stone and protected by chance from the gnawing tooth of time. And from these posterity will construct for us a history in which we will appear, perhaps, as the straggling vanguard of civilization instead of heirs of all the ages. They may dig up a petrified dude and figure out that we were a species of anthropoid ape—learnedly proclaim us as "the missing link!" Suppose that by some mischance a picture of the new woman in bloomers and bestride a bike should be preserved: Would posterity accept her as its progenitor, or class her as a *lusus naturæ*—perchance an hermaphrodite? A few coins will doubtless be discovered—if the excavators avoid the Texas treasury—and triumphant Populism take it for granted that 'twas on these curious discs that our "infant industry" cut its teeth. The "In God We Trust" inscription may be regarded as a barbaric hoodoo to prevent infantile belly-ache or the evil eye, but the dollar mark will be entirely unintelligible to a people so many thousand years removed from the savage superstition of metallic money. Of course woman will have ruled the world so long that "tyrant man" will be regarded as a sun myth, and the Goddess of Liberty on our coins be mistaken for portraits of our female monarchs. Thus will Cleveland and McKinley, like Hippolyta and other amazons of old, be passed down to remote posterity in petticoats. If the electrotype from which the New York *Journal* prints its portraits of Mark Hanna should be found among the *tumuli* of Manhattan Island, it were well worth remaining alive until that time to hear the curious speculation of craniological cranks. Should the paleologists unearth the *World* building, they will find in the basement an imperishable object about the size of a bushel-basket, which will puzzle them not a little, but which his contemporaries could readily inform them was the gall-bag of Josef Phewlitzer's circulation liar. The discovery of Editor Dana's office cat nicely embalmed may get us accredited with the worship of *felis domestica* alias cream-canner, as a "judgment" for our persistent slander of the ancient Egyptians. But seriously, is it not a trifle startling to reflect of how little real importance all our feverish work and worry is, and how small a space it is ordained to occupy in the mighty epic of mankind! Here we have been fretting, fuming, and even fighting for months past to "save the country," only to learn that it will in nowise stay saved—is hastening rapidly on to the tomb of the world's history, will pass in turn thro' that gloomy sepulchre of countless nations into the great inane, the eternal void, the all-embracing night of utter nothingness! With all our patriotism and scannel-piping, our boasting and our battle-fields, our solemn Declarations and labored Constitutions, we are but constructing a house of cards.

> "The cloud-capped towers, the gorgeous palaces,
> The solemn temples, the great globe itself,
> Yea, all which it inherit, shall dissolve,
> And like this insubstantial pageant faded,
> Leave not a rack behind. We are such stuff
> As dreams are made of, and our little life
> Is rounded with a sleep."

We devote our energies to the propagation of a religion which Reason, that pitiless monarch of the mind, tells us must as inevitably pass as did those of Isis and Bel and Cybele, leaving in the earth's all-absorbing bosom only a few shattered altars and broken fanes. We are striving to win and wear the immortelles, only to be told that mighty empires have passed from the memory of mankind, and proud kings who may have ruled the world, sunk into the far depths of Time and been forgotten. We divide into classes industrial and sets social and give Pride free rein to vaunt herself, knowing that the hour will surely come when not even a Hilprecht can distinguish between the prince's ashes and the pauper's dust—can e'en so much as say, "This cold dead earth, o'er which lizards crawl and from which springs the poisonous worm and noxious weed, once lived and loved." We busy ourselves about the style of a coat or the cut of a corsage; we dispute anent our faiths and plan new follies; we struggle for wealth that we may flaunt a petty opulence in our fellows' faces and win the envy of fools— and the span of Life but three score and ten, while a thousand years are but as one tick of the horologe of Time! We quarrel about our political creeds and religious cults, as tho' it made any difference whether we wore white or yellow badges, sacrificed at the shrine of Jupiter or worshipped in the temples of Jehovah. Why so hot, little man? Look up! Thou seest that sun? 'Tis the same that shone on this debris when it was the throbbing metropolis of a world. The self-same moon that looks so peacefully down smiled on the midnight tryst in Nippur's scented groves or Babylon's hanging gardens; the same stars that now fret heaven's black vault with astral fire winked and blinked 11,000 years ago while the sandaled feet of youth, on polished cedar floors, beat out the rhythmic passion of its blood. There too were the heaven of requited love and the hell of breaking hearts; there too were women beauteous as the dawn and ambitious men, grasping with eager hands at what they fondly thought were the ever-fadeless bays; there too were crowned kings and fashion's sumptuous courts, chanting priests and tearful penitents—the same farce tragedy of Life and Death. And now an unsightly heap of rubbish marks this once bright theater in which prince and pauper each played his part— marks it, and nothing more. But the sun shines on, and the stars, and the silver moon still draws the restless wave around a rolling world. How small we are, how ephemeral, how helpless in God's great hand! Is it not strange that we do not cling, each to the others, like shipwrecked mariners riding the stormy waters on some frail raft and looking with dilating eyes into the black abyss?—that we waste our little lives in wild wars and civic strife?—that all our souls are concentrated in that one word, selfishness?—that we have time to hate? If History be Philosophy teaching by example, what lesson does Prof. Hilprecht bring us from the chronicles of those kinds who died 5,000 years before that garden was planted "eastward in Eden!"

A CRUSADE OF CALUMNY.

The brutal post-election assaults of the Republican and mugwump press on Mr. Bryan and those who followed his banner, is mournful evidence of the decadence of American manhood. Having accepted the arbitrament of the ballot, we should be accorded the "honors of war" instead of persistently Weylered. When brave men sheathe the sword the quarrel's done; to assault an opponent who is *hors du combat* bespeaks the cowardly cur. The dunghill rooster and McKinley editor are the only bipedal animals on earth contemptible enough to insult a fallen foe. During the campaign we expected to be belittled and belied by the opposition orators and editors—to be deluged with the malodor of polemical pole-cats—and were not disappointed; but what object they have in continuing their crusade of calumny after capturing the spoils, is beyond my comprehension. It must be because they are built that way—because their campaign of conquest has made them so corrupt that lying adds zest to life, so embruted that they enjoy their own bestiality. Conspicuous among the blatant jacks now vigorously flaunting their cowardly heels in the wounded lion's face is that lantern-jawed libel of God's masterpiece who is making a futile attempt to fill the editorial toga once worn by the mighty Horace Greeley. Speaking of the Bryan campaign, the New York *Tribune*—one of the hungry dogs that ever hang about Dives' door—says with ponderous gravity:

The thing was conceived in iniquity and was brought forth in sin. It had its origin in a malicious conspiracy against the honor and integrity of the Nation. It gained such monstrous growth as it employed from an assiduous culture of the basest passions of the least worthy members of the community. It has been defeated and destroyed because right is right and God is God. Its nominal head was worthy of the cause. Nominal, because the wretched, rattle-pated boy, posing in vapid vanity and mouthing resounding rottenness, was not the real leader of that league of hell. He was only a puppet in the blood-imbued hands of Altgeld the anarchist and Debs the revolutionist and other desperadoes of that stripe. But he was a willing puppet, Bryan was, willing and eager. Not one of his masters was more apt than he at lies and forgeries and blasphemies and all the nameless iniquities of that campaign against the Ten Commandments. He goes down with the cause, and must abide with it in the history of infamy. He had less provocation than Benedict Arnold, less intellectual force than Aaron Burr, less manliness and courage than Jefferson Davis. He was the rival of them all in deliberate wickedness and treason to the republic. His name belongs with theirs, neither the most brilliant nor the most hateful in the list. Good riddance to it all, to conspiracy and conspirators, and to the foul menace of repudiation and anarchy against the honor and life of the republic.

There is much more of it; but my readers will doubtless find the foregoing amply sufficient. It is offered as a fair sample of the impudent post-election utterances of the McKinley organs. Thousands of columns of that kind of slop have been spewed forth by editors posing as "public educators," and whose bellies are still plethoric with bile. It provokes the contemptuous pity rather than excites the anger of intelligent people. It is impossible for such foul-mouthed blackguards to insult well-bred American sovereigns; still it is well to understand with what kind of cattle we have to deal, that we may waste no courtesy upon them in the next campaign. Such utterances prove conclusively that the consideration shown them by Mr. Bryan was a mistake—that " 'tis a waste of lather to shave an ass." In treating his opponents with Chesterfieldian courtesy and assuming that they were patriots honestly holding erroneous opinions, he was casting pearls before creatures whom it were fulsome flattery to characterize as swine. By employing legitimate argument he provoked their unappeasable anger, and the further they get from the election the greater their fury. In appealing to their honor and understanding, he addressed himself to the non-extant. Perhaps, after all, Mr. Bryan was too inexperienced for the presidency. He ingenuously judged his opponents by himself—supposed them honorable when they were really infamous. He could not comprehend that courtesy was utterly wasted on even the most contemptible of those unclean creatures called into being by the inscrutable wisdom of God. It appeared to him impossible that editors like Reid and Watterson, Belo and Pulitzer, while posing as tribunes of the people, could be corrupt to the heart's core—could be vulgar as buzzards and vicious as bulls. And so he appealed to the reason of the people and ignored the coarse insults of the opposition—refused to sling slime with the lepidosauria, to fight the devil with fire. He bore himself in battle with all the gracious courtesy of an Arthurian knight; and, while realizing that he had been o'erthrown by fraud—had been struck in the back with a golden dagger by base conspirators—accepted the adverse decision without complaint and left the lists with clean hands, carrying with him the love and admiration of all capable of appreciating creation's lords. The champion of a party with an empty treasury and basely deserted in its hour of peril by those whom it had long delighted to honor; handicapped by a malevolent traitor-breeding administration and opposed by the tremendous resources of a money power as destitute of conscience as of patriotism—such was the trying position in which Mr. Bryan was suddenly placed. The battle which he waged against these overwhelming odds will pass into history as the mightiest struggle made by one man for human rights since Rienzi contended single-handed with the gilded robbers of Rome. Self-poised as Washington, eloquent as Webster, courageous as Jackson, honest as Lincoln, and the equal of a thousand McKinleys in intellect— such will be the estimate of W. J. Bryan by the Carlyles and Macaulays of the Twentieth century. And this is the man upon whom the *Tribune* and other journalistic peons and Wall street panders are emptying their stink-pots, just as they emptied them upon Lincoln and every other patriot who has dared proclaim that the people have rights which even the money-power is bound to respect. "Fool, knave, demagogue, anarchist, clown, idiot"—these are a few of the epithets applied by New York's boodle press alike to Bryan and Lincoln. Never did a man of sterling integrity offer for the presidency but had to run the brutal gauntlet of New York's journalistic bravos. Think of such a man as Bryan—a man as rigidly honest as that ill-starred Roman who proposed to coin his heart's blood into drachmas rather than despoil the poor—being declared "apt at lies and forgeries and blasphemies and all the nameless iniquities against the Ten Commandments!" And this by a disreputable journalistic misfit and political Jonah who four years ago sought to attain the vice-presidency by means of votes bought in "blocks-of-five!" Out upon you, you cadaverous hatchet-faced Anglomaniacal parvenu—you canting hypocrite rolling your watery eyes to heaven and mouthing of God and the Commandments while striving to steal by means of malicious lies the good name of honest men! If we had no better Americans than you, we'd be the very humble subjects of Albert Edward and John Brown's beery relict, or the barefooted, dog-eating peons of Dictator Diaz. Haven't you got gall to assume that a party which contains you and 8 million other disreputable niggers and unmanly mongrels represents the intelligence and integrity of the most enlightened land upon which shines the sun! Hadn't you best get on the port side of yourself and make a cautious inspection of your panties after denouncing a majority of the native-born white men of America as repudiators of their honest debts and conspirators against the life of this Republic? There are many good men in the Republican party, but they didn't elect Mr. McKinley. His popular plurality, of which you are so proud, represents the votes of niggers who will steal anything they can carry—who will barter the sexual favors of their wenches to white Republicans for half the money they demand for their ballots. It represents the venal suffrages of illiterate paupers imported from Southern Europe by Mark Hanna and other leather-lunged "protectors of American labor." Take out the nigger vote and Bryan has a popular plurality; take out the votes of Slavs and Huns, of Poles and Sicilians, of the Italian Lazzaroni and other beggarly scavengers of Europe's back alleys—who went as one man for McKinley—and Bryan is elected with votes to burn. These are the critters who smashed the "league of hell," the "conspiracy against the honor and life of the Republic"— entered into by men whose fathers were the first defenders of Freedom's flag! I have no bricks to cast at intelligent men of foreign birth whose honesty and industry lend dignity to the land of their adoption; but as we are here discussing the relative worth of the personnel of the two great parties, it is not amiss to call attention to the fact that those states containing the largest contingent of undesirable Europeans rolled up the biggest majorities for McKinley—that this one element of the Republican party furnishes more than 58 per cent. of our paupers and nearly 57 per cent. of our criminals. To these malodorous factors in the "preservation of the national honor"— the buck niggers and assisted emigrants—must be added a third, fully as foul. I refer to those conspirators who nominated Palmer for the express purpose of deceiving the people and electing McKinley. The man who resorts to political skulduggery, who deliberately practices deception, is a thief at heart and would not scruple to rob a corpse if sure he wouldn't be caught. Doubtless many gentlemen voted for McKinley—men who are infinitely better than their party. For these I have no word of criticism—their chagrin at being caught in such disreputable company is sufficient punishment. It is eminently fitting that Whitelaw Reid be organ-grinder for such an aggregation—the piano in a bawdy-house should be played only by a pimp. The honesty, patriotism and intelligence of this nation must be sought among its native-born citizens, and those naturalized Europeans who have made a careful study of our institutions and are striving earnestly to preserve the primal principle of the Republic— the greatest good to the greatest number; and it was from these classes that Bryan drew his support. The niggers and Huns, the vote-peddlers and men with axes to grind at expense of government, and those political shysters who attempted to bunco the people out of their ballots by means of the Palmer-Buckner green goods game, had no place in the Democratic procession. Mr. Bryan was the choice of two-thirds of those who create the nation's wealth—who support the government in peace and defend it in war. Had an educational test been generally in force, not a single state could have been carried for McKinley. Yet, having assisted in marshalling the ragtag and bobtail of Europe and Africa to the battle of ballots, where the nigger crap-shooter or the Hungarian helote is potent as the noblest patriot; having helped deliver Columbia into the hands of professional despoilers, the *Tribune* has the colossal impudence, the monumental nerve to add insult to injury by denouncing the very men who have made this the greatest nation on the globe, as its most dangerous enemies. If I might presume to give the *Tribune* and other papers of that ilk a little advice, I would "tell 'em to don't." The Republican boodlers should enjoy their stolen fruits without unnecessary ostentation. The people realize that they have been swindled; but, while inclined to let it go at that—as they did in 1876—they do not much relish being abused. We were frankly told during the campaign that if Bryan was elected, his inauguration would not be allowed. We know that McKinley was not elected in conformity with the laws of the land—that he should be put in the penitentiary instead of the presidency. The West and the South are a trifle quick on the trigger; hence it were the part of wisdom to jolly them up instead of making a bid for trouble. Mr. Bryan might become tired of being systematically insulted by such intellectual tomtits as the *Tribune* man, and announce that, having been rightly elected president, he proposed to occupy that office. Persistent abuse of his followers enhances his power—and there are already in the West and South a million men who would shoulder Winchesters and follow him to Washington. If he is the "rattlepated boy" and disreputable demagogue the *Tribune* would have us believe, it were good policy not to monkey with him overmuch at this stage of the game. He might precipitate a little *contretemps* that would knock so much wind and water out of speculative values that the *Tribune* would find pimping for the plutocracy no longer profitable. This is emphatically one of those cases wherein "the least said is soonest mended." Never awaken a sleeping bulldog with a kick in the ribs just for the pleasure of expectorating tobacco juice in his eye. The South once became aweary of the infernal impudence of the East, and would have whaled h—l's bells out of her in a hundred days had not Grant's Westerners spoiled our sport by getting between us and the impuissant blue-bellies and given us the bayonet. When the East rides both the South and West, she should warble a soothing roundelay instead of berating us in choice billingsgate.

THE AMERICAN PRESS.

Its Hypocrisy and Cowardice.

"Lord, Lord, how this world is given to lying."

And yet the greatest liar desires to be thought truthful, just as the most cringing coward poses as the avatar of courage, the most abject slave of custom the beau-ideal of manly independence.

Truth, courage, independence—the three cardinal virtues of manhood, chief attributes of a godlike soul, triune, transcendent, synonymous, yet not the same.

Have you ever carefully considered the claim of the American press to these three great moral excellencies? Truthful? Is the American press truthful? Does it even attempt to be so? to separate fact from falsehood; to sustain the one and crush the other regardless of partisan creed or personal greed? Courageous? What has the American press done during the past decade to entitle it to flaunt these badges of honor in the face of the world? By what right does it assume the titles "public educator," "guardian of liberty," "tribune of the people?" What has it done to validate them? Can you think of a single instance wherein this self-styled "leader" has led in any movement calculated to benefit mankind?

Is it not true that the American press, instead of being a leader in the march of progress, is but a blatant camp follower? Is it not true that its most assiduous study is to get on, not the right side of a question, but on the popular side—the side that will put the most money in its purse? Is it not a fact that instead of moulding public opinion, it is moulded by it as clay is fashioned by the hand of the potter? Is it not a fact that it will follow the crowd tho' it lead to the devil? Is it not a fact patent to all the world—a fact most pitiful, shameful, infamous—that its every utterance is predicated on policy, and that it will no more denounce the wrong or defend the right in any case or cause until assured of popular approval than the cur dog will attack a catamount unless hounded on by his master?

Truthful as a Cretan! Courageous as Falstaff! Independent as Uriah Heep!

Of course there are exceptions to this rule; there are to most rules. There is occasionally a paper that prints the honest views of an honest editor. There is occasionally a paper that scorns to wear the label of creed or party and accept as truth incontrovertible, wisdom infallible, the decisions of ecumenical councils and partisan conventions. There is occasionally a paper that does not wait until the popular verdict is signed, sealed and delivered before daring to express an opinion; that panders to the prejudice of no party clique, class or creed. To them be all honor! May their tribe increase! They are the noblest work of human hands—and the rarest.

Instead of being, as it proudly asserts, the advance courier of civilization, the American press is a brake on the wheels of progress, a strait-jacket on society that prevents it from expanding, from attaining a symmetrical development. Its influence—such as it has—is used to aggravate all social deformities, to make them permanent. Its boasted conservatism is the curse of the age, the Old-Man-of-the-Sea about the neck of the social Sinbad. The American press is the sworn enemy of every man who would better his fellows; who would lift civilization to higher planes. It would have clamored for the torture of Galileo, the death of Socrates, the crucifixion of Christ.

It is the press that stones the prophets of progress. It is the weight that bears down the safety-valve of society, while the furnace fires rage ever hotter and hotter, the pressure in the boiler grows greater and greater, and the very earth quivers beneath the restless throbbing of the mighty machine, groaning with an agony of gathering power that sooner or later must tear it to shreds. Every advance in the march of civilization, every step in the procession of progress is accomplished, not with the aid, not under the loving guidance of the press, but despite its vigorous, ofttimes vicious protests.

Let the wisest, purest man in the world, the most unselfish friend of humanity the century can boast, dare to call in question the dogmas of a political party, and forthwith the newspapers wearing its collar strike his trail, remorseless as Siberian blood-hounds, persistent as red Indians, brutal as calumny! He has attacked "party principles" and deserves no mercy! He has dared to call in question the infallibility of the national convention—an *omnium-gatherum* made up chiefly of antiquated political hacks, tin-horn statesmen and patriots for plunder! Sacrilegious wretch! Nail him to the cross! Proclaim him an enemy of his country! besmirch his reputation! Call in question his sanity! Work, oh my brethren! bury him in a sea of filth, lest he lead the people from the true faith and we be left to follow the crowd on crutches!

The conservative press can learn nothing new from professors not graduates of its school. If they teach that water is wet the theorem must be carefully compared with the last party platform before it can be entertained for a moment.

But what of the non-conservative press? Shall we turn there for hope? Yea, in heaven's name, though disappointment make the heart sick. What has it to offer? Catholicons, panaceas, each warranted to cure all social and industrial ills "while you wait." Co-operation will save the world if somebody will but hold the patient's nose and pour the medicine down its throat! Government ownership of land, or railways, or banks, is all that a valetudinarian society needs to transform it into a Hercules with a snake in each hand! Socialism, communism, prohibitionism, greenbackism, Henry Georgeism, *ad infinitum, ad nauseam*. God help us! May the great Demiurgus deal tenderly with the earnest crank and have pity on the damphool. But it is not *laissez faire;* it is not conservatism, so-called. Let us be grateful for that. Though it is stupidity, it is not the hopeless, helpless, house-dog kind that characterizes those papers that can only drink out of gourds inscribed with the party trade-mark. It recognizes that something must be done—something quite different from hooting the hoots of Republicanism; something far otherwise than parroting the Ave Marias of "Jeffersonian Democracy," or there will ere long be his Satanic Majesty to pay and an embarrassing stringency in the money market; that the conservative nigger must be clubbed off the safety-valve or the pent-up forces will soon blow our boasted American civilization at the moon, and it offers such remedy as its narrow visual range can espy, such as its scant knowledge of social therapeutics can suggest. If it cannot allay the fever that is burning and blazing like hell-flames in the veins of the great social organism, it may, by constant irritation, bring it to an earlier and consequently less disastrous climax than would otherwise be the case.

* * *

One of the ludicrous features of the position of the American press is its abiding faith in its own puissance, despite the many object lessons it has received to the contrary. It honestly believes that as a world power it outranks potentates and princes, is second only to Providence. It is firmly convinced that in politics at least it is a curative autocrat—that it maketh all things, and without it is nothing made that is made.

But what are the facts? There are probably not a dozen papers between the Arctic Ocean and the Austral Sea competent to elect or defeat a candidate for any office from President of the Republic to pound-master of a precinct. Certain it is that there is not within the broad confines of the State of Texas a single journal that can do as much to shape an election as can the proprietor of the most disreputable dive in the city where it is published.

This is no fancy sketch; it is true as the Synoptical Gospels. Many a ward heeler and saloon rounder is more potent in politics than any diurnal publication between the Sabine and the Rio Bravo. There is not a paper in the State with influence enough to close up a disreputable doggery or dance house whose existence is a plain violation of both the letter and spirit of the State law and municipal ordinances! And what is true of Texas is true, in greater or less degree, of every State of the Union.

Influence? The influence of the American press is of the negative kind. It can and does keep good men out of politics, out of works of reform, because such men are nearly always sensitive, and dread like death even a public criticism which they heartily despise. The people are not like sticks and stones, *sans* eyes, *sans* ears, *sans* sense. They are fully alive to the fact that the newspapers are not philosophical impartial tribunals, but organs of partisan prejudice, attorneys engaged to promote special interests. The people no longer accept the opinions furnished them cut and dried by the papers, because they know that they are not honest opinions. They no longer accept the dicta of the press, because they know full well that editors have exchanged the ermine of the bench for the wig of the barrister.

And this is the Archimedean lever that moves the world! This is the "sentinel on the watch-tower of liberty," the dynamics of progress! This it is that presumes to criticise potentates and powers, principles and politics; that opposes to the death every innovation until it is accomplished, then, if it prove popular, calmly takes to itself the credit and hurls foul scorn at all dissenters! This it is before which brave men are mute and honest men, fearing unmerited dishonor, open not their mouths! This it is that men try to propitiate as they would an ignorant, brawling woman; whose anger they avoid as they would the blind fury of a mob; beneath whose criticism the sensitive soul writhes in torture such as Dante pictured of the damned. And yet the anger of the press amounts to nothing more than a thunderous report and the villainous smell of sulphur. Men have defied it and lived—lived beyond prison walls, loved and respected.

It may be that under existing social conditions it is impossible that the press should be better than it is. No publisher can be blamed for declining to steer his paper into inevitable bankruptcy. It may be that the press has but adapted itself to social conditions which it did not make and is powerless to alter.

But while that fact, if fact it be, may extenuate its frivolity, it does not excuse its offensive self-righteousness, its arrant hypocrisy, its attempt to shackle every man who would make social conditions better, politics purer. If it find it impossible to lead; if it find it necessary to servilely follow, to become a foul pander to partisan prejudice, a pleader of special causes instead of the umpire of national polity, it should drop its high pretensions.

The standard of intelligence, like the standard of professional ethics, is too low in journalism. While the American press is arrogating to itself superior wisdom; while it is presuming to give counsel to the world's wisest with the calm assurance of preternatural prescience, it is a mournful fact that American newspaper men are, as a class, below, and far below in intelligence, any other professional class, any commercial class in this country.

Look at a State convention of lawyers, doctors, bankers, commercial travelers, manufacturers—what you will; then look at a State press convention, and mark the contrast! The former is to the latter as Hyperion to a Satyr. Thoughtful, intelligent faces predominate in the former; stupid, shallow, conceited physiognomies in the latter. "A fool newspaper man," has well nigh passed into a proverb.

That the journalistic standard of intelligence is below instead of above the average of professional and commercial standards every close observer will bear willing witness. That such should be the case, every man capable of reasoning from cause to effect will say upon a moment's reflection. Money, in America, attracts brains as the magnet attracts the needle. The intelligence of the country is drawn to the gain-getting avocations and journalism is not one of them. In fact, the poverty of the press is as proverbial as its pusillanimity, of which it is both the mediate and immediate cause. The higher intelligence of the American people is not devoting its energies to scandalmongering, chronicling prize fights and expatiating on the beauties of ball dresses. The bright young men of this land are not falling over each other in their mad haste to capture the editorial "we" and give unsought advice on matters of which they know nothing. They are turning their attention to merchandising, banking, speculation, transportation, to law and medicine, to avocations that pay, leaving journalism to those who make up in "gall" what they lack in "gumption." Gambling, baseball, the pulpit and the stage divide with the sanctum those aspiring intellects that mount above the plow but cannot reach the counting-room.

Will Carleton's old farmer, who thought his young hopeful would make a capital editor because he was fit for nothing else, was evidently a close observer. The fact that Jim was "built of second-growth timber;" that his judgment was small and his appetite abnormal, especially qualified him to shine at a State press convention. He would doubtless have been elected President of the association on the first ballot. Of course there are exceptions to this general rule. American journalism can boast its Greeleys as the stage can its Barretts, the pulpit its Beechers; but the number of really brainy men in editorial harness, as compared with those in other occupations, is ludicrously small.

Such American journalism is, but such it should not be. Journalism should be to all other avocations what philosophy is to science. It should be the crucible in which all things are tried by Promethean fire; the laboratory in which principles and politics, measures and moralities are analyzed with painstaking patience, with absolute fairness, and stamped with their true worth.

Journalism and practical philosophy should be synonyms. The editor should be the high priest of civilization; the sanctum should be the sanctuary of justice, the temple of holy aspirations, the alma mater of noble thoughts. Will it ever be so? It may be. That journalism appears to be sinking down to more fearful depths, does not extinguish hope. Even the church lapsed from virtue, and instead of the avatar of love and law became the personification of hate and discord. It touched the deepest depth, and then the divine spark in man rebelled against the degradation, and brave souls led it back toward the sun-kissed heights.

Let us hope that American journalism has reached its nadir, and that henceforth its tendency will be steadily upward. There are portents that proclaim it cannot much lower go. Public opinion is already turning upon it angry, scornful glances. Already may be observed an occasional effort to mount; already the truth is sometimes blurted out with a sullen defiance of party platforms and policy, with a contempt of partisan prejudice, here and there an editor whose pen is not guided by the hand of a peon—whose proud spirit is turning fiercely at bay. Here and there is being planted a standard a little way up the mountain-side, and from its shadow rings sharp and shrill, above the buzz of barristers and the stale platitudes of partisan polemics, a clarion call inciting the servile press to exchange the shackles for the sword—to stand erect in its might and majesty, and lead where honest men dare follow.

OBSCENE CONVERSATION.

I can understand the man who frequents houses of ill-fame; I can apologize for a man like Lincoln who tells a fragrant story to illustrate a thesis or enforce an argument; but I cannot comprehend the degradation of that mind which, like a scurvy fice, finds pleasure in wallowing in the filth of obscene conversation. Animalism may drive a weak man into excesses which his conscience condemns; but that the mind itself should find pleasure in feeding on corruption, evidences a mental obliquity and moral perversity that staggers belief. To their eternal shame be it said, American men are the most foul-mouthed animals on earth. The obscene exclamation is fast supplanting the "good round Anglo-Saxon oath." The retailing of vulgar stories constitutes the feature of their social conversation, doggerel verses too foul for print in the most disreputable journals attain a vast sub-rosa circulation, and pictures so vile as to be monstrous find a ready sale in so-called respectable circles. Taste for this class of art and literature must be acquired like that for tobacco and opium, for, whatever be the inclinations of the flesh, the mind naturally worships the pure. Our young men appear to think a vulgar mouth an evidence of manliness, as they once thought the ability to drink and smoke distinguished the dashing cavalier from the common herd. Like Gil Blas, they are eager to be thought gentlemen of intrigue, and so cultivate a taste which stamps them at once as proletarians—dangerous only to grisettes and Bowery girls. The accomplished roue would as soon die with a bullet in his back as an obscene publication in his pocket. The most daring Don Juan I ever knew would not listen to an anecdote that was not chaste as ice. His cheeks would flame like a school girl's at a vulgar word. The imprint of Hell was upon his heart; but it was the Gehenna of fire, not the Valley of Hinnom. Nor is it the young men alone who are given over to grossness; the gray-beards are equally guilty. Coming up from Galveston a few nights ago, a party of four professional men—than whom few stand higher in the South —occupied the smoking-room of the Pullman. Two were old, two young. They discussed politics as a matter of course—and business. Then they talked of their families. The young men were newly married, the old had grown daughters—four happy homes. From this sacred subject they drifted to obscene "yarns," and for two hours Youth and Age vied with each other in the province of vulgarity. I felt as tho' these educated and unquestionably able men had been transformed into Gulliver's Yahoos before my eyes A railroad cigar makes a good disinfectant, and I concluded to stand it. A preacher must not altogether avoid the slums, but study life in all its phases. I looked at these men and wondered why Almighty God allowed lips so foul to touch those of pure women. In the smoke of my cigar I saw a vision. Standing beside the young men were their brides with faces ghastly pale, gazing horror-stricken upon their shattered idols. Near the old men were two imperial dames with silver threaded hair, vainly striving to shut from the ears of shame-faced maids the coarse obscenities of their sires. The quartette suddenly observed their visitors, and, springing to their feet, stood with bowed heads and burning brows. Timidly they put out hands to their loved ones, mumbling unintelligible apologies; but the latter drew back in alarm, stood for a moment with heaving bosoms and wildly dilating eyes, then turned with a shriek and fled into the darkness. Perhaps the phenomenal success of publications given o'er to sensationalism and scandal-mongering is an encouraging sign—an evidence that Vice is coming down out of the realm of sentiment, of poesy and song, where it endangers the very elect, singes the wings of angels; that in time it will become so grossly materialistic as to be attractive only to stable boys and scullions. When Launcelot lays aside the lute for the coarse compliment, foregoes the bewildering anacreontic and puts a "personal" in the paper requesting Guinivere to meet him in the park, we may well hope that the pure in heart are safe. Only buzzards are trapped with carrion.

JINGOES VS. JABBERWOCKS.

As we heard a very great deal during the last decade about Jingoes and Jingoism, it might be well to consider what these terms really signify, together with the political status of those by whom they are so glibly employed. An opprobrious epithet applied to a person by a social blackguard or political Judas Iscariot, might well be considered a compliment. It is much safer to estimate a man by the character of his foes than by the clamor of his friends. "By Jingo," a milk-and-cider cuss word, is a corruption of "By St. Gingoulph," the latter proving too big a mouthful for ordinary every-day use. In the cant vernacular of the Mugwump's "mother country," a statesman who favored a foreign policy with whiskers on it was called a Jingo by the ultra-conservatives, the origin of the term being usually attributed to some doggerel verses written by a worthy predecessor of Poet-laureate Austin during the Turco-Russian unpleasantness. One couplet runs—or rather wobbles along —in this wise:

> "We don't want to fight, but by Jingo if we do,
> We've got the ships, we've got the men, we've got the money too."

Our own blessed ultra-conservative—or Anglomaniacs —borrowed the term from their British cousins, together with the rest of their ideas, and now roll it as a sweet morsel under their tongues, because "it's so English y' knaw." When you find a man talking about Jingoes and Jingoism, you're pretty apt to find a critter using the nawsty broad Henglish ha, smoking a black pipe on the street, and turning up his twousahs at the bottom, a la the anthropoidal purchase of the Vanderbilts. A Jingo, according to the couplet which I have quoted, is simply a patriot who earnestly desires peace if it can be had with honor; but who doesn't propose that his country shall be transformed into a cuspidore and its flag into diapers by any prince, potentate or power in all the great Universe of God. He longs to recline beneath his own vine and fig tree, with none to molest him or make him afraid; and to assure that blessed tranquility, he feeds a few slugs to a double-breasted shotgun and invites marauders to keep off the grass. He "don't want to fight"—prefers Persian pink to villainous saltpetre, truffles to hard tack, the smiles of lovely women to grim-visaged war. He doesn't carry a cypress shingle on his shoulder nor trail the narrative of his Albert Edward on the shrinking earth; but, like Sancho Panza, he will not permit his face to be handled with impunity. The Jingo is a man who has escaped the denationalizing curse of foreign commerce, the damnation visited upon political pride by the almighty dollar. He still entertains the idea that this state is the best for the country, and his country the equal of any on earth. He never forgets that the national flag is his oriflamme—that it represents his father's blood and his mother's tears, the honor of his home and the glory of his manhood. It is the Iliad of his nation, the history of his family, and was written by the sword of Liberty in letters of flame. He regards an insult to the flag as a personal affront, and a stain on his country's escutcheon as a reflection upon his own character. National integrity represents not his honor alone, but the fame of his sire and the future of his son. In these degenerate days, when

> "The nations do but murmur, snarling at each other's heels,
> And the jingling of the guinea helps the hurt that honor feels,"

it is not surprising that the patriot should occasionally lose patience, curse the meanness of spirit that shapes the national polity, and demand that the "snarling" over gross affronts be exchanged for the fierce protest of the six-pounder—that the jingle of servile gold be drowned in the crash of sovereign steel. James G. Blaine, a statesman of the first rank, self-poised as a star, accepted by the world as typical of all that is best in the American people—a patriot who loved every acre of the sunny soil on which falls the shadow of Freedom's flag—was called "Jingoism incarnate." Blaine was neither dreamer nor demagogue. While practical as Cato, he was just as Aristides. He believed that nations, like individuals, should treat each other with manly candor and ever place honor above expediency. He recognized that the United States is the most powerful—as it is the wealthiest—nation in the world and saw no harm in felicitating the people who made it so upon that fact. He despised a bully, but insisted upon a foreign policy of sufficient vigor to make the national ensign respected on every sea. To preserve peace and foster commerce he would go so far as consistent with his country's dignity; but further he would not fare, tho' confronted by an embattled universe and the certainty that the nation he loved would be wiped from the map of the world.

"Every medal has its reverse"—there are two sides to every shield. The Jabberwock is the antithesis of the Jingo. He must be numerous, else the earnest patriotism and modest national pride of a man like Blaine would not become the subject of general remark. These two illegitimate words were unknown to Webster, the great lexicographer being gathered to his fathers before they obtained lodgment in our language. In his day the Jabberwocks (signifying morbidity of the brain complicated with St. Vitus' dance of the jaw-bone) were designated as Tories, Traitors or Monarchists; the Jingoes as Patriots, Sons of Liberty or Minute Men. We have changed our political nomenclature in conformity with the prevalent craze for the bizarre—made it more picturesque if not so expressive; but the Jingo is still a patriot, while we recognize in the Jabberwock a Tory *in esse* and a traitor *in posse*. The latter, disguised by whatsoever name—as a Conservative, Mugwump or Anglomaniac— is a lineal descendant of those American Royalists who sneered at Washington, defamed Jefferson, lied about Hancock, denounced Adams, and lent aid and encouragement to the enemy while our forefathers were starving and freezing at Valley Forge. Their scabby progenitors constituted the Peace Party in 1812-14, when John Bull was insulting our national banner on the high seas and impressing our sailors; and again in 1848, when American patriots chastised Mexican insolence and annexed an empire. They belong to that breed of unclean buzzards that has befouled the eagle's nest, and puked on every gleaming star in Old Glory's field of blue. They have ever been the chief beneficiaries of the Republic and its most active enemies. When John Bull attempted to bluff Uncle Sam out of his boots in the Venezuelan embroglio, they declared that war must be avoided at any cost. It was the same cowardly yawp, the same doleful prophecy of certain defeat that greeted the Continental Congress, that rung in the ears of Madison and Polk, of Lincoln and Davis—the same old plea of aristocracy-worshipping Mugwumps and anæmic Anglomaniacs that somebody was going to lose a dollar if Uncle Sam declined to get down and run his nose in the dirt. The Jabberwock gathered himself numerously together and revived the Peace Party of crazy King George's most dutiful subjects, assured his blessed "mother country" of his profoundest regard, prated of the "eternal debt of gratitude" we owed her for having twice compelled us to kick her bustle through her belly-band, slandered his fellow-citizens, sniveled over the prospective collision like a bottle-fed kid with a blistered basement, and otherwise conducted himself as did his servile ancestors when old Bunker Hill was crowned with flame, American seamen fighting their guns below the water-line for the honor of our flag and Jingo Jackson writing history with lead at New Orleans. Just now he is opposing whatsoever may directly or indirectly aid the Queen of the Antilles to free herself from the infamous tyranny of the Christian Turk. Why? Because the miserable parody of God's masterpiece is built that way. Because war, or the probability of an international collision unsettles speculative values, squeezes the wind and water out of stocks, and—like Pedro Garcia—he carries his soul in his money sacks. He has nothing in common with the spirit of liberty and cares never a copper for the rights of man or the slaughter of innocents at home or abroad; but regards as grossly criminal whatsoever interferes for a moment with his accumulation of cash. He is invariably some fellow who inherited wealth or is fattening on the fruits won by the toil of his fellowmen; else a pitiful dependent of such parasite who echoes, parrot-like, the words of his owner. Crafty as a fox and cold blooded as a fish, cowardly of heart and servile of soul, he takes refuge behind a Mokanna veil of sanctified "conservatism" and spews his spite upon every man who suggests that national honor is worth considering—that forbearance can cease to be a virtue so long as gilt with gold. He would not have the nation go to war, because "it is not prepared;" and it is never prepared, because he prevents it building an efficient navy and providing munitions of war with which to equip an army. Having deliberately tied the hands of the Giant of the Occident, he advises him that, being helpless, he should meekly submit to insult.

It by no means follows that all who clamor for war are patriots, that all who advise peace are knaves. I am simply contrasting those who, like the Conscript Fathers, are ever ready to sacrifice life and fortune for honor and freedom, and that all too numerous class whose god is the dollar and whose bogey is death. Chauvinism is a grievous fault; but 'tis the fault of a sovereign, not the vice of a slave. The most vainglorious swash-buckler that ever shrieked for canned blood is preferable to the Peace Party tear-jug who, when cuffed at one end asks to be kicked at the other. Between the exaggerated Jingo and the ultra Jabberwock there is ever the same difference that exists between the lynx and the louse—one always wants to fight, it cares not what; the other ever wants to feed, it cares not where. Commerce is a matter of grave importance; but to get gain—to feed and lie dormant—is not the all-in-all of earthly existence. Those orators and editors who object to any action on the Cuban question by Congress lest it "unsettle trade" and possibly occasion the loss of a few ha'pence, are so deficient in national pride, so guiltless of private shame that should nigger babies be born in their families their only concern would be to learn where they could sell them. When a nation takes its hand from the sword-hilt to put a penny in its purse the end of its glory is near. We laugh at Lycurgus for having made money of iron that luxury might not corrupt the people and debase the national pride; yet every grand empire and aspiring republic that has passed from earth was slain with a dagger of fine gold. So perished Greece and Rome—raised to the skies by the swords of Jingoes, cast down to hell by the itching palms of Mammon's helotes.

The very men who have most to say about Jingoism when sympathy is expressed for the Cuban insurgents, groan the loudest and longest over the misery of the Armenians. Day and night they call upon the Christian powers of Europe to annihilate the unspeakable Turk, while the still more unspeakable Spaniard is committing darker crimes at our very door. The Armenian outrages are perpetrated for the most part by roving bands of mountain robbers, who bear much the same relation to the Sublime Porte that the murderous Apaches once did to the American president, while those in Cuba are the systematic work of the Spanish soldiery. Why does the Jabberwock weep for the woes of the Orient and regard with complacence those of the Occident? Simply because war between European nations would make to his profit, while one to which Columbia was a party might deplete his purse or imperil his person. Hence the facility with which he swallows impossible stories of Islam's cruelty, while protesting that the Cuban butcheries of non-combatants are the vain imaginings of press correspondents. He's the soul of philanthropy when it yields dollars without danger; but when the balance promises to be on the other side, he's "strictly business" and loudly preaches non-interference. I do not assume that all the horrors which make Cuba a hell are committed by Spanish hirelings; for when thro' impuissance of the governing power, a country is given up to unbridled anarchy, armed bands of thieves and thugs, owning no allegiance but to Lucifer, hold high carnival; but I do say that according to the testimony of Weyler himself it is high time for America to interfere in the name of humanity. Spain is privileged to crush the revolt of a colony if she can do so in accordance with civilization's recognized canons; but she is not priviliged to set up a perennial slaughter-house under the very nose of this nation, then insult us with her infernal insolence if we fail to police every mile of our seaboard to prevent our citizens doing for the struggling victim of her insatiate greed and supernal gall what La-Fayette, Baron de Kalb and hundreds of other brave souls did for Columbia when British bayonets were at her breast. The plea set up by the so conscientious "conservative" that we owe Spain a debt of gratitude that should cause us to withhold our hand, is the sheerest guff. It is true that her monarchs, anxious to extend their empire and enhance their revenues, aided somewhat the Italian Columbus, who paved the way for the discovery of this continent; but what did the Spaniard ever do for the Western world except rob its copper-colored kings and mix syphilitic blood with that of the equally "haughty" and almost as indolent savages? Spain encouraged us in our rebellion against an easier task-master than she was ever known to be; not that she loved liberty more, but that she esteemed England less. For the loan of $70,000 and a few old flint-lock muskets, she has our thanks, but not our co-operation in her cruelties. France was our active ally, both on land and sea; but we could not reward her services by leaving Mexico at her mercy. The very aid and encouragement Spain extended to a revolted colony of England precludes the plea that we are not privileged to assist struggling Cuba, but must stand idly by while she, like Galgacus' Romans, transforms a garden into a desert and calls it peace. To merely recognize the belligerency of the Cubans were as idle as to tender moral support to a man beset by savages. Senator Mills is the only public man with sufficient courage to defy the canting "Conservatives" and Pecksniffian Mugwumps and go to the root of the matter. We must either close our ears to Cuba's cry for assistance or we must go to her side with the naked sword. There are but two ways to deal with the Spanish Don. One is to ignore his barbarities, and the other is to break him in twain and feed the better half of him to the buzzards.

THOMAS CARLYLE.

Of a recent edition of Carlyle's "Heroes and Hero Worship," it is said that 100,000 copies are already sold. The work has been on the market many years, and this continued popularity is indeed encouraging. It argues that the taste for the legitimate, the sane in literature, has not yet been drowned in the septic sea of *fin de siècle* slop—that, despite the enervating influence of an all-pervasive sensationalism, or sybaritism, there be still minds capable of relishing the rugged, strong enough to digest the mental pabulum furnished by a really masculine writer. Carlyle ranges like an archangel thro' the universe of intellect, overturning mountains to see how they are made—now cleaving the empyrean with strong and steady wing, now shearing clear down to the profoundest depths of Ymir's Well at the foundations of the world. That his followers continue to increase argues well for the age, for he is a man whom weaklings should avoid if they would not be sawed in twain by mountain chains, forever lost in pathless limboes or drowned in the unmeasured deep. Even the strongest must, perforce, part company with him at times, else follow with the eye of faith, for his path oft leads up into that far region where mortals can scarce breathe, over Walpurgis' peaks, through bottomless chasms and along the filmy edge of clouds.

The admirers of Carlyle—may their tribe increase!—are indignant because one Edmund Gosse, in his introduction to the late edition of "Heroes and Hero Worship," alludes to the lion of modern literature as "an undignified human being, growling like an ill-bred collie dog." They take Mr. Gosse too seriously—dignify him with their displeasure. James Anthony Froude—a literary gun of much heavier calibre than Mr. Gosse appears to us from this passing glimpse—once wrote, if I remember aright, in a similar vein of the grizzled sage; but the unkind critique has been forgotten, and its author is fast following it into oblivion, while the shade of Carlyle looms ever larger, towering already above the Titans of his time, reaching even to the shoulder of Shakespeare! Gosse? Who is this presumptuous fellow who would take Carlyle in tutelage, foist himself upon the attention of the public by making a peep-show of the great essayist's faults? There is, or was, a pugilist named Gosse, or Goss; but as he did not deal foul blows to the dead, this must be a different breed of dogs. Sometime since there lived a little Englishman named William Edmund, or Edmund William Gosse, or Goss; but I had hitherto supposed that, becoming disgusted with himself, he crawled off and died. As I remember him, he was a kind of half-baked poetaster or he-bulbul, a Johannes Factotum in the province of dilettanteism, a universal Smart Alec who knew less about more things than any other animal in England. He was one of those persistently pestiferous insects tersely called by Carlyle "critic flies"—a descendant of that placed by Æsop in St. Paul's cupola. They presume to judge all things, great and small, by their "half-inch vision"—take the measure of cathedrals and interpret to the world the meaning of brainy men! Unfortunately, the "critic fly" is confined to no one nation—is what might be called, in vigorous Texanese, an all-pervading dam-nuisance. Mounted upon a mole, pimple or other cutaneous imperfection of an intellectual colossus, it complacently smooths its wings and explains, with a patronizing air, that the big 'un isn't half bad; but sagely adds that had it been consulted, his too visible imperfections would have been eradicated. We dislike to see an insect leave its periods and semi-colons on the immortal marble; but it were idle to grow angry with a Gosse. This must be the English literary exquisite whom Americans have hitherto incidentally heard bellowing before the tent of this or the other giant and taking tickets—I mean the prig, not the pug. He is comparatively youthful yet, and can, on occasion, digest a good dinner. Perchance when he is well past four-score, worn with long years of labor compared with which the slavery of the bagne were a blessing, and half-dead with dyspepsia, he too, will "growl like a collie dog;" but never a copper will the great world care whether he grumbles or grins. Should he even get hydrophobia, that fact would scarce become historic. The public marks and magnifies a great man's foibles, but forgets both the little fellow and his faults. Jeanjean may hide from the battle in a hollow log, and none hear of it; but let a Demosthenes lose his shield and the world cackles over it for two-and-twenty-centuries. To digress for a moment, I believe the story of Demosthenes' cowardice as damnable a lie as that relating to Col. Ingersoll's surrender. Even in his day human vermin sought to wreck with falsehood those they feared. The world—unwisely I think—interests itself in the personality of a genius, and somewhat impudently invades his privacy. A young man may muster up sufficient moral courage to lie to his callers, and thus preserve the proprieties; but an aged valetudinarian who wants to get into a quiet nook and nurse himself, may show scant courtesy—even brush the "critic fly" of the genus Gosse out of doors with a hickory broom.

Carlyle belonged to "the irritable race of poets," albeit he seldom imitated Pope's bad example and tortured his rugged ideas into oleaginous rhyme. There is a strange wild melody in all his work—what he would call "harmony in discord" suggesting that super-nervous temperament which is inseparable from the highest genius, and which degenerates so easily into acute neurosis—that "madness" to which wit is popularly supposed to be so "near allied." Such natures are aeolian harps acted upon, not by "the viewless air," but by a subtler, more impalpable power, which comes none know whence, and goes none know whither—one moment yielding soft melodies as of an angel's lute borne across sapphire seas, the next wailing like some lost soul or shrieking like Eumenides. The "self-poised," the "well-balanced" man, of whom you can safely predict what he will do under given conditions; the man who never bitterly disappoints you and makes you weep for very pity of his weakness, will never appall you by exhibitions of his strength. He may possess constructive talent, but never that creative power which we call genius because it suggests the genii. "No man is a hero to his valet," says the adage. Carlyle assumes this to be the fault of the latter—due to sawdust or other cheap filling in the head of the menial. Yet, may not the valet be wiser in this matter than the world? The hero, the greatest genius, is not always aflame with celestial fire, impelled by that mysterious power which comes from "beyond the clouds"—may be, for most part, the commonest kind of clay, a creature in nowise to be worshipped. The eagle, which soars so proudly at the sun, will return to its eyrie with drooping wing; the condor, whose shadow falls from afar on Chimborazo's alabaster brow, cannot live alway in the empyrean, a thing ethereal, and back to earth is no better than a carrion crow. To genius more than to aught else, perhaps distance lends enchantment. While we see only the bold outline of the Titan, we are content to worship—nay, insist upon it; but having scrutinized him inch by inch with a microscope, we realize that familiarity breeds contempt. Well does Christ say that a prophet is not without honor save in his own country—which is the origin of the hero and valet adage. I cannot understand why the world insists upon seeing le Grand Monarque in his night-cap and Carlyle in his chimney corner. With the harem of Byron and the drunken orgies of Burns, the poaching of Shakespeare and the vanity of Voltaire it has nothing to do—should content itself with what they have freely given it, the intellectual heritage they have left to humanity, and not pry into those frailties which they fain wolud hide. If Goldsmith "wrote like an angel and talked like a fool," it was because when he wielded the pen there was only a wise man present, and all are affected more or less by the company they keep. We care not whether the gold in our coffers was mined by saint or sinner, so that it be standard coin; then what boots it what manner of men stole from heaven that Promethean fire which surges in the poet's song, leaps in lightning-flash from the orator's lips, or becomes "dark with excess of bright" in Carlyle's Natural-Supernaturalism? Judge ye the work, and let the workman "growl like a collie dog" if it ease his dyspepsia!

That Carlyle was "an undignified human being," I can well believe; for he was the wisest of his day, and dignity is the distinguishing characteristic of the dodo and the donkey. If Mr. Gosse esteems it so highly, he might procure a pot of glue and adorn his vermiform appendix with a few peacock feathers, else take lessons in posturing from the turkey-gobbler or editor of the Houston *Post*. Had Carlyle been born a long-eared ass, he might have been fully approved—if not altogether appreciated—by Gosse, Froude and other "critic flies." When Doctor Samuel Johnson was told that Boswell proposed to write his life, he threatened to prevent it by taking that of his would-be biographer. It were curious to consider what "crabbed old Carlyle" would have done had he suspected the danger of falling into the hands of a literary back-stairs Mrs. Grundy like Edmund Gosse! In his "Heroes and Hero Worship" he treated his colossi far otherwise than he in turn has been treated by Gosse and Froude. He first recognized the fact that they were colossi, and no fit subject for the microscope. We hear nothing from him to remind us of Lemuel Gulliver's disgust with the yawning pores and unseemly blotches of the epidermis of that monster Brobdingnagian maid who set him astride her nipple. He reverenced them because they possessed more than the average of that intellectual strength which is not only of God, but is God; then considered their life-work as a whole, its efficient cause and ultimate consequence. He does not appear to have thought to inquire whether they had dyspepsia, and how it affected them, being engrossed in that more important question, viz., what ideas they were possessed withal, how wrought out, and what part these emanant volitions of the lords of intellect played in the mighty drama of Human Life.

It is not my present purpose to review Carlyle's literary labors—that were like crowding the Bard of Avon into a magazine article. For 300 years the world has been studying the latter, and is not yet sure that it understands him;

yet Shakespeare is to Carlyle what a graded turnpike is to a tortuous mountain path. The former deals chiefly with the visible; the latter with the intangible. The first tells us what men did; the last seeks to learn why they did it. Carlyle is the prince of critics. He is often lenient to a fault, but seldom deceived—"looks quite thro' the shows of things into the things themselves." Uriel, keenest of vision 'mid all the host of heaven, is his guardian angel. To follow him into the sanctuaries of great souls and become familiar with all their hopes and fears; to pass the portals of master minds and watch the gradual evolution of great ideas in these cyclopean workshops; to mount the hill of Mirza and from it view the Tide of Time rushing ever into the illimitable Sea of Eternity, and comprehend the meaning of that mighty farce-tragedy enacted on the Bridge of Life, were scarce so easy as listening to the buzzing of the "critic fly" or dawdling over a French novel on a summer's day.

Carlyle is frequently called a "mystic," and mystagogue he certainly is—a man who interprets mysteries. If the average reader urge that his interpretation is too oft an *obscurum per obscurius,* he might reply, in the language of that other woefully "undignified" and shockingly impolite human being, Dr. Johnson: "I am bound to find you in reasons, Sir, but not in brains." Carlyle was regarded by those writers of his day who clung to and revered the time-worn ruts, as chief of the "Spasmodic School," the members whereof were supposed to be distinguished by "a strained and unnatural style." This "School," which was satirized by Aytoun while editor of *Blackwood's Magazine,* was thought to include Tennyson, Gilfillan and other popular authors of the time. I incline to the view that no writer of whom we have any knowledge exhibits less affectation in the matter of style than does the subject of this essay. It is rugged and massive; but so is his mind. It were impossible to imagine the author of "Sartor Resartus" and "The French Revolution" expressing himself in the carefully rounded periods of Macaulay, whose prose is half poetry, and whose poetry is all prose. Carlyle seems to care precious little what kind of vehicle he uses for the conveyance of ideas so long as it does not break down. All his labor "smells of the lamp;" but "the midnight oil"—of which our modern "ready writers" evidently use so little—was consumed in considering what to say rather than how to say it. Not even Shakespeare possesses so extensive a vocabulary. The technical terms of every profession and subdivision of science come trippingly to his tongue. But even the dictionary is not large enough for him, and he extends it this way and that, his daring neology creating consternation among the critic flies and other ephemera. He wrote as he thought, hence his style could not be other than natural. That of Aytoun was formed in the schools, principally modeled by masters— made to fit a procrustean bed—and was, therefore, eminently artificial. If we apply the term "unnatural" to the matter instead of the manner of Carlyle and Tennyson, then away with genius, for intellectual originality is tabooed!—no man is privileged to think his own thoughts. That is the law nowadays nowhere except in the sanctum of the Gal-Dal *News,* where Col. Jenkins takes the editorial eyas and teaches it to soar in exact imitation of himself.

Whether by the "Spasmodic" method or otherwise, Carlyle dragged more true orients out of the depths than did any of his contemporaries; and that is saying much, for "there were giants in those days," and they were neither few nor far between. The intellectual glory of the first half of the present century was scarce eclipsed by the Elizabethan era. It was in very truth "a feast of reason and a flow of soul." Goethe and "Jean Paul" were putting the finishing touches to their work while Carlyle, then a young man, was striving to interpret these so strange appearances to the English-speaking world, to hammer some small appreciation of German literature into the autotheistic British head. Tom Moore, sweetest of mere singers, and Lord Byron, prince of poets, were but five and seven years respectively his seniors. He saw the beginning and the end of their literary labors, as of those of Macaulay and Mill, Darwin, Disraeli and Dickens. Much of his best work was done ere the death of Walter Scott, and he might have played as a school boy with the ill-fated Shelley. He had just begun his long life-labor when Longfellow and Tennyson, Hugo and Wagner came upon the scene, and together they wrought wisely and well in that mighty seed-field which is the world! What a galaxy of intellectual gods!—now all gone, returned home to High Olympus— the weird land left to the Alfred Austins, the William Dean Howells and the Ian McLarens! Gone, but not forgotten; yet the world will in time forget—even the amaranthine flowers must fade. Of them all we see but one star that blazes the brighter as the years run on, and that one long mistaken for a mere erratic comet *sans* substance, or unformed nebulae hanging like a splotch of semi-luminous vapor in a great void. Year by year the voice of Carlyle rings clearer and clearer from the "Eternal Silence." And as we listen with rapt attention to the music of the spheres becoming audible, intelligible to our dull ear—the Waterloo and Lisbon earthquakes, the Revolutions and Warring Religions, all the glory and shame, the wild loves and bitter hatreds of humanity—even Birth and Death—but minor notes in the Grand Symphony, the Harmony of Infinitude, the little man who has undertaken the management of the microphone, without suspecting its significance, distracts us with the unwished for and utterly useless information that the Voice coming from beyond Time and Space, out of the Everlasting Deep, once "growled like a collie dog!"

SEXUAL SINS OF AMERICAN SOCIETY.

Rev. Chas. Parkhurst has drawn down upon his devoted head the ire of the St. Louis *Mirror* by saying that one-half the husbands and wives of New York are unfaithful to their marriage vows. The *Mirror* remarks:

> There are more men true to their wives than are not. The unfaithful husbands are conspicuous. Not one-half the men, not one-tenth in any city are untrue to their wives. They have not the time for the most part. They have not the money, because that is a luxury that costs dearly. And above all they have not the inclination. * * * * It is all bosh to say that unfaithfulness prevails among society women. They are as faithful as the wives of the poor. Their position would enforce faithfulness, if their moral sense did not. They are observed. American society women are unromantic. One might almost proclaim their virtue upon the poor ground that their blood is snow-broth. * * * * The vast majority of men are not Priapians rampant. Only a man whose mind is a Tenderloin district and his soul an unclean "circus" can maintain that any appreciable number of married women in any station of life are sluts.

I dearly love a cheerful optimist—a man who can fix his gaze on a will-o'-wisp, or glow-worm in the blackest midnight, and persuade himself and others that it is high noon—that the world is "dark with excess of bright." Sure, 'tis better to laugh than to be sighing—Democritus is preferable to Heraclitus. It is more pleasant to seek and commend virtue than to hurl anathemas at vice. Why, it may well be asked, should a man gaze into a cesspool when he may look at the stars? Why explore the foul sewers of a great city when he may sun himself in its pleasant parks? So said the people of Paris, until disease and death reminded them that, however they might close their eyes thereto, there was an under as well as an upper world—that a sanitary officer is not necessarily a nuisance. If Bruneseau was called the most intrepid man in France for having explored and purified the Parisian cloacae that the public health might be preserved, may not the man who seeks to edulcorate the moral Gemoniae of America be entitled to equal honors?

The optimist is a good gift, for which we should be duly grateful. He is the brass band in the political torchlight procession, the hallelujah at the Methodist campmeeting, the Weylerian press agent in Ahriman's war upon the powers of Darkness and the Devil. Overtaken by the deluge, he would not drown, but, like a champagne cork, bob serenely to the surface of that circumambient sea. Were old Sol to go out of business, he would proclaim it a blessing and prove it by sunstroke statistics—would insist that enough light and heat could be extracted from our stock of canned cucumbers to supply mankind until time shall be no more. The optimist points the small, the pessimist the large end of the telescope at the enemy. What one considers merely a sick house cat the other takes for a royal Bengal tiger; hence, while one is ever hopeful, the other is always sad at heart. Dr. Parkhurst sees too much and Mr. Reedy too little of the world's wickedness; due no doubt to a radical difference in age and temperament. Parkhurst's ravelled rope whiskers have grown grizzly in the unsavory but necessary occupation of moral night-soil man. The hypocrisy of his parishioners and the phallic revels of the red-light district have soured his soul and given him dyspepsia. It is quite natural, under the circumstances, that he should believe in original sin and doubt the perseverance of the saints. He mistakes sociability for lewdness and a little harmless lallygagging for a *liaison*. He has come to the conclusion that the human race is rolling down hill to hell, and is trying to hold it back by the coat tails and making a brake of his boot heels. He cries aloud and spares not—has become the Jeremiah of his day and generation. The *Mirror* man is a rosy-cheeked youth, known to his *intimes* as Willie, and might be easily mistaken for the son or younger brother of W. J. Bryan. He looks at life thro' the rose-tinted glass of his study window and the mellow radiance of Arthurian romance. "To the pure all things are pure", and the Adonis of the Cyclone City has not yet fallen into the tigerish clutch of Venus Pandemos, or sunk beneath the brutalizing wand of Circe. He still believes that doctors find babes in hollow trees and peddle them about the streets in baskets. To him every man is St. Anthony, every woman a sacred mystery—the very habitues of Pine street are moving poems, celestial symphonies. To him the only wicked people in the world are those who reject the monetary wisdom of G. Cleveland for the financial heresy of Adam Smith, the economic omniscience of Mark Hanna for the maudlin idiocies of John Stuart Mill. It is a great pity that youth's sweet dream of innocence cannot last thro' life—that there comes a time when the shameful fact is driven home to e'en the most unwilling heart that the world is full of incontinent husbands and unfaithful wives.

We will find the truth anent American morals midway between Parkhurst's pessimistic croak and the *Mirror's* optimistic song. What proportion of married women "go wrong" no man can know; for this evil, like the iceberg, shows but little on the surface. Let any Lovelace of long experience, and formed to please a woman's fancy, but pause and reflect how few of those he knows to be unfaithful wives are so regarded by the world. Women of professed respectability do not keep an assignation accompanied by a brass band, nor advertise their amours in the public prints. There are millions of wives who are, and well deserve to be, as far above suspicion as Cæsar's spouse; but could all the husbands in even the eminently virtuous St. Louis be wafted above the city like Don Cleofas, and look with magic vision thro' every roof and wall, the divorce courts and funeral directors would experience a business boom. It may be true, as the *Mirror* urges, that society women are faithful as poor men's wives. The great middle class is and has ever been the chief repository of the nation's virtue. A century or so ago, when the mass of the American people led useful and laborious lives, were permeated with a true religious spirit and enjoyed homely plenty, there were few nymphs du pave, and even a Hester Prynne was regarded with almost universal horror. Healthful toil and frugal fare are virtue's guardian angels. They exorcise the demon Asmodeus and evolve a rugged and continent race; but such grinding penury as millions feel in our modern cities "freezes the genial current of the soul" and blunts the moral sensibilities. Not necessity alone, but ignorance and evil environment, make panders of men and wantons of women. Solomon assures us that "Pride goeth before destruction"; but I say unto you that when pride is crushed out of man or woman by a load of rags and wretchedness, damnation is even at the door. Pride is the sheet-anchor of morality, the dynamics of noble deeds. When love fails and hope flies, pride still lingers, the savage rear-guard of a human soul, and dies in the last ditch. Solomon was an ass. Think of the millions of kingly men who but for the power of pride would to-day be driveling drunkards —of the women pure as the flowers that bloom above the green glacier, who else were wantons! For legions in every land pride stands with drawn sword between appetite and infamy, between desire and dishonor. But I shall not quarrel with the shade of Solomon. By an heroic effort, and an occasional lift from the lord, he was able to remain reasonably faithful to one thousand women of all colors and kinds, albeit we learn from the Canticles that he was particularly partial to coons. I infer from this that he was a republican in politics. While penning his brief essay on pride, he may have been distracted by the arrival of a fresh consignment of wives from the Congo country, or the report of his seneschal that some neighboring monarch had plundered his smoke-houses during the night. Despite Bro. Parkhurst's tearful complaints, I opine that the average New York hubby would not stray far from his own fireside were it a duplicate of Solomon's, and we could scarce expect the average man to be either wiser or better than Israel's consecrated king.

While poverty assails virtue on one side with the plea of necessity, luxury attacks it on the other by inflaming the passions. The female favorites of fortune usually belong to the Cyrenaic sect—consider pleasure the greatest good. That their blood is not "snow-broth" is evidenced by the many scandals, which, despite all efforts at repression, find publicity. They are of the same blood and bone as their sisters in humbler walks of life, are better fed and groomed, have more leisure—and "Satan finds some mischief still for idle hands to do." If they be "unromantic," as the *Mirror* says, so much the worse, for unromantic people are ever animalistic. Marius and Cosette may dream away a hundred sensuous summer nights hidden in the boskage, satisfied with their own fond imaginings; but rob them of the halo of romance, destroy the airy Nepheloccygia in which they live and love, and there's naught left but a solfatara of lust. Romance is not alone the corolla of love; it is the very incense of virtue. So long as it envelops man and woman, they wander far above the crass animalism of the world. Banish it, and you either abolish sex or reduce the commingling of men and women to the level of brute beasts. Society women are "observed" more than others, 'tis true, for to be seen of men and envied of women seems to be the chief object of their existence; but it is likewise true that they are by custom allowed a larger liberty than are the wives of workingmen. Not even the French matron is so free to flirt with gentlemen friends, to go and come with escort other than her husband, as our fair devotee of fashion. Hubby grubs away at moneygetting and sends her to the mountains or seaside for the summer to enjoy herself—and any kind of weather would indeed be dreary to the average society dame if she could not have a gallant or two traipsing at her heels. The society woman is indeed "observed." She is observed boating, bathing, bikeing and strolling in leafy dells on moonless nights with noted "mashers," while her hubby is worrying thro' the summer in a distant city. She is observed at the opera, while her matrimonial mate is soaking his bunions at home—taking lunch with her escort afterwards; disporting herself at balls until late hours, then carried home in a closed carriage much the worse for wine. And the more she is observed, the more suggestive becomes the lament of the despoiled Lucrece:

> "O Opportunity, thy guilt is great!
> Thou makest the vestal violate her oath.
> Thou blow'st the fire when temperance is thaw'd:
> Thou smother'st honesty, thou murder'st troth;
> Thou foul abettor! thou notorious bawd!
> In thy shady cell, where none may spy him,
> Sits Sin, to seize the souls that wander by him."

The morals of le beau monde is frightfully low, else we would not find in every city women notoriously corrupt as Sycorax, moving in the "best society." Money covers a multitude of sins, and the woman of great wealth may have as many lovers as she likes without impairing her social position—so long as her husband doesn't "raise a roar." Even a divorce "for cause," and opera bouffe duel among her admirers afterwards, does not always succeed in driving her from the sanctum sanctorum of swelldom. Nay, such a trifling *contretemps* is apt to increase her popularity in "polite society"—on the principle, I presume,

that "like takes to like." Let a seamstress be so much as
suspected of a *liaison* and she's branded as a slut by her
"set" and "guyed" on the street by gamins; but the debaucheries of a female Astor, or the foul leavings of a
he-Vanderbilt, are considered as things almost sacred.
These slimy lepidosauria have mounted so high on steps
of gold that they are worshipped as were those obscene
gods who made lechery a virtue and drunkenness divine.
There are doubtless good women in the fashionable world;
but, like old Dog Tray, they are caught in very suspicious
company.

Taken all in all, the American people are the purest
found on this planet. Our poor have not yet become so
degraded as those of Europe, nor have our rich descended
to the unspeakable abominations which have so long disgraced the "hupper suckles" of old England. The *Mirror's*
assertion that American husbands have not time to be
unfaithful, will strike the average reader as very funny;
but the fact is that of all men they are the busiest, and it
is the drones, the "gentlemen of elegant leisure" who are
most addicted to debauchery. Even our great millionaires are deeply engrossed in business, grasping right and
left for a few more grains of gold. Wealth, not women,
is the dominant passion of the sons of Uncle Sam; still,
they are human—"abounding in pleasant faults"—and not
much addicted to overdoing the part of Adonis. The idea
of the *Mirror* that American husbands are continent because "they have not the money" to be otherwise, must
be dismissed as the merest moonshine. The money expended by these same men every year for cigars and
liquors alone would deck every bawd with diamonds. The
wealth-producing power of the American is the wonder
of the world; but he is no miser. He values money only
because of the pleasure it brings. He is the spendthrift
par excellence of the universe. Yet despite this fact the
path of the average prostitute lies thro' the vale of Poverty and ends at the potter's field. "The weariness that
lies awake for hire" has little attraction for the average
American husband. It is "the hell of a fellow" and the
foul-mouthed hoodlum, the precocious "kid" and the be-
sotted bum who support the bagnio. The wife who is
"led astray" invariably supplied the string; but she is
usually sufficiently exacting in her tastes to make the
male frequenter of Boiler avenue innocuous in society. A
good woman, refined enough to be modest and sensible

enough to be discreet, may travel this land alone, safe from insult, for nowhere else in the world have men so high respect for a noble woman. The very ditches and delvers are her knights-errant, and woe betide the brute who would deflower her by force, or that gallant who gets prematurely "gay." But high as my opinion is of American husbands, I confess that their virtue is of that kind which "rejoices in temptation." I go surety for no man assailed by the cestus. Despite long centuries of civilization and the lessons of religion, man is still a savage—the moral law has not yet reduced his animalism to subjection. I suspect that if any large proportion of benedicts are faithful it is not altogether their fault. The gentle reader will please bear in mind that I am in nowise responsible for the frailties of my fellowman—my duty's done when I set him a good example. I did not make the bipedal brute, else had less mud been employed in his manufacture. I heartily approve of the late Bill Nye's reflections on the "rewey;" but am dreadfully afraid the "single standard of morals" will long remain an iridescent dream. Thus far its chief agitators have been people well past their grand climacteric, busy old maids and envious eunuchs. It is well to ever bear in mind that man is by nature a Mormon.

THE MODERN SPHINX.

An Oedipus Wanted—Apply Early.

"We are beset with problems. The characteristic symbol of the age is the question mark. Our patron saint is the sphinx."

These be not the words of "Vocal Willie," "Pitchfork Tillman" or "Anarchist Altgeld;" but the line with which Rev. Geo. Hodges, dean of the Theological School, Cambridge, opens a series of profound lectures on the tendencies of the times. I have not read all the dean's discourses; but the statement made by a careful reviewer that he "disavows any intention of speaking with authority" on these intricate questions, makes me eager to do so. I always feel ill at ease in the presence of Omniscience—long to sneak out and commune with mere mortals who are not altogether infallible. That is why I avoid

those reformers who know it all, the purveyors of panaceas
—those who propose to remodel our entire social system
and drag the industrial millennium in by the ears. I am
a purblind crepuscular animal, and cannot stand the glare
of that great white light which beats upon the thrones of
those sociological demi-gods who consider a rejuvenescence
of the Golden Age,

> "A warke it ys as easie to be doone
> As tys to saye, Jacke! robys on."

I have noticed that the closer a man examines those
complex social questions with which we are confronted,
that the more brain power he brings to bear upon them
the less inclined he is speak *ex-cathedra*. It is usually
the fellows who absorb their information from the prescription department of a political party, and the feculent
vomitings of a partisan press, who are most eager to relieve
the Almighty of his occupation and assume control of the
universe. These are the Magi who point the way from the
dark valley of Doubt to the sunny mountains of Certitude
to men who have labored long and earnestly to familiarize
themselves with every phase of the social contract; who
have striven with all their strength to trace each effort to
its efficient cause. To the ne'er-do-well, the street-corner
psilogist and other empty gab-traps and chronic failures
it is easy enough to say, "Physician, heal thyself;" but
there is another class well nigh as noisy and equally ignorant, with which it is more difficult to deal. I refer to
those who have accumulated more or less cash by trading
in tape and tripe, selling soap or sad-irons, harvesting hooppoles or planting hogs, loaning money at usurious interest
or sitting on their hunkers while others built towns and
cities around their realty holdings. Having managed to
keep the skin of their bellies from flapping around their
backbones like a wet dish-clout about a wire clothes-line,
they imagine themselves filled to the muzzle with monetary
wisdom—assume to speak authoritatively on subjects anent
which they know as little as any other breed of gibbering
parrots who have managed to get their beaks into the almand-box. In one respect at least, I am like the Lord—
being no respecter of persons; hence even the studious and
painstaking economists need not hope to escape criticism.
They are too much addicted to saving the world by the science of definition—resembling those who "by geometric
scale do take measure of pots of ale." They give us long

disquisitions on the "law of rent," the "law of interest," the "origin and use of money," etc.; all of which is very curious and entertaining for those who have time for it, but is emphatically that philosophy which bakes no bread. When first informed of the existence of the "law of interest," the world must have felt much as did Moliere's M. Jourdain, who was surprised to learn from his professors of languages that he "had been talking prose all his life without knowing it." Taking the social machine apart simply to name its component parts were much like analyzing an apple that the schoolboy may know what he is eating. What the latter wants is to have pointed out to him the path to the orchard that he fill his "pod" with fall pippins. The people ask for dumplings and are given an essay on digestion. "Knowledge is power," say the old copy-books; but that depends. The knowledge that labor is the creator of all wealth has enabled no slave of toil to help himself out of the hole. When Tennyson said that "knowledge comes but wisdom lingers," he must have been contemplating the economic metaphysicians. But perhaps I do the professors of political economy an injustice. When a man of mediocre mind is seized with a fervent desire to know God he joins church, "gets religion," becomes a phrenetic defender of some foollish faith, and is ready to persecute those who hold other opinions; but the wise man is not so easily satisfied. He explores the history and weighs the evidences of all religions; then, instead of saying, "Here is God," seizing a bull-whip and driving his brethren to the Throne of Grace, he tells us how this or the other religious customs arose and what effect it has had upon the human race. This is eminently unsatisfactory; but shall we blame him because despite his persistent research, he has nothing better to offer? It is easy enough for the sciolist to be a partisan—to profess that faith which "removes mountains"—pitching them headlong into the fertile plain, foolishly enough, we think. The ignorant man finds no difficulty in taking Davy Crockett's advice. He is ever sure he's right, always ready to go ahead; but for the man of clear, analytical mind, who insists upon examining both sides of the shield before so much as hazarding an opinion that it is a shield and not some cunning pasteboard imitation thereof, it may be quite a different matter. Perhaps in dealing with social problems we can do no other than "go it blind" and trust to Providence. A clown in Hamlet's place would have quickly determined where lay his duty and done it. Of course he would, in all human probability, have done the wrong thing in the right place; but "the native hue of resolution" would not have been "sicklied o'er with the pale cast of thought" and lost the name of action. While the economic Hamlets soliloquize, the people pin their faith to the patent medicines hawked with so much lung power by this or the other coterie of place-hunters. All things considered, it is not so much wonder they often go wrong as that they ever get right.

Dean Hodge's remark that "Our Patron Saint is the Sphinx," must be condemned as a metaphorical miscarriage; still we may easily divine his meaning. The Texas editor who alluded to the flight of a disreputable character from the community as having "filled a long-felt want" succeeded in making himself understood, which is more than can be said for some of our grammar-sharps. The Sphinx which proposed a riddle to the Thebans and slaughtered such as failed to return a correct answer, could scarce be called a Patron Saint—unless, indeed, the fool-killer be so considered; still she may be taken as truly representative of the condition which confronts us to-day. The Sphinx of Time is propounding to this nation a riddle which it must solve, and that soon, else be destroyed. And up to this time no Oedipus has arisen, or seems likely to arise, whose wisdom will stand between us and destruction. Nay, should he appear upon the scene, how could the Sphinx hear him, deafened as she is by the persistent clamor of the Jack Cades and Cagliostros—each perched on some political platform or foolish editorial tripod, and playing at Liberty enlightening the world—by the aid of gas? If I might presume to drop a few words of advice into this polemical chaos, like sperm oil on the waves of a tempestuous ocean, I would say: Keep cool. Remember that no political party has a corner on the patriotism and intellect of the universe. Even a Democrat is not first cousin to the Demiurgus, nor a Republican necessarily an ass—however impossible the latter proposition may appear to the careful students of cause and effect. We must first free ourselves from partisan prejudices if we would hope to deal wisely and well with vexatious social problems. What can we expect from a party platform built expressly to please either the plutocrat or the *fœx populi?*—of a Congress which makes no secret that it is governed altogether by "party expediency"—is not considering the general welfare, but playing a game of political chess—with the public flesh-pots for pawns? It has been said, and truly so, that "in a multitude of counsel there is wisdom;" but the American people do not come together in council, do not deliberate calmly. Each grabs a parcel of made-to-order "opinions" and attempts to shove it bodily down the throat of his brother. If he declines to gulp it down like a hound-pup feasting on hot pancakes, he's either a "peon of the money power" or a "repudiator," a "parasite" or a "popocrat." That is what we are pleased to call a "campaign of education"—that's the "multitude of counsel" from whose cumulative brain-power we expect to see emanate a full grown Minerva. Lincoln's remark to the effect that "you can't fool all the people all the time," has puffed us up with our own importance. Lincoln was right; you cannot fool them all the time—you cannot so much as persuade the half of 'em to apply the soft pedal to themselves and give you a hearing—unless you consent to hoot the jejune hoots that tickle the untrained ears of the majority. Fool them! You might as well try your sophistry on a stampede of buffalo bulls—which stick tail in the air, shut eyes and run over you, bringing up in a fat pasture or at the bottom of a precipice, as it may happen. Impartial consideration of any economic thesis whatsoever is out of the question for the simple reason that each individual assumes to know it all—insists on teaching instead of being taught. Government is simply a vast co-operative concern in which all are interested. If the stockholders in any private enterprise, however great, divided into warring factions and fought for its employments without regard to fitness; if they made a pickleherring or ninnyhammer general manager, and in their councils each opposed a business proposition for the simple reason that it did not originate with his office-seeking set, the corporation would quickly become bankrupt. That government is able to meet its bills is due to the fact that it is an assessment concern—is empowered to make its stockholders foot the losses occasioned by their own egregious folly. Like the horse-leech's daughters, its continual cry is "more!" and it saps the very life blood of labor. Instead of earnest, dignified discussions, such as distinguishes the directors of a bank or other business, we hold political scalp-dances—and it is bankrupting us to pay the piper. Imagine the board of control of a great department store determining a business policy by means of a brass-band and torch-light procession! Yet that is the way in which this nation, the greatest corporation on earth, decides economic propositions. It might be well to blow less brass and employ more brains.

We are indeed "beset with problems;" but by far the most important—one which may be said to embrace all others—is simply this: How can we secure a more equitable division between labor and capital of the annual increment of wealth, and assure to every able-bodied individual in this land an opportunity to earn an honest living? This is a problem that is pressing upon us with ever increasing power. It is the riddle which the modern Sphinx propounds to the American Thebes, and woe betide us if we blunder in our answer! Upon its proper solution depends not only peace and the perpetuity of representative government, but perhaps our very civilization itself. I am well aware that many well-fed people consider it a crime to call attention to this fact; even deny the proposition altogether, brand it as "sensationalism"—shove their heads into the sand, and leave their tail-feathers temptingly exposed to the fury of the coming cyclone. The French aristocrats declined to acknowledge the approach of the Revolution; but unfortunately, you can't snub an earthquake nor induce an active buzz-saw to wait for an introduction. There be people who curse the weather clerk for predicting storms instead of halcyon days, forgetting that but for his watchfulness picnic millinery might get wet and proud ships be cast away. It were foolish to shoot the sentinel for sounding an alarm on the approach of the enemy instead of making the welkin ring with the criminal cry of "All is well." It were best that we should all be honest with ourselves—that those people who live on "Easy Street" occasionally look elsewhere than into their own well-furnished back parlors—to open their ears and consider well whether the hoarse rumbling be but the car rattling o'er the stony street or the cannon's opening roar. Labor being the Atlas upholding our world, it were the part of wisdom to inquire from time to time how he come on with his contract—especially when he complains audibly that his burden is too grievous to be borne, manifests a disposition to take his pack for a football and play a game scarce relished by the grand-stand.

I have no incentive to magnify the danger with which this nation is confronted. I have never been a candidate for office, nor had a governmental ax to grind. As an employer I am not especially interested in the advancement of wages to the curtailment of my profits. Readers of and advertisers in magazines usually belong to what is known as the "conservative class"—those who strenuously object to anything savoring of "agitation," who agree with Pope that "whatever is is right." Still I cannot see that aught is to be gained—while certainly much may be lost—by self-deception. An agitator is not necessarily a public enemy; else must we denounce the Conscript Fathers, condemn the labors of Luther and approve the crucifixion of Christ. Only through agitation is progress possible. It is the law of life. Without it the seas would become mighty pools of putrescence. A prominent pulpiteer recently delivered himself as follows:

The laborer should be content in that sphere where God has placed him. His condition is better than ever before. It has greatly improved during the last 100 years. But for the Bryans and Tillmans and Debs, he would be docile enough.

These have long been the platitudes of Dives. If true, it is only necessary to execute the Bryans and Tillmans and Debses as fast as they appear and snap our fingers in the face of the Sphinx. But they are not true. It is rank blasphemy to assume that God is responsible for the hunger and wretchedness existing in a land capable of supporting in comfort, even in luxury, five times its present population. It is not true that the condition of labor "is better than ever before," or that "it has greatly improved during the last one hundred years." I brand that statement, which comes so trippingly to the lips of the apostles of *laissez faire,* as a foolish falsehood. The past century has transformed the workman from a sovereign into a slave. Then he need ask no man's permission to provide himself with food and raiment; now he must lay down his tools and starve at the beck of a boss. He can, when permitted to employ his strength and skill in the production of wealth, enjoy many comforts denied his grandsire—comforts of his own creation; but who would not prefer independence with homely plenty well assured, to the constant fear of being transformed into a pitiful tramp and compelled to beg his bread? Who would not rather be lord of his own life than the trembling creature of another? The condition of labor has not "greatly improved during the last hundred years" even for those whose souls are formed for servitude instead of sovereignty. The addition of the word "tramp" to our vocabulary is itself suggestive. A century ago—before the condition of labor had so "greatly improved"—such industrial vagabondage was unknown. Men did not then commit offenses against the law for the express purpose of securing shelter from the cold behind the walls of a calaboose and being fed on prison fare. I do not want to see the workingman rendered too "docile," for docility is the nature of the lap-dog. When it becomes the distinguishing characteristic of the Caucasian, he will begin supplying the African "coon" with liveried lackeys. How comes it that docility is demanded of men who have twice played Samson to Britain's royal beast—who in a single century have made this the wealthiest nation in the world? "Docile?" I like your impudence! To whom, forsooth, should the giant "bend the pregnant hinges of the knee?" To whom shall Labor—having filled the land with fatness over which it stands guard with the sword of Gideon—humbly apply for the privilege of existing upon the earth?

The condition of the laborer should have "greatly improved during the last hundred years," for his productive power has multiplied. It is estimated that the average wealth-creating power of the individual has more than quadrupled since the adoption of the Constitution. Has the reward of the workman increased in equal ratio? If not, there's something radically wrong with our industrial system, and the man who does not seek earnestly to discover and remove the evil is in league with the Devil, I care not how earnestly he prays to the Lord. The minister who prostitutes religion in the interest of proscriptive right entrenched behind a system of brutal wrong, is an infernal hypocrite who should be plunged fathoms deep in hell. There is not a man capable of successfully passing a *lunatico-inquirendo* but knows full well that the reward of the worker has not kept pace with the wonderful enhancement of his productive power, and it is this universally recognized fact which constitutes our chief danger today—is the riddle which we are called upon to read.

Let us take a cursory glance at existing conditions; not from the standpoint of plutocrat or pauper, employer or employe, but from that of the patriot eager to promote his country's honor—to steer the nation clear of those rocks upon which so many proud empires that imagined themselves immortal have been hopelessly wrecked. According to a special report made by Carroll D. Wright of the U. S. Census Bureau, there were 22,735,661 persons employed in gainful occupations in 1890, of whom 3,523,730 were unemployed for three months or more, and 1,139,672 during the entire year. Those 22,735,661 people create all our wealth—clothe, feed and house the nation; hence each must provide for approximately three people. This means that during at least three months of the year 1890, more than ten and one-half million Americans were deprived of the usufruct of industry, more than three and a half million during the entire twelve months. And all authorities unite in calling 1890 "a normal industrial period!" It is estimated by competent authority that during 1893 and six months of 1896 the number of unemployed was fully double the foregoing figures—that seven million wealth producers were idle and more than twenty-one million Americans deprived of the fruits of industry, their legitimate support! Yet we are told that if the Bryans, Altgelds and Debses could be suppressed, all would be well—that this grand army of unfortunates would continue to suffer in silence and with lamb-like docility; that the Deity would be delighted and Dives in no danger! Robespierre was the creature, not the creator, of the Revolution. And what is the reward of those so fortunate as to have employment? This is a gold-standard, high-wage country, the Paradise of working people, the Utopia where the condition of labor so "greatly improved during the past one hundred years;" hence we may expect to find every employed workman fairly wallowing in wealth, lolling during his hours of leisure in sybaritic luxury. In 1890—a good year, and before that tremendous slump in wages from which the country has not yet recovered—the American manufacturing industries employed on an average 4,050,785 operatives (exclusive of officers and clerks) and paid them $1,799,671,492. If we figure 300 working days to the year, we have for the finest skilled and most productive labor in the world an average reward of $1.48; but as 313 days constitute the working year of such shops as shut down on Sunday, while many run the entire 365, we may safely assume that the average earnings of four million American operatives during a "normal year" does not exceed a dollar a day. Debs declared some months ago that thousands of men, recognized as good operatives, were then working in American mills for 50 cents a day; and as the statement has never been disputed, even by those who proclaim him a *gibier de potence,* or at least a dangerous demagogue, I take it that the assertion was literally true. When we deduct for time lost through sickness and lockouts, we may readily see what chance even the skilled laborer has for his life in this land of "Liberty, Fraternity and Equality." Yet we read in ponderous essays—penned by this or the other possessor of "fair round belly with good capon lined"—that if he would practice economy and leave the wretched agitators alone, he might get rich as grease!—that in this blessed land every deserving man has an opportunity to become a plutocrat, perchance president! The hundred or so boys actually born stark naked in log cabins half a century or more ago—when the world was much nearer industrial equality—and who have been cast to the surface of the ever-restless political sea, struck oil, married a competence, wrecked a railroad, swindled an orphan or stolen a valuable idea from a confiding inventor, are offered in evidence. Think of preaching economy to a man who is striving to pay house-rent, feed and clothe a family on $5 a week— and half the time out of work!—of telling the wretch who toils for 50 cents *per diem* that he should "live well within his means and lay up something for a rainy day!" I sometimes wonder that the workingman doesn't grow weary of being hectored by these wooden-heads and shut off their wind. We have entirely too many silk-stocking theorists dabbling with this labor problem—men who never trained with the tin-bucket brigade, who know not what it is to tramp from boss to boss, asking the privilege of earning his bread. No man is competent to speak for American labor who has never regarded "the primal eldest curse" as a gracious gift of God—who has never been denied the poor privilege of eating bread in the sweat of his brow. Here in the West and South, as in all new countries—where man produces in a more primeval manner, giving little of his produce to capital—labor retains something of its old-time dignity and receives a better reward; but the foregoing is a true pen-picture of the condition of a vast majority of those Americans who work for wages.

With so large a contingent hovering ever on the verge of starvation's hell, and the farmers sympathizing openly with the strikers who defy the laws, wreck property and destroy life, were it not well to treat the sphinx seriously and cast about earnestly for an answer? It is customary to rely upon general education as the preservative power *par excellence;* so we proceed to fill mens' heads with a clear conception of their power and their hearts with ambition, then expect them to be patient on empty bellies—to remain "docile" under the fire-whips of want while idleness ostentatiously wastes. By public education we continually increase the furnace fires; by making the battle of labor more bitter we augment the weight on the safety valve, then calmly assume that we have made explosion impossible! Only an ignorant people, like those of Mexico, India or Persia, will patiently suffer the pangs of abject poverty in the midst of plenty. Our public school system is the sulphur, our hard industrial conditions the niter, of that social gun-powder to which the ostentation of our multi-millionaires is applying the match. Suppose that the "era of progress and prosperity" promised by the Republicans should fail to materialize, and 1897 be an exacerbation of 1893: Could we depend on the "docility" of more than seven million idle and desperate wage-workers—the farmers meanwhile asserting that they would burst no blood vessels hurrying to the defense of Dives? Suppose that Debs is supplanted by a Danton in our Faubourg St. Antoine, that a Little Corporal succeeds Coxey? Of course I will be called an "alarmist"—such was the fate of John the Baptist, who declared that the baptism of water would be followed by one of fire. It was the fate of those who advised the rantankerous abolitionists that they were forcing this nation into a civil war that would cost more treasure, blood and tears than all the d—n niggers from Ham to Ida Wells were worth; of those who told the impudent French aristocrats that they were dancing on a mine of dynamite which would assuredly slam them against the shrinking face of the silver moon. It is the goose-gabble which offends the ear of every man who sees a little further into the future than does the eminently "conservative" jackassicus who goes about with his eyes shut, proclaiming that there can be no upheaval of the nether fires so long as he is here to keep the universe in order. I trust that every industrial promise made by our friends the enemy will be fulfilled; but we must not suffer ourselves to be misled by temporary spasms of prosperity into the belief that the Sphinx has winged her way elsewhere. She has propounded her fateful problem, announced the penalty, and while she may be soothed to slumber for a time by a periodical business revival, sooner or later she will enforce her edict.

How can we secure a more equitable division between labor and capital of the annual increment of wealth, and assure to every able-bodied individual in this land an opportunity to earn an honest living?

That is the most important problem submitted to the

arbitrament of human wisdom since the beginning of the world. It is a mighty interrogation point thrown up by human progress, and cannot be answered from the musty tome of precedent, for in all history present industrial conditions have no parallel. Solve it, and pauperism will practically disappear. The giant spectre of crime will shrink as did the fisherman's genie of the flask, for necessity will not goad the one nor pride tempt the other to defy the laws of man and mock the will of God. Half the burden of human misery will disappear like a miasmic mist before the beams of morning, the waters of Bimini renew the youth of those aged and broken before their time, and smiles shine with a celestial radiance on faces now wet with tears. Why should it not be so? Are we, the wisest of God's creatures, too dull to utilize to the utmost his gracious gifts. Must the fertile fields lie fallow, the fecund mines untouched beneath our feet, the tall timber stand, the cattle remain unsold, the sheep unshorn and the fish uncaught, while millions of men with hearts of oak and muscles of iron remain idle and see Want and Wretchedness stalk like grisly phantoms through the world—laughing perhaps at ponderous lectures on the evils of over-production?" Have we not wisdom and honesty enough to work together and fairly divide the joint product at the end of the day? Does God create only fools and knaves? "Come, let us reason together."

No, I shall not presume to take the initiative—to tell the world exactly what it must do to be saved. "I am Davus, not Œdipus." I suggest, however, that we leave all our pet panaceas to the janitor for safe-keeping, or hang them on the hat rack before entering the hall. We have had all kinds of tariffs and all manner of moneys, but the Sphinx remains minatory. We have heard considerable from the gentleman who would abolish interest; but while the government may accord me the free use of its "rascal counters," my neighbor will not allow me the use of his property, without hope of reward, and that is really what I want. The man who is going to redeem the world industrial by a "powerful Christian awakening"—an universal altruism— has long been abroad in the land; but I have not yet noted that Christianity, howsoever much awake, induces a man to tender me the big end in a horse-trade. Co-operation, so-called, has proven a *chateau en Espagne,* while communism places the industrial giant and the scurvy pigmy on a parity. Doubtless something may be accomplished by wise tariff and monetary legislation, warfare on monopolies of this or the other article, and regulation of common carriers, while a religious revival that will give us a clearer conception of *meum et tuum* were not to be despised; yet these do

> —"but skin and film the ulcerous place,
> Whilst rank corruption, mining all within,
> Infects unseen."

They do not reach the root of the trouble, which is simply this: Labor, broadly speaking, can no longer produce without the co-operation of large capital, and to secure such co-operation it must yield whatsover proportion of the product capital has the impudence to ask. The natural order is reversed in our industrial world today—the creature hath become lord of its creator. It may be the inevitable penalty of that differentiation of effort and consequent increase in productive power which we call progress; but if so, we must sorrowfully admit to the Sphinx our inability to answer. The temptation to launch forth into a long—and perhaps unprofitable—lecture at this point is nipped in the bud by the inelasticity of our column rules; but at the risk of creating a stampede—if not indeed a riot —I suggest that we all procure the complete works of Henry George and give them not only a careful but an unprejudiced perusal. I do not premise that he has discovered the alkahest of the ancient alchemists or has the philosopher's stone concealed about his person; but a man who has devoted a score of years to the patient study of this problem should be accorded a patient hearing—especially by those wise-acres who, to save their immortal souls, could not so much as name half a dozen standard economic authors. He is entitled to a hearing if on no other ground than that he is the only man of superior mind who has had the moral courage to really face the problem. Whatever may be said of his economic theorem, the fact remains that he is the most powerful logician in the world today. He is to polemics what Ingersoll is to oratory. He has unhorsed all his critics and trampled them into the subsoil —despite the axiom that "thrice armed is he who hath his quarrel just." His paramount position is alarming to people bred to our way of thinking; but no more so than was that of the supreme court of Vermont, which, at the beginning of this century, refused to surrender a fugitive slave "unless the master could show a bill of sale from the

Almighty." At that time the people of every section denounced the decision as anarchical and infamous; today the slaveholders themselves admit the justice of the decree. Every proposition that is new is necessarily strange, and quite apt to excite the ridicule or disgust of those whose mentality flows along time-worn ruts. It required five centuries for the Christian faith to secure a firm foothold, so eminently "conservative" were our idol-worshipping ancestors! As the wise men of the various political sanhedrins and ecumenical councils have signally failed to unravel the industrial riddle, it might not be amiss to call the Napoleon of economic controversy into court and consider whether he be the Oedipus raised up by Providence to knock the threatening Sphinx off her perch. At least we should hear before condemning him—if only to escape the withering scorn of Byron, who declares that "The man who will not reason is a bigot, and the man who dares not is a slave."

BRADLEY-MARTIN BAL-MASQUE.

"Apres Moi le Deluge!"

Mrs. Bradley-Martin's sartorial kings and pseudo-queens, her dukes and DuBarrys, princes and Pompadours, have strutted their brief hour upon the mimic stage, disappearing at daybreak like foul night-birds or an unclean dream—have come and gone like the rank eructation of some crapulous Sodom, a malodor from the cloacae of ancient capitals, a breath blown from the festering lips of half-forgotten harlots, a stench from the sepulchre of centuries devoid of shame. Uncle Sam may now proceed to fumigate himself after his enforced association with royal bummers and brazen bawds; may comb the Bradley-Martin itch bacteria out of his beard, and consider, for the ten-thousandth time, the probable result of his strange commingling of royalty-worshipping millionaire and sansculottic mendicant—how best to put a ring in the nose of the golden calf ere it become a Phalaris bull and relegate him to its belly. Countless columns have been written, printed, possibly read, anent the Bradley-Martin ball—all the preachers and teachers, editors and other able idiots pouring forth voluminous opinions. A tidal wave of printer's ink has swept across the continent, churned to atrous foam by hurricanes of lawless gibberish and wild gusts of resounding gab. The empyrean has been ripped and the tympana of the too patient gods ravished with fulsome commendation and foolish curse, showers of Parthian arrows and wholesale consignments of soft-soap darkening the sun as they hurtled hither and yon through the shrinking atmosphere. A man dropping suddenly in from Mars with a Nicaraguan canal scheme for the consideration of Uncle Sam would have supposed this simian hubbub and anserine to-do meant nothing less than a new epocha for the universe, it being undecided whether it should be auriferous or argentiferous—an age of gold or a cycle of silver. Now that the costly "function" has funked itself into a howling farce, an uncomfortable failure, and the infucated revellers recovered somewhat from royal katzenjammer, we find that the majestic earth has not moved an inch out of its accustomed orbit, that the grass still grows and the cows yet calve— that the law of gravitation remains unrepealed, and Omnipotence continues to bring forth Mazzaroth in his season and guide Arcturus with his sons. Perchance in time the American people may become ashamed of having been thrown into a panic by the painful effort of a pudgy parvenu to outdo even the Vanderbilts in ostentatious vulgarity. Rev. Billy Kersands Rainsford cannot save this country with his mouth, nor can Mrs. Bradley-Martin wreck it with her money. It is entirely too large to be permanently affected by the folly of any one fool. Preacher and parvenu were alike making a grand-stand play. Now that the world has observed them, and not without interest, let us hope that they will subside for a little season.

This Dame DuBarry extravaganza was not without significance to those familiar with history and its penchant for repetition; but was by no means an epoch-maker. It was simply one more festering sore on the syphilitic body social —another unclean maggot industriously wriggling in the malodorous carcass of a canine. It was another evidence that civilization is in a continual flux, flowing now forward, now backward—a brutal confession that the new world aristocracy is oozing at present through the Armida-palace or Domdaniel of DuBarrydom. The Bradley-Martins are henceforth entitled to wear their ears interlaced with laurel leaves as a sign of superiority in their "set." They won the burro pennant honestly, if not easily, daylight being plainly visible between their foam-crested crupper and the panting nostrils of the Vanderbilts. They are now monarch of Rag-fair, chief gyasticuti of the boundless realm of Nescience and Noodledom. Mrs. Bradley-Martin has triumphed gloriously, raised herself by her own garters to the vulgar throne of Vanity, the dais of the almighty dollar. She is now Delphic oracle of doodle-bugs and hierophant of the hot stuff. Viva Regina! Likewise, rats! Like most of New York's aristocracy, she is of even nobler lineage than Lady Vere de Vere, daughter of a hundred earls, having been sired by a duly registered American sovereign early in the present century. His coat-of-arms was a cooper's adz rampant, a beer-barrel couchant and the motto, "Two heads are better than one." By wearing his neighbors' cast-off-clothes and feeding his family on cornbread and "sow-belly," he was able to lay the foundation of that fortune which has made his daughter *facile princeps* of New York's patricians. John Jacob Astor, who acted as royal consort to the cooper's regal daughter in the *quadrille d' honneur,* is likewise descended from noble Knights (of Labor) and dames of high degree. He traces his lineage in unbroken line to that haughty Johann Jakob who came to America in the steerage, wearing a Limburger linsey-woolsey and a pair of wooden shoes. Beginning life in the new world as a rat-catcher, he soon acquired a gallon jug of Holland gin, a peck of Brummagem jewelry, and robbed the Aborigines right and left. He wore the same shirt the year 'round, slept with his dogs and invested his groschens in such Manhattan dirt as he could conveniently transport upon his person. Thus he enabled his aristocratic descendants to wax so fat on "unearned increment" that some of them must forswear their fealty to Uncle Sam and seek in Yewrup a society whose rough edges will not scratch the varnish off their culchah. Mrs. Bradley-Martin does not exactly "look every inch a queen," her horizontal having developed at the expense of her perpendicular, suggesting the rather robust physique of her father's beer barrels. Still, she is an attractive woman, having the ruddy complexion of an unlicked postage stamp and the go-as-you-please features of a Turkish carpet. Her eyes are a trifle too ferrety, but the osculatory power of her mouth in auld lang syne must have been such as to give Cupid spinal curvature. Her nose retreats somewhat precipitately from the chasm; but whether that be its original pattern, or it has been gradually forced upwards by eager pilgrims to her shrine of adjustable pearls, is a secret hidden in her own heart. Like Willy Wally Astor, she finds the customs of this country too crass to harmonize with her super-sensitive soul, and spends much time dangling about the titled slobs "on the other side." Some time ago she purchased the epicene young Earl of Craven as husband for her daughter, in the humble hope of mixing cooperage and coronets, and may yet be gran'ma to some little Lord Bunghole or fair Lady Firkin. As a "pusher" in society she can give points to Mrs. Potter Palmer or the wife of a millionaire pork-packer. Although she has "seen" the bluff of the notorious Smith-Vanderbilt-Belmont female and "raised" her out of her bunion repositories, she has probably not yet reached the summit of her social ambition. Bred to shabby gentility, Miss Alva Smith proceeded to "splurge" when she captured a Vanderbilt. She had probably never seen a hundred dollar bill until permitted to finger the fortune of the profane old ferryman who founded her husband's aristocratic family. She was a parvenu, a *nouveau* rich, and could not rest until she had proclaimed that fact by squandering half a million of the man's money whom she subsequently dishonored, on the ball which Mrs. Bradley-Martin set herself to beat. Having been divorced "for cause," she proceeded to crown her gaucheries by purchasing for her ligneous-faced daughter a disreputable duke who owes his title to a grand-aunt's infamy—is the descendant of a plebeian who rose to power by robbing dead soldiers and prostituting his sister to a prince. Mrs. Bradley-Martin has trumped two of her rival's cards—and a social game, like seven-up, "is never out till it's played out."

The denunciation of the ball by Dr. Rainsford proved him not only a notoriety-seeking preacher, but a selfish parasite who lacks sufficient sense to disguise his hypocrisy. It contained not one word of protest against the amassing of enormous fortunes by the few at the expense of the many, not a single plea for justice to a despoiled people, not one word of Christian pity for their woes. It was simply a warning—foolishly flung from the housetop instead of whispered in the closet—that such reckless waste would breed discontent in the home of want—would "make demagogues and agitators dangerous!" Dr. Rainsford would not alter, but conceal, existing conditions. His theory is that robbery is all right so long as the people do not rebel, thereby imperiling the system by which they are despoiled. From his fashionable pulpit and sumptuous home he hurls forth his anathema-maranatha at those who would presume to abridge the prescriptive rights of the plutocracy—who doubt that grinding penury in a land bursting with fatness is pleasing to the All-Father! He would by no means curtail the wealth of Dives or better the condition of Lazarus; but thinks it good policy for the former to refrain from piling his plate so high in the presence of the hungry plebs, lest the latter cease crying for crumbs and swipe the tablecloth! Dr. Rainsford is a paid servant of Dives, his duly ordained Pandarus. His duty is to tickle his master's jaded palate with spiritual treacle seasoned with Jamaica ginger, to cook up sensations as antidotes for *ennui*. If the "agitators" cause a seismic upheaval that will wreck the plutocracy, what is to become of the fashionable preachers? Dr. Rainsford would not abolish Belshazzar's feast—he would but close the door and draw the blinds, that God's eye may not look upon the iniquity, nor his finger trace upon the frescoed walls the fateful *Mene Mene Tekel Upharsin!* Save thy breath, good doctor, to cool thy dainty broth; for, mad with pride, thy master hears nor heeds the gabble of the goose beneath his walls, nor the watch-dog's warning. Gnaw thy bone in peace, for the people, schooled to patience and amused with panaceas, will scarce resent the trampling of one more parvenu upon their necks, be she ever so broad of beam. If some years hence they should rise against the robbers, led on by "dangerous demagogues," repine not, for every dog, sacerdotal or otherwise, can but have his day.

Turgid Talmage must likewise unload; Talmage, who presumes to teach not only theology but political economy; who interlards his sermons with strange visions of heaven, dreams of hell, and still more wonderful hints on how to make a people terrestrially prosperous. He, like thousands of "able editors," apologizes for such vulgar extravagance by urging that it "puts money in circulation, makes business better, and helps the people by supplying employment!" Has the world passed into its dotage, or simply become an universal asylum for idiots? If wanton waste makes business better, then Uncle Sam has but to squander in *bal-masques,* or other debauchery, his 75 billions of wealth to inaugurate an industrial boom! To gratify their taste for the barbaric, to advertise themselves to all the earth as the eastern termini of west-bound equines, the Bradley-Martins wiped out of existence $500,000 of the world's wealth, leaving just that much less available capital for productive enterprises. They might as well have burned a building or sunk a vessel of that value. It is urged that "labor was employed and paid." Quite true; but tell me, thou resounding ministerial vacuum, thou unreflecting editorial parrot, where is its product? What has society to show for the expenditure of this energy? A hole in its working capital—a hiatus in its larder caused by employing and sustaining labor, not to produce but to destroy. Prodigality on the part of the rich personally benefits a few parasites, just as the bursting of a molasses barrel fattens useless flies; but waste, by reducing the amount of wealth available for reproduction, breeds general want. A thousand editors have screamed in leaded type that it were "worse for the wealthy to hoard than waste." Thou lunatics, go learn the difference between a car and its load of cotton, a bolt of muslin and that wherewith it is measured, a nation's wealth and its exchange media. What does a man with the wealth he "hoards?" Does he not seek to make it earn an increment? Concentration of capital may be bad for the people, but destruction of capital takes the tools from their hands and the food from their lips. The court of Louis XV., which American snobs have just expended half-a-million trying to imitate, likewise, "made business better" by wasting wealth—Madame DuBarry posing as "public benefactress," and receiving no end of encomiums from Paris shop-keepers, jewel merchants and mantua-makers. Much money was "put in circulation and labor employed" in furnishing forth the transient splendors of players and prostitutes; but somehow France did not prosper. Finally not even the pitiless screws of the tax-farmer could wring blood from the national turnip. The working capital of France was so far consumed that her people stood helpless, perishing of hunger. Finally Madame DuBarry was supplanted as "public benefactress" by one with an even sharper tang to her tongue, namely, *la Belle Guillotine,* who blithely led the *quadrille d'honneur,* with a Robespierre for consort, to music furnished gratis by the raucous throats of ragged sansculottes. Instead of lords and ladies treading the stately minuet in Versailles saloons adorned with beauty roses, the bare feet of hungry men beat time to the fierce Carmagnole on Parisian pavements.

It is not a little suggestive that the participants in this foolish fandango should have turned for inspiration to the court of Louis XV., whose debauchery and depravity, the historian declares, had not been paralleled since the year of

Tiberius and Commodus—that the Bradley-Martin "function" should have been copied from the extravaganzas of a harlot! What glorious exemplars for New York's Four Hundred!—a dissolute king, and a woman thus apostrophized by Thomas Carlyle: "Thou unclean thing, what a course was thine: from that first truckle-bed, where thy mother bore thee to an unnamed father; forward, through lowest subterranean depths, and over highest sunlit heights of harlotdom and rascaldom—to the guillotine-axe, which shears away thy vainly whimpering head!" Of the 350 male revelers more than 100 were costumed as Louis XV., while but three considered Washington worthy of imitation. Was this the result of admiration in New York's "hupper sukkles" for this wretched *Roi Faineant,* or King Donothing, whose palace was a brothel, and whose harlots stripped his subjects of their paltry earnings and left them to perish? Louis XV., who permitted his country to be ruined, its revenues squandered, its provinces lost, and half-a-million men sent to an untimely death that a prostitute might be revenged for an epigram! Is that the kind of man our money lords admire? Louis lived until the *fleur-de-lis* of France was struck down in every land and dishonored on every sea, then died, deserted by his drabs, cursed by his country, and was consigned to the grave and the devil as unceremoniously as tho' he were a dead dog! And now more than 100 men who have stripped the people to enhance the splendor of palaces, don the royal robes of this godless rake and do homage to bogus DuBarrys! Small wonder that Dr. Rainsford feared such colossal impudence might serve to remind Americans how France got rid of royalty; might evoke a hoarse growl from the many-headed monster; might cause some "dangerous demagogue" to stir—perchance a Danton! Fit patron saint for our own plutocracy is this swinish king, once called *Bien amie,* the Well-beloved; but after some 30 years of Bradley-Martinism, named *Ame de boue*—A soul of mud! How much our super-select society resemble the Madame DuBarrys, the Duc d'Aiguillons and Abbe Terrays, who made the court of Louis a by-word and a reproach, his reign a crime, himself a hissing and a shaking of the head of the nations!

Suggestive indeed that at the swellest of all swell affairs in the American metropolis there should appear, according to the press dispatches, "ten Mme. de Pompadours, eight Mme. de Maintenons, four Mme. de la Vallieres, and three Catherines of Russia." Good God! Has our "best society" come to such a pass that its proudest ladies delight to personate notorious prostitutes? "There was no Racine or Moliere, no Charlotte Corday or Mme. de Stael"—the men posed as profligate kings, the women as courtesans! Yet in that same city young Mr. Seeley is arrested for looking at a naked dancing-girl, and "Little Egypt" has to "cut it" when she hears the cops! And what is the difference, pray, between a Pompadour and a Five Points *nymph du pave?* Simply this: The one rustles in silks for diamonds, the other hustles in rags for bread, their occupation being identical. New York was Tory even in Revolutionary times. From its very foundation it has been at the feet of royalty and mouthing of "divine right." It is ever making itself an obtuse triangle before the god of its idolatry—its knees and nose on the earth, its tail-feathers in the air; but we had yet to learn that it considered "that divinity which doth behedge a king" capable of sanctifying a woman's shame, transforming a foul leman into an angel of light! Catherine of Russia was an able woman, but a notorious harlot, foul as Milton's portress of hell; a woman who, as Byron informs us, loved all he-things except her husband. Is that why the masqueraders preferred the character of Empress Catherine to that of Martha Washington? Did they consider it more in keeping with the company? Strange that each Russian empress was not attended by a few of her favorite grenadiers, with "the fair-faced Lanskoi," her boy-lover, thrown in as *lagniappe.* More than 100 Louis XVths and only 10 Pompadours! What a pity! But we may presume that each Pompadour, like the frail original, was "in herself a host! Eight Maintenons, four Vallieres, and only one Louis XIVth present to look after his personal property! How proud a genuine American gentleman—one untainted with royalist fever—would have felt to see his wife or daughter posing as the leman of Lanskoi, of Louis XVth, or le Grande Monarqe—of whom Three-Eyed Billy of England once said that he selected young men for his ministers and corrupt old cats for his mistresses!

Half a million dollars gone up in frippery and flowers, and the bedizened gang didn't get half the fun out of it that a party of country-yaps will extract from a candy-pulling or a husking-bee. The Pompadours and DuBarrys didn't know how. Louis XVth went around by himself in droves, stiff and uncomfortable as a Presbyterian Sunday-school, wishing everytime his rapier galled his kibes or tangled his royal legs that he had remained comfortably dead in that dog-hole at St. Denis. There was entirely too much formality for fun. The next time New York's toad-eaters give a *bal-masque* they should disguise themselves as American sovereigns and their consorts. Of course it will be a trifle difficult for them to play the part of respectable people; but they will find even awkward effort in that direction refreshing, and calculated to inspire them with respect for their country's flag.

CONSTRUCTION VS. DESTRUCTION.

The editor of the Iconoclast knows too much to have his bridle off. He is the most dangerous person at an editorial desk in the United States. Pagan Bob and this erudite blasphemer are of the same stripe. Catholics are reading his screeds by the wholesale, and we are astonished to see some Catholic editors still using them as a weapon. It will burn the hand that wields it. We need builders, not iconoclasts.—The Angelus Magazine.

Och! Wurra! wurra! Just listen to that now! My Cincinnati contemporary puts the whole Protestant world under lasting obligations—by demonstrating that its editors have no monopoly of nonsense; that a Catholic ink-slinger can be almost as great a dunderhead and myopic bigot as our own Brer Cranfill. But *The Angelus Magazine* is very young, and probably its editor also These be journalistic faults, which, by God's grace, it may outgrow. The Iconoclast always treats its youthful contemporaries kindly, for it realizes that whom the gods right dearly love are apt to die in their swaddling clothes. They are too good for this gross earth; hence the angels steal 'em, leaving us to spill the scalding sob on a few dusty patent medicine cuts, railways ads, and other pathetic evidences of their morality. Furthermore, the Iconoclast delights to set a good example in Christian charity and brotherly kindness for its religious contemporaries. That's what it is here for. *The Church News,* of Washington, D. C., wants it debarred from the reading-room of the Carroll Institute, lest it break the pastoral staff of the Pope, blow the Vatican across the yellow Tiber and proclaim the gospel according to Ingersoll in the pulpit of St. Peter's. It occurs to me that my zealous contemporaries are far too easily frightened—are in imminent danger of making themselves ridiculous. The American Catholics do not hold their faith so lightly that any one man may relieve them of it and march them into the camp of the A. P. A. The Cincinnati youth and Washington editor should observe with what serenity the Pope regards his terrible Texas enemy, and make a reasonable attempt to rally. So long as Leo doesn't lose his nerve, there's at least a faint hope that the Church of Rome—that everlasting rock upon which the fierce storms of so many fateful centuries have beat in vain—may come safely through this awful crisis, may even survive by a year or two the Texas Iconoclast. Those little fellows who become alarmed lest somebody wreck the Catholic Church, remind me of the little girl who feared that her dog Fido might bite the army of General Lee. With their stub pencils and paste-pots they fly to the protection of the Mother Church—as Chinamen at an eclipse beat on tin pans to prevent some imaginary monster eating up their moon. Peace, good sirs; Fido is not going to bite the army, nor will the Iconoclast hurt the Pope. The hearts of these alarmed editors are all right; but they need new machinery in their heads. If Catholics read the Iconoclast, they do so well knowing that its editor is not, and in all human probability will never be a communicant of that church. Up to the present writing they have not been ordering their theology from Waco, any more than they have been receiving their politics from Rome. Baptists and Methodists likewise read it, their ministers not infrequently taking it as text and discoursing thereon with a zeal that registers 200 in the shade. I am, perhaps, the only duly ordained minister in Texas who doesn't read it. The Iconoclast is "dangerous" only to humbugs and hypocrites—to "all that loveth or maketh a lie." This statement may not, however, greatly comfort one who so flippantly accuses me of blasphemy, and advertises me as a member of the Ingersollian cult. I might with as much propriety accuse *The Angelus Magazine* man of murder and write him down as a Mormon. Strange as it may appear to those not handicapped in their utterances by "the grand thaumaturgic faculty of thought," the world has need of iconoclasts as of builders, can in nowise proceed without them. Of what use, prithee, are your popes and priests, or your ready-writers for sectarian papers, if they shatter no eidolons set up by the Evil One, destroy no tares sown by the Devil? The prophets of ancient Israel were quite vigorously engaged in the iconoclastic industry. Mahomet took a rather effective fall out of the idols of Araby—the "gods with flies on them." The unsafe building must come down to make place for a better, the old falsehood must be eradicated ere the new truth can take root. The destroyer and builder are interdependent, one useless without the other. Thus in the Hindu mythology Vishnu the preserver and Siva the destroyer are but different emanations of Brahma, or the All-in-All. All creative gods are destructive deities. Mortal man can bring nothing into being, either in the realm spiritual or material, except at the expense of something else. You cannot even give life to a dude without spoiling the ingredients of a respectable puppy, nor advance a new idea without displacing an old. Yet my Cincinnati friend wants only builders. In other words, he wants Jehovahs, who can succeed in the manufacturing business with a hiatus as a raw material. He must excuse me—I'm not the architect of Chauncey Depew. Christ destroyed old faiths, and the Church of Rome stands to-day upon the wreck he made of Pagan creeds—upon the broken altars of Jove and Baal, of Isis and Ashtaroth, the desecrated shrines of "the unknown god." The Almighty appears once as creator, and thenceforth as annihilator. He got quick action on Ananias, but is probably reserving the *Angelus* man "unto the day of wrath." He might as well drown the earth again as make falsehood instantly fatal. The English kings once held to the theory that the people had no rights which sovereigns were bound to respect, but the Catholic barons gave it a dose of iconoclastic medicine at Runnymede. Washington's Continentals had to clear away the monstrous doctrine of "divine right" before they could build a republic. Lincoln also spoiled a "divine institution," called slavery, and wrote his iconoclastic thesis with fierce whirlwinds of fire; yet the same hammer that shattered the Confederacy welded into homogeneity a mighty nation. When the A. P. A. attempted to divide this people on religious lines and exclude Catholics from office because of their creed, Uncle Sam concluded it time to do the Siva act, so he slammed the Ape against the face of nature a few times, then rammed its head into the earth and neglected to erect a monument sacred to its memory. So much for "iconoclasm"—a word no longer signifying in American literature the desecration of a shrine, but the abatement of a nuisance. For years I have heard the cry that the world needs builders, not iconoclasts; and it has invariably come from those who have builded nothing, who don't know the difference between an assault on things sacred and an antidote for the itch, who object to having humbugs exposed lest they find their own breeches at half-mast in a Dakota blizzard.

PASSING OF THE STUFFED PROPHET.

Cleveland's Place in the American Pantheon.

Now that Grover Cleveland is a political has-been—it but remaining for Uncle Sam to give him his conge—it becomes possible to make a correct estimate of the man. Shorn of the dazzling halo which doth behedge a president; withdrawn from the chevelure of incense offered on the altar of authority by professional toad-eaters; no longer apotheosized by those who servilely flatter that thrift may follow; no more a mark for the shafts of malice, the object of studied misrepresentation by political enemies, Cleveland stands forth in his proper person and the world may see and know him as he actually is. It is customary to make an epicedium an eulogy, and I should much like to lay a few Texas field flowers on Cleveland's political sarcophagus; but funeral orations and epitaphs are usually falsehoods, and it is the duty of the Iconoclast to confine itself to the actual, whether dealing with the quick or the dead.

Cleveland will unquestionably occupy an important niche in the history of this nation; but those who, standing in the shadow of his adventitious greatness, would place him on a level with Washington and Lincoln, will find that their pride-blown demi-god shrinks like a terrified jelly-fish or flannel bathing suit as he recedes into the shadows of the centuries. To a thoughtless man an arc light by which he stands may seem greater than a star; but place them equi-distant, and the one is swallowed in the maw of immensity, the other floods him with astral fire. Cleveland's admirers delight in referring to him as a "strong man;" and it is true that he exhibited some of the characteristics of those other strong men, Caesar, Cromwell and Napoleon; but these be not men we would care to place at the helm of a republic, whose strength is supposed to lie in the people. Lincoln was a strong man; but his strength was exerted to promote, not to pervert, the will of the people. He aspired to wisely serve rather than to tyrannically rule, and was therefore strong with the strength which should ever characterize our chief magistrates. It must be confessed that Cleveland's strength was exerted from first to last, not to foster local self-government, not to preserve and enlarge the privileges of the American citizen, but to enhance presidential prerogatives—to transform the chief magistrate from what Mr. Bryan correctly if somewhat coarsely calls a "hired man," into an absolute monarch. As "the evil men do live after them," Cleveland is likely to occupy an interesting page in American history—as well as crazy King George. It will require years of careful education to overcome the dangerous centralizing tendencies born of his administration—to worm the idea out of the fat heads of monarchy-worshipping Anglomaniacs and boneless Mugwumps that there is such a thing as "presidential prerogative." Prerogative is the malodor which rises from the rotten cesspool of "divine right." It was shot out of our atmosphere by the men who tickled the bustles of Burgoyne's Britishers with their bayonets and gave Cornwallis' redcoats hours to get their impudent carcasses off the American continent. The president of this republic is commissioned to perform certain clearly specified duties, and if he transcend his constitutional instructions is answerable to our courts—may be imprisoned like a common criminal or jerked to Jesus by the public hangman. Whenever you hear a man advocating "presidential prerogative" ·kill him; for he is an enemy to his country, a political pervert, a natural serf, and if suffered to live may breed Mugwumps, Anglomaniacs, and other cowardly vermin to crawl about an unclean throne—to peep about the huge legs of some Occidental Caesar.

Cleveland is a "strong man" exactly as the hog is a strong animal. Stubborn without courage, persevering without judgment and greedy without gratitude, these unpleasant characteristics Cleveland and the hog have in common. There are several other points of resemblance; but I have no desire to be hard on the hog. To his eternal credit be it said that the porker is content with his penfold, and has never aspired to defile the White House with his filth, to discredit the presidency with his folly. I have said that Cleveland is in some respects like Napoleon. There is a mutual ambition to rule regardless of human rights. Both manifest a contempt for the higher culture, an abnormal egotism, a base ingratitude, a foolish belief in fatalism; but while Napoleon rose to eminence by the dynamics of a commanding intellect, Cleveland was cast up by accident. Julius Caesar was ambitious; but he had the advantage of Napoleon in that, while a genius, he was also a gentleman. Domineering he was; but to him the glory of his country was dearer than life or crown. Instead of making the Imperial City a satrapy of Armenia because Aeneas came from ancient Ilium; instead of sending congenital bootlicks abroad as ambassadors to belittle the Latins; instead of tying his country's hands by a cowardly and inequitable arbitration treaty with an ancient enemy, he made the world to rock beneath the martial tread of Rome, the forum the court of arbitration for the earth, and princes to bow the knee wherever his eagles flew. Even American sovereigns might shift the cares of government to the shoulders of one whose charity was broader than his ambition, whose mailed hand was the symbol of eternal justice, whose intellect was his country's noblest jewel—might entrust their political fortunes to a man who was a Tacitus in the studio, an Aristides in the purple, an Apollo in the forum and a Mars in the field. Caesar and Napoleon treated the people's representatives with almost Clevelandesque discourtesy; but neither sent a substitute—a hired assassin—to the front to do his fighting, while he played pinochle for the beer and wallowed around in fourth-class bawdy-houses with disreputable widows.

Of all the "strong men" Cleveland most resembles Cromwell; still he is to the Lord Protector what the shadow of a shade is to the substance. The minds of the two men conform in many respects to the same mould; but where Cromwell is courageous for his God, Cleveland is only obstinate in behalf of his own egotism. The intellect of each is vigorous and tenacious, but narrow; and you may rake history with a fine-tooth comb without finding two others elevated to high office by civilized nations who are so grossly ignorant. Cromwell's book-learning was confined to the Bible; Cleveland's has an even narrower boundary. The latter has absolutely no conception of English literature. The only Horace he ever heard of is surnamed Boies, while Troy suggests to his mind only collars and cuffs. It is dollars to doughnuts he couldn't tell who invented the electric telegraph or built the first steamboat. It is stated on respectable authority that at the time of his first inaugural he had never read the constitution of the United States. How that may be I do not pretend to say; but his frequent violations of the fundamental law of the land gives to the statement a strong vraisemblance. Cleveland probably knows less about more things than any other man in America who can read and write; yet he is ambitious to be thought learned, and, like the editor of the Gal-Dal *News*, searches the dictionary for archaic and obsolete words of resounding length with which to adorn his labored lucubrations and make the ignorami wonder how one small head can hold so much. "Innocuous desuetude" is a fair sample of his linguistic damphoolery. An essayist, a magazine writer, whose clientele embraces only the educated, may be permitted, when drawing fine distinctions, to indulge in sesquipedalianisms, and even borrow untranslateable illustrations from other languages; but what must we think of a president who employs in a message, intended for *hoi polloi* as well as the *illuminati*, words which not one suffragist in ten can understand? We must place him on the same form with the pedantic editorial ass who flaunts boarding-school French, dog-Latin and exaggerated euphuisms in the columns of a nickel newspaper. Cleveland knows nothing of the nation he aspires to rule; nothing of its past, nothing of its present. How can he? He has not read a dozen books, has not seen a dozen cities. Such political education as he has was acquired from the slums of Buffalo and New York Bankers. Of the interest and needs of the great middle class, upon whose shoulders rest the government, in whose hands is the nation's destiny, he knows absolutely nothing. His only accomplishment is a certain expertness with rod and gun; albeit his so-called duck-hunts might more properly be called periodical drunks. He has no ear for music, no eye for art. He couldn't distinguish between Yankee Doodle and Dixie, or tell a plaster cast of Muckle-Mouthed Meg from a Carian Venus de Medici. Instead of making the White House the resort of authors, poets, painters, philosophers and scientists, it is the rendezvous of female necromancers and nigger mascots. Jefferson's delight was philosophy; Lincoln recuperated from his bloody cares with Artemus Ward's Wax Wurx; but Cleveland delights in fishing and fortune-telling. His idea of a "feast of reason and flow of soul" is something that can be gotten into a gut. The spiritualists assert that both of his administrations were directed by a female medium whom he frequently consulted. About three years ago this spook-compeller was touring the country and extensively advertising herself as Cleveland's confidential adviser, directress-general of the nation's destiny. The Blavatskyites claim him as a communicant. Whether this be true I know not; but that, like most **ignorant people, he is** grossly superstitious, there is ample evidence. He is a confessed fatalist, and fond of alluding to himself as "a man of destiny." He once appointed to an important army post a man of whom he had never heard, because, as he confessed to Senator Cockerill, he chanced to see the name in print and "had an impression" that he was the right party for the place. He was so pleased with the prophecy of a corrupt "coon" that he would be re-elected in '92 that he tried to make him minister to Bolivia, and being sat upon by the Senate, kept the ebon-hued Delphic oracle dangling about his court as a confidant.

Of course these may be the idiosyncrasies of genius, like Dr. Johnson's coffin-tapping in his search of the Cock-Lane ghost; but without aid from the occult, how can we account for Cleveland's sudden acquisition of a seven-figure fortune? He came to the White House with less coin in his pocket than Job's turkey had grain in its crop, and quickly blossomed forth as a plutocrat. A fortune-teller would—for a couple of dollars—locate for him the lost mine or the buried cash of the erstwhile Capt. Kidd. A magician might transmute his crapulous perspiration into pearls, or lend him Aladdin's lamp; but without supernatural aid how can an absolutely honest man become a multi-millionaire in eight years of office-holding at a salary of $50,000 per annum? Of course there are ways by which a president can make money without conspiring with bond syndicates for the sale of public securities at millions below their market value. Where the evidence of malfeasance is solely circumstantial, howsoever strong, we must, in conformity with legal usage, give the official full benefit of the doubt. Mr. Cleveland may have enacted the role of ninny rather than of knave. The plotters may have "worked" him without the necessity of taking him into partnership and sharing the swag. That Cleveland permitted speculators to employ the social pull of the presidency to boom real estate, and received $130,000 as his share of the profits on one deal in which he had not invested a dollar, even Cuckoodom does not deny. That none of his predecessors furnished a precedent for the Red Top transaction is doubtless due to the fact that they were gentlemen, and could not be used for speculative purposes. But what matters the example of a mere American to the King of Mugwumps? Is not His Royal Highness, the Prince of Wales, much given to the sale of his august society? And if the prince accepts a fat fee for spending an evening with a parvenu, should not his admirer have something handsome for residing at Red Top long enough to put pride-blown values in building lots? Cert! Cleveland's rapid rise from poverty to affluence may have been due to inherent crassness, to more than Boeotian ignorance, to his failure to apprehend the difference between dollars and dignity, rather than to absolute dishonesty. Be that as it may, he enjoys the doubtful distinction of being the first chief magistrate to leave the office richer than he entered it. That this was in nowise due to superior business acumen is evidenced by the fact that he was practically a pauper at eight-and-forty, and by the further fact that from the day he left the White House to the day he re-entered it he didn't make a dollar. In these times of ostentation it is customary to select for the higher governmental offices, such as members of the cabinet and ministers, men of large private means, it being tacitly understood that the honor costs more than it comes to. Presidents have hitherto left the White House with depleted purses; yet eight years in that office made Cleveland a multi-millionaire.

It is popularly supposed that men raise themselves to the chief magistracy by inherent merit; but that is an egregious error. Take any executive office, from grand-panjandrum of a 2x4 town to the presidency, and you will find a second-class man behind the fasces of authority four times in five. Observe the second-growth timber of which Texas makes "heroic young Christian governors!" What would a physiognomist say of that fact—two fishballs, a seed wart and a pucker sketched on the clammy hide of a coyote? Note the wooden-headed yaps who squat like mowing apes on the supreme bench of New York, deciding it to be "not laudable" for Jewish religious societies to meet on Sunday—the crooked roots and rotton limbs of which Illinois makes legislators. Webster, Clay, Conkling, Blaine, Greeley, Sherman—con the long list of mental giants who failed for an office which time after time has gone to unknown men of little minds. How many Americans knew aught of Hayes or Harrison, Garfield or Cleveland before they were put forward as political gonfaloniers? You can count on your fingers those who won name and fame before reaching the presidency, and five of these had attracted attention, not in the council, but the camp. McKinley was known only by his name having been tacked to a vicious law which he did not draft—not that his heart was unwilling, but that his head was too weak. Great men usually defeat each others' presidential aspirations. While Agamemnon storms and

Achilles sulks, Patroclus—the "fool positive"—leads forth the legions.

Like so many of his predecessors in office, Cleveland was not born great, nor did he achieve greatness; it was thrust upon him by the god of mischance—by that bull-luck which he denominates destiny. From all that I can gather of his early life he was a slow, phlegmatic child who learned the simplest things only by a laborious effort which he was inclined to shirk. At seventeen he had barely succeeded in mastering the Three R's, and was packed off to an uncle at Buffalo, who supported him for several years while he studied law, and for sometime thereafter because he could not make a living. He spent some little time teaching blind children their letters—and has been a guide to the sightless ever since. His profession failing to yield him a livelihood, and his uncle being unable or unwilling to house a great hulk of three-and-twenty free of cost, he took to peanut politics and obtained a small office by grace of the "push." The tough element of Buffalo controlled municipal and county politics. It finally made him sheriff, then mayor, apparently for the same reason that the same element in Galveston sent Miles Crowley to Congress—to show its contempt for the "silk stockings." Then the country Democracy dug up the tomahawk and went for Tammany The chasm had to be bridged before the gubernatorial election or the party was in the nine-hole. Cleveland had continued to play at pinochle and peanut politics—did not so much as send a substitute to the political strife. Old John Kelly discovered him and offered the unbranded maverick to the country Democracy as a compromise gubernatorial candidate. Under ordinary conditions he would have been beaten; but that providence which watches over drunk men and fools still had him under its protection. Conkling and Me Too Platt, by putting the gaffles into President Garfield, ruptured the Republican party from narrative to neckband, and the Democrats won in a walk. Had their candidate been a Chinese joss or wooden Indian he would have got there just the same, and by as big a majority. Cleveland was considered an available candidate by the warring Democratic factions for the self-same reason that a juror is accepted—he knew nothing of the case in court. Had he been addicted to the thinking habit he must have expressed an opinion; and had he done so he would not have been made governor—might have been hanging malefactors and chasing Widow Halpins in Erie county to-day. As New York was considered the pivotal state, the governorship put him in line for the presidency. The Democratic candidate must be depended upon to carry New York, and Cleveland had swept it like a cyclone—thanks to Conkling. Thus a few years after this fellow was fiddling around the chicken-courts of Buffalo, picking up an occasional five dollar (trade) fee as counsel for female vags, he was elevated by accident to the chief magistracy of the mightiest nation that ever graced the tide of time.

It is unnecessary to tell any true disciple of Blackstone that Cleveland is unlearned in the law, for no man having the faintest hope of rising in that profession will become a shrievalty candidate. Your thorough-paced lawyer is something of an aristocrat, not to say a snob. From his lofty —but narrow—pinnacle he looks down patronizingly upon more useful professions. It is claimed by some sociologists that the practice of law, while sharpening the vulpine faculty, atrophies the broader intelligence. Whether that view be correct is not my present concern. If not eminently successful, your lawyer (I am speaking only of ornaments of the bar) may regret at times that he did not take to medicine, the army or navy, as almost equally respectable and usually more profitable; but the eviction of widows for non-payment of rent, the strangling of malefactors, the levies and distraints of the constabulary he regards as occupation for quite another class. Having been a public hangman, Cleveland stands condemned *ex-officio* as a shyster in the legal profession. From counsel for courtesans to sheriff of a notoriously corrupt county; from sheriff to mayor of a feculent sink-hole of political iniquity; from mayor to governor by the grace of old John Kelly—keeper of the reliques of St. Tammany; from governor to president, for reasons purely geographical, and behold this able-bodied sponge on an impoverished relative is permitted to parcel out a nation's patronage, to say to the senators and representatives of more than forty sovereign states, "I object." This creature of blind chance, this sport of chaos, this bubble cast up by a political Malebolge, this egesta of the boozing-kens and honk-a-tonks of Buffalo, was now able to laugh to scorn the will of a majority of the senate and house of representatives, composed largely of men grown gray in the nomorhetic work of the nation— men who will know more when they are dead than his fat head can ever hold. And object he did. In the first year of his incumbency he vetoed more bills than had all his predecessors combined. There was an exhibition of egotism, of transcendental gall, to amaze the gods. Other presidents considered the people's representatives as rational beings who knew what their masters desired; Cleveland treated congress as an unruly kindergarten and his cabinet officers as mere clerks. Being the first Democratic president elected since Buchanan, he calmly assumed that he was the heaven-sent Messiah, not only of his party but of the nation, his will was the supreme law of the land. As he began so he continued; or rather say his impudence increased from year to year in a ratio of geometrical progression. During his second term he developed unmistakable monarchical tendencies. He entered into a compact with England and Germany to keep the Samoans subject unto a king. He tried to reinstate a saddle-colored harlot as queen of Hawaii. He planted his ponderous corporosity in the path of the Cuban Republic. He ordered the invasion by federal troops of a sovereign state in defiance of the constitution. He suffered Bootlick Bayard to go unrebuked for declaring in effect that he was a dictator, and that a dictator was necessary to the proper government of the unruly American people. He attempted to dictate the platform of his party in the interest of England, and not being permitted to do so, employed all the power and patronage of his office to destroy an organization that had twice made him chief magistrate. That is this great man's idea of gratitude. It is likewise an apt illustration of his insolence. The creature would give law to its creator—the ex-hangman calmly assumed to be wiser, better, more patriotic than his party. If there was a wire running to the Throne of Grace he'd issue orders to Almighty God, remove Christ Jesus as a Communist and give some Massachusetts Mugwump his job.

Inordinate gall and base ingratitude are Clevelands's integrants, his component parts. The uncle who had befriended him died and left a poor daughter in straitened circumstances. In the day of his prosperity Cleveland suffered to be sold over her head the house in which he had fattened at the expense of her father. She appealed to him for help and he gave her the horse-laugh. It is said that all sins may be forgiven except blasphemy against the Holy Ghost. I move to amend by striking out Ghost and inserting ingratitude. Ghosts, holy or otherwise, do not have to hang around where their feelings are liable to be hurt; but the ungracious human fice that will not fight for those who have fed it deserves the triple-heated tortures of hell. Cleveland kindly permitted his sister to act as his housekeeper until he found a wife, then gave her the bounce. He has a brother, but his footstep is never heard in the corridors of the White House. His relatives know him —and come not near him. But enough! If you want a disquisition on Cleveland's ingratitude that will make your hair curl, go to Gorman, who, having elected him, called at the White House three days after the inaugural expecting to be drowned in a sea of sirup—and got the door slammed in his face. Go to Bissell, to Mills, to Voorhees—to any man who has ever done Cleveland a personal or political kindness. Invariably those who have served him best have been treated worst, while those who have done naught but fawn and flatter that they might feed on public fodder, bask in the sunshine of his favor. I have compared Cleveland to Cromwell; but I think an apology is due the Lord Protector. Cromwell was savage as a she-wolf to powerful foes, but Cleveland is mean to relatives and friends. When a stranger grossly insulted Cromwell and was bundled off to prison, the object of his wrath released him and gave him a dinner; when a congressman criticises Cleveland the latter avenges his outraged dignity by vetoing measures of local interest to his constituents. Cromwell retained his personal enemy at the head of the British navy because of his great ability. Cleveland unceremoniously kicked his old law partner, Bissell, out of the cabinet for having suggested that he might resign in a few months. Neither of these upstart ignorami was satisfied with a divided authority; each strove to draw unto himself the entire power of the state. Cleveland did refrain from adjourning congress at the point of the bayonet for declining to do his bidding; but his forbearance seems to have been due more to that cause which led him to send a substitute to fight the battles of a care-free young bachelor than to any respect for the constitutional rights of the people or the dignity of their representatives. He could not play the Cromwellian game to the limit because he lacked physical courage. The war substitute is not the only evidence that, despite the philsophy of the Melancholy Dane, a man may be white-livered who doesn't lack gall. Cleveland never appears in a crowd unless surrounded by a cordon of armed detectives. It requires a company of 26 police to keep the bities off him at the presidential mansion. When Cæsar the tyrant was warned of his impending assassination he replied with a scornful laugh; when our popular idol gives a reception to those who delight to do him honor, armed men stand ready to protect his precious life, and the crackling of a parlor match will make his coward lips from their color fly. At one of these "functions" he had 50 uniformed police in the East Room; but Washington guyed him so unmercifully that he has since relied upon the secret service and the enforced presence of officers of the army and navy for temporal salvation. Yet he professes to be a fatalist and prates of destiny —which proves that he doesn't know the Norns from an accident insurance association. Think of a "man of destiny" taking such heroic precautions against death!—of a fatalist trying to dodge his lethal day! Yet we hear much from the Mugwumps of Cleveland's consistency. He is consistent very, I don't think. When first elected he declared that no man should occupy the presidency more than one term; yet he has been three times a candidate, twice elected, and is already plotting to get himself returned in 1900, despite a hundred years of precedent. He is of the opinion that the country will then turn to him and tearfully implore him to succor and to save. If it does, the South and West will part company with the Eastern cuckoos. They have had all the Cleveland in theirs they can stomach. If they must have a dictator they'll take a man like Diaz—one who runs less to bowels and more to brains.

I freely concede that all Cleveland's intentions may have been upright. I am not of those who regard him either as Anti-Christ or angel. I think he would average up very well as a Chicago alderman or Dallas editor. If honest, the dreadful blunders of his administrations should be forgiven if not forgotten. That he has disrupted his party and bankrupted his country may be the misfortune of his head rather than the fault of his heart. If, as Schiller assures us, the gods themselves are powerless against stupidity, could we expect Cleveland to rise superior to himself? If we employ a blacksmith to make a watch we have no right to complain of his work. From first to last Cleveland was unfortunate in his surroundings, and the strongest men are largely moulded by environment. His uncle's mistaken kindness in supporting him in idleness after he had grown to man's estate disqualified him from earning a respectable livelihood. Perhaps he should be commended for having become a pothouse politician instead of a foot pad. His associations at Buffalo were brutalizing. His rapid rise from saloon bum waiting to be "asked," to political eminence, gave him an exaggerated idea of his own importance. From the day he entered the gubernatorial mansion at Albany to this good hour he has been surrounded by Anglomaniacs, title-worshippers, tuft-hunters and devotees of Mammon—those to whom money and place are everything, and genius, manhood and national honor nothing. Half a century of bachelorhood and unbridled debauchery has stifled all the finer feelings that may have been native to his blood. Thus we find him chuckling in high glee over the manner in which the vultures of the press watched his young and beautiful wife for signs of embonpoint, and when discovered, speculated on whether the unborn pape would be a girl or a boy. It filled his crass corporosity with elephantine pride to have reporters detailed by the "great dailies" to count and dilate upon the texture of the diapers, to pump the nurse-maid and family physician and inform an anxious, almost awe-struck universe, when the heir-apparent might be expected. I can only wonder that he didn't invite the general public to the accouchement and charge admission. It would have been just as legal and fully as respectable as some of the other methods he adopted for making the presidency pay. We have in the South, I confess, a considerable coop of cuckoos who considered Cleveland's course as quite the proper caper —people who would feel highly flattered to see before-and-after portraits of their own wives in the public prints; but a genuine Southern gentleman would have pumped those parturition reporters so full of buckshot that their cuticle wouldn't have held corn-cobs. Cleveland was controlled, not by public opinion, not by his legal advisers, but by his kitchen cabinet, fortune-tellers and colored mascots. He was flattered by sharpers and fawned upon by fools until he became lost in the awful gloom of his own supposed greatness, isolated in the everlasting night of what he didn't know. He should be treated for ossification of the heart and fatty degeneration of the head.

TRILBY PARTIES AND PIETY.

EMOTIONAL RELIGION RESPONSIBLE FOR PROSTITUTION.

The Methodists of Bath Beach, N. Y., are doing what they can to make religion both pleasant and profitable. They needed money for their church, but somehow the tearful appeals of the preacher did not cause the contribution basket to become sag-bellied. All the good brethren loved Jesus; but the McKinley tidal wave of progress and prosperity was rolling over Bath Beach, and it is much easier to hang up the premiums on a celestial insurance policy than to stand off a grocery bill. When times are hard a man's first stroke of economy is to cut down his monthly allowance to his lady and his Lord, his last a reduction in the quality of his liquor. The financial crisis of the church became acute before a man rose equal to the occasion. Finally Deacon Peter Moore put his wits to work, and now the M. E. church of Bath Beach has money to burn. Peter, who appears to be the rock upon which the Lord has built the M. E. church at that point, gave a "Trilby party." He selected two dozen young lady members of the sanctified flock who rejoiced in shapely feet, divested them of shoes and stockings, exposed the dainty pedal extremities beneath a screen to the gaze of the admiring multitude, and sold each a pair of tootsie-wootsies at auction to the highest bidder. The dispatches state that "the young men of the congregation bid recklessly." I don't doubt it. Such a divine revelation as that were enough to fill even a wooden man so full of religious fervor that he would sell his extra pair of pantaloons, pawn his overcoat and cheerfully give receipts for the spread of the gospel, the promulgation of saving grace. I am pleased to learn that one pair of underpinning especially Trilbyesque, the toes whereof were tied with blue ribbon bows, brought a fancy price. Such a blending of the red, white and blue could not but appeal with a weird power to any rightly constituted American patriot. Under such circumstances the man who would not contribute his last copper to the end in view were fit for treasons, stratagems and spoils. It is to be taken for granted, of course, that the pedalic symposium had been duly chiropodized, perfumed and was redolent with the odor of sanctity. Verily Deacon Peter Moore hath a large, juicy head; is a veritable genius. What a pity McKinley didn't give him the treasury portfolio!

There are few things more attractive to the average man than a shapely pair of feminine feet. Even when their glories are half-hidden in silk stockings and glove-fitting kids he abases his soul in the dust before them and lets the high heels trample on his heart; but when relieved of impedimenta, he feels an irresistible impulse to get hold of and fondle them, to trace love-letters in the tangle of blue veins on a field of alabaster, and tell off the little pig story on the pearly toes. Little Billee was just like all his brothers—the beauty of Trilby's foot made him forget the malformation of her morals and the resounding emptiness of her mind. Still, a man in search of a wife may get some valuable pointers at a "Trilby party." He may there obtain in advance an inkling of what he's going up against. Cold hands indicate a warm heart, but cold feet signify that there's going to be trouble in the family. Half the domestic infelicity and resultant divorces might be avoided were bridegrooms-elect permitted to take the temperature of their fiancees' feet. Many a man who can give Job points on patience and Moses on meekness, will rise up and blaspheme all the saints in the calendar when, in the stilly watches of a winter night, a brace of icebergs insinuate themselves beneath the narrative of his nightshirt and begin a tour of exploration up his spine. I don't wonder that Deacon Moore's scheme was a scintillating success. Had he notified me in time I would have been on hand with a wad of greenbacks as big as a cotton bale—would have purchased everything in sight and thereunto appertaining. I would have had those blue-ribbon bows made into a necktie and worn it when I went in quest of the most beautiful woman in the world. The opportunity to luxuriate in the loveliness of four-and-twenty pair of naked feminine feet comes but once in a lifetime, and I got side-tracked in the shuffle. But doubtless Deacon Moore is not yet done. Having become the chief exponent of Trilbyismus, he must not hesitate to play the game to the limit in the name of the Lord. The young ladies of Bath Beach, having made so good a beginning, cannot well refuse to do as much for religion as their great exemplar did for art. Having taken Trilby as their criterion in modesty, their guide in morality, the next time the church needs money we may expect them to be auctioned off *in puris naturalibus*. Doubtless the young men of the congregation would bid even more recklessly on the "altogether" than on a collection of corns and crop of bunions offered them at auction in the name of religion.

A "Trilby party" may be a good thing in its place, but its place is a sub-cellar in the most disreputable corner of Hell's Half Acre. The heroine of Du Maurier's trashy novel is a grimy Parisian grisette who hangs about the Latin Quarter, posing naked for a crowd of half a hundred artist hoodlums, who, after sketching her figure, help her on with her clothes —"placing each garment in its proper place and deftly buttoning it." She confesses to having been criminally intimate with three men and offers her damaged wares to a fourth, and this without having been driven to degradation by need or hurried thither by passion. She breaks the Seventh Commandment "in a gay spirit of camaraderie," just to be accommodating—because of "the difficulty of saying nay to earnest pleading." Is that why she has been apotheosized in a thousand pulpits?—why female church members are so anxious to imitate her? Why is it that we have no Mary Magdalen parties? When "a woman of the city who was a sinner" reformed and was forgiven, did she cease to be interesting to the super-sanctified? Does it require a suggestion of sexual sin, unpardoned and unrepented, to popularize a name in religious circles? For every effect there must be an efficient cause, and in this case it is not far to seek; for the Protestant religion has become little less than a perverted sexuality, the Methodist and Baptist churches the most striking example of its debasement. Of course it were impossible to make this appear to the shouters and sanctifiers; but a little reflection will convince any close student of both psychology and physiology that it cannot be otherwise—that sensational religion is responsible for a large per cent. of our prostitutes. The Jews are frequently alluded to by their critics as a "lustful race," and we are assured by the A. P. A. that the Catholics are "ignorant." It is from lustful races and ignorant people that we naturally expect the great army of courtesans to be recruited; but, boasting a more temperate blood than the Jew, a wider intelligence than the Catholic, Protestantism furnishes nearly all the prostitutes! This fact has been demonstrated so often that the man who denies it simply signs a certificate to his own irremediable idiocy or hopeless dishonesty. When a dirty social scandal occurs everybody is surprised if the woman in the case chances to be a Catholic. I have frequently called the attention of Protestants to this fact. When compelled by indisputable evidence to admit the superior chastity of the Catholics, they have attributed it to the restraining influence of the confessional. If this be true, it seems to me that the confessional is a pretty good thing and should be universally adopted; but such is not the case. That lying is a sin the Bible teaches; but that it is by no means as serious as adultery may be inferred from the fact that it is not prohibited by the Decalogue; hence it were idle to urge that a woman capable of fornication is incapable of falsehood. The first fault not only connotes but includes the last, is a falsehood by itself considered.

Religion and music belong not in the realm of reason, but

are expressive of the emotional in man, and the emotional—even the highest—is a refinement of the physical. Both have been employed from time immemorial to play upon the passions. The early Greek authors noted the power of music to make men savage and sensual. The battle-hymn breeds murder in the heart; the Lydian strain suggests the temple of Mylitta. The gust for blood is cousin-german to the gust for beauty, and none can say which is the most savage. Shakespeare and many other authors have noted the deleterious effect of music on female morality. In our own day we have seen women of alleged respectability clamber upon the stage and passionately embrace a crummy male pianist, while performances of equal merit by musicians of their own sex evoked only an icy admiration. The world has had some eloquent lady preachers; but none have been able to win that adoration from women which they yield to every he-pulpiteer, from the vulgar Sam Jones to the jejune Talmage and libidinous Beecher. This is simply because there is a strong suggestion of sex in both religion and music, a suggestion that has been developed to the danger point by several Protestant denominations. This abnormal excitement, this exacerbation of the nerves, this continual appeal to the emotions, produces that morbid condition of the mind and body so inimical to continence, which so easily degenerates into nympholepsy or nymphomania. Thus it is but natural that from earliest times music should have been a leading feature in religious rites. I do not mean by this that either is an evil by itself considered; it is against their perversion that I protest.

There is an unmistakable tendency on the part of Protestantism to leave those lofty heights to which it attained in a purer age, and revert to the phallic revel. Emolliated by wealth and luxury, the old spirit of heroism is dying out of it, leaving the sensual in full possession. Nor is this decadence confined to a particular faith; it affects, more or less, men of all creeds and those who belong to no cult. The emotional in man no longer finds expression in a crusade of the Holy Sepulchre or the austere life of the Puritans, in Demosthenic eloquence or Miltonian poetry. In that old land where Saxon steel once rang against Saracen sword the Christian is trampled beneath the brutal heel of the Turk, but steel-clad Europe stirs not. From the loins of Christendom there spring Talmagian blatherskites and Parkhurstian police inspectors, but no Peter-the-Hermit or Richard Coeur de Lion. No more are heroes wafted to Valhalla's halls by Valkyrian hymns; no longer does youth listen with bated breath to the Wondrous Tale of Troy, or manhood feel the music of the battery beating in its blood. Mars, that virile god at whose high altars the world once worshipped, now stands discredited, his field a tennis-court, his temple a Sam Jones tabernacle or *maison de joie*. Human rights are no longer worth a battle, nor national honor the expenditure of boodle. Even America, the sum and crown of things, is fast adopting the Machiavellian policy—now relies upon vulpine diplomacy rather than the justice of her cause, her heart of oak and almighty arm. Once jealous in honor and quick to resent an affront with a blow, she now whines like a sick girl about the barbarity of war, and asks a board of arbitration to estimate in dollars and cents the gravity of an insult. Instead of "mounting barbed steeds to fright the souls of fearful adversaries," Uncle Sam now "capers nimbly in a lady's chamber to the lascivious pleasing of a lute." Year by year we are drifting further from the stern integrity and high purpose of our fathers toward that sybaritism which marked Rome's decline, and those sexual abnormalities that are the curse of Asia. From imperial Byron with his titled mistresses to Oscar Wilde and his nameless infamies; from the sword of Washington to the cowardice of Cleveland; from the eloquence of Massillon to the pruriency of Parkhurst—yet we dare turn our faces to the throne of God and pray for saving grace!

This decadence is reflected in our politics, art and literature, but more especially in our religion. The preacher is becoming ever more a phallic priest. He explores the slums of great cities for offal to carry to his congregation. His sermons tend ever more and more to sensuality, because he appeals ever less and less to the laws of logic, seeks only to excite the emotions to unhealthy activity. The result is neurasthenia, manifesting itself sometimes in fierce fanaticism, hysteria or "jerks"; but more frequently in an undermining of the moral concept, obfuscation of the mental faculties and perversion of the procreative passion. A love of God born of the normal head and heart is the highest and holiest of human emotions; but a half-crazed adoration begotten of diseased nerves is apt to be carnal enough—to mistake the minister for the Almighty. Thus it is that popular revivalists can truthfully proclaim that "there is no relation between morality and religion." This may explain why relatively more preachers than of any other class of professional men get into trouble through excessive mulierosity. The position of a doctor of medicine is not nearly so Josephean as that of a doctor of divinity. It is well to bear in mind that civilization, bearing all things with it, moves in a circle, and that the earliest religious cults of which we have knowledge were grossly carnal. To this day the procreative organs are objects of religious worship to millions. Within historic times prostitution was not only considered pleasing to the gods, but made obligatory. Judaism was polygamous, and the Bible abounds with stories of debaucheries by the beloved of the Lord. The Mohammedan is allowed four wives here and houris galore hereafter. The Christian religion is grounded upon the Immaculate Conception. Sexualism is the law of life, a thing natural, necessary to the conservation of the race, and there is nothing in the Christian religion proper that makes for its perversion. After an existence of fifteen centuries the corruption of its priesthood was urged in extenuation of Luther's revolt, yet from this so-called Reformation there sprung numerous societies infamous because of their sexual immorality. Mormonism, the latest independent religion to develop, is a synonym for sensuality. There is a tendency to free love on the part of the sanctificationists and other late diversifications of Protestantism. The immorality of church choirs has passed into a proverb. To the members of the emotional churches the Lord is becoming ever less and less, their sensation-mongering ministers ever more and more. Deny Christ, insult the Virgin and blaspheme the name of God, and they'll forgive you; but insinuate that their little ticky-tailed preachers are a set of blatant asses who ought to go braid their ears, and they'll boycott you simply because they dare not crucify. While the Presbyterians and Episcopalians are not much more tolerant than are the Baptists and Methodists, they are less addicted to the whoopla style of evangelism, and are therefore doing less to fill the land with nerve diseases and enhance the population of the redlight district.

We are getting back very fast to the starting point—to that religious state wherein the priests were panders, and virginity solemnly sacrificed in the face of heaven as a first-fruit offering to the powers of Lust and Fecundity. The churches now resort to devices for raising money that would have set worldlings in the stocks a century ago and put women in prison as disreputables. Had young Mr. Seeley given his bachelor blow-out under the auspices of religion, charged a dollar admission and donated the receipts "to the cause," he would have found no end of apologists and defenders. Did not the pulpiteers praise Trilby?—accept St. Du Maurier as the apostle of the divine cult of female modesty? And does not St. Du Maurier assure us that only clothing is sensual—that "nothing is so chaste as nudity?" What then? Should not the Campbellites of Lampasas, who sold old maids at auction, have disrobed them first that their calikers appeal not to the carnal? Should not the Epworth Leaguers of Suffern, N. Y., who gave a leg-show to raise money for an impecunious minister, have first removed their hosiery? Should not the young ladies in various places who have given fancy dances and high-kicking exhibitions to fill church coffers have done so costumed *a la* "Little Egypt"—simply in a pair of anklets? If Trilby was a nice party whom it is proper for respectable young ladies to ostentatiously imitate in some respects, why not in all? But perchance the church will yet come to that—especially if the hard times continue. Under the tuition of St. Du Maurier, they may yet give "altogether" exhibits—with blue ribbons tied around the waists of their stock-in-trade, instead of about its toes. They may yet establish a Succoth-Benoth for the relief of bankrupt congregations and the spread of the gospel. I nominate Deacon Moore as keeper of the "Tents of the Maidens" and permanent auctioneer. The Catholic church once preserved the Christian religion amidst the wreck of civilization; but whether it will be able to save it from the ever rising tide of diseased emotionalism remains to be seen. As a candle sputters most vigorously when on the point of expiring, it is possible that the emotional creeds are even now frying themselves in their own fat; that we will have a little more of the "Munster Baptist" business, and then a renaissance of decency, if not a remarriage of morality and religion and a general return to reason.

EVIDENCES OF MAN'S IMMORTALITY.

Unless you accept the testimony of the Bible as conclusive, what evidence have you of God's existence and man's immortality?—Gladstone.

The same evidence that we would have of the existence of the ocean were one drop of water withdrawn, of the life of a forest, were a single leaf to fall. The Bible did not create man's belief in God's existence and his own immortality, but of this belief, old as Zoroaster, ante-dating Babylon, was the Bible born. It is simply an outward evidence of man's inward grace. I do accept the testimony of the Bible, but only as one of a cloud of witnesses. In questions of such grave import, we cannot have too much evidence; hence it is strange indeed that any one should make the Bible the sole foundation of his faith, should take his stand upon an infinitesimal portion of what the world knew in ages past. The Bible is but one of many sacred books in which man has borne witness that he is the favored creature of an Almighty Being, but one voice in a multitude singing hosannas to the Most High, a single note in the mighty diapason of the universe.

A hundred men are shipwrecked upon an island in the Arctic ocean. By day and night they dream of absent friends, of mother, wife and child, the pleasant meadows or the sunny hills of their distant homes. Hourly they scan the horizon with eager eyes. Daily they ask each other, "Is there hope?" All former animosities are forgotten, for they are brothers in misfortune. One declares that the island lies in the pathway of a regular line of steamers, and that they must soon be rescued. This view is approved by many, and their hearts beat high with hope. Their sufferings are borne with cheerfulness, their hardships appear trivial, for their probation is soon to pass and they will be at home. Another avers that they are too far north to be reached by the ocean liners, but that a whaler will soon be due in that vicinity, and all will be well. This view is approved by some, and thus there are two parties confidently expecting succor, but from different sources. A third studies the map, notes the advanced season, inspects the food supply and shakes his head. "We shall be lost," he says; "desire has misled your judgment; you do but dream." Do the two parties that entertain hope strive, each to disprove the theory of the other, and unite in persecuting the dissenter? No; they reason together, each anxious to ascertain the truth, knowing that it will profit him nothing to believe a lie. Suddenly a cry is heard, "A sail!" Do those who put their trust in the whaler turn their backs to the sea and say, "Oh, h——l! that's only one of those regular steamship heretics! no rag of canvas will he discover!" Do those who were destitute of hope decline to look? No; all rush to the shore, and strain their eyes to penetrate the mist, little caring whether it be whaler or steamer, so they do but see a ship. When one makes out the vessel, he is not content until the eyes of others confirm his vision, and all look, not with the jealous hope that he may be wrong, but with an earnest prayer that he may be right. That island is this little earth, its shipwrecked mariners all sons of men; yet how different we set about determining whether, from out the everlasting sea that encircles us, there comes indeed a Ship of Zion to succor and to save!

What one man believes or disbelieves is a matter of little moment; for belief will not put gods on High Olympus, nor unbelief extinguish the fires of Hell. Man can neither create nor uncreate the actual by a mental emanation. If Deity exists, he would continue to exist did a universe deny him; if he exists not, then all the faith and prayers and sacrifices of a thousand centuries will not evolve him from the night of nothingness. There is or there is not a life beyond the grave, regardless of the denial of every Atheist and the affirmation of every prophet. Then what boots it whether we believe or disbelieve in God's existence or man's immortality? Nothing, in so far as it concerns the factual; much, in that upon our hopes and fears is based our terrestial bane or blessing. Banish all belief in God, eliminate the idea of man's responsibility to a higher power, make him the sole lord of his life and earthly good his greatest guerdon, and you destroy the dynamics of progress, the genius of civilization. Man has a tendency to become what he believes himself to be. Consciously or unconsciously, he strives with less or greater strength toward his ideal; hence it is all-important that he consider himself an immortal rather than the pitiful sport of Time and Space; a child of Omniscience, rather than the ephemeral emanation of unclean ooze. Had man always considered himself simply an animal, his tendencies would have been ever earthward; believing himself half divine, he has striven to mount above the stars. True, many great men have been Atheists; but they were formed by ancestry and environment permeated by worship of Divine power. Without a belief in his own semi-divinity to lead the race onward and upward, the conditions which produce a Voltaire or Ingersoll were impossible. Civilization is further advanced than ever before, and Atheism more general; but those who employ this fact as argument against religious faith forget that a body thrown upward will continue to ascend for a time after it has parted from the propelling power. Atheism is in nowise responsible for human progress, for Atheism is nothing—a mere negation—and "out of nothing nothing comes." A belief in God affords man a basis upon which to build; it is an acknowledgment of authority, the chief prerequisite of order; but in Atheism there is no constructive element. While it may be no more immoral to deny the existence of Deity than to question the Wondrous Tale of Troy, history teaches us that, considered from a purely utilitarian standpoint, the most absurd faith is better for a nation than none; that the civic virtues do not long survive the sacrifice; that when a people desert their altars their glories soon decay. The civilization of the world has been time and again imperiled by the spirit of Denial. When Rome began to mock her gods, she found the barbarians thundering at her gates. When France insulted her priesthood and crowned a courtesan as Goddess of Reason in Notre Dame, Paris was a maelstrom and the nation a chaos in which Murder raged and Discord shrieked. Today we are boasting of our progress, but 'tis the onward march of Jaganath, beneath whose iron wheels patriotism, honesty, purity and the manly spirit of independence are crushed into the mire. We have drifted into an Atheistical age, and its concomitants are selfishness, sensationalism and sham. The old heartiness and healthiness have gone out of life, have been supplanted by the artificial. Everything is now show and seeming—"leather and prunella"—the body social become merely a galvanic machine or electric motor. In our gran'sire's day "the great man helped the poor, and the poor man loved the great;" now the great man systematically despoils the poor and the poor man regards the great with a feeling of envy and hatred akin to that of which the French Revolution was born. Character no longer counts for aught unless reinforced by a bank account. Men who have despoiled the widow of her mite and the orphan of his patrimony are hailed with the acclaim due to conquering heroes. Our most successful books and periodicals would pollute a Parisian sewer or disgrace a Portuguese bagnio. The suffrages of the people are bought and sold like sheep. The national policy is dictated by Dives. Men are sent to Congress whom God intended for the gallows, while those he ticketed for the penitentiary spout inanities in fashionable pulpits. The merchant who pays his debts in full when he might settle for ten cents on the dollar is considered deficient in common sense. The grandsons of Revolutionary soldiers, who considered themselves the equal of kings and the superior of princes, wear the livery of lackeys to obtain an easy living. Presidents save seven-figure fortunes on five-figure salaries and are applauded by people who profess to be respectable. Governors waste the public revenues in suppressing pugilistic enterprises, begotten of their own encouragement, only to be re-elected by fools and slobbered over by pharisees. Bradley-Martin balls are given while half a million better people go hungry to bed. Friendship has become a farce, the preface of fraud. Revolting crimes increase and sexuality is tinged with the infamy of the Orient. Men who were too proud to borrow leave sons who are not ashamed to beg. In man great riches are preferable to a good name, and in woman a silken gown covers a multitude of sins. The homely virtues of the old mothers in Israel are mocked, while strumpets fouler than Sycorax are received in society boasting itself select. Why is this? It is because the old religious spirit is dormant if not dead; it is because when people consider themselves but as the beasts that perish, they can make no spiritual progress, but imitate their supposed ancestors. Religion is becoming little more than a luxury, the temple a sumptuous palace wherein people ennuied with themselves may parade their costly cloths, have their jaded passions soothed by sensuous music, their greed for the bizarre satiated by sensational sermons.

This being true, the question of evidence of God's existence and man's immortality becomes the most important ever propounded. The devout worshipper points to his Sacred Book; but we have had Sacred Books in abundance so far back as we can trace human history, yet the wave of Atheism, of Unbelief, rises ever higher and higher—threatens to engulf the world. After nearly nineteen centuries of earnest proselyting less than a third of the world has accepted Christianity, and in those countries professedly Christian, Atheism flourishes as it does nowhere else. Of more than seventy million Americans, less than twenty-four million are church communicants, and it is doubtful if half of these really believe the Bible. Beecher criticised it almost as freely as does Ingersoll, while a number of prominent preachers of the Briggs-Abbott brand are even now explaining, in the pulpit and the press, that it is little more than a collection of myths. The people are drifting ever further from the Book of Books, and the pulpit appears ambitious to lead the procession. It is idle to urge that man should believe the Bible; for man should believe nothing, man can believe nothing but what receives the sanction of his reason. He is no more responsible for what he believes or disbelieves than for the color of his eyes or the place of birth. He may deceive the world with a false profession of faith, but can deceive neither God nor himself. The mind of even the worst of men is a court in which every cause is tried with rigid impartiality, with absolute honesty. A fool may mislead it, a child may convince it, but not even its possessor can coerce it; hence to command one to "believe," without first providing him with a satisfactory basis for his faith, were an idle waste of breath. A man is no more blamable for doubting the existence of Deity than for doubting aught else that may seem to him absurd. He doubts because the evidence submitted is unsatisfactory, or his mind is incapable of properly analyzing it. Probably none of the Sacred Books ever yet convinced an intelligent human being that there is aught in the universe greater than himself. I do not mean by this that the Bible and the Koran, the Zend-Avesta and the Vedas are all false, but that there is lack of sufficient evidence that they are true. Those who accept them do so because they harmonize with their own half-conscious religious conceptions, because their truth is established by esoteric rather than by exoteric evidence. All attempts to supplant Buddhism and Mohammedanism by Christianity have proven futile, and that because the former do while Christianity does not voice the religious sentiment of the Orient, a sentiment which exists regardless of their Sacred Books, and of which the latter are but indications. You can no more demonstrate the truth of the Bible to a Hindu than you can demonstrate the truth of the Vedas to a Christian, for in either case outward evidence is wanting and the subject is not *en rapport* with the new doctrine. It is not infrequently urged that evidence sufficient to convince Mr. Gladstone should likewise convince Col. Ingersoll. And so it doubtless would in a court of law; but in matters spiritual what may appear "confirmation strong as proofs of Holy Writ" to the one may seem an absurdity absolute to the other. Neither had the pleasure of Moses' acquaintance. All witnesses of his miracles have been dead so long that their very graves are forgotten. There is nothing in the accounts, however, violative of Mr. Gladstone's conception of Deity, hence he finds no difficulty in accepting them. To Col. Ingersoll, however, there is something ridiculous in the idea of the Creator of the Cosmos become a bonfire and holding a private confab with the stuttering Hebrew. He demands undisputable evidence, it is not forthcoming, and he brands the story as a fraud. For the same reason Mr. Gladstone accepts the miracles of Moses he accepts Christ as the Savior; for the same reason that he denies the burning bush, Col. Ingersoll denies Christ's divinity. The story of a suffering Savior appeals directly to Mr. Gladstone's heart, but it gets no further than Col. Ingersoll's head. The one tries it by his sympathies, the other by the rules of evidence that obtain in a court of law. In summing up, Col. Ingersoll might say: It has not been demonstrated to the satisfaction of this court that Jesus ever claimed to be "the only-begotten Son of God." The testimony to the effect that he raised the dead, walked upon the waves, came forth from the grave and ascended bodily into heaven, appears to be all hearsay, and by witnesses of unknown credibility. If we consider the impression made upon his contemporaries, we find that his miracles and resurrection failed to convince those best qualified to analyze evidence. He seems to have been regarded as nothing more than a popular religious reformer or schismatic. From the New Testament we learn that he did not found a new faith, but lived and died in that of his fathers—that it is impossible to follow the instruction of Jesus without becoming in religion a Jew. As he was the sixteenth savior the world has crucified, his tragic death does not prove him divine. As immaculate conceptions were quite common among the Greeks and Romans, with whom both he and his immediate following came much in contact, I incline to the view that he entered the world in the good old way.

Granting the correctness of such a conclusion, it does not necessarily follow that Jesus was not heaven-sent, or that he was in any way unworthy the love and veneration of the world. The proposition of the eloquent Father Brannan that Jesus was either in very truth the only-begotten Son of the Father, or an impious fraud deserving execration, is only tenable on the supposition that the language attributed to him by New Testament writers is properly authenticated. When we remember that the art of printing had not then been invented; that Christ wrote nothing himself; that the record of his life was probably not composed until he had been long dead; that the besetting sin of the East is exaggeration; that it was the custom of the Greeks, in whose language the New Testament was first written, to assign a heavenly origin to popular heroes, we must concede that there is some reason for doubt whether Jesus ever claimed to be other than the son of Joseph the carpenter. Granting that his life and language are correctly reported, that he was indeed Divinity: The fact remains that a vast majority of mankind decline to accept him as such; that while the church is striving with so little success to raise his standard in Paynim lands, Atheism is striking its roots ever deeper into our own. The church should recognize the fact that no man is an Atheist from choice. Deep in the heart of every human being is implanted a horror of annihilation. A man may become reconciled to the idea, just as he may become resigned to the necessity of being hanged; but he strives as desperately to escape the one as he does to avoid the other. Does the church owe any duty to the honest doubter, further than the reiteration of a dogma which his reason rejects? When he asks for evidence of God's existence, Judaism points him to the miracles of Moses, Christianity to those of Jesus, Mohammedanism to the revelations of its prophet; and if he find these beyond his comprehension or violative of his reason, they dismiss him with a gentle reminder that "the fool hath said in his heart there is no God." He retorts by accusing his critics either of superstitious ignorance or rank dishonesty, so honors are easy. He is told that if he doesn't perform the impossible—work a miracle by altering the construction of his own mind—he will be damned, and is touched up semi-occasionally by the pulpiteers as an emissary of the devil. Being thus put on the defensive, he undertakes to demonstrate that all revealed religions are a fraud deliberately perpetrated by the various priesthoods. He searches through their Sacred Books for contradictions and absurdities, and not without success; proves that their God knew little about astronomy and less about geography, then sits him down "over against" the church, like Jonah squatting under his miraculous gourd-vine in the suburbs of Ninevah, and confidently expects to see it collapse. He imagines that in pointing out a number of evident errors and inconsistencies in "revealed religion" he has hit Theism in its stronghold; but he hasn't. He has but torn and trampled the ragged vestments of religion, struck at non-essentials, called attention to the clumsy manner in which finite man has bodied forth his idea of Infinity—has made the unskillful laugh and the judicious grieve. In an ignorant age the supernatural appeals most powerfully to the people; hence it is not strange that revealed religion, so-called, should have been grounded upon the miraculous; but the passage of the Red Sea, the raising of Lazarus and kindred wonders are not readily accepted in an enlightened era, and are utilized by scoffers to bring all religion into contempt. We can scarce conceive of God being reduced to the necessity of violating his own laws to demonstrate his presence and power. While it were presumption to ask any church to abate one jot or tittle of its dogma, it seems to me that all would gain by relying less upon the "evidential value of the miracles;" that a broader, nobler basis can be found for religious faith, one more in accord with the wisdom and dignity of the great All-Father than tradition of signs and wonders in a foreign land in the long ago. Had God desired to personally manifest himself unto man, to deliver a code of laws, to establish a particular form of worship, it is reasonable to suppose that he would have done so in a manner that would have left no doubt in the mind of any man, of any age or clime, anent either his divinity or his desires. That he has not done this, argues that all "revealed religions" are but the voices of the godlike within man, rather than direct revelations from without. All religions are fundamentally the same, and each is the highest spiritual concept of its devotees. Whence came the gods of the ancient Greek and Egyptian, of the Mede and Persian? If they were made known by direct revelation, how came they to be false gods? If they were the result of a spirit of worship inherent in all men, who implanted that spirit? If God, he must have done so for a purpose, and what purpose other than to enable man to work out his own salvation? Would we not expect him to operate through this spirit for universal guidance, rather than leave the world in darkness while he retired to an obscure corner thereof and practiced legerdemain for the edification of a few half-civilized people? If we adopt the internal instead of the external view of the origin of Judaism and Christianity, all the other Sacred Books range themselves about the Bible and with it bear witness that man is the creature of Design and not a freak of Chance. We bring to confirm the teachings of Moses and Christ and the wise Zoroaster, the loving Gautama, the patient Mahomet, the priests and prophets of every clime, the altars of every age, the countless millions, who, since man's advent on the earth, have worshipped the All-in-All. If this be not basis broad enough for man's belief, add thereto the story of God's wisdom written in the stars and the never-ceasing anthem of the sea; the history of every consecrated man who has died for man, whether his name be Christ or Damien; the song of every bird and the gleam of every beauty; the eternal truth that shines in a mother's eyes, the laughter of little children and the leonine courage of creation's lord; every burning tear that has fallen on the face of the dead, and every cry of anguish that has gone up from the open grave to the throne of the Living God. Were not this "revelation" enough? Yet 'tis but the binding of humanity's Sacred Book, of that Universal Bible in which God speaks from the age and from hour to hour to all who have ears to hear.

The fact that man desires immortality is proof enough that he was not born to perish. 'Tis a "direct revelation" to the individual, if he will but heed it—will get out of the grime of the man-created city, with its artificialities, into the God-created country, where he may hear the "still small voice" speaking to that subtler sense, which in animals is instinct, in man is inspiration. There is no error in the ordering of the universe. It was not jumbled together by self-created "force," operating in accordance with "laws" self-evolved from chaos, on matter which, like Mrs. Stowe's juvenile nigger, "jis growed." It is the work of a Master who "ordereth all things well." Beauty might be born of Chance, but only Omniscience could have decreed the adoration it inspires. Hate might spring from the womb of Chaos, but Love must be the child of Order. Pain might be begotten of monsters, but only Infinite wisdom could have invented Sorrow. Nature does not put feathers on fishes, fins on birds, nor give aught that lives an impossible desire or an objectless instinct. Then why should man desire immortality, why should he fear annihilation more than the fires of Hell? During a third of his life he is unconscious, and annihilation is but an ever-dreamless sleep. Whether he sleeps the sleep of health or that of death, an hour and an eternity are the same to him; yet he desires the one and dreads the other. If man's fierce longing for immortal life is not to be gratified, then is the whole universe a cruel lie; its wonderful arrangement from star to flower, its careful adaptation of means to ends, the provision for the satisfaction of every sense, an arrant fraud, a colossal falsehood. If there be no God, then is creation a calamity; if there be a God and no immortality for man, then it is a crime.

God does not reveal himself to beasts, nor to men of brutish minds. How can those who have no ear for music, no eye for beauty, hear the melody of the universe or comprehend the symmetry of the All? What need have those for immortality to whom love is only lust, charity a pander to pride, a full stomach the greatest good and gold a god? It is these who become "motive grinders," dig genius out of the earth like spuds and goobers, and achieve perpetual motion by making the universe a self-operative machine needing neither key nor steam generator to "make it go." They pride themselves, sometimes justly, on their reasoning powers; but the product of their logic-mill is like artificial flowers, as unprofitable as the icy kiss of the Venus de Medici. Of that knowledge gleaned in the Vale of Sorrow they know nothing; of that wisdom which cannot be demonstrated by the laws of logic they have no more conception than has a mole of the glories of the morning. They are of the earth earthy. To make them understand a message God would have to type-write it, add the seal of a notary public and deliver it in person. They hear not the silver tones of Memnon, heed not the wondrous messages that come from the dumb lips of the dead. They search thro' musty tomes and explore long-forgotten languages to prove the rhapsodies of some old prophet false, while the grave of the babe that was buried yesterday is more than a prophecy—is an Ark of the Covenant.

"KING CHARLES THE MARTYR."

Anglomaniacism Run Mad.

It is a trifle difficult for an American to discuss in polite language the recent canonization of Charles I. by the Episcopalians of this country. One scarce knows whether to laugh at the ridiculous mummery or be angry with the miserable toad-eating unamericanism of the Episcopal prelacy. It is by no means easy to contemplate in a spirit of toleration, the existence in this country of a church that has ever been the pliant tool and obsequious apologist of tyranny. Episcopalianism in America is like the presence of a pebble in the works of a watch. It is a foreign and disturbing element, and could, like polygamy, be prohibited by law without doing violence to our fundamental principle of religious freedom. Neither individuals nor governments should be expected to ignore the law of self-preservation, and to republican institutions Episcopalianism is a perennial fount of poison. It is the fecund mother of Tories, Anglomaniacs and traitors. From the time when this church was born of the lustful bowels of that royal brute, Henry VIII., to this good hour, it has been the uncompromising foe of freedom. True, it has produced a few American patriots—men who were better than the church to which they belonged; but its tendency is no more toward human liberty than that of Anarchism is toward human law. Scratch a title-worshipper, an Anglomaniac or a snob, and you are pretty apt to find an Episcopalian. Had Charles' beatification, canonization or whatever it may be called, been the horse-play of some obscure prelate of A. P. A. proclivities, it would have merited no attention beyond a *lunatico inquirendo;* but such was not the case. It occurred in Philadelphia, with two bishops officiating in full canonicals, while other prominent prelates sent regrets, assuring the mimers that they were "in cordial sympathy with the occasion." We must accept the unveiling of the portrait of "King Charles the Martyr" as expressive of the religious views and political tendencies of American Episcopalians, hence it may be well to inquire: Who was this "King Charles the Martyr," whose life is so solemnly recommended to Americans as worthy their emulation? He was the victim of that very "Reformation" inaugurated by pious King Henry VIII.—at once defender of the Catholic faith and chief of schismatics. He was devoured by the legitimate spawn of that illegitimate monster begotten in Henry's bedchamber and known to history as the Church of England. He was a king who persecuted Calvinists because they would not conform to the Cranmer-corrupted rites of Rome, and persecuted Catholics because they would not accept him as their pope. Although Ireland was true to the House of Stuart, and in every great crisis the mainstay of its throne, he was more cruel to Ireland if possible, than was Cromwell. In religion he was a nondescript, in politics he was a petty tyrant and a professional perjurer. What a pity the solemnly blessed portrait of "King Charles the Martyr" was not accompanied by a few descriptive lines from Macaulay, as passport to the association of Saints. Macaulay, be it remembered, detested "Popery," and described the Anglican Church as the crowning glory of Protestantism; hence we may suppose he was lenient as possible to the royal head of the Anglican hierarchy. He says in part:

We think his sentence describes him with perfect justice as "a tyrant, a murderer, and a public enemy." * * * * They had to deal with a man who made and broke promises with equal facility, a man whose honor had been a hundred times pawned and never redeemed. * * * * The Puritans were imprisoned. They were whipped. Their ears were cut off. Their noses were slit. Their cheeks were branded with red-hot irons.

Yet when these same Puritans, many of whom did so much to make America what it is, brought the author of these hellish outrages to the block, he became a "blessed martyr" in the eyes of the Anglomaniacs whom we permit to fatten beneath freedom's flag! This is the man who trampled beneath his feet the constitutional rights of our fathers; yet before his portrait an audience of fashionable Americans prostrated themselves while Bishops Coleman and Perry prayed the good God to make us all like unto "Thy servant and martyr, Charles." How do the descendants of the Puritans relish having such an insult flung into their faces by the spawn of those Tories who were prating of "divine right" and preaching the doctrine of "non-resistance" while the streets of Boston were slippery with patriotic blood? How do American Catholics relish this apotheosis of the royal master of Laud and Strafford—the kite and vulture who together preyed upon the vitals of Ireland? Of all the monarchs who have swayed the English sceptre, of all the men who have posed as religious hierarchs, "King Charles the Martyr" was perhaps the meanest. He was true neither to friend nor foe. He had "just ability enough to deceive and just religion enough to persecute." He was selfishness personified, ready at any time to give up his favorites to the vengeance of his foes in return for a parliamentary grant of gold. Persecuting Puritans and Catholics impartially, he was unable to determine his own religious convictions. I could never work up much admiration for the English "Gospelers." At this distance they appear to have had a virulent attack of pseudo-religious *mania a potu;* but I have been ever grateful to Cromwell for bringing that sublimation of selfishness, that incarnation of cruelty, "Charles the blessed Martyr," to the block. As a liar he outranked Ananias; in treachery he could give Iscariot instruction; as a hypocrite he was equalled only by Bishop Cranmer, the first primate of Episcopalianism.

When we consider the history of the Church of England—known in America as the Protestant Episcopal Church—we can scarce wonder that its devotees should beatify a brute, that Charles I. should be accorded a place in its calendar. Conceived in sin and brought forth in iniquity, it still bears unmistakable impress of its parentage. Begotten between incestuous sheets, it has been nurtured from its birth on the fruits of robbery and the milk of perfidy. Upon its unclean altars tens of thousands of human beings of both sexes and all ages have been freely sacrificed. The best and bravest of England's children have been passed thro' the fire to glut the pitiless maw of this modern Moloch. William Cobbett, himself a communicant of the Anglican Church, confesses in his "History of the Protestant Reformation," that it was "established by gibbets, racks and ripping knives." A cross between perverted Catholicism and fanatical Calvinism, it inherits the virtues of neither while rank with the vices of both. Its father was a wife-butcher, its mother a bawd —and an evil tree cannot bring forth good fruit. Doubtless we have in America many worthy people who are Episcopalians; but they are communicants of that church only because ignorant of its origin. I have neither time nor inclination to write a history of the Church of England—to trace Episcopalianism from its genesis to the enrollment of Charles among its "blessed Martyrs" by alleged Americans; but in view of the Philadelphia episode, a few words of explanation may not be out of place. To fill in the outlines were too much like writing the annals of a combination slaughter-house and honk-a-tonk. The Anglican Church came into being because the Pope would not divorce Henry VIII. from a virtuous wife that he might marry Anne Boleyn—his own daughter by a disreputable drab! Because the Pope would not play Pandarus to Henry's unholy passion, the latter proclaimed himself the head of the Catholic Church in his Kingdom, made Cranmer his primate and Thomas Cromwell his vicar-general or chief gyasticutus. In the whole world there was but one man more brutal than Cranmer, and that was Cromwell; but one constitutionally meaner than Cromwell, and that was Cranmer; but one more bestial than either, and that was King Henry. And upon these three pillars rests the entire superstructure known as the Anglican Church, or Protestant Episcopalianism! Should Oofty Goofty, the Yellow Kid and the editor of the Houston *Post* essay a revision of the Code Napoleon or Justinian Pandects, it would be neither so impudent nor ridiculous as the attempt of this gallows-faced triumvirate of black-hearted rascals to bring about a religious "Reformation." Having in the meantime gotten Anne Boleyn with child, Henry secretly married her before obtaining a divorce, or even a semblance thereof, from Catherine, thereby becoming a bigamist as well as an adulterer. Henry had been criminally intimate with Anne Boleyn's mother, and we have it on the respectable authority of Dr. Bayley that she warned him previous to the marriage that his intended was his own daughter. Cranmer, who divorced Henry from Catherine, subsequently relieved him of Anne by declaring the marriage—which had been a second time solemnized—was of no effect, thereby bastardizing Elizabeth, the too early fruit of the union. In this view both houses of parliament concurred, alleging the invalidity of his marriage with Anne "because of certain just and lawful impediments." These "certain just and lawful impediments" were urged by both Cranmer and the King, but they do not appear to have worried the pious pope of the Anglican Church until he caught daughter-wife dallying with the gentlemen of his household when she was charged, among other frailties, with incest with her brother, and promptly beheaded. The next day Henry was happily wedded to a new wife! And from such a source sprang the Anglican Church, which numbers Charles I. among its "blessed martyrs," and has Bishop Coleman and Perry for apologists! The Episcopalians indignantly deny that Anne Boleyn was Henry's daughter; but that she was so, and that both she and Henry knew it at the time of their marriage, there is indisputable documentary evidence. Lady Elizabeth Boleyn, Anne herself, Cranmer and King Henry confessed the consanguineous relationship. Probably Lady Boleyn did not know to an absolute certainty who Anne's Father was, any more than Anne knew for a surety who Elizabeth's father was; but in cases of this kind we must, perforce, accept the testimony of the mother as final. Lady Boleyn's daughter Mary was likewise the Anglican pope's leman; but one possible case of incest more or less on the part of such a great religious "reformer" is a matter of small importance. With the subsequent marriages, divorces and beheadings of the apostle of the Anglican faith we need not concern ourselves. They are familiar to everybody but Episcopalians.

Bigamy, incest, uxoricide and adultery are not the only crimes of which the founder of this new faith stands convicted. For nearly nine centuries England has been a Catholic country. The Church of Rome had transformed the English race from a race of barbarous root-diggers, who fled like scared rabbits before the legions of Cæsar, into a nation at once civilized, prosperous and powerful. Crime and pauperism were practically unknown. It was the boast of an English king that jewels hung upon the trees by the roadside were safe as tho' encased in vaults of stone and iron; that within his realm there was no beggar, none suffering for shelter or bread. Beef, pork and mutton were described by pre-reformation historians as "the meat of the poor." This was the age in which Albion received the name of "merrie England," in which she won that reputation for hospitality and good cheer which for more than 300 years has been but a shadow of a shade. It was during this epoch that Ireland became famous as the seat of learning to which the crowned heads of Europe sent their sons. A considerable portion of the arable land of the two islands was owned by monasteries, their tenants enjoying almost freehold privileges. These monastic institutions educated the youth and cared for the aged. This was not alone their pleasure; it was their legal duty, for it was at that time recognized that the landlord held natural resources in trust; that every person, howsoever poor, was entitled to a subsistence from the soil. Judged by our present economic ideas, the system was bad; but with all our wisdom we have as yet been unable to put a system in practice that produced such beneficial effects. Good or ill, the system was there, the people had become accustomed to it, and the most callow kindergarten statesman knows that it is suicidal to violently subvert immemorial custom. Henry, having proclaimed himself the Anglican pope, despoiled the monastic institutions of their land, robbed their churches and divided the booty among his favorites, leaving no provision for the education of youth or the sustenance of age, thereby flooding the Kingdom with ignorance, beggary and crime. Dr. Sharpe declares that the despoliation of the religious houses of London "caused the streets to be thronged with the sick and poor." Such was the immediate fruit of the Protestant "Reformation." From beef, pork and mutton being the "meat of the poor," labor in England began to live on black bread and water, in Ireland on water and boiled potatoes. During his lifetime this incestuous monster, aided by Cromwell and Cranmer, cruelly persecuted all those who refused to recognize his spiritual as well as his temporal supremacy. They invaded convents and tore down altars to secure gold and silver with which they were ornamented, ransacked chests and destroyed valuable books for the sake of the gilt binding. The monastery of St. Austin, called the Apostle of England, was plundered, the tomb of Thomas-a-Beckett despoiled of the pious offerings of pilgrims, and the sainted dust of the dead were hurled to the four winds of heaven. Protestant and Catholics were tied together in pairs, one of each, back to back, dragged through the streets and consigned to the flames as heretics. Priests and priors were hanged, drawn and quartered, their hearts and entrails cast into the fire, their bodies parboiled, their hands nailed up before the doors of monasteries as a warning that the paramour of Anne Boleyn would permit no trifling in matters of piety. Sir Thomas More, the most learned lawyer in the Kingdom, and Bishop Fisher, who had been the privy councillor of Henry's father, suffered death for declining to accept this bloody-minded butcher as God's vice-regent on earth! But enough! A magazine ten times the size of the Iconoclast would be thrice filled by printing in the smallest possible type the names of those who suffered death for no other reason than a positive refusal to apostatize. We may dismiss Thomas Cromwell, the new pope's vicar-general, in a paragraph: He was simply another brutal, ignorant Jack-the-Ripper. He seems to have been a servant in the household of Cardinal Wolsey, and by treachery to his old master recommended himself to the good graces of Henry. But Cranmer was a man of a different stripe—intellectual, foxy, ambitious. He is another "blessed martyr" of the Episcopalians. I will not trust myself to paint his portrait, for I despise the unctuous old scoundrel so heartily that I should do him injustice—if it were possible to heap upon the head of an imp of hell unmerited ignominy. I leave that labor of love to Macaulay, the hater of Catholicism, the eulogist of the "Establishment," the sweet singer of the glory of Elizabeth, England's virgin (?) queen, feeling assured that he will let him down as easily as his conscience will allow:

Cranmer rose into favor by serving Henry in the disgraceful affair of his first divorce. * * * * He attached himself to Cromwell (Thomas) while the fortunes of Cromwell flourished. He voted for cutting off Cromwell's head without a trial when the tide of royal favor turned. He conformed backward and forward as the king changed his mind. While Henry lived he assisted in condemning to the flames those who denied the doctrine of transsubstantiation. When Henry died he found out that the doctrine was false. He was, however, not at a loss for people to burn. The sanguinary intolerance of a man who thus wavered in his creed excites a loathing to which it is difficult to give vent without calling foul names. Equally false to political and religious obligations, he was first the tool of Somerset, and then the tool of Northumberland. When the former wished to put his own brother to death, without the semblance of a trial, he found a ready instrument in Cranmer.

And of such material are Episcopalian martyrs made. This is the party that helped Henry VIII. establish the Anglican Church; this is the saint to whom our Episcopalian brethren are indebted for their Book of Common Prayer! This is he "of glorious memory," who, before the Anglican priesthood were permitted to marry, imported a wife from Germany, nailed up in a box, and while primate of the new church kept her concealed in his palace. Mary, Henry's legitimate daughter, was a Catholic. Fearing that if she ascended the throne she would compel them to restore the property of which they had despoiled the "Popists," the Godly, headed by Cranmer, attempted to change the succession, well knowing that to do so meant civil war. Failing in this, Cranmer and the rest of the canting crew, crawled to Mary's feet like abject curs. Cranmer recanted as a matter of course. Entirely of his own volition, he made six recantations in six weeks, each more pitiably abject than its predecessor. He declared that the doctrine he had enforced with gallows' ropes and branding irons and disemboweling hooks was false as hell, asked Mary's forgiveness and the prayers of the Pope. Finding that Mary was determined to make an example of him, he recanted his six recantations and died "a blessed martyr." The church planted by Henry VIII. and Cromwell and Cranmer—triune of infamy!—was tenderly nurtured by "Sainted Edward VI.," "Good Queen Bess" and "King Charles the Martyr." I am not writing a complete history of England just at present; but I'll just spike the gab-traps of those pious Episcopalians who have so much to say about "Bloody Mary." Like most other Protestants, I was taught early to believe that Queen Mary had scrambled Episcopalian brains for breakfast and slept with her bed floating in a vast tank of Puritan blood. True, "Bloody Mary" burned old Cranmer; but as he was headed for hell anyhow, it was a mercy of acclimation. She made matters uncomfortable for several other people; but during her entire reign she caused fewer deaths for opinion's sake than did "the sainted Edward" in a single year. Where Mary let a drop of blood in the name of Catholicism, Elizabeth spilled a pint in defense of her own spiritual supremacy. Such is the testimony of the public records of England. I am not the apologist of either Queen Mary or St. Dominic. Catholic persecution is far more inexcusable than Protestant persecution, for the simple reason that the Mother Church is old enough to have learned wisdom. Its priests are usually learned men, and we have a right to expect better things of them than of the fanatical blatherskites who, like Sam Jones, were educated in a mule seminary, and who spout their religious theses from the tops of tubs. We can forgive Calvin for burning Servetus, for we can expect nothing better of a God-intoxicated savage with a scant thimbleful of sense; but Cranmer was a man of a different kidney, one who had brains and erudition in abundance. Luther was a man of some learning, but of disordered intellect. Were he living today, he would be adjudged insane and sent to the asylum. The assumption that he was crazy is the mildest construction that can be placed against his performances. Having rebelled against Rome because of its "indulgences," he proceeded to grant a more remarkable indulgence than the worst of Catholic prelates ever dreamed of. He authorized Philip of Hesse to have two wives at the same time— "in order to provide for the welfare of his body and soul, and to bring greater glory to God!" Although Luther did and Cranmer did not sanction polygamy, no one who has carefully studied the character of the two men will believe for a moment that Henry could have made of the first an obsequious pander to his passions. Luther was a religious crank, an ill-balanced, irresponsible enthusiast; Cranmer was a subtle plotter, an unprincipled scoundrel. And the difference between the representative men of the opposing sects extended to their disciples. The Puritans persecuted because they were, as a rule, ignorant men who had been wrought up into a religious frenzy; the Anglican Church persecuted with a view to political power and pecuniary profit. I have said that Luther was crazy; but his opinion of Henry VIII. well-nigh destroys that hypothesis. He declared that the founder of the Anglican Church was "a pig, an ass, a dunghill, the spawn of an adder, a basilisk, a lying buffoon, a mad fool with a frothy mouth and a w——hface"—which demonstrates that, like Hamlet, he could tell a hawk from a heron-saw when the wind was in the right direction.

"Bloody Mary"—whose victims numbered less than 300 all told, including Cranmer and numerous other rogues whom the world could well spare—was succeeded by Elizabeth, Anne Boleyn's scrawny brat. To her dying queen she swore to adhere ever to the Church of Rome, and prayed that the earth might open and swallow her up if she broke her vow. Her coronation oath made her defender of the Catholic faith, yet she was scarce seated upon the throne ere she apostatized. It must be comforting to Episcopalians to reflect that for five-and-forty years their church had a she-pope, a vinegar-hearted old virago who turned her palace into a den of vice. Faunt says at her court "all enormities reigned in the highest degree." Lingard avers that she assigned to her favorite paramour "an apartment contiguous to her own bedchamber, and by this indecent act proved that she had become regardless of her character and callous to every sense of shame. The court," he naively adds, "imitated the manners of the sovereign." And for nearly half a century this was the Anglican Vatican—with Dudley, Raleigh, Blount, Oxford, Anjou, Simier, Hatton, *et id genus omnes* as College of Cardinals! Under such happy auspices the H'english Church was brought to its present state of perfection—flourished like a green bay 'orse! Old Liz seems to have persecuted Puritan and Catholic with rigid impartiality, and a cruelty scarce equaled by

Cranmer. Her favorite method of dealing with men who denied her spiritual supremacy was to hang them up until half dead, then rip out their bowels with grappling hocks. This was "Good Queen Bess," that "Virgin Queen" to accommodate whose sexual idiosyncrasies parliament decreed that any brat she might happen to have, by whatsoever syndicate of sires, should succeed to the sceptre. But the act was useless—the cake had too many cooks. In those days a man couldn't loll around in slippers and dressing gown on Sunday morning and peruse the papers. So deeply consecrated was the Queen for his immortal soul that if he failed to show up at her church she fined him 20 pounds for the first offense, and kept doubling the dose. If that failed to bring the contumacious sinner to time she sawed off his head and flung his internal economy into the fire. Her pursuivants burst into private houses at any hour of the day or night and ransacked them from top to bottom for "Popish" paraphernalia, and woe betide that unlucky wight whose possessions suggested the Papal See! She crammed the prisons with recusants, confiscated their estates and kept the rack, the gibbet and the persuasive bowel-hooks in constant operation "for the greater glory of God!" Corbett says:

One greedy and merciless minion after another was sent to Ireland to goad that devoted people to acts of desperation, and that too, not only for the obvious purpose, but for the avowed purpose, of obtaining a pretense for new confiscations. The "Reformation" from its very outset had plunder written on its front; but as to Ireland it was all plunder, from the crown of its head to the sole of its foot. This horrible lynx-like she-tyrant could not watch each movement of the Catholics there as she did in England. She could not harass them in detail; therefore she murdered them in masses.

This is but a glimpse of the portrait of "Good Queen Bess," as drawn by the pen of a Protestant. That this little sketch of the founders of Episcopalianism might be eminently conservative, I have excluded the testimony of Catholics and Puritans, the objects of their persecution. It is doubtful if all the savage atrocities perpetrated by the followers of Knox and Calvin, added to all the cruelties chargeable to the Catholics in every age and clime, would equal the outrages sanctioned by this red-headed old harlot in less than half a century. There have been bone-breakings and tongue-borings and burnings by Puritans and by Catholics; but they were the result of mistaken zeal; those perpetrated by the Anglican Church have not that excuse. It were an insult to common sense to urge that an old wife-butcher like Henry, a bawd like Elizabeth, a liar like Charles had any genuine regard for religion or morals. What Puritans and Catholics inflicted they were willing to suffer —and frequently did suffer—rather than recant; but look at Cranmer and the rest of that unclean crew who have persecuted in the name of the law-established Church of England—not a man of whom but was ready to recant at a moment's notice to save his worthless neck, or for his pecuniary profit! Queen Mary was always a Catholic. To preserve her faith she defied her unnatural half-brother and her still more unnatural father. The one threatened her life, the other disinherited her; but to her life and crown were as nothing to the chrism and the cross. Elizabeth was a devout Protestant when Edward VI. was persecuting Catholics, and an equally devout Catholic when Mary was persecuting Protestants. Branded by Parliament as an illegitimate, and tacitly acknowledging herself a strumpet in consenting to the act of "natural" succession, this old heifer was for nearly half a century the "Anglo-Saxons'" first lady of the land! No wonder Englishmen assume airs of superiority—that Episcopalianism has become such a hot favorite with our own Anglomaniacs. It is not every church that can trace its lineage back in an unbroken line to the amours of Anne Boleyn and 'Andsome 'Arry! Every man to his taste; but I prefer crazy Luther, who says he slept with the devil, to Henry, who wedded with his daughter; St. Dominic's thumbscrews for heretics to "Good Queen Bess'" disemboweling hooks. I really don't care to mix up with a family of religious reformers in which a fellow is likely to discover that he's his own grandfather.

Elizabeth shone like Luna, by borrowed light. The glories of her age are not her glories. During her reign English literature reached its zenith and gilded her throne with an adventitious glory. It was the high noon of intellect; but it was the twilight of religion and the midnight of morality. The Augustan Age was not that of Rome's political glory or commercial greatness, but the beginning of her decay. Those brilliant minds that made the times of Elizabeth memorable were the fruitage of kindly Catholic culture. You may trace British literature from the days of Alfred, step by step, onward and upward, to that imperial height where Shakespeare lifts his brow, bound with the anademe of immortality—but beyond him is the blank abyss! The fruit of the Elizabethan Era was Apples of Hesperides, but the tree was dead! The accursed "Reformation" of King Henry had pauperized the once fruitful soil and withdrawn the kindly dews; it lifted its leafless branches into a leaden sky and struck its withered roots into rocks and ashes. The founders of the Anglican Church left England bankrupt, both in money and brains. When Henry VIII ascended the throne it was a powerful and prosperous nation; by the time it was done with "Charles the blessed Martyr" it was little better—if we may believe Lingard, Cobbett, Lever and others—than a congeries of criminals, beggars and bawds. It declined in wealth and power until the Puritans kicked the immortal ichor out of the "Establishment." Under the Lord Protector it regained somewhat of its old-time political prestige, only to sink still lower when the Anglican religion was re-established. The regime of "Old Noll" was doubtless fantastic, cruel and despotic; but he made the flag of England again respected in every land and on every sea. If he devastated Scotland and Ireland, he humbled Holland and Spain. He was the father of England's maritime greatness and of her colonial empire. We hear a great deal of "glorious Queen Bess;" but what she contributed to England's greatness other than, by her meddling, to provoke the so-called "massacre of St. Bartholomew" in France, and by her treachery, to bring the Spanish Armada down upon her poverty-stricken shores and escape destruction only by the intervention of a storm, I do not now remember.

If the reign of the Puritans was savage, it was because the long-continued cruelties and innate cussedness of the Anglican church had made men mad. Those who had had their ears clipped and their noses slit; those whose property had been confiscated and their relatives butchered by Charles, could scarce be expected to cast bouquets at him and his henchmen when they got the inhuman hyenas grabbed. The Episcopalians have no cause to complain of the Puritans. They were the natural sequence, the inevitable result of Henry's "Reformation." When he broke away from the authority of Rome he unloosed a power which he could not control. By his rebellion against the Pope he proclaimed the right of private judgment. He started the avalanche but could not stop it. If one man might ignore the spiritual authority of Pope Clement, others might, with even greater propriety, deny the spiritual supremacy of King Henry. Finally his bastard Catholico-Protestantism degenerated into Puritanism, and the throne of Britain, like Frankenstein, was destroyed by a monster of its own making. Had old Henry kept his concupiscence under control, there would have been no Protestant Episcopal Church to transform American hermaphrodites into Anglomaniacs, no illegitimate Elizabeths or "blessed Charles the Martyr." Protestantism and Catholicism would have met in a fair field in Britain as they did in America. Men would have adopted one or the other, instead of a compound of both, acceptable to neither Deity nor Devil—a religious mulatto or moral mule. Tens of thousands of lives would have been saved. England would not boast a few great fortunes, offset by a million registered paupers; and Ireland, fruitful as the gardens of the gods, be a synonym for poverty and suffering. I trust that Bishops Coleman and Perry will pardon the suggestion that, as Anne Boleyn's beauty was the inspiration of Episcopalianism, its divine revelation, so to speak, and as she was the first to die for its sake, she should have the post of honor in its hagiology.

THE SINGLE TAX.

Is It a Panacea for Poverty?

The advocates of the Single Tax on land values are the only politico-economic reformers who have attempted to fully meet the unsatisfactory industrial conditions with which we are confronted, the only ones who seem to realize that the disease is fundamental and therefore, beyond the reach of any tariff edulcorant or monetary emollient. They alone appear to comprehend the self-evident truth that, no matter what may be our exchange media, the political complexion of congress and president, and our policy regarding imports, the rich and poor must continue to drift further apart until a radical change is effected in our industrial system itself. This, together with the fact that Henry George, the chief exponent of the Single Tax, is the ablest man of his time, should secure for the theory a courteous consideration. The man who dissents from the political doctrines of Gladstone, the religious teachings of Cardinal Manning, or the economic theories of Henry George, should do so with becoming diffidence. One of the most discouraging signs of the times is the decay of that spirit of reverence with which men of genius were once regarded. While the worst of democracies is preferable to the best of monarchies, government by the people has its inherent and ineradicable drawback. A political system in which "everybody is good as anybody" unmuzzles brawling ineptitude and gives tacit encouragement to impudence. Instead of a bump of reverence, the American *Zeitgeist* has a hollow in its head. Nescience insults Knowledge, the people stone the Prophets of Progress and bow down before such political thugs as Hanna, such economic doodlebugs as Atkinson. The blind lead the blind, and with blare of partisan trumpets and noisy polemical clamor, both go over the brink. To accept unquestioned the *ipse dixit* of any man, however wise, were intellectual slavery; but those who can oppose nothing better than the idle jeers of raucous throats to the thunders of Omnipotence should avoid theomachy. In the presence of such men as Quesnay, Turgot and George, the opponents of the Single Tax should remember that they are peeping about the huge legs of intellectual titans. We are all vitally interested, did we but know it, not in proving the Single Tax theorem wise or unwise, but in determining its true economic status— deciding in all candor whether it be indeed a Nehustan lifted up in the industrial wilderness upon which we may look and live. The lessons of history—"philosophy teaching by example"—proclaim that there is danger ahead; that the many will not always consent to want while others waste; that some relief must be had, and that soon, else our laws, our liberties, our civilization itself, cannot be long preserved. The man who points the way to such relief is our greatest benefactor—does more to promote the moral and material well-being of mankind than have all the priests and prophets from Melchizedek to the present day. The man who makes it possible for all to earn a comfortable livelihood removes the efficient cause of poverty and crime. We know from sad experience, oft repeated, that the great political parties are contending over carefully cooked-up "issues" rather than important economic ideas; that tariff and currency juggling are but as the beating of Chinese tom-toms to avert an eclipse. After years of patient research, Mr. George offers what he insists is a radical and sufficient remedy for our industrial ills. Every man capable of understanding what is for his own best interest will sincerely hope that the remedy offered will prove equal to the emergency; but if it will not, it were well that we should know it quickly that we may cast about for wiser methods of bettering our bad condition. Next to knowing how to do a thing is knowing how not to do it. The people are now sitting in judgment on the Single Tax, and as a court is more apt to render an equitable decision after hearing all that can be urged by counsel for and against, I beg to submit what appear to me a few legitimate objections. The role of *advocatus diabolus,* like that of heavy villain in the play, while unpopular, is absolutely necessary. I had intended to make, in this issue, an exhaustive analysis of the Single Tax; but want of space confines me to a cursory examination of a few salient features. As the Iconoclast probably reaches many who do not habitually read Single Tax literature, and the determination of truth is my only object, I cheerfully offer Mr. George the use of my columns for rejoinder.

* * *

It is the theory of Mr. George that landlordism is the curse of this country—that the enormous wealth of the few and the pitiable poverty of the many are chiefly due to monopoly of natural resources. In his opinion, the land-owner appropriates all the fruits of labor in excess of what it can produce on land which, by reason of sterility or undesirable location, has no commercial value. The improvement in machinery and consequent multiplication of the laborer's productive power but enhances in equal ratio the price he must pay for access to the natural resources of the earth. He would abate this monopoly by transferring land values from the individual to the community, and compel the landholder to pay rent to the government in proportion to the desirability of his holdings, such rent to be taken in lieu of all other forms of taxation. He urges that as all men are born with an equal right to the land, private ownership is a violation of natural law; that as the community, rather than the individual, creates land value, it may, with perfect equity, appropriate it. The effect of such a system would, in his opinion, be to compel the release of unused land, thus affording to all easier access to the bounties of nature, thereby enhancing the production of wealth and effecting a more equitable distribution. Such *in nuce,* is Single Tax, which has become almost a religion with thousands of intelligent people, who see therein not only a remedy for our industrial ills, but the mandate of Divinity.

* * *

In my opinion, the Single Tax is the antithesis of a paradox—apparently true, but really absurd. To say that all men are born with an equal right to natural resources is to state a general truth; but one of more practical importance, either in ethics or economics, than that the sky is blue or water is wet. We do not recognize God in our constitution, nor can we safely recognize him in our economics. God is all-wise, God made man, man is a land-animal. From these premises it follows, as an illative consequence, that whatsoever abridges his free access to the land is, to that extent, an abrogation of his natural rights and an insult to Omniscience. The same all-wise God made the panther, and the panther is a carnivorous animal; therefore, it has a natural, an inalienable right, to kill and devour anything, from a cotton-tail to a Single-Taxer. Mr. George complains that critics of his system lose sight of fundamentals—are confused and misled by the complexities of modern society; yet there is one great fundamental which he has not yet found. Man is a gregarious, not an anchoretic animal. Society is both natural and necessary; but it can in nowise exist without a material abridgment of the "natural rights" of the individual. Labor must be applied to land before it will yield subsistence, and to apply it profitably requires organization. While land is the creation of God, the social organism is the creation of man, in which the newcomer can plead no natural rights. He is entitled only to such place therein as he earns. Mr. George complains that all land titles are founded in force and fraud—that not one of them can be traced back to the Creator. Quite true; but it is by force and fraud that man dominates the lower animals, which have as good a "natural right" as himself to the enjoyment of life, liberty and the pursuit of happiness. It is by force and fraud that he makes the horse to carry him, the cow to feed him and keep his babes from between the ravenous jaws of such wild beasts as seek to exercise their "natural rights" Self-preservation is the first law of all things that live, from the mite floating in a sunbeam, to civilized men and nations of men. It is the basic principle of all law; hence it is idle to complain that *meum et tuum* is a decree of force. Were Mr. George and I set adrift upon the ocean or lost in the desert, the hour would soon come when the stronger, whether because of brawn or cunning, would devour the other. For the same reason that the white man deposed the Indian landlord, and the American the British, Mr. George would have society depose the individual. Repulsive and unchristian tho' it be, the law of progressive life is the survival of the fittest, and the inevitable correlative of that law is the paramount right of the strongest. Deny it, and you make England a den of savages and America a desert. But discussing the ethics or economics, like discussing forms of baptism, is a species of mental calisthenics that winnows no corn. We need concern ourselves only with the probable effect of the Single Tax system.

* * *

I do not plead that landlordism is never an evil; it is frequently an outrage. Because a flying Dutchman, who wore the same undershirt the year 'round and subsisted by rat catching, chanced to make his roost on Manhattan Island, his worthless spawn—whose syphilitic carcasses are not worth a cent a pound for soap grease—are permitted to squat on their hunkers and compel industry to pour into their coffers the greater portion of its product; but before condemning our land system *in toto,* it were well to inquire whether this be the rule or the exception. Nor must we forget man's fallibility; that every law he has framed and every system he has devised have wrought occasional injury and injustice. Nor must the Single Taxer forget—what is most difficult for any man to remember—that he, too, is fallible, and taking issue with the cumulative wisdom of the world. We find, on examination, that while a few have been enormously enriched by the increase of land values to which they contributed little, many who contributed much have become impoverished; that the American land-owner, collectively considered, instead of being an all-devouring octopus, receives but a beggarly return on his investment. We find that there has never been a time since the organization of this government when the "unearned increment," of which we hear so much, and which Mr. George proposes to confiscate for the public benefit, would pay the taxes laid upon the land! By "unearned increment" I mean—and understand Mr. George to mean—the increase in market value of landed property. Take the land tax that has been paid during the past 100 years, compound it annually at the prevailing commercial rate, subtract the present market value of every foot of American soil exclusive of improvements, and you'll have enough left to buy all the royal vermin of Europe. Government is already taking the "unearned increment," and taking it twice told; hence, instead of the landlord being a leech on society, society is a leech on the landlord. Of course the landlord as landlord produces nothing; the mulct is taken from the product of labor as applied to land. The owner of a railway, a factory or a million gold dollars produces nothing as owner, the increment arising solely from use. Land must yield the owner a rental somewhat in excess of taxes and cost of superintendence, else he would release it. Rent is simply interest paid upon land values by the user. As the earth was evidently made for the use of all, is that system defensible which enables one man to compel another to pay him for using any part thereof? As the community creates land value, may it not properly confiscate it? Let us see: I move far beyond the confines of civilization and there make myself a home. Other settlers follow until there is a community of a hundred families. Men congregate for mutual aid and society, and my land becomes the center of the settlement, and therefore the most desirable. Homes spring up around me in an ever-widening circle. When we have endured all the privations of pioneers; when we have driven off the Indians and slaughtered the wild beasts; when we have become sufficiently numerous to maintain a blacksmith and a doctor, a school-master and a preacher, and are beginning to enjoy somewhat of the sweets of civilization, Mr. George concludes to make his home among us. But he is not willing to take his place in the outer circle—he wants to get in the center. As I am growing old and can no longer use all my land, I offer to part with a "forty" for a consideration. Or I will lease him the land for a sum which, in the opinion of homeseekers, marks the difference between its desirability and that of the best land still open to settlement. Mr. George demands to see my title to the land—signed by the Almighty and countersigned by the Savior! He tells me that, being a land-animal as well as I, he has an equal right of access to the earth. He assures me that the desirability of my land is due to the presence of the community, and that the benefits received and contributed by the new settler are coequal. He secures the passage of a law confiscating all ground rent, and thus begins where I leave off after the isolation, dangers and trials of half a life-time! The land-value of a community having 1,000 industrious citizens may or may not be doubled by the influx of 1,000 immigrants. How much would the addition of a thousand worthless niggers add to the desirability of land on Fifth Avenue? Why, the bottom would drop out of values! Land values do not depend so much on density as upon character of population.

* * *

But granting that private ownership is indefensible from an ethical standpoint: It is in existence, and it now remains to be seen to what extent it despoils labor. Rent is appropriated by the owner, whether he use or lease. In 1890 the estimated market value of all American land, together with the improvements thereon, was 39 billions. These improvements constituted everything adscititious, from the buildings of New York city to the barbed-wire fence around a Texas ranch; hence we may reasonably conclude that the value of the land alone did not exceed 25 billions. This at 4 per cent. rental would yield a billion dollars—and we have billion dollar congresses! That land values do not yield an average return of 3 per cent., will appear on a moment's consideration. For various reasons land is the form of investment most popular with the people. It is usually considered safest, and the veriest tyro in economics knows that investment considered safest yields the smallest increment. Thus, government can borrow money at 2 1-2 and great corporations at 3 and 4, while private individuals must pay from 5 to 15. A certain dignity and additional political privileges pertain to land-ownership. You can sell a man land that has not budged a peg in value for 50 years, and which he knows will not yield him 3 per cent. above his taxes, when you cannot borrow his money on gilt-edge security at 6. Banks may break, merchants fail, corporations collapse and government be subverted, but the land is always in evidence. It can neither burn up nor blow away. The earliest economists noted that land-owners were content with smaller returns than any other class of investors. Most men are earth-hungry, desire to possess land for possession's sake—to feel that upon this mundane sphere there is a spot where they are absolute master. Here in Waco it is much cheaper to rent than to own a home; yet men are eager as ever for the shade of their own vine and the shelter of their own roof. The great financiers have ever considered the soil as the poorest possible investment. The mortgage companies do not want land. When they slip a segment of the earth's surface from under you in lieu of money loaned, they throw it on the market. Were the landlord the chief of robbers, they would gobble up all the realty they could get. They do not appear to care to "monopolize natural resources" and compel the slave of toil to give up his last groschen or "get off the earth." The great money lords will buy bonds at 2 1-2 to 3 per cent., when in every state hard-pressed landlords are offering to sell at a sacrifice. If the man who wants the use of land, whether to plant hogs or grow a business block, will lease and loan his money—will pay rent and draw interest—he will save it five times in six. You can get at least 6 per cent.

for your money and dodge taxation, while not one acre in a dozen nets the owner so much. Granting that the average ground rent is 3 per cent., 750 millions is the annual toll taken by the landlord from labor. An enormous sum, 'tis true; but not an ounce in the pound, a gill in the gallon, an inch in the yard of the annual product of the people, hence it cannot be the all-efficient cause of labor's rags and wretchedness. It must be borne in mind that the foregoing figures include the rent accruing to the owner through personal use of his own property. It includes the rent of the land I occupy and use, as well as the rent I take of my tenants. Few people draw a proper distinction between the landlord and the capitalist—between what is paid for the use of natural resources and what is paid for the use of man-created wealth. This confusion arises from the fact that the capitalist is usually to some extent a landlord, the landlord to some extent a capitalist. What is paid for the use of improvements is properly interest.

The three factors in the production of wealth are land, labor and capital. The latter may properly be classed as a factor, as without it man is reduced to primitive methods of production. The landlord increases in wealth but slowly, labor is often on the verge of starvation, but the capitalist is able to give Bradley-Martin balls and buy dukes for his daughters. This argues that he despoils the other two factors of production. How does he do this? Much as Joseph, the first monopolist of whom history makes mention despoiled the ancient Egyptians. He has cornered, if not the subsistence of the country, what amounts to the same thing. He is master of our tools of trade—of the money, machinery and transportation facilities. No matter how much land and muscle you may have, without the co-operation of capital you cannot profitably produce. It is an easy matter to obtain the use of land; the trouble is to obtain the use of capital. The Single Taxers insist that but for this dog-in-the-manger of a landlord, labor would quickly create such an abundance of capital that its use could be had for the asking; that it would be humbled by the law of supply and demand. From 1850 to 1890 the per capita of wealth in this country trebled; yet there was never a time when the landlord and the laborer were more at the mercy of the capitalist. Change in methods of production—the substitution of the costly factory for the shoemaker's awl and hammer, the cable-car for the meek-eyed mule, the lightning express for the lumbering stage-coach

—has enhanced the demand for capital faster than it has been produced. Not only has this change from the simple to the complex opened new avenues for the employment of capital, but made it possible for it to control production and prices, to fix the land rent and the wage rate! The capitalist was of comparatively small importance when each community was a microcosm, its bread-stuffs supplied by its own farmers, its manufactures the product of its own independent artisans; but the world is now practically at the mercy of transportation companies, manufacturing syndicates, monetary combines—Dives juggles the markets of the earth and plays the antipodes against each other. The independent *entrepreneur* must pay wages, rent for land occupied and interest on capital invested, and this from what is left of the selling price of his product after the transportation companies and factors have taken toll. If the transportation companies interested in the "long haul" fail to freeze him out, and the interest does not eat him up, the trust that affects his particular line takes him in hand and Standard Oils him—crushes him by cutting prices below a living profit, and then recoups at the expense of his customers. The American farmer must sell at a price fixed in Liverpool, buy at one fixed by American combines, and what he has left is sopped up by the interest on his mortgage and by taxes levied to educate the brats of beggars, pay preachers $5 a minute to make legislative prayers, and mugwumps like Bayard $17,500 per annum to misrepresent him abroad.

* * *

How would the Single Tax afford people easier access to the earth—enable them to so multiply capital that it beg for employment? Under the present system when you have acquired a piece of land it is exchangeable wealth, enables you to command any other form of wealth in the world. If you exchange gold or labor for land you can exchange land for gold or labor; and wherein is the giving of value for value any more to be decried than the giving of nothing for nothing? I am told that if one does not have to purchase land he may put his capital or labor in improvements. Quite true; but he may do that as well under lease from the private owner as under lease from the government. If a change from private to public landlordism would reduce the rent, that were a point in favor of the poor; but if it does this how will it compel the release of land now held for speculative purposes? If we are to meet all governmental charges, both general and local, from ground rent, and it amounts now to but 750 millions, it must be doubled instead of reduced. And how will the man who cannot pay $5 an acre rent, manage to pay $10? True, he will be relieved of all other taxation, both direct and indirect; but will this offset a raise of $5 an acre on a forty-acre farm? The tenant pays very little direct taxes. By chewing gum and drinking Prohibition "peruna" he can avoid the exercise. He is not likely to impart many luxuries from foreign lands. The direct, internal revenue and tariff tax may touch him annually for $10, while a raise in rent of even $1 an acre on a cotton-patch he can plow with one pair o' mules, would fleece him of $40. Is that making any Progress out of Poverty? For years past farmers who are out of debt—who are their own laborers and landlords—have been able to save but little, even with the "unearned increment" thrown in as *lagniappe*. I recently visited Illinois—the "Garden State"—and there found many freehold farmers in worse condition than they were five-and-twenty years ago; plenty of urban property, upon which stiff taxes had been paid for two generations, that would not bring as much as when I was a boy. Everybody must pay rent under the new dispensation, a rent sufficient for all needs of government. I much fear a new and greater Coxey's army would soon march on Washington, and do something more desperate than get on the grass. Imagine Mr. George going forth to expostulate with the exasperated people—explaining that inasmuch as all wealth comes from the land, the burden of government must fall upon the land, and that it were cheaper and better that it be direct in its incidence. The entire army of malcontents could not confute his argument; and I don't believe it would try to—until after the inquest. I opine that Mr. George has refined his logic too far for any practical purpose in assuming that land is the source of all wealth. Technically this is true; but only technically. One great trouble with the Single Taxers is their ambition to save the country by the science of definition. Logomachy will never make two pieces of pie to grow in place of one sun-burned potato. The product of the land is, for the most part, merely potential wealth. The taxes taken by government are estimated in money, but are in reality a portion of labor's annual product. They are so many pounds of sugar and soap, so many barrels of molasses and bourbon, so many watches and wagons. The raw material for all these things comes from the soil, and they are made on the earth's surface, to be sure; but while the prime factors in the production of a $10 log are labor and land the prime factors in its transmutation into a $500 suit of furniture are capital and labor. Government might as well ask a horse for furniture as to require it of the land and the logger. They have not produced any furniture; they have only produced a log. Mr. George's government would resemble the country editor who's trying to run a paper on cord-wood and cabbage. But the land occupied by the furniture factory would be taxed! Quite true; but a factory producing a million dollars' worth of goods per annum may occupy land of less value than a 10-acre farm. The man who produces 5 bales of cotton may pay more rent than the man who manufactures 500 into muslin. Mr. George is going to the wrong place for this revenue. But he is a professing Christian, and doubtless thoroughly scriptural, for the Bible says that "from him who hath not shall be taken even that which he hath." You may theorize until the cows come home, but you cannot extract sunbeams from cucumbers nor blood from turnips. Taxation being but a toll taken from the product of each, government may appropriate a part of the farmer's potatoes, but cannot pull his leg for a piano. Without land to produce raw material, there could be no wealth; ergo, land is the source of all wealth and the one proper subject for taxation. Without rain the land would be sterile; but for the ocean there would be no rain; ergo, the ocean is the source of all wealth, and will please step up to the captain's office and settle.

* * *

Wealth consists of things adapted by labor to the wants of man. It is upon the brawn and brain of the human race that society, government, rests. The land, like the atmosphere, like time and space, is merely an incidental, economically considered. You can no more tax the land than you can tax the moon, which, like the "cat" of the Single Taxers, is by no means where it appears to be, the line of vision being oblique. I may have 50,000 acres of land, and all the tax-chasers this side of Sheol cannot collect 50 cents from it. They can confiscate a portion of what labor produces thereon. If it produces nothing they can fine me for possessing it; but to meet this mulct I've got to produce—or steal—something desired by others.

Ever since I can remember this country has been full of people who were "land poor"—people who were working themselves to death to pay taxes on land that nobody seemed to have any use for. Millions of dollars are paid into the treasury every year by holders of unused land—unused simply because nobody will buy or lease. Under the George system all taxes will be taken off idle land and placed on that in use. Why does fertile land often lie idle in states like Ohio and Illinois? Rent so high nobody can afford to pay it? Oh no! We have seen that it is cheaper for a man to rent land than to own it. Idle land presses for employment just as do capital and labor. When its owner cannot get much, he will take little. Rent can never remain exorbitant in a community where there is always considerable idle land. It would undoubtedly do so if one man, or a syndicate of men, owned the earth. In that case the landlord would dictate to both capital and labor; but such a condition does not, never did, never can exist except in the uneasy dreams of the Single Taxers. I defy any man to organize a landlords' league sufficiently powerful to raise the average ground rent one iota in a single American state. "Land monopoly!" What is a monopoly? It is, says Webster, "exclusive possession." Who has exclusive possession of the earth? Nobody. Some millions of people, each acting independently and for his individual interest, own the arable land of America—and to the south of us, a few hours' sail from New York, Galveston and San Francisco, is a vast and fertile continent where land may be had for the asking. True, it is not provided with macadamized streets and cable-cars. There is no great Baptist university or "reservation" within easy reach. It is wellnigh as wild as was Virginia when our ancestors struggled in there from everywhere. If the Single Taxers will migrate thither and take chances with the Aborigines, British and other wild beasts for a century or so, I will not question the right of their descendants to charge newcomers somewhat for the privilege of enjoying the blessings of a civilization founded by their fathers. If the world were peopled up to something like its ability to sustain life, Mr. George's system would deserve more serious consideration; but the land-owners cannot grievously oppress labor or dictate to capital until they form an effective "combine," or the demand for land exceeds the supply. Can high wages exist when the supply of labor exceeds the demand? Can high rents exist when there are not men enough living to utilize half the land? Is population increasing so rapidly that we need take thought for the future? During the present century there has been a vast gain in America, but a marked decline in many foreign countries. London has risen, but Babylon has fallen. San Francisco and Sydney are of the present, but Memphis and Palmyra are of the past. Not for ages hence will the fears of Malthus be realized, nor will the great-grandsons of Henry George live to see a "monopoly of land." It is idle to urge that the poor cannot emigrate from where land is dear to where it is either cheap or free, for it is ever the poor who do emigrate. America has been peopled by the poor. Wonderful improvements in transportation facilities are rendering the people ever more mobile. The iron horse and the steamship are rapidly bringing the most distant parts of the earth within reach of the markets, thereby rendering monopoly of natural resources more difficult—steadily increasing the power of the capitalist at the expense of the landlord.

* * *

I have called the Single Tax the religion of its devotees; but they have evidently not yet formulated it into an exact dogma. Their editors and apostles explain it differently, while of the hundreds of letters I have received on the subject, scarce any two agree in their confession of faith. I will give a couple of extracts, selected at random. Mr. R. S. McMahon writes me from New Iberia, La.:

When Waco was a Cross-road Town was rent the paramount question? No! While there was less wealth produced per capita than now, the share which went to labor and capital was both proportionately and actually greater than now, and the share which the land-owner (as land-owner) was able to exact, was trifling as compared with rents in Waco, to-day. Was not interest higher when Waco was young? and is not interest always higher in young communities? Were not wages higher then, than now?

Mr. A. Freeland writes me from Waco:

Says the common laborer, squatting on free land at the margin of production can produce $1 per day: He pays no rent, it is all his. On the cheapest owned land, by reason of roads, nearness to neighbors and markets, he produces $1.10 per day, but 10 cents goes for the rent. On $10 per acre land labor produces $1.20 per day, but, on account of superior advantages, pays 20 cents rent. On $100 per acre land he pays 30 cents. On $100,000 per acre land he produces $1.60 per day and pays 60 cents rent, leaving in each instance and on all grades of land, $1 per day above rent.

According to one writer, the laborer is infinitely better off on free or cheap than on dear land; according to the other, his reward is the same whether he occupy "free land at the margin of production" or that valued at $100,000 per acre. Mr. Freeland is clearly in the wrong; Mr. McMahon only partially in the right. The man occupying land having no commercial value is troubled with neither rent nor taxes. He can produce as much as the occupant of land worth $100 per acre, but it requires more labor to market his product. He will overcome this inconvenience as far as possible by turning his bulkier products into live stock. He will earn less and save more than the man more happily situated; but his gain in wealth will mark the discomforts of his isolation. It is the price he must pay for the lack of society, schools, churches and the thousand and one things that make life worth the living. He cannot attend the meeting of the Single Tax League nor see Lillian Russell ride the elephant. A man must in some manner pay for all the conveniences afforded by civilization; and it is the fact that money can be saved by foregoing them that entices men to "the margin of production"—makes of them pioneers. Mr. Freeland would "have his cake and eat it too."—When Waco was a "crossroads' town" its citizens were, to some extent, suffering the discomforts and reaping the profits of pioneers. They had poor educational facilities and worse streets than at present—if the latter be possible. When they wanted to go to San Antonio or New Orleans, they had to mount Shanks' mares or straddle a mule. They had to take their mint juleps without ice and worry along without the Iconoclast to point the way. If "there was less wealth produced per capita," it was because there was less capital—because our methods of production were more primitive. If wages were not higher on the frontier than in old civilizations, who would exchange the pleasures of the one for the perils of the other? Interest is usually if not always higher in young communities than in old, and for the very good reason that the great basis of credit, land values, is practically non-extant. The greater the risk, the higher the interest rate. As a frontier community develops into a populous state the interest rate falls because there is less risk, and rent rises—actually but not relatively—because all the new advantages and comforts must be paid for. The decline of the interest rate synchronously with the rise of rent is a favorite argument with the Single Taxers, but really one of their weakest. It is a case in which they see not only the "cat" but a litter of kittens—but see 'em with their eyes shut. They forget that it has been but a little while since the original American colonies constituted the western frontier, could only tempt capital from Europe by promise of large reward. When money is going begging in Boston at 4 and in Edinburgh at 3 per cent., Texas can scarce obtain it at 8. Why? Because our land values are still small, and we have a homestead law enacted by whining hypocrites as a fence for thieves, a citadel for fraud. How much has the interest rate fallen in the United States during the past 50 years? The present legal rate in the various states ranges from 6 to 10, with an average of about 7; contract rate from 6 to the ceiling; commercial rate fully 10 per cent. It has been but a few weeks since there was a case in court in Tarrant County, Texas, to recover money loaned at 10 per cent. a month! "What a fall was there, my countrymen!" And it must not be forgotten that we are paying interest on more than three times as much wealth per capita as we were 50 years ago! Suppose that the rate is approximately the same: Where we paid $1 interest per capita then, we pay $3 per capita now. If anybody sees that cream-canner he will please shy a boot-jack at it.

* * *

As rent rises taxation shadows it—clipping away the "unearned increment" to provide police, lights, fire protection, paved streets, schools, sanitation, etc., for the honorable gentleman who usually leaves his landlord about six months in arrears. A man may lock a bushel of money in a safe or loan it out at 2—or 10—per cent. a month, and dodge taxation; Jay Gould may have 75 millions of personal property and be assessed at that many thousands; the merchant may return his stock at a tenth its value; but the landlord cannot renege. He has to come to taw, and not only take his medicine but lick the spoon and swallow the label. The capitalist has him by the head, the government by the heels, and it's pull Dick, pull Devil, while a coterie of tenants who ain't half worth killing spout communism and dance the Carmagnole on his liver-pad. Fifty years ago many parts of Europe and some portions of America were as densely populated as they are at present, the people more at the mercy of the landlord because less mobile; yet the word "tramp" had not been added to our vocabulary. Nobody complained of lack of opportunity to earn a living. The hired man usually got "forehanded," and became a landholder. There were practically no multimillionaires and no able-bodied mendicants. I am not yet too old to tread the mazes of the fandango, yet can remember when a seven-figure fortune was considered remarkable. It has not been a great while since Charles Dickens declared that the appearance of a beggar on the streets of Boston would have created consternation; yet rent was relatively higher in Beantown then than now, rapid transit having materially reduced the surcingle of the urban landlord. Now you cannot walk the streets of a frontier town, where land may be had almost for the asking, without being beset on every side with tearful pleas for the price of a plate of soup or chilled-steel sandwich. The Single Taxers would not only make us all tenants of government, but make transportation, light, water and telegraph facilities public property. Hence we may infer that the capitalist is enjoying a very comfortable mouthful while the landlord is absorbing a square meal. Which argues that, if "corporations have no souls," the "land monopoly" is not destitute of the milk of human kindness. If the landlord possess the power to despoil both the laborer and the capitalist—to compel them to yield him the bulk of their earnings or drive them into the ocean or off the earth—how comes it that men occupying land of little value, and that often upon lease, can form combinations that fix the price of the land-products? A man possessing $100,000,000 may occupy a flatboat anchored in mid-ocean, yet take a heavier toll from the annual product of labor than can the man who owns 1,000 acres of land in the heart of Ohio. The American landlord and the American laborer are paying heavy tribute to men who reside in Europe on land that would not grow bunch-grass. The American landlord has no more power over them than tho' they made their home in the moon or existed in the atmosphere. The relatively rich and poor we have had with us since the dawn of history; but not until the change in productive methods, making necessary the co-operation of vast capital did we see scores of men become suddenly richer than sceptred monarchs, while others, able and willing to work, were compelled to beg their bread. The foregoing are a few reasons why I am inclined to doubt the efficacy of the Single Tax. If Mr. George can prove them fallacious, can demonstrate the practical worth of the Single Tax system, I will heartily congratulate both him and the country.

THE MEANEST MAN IN AMERICA.

Every little while some daring student of sociology, delving into the moral slums, discovers what he conceives to be the meanest possible man. There are at present half-a-hundred candidates for this distinction, and the Iconoclast is requested to settle the vexatious problem of precedence. Fortunately it is in a position to do so, to determine the matter beyond the peradventure of a doubt. It is first necessary to understand what we mean by the word "man." Plato assures us that man is a two-legged animal without feathers; but this description is too indefinite. It would include Gulliver's Yahoos, as well as that species of unclean simians who write insulting letters which they fear to father. It would dignify with the name of man all the imps of hades, and even that Warren, O., monster who sends foul anonymous screeds to lady authors in the South. The devils may have once been men, and even angels, for aught I know; but to urge that the author of anonymous letters of an insulting character, whether addressed to men or women, was begotten by an Indian pariah of a colored prostitute in the penetralia of Perdition were to libel a race, slander a trade and calumniate a country. Such cattle are not men, but parodies on God's masterpiece—are but as the beasts that perish; hence cannot be considered in our search for the meanest of the *genus homo*. The Warren, O., abnormality was probably hatched by a gila monster in some miasmic marsh from the addled egg of an aspic, and is hiding in the umbrage to avoid a load of buckshot while it vents its empoisoned slime upon Southern women. So wretched a creature cannot be America's meanest man, being barred from that bad eminence by lack of brains. It requires a man capable of ratiocination to become *facile princeps* even in the dark realm of rascality.

Some are inclined to think the doubtful honor should be conferred on Dr. Parkhurst, who hired half-starved women to dance the hoochee-coochee, and befuddled them with beer, that he might complain of them to the police and get much gratuitous advertising in the daily press; but they do mistake: it was but an application of Vidocq's principle,—

"set a rogue to catch a rascal"—and the reverend gentleman rose for once in his career to the exalted level of a bum detective in the redlight district. Nor can it be conceded that the manager of an old line life insurance company who attempted, by the emission of tons of lying literature, to convince the victims of his conspiracy against the people that a vote for Bryan was a vote to halve the value of their policies, is the meanest of men, for brazen liars and conscienceless robbers abound. Life insurance presidents who pocket salaries of $75,000 per annum wrung from the thin purses of sweat-stained masses, are not the only scoundrels fattening on the substance of the poor. Even G. Cleveland, who saved a seven-figure fortune out of a five-figure salary during the darkest days of his country's distress, and then had the transcendent impudence to stand up at a mugwump banquet whose cost would have shamed a Roman sybarite—and was borne by men who had profited by his malversation—and whine about the "dishonesty" of a people he had impoverished, is no worse than many other patriots for revenue only with which this country is cursed. Some incline to the view that the meanest man is a woman, and that her crowning act of atrocity consisted in having the historic spoons of Dolly Madison remodeled and adorned with the Cleveland crest; but if we assume that vanity in woman is a cardinal sin, there is small hope of salvation for the gentle sex. Tennyson assures us that "as the husband is the wife is;" hence Mrs. Cleveland's scandalous act of vandalism was the natural result of long association, not with America's meanest, but most ignorant man.

If the question were left to a vote of the people, they would doubtless decide that Russell Sage is America's meanest man, and he certainly has strong claims to that unenviable distinction. He is the multi-millionaire who, when attacked by a dynamiter, pushed a clerk between himself and danger, then declined to pay his unfortunate substitute for the injuries he received. The wife of his nephew, fearing they would be unable to save from their joint labor the sum of $50 to meet the mortgage he held on their little home, became crazed with grief and hanged herself. But there are other misers with hearts as mean and souls as small. Rich men have been known to wear the cast-off clothes of their neighbors, while Sage indulges in the luxury of $4 hand-me-down suits. Other worshippers of the golden calf have filled their bellies with warm water to cheat themselves into the belief that they had been to dinner and save the price of a sandwich, but Sage dines almost every day. The report that he has been caught stealing from himself, and that he debated long and earnestly whether it was cheaper to go lousy or purchase a fine-tooth comb, is probably a canard. As a miser, Sage averages up fairly well with Texas' W. L. Moody, or even with Doc Talmage, now so eloquently urging that relief be sent to the famine-sufferers of India, while contributing nary a nick. I remember when the reverend doctor was requested to deliver a lecture to raise money for the relief of starving Americans, and he cheerfully agreed to do so—if paid $300 cash in advance!

The meanest man is a resident of Massachusetts. All other candidates for chief place in the infernal pantheon are white-winged seraphs by comparison. A fragment of pitch from the foundations of Erebus, or a segment of that darkness which Moses laid upon the land of Egypt, would make a white mark on his soul—but would have to be whittled to an infinitesimally small point ere it could be applied, for his ego would rattle in the shell of a mustard seed like a bird-shot in a tin wash-boiler. It was said of old that all sins may be forgiven except a sin against the Holy Ghost. Just how such an offense might be committed has long remained a mystery to most; but this acme of human cussedness has succeeded in placing it to his discredit. The Holy Ghost is simply that divine essence increate which prompts men to noble deeds, and those sin against it who are guilty of ingratitude. It is the most heinous crime in the calendar, and those capable of committing it are already lost beyond recall. Even the blood of Christ and the grace of God will not make angelic pinfeathers sprout on the shoulder-blades of the ingrate. The ungracious fourlegged fice is blamed for snapping at the hand that feeds it; but I have found one born in the shape of man, who befouls the memory of his benefactor, pukes upon the bones of his patron. His name is Spenser B. Meeser, and he is pastor of the First Baptist Church of Worcester, Mass. What state produced him, how and why, I know not; but howsoever he arrived, he is here. Behold him!—if not the wisest or the brightest, assuredly "the meanest of mankind." Observe him well, for it has required six thousand years to produce him, and the world may never look upon his like again. The present is said to be an embodiment of all the past. If this be true, then Meeser is a conservation of all the ulcers on the body social for sixty centuries. We are told that nothing is created in vain; but I'm inclined to suspect that the hand of Providence slipped when this fellow put in an appearance. On no other hypothesis can I account for the brain of a buzzard and the heart of a hyena being present in the body of a human being. If nature mistreated him in the making, then his shortcomings should be pitied and pardoned; but if it really furnished him with human viscera, he deserves to be held up to the withering scorn and eternal contumely of a world.

The man whose corpse this fellow has insulted, and whose memory he would defame, was no common clod, but America's greatest philanthropist, Stephen Girard—a name graven in letters of gold on the great heart of humanity. For five and sixty years this good man has been in his honored grave; and that the memory of his princely deeds might be perpetuated, those he befriended—and their name is legion—erected with loving hands and grateful hearts a marble monument. But there is one who owes to the generosity of Stephen Girard all that he is or can ever hope to be, who participated not in this labor of love. Not only this, but he grew angry and insolent when asked to contribute a mite from his comfortable salary of $3,500 per annum, coarsely declared that he could not afford any further "charity," and added that "his views touching Girard and the religious side of his nature would not permit of his doing honor to the man!" From whom, in the name of that Christ who forgave Mary Magdalen and those who crucified him, came this reply. From Rev. Spenser B. Meeser, who for years was fed and housed, clothed and educated at Girard's expense! The ignorant adder, warmed in a good man's bosom, stung its benefactor; but who could have expected such a return from a saintly Baptist preacher? Who and what is this Sir Oracle who thus prates of "charity" to old Stephen Girard, and presumes to sit in judgment on his soul? He belongs in the same category with that crowd of God-intoxicated fanatics who shrieked and howled in the streets of Jerusalem for the crucifixion of Christ. Nay, I do wrong those who demanded the release of the bloody Barabbas, for they had not been sheltered in helpless infancy from summer's heat and winter's cold by the labor of Christ. They had not sat at his board and eaten his bread. Nor is it recorded that they derided him when he lay cold in death. No, Mr. Meeser, you do not belong in that crowd; for they warred upon the living whom they considered an enemy, you upon the dead who was your benefactor when else you were friendless. You approach nearer to the character of Judas Iscariot. But perchance I should apologize to that infamous apostate also for making such a comparison. He was paid handsomely for his crime, while your ingratitude is purely gratuitous. He yielded to the pressure of a powerful priesthood; you sought an opportunity to expose the poverty of your soul. Judas repented and hanged himself; you still live despite the plenitude of hemp. Granting, for the sake of argument, that Girard had committed all the cardinal sins: Does it become you, a charity child, nurtured by his bounty, to play the accuser? Whatsoever he was to the world, to you he was a guide, philosopher and friend. If you could not commend, a sense of decency should have set upon your lips the seal of silence. "The religious side of his nature" is what gives you a pain in that thing you call a Christian conscience; yet if you do but follow the teachings of the New Testament one-half so well, you may sit at the right hand of the Savior.

"Faith, Hope and Charity—and the greatest of these is Charity." Listen to this from St. Paul, and let it saturate your pharisaical soul—if you've got a soul: "Though I speak with the tongues of men and of angels, and have not Charity, I am become as sounding brass, or a tinkling cymbal. And though I have the gift of prophecy, and understand all mysteries, and all knowledge; and though I have all faith, and have not Charity, I am nothing."

Do you catch the sequence of St. Paul's observations? You may yawp in your $3,500 pulpit until ice forms in Perdition, you may sing psalms until the cows come home, and agonize in prayer until your collar limps and you break a lung; you may visit all the sisters once a week and paddle about in the baptismal tank until you develop dorsal fins and web feet; you may believe the Bible from Alpha to Omega and the Baptist credo from A to Izzard; but if you have not Charity such as dwelt in the heart of old Stephen Girard, you are no more than a cracked cymbal at a tencent circus, or a hiatus in a hole. You're the cube-root of a vacuum, the net product of nothing. St. Paul says so, and the gentleman from Damascus was usually correct in his conclusions. Yet from the turtleshell of your pitiful self-righteousness, you peer forth at Charity incarnate, call it irreligious, and mumble that you—sweet-scented slug of sanctified slobber!—cannot honor such a man. Small wonder that infidelity is on the increase, for who could believe that a self-respecting God made you in his own image?—that he ever sent his Son to die for your salvation!

At the time of his death Stephen Girard was, despite his munificent ante-mortem charities, the wealthiest man in America, and calumny itself has never hinted that he obtained a dollar dishonestly. He left $500,000 to the city of Phila., $300,000 to the state of Penna., and valuable property to the city of New Orleans for public improvements; princely sums to hospitals and asylums, and to provide the poor of Phila. with winter fuel, and the residue of his vast estate for the building and support of a college for orphan boys. "Applicants for admission must be poor white male orphans between the ages of 6 to 10 years. They are provided for and educated free of cost." We learn from this proviso that when Rev. Spenser B. Meeser entered the hospitable doors of Girard College he was a poor male orphan under ten years of age; also that he was white —impossible as that fact may now appear. And this charity child quartered on Girard's generosity, every ounce of bread that went into his poor lank belly paid for out of his purse, is now the pompous Yankee parson who, preaching the "judge not lest ye be judged" doctrine of Jesus—for $3,500 per annum—declares himself "not in sympathy with the movement" to commemorate the noble deeds of his benefactor, that his religious mulligrubs "will not admit of his doing honor to the man!" I'll pay $5 for a photograph of that fellow to place in my museum of monstrosities. When he dies he ought to be preserved in alcohol with centipedes and tarantulas in some toxological institute. If it be true that the breath of some creatures is poison, it is a wonder that Meeser doesn't kill his congregation.

When Philadelphia was plague-swept was it the sanctiloquent Baptist preachers who ministered to the sufferers? Not on your life!—the last mother's son of 'em went pounding down the turnpike like the devil beating tanbark. They could all read their titles clear to mansions in the skies, but were not anxious to emigrate. They preferred to serve the Lord on earth a little longer—when they could do so safely and for a good salary. Old Stephen Girard—this "irreligious" man who was supposed to have no treasures laid up in heaven—devoted himself day and night to the relief of the suffering. Husbands abandoned their wives and mothers their babes, so fearful was the pestilence, so busy the dark angel of death; but the man whom this infernal pharisee declines to honor, never faltered. America's wealthiest man, with neither kith nor kin to hold him by the heart-strings in the stricken city, refused to seek a place of safety, became a common nurse and through the long hot days and fever-laden nights toiled from house to house and from room to room, beating back the pestilence, seeking to succor and to save. To those who lay sick with that loathsome disease deserted by those most dear, vainly seeking with fevered eyes the faces of relatives and friends, that "irreligious" man must have seemed an angel of mercy. Any man may be a hero when surrounded by the pomp and circumstance of war—when the cheers of contending thousands, the roar of batteries and the crash of steel breeds murder in the blood; but picture to yourself this grim old man, pacing the floor of a poor tenement house among the dead at the midnight hour and crooning a lullaby to the nameless babe breathing out its life upon his bosom! Look upon it—if thou cans't see through a veil of tears; then turn and contemplate the canting pharisee who cannot obtain the consent of his sanctified soul to honor this Good Samaritan! What says the Son of Man? "Go thou and do likewise." I tell thee, Meeser, a ministering angel will that old man be when thou liest howling. Was he indeed an Atheist? Was this done for pure philanthropy and without hope of heaven? Was there no faith to sustain him in his time of trial?—naught for him to lean upon but his own unselfish love? And did that bear him up triumphantly when preachers fled and the courage of Christians failed? Was he better in his unbelief than those who relied upon the Lord? "Love thy neighbor as thyself." So reads the law; but Stephen Girard went beyond the statute.

> "Why drew Marseilles' good bishop purer breath,
> When all nature sickened and each gale was death?"

The answer is recorded in Holy Writ; but when we turn to the city of Philadelphia, we find a man as tender, as loving and as true who fears not the fires of hell, hopes not the rewards of heaven. If high honor be due those who to 'scape the wrath of God and win the immortal Crown take up the Cross, how much more should be meted to that man who, seeing at the end of life's fitful fever only an ever-dreamless sleep, performs works of equal worth! Hads't thought of that, my Meeser?—that Stephen Girard needed not the thunders of Sinai to drive him in the path of duty?

—that he could stand Godless and hopeless in the conflux of two eternities and play the man!—as firm in love as Lucifer in hate—bidding defiance to destiny! To me there is something appalling in such a sight. A man engulfed in the wide-weltering chaos of Infidelity, shut in by the black night of unbelief, yet weaving of the gold and lilies of his own hopeless heart a robe of godhood.

If the life of Stephen Girard was not applied religion, then is religion a lie. He was not a sectarian, and does not appear to have held a very high opinion of preachers. Perhaps he had the misfortune to encounter the prototype of Mr. Meeser, and, judging the stock by the sample, concluded it best to keep them out of his college. Their bickerings, quarrelings, even riotings in Philadelphia, together with their cowardly desertion of their flocks in time of danger, were not calculated to increase his respect for "the cloth." He does not appear to have warred upon religion or attempted to turn any man from his faith. He was a self-sufficient man who believed as he pleased and allowed others the same liberty. He requested his employes to attend divine services and himself gave liberally of his means to various denominations. He did not object to prayers and religious lectures in his college, but excluded the sectarian clergy because of their disposition to "spute" anent points of doctrine. He appears to have acted on the idea that,

"In Faith and Hope the world will disagree,
But all mankind's concern is Charity."

If we may judge a tree by its fruit there is small danger that Stephen Girard missed salvation. If he be indeed in hell, I pray the good Lord to send Meeser elsewhere, for to be compelled to associate through all eternity with a creature so contemptible were to add insult to injury and devise a deeper damnation than spike-tailed devils and burning brimstone. I'd rather be in hades with Girard than have to breathe the same atmosphere with his defamer. I'd rather be a hungry hyena and rob graveyards in a lazar colony than an impudent preacher guilty of base ingratitude. I'd rather be a maggot in the carcass of a mule than a minister who damns his fellow-men for not seeing the plan of salvation through his smoked sectarian microscope. I'd rather be an itch bacillus in a suppurating sore than a sanctified simian straddling about on its hind legs and flinging filth at the corse of the man who paid for the meat on its bones. Yes, I have found the meanest man in America. His existence confutes the theory of the survival of the fittest and suggests that mankind is merely a malodor. His character casts a shadow on the sun. He has cirrhosis of the soul. His heart is a green worm that feeds on gall. His bowels of compassion are petrified. If his milk of human kindness were churned, the product would be limburger cheese. He has moral strabismus and carries his brains in his belly. His odor of sanctity would give a pole-cat convulsions. He perverts the doctrine that "faith without work is dead." To sit beneath the drippings of his sanctuary were like getting caught in a cataclysm of sheep dope. Massachusetts is welcome to Meeser. We have one tree in Texas on which we have hanged 37 better men—and they are all in hell.

JUDGE LYNCH AND THE LAWYERS.

One J. S. Hogg, attorney-at-law by trade, has been taking what he evidently considers a terrific fall out of Judge Lynch. He picks this preter-jurist up by the slack of the pantelettes and wraps him around the periphery of a gumstump with an armipotence that fills the quivering atmosphere with fragments of "liver and lights" and the pungent odor of toasted tripe. Hogg is a roasting-mill for your gridiron when he does the Ingalls act—or thinks he is, which is just as satisfactory to his soul. When the "storm tossed" lashes himself to fury and begins to fulgerate, he's pre-eminently a hot potato. When he assumes the role of malefactor and begins to spout fire, Philaris' brazen bull were an ice-box or the chilly kiss of a Boston school-marm by comparison. There is an explosive force to his dehiscience that would shame a dynamite shell. He's past grand master of the science of anacamptics, and can, with one blast upon his bugle-horn, awake the slumbering echoes from Sabine's slimy ooze to the Rio Bravo's glistening sands. Hearken to the deep-toned dreadfulness of Texas' only Hogg:

"Judge Lynch is the most contemptible, the most villainous, the most cowardly of all the red-handed murderers whose souls ever roasted in the log-heaps of hell," etc., etc.

Bravo! Old Balaam, the prince of curse-peddlers, could scarce have done better. The trouble with Hogg, however, is that he has no concept of proportion, the positive and comparative having been eliminated from his vocabulary to make room for the super-superlative. It has been said that he cannot distinguish between buttermilk and bordeaux, between corn-pone and pound-cake—that whatsoever he can get through his neck is welcome gastronomic grist; and I much fear that his estimation of men and measures is faulty as his idea of edibles. In the opinion of this adipose limb of the law, those who hanged the bank-robbers and assassins at Wichita Falls; those who burned a buck nigger for ravishing a 3-year-old babe at Paris; those who executed a black beast for having forcibly debauched a white maid near Bryan, are infinitely worse than the fiends they put out of the world. In other words, it is more "contemptible" to unlawfully slay a professional assassin than it is to unlawfully slay a worthy citizen. It is more "villainous" to send a rape-fiend hence without due process of law than to take an infant from its cradle and sacrifice its life to lust. It is more "cowardly" to string a negro up in the face of heaven than to pounce upon an unprotected maid, defile her and inoculate her with a loathsome disease! Disliking to say anything disrespectful of a man whose intentions it believes to be good, the Iconoclast refrains from comment. It is of the opinion that a majority of the participants in the affairs above referred to are undeserving of such severe denunciation. They did not go about their work "masked and in the darkness of the night," as Mr. Hogg imagines is the invariable practice of punitive mobs, but with uncovered faces and in the broad open light of day. They believed that when such desperate criminals are caught red-handed, the proper thing to do is to crack their necks with the least possible delay, instead of saddling themselves with the expense of long and tedious trials and affording various learned lawyers an opportunity to pad their weasel-skins by perverting justice and turning the offenders loose upon the land. I grant you freely that there should be no such thing in this land as mob-law; but instead of attempting to blow Judge Lynch off the earth with what Casca calls "a deal of stinking breath," it were the part of wisdom for Attorney Hogg to inquire diligently what brought him thither. I fear that a critical examination of the matter will demonstrate that mob-law is due chiefly to the lawyers—to the very class loudest in its condemnation. They shape our laws, and take precious good care in doing so not to deprive themselves of their occupation by making statutory intent too plain and court procedure too simple. Having secured a criminal code which it requires an expert to interpret—a labyrinthic maze inturbidated with a ridiculous terminology—the lawyers are preparing to entangle an innocent man in its meshes or secure the release of a Jack-the-Ripper as goes the professional fee. Of course there are honorable exceptions to this rule, for it is not absolutely necessary that a lawyer should be a rascal. Some there be who would scorn to accept a fee from the blood-stained hand of a criminal; but candor compels the confession that they are in nowise numerous. No matter how honorable he be in his private capacity, the average lawyer is professionally ambidexterous, and, within the court-room, morally ambilevious; he is not only ready to accept service under any flag, but to strike foul blows to win his fight. I do not mean by this that he will pack juries and suborn witnesses; but that he will employ all those arts recognized by his too liberal code of ethics to mislead the court and shield his client. If justice will acquit his client then he would have justice "tho' the heavens fall;" if justice would hang or imprison his client, then he becomes a conspirator against the peace and dignity of the commonwealth. We will say that Smith meets Jones on the streets of Tyler, by gross insult provokes an assault, then shoots his assailant dead. He employs as counsel Messrs. J. S. Hogg and J. M. Duncan, both of whom are now tearing their lingerie to tatters because of the activity of Judge Lynch. These distinguished attorneys promptly set up the plea of self-defense. The county is raked with a fine-tooth comb to secure a dozen fat-headed aphides who have formed no opinion about the case simply because not blessed with "the grand thaumaturgic faculty of thought." A week is expended in securing this museum of mental misfits, and another in badgering and browbeating witnesses, who become so confused that they would contradict themselves in attempting to state their names, ages and occupations. The jury is overawed by Hogg's pomposity, befuddled with Duncan's sophistry, and impressed with the idea that the dead man was a dangerous character who was seeking to slay defendant instead of trying to tweak his nose as offset to a gratuitous insult. Then it is locked up—having but a shadowy conception of lawyer-made law and utterly unable to analyze attorney-distorted evidence. What can you expect of such a tribunal? Has not the blundering of petit juries passed into a proverb? Do you not know of a dozen men formally tried and solemnly acquitted who should have been hanged or put in the penitentiary? Can you not cite a score of cases in which poor devils charged with trifling offenses were given the extremity of the law, while men guilty of capital crimes received lighter sentences? Do you not know that it is more dangerous for a beggar to steal a mule than for a plutocrat to kill a man? The Smith-Jones jury probably agree to disagree simply because the miserable blockheads can not tell what the devil the contention is all about; in which case the pitiful farce must be played over again—at the expense of the people. The next time the defendant is convicted of manslaughter and given two years in prison instead of ten minutes on the gallows. On some flimsy pretext a motion is made for a new trial. Perchance one of the jurors went to sleep during a tedious wrangle over the admission of unimportant evidence; or some one in the crowd may have passed him a bottle of Prohibition bitters. The motion must be argued. If overruled, an appeal is taken on some fool technicality. More delay. Finally the case is reversed and remanded. Smith can now be tried only for manslaughter, having been formally acquitted of deliberate murder. New trial; mistrial; change of venue; case continued from term to term until important witnesses die or disappear. The public loses interest in the case and forgets the dead man's family. Smith has joined church and is leading an exemplary life. The public becomes sorry for the defendant and when he is finally acquitted, crowds around to congratulate. And the name and fame of Hogg and Duncan are exploited far and wide as "great criminal lawyers"—men whose services other vicious hoodlums may find invaluable. And the next time a murder occurs under like conditions, the people, remembering the incompetence of courts, take the law into their own hands. And the mistake they make in hanging the homicide instead of stringing up Duncan and Hogg, whose skill in protecting criminals encouraged him to commit the crime. They are guilty before God; for had Smith been hanged as he deserved, the second murder had not been committed. Yet Duncan indulges in mandragora moans and Hogg puffs himself up like some bloated *bufo vulgaris* and denounces the people as contemptible cowards—whose pernicious activity has deprived him of a fat fee. They are cowards, says he, because they have killed "an unarmed prisoner" —just as though sheriffs conducted executions by releasing the condemned men and providing them with loaded muskets! When Mr. Hogg roasts a hare he does so while it's running. It has been said that the shortest route to a man's pericardium is through his purse—and every rape-fiend lynched, every murderer hanged by the mob takes a shingle off some lawyer's house. Doubtless mobs sometimes make mistakes; but in this particular they may well challenge comparison with the courts. As a rule Judge Lynch will harm no man unless his guilt be established beyond the peradventure of a doubt. With him it is simply a question of identity and evidence. There are no delays, no loop-holes in his law, no technicalities and continuances, no foolish red-tape and no lawyer's fees. How is it in our criminal courts? On one side is the prosecuting attorney eager to convict, no matter if the prisoner at the bar be innocent as a babe newborn, for both his fee and professional reputation are concerned; on the other side is the counsel for the defense, intent only on securing an acquittal, tho' he knows his client to be guilty of every crime in the calendar. The defendant is alternately painted as an angel of light and goblin damned, the lawyers pro and the attorneys con seeking to "make the worse appear the better reason" to a dozen sleepy dunderheads, who view the proceedings with eyes that bespeak the intelligence of a string of burnt holes in a blanket. It is not an attempt to determine right and wrong, but a tourney between opposing counsel, the prisoner the bone of contention and ignorance officiating as umpire. And so it is that the courts, which should be the pillars of order, become the nidi of anarchy. Statutes exenterated by technicalities and courts eviscerated by red tape, constitute the *raison d'etre* of Judge Lynch —and he will never be debauched by denouncing the effect while the cause is permitted to remain. We have mob-law because we have lawlessness, and we have lawlessness because we have too many criminal-shielding lawyers. Every criminal statute needful could be printed within the compass of this little paper and made so plain that judges need rely no longer on "precedent," but adhere to the strict letter of the law. The courts should be stripped of all circumlocutory customs and made in truth temples of justice instead of tilting-grounds for smart attorneys. The unit rule should be abolished in the jury room, a two-thirds vote made sufficient for a verdict, and intelligence instead of blank ignorance called to the box. As I have frequently suggested heretofore, it might be well to elect our jurors as we do other county officials, and make their vote in every case a matter of record, thereby fixing upon them more than a transient responsibility, and securing for such important service men in whose honesty and intelligence the people had formally expressed their confidence. As matters now stand, when a man of average intelligence finds himself on the jury, he is distracted by thoughts of his neglected business and can not give his undivided attention to the case. He is driven to a disagreable duty for which he is in nowise qualified, and is inclined to compromise that he may be the sooner released. An elective jury would save the public great aggravation, expedite the business of courts and materially reduce the cost. Experience would soon enable them to properly analyze evidence and make them impervious to attorney-sophistry. Such a jury would constitute an elective bench of judges, be subject to impeachment and removal, and would be careful not to render verdicts which the court of appeals would reverse. Any attorney will tell you that if he has a good case, he would prefer to submit it to the judge, because that official is usually capable of determining it wisely and well and it is to his interest to do so; but that if he has a bad case, he wants a jury, and the more stupid and irresponsible the better. The jury is so interwoven with our institutions that to altogether abolish it were probably unwise, certainly impossible at present; but instead of keeping pace with our civilization, the system has retrograded until, instead of being "the bulwark of our liberties," as once appropriately called, it has become the shield of criminals and the nursing mother of anarchy. It was once the custom to select as jurors "good men and true" who were supposed to know most, rather than those who knew least about the case, and they were at liberty to decide the matter without the assistance of contending attorneys or the taking of other testimony than what themselves could furnish. If they failed to agree, the dissidents in the minority were discharged and other reputable men of the immediate neighborhood called in. This was repeated until a verdict was reached, and the punishment decree followed as swiftly as in the days of ancient Israel. A man accused of crime was then tried by a "jury of his peers," or men who were more than his equals; he is now tried by a jury of jackasses. There should be no attorneys employed to prosecute, none retained to defend in criminal cases; but a skillful lawyer should be attached to the court to see that all important evidence is properly laid before the jury, while the judge interprets the law. To such a court the people would turn with respect and confidence and we would soon hear the last of Judge Lynch. Punishment, to have a repressive effect upon the criminal class and satisfy the public sense of justice, must follow sure and swift upon the commission of a crime. Statesmen take cognizance of the world as it is rather than indulge in Ernulphus-curses, because it is not all they imagine it ought to be. An eye for an eye, a tooth for a tooth, and a life for a life, is not only the law of Moses, but is a statute deep-graven on the heart of humanity by the burin of the Almighty. When one commits a dreadful crime, the public conscience demands that he speedily die the death; and where courts notoriously fail to execute this mandate, uprisings of the people and mob-violence may be expected. What Hogg and Duncan so vigorously condemn is the result of society's inherent sense of justice, of pity for its outraged member and lack of confidence in the courts. The contemptibility, the villainy, the cowardice and the disregard for life of which they complain are the attributes of those attorneys who prostitute their talents to preserve intact the forfeited neck of the felon—who are willing, for a money consideration, to turn such monsters loose upon the community. When a lawyer begins to berate mob-violence, to brand whole communities with the stigma of Cain and consign them to "the log heaps of hell," it were well to ask him if he ever shielded a criminal from the sword of Justice, thereby not only provoking but making necessary the very deeds he condemns. And if he can not return a negative answer he should be advised to poultice his impudence. The people of this county are neither "contemptible," "villainous" nor "cowardly"—if they did twice make Hogg chief magistrate. They will respect the laws and the courts when and only when they are worthy of respect. Of course, I will be told that laws and courts are creations of the people, who are responsible for their imperfections, and who should reform instead of defying them. This is theoretically true, but practically false. The people demand various general laws, and they are enacted, and satisfactory penalties provided; but the lawyers prescribe methods of court procedure and make their enforcement a costly and difficult matter. The general public has just about as much to do with the practical workings of our jurisprudence as it has with the science of medicine. How will the general public so reform the judiciary that a millionaire murderer may be tried, convicted and executed within ten days and at a cost of a few hundred dollars, when it can not so much as get a decent fee-bill enacted after making it an imperative platform demand? How will it deprive several thousand lawyers of their perquisites in criminal cases, when it can not compel a few stall-fed county officials to either resign or serve for a reasonable consideration? Could we expect the self-righteous Hogg and the begodly Duncan to favor a reform in our judiciary that would leave criminal lawyers without occupation and consociate our courts with common sense? The public, be it remembered, with more tongues than the hydra, more eyes than Argus, more hands than Briaerus, is dumb and blind and helpless, sprawling this way and that on its multitudinous legs in the wake of various leaders who travel in a circle—in the center of which are the political flesh-pots. The public is seldom agreed as to what it does want, but is quick to determine what it does not want—and it does not want a rape-fiend or assassin to live one minute longer than necessary to determine his guilt and get a rope around his goozle. Like a blind horse, it may be led to water, but making it drink is a different matter. Until the courts can crack a criminal's neck while his offense still rankles in the public breast, Judge Lynch may be expected to do business despite all denunciation. There be some who seem to entertain the mistaken opinion that the people were made for the criminal and the criminal for the lawyer, on the principle that every bug must have smaller bugs to bite it. The lawyers, being pretty good fellows, non-professionally considered, will not, I opine, take serious umbrage at this indictment or attempt to argue it before that august tribunal we call the people, realizing, as it certainly must, that it were safer to promise reformation and cast themselves upon the mercy of the court. They have fallen into the bad habit of worshipping "due process of law" because it yields victual, forgetful that it is in nowise worthy adulation unless it yields also protection to the people. Of course certain would-be John the Baptists will rise up in the wilderness and denounce me as an advocate of lynch law; but remembering that Cicero assures us "even flies have their spleen," I will make a prayerful effort to survive. I am not an advocate of mob-violence; but I do say that no honest man in Texas fears Judge Lynch a little bit, while to the criminal class he is a greater terror than all our courts. If the man who religiously respects the persons and property of other people lives until he is made the central figure of an impromptu necktie sociable, he'll make old Methuselah appear a veritable mammothrept. In some way the public must be protected from the vicious, and Judge Lynch is like to hold his ægis over his people until a potent substitute is provided. I would prefer that all necessary hanging be done by sheriffs duly ordained; but to save me I can not add aught to the ostentatious tear-jugs of Hogg and Duncan because a few desperate criminals have been sent to hell by an irregular route. Perhaps my sob machinery would work smoother and my snuffle glands give down more voluminously if I could remember only the criminals and forget their victims.

THE RAPE FIEND REMEDY.

When I suggested some years ago that we would yet be compelled to drive the negro out of this country or drive him into the ground, the northern press in general and the Ohio press in particular, reared up on its hind legs and hurled at me sizzling wads of reproach. I am not a little curious to know how the people of Urbana now regard the suggestion—whether the thousand and one women who have since been defiled by black fiends, as well as the immediate friends and relatives of these unfortunates, are inclined to join that indignant Cleveland dominie in denouncing the forcible expulsion of blacks as "a damnable crime conceived in the brain of a Texas brute." It was said of old it is easy to bear the sorrows of others; but if we leave the disposal of the blacks to those men whose homes they have forcibly dishonored, will they receive a lighter sentence than banishment? If they decide that the blacks shall be permitted to remain, then I withdraw my suggestion and beg the pardon of that civilization which it is said I have "insulted."

The "coon" has ever been a curse to this country. He has caused an amount of sorrow, suffering and shame which only Almighty God can measure. From an economic standpoint he has cost this country more than all the wars it has waged, added to the ruin wrought by flood and fire. He is, and will continue to be, an industrial stumbling-block, a political ulcer, a social scab, a moral nightmare so long as he is permitted to remain. His presence here is a ten-fold greater curse than all the apocryphal plagues laid upon the land of Egypt. He is a perpetual pestilence, an inexhaustible fount of political putrescence and moral poison. It is said that Ham was cursed with blackness because of his impudicity—his utter disregard of the laws of decency; and that characteristic has been transmitted unimpaired to his descendants of the present day. The negro is a lazy, lying, lustful animal, which no conceivable amount of training can transform into a tolerable citizen. He lacks the fundamental elements of manhood. Ye cannot gather grapes of thorns or figs of thistles; ye cannot hatch nightingales of goose eggs; ye cannot make a gentleman of a jackass or one of nature's noblemen of a nigger. The Ohio people propose to make rape a capital crime and apply the death penalty. Such statutes are impuissant, afford absolutely no protection. Such is the law of the South, and it is ably supplemented by Judge Lynch; yet no white woman is safe in her home, no white maid is secure beneath her father's roof unless shielded with a six-shooter. Even babes have been debauched, and we dare not leave toddling innocence or decrepit age beyond the reach of the white man's rifle. In days agone the red Indian hung like a circle of hell-fire on our frontier; but he was an angel of mercy compared with the Ethiop. His gust was for blood, not beauty; he destroyed, but seldom debauched. The Indian was an evil with which we could contend—an evil which we could and did crush out with unfaltering courage; but the negro is a pestilence which walketh in darkness and becomes more deadly with our every effort to strike it down.

Our Northern neighbors do not understand the negro. Plenty of sloppy sentimentalists who have absorbed "Uncle Tom's Cabin" and reams of kindred "rot" think that they do, but they don't. His mentality is in nowise akin to that of the white man. It is murky as his hide and resembles that of a hog. I mean no offense to the porker by comparison. You can teach a hog almost anything except to control his appetite, in which respect he is cousin-german to the "coon." Leave your garden gate ajar for a moment, and Mr. Hog meanders in. Your dogs half devour him;

but at the first opportunity he returns—returns, well knowing that it means a cruel clubbing and a cataract of curs. He is cowardly as a heifer calf, or that Warren, O., lazar who writes insulting anonymous letters to Southern ladies; but his belly rules his brain. A dozen times he is driven thence with a dog swinging to either ear and half a dozen more hanging to his bleeding hams; but a dozen times he returns in the hope of getting one more mouthful before squealing in vain for mercy. Such is the character of the "coon." He well knows that if he assaults a white woman the chances are as 10 to 1 that he will be killed like a hydrophobic cur. He is cowardly to the last degree and has no intention of committing such a crime; but the opportunity offers and in the fever of his brute desire he forgets that there is such a thing as death. Examine the daily press, and you will find that the courts are imprisoning and hanging negro rape fiends—that Judge Lynch is after them with the torch, the rifle and the rope; and you will find also that there is a steady increase in this character of crime. The fact that a negro has been hanged, or even burned alive for ravishing a white woman, makes others fearful, but it also suggests to their foul minds the crime itself. To a negro a white woman is as Dian to a Satyr or Athena to old Silenus. That one of these superior creatures has actually been enjoyed by a lustful black sets them all adreaming and makes them dangerous. A white woman is found unprotected; all visions of the rope or the stake vanish, drowned in the hell of desire, and Judge Lynch claims another victim—thereby spreading the foul infection. What can be done with such cattle? The evil is irremediable so long as the blacks are permitted to remain. Have we the moral right to apply such a drastic remedy? I answer yes—that we would be amply justified in slaughtering every Ethiop on the earth to preserve unsullied the honor of one Caucasian home. Show me the man who would purchase the lives of an hundred million blacks with the defilement of his wife or daughter—and give me a gun. Yet the daughters of white men are debauched by Ethiops every day. The rights of the Caucasian are paramount and, in case of conflict, extinguish those of the inferior race. Where the honor of white women is concerned, the Ethiop has absolutely no rights which we are in duty bound to respect. Of course, it will be urged that the good blacks should not be made to suffer for the sins of the bad. I answer that the good are few, the bad many, and it is impossible to tell what ones are not dangerous to the honor of the dominant race until the damage is done. When we see a wolf we do not pause to inquire if it will slaughter sheep, for we know that such is the general tendency of its tribe. There was a time when the negroes were, to some extent, worthy of our trust. It was when they were held in bondage and not permitted to roam abroad. Perhaps they were as immoral then as now; but they recognized their racial inferiority, and no more coupled white women with the idea of evil than the owl aspires to mate with the eagle. Emancipation, the elective franchise and a smattering of education are responsible for their present acts of infamy. When Fred Douglass, the saddle-colored miscegenationist, died, nigger preachers at Dallas declared in memorial addresses that all black men wanted white women, a fact which shows the drift of the darky's thoughts and the danger. The negro has heard that in England and other degraded European countries no social distinction is made because of color, and conceives that he is being robbed of his sexual rights. He sees his women courting, and not without success, the favors of white men, and, like Iago, he demands "a wife for a wife." In short, his yearnings by day and his dreams by night are for forbidden fruits, and, like the drunkard, he misses no opportunity to gratify his appetite, tho' he knows indulgence means damnation.

I would not wrong the Ethiop race—would not forcibly expel it and leave it to perish. The white man is responsible for the presence of the black man in America. Frugal Yankee traders and witch burners—the blessed Covenanters who enacted New England's blue laws—captured him in his native wilds and sold him to us to be a hewer of wood and a drawer of water. Having stuffed their pockets to the bursting point, built fine churches and employed impudent preachers of the Beecher brand with the profits of the slave trade, these sanctified thieves with Sunday faces and cerulean equators, despoiled us of the very property for which we had paid them, and made it our political peers. And we submitted to the infamy at the point of the sword, because we had found slavery unprofitable and did not then appreciate the deep damnation thrust upon us by the new conditions It was not until "reconstruction" days that our eyes were opened. But we must let the dead past bury its dead and face the future. The question now is, how can we get rid of the niggers? Fertile land sufficient to colonize them all can be had in Africa for the asking. We should send them thither at our own cost and provide them with whatsoever may be necessary to make a crop. The entire cost need not exceed 200 millions, and their expulsion would, in five years, add ten times that amount to the taxable values of the Southern states. The hiatus would be quickly filled with worthy white immigrants, who now avoid the South because of the negroes, and by the natural increase, hence the expulsion regarded from an economic standpoint, were good policy. We owe the negro nothing. We found him a naked, snake-worshipping savage, and conferred upon him all the polish of civilization that he is competent to receive. We have taught him the use of tools, opened to him all the avenues of knowledge and supplanted his serpent fetish with the Christian faith. True he will, in one or two generations, subside again into savagery if withdrawn from Caucasion association, such having ever been his history; that is neither our coat nor our cake. Having lifted him out of the serbonian bogs of savagery, we are under no obligation to bear him ever on our shoulders. It were charity to do so, doubtless; but charity begins at home, and our first consideration should be the safety of our wives and daughters. If the man who provides not for his own household be worse than an infidel, what must he be who fails to protect its purity to the fullest extent of its power?

The strangest feature of this whole affair is the fact that whenever the negro is seized with the migratory fever, the Southern press opposes it. Sambo is begged to remain "among his friends in the South," to imperil the honor of our women while his lewd wenches corrupt our sons. What the devil we want with the "coon"—unless it be to call us "colonel" in exchange for our cast-off clothes—I cannot comprehend. Perhaps we have become "wonted" to the nigger —like the Scotch to the itch and the Spanish to the infamous malodor of leeks. The Southern people are inclined to contemplate the negro, not as he now is, but as he was in ante-bellum days, when he loved "massa, missus an' de chillun" and served them faithfully. But those old days are dead, as well as the old darkies, and new conditions bring new duties. There is a soft spot in my heart for "Uncle Remus" and the "ole black mammy" with her crooning lullabies and corn-cob pipe; but we are confronted now, not by these faithful servitors, but by the elective franchise "coon" whom it is becoming ever more and more necessary to kill. Of course, the plan of expulsion will be pronounced "impracticable" by those wiseacres who imagine nothing can be done which has not been done for a century or so, and by those Republican politicians who need the black in their business; but if the women of the South, who stand ever in dread of a fate worse than death and damnation, had the "say," there wouldn't be a Senegambian between Cape Hatteras and San Francisco by the end of the century. I am, as a rule, opposed to petticoats in politics, but every decent woman in this nation should, if not for her own and her daughter's sake, then for the sake of her imperiled sisters of the South, demand the speedy expatriation of the negro, the banishment of this black shadow of lust and brutality from the land. Let them bear in mind that it is an evil which no law can lessen, which the blind fury of mobs cannot abate. Death by the rope, says the law, death by the faggot, says Judge Lynch; but slaves to the hell-born harpy of lust and drunk with the beauty of the daughters of men, these beasts from Afric's jungles transplanted into our civilization like the worm o' the Nile between Cleopatra's glowing breasts, continue their damnable work. O that I dared picture to the maids and matrons of America this abomination of desolation in all its hellish hideousness—the little children sacrificed to glut the appetite of apes; the young women whose future has been wrecked, the wives whose happiness has been ruined, the gray-haired gran'dames who have been beaten and foully abused, the innocent maids who have been murdered. Not even the dead are sacred in the sight of these monsters who have learned to walk upright in the shape of men. If I might do this—if I might recount the particulars of crimes that have been perpetrated in America within the month by this accursed race, the shame and suffering it has wrought, e'en the women who weep for the woes of the condemned wife-butcher would cry out, not that the blacks be mercifully banished to a foreign shore, but that every living thing containing one drop of Ethiop blood be instantly executed.

THE SIGNS OF THE TIMES.

"God help the rich! the poor can beg," appears to be the motto of those economic pollywogs and political peewees to whom an inscrutable Providence has given control of this government. And perhaps the saying is not so foolish as one might at first imagine; for history has a bad habit of repeating itself, and the day may not be distant when the rich will have more occasion for pity than the poor. To the careful student of sociology, there are many and unmistakable signs that we are rapidly nearing the patience limit of the common people—that the hour draws on apace when they will decline to be longer hoodooed and humbugged by fake panaceas for poverty cooked up by place-hunting politicians. And then? Well, strange things have happened when the toiling millions became maddened by misery and frantic with hope deferred. Conditions in France during the closing years of last century were not materially different from those existing in America today: —it was a greedy and impudent aristocracy vs. a patient and long-suffering people, and when the latter could endure their privations no longer the former went to the wall, and there was little left of them but hide and hair. Deprived of property and imprisoned, guillotined and trampled beneath the iron-shod feet of the people they had learned to despise:—one would imagine after this terrible rebuke, written in fire and blood, the lily-handed few would never again tempt the murderous wrath of the "many-headed monster;" but the curse of greed, the lust for gain, the thirst for power, blinds men to danger and drives them on to their doom.

Hold yourself down a moment, my ultra-conservative friend, until I can work the idea into you that I am not an "anarchist," or any of those dreadful things that flit like monstrous nightmares thro' the stertorous dreams of multi-millionaires, and terrify the waking hours of those who humbly serve in the house of Dives and board themselves. Let us understand each other: I am not of the army of vicious idlers who rail at those who by industry and frugality have become rich. I only regret that their honest prosperity is the exception to the rule. There is a third of a century of hard work behind me, and while not a man of wealth, my income is sufficient for my wants. Now what are you, that look into your leather spectacles and see only the rose pictures painted there by the aristocrats? In ninety-and-nine cases out of a hundred you are a pitiful hanger-on to the bedrabbled skirts of a pseudo-respectability, echoing parrot-like ideas of the plutocrat, and condemning the honest workingman who cannot conceal his poverty. It is by the aid of such as you that the plutocracy retains its power to despoil the people. It makes of you a cat's-paw to rake the chestnuts out of the coals, and despises you, as a matter of course. I am not inciting a revolution or fostering the spirit of unrest, as has been so often asserted; I am simply calling the attention of Dives to the irrefragable law of cause and effect that he may stand from under the avalanche. He is too much inclined to look into his ledger and cry, "all's well," because the balance is on the proper page, quite forgetful of the fact that he may have money in his purse and a square meal concealed about his person, while a dozen of his neighbors are hungry, dead-broke and desperate. I am not posing as a philanthropist who has nothing to do but weep for the world's woes; but I dislike to see men taking a siesta on the muzzle of a loaded volcano which may get action any moment and spread their *disjecta membra* over the shrinking face of the gibbous moon. Being a man of quiet tastes, I have no desire to see an upheaval of the fires of hell—the "submerged tenth" floating to the top and inspiring a Reign of Terror. Nor do I care to see the people become so poor that the average lover of classic literature will be unable to fish a dime out of the front elevation of his pantellettes with which to purchase a copy of my truly valuable paper. For these reasons, if for no other, I am anxious to see the condition of the working people so improved that they will be contented and prosperous. But just so sure as death and taxes, there's trouble ahead for Dives if Lazarus be left much longer to the care of the dogs. This is not a "calamity wail;" it is a solemn warning by one who knows better than does the average scribe the temper and condition of the working people. The average editor assures you the masses will do—what he imagines they should do! I tell you that if the pressure is not soon relieved they are likely to do what they should not do. In nearly every avocation where men eat bread in the sweat of the brow I have studied the wealth-creators of this country; not from the standpoint of the kid-glove journalist or economic dilettante; but from that of the man whose own hands hardened on hoe or halyards, wielded the hammer or swung the steel. I ought to know the workingman, for I am master of four trades and can "follow copy" on as many more. I have studied him in his comings and his goings, in his hopes and fears, his struggles and disappointments; and I say unto you that his heart is bitter to-day with the bitterness of death, and in his dissatisfaction there lurks a danger more to be dreaded than foreign foes or the pestilence that walketh in darkness.

When coal miners must brave the dangers of their trade for 70 to 90 cents a day and are employed scarce half the time; when skilled factory operatives receive only 50 to 60 cents; when experienced clerks can be hired in shoals at $2 to $5 per week; when farmers must put their wives and daughters in the field because unable to hire help willing to work for little more than board, clothes and tobacco; when a million men are unable to find employment at any price, relief must come if we would keep the smell of sulphur out of the atmosphere. There are bitter complaints in Texas of "hard times;" but Texas is an industrial paradise compared with some sections of our common country. When the working people are able to fairly live, they are conservative, patriotic and constitute the strength of the state; but when, toil as you may, save as they can, they find their condition becoming ever more desperate, while the wealth created by their labor goes to the enrichment of others, they become dissatisfied and dangerous. If the ruling class can divide and subdue them, they degenerate into spiritless lazzaroni; but if the people triumph in the struggle, then woe to those who have reaped where they have not sown and gathered where they have not strewn.

It is a favorite argument of the professional optimist, whose cackle is making the world weary, that the common people of this country cannot become dangerous, as they are the masters and government what they make it. That is a foolish conclusion drawn from a false premise. Government is not what the people make it, but what the money power elects to have it. The former are divided among themselves, following all manner of false prophets, the latter is organized, united, and whatso it wants it gets. "Love is potent, but money is omnipotent," say the French; and certain it is that in a country where any biped may vote that wears breeches, a 20 million "educational fund" is not without effect. If it be true, as was said of old, that "every door opens to a golden key," the people may be pardoned if they lose hope of relief from robbery through legislation. When United States senators gamble in commodities upon which they are legislating, and four years in the presidency suffices to transform a beggar into a plutocrat and increase the bonded debt for the benefit of a kitchen cabinet, is it wonder that the people begin to lose confidence in the efficacy of the ballot? Optimize as you may, the stubborn fact remains that time and again portions of the working people have become dangerous—have reached the rifle and torch stage of revolt —and in almost every instance they have had the sympathy of the majority. Hungry men are always dangerous—no man can be a patriot on an empty belly. If it be true that "men will not take up arms in defense of a boarding-house" they are not likely to do battle for a squalid barn—to fight for a flag beneath which they cannot obtain bread.

In a recent speech Congressman Bailey asserted that the farming class could ever be relied upon to suppress the turbulence of the cities. My young friend is evidently unfamiliar with the recent history of the man with the hoe. The farmers were so much in sympathy with Coxey's semi-military demonstration that the governors of states thro' which the "army" passed dared not oppose its progress. So tense was the strain at the time that it was feared that an effort to disperse the Coxeyites by federal force would cause a general uprising of the wage-workers, and that the farmers would refuse to give assistance to the federal government. Had Coxey been a Napoleon, instead of a crack-brained noodle; had he led, let us say, 100,000 striking miners to Washington to demand redress, instead of a ridiculous horde of Hungry Willies, a clash with the federal soldiery would almost inevitably have occurred, civil war would have ensued, and when we came to count the cost, many a multimillionaire would have been among the "missing."

The panic of '93 safely passed; but it left industry on a lower level. The business depression continues, with but little abatement. The political situation has changed from bad to worse. The working people were promised an advance of wages if the Republicans were successful at the polls. Instead of an advance, there has been a general reduction, and as I write this probably 150,000 men in the various trades are out on strike simply because their earnings were not sufficient to provide their families with the necessaries of life, and it is estimated that a million more are idle who have no job to leave. Men who voted and worked for McKinley, who pilgrimed to the Canton shrine and wore out their feet in torch-light processions, are now trampling Republican badges into the dust and venting their anger on the president's portrait. And what is the dominant party doing for the relief of the people. It is shoving up the tariff—giving the country the same old dough pill that has been so often tried without beneficial effect. Shoving up the tariff to raise wages—in a country whose wage scale is fixed by industries that cannot be protected because they produce for export!

Steady there! I'm not going to write a tariff editorial. Life is too short to gnaw stale bones that every dog has mouthed and mumbled; but I can demonstrate to you while you hold your breath that the man who argues that a protective tariff makes for high wages is an ass, and the one who believes it is an idiot. Now fill your lungs and hold on to yourself: The price of labor, like the price of putty, is governed by the law of supply and demand. When there are more men than jobs, wages will be low; when there are more jobs than men, wages will be high. Then the beneficiary of a protective tariff may be able to pay higher wages than without it, but as selfishness is the law of trade, he will not do so unless compelled, and there is nothing in a protective tariff to make either more work or fewer men. True, it may build a few factories and open a few mills; but for every man it puts on the payroll it cuts off two or more in unprotected industries, thereby increasing the pressure for employment and decreasing the wage rate. A nation pays for its imports with its exports, trade being nothing more than an exchange of commodities; hence whatever has a tendency to prevent European products coming to America has a like tendency to prevent American products going to Europe. Protection for the manufacturer limits the foreign market for our foodstuffs and fibres by preventing the importation of those things in which we must accept payment, and just as our market is curtailed, our working force is decreased. Not only does a protective tariff strike at the employment of the farmer and stock raiser, but at that of the railroader, the stevedore, the sailor, and all others necessary to the exchange of the produce of one continent for that of another. A protective tariff is a conspiracy against both high wages and cheap living. It plays both ends against the middle—and the workingman's the middle. And that is the only remedy the Republican party has to offer for industrial ills so grievous that they threaten the very existence of government! How many times more will the country consent to swallow the protective tariff panacea before it learns in the school of experience that it is rank poison—that low wages and idle labor are the logical sequence of Republican therapeutics?

An eastern journal suggests that "the Iconoclast should preach economy to the workingman instead of encouraging his complaints," that "he should be content with a little less luxury." I stand reproved, submit my neck to the goose-yoke with the best possible grace. The workingmen are doubtless grievously at fault. Many of those who receive the princely stipend of $3 or $4 a week for factory work, lavish it all upon their families and fairly riot in luxury, instead of laying by slathers of ducats for the proverbial rainy day. Perhaps not one in a hundred of the million idle men are saving a cent. Doubtless the man whose reward for a year's labor is $150 worth of cotton, ought to keep out of debt! Clearly the poverty of these fellows is due to their own improvidence and they deserve no pity—"the fool and his money are soon parted." The workman is evidently going too rapid a gait. He must apply a Westinghouse to himself—must learn to court the drowsy god on the soft side of a pine plank with clouds for coverlet, attire himself in cotton bagging and live on locusts like Blessed John the Baptist. By so doing, he might accumulate enough in a long and industrious lifetime to purchase his own hemlock coffin in which to go to hell, instead of arriving thither as an assisted immigrant, duly tagged by the county undertaker. So fed and clothed and housed, he would probably meet with the unqualified approval of those who live on the fruits of his labor—who toil nor spin, yet make the glory of Solomon ashamed. Doubtless there is some waste among the workingmen; but a majority of them live lives of bitter self-sacrifice. If the average rate be $1 a day, the workman could not in 1,000 years earn the cost of the Bradley-Martin ball, and it would require twice that time for him to pay for a palace in which a plutocrat lives who has never yet created wealth equal to the diaper in which he was tied up to be weighed.

It is not a closer economy on the part of the working people that is wanted, but a more equitable distribution of the wealth annually created by brawn and brain. The United States contains some 70 million people, yet 40 thousand own more than one-half of all its wealth. Think of it! Fewer people than live in the little town of Dallas, Tex., own more than one-half of all the wealth between the two oceans. Less than a quarter of one million of our 70 million people own 80 per cent. of everything you can find between Boston Harbor and San Francisco Bay, between the Great Lakes and the Gulf! There are in America a dozen people worth a hundred million or more apiece; a hundred more worth twenty-five million and upwards each. Now as a man is entitled only to the wealth which he creates, and to that which is created and freely given him by others, it follows as an illative consequence that each and every one of these hundred-odd colossal fortunes is a flagrant fraud. Had a man begun the creation of wealth on the day that Christ was born and continued it unremittingly until this present hour, and not an atom of his handiwork had perished, the net result would not be worth 100 millions of money in any market; hence it follows that families which have in one or two score of generations accumulated such colossal fortunes have, in some manner appropriated the earnings of others and are public enemies. But were it possible for a man to honestly own a hundred millions of money, the possession of such vast wealth when millions of worthy people are suffering the pangs of want were an infamy instead of an honor. When the day of reckoning arrives let Dives retire to his costly temple and devoutly pray, "the mercy I to others show, that mercy show to me." Were all poor there would be no complaint. It is the evidence ever before the people's eyes that they have created wealth beyond the wildest dreams of avarice, yet are compelled to suffer the extremities of want; that they have but bowed their backs to other men's burdens, have sown that others might reap, denied themselves that others might enjoy, that breeds murder in the blood. In a land fruitful as the Garden of the Gods, yielding in abundance whatsoe'er is necessary to the comfort of mankind, the American workman, whose productive power is the wonder of the world, should be able to create wealth enough in twenty years of toil to maintain himself and family to the latest day of their lives. And so he does; but of this he receives but a scant subsistence, the remainder going into the coffers of the millionaires. So he toils on year after year, until his step falters and his aged hand weakly fumbles the tools that once beat so merrily to the lying song with which Hope beguiled his youthful heart. The remedy? "That's another story;" perhaps I'll have something to say about it in September. I simply take the stage at this time to observe that there's something radically wrong with an industrial system which compels the many to toil for the enrichment of the few, and to add, *sotto voce,* that the working people are getting d——d tired of it all, as well as aweary of the broken promises of politicians with a mouth for pie. For something like a hundred years they have been trying pretty much all kinds of parties, platforms and policies, and the further they go, the worse things get; so they are likely to conclude that, as none of the office-holding M. D's seem able to do the patient any good, it were an act of mercy to hit it in the head with a hatchet, and thus end its agony. It does not require a microphone to hear the hoof-beats of "the man on horseback."

A COUPLE OF HIGH-TONED KIDS.

Kunnel Josef Phewlitzer of the New York *World* and St. Louis *Post-Despatch,* has discovered that the Duchess of Marlborough, *nee* Vanderbilt, and Mrs. Harry Payne Whitney, are in what we modest country-folk call a "delicate condition;" also that both young matrons will be delivered this month—without mishap, let us hope. What a wonderful nose for news that man has, to be sure!—wonderful in fact, that I can imagine him wishing for the ability to walk on the windward side of himself. I presume that both ladies have a perfect right to be in the interesting fix in which they find themselves. They have been married, let's see—but no matter; they can shove up the date-line a few days, as Phew-litzer does on his European dispatches, should they find that the law of nature doesn't correlate with their marriage chronology. I 'spose it's all right; at any rate it's no affair of mine, hence I shall not worry about it this hot weather, with the Texas Democracy in session and the cotton needing rain. Phewlitzer makes a three-column illustrated "spread" of his discovery, throws bouquets at his own churnalistic oonterprise—then speculates on whether the unborn babes will be girls or boys. Right there is where Josef gives it dead away that he's no up-to-date journalist. What's the use of our boasted science if it's not to be employed in the harvesting of useful information? How comes it that he didn't have the ladies X-rayed, and thereby set the minds of his readers at rest regarding the sex of the unborn babes? There is every indication that they would have submitted to the operation with alacrity, and this would have enabled him to add a couple of highly interesting, as well as instructive, illustrations to his rather startling collection. He signally failed to improve his opportunities, to work the item for all it was worth. He didn't even inform us whether the babes will be brought up at the breast or nurtured on a bottle. I can scarce wonder that the circulation of the *World* has taken a sudden drop from eleventy-seven to seventy-eleven billions, while that of the *Pee-Dee* has slumped in proportion. Think of a progressive and eminently practical people giving up their good dough for an antediluvian daily that indulges in idle speculation instead of scientific certitude. Evidently Josef has become a back-number journalist, has passed his perihelion. Still he is interesting as far as he fares. He gives us a picture of the cradle awaiting the coming of the Marlborough kid, and tells us how much it will be worth in cold cash—granting, of course, that it comes as live freight and safely survives whooping-cough, measles, mumps, and the many other ills that infantile flesh is heir to. He volunteers the information that while the Whitney youngster will have the most money it will possess no title, quite overlooking the fact that it will be born a sovereign, the other a subject. And the public, awakened from its midsummer siesta by all this bawling over a brace of unborn brats, looks at the bloomin' Jook, and at poor little Harry Payne Whitney tottering about under his threedecker name and his daddy's dollars, shakes its head incredulously and returns to its slumber, to dream, perhaps, that the world is being populated by painted dunghills whom it imagined impotent. The *World* and *Pee-Dee* solemnly assure us that "the finest possible layette has been provided" for each of the young pilgrims. Layette is probably an imported euphemism for those three-cornered affairs and other fixin's so handy to have in the house when there's a baby about. Mr. Dingley neglected to have such words made dutiable as useless luxuries of purse-proud lollipops. The Duchess of Marlborough is the daughter of W. K. and Mrs. Whitney, the daughter of Cornelius Vanderbilt. Old man Whitney has boodle to throw at the birds, and young Whitney is a nephew of old Payne, the Standard Oil multi-millionaire; hence the youngsters in question will have much more elaborate layettes—or layouts, as we say in Texas—than the average infant. They will be triangled with the finest bird's-eye linen, dandled on the dimpled knees of French nurses, and have paregoric seasoned with aromatic syrups slid into them out of silver spoons, while the common run of kids are swathed in second-hand flour sacks, the XXX still visible that none may mistake them for mavericks, and left to prosecute their arduous search for carpet tacks, bits of broken glass and other edibles. But the poor man's offspring, when grown to manhood, will have the satisfaction of knowing that his mother, instead of exploiting her potential maternity in the daily press, sought to conceal it by keeping out of sight, admitting it only with modest blushes to her dearest female friends. And he will have the further satisfaction of knowing that his father would have blown the vulpine brains out of any reporter who presumed to pry into his domestic affairs and set the world gabbling about the condition of his wife. It does seem that our would-be aristocrats, on both sides of the sea, are destitute of common modesty as a muley cow. When one of its female members is to be married, she proceeds to take the world into her confidence. The press reporters are shown her "lingerie," and the public given a minute description of every costly rag she wears on her bridal tour, from her gray traveling dress and gloves to her lace-trimmed chemise and silken undershirt. She actually seems to think the public cannot sleep o'nights until it learns the exact cut, color and material of the panties she will wear at the wedding, and the make of the "nighties" she will sport during the honeymoon. The moment the "happy couple" imagines it has succeeded in making a family increase probable, it can no more hold its cackle than can a yaller hen. The discovery of the law of cause and effect seems to demoralize its mentality and wreck its modesty. It rests not until it gets an account of its wonderful doings in the dailies. Ostentatious preparations are begun for the great "event." Everybody who belongs to the "set" is notified that they may make prenatal presents. The reporters who had the felicity to describe the bride's underwear, are again called in that they may dilate upon her expected infant's duds. The affair is discussed with as much *sang froid* as the price of putty or the cotton prospects. The "genealogical tree" is re-examined, generation by generation, from the old rat-catcher, ferryman, scavenger, professional pimp or railroad wrecker who laid the foundation of the family fortune. The condition of the prospective mother is freely discussed by papers professing to be decent, and apparently with her approval and the help of her husband. All the sacred mystery of motherhood is sacrificed by the family to the prurient desire to be discussed. And discussed it is—chiefly by barrel-house bummers and variety-dive bawds who bandy the names of fashion's fools back and forth over pots of stale beer. I cannot understand the crassness of these *soi-distant* aristocrats. Of course I know that a majority of them have sprung like jimson weeds from the very sewage of society—that most "proud titles" can be traced to Pandarus and most great fortunes to Fagin; still we might hope that even noblemen spawned by pimps, and plutocrats begotten by thieves, would learn to imitate the modesty of the common people—to "assume a virtue tho' they have it not," and cease to offend the public sense of decency by brutal exhibitions that would sicken Doll Tearsheet. Nor can I understand how the press, which enables these coarse creatures—these gilded heaps of guano—to flaunt their vulgarity in the faces of decent people, profits thereby, unless indeed it sells them space, just as it does the purveyor of abortion pills and private disease panaceas; for certain am I that the American people care never a continental about the pattern of Miss Plutocracy's wedding underwear, nor whether the gangle-shanked, goose-necked Vanderbilt girls mother one babe or a million. They may be pleased to learn that young Harry Payne Whitney has reached the age of puberty, that it is possible for the Jook to grow a beard and thus hide from his long-suffering fellows at least part of his face. If the arrival of an heir to the title which old John Churchill purchased with his sister's shame, or the decoration of young Whitney's mewling infant with a velvet diaper secured with jewelled pins would affect the price of cotton or corn, Phewlitzer might be able to work up considerable interest in those events; but as nothing of the kind is expected, the people quite naturally wonder why these flamboyant plutocrats don't take a tumble to themselves and do their breeding without the aid of a brass-band. It is impossible to determine until after the lapse of a third of a century or so whether the birth of a babe be of any particular importance; so there is really no occasion to become excited, as all babies look much alike, whether born heir to millions or to a rag-picker's route—little blear-eyed balls somewhat resembling a raw beefsteak. I trust that the youngsters in question will arrive all right and enjoy the finery provided for them; also that they will prove more worthy than their ancestors and surroundings would lead a student of sociology to expect. The best of children when handicapped with petty titles or vast fortunes, usually develop into dawdling dudes, live useless lives on the labor of others, and leave the world poorer by the exact cost of their keep. There may be a man-child born this month who will be the glory of his generation; but he is far more likely to make his appearance in a log-cabin or cheap cottage than in the Whitney mansion or Blenheim palace. It is worthy of remark that when society cackles loudly over the birth of a babe, the world seldom weeps at its burial. The Shakespeares and Miltons, the Grants and Napoleons, the Lincolns and Hamiltons creep into being unnoticed by other than the immediate neighbors—the Phewlitzers of the press being too busy admiring costly cradles and cut-glass nursing-bottles to take cognizance of the advent of the world's colossi.

THE HENRY GEORGE HOODOO.

A Ram Dass Worshipped as a Deity.

I seem to have gotten into a world of trouble with the Single Taxers, hence all the gladness has gone out of my life, and I may never smile again. Some time ago I was so indiscreet as to courteously state what I humbly considered some insuperable objections to their proposed system, and ever since I have been the geographical center of a cyclone of sphacelated cabbage and a cataclysm of dead cats. I deserve it all, for I was well aware that the dogmas of George were more sacred than the doctrines of Jesus, and that to question the infinitude of his wisdom or his economic impeccability was a sin unpardonable. From Dan to Beersheba and from H—alifax to Breakfast, Single Tax editors and orators are remorselessly punishing my "presumption," while every mail brings me scores of essays from the faithful, informing me that I am an "ijiut," "a ass," "an igeramus," and other dreadful things unknown to any well-ordered natural history. Truth to tell, I had begun to seriously suspect there must be something wrong with me, else I would not have wasted time crucifying an economic mooncalf that was rapidly dying of its own accord. Sweet gentlemen, for the love of God be merciful to an "ijiut," "a ass" and "igeramus," for how can so weak a creature meet in the rude shock of war the jawbone thunderbolts and 'gray goose-quill excaliburs of the terrible Single Taxers? Forgive my sins, dear sirs, cosset me once more on your heaving briskets and regale me again with the unctuous milk of approval and the honey of adulation with which you were wont to tickle my esurient palate in the good old days when I insisted that Henry George should have a respectful hearing. Your master has no cause to complain of the Iconoclast; nor does he so, that I have ever heard. This paper has ever treated him with marked courtesy and consideration. While unwilling to concede that he is a Pallas in pants, and his Progress and Poverty the national palladium, it has admired his honesty and earnestness, and urged that everybody read his books and pass upon his economic plan without partisan prejudice. It seems to me that I have treated the Single Taxers as fairly as they could ask, and if I now proceed to state a few plain truths about them and their faith, they will have no just cause to complain. Should they think differently, they are royally welcome to "chew the rag." Frantic denunciation of dissidents and indecent exhibitions of Boeotian ignorance permeated with Gascon impudence are not calculated to make converts, but seem to be the favorite Single Tax methods of "refuting" argument. It is a bad cause that must take refuge in discourtesy. I regard jackassierie as a misfortune rather than a fault, to be pitied rather than denounced; for if God does not give a breeches-wearing biped the instincts and intellect of a gentleman, it were idle to expect him to act like one. Nor do I assume that there are no courteous and cultured people among the Single Taxers simply because it has been my misfortune to find in that faith so many impudent Smart Alecs and irrepressible damphools. The man who takes issue with a political thesis or religious tenet invariably sees the seamy side of the party professing it, and should remember that "every medal has its reverse."

Henry George is a man of much natural ability, who has revived and elaborated an idea of the old French philosophers in the mistaken hope that it would relieve the woes of the world, and his postulates must be examined with as much freedom as those of Mill or Montesquieu, despite the foolish yawp of those whose matin hymn and vesper prayer reads, "There is no God but George, and may those who dare to doubt be anathema forevermore." Despite his long and arduous struggle, he has obtained no standing of consequence in either politics or economics, and that because his teachings are violative of the public concept of truth. Like most brilliant men, he is not well-balanced. What the world terms a "great man" is usually a mental abnormality—some one feature of his intellect developed at the expense of others. Thus Ingersoll is probably the most eloquent man in the world to-day; but his creative faculty is so weak that he must content himself with garlanding the prosaic ideas of others. He is a magnificent word-painter, but others must supply the pigments. He is, if I may be permitted the solecism, simply an echo filtered through an aeolian harp. George's head would furnish brains for a hundred Ingersolls, but he is much farther off the mental equipoise. As a polemic he stands without a peer. No other living man could have made so absurd a theory appear so plausible, deceived hundreds of abler men than himself. I would as soon undertake to convince intelligent people that the poverty of the masses is due to the mountains in the moon. But he is only polemic, in nowise a philosopher. He is credulous as Moses Primrose, through whose worthless green goggles he seems to be ever gazing. He mistakes the plausible for the actual and by his sophistry deceives himself. Of this self-deception is born his earnestness, and history has amply demonstrated that, no matter how ridiculous a proposition, if a man believe it with his whole soul, he will not only make converts, but often awaken a fierce enthusiasm, even an unreasoning fanaticism which assumes the absurd to be self-evident because "the master said it." It was thus that John Knox transformed hospitable Caledonia into a nest of intolerant and canting Covenanters, and Mahomet made the easy-going Arabians a brood of murderous bigots. In the pathway of a Peter the Hermit, or a Henry George, preaching his "crusade" with faith believing, everything inflammable takes fire, and once aflame, argument were useless—the craze must run its course. Hence it is that we find the disciples of Henry George paying him almost divine honors —branding doubt as "presumption" and denial as blasphemy. Hero worship is well enough in its way, and I have no objection to American sovereigns singing Gloria in Excelsis to one of themselves, for does not Hardenberg assure us that "Bending before men is a reverence done to heaven's revelation in the flesh?" Henry George and "Count" Cagliostro are the only two men of modern times who have been devoutly worshipped by their dupes; and in some respects the Single Tax folly of the one resembles the Egyptian Masonry foolishness of the other. It is to the credit of Mr. George's heart, but not at all complimentary to his head that he is an honest fanatic, while Cagliostro was a conscious fraud. George's career suggests that of Francis Schlatter, the "divine healer." He is a well-intentioned man, who confidently believes that he can work miracles—can reverse the law of cause and effect and make the poverty-stricken millions prosperous by revoking the taxes of the rich and increasing the burdens of the poor. He would equalize the conditions of Dives and Lazarus by removing the tax from the palace of the one and laying it upon the potato patch of the other. When Progress and Poverty first appeared, I believed it inspired by the plutocracy, 250,000 of whom own 80 per cent. of the taxable wealth of the country, while the land is largely in possession of the great middle class. I could not understand how a man possessing common sense could fail to see that removing taxation from a class of property chiefly in the hands of the rich and placing it altogether on property chiefly in the hands of the comparatively poor, could fail to benefit the millionaire at the expense of the working-man; but I did not then realize that Mr. George was a monomaniac. The cruel outrage which he is striving to perpetuate upon the poor is the result of a strange misconception of the fundamental principle of economics. Unfortunately Mr. George was mis-educated; if it can be said that a man of distorted vision is educated at all. The Single Tax monomania seems to have taken hold of him before he began a serious study of economics, and thenceforth his investigations were dominated and their legitimate fruition defeated by this morbid idea sprung from the corpse of an intellectual mooncalf once galvanized into a semblance of life during the most artificial and unprofitable era of France. He seems to have devoted all the powers of his mind, not to judicial investigation, but to the manufacture of apologetics for his preconceived opinions. Conceiving land to be "monopolized," the next step was to assume, without a show of reason, that land monopoly is the mother of all other economic monstrosities—just as tho' it makes any difference how Anthaeus gets his feet upon the earth so long as he has to seek the co-operation of the capitalist in production and suffer him to fix the price at which he must buy and sell. How will you smash the cotton-seed oil trust, for instance, by compelling planters to lease their crop-land to the government? With coal fields leased to the operators by Uncle Sam, how will you prevent Hanna organizing a pool, limiting production, raising prices and reducing wages? How will you prevent the Standard Oil company forcing weaker concerns to the wall by the simple expedient of selling below the cost of production. But it is not my present purpose to goad the Single Taxers into another conniption fit, but to let them wrestle for a few months with the heretofore demonstrated fact that, as the only excuse for the existence of their cult is to appropriate for public use the "unearned increment," it might as well get off the earth, as said "unearned increment" is already taken for public use under our present system of taxation. The increase in value— the "unearned increment"—of all the land in the United States during the past three years will not equal the taxes paid upon it in one year. As Zanga would remark, "First recover that, then thou shalt know more." It is well to administer spoon-meat to infants *poco a poco*. Mr. George declares that a tax on man-created wealth is a fine on industry which has a tendency to discourage production; so he would lay the entire tax on God-created land, kindly permit industry to pay it from man-created wealth and prosper! As the able editor of the *National Single Taxer* would say, "There's nothing complex about that proposition." And the fact that he can understand it is *prima facie* evidence of its simplicity. Figure it as you will, adjust it as you may, a tax is "a fine on industry" and will remain so until you get blood from turnips or wealth from tramps. As the present rental of every acre of ground in use between the two oceans would not defray the expense of government, federal, state and municipal, the Single Tax would compel a radical advance in ground rent and make it impossible for us to successfully compete with other countries in the fibre and foodstuff markets of Europe. The fact that land is the primal source of all wealth has strangely confused my Ft. Hamilton friend. Land does not produce wealth; it simply affords man an opportunity to produce it. A tax is simply a toll taken of labor's product and to be equitable, it must fall with equal incidence on all, whether it be the product of a cheap farm or a costly factory. The red shirted miner toiling on ferriferous land of little value, produces iron ore worth $1. The smelter and mill transform it into bars worth $5. The factory makes it into watch-springs worth $5,000. Government must compel each to pay toll in proportion to the amount of wealth he has produced—and that is the only equitable law of taxation.

Mr. George began under very favorable conditions the propagation of his cult. The history of this and other nations had taught observant men that our industrial ills could not be cured by the bread boluses of the old political parties—that sooner or later the country must resort to a more radical remedy, else hear the *"ca ira, les aristocrates a la lanterne"* of a new revolution. Mr. George's system being radical and far-reaching, quite naturally attracted the attention of those who saw the insufficiency of the old political nostrums, so often proven abortive by experience. The study of economics had not then become popular in this country, men judged of party measures chiefly by the light of individual experience. They knew from observation that tariff and currency juggling do not go to the root of the evil, do not make it the easier to earn a living; so they listened attentively to the great propagandist of the Single Tax. The scheme for dragging the golden age in by the ears was plausible, even forcefully presented, and many really intelligent men were converted. The cult was a novelty, a novelty captures all the "cranks," and Mr. George soon found himself the Grand Coptha of a rather numerous and very noisy crowd of "Crusaders." For a time the trained economists paid little attention to him, regarding him as a kind of Jack Cade and his cult unworthy of serious consideration, while those who did attack his views hardly sounded their fanfare before they were unhorsed. Mr. George had expended years preparing for the tourney and came to the lists armed capapie—to put the gaffles into such polemical dunghills as the Duke of Argyll! As he ate up the imprudent amateurs his heresy came more into repute and spread like the holiness fake at a Methodist camp meeting. He became the "fad" and men who couldn't tell the Republican platform from the Odes of Anacreon, the law of rent from the law of gravitation, hastened to sit at the feet of this new Gamaliel. "One God, one Farinelli!" cried the profane princesses; but Farinelli wasn't "in it" with the apostle of the faith that was to raise the landless man out of the Slough of Despond by raising his rent. That the average George convert became an immovable Ephraim joined to his idol, is not strange when we consider that the impotency of the remedies proposed by the old political parties could be so easily proven. As one must have some political faith, the Single Taxers can scarce be blamed for clinging tenaciously to a doctrine, which, altho' discredited by common sense, has not yet been proven fallacious by the *experimentum crucis;* for even insisting, after a critical survey of Cleveland and McKinley, that their Toomtabard George is a Jupiter Tonans—even a Ram Dass, with "fire enough in his belly to burn away the sins of the world," it must be conceded that the world-power has even been composed of one-idea people—those who believe more in a minute than they can prove in a month. We are progressing backwards at present, simply because we have so many philosophic Hamlets who don't know how. A Cromwell or a Francis, even a Debs or a George with one unhealthy idea in his head which he proposes to reduce to practice or break a tug in the attempt, were worth a thousand namby-pambys who are sure of nothing and can only swing round in the current like dead eels in an eddy. One-idea men are apt to be revolutionary; but even revolution were preferable to dry rot. It were better to keep moving even tho' the goal be somewhat uncertain than to sit patiently down beneath grievous abuses and petrify. It were better that the doctors do something than nothing when the patient sick unto death, even tho' they resort to the drenchings of Sangrado or the Mumbojumboism of George. It were better to launch boldly out on the sea of experimentalism and trust to the winds and waves to bear us to the Isle of Bimini than to putter around in unprofitable goose-ponds, playing minnows for sperm whales and bullfrogs for Alboraks while Sansculottism grows ever more savage. As between Georgeism and Donothingism I would, if compelled by adverse fate to make a choice, chain my fortunes to the former—just as I would have followed Robespierre rather than eat hay that the harlots of *les roi faineants* might bedeck themselves with diamonds—and have their bawdry reblazoned at Bradley-Martin balls.

But, fortunately or otherwise, we will have no opportunity to test the breakers with Henry George at the helm. There is every indication that his cult has had its day and is rapidly going to join the many other isms, political and religious that have been swallowed up like cast-off clothes and other exviae by the great "mother of dead dogs." It is curious to reflect how many once popular highways to heaven and turnpikes to the terrestrial millennium are now weed-grown and forgotten. Every age has its panaceas for woes temporal and woes spiritual, high-flaming, loud-sounding, yielding tithe of the first fruits and fat of the land to their high-priests; but so few of them do more than relieve their chief propagandists of the necessity of ditching and delving and assure them a three-line notice in biographical dictionaries. Change is the order of the universe, and the political reformer who is a candidate for President, or even mayor of New York to-day, is gone to-morrow, heaven alone knows whither. His crusade languishes, flickers, expires, and the world, that once played Sweet Alice to his Ben Bolt, knows him no more forever—follows hard upon the heels of some new reformer with a maggot in his head, until he in turn is swept with his pamphlets, credo and crusade into the rubbish heap and eternal night of oblivion. So wags a weary world, round and round in the same circle of industrial doldrums, instead of spinning, as Tennyson would have it, "through the ringing grooves of change." What the deuce "ringing grooves" have to do with "change" I know not; but the great Alfred may have served as cash boy in a department store. The Single Tax party will not long survive its creator, for he is the breath in its nostrils and makes its heart to beat. Nay, if he tarries long, it will beat him to the tomb, for already it has passed from lusty manhood to the lean and slippered pantaloon. The cult seems to be acquiring a few new recruits, and those not of the mental calibre of its charter members. Conditions for the propagation of empiricism are more favorable than ever before, for the industrial problem is pressing with ever greater force, there is a general weakening of party fealty, a desire to train under a more promising flag. The opportunity is even now for the birth of a new party, springing Minerva-like, from the brow of American Jove; but Mr. George cannot work the combination. In fact, the public is becoming just a trifle tired of him, as it does of all men who have slipped their trolley-pole. Single Tax papers now run largely to "boilerplate" and are not so ably edited as in the erstwhile. If I mistake not, Mr. George was unable to keep one of these expounders of his doctrines from running upon the financial rocks. Certain it is that those which still linger have but limited circulation, and are managed by men who seem to exist by chewing the fag end of hope deferred and sucking the juice. The Single Tax is evidently passing, just as the impot unique disappeared a century since. Perhaps in another hundred years some new reformer will resurrect it and again set the forks of the creek afire, for we are told that history repeats itself; but struggle as it may, it must yield, so often it appears, to the irrefragable law of the survival of the fittest. With a century upon it, the Wealth of Nations is still young, while Progess and Poverty is already old. This is because the first is true and truth is eternal, while the latter is an idle dream and cannot last. Forgetful of the proverb that "everybody knows more than anybody," Mr. George took issue with the cumulative wisdom of the world. That's why he is a reformer who can't reform. Alas, poor Yorick!

THE LAST OF OUR LIBERTIES.

When an American citizen is not permitted to have his mail directed to whatsoever postoffice he pleases and delivered to whosoever he likes; when he is not allowed to request a fellow craftsman to refrain from working for starvation wages; when he is forbidden by the courts to walk on the public highway, and is shot in the back on the plea that he is imperiling the lives of his assassins, it would seem that we have precious little left of our boasted "right to life, liberty and the pursuit of happiness." The human battle at Latimer, Pa., was the most horrible affair that has ever disgraced American history. A party of half starved miners, finding their wages insufficient to provide themselves and families with the simple necessaries of life, had quit work, hoping that their wealthy employers might be coerced by their idleness into according them a living in exchange for their labor. Never had a great strike been conducted with so little violence—altho' a majority of the workmen and their families were actually suffering for food and clothing, life and property were almost universally respected. A party of these poor fellows were trudging peaceably and unarmed along the public highway when they were halted by a super-officious sheriff, accompanied by a hundred or more heavily armed deputies. He undertook to read the riot act to them —why only he and heaven know, as they were perpetrating no violence, committing no crime. Being for the most part Hungarians and Italians who spoke little English, they could not comprehend, but crowded about the sheriff, staring inquiringly into his face. And the poor miserable creature miscalled a man, conceived the fool idea that "his life was in danger," that he was "about to be trampled to death" under the very muzzles of his own guns, before the eyes of his well-fed deputies, who could have put them to flight with their fists. "His coward lips did from their color fly"—his white liver turned green with craven fear—his chicken heart melted in his mouth—his currish blood curdled in his carcass, and in a voice hoarse with fear, husky with baby tears, he bawled out the order to fire. The miners hear the click of the gun-locks—they see the long line of rifles raised to the shoulder and divine their danger—but alas! too late. They turn to flee, terror-stricken, and a murderous volley is poured into—their backs!—then another! Two and twenty lie dead, fifty more are writhing with grievous wounds, pleading for mercy—"the poor people who have to work" are slaughtered like sheep in the shambles, and for no other crime than walking unarmed on the public highway—huddled together because "misery loves company." The sheriff and his deputies, having done their dastardly work, slink off like so many unclean jackals and ragged little children come creeping forth to peer into the ghastly faces of their fathers, while gaunt women bewail their widowhood in a foreign tongue, or kneel in the dust with clasped hands and faces of blank despair beside their still bleeding dead. Gracious God! what an ending to many a happy dream! what a breath from hell, blasting so many humble homes! What are the thoughts of that dark-eyed daughter of Italia, crouching like a lioness over the corpse of her lover?—of that Hungarian woman striving to staunch with her ragged skirt the life-tide of her lord while her almost naked children cling about her knees? Does she remember the day when an oily-tongued agent for the mine operators visited their humble shack and told them of the great country beyond the setting sun where the common people bear rule—where the lowliest laborer is a sovereign and the superior of Europe's haughty lords? Does she remember how they dreamed and planned, how they looked forward to long years of happiness in "the land of the brave and the home of the free," the "refuge of the world's oppressed?"— how they toiled and saved to pay their passage to a country where a child born to them might become President? At last they took ship, and day by day strained their eyes to catch a glimpse of that western haven which was to be the portal of their heaven, and when they landed they could have kissed the land where "all men are equal before the law." But the fond dream soon faded, they were more hopelessly enslaved than in the fatherland, compelled to live on less, answerable not to some haughty but generous nobleman, but to a grasping, insolent and ignorant parvenu, willing to coin their heart's blood into boodle. And this is the end! The husband of her youth, already grown grizzly in the fierce struggle for existence, shot down by his "fellow citizens" because he chanced to walk on the public highway and there met a coward whose strange words he could not understand, lies dead in her arms, while around her his hungry orphans wail! I say he met a coward; but perchance I do Sheriff Martin too much honor. Cowards are born, not made; and if he inherited cowardice from a mongrel sire, or drew it in with his mother's milk, he should not be unduly blamed. Did he give that order to fire because he was frightened, or because he was instructed by the mine operators to "make a killing" that would terrorize the ill-fed and unarmed miners into submission to their hard terms? Is Sheriff Martin a cringing coward or a subsidized assassin? From the testimony before me I cannot tell; but I learn that the mine operators "consider that the killing had a good effect." I learn from to-day's (September 21) dispatches that "a majority of the miners have returned to work, and that, with but one or two exceptions, at the old terms"—that "the backbone of the strike is broken"—since upwards of 70 inoffensive men were shot in the back! Napoleon learned long ago that a few well-directed volleys would break the backbone of almost anything, and the mine operators appear to have profited by his experience. The same dispatches state that the sheriff and a number of his janizaries have been arrested—the sheriff who pleaded in extenuation of his crime that his victims "were most all foreigners." They were foreigners brought here by the mine operators in defiance of the contract labor law, starved and abused until they laid down their tools—then shot at until they took them up again. What will be done with the assassins? O, they will "be subjected to a rigid examination"—to satisfy the public and avoid international complications. They will have behind them the powerful influence of the mine operators, whom they have served so well, and the plutocratic newspapers and mugwump magazines will see to it that all who demand that they be properly punished are denounced as "anarchists." But one thing is sure as that there's a God in Israel: Every one of those assassins should be stood with his face to a brick wall and a pound of lead blown through his back. True, "the deputies obeyed orders;" but a man who will obey an order given by a frantic fool or hired assassin to slay inoffensive people, should not be permitted to halt four-and-twenty hours this side of hell. I am told that "the sheriff and most of his deputies are Americans." It's an infamous falsehood—no American ever did such a deed. A mongrel cross between a lousy yahoo and a mangy she-wolf were not capable of committing such a crime. They are not Americans, but unnatural monsters who committed their cowardly crime in this country, and Columbia can purge herself of the damning disgrace only by blowing the last one of them to fragments or hanging him in a hair halter higher than Haman. I once said that the workman was at least allowed liberty to starve to death; but even that poor privilege is now denied—if he attempts it he will be shot to death.

VICTOR HUGO'S IMMORALITY.

Philadelphia's school board has barred Victor Hugo's "Les Miserables" from the list of books to be used in the High School in the teaching of French, as a book not fit for girls. What would not one give for a diagram of the heads of these educators? It must be a nasty mind which can find anything immoral in that book as a whole. One may take a chapter out here and there, and show it to be broad or coarse, divorced from the context, but the whole effect of the book is moral. The mind of the man who can say that "Les Miserables" will not tend as a whole to make a girl more womanly, a boy more manly, must be poisoned by the miasma from a filthy heart. What and who in it are immoral? Not Valjean! Not Fantine even, nor Cosette! Not

Marius! Not Javert, the detective! Is the chapter on Cambronne's surrender the offending fragment of the great literary masterpiece? That chapter is the sublimity of disgust! There never was anyone hurt spiritually or morally by the great French masterpiece of fiction. The man who can say the book is defiling, would draw defilement from the fount of Castaly. The Philadelphia School Board has declared itself an aggregation of asses. "Les Miserables" is the greatest poem of divine humanity that this world has known since Shakespeare wrote "Lear." But I suppose "Lear," too, is immoral. I suppose everything is immoral, from "Oedipus, the Tyrant," to Hall Caine's "Christian," that teaches that men are born of woman, and that love will have its way, even unto all bitterness. It is eminently fitting that "Les Miserables" should be condemned as immoral in the most immoral city in the United States. A Philadelphian may be depended upon to see immorality in one of Raphael's Madonnas.—*St. Louis Mirror.*

My esteemed contemporary should bottle up its indignation, there is absolutely nothing to be gained by lambasting idiots, by criticising cretins. Editor Reedy is but casting his pearls before swine—is talking to people who, having eyes see not, having ears hear not, and whose cerebra are filled with sawdust. They are like unto a lot of sheep that follow the master ram, not because they comprehend or care whither he is going, but because they smell him, and point their proboscidi in his direction as naturally as the needle lines the pole. It was Jean Paul—was it not?—who discovered that if a cane be held horizontally before the lead ram of a flock, compelling him to saltate, then removed, the thousandth ewe lamb will jump at that point just as did the pioneer. So it is with a pietistical and puristical people —they will follow some stupid old bell-wether because uteerly incapable of independent thought, of individual ratiocination. When "Les Miserables" first appeared some literary Columbus made the remarkable discovery that it was a French book; that it was shot full of "slang," the expressive *patois* of the race; that it was liberally spiced with ergot, the vernacular of vagabonds. Hugo's immortal masterpiece has not yet recovered from this discovery—the thousandth ewe-lamb is still blithely saltating over the blackthorn. It is as useless to contend against the purist fad as against the holiness fake. Like a plague of army worms or epidemic of epizootic, it must run its course. Preternicety of expression, an affectation of euphemism, has in every age and clime evidenced moral degeneration and mental decay. When people emasculate their minds, they redouble their corporeal devotion at the shrine of Priapus, for Nature preserves the equipoise. Every writer of virility is now voted obscene, every man who strikes sledge-hammer blows, at brutal wrong intrenched in prescriptive right is denounced as immoral. "Les Miserables" not fit for young ladies' reading!—and this the epocha of the New Woman, of the single standard of mind and morals. While woman is insisting that she is every way man's equal, entitled to share with him the worship of this world, Detroit is putting bloomers on the statues of Dian, Boston refusing the Bacchante, Waco draping the marble figure of a child exhibited at her cotton palace, Anthony Comstock having cataleptic convulsions, "Les Miserables" excluded from Philadelphia high schools and the Iconoclast denounced by certain bewhiskered old he-virgins as obscene! And so it goes. This world is becoming so awfully nice that it's infernally nawsty. It sees evil in everything because its point of view is that of the pimp. Its mind is a foul sewer whose exhalations coat even the Rose of Sharon with slime. A writer may no longer call a spade a spade; he must cautiously refer to it as an agricultural implement lest he shock the supersensitiveness of hedonists and call down upon his head the Anathema Maranatha of men infinitely worse than Oscar Wilde. What the *Mirror* means by "Cambronne's surrender" I cannot imagine, unless Editor Reedy was indulging in grim irony. I present extracts from the account of Cambronne, which he suspects may have given the pietistical Quakers a pain. It is the finale of Hugo's matchless word-painting of the Battle of Waterloo:

"A few squares of the guard, standing motionless in the swash of the rout, like rocks in running water, held out till night. They awaited the double shadow of night and death, and let them surround them. Each regiment, isolated from the others, and no longer connected with the army, which was broken on all sides, died where it stood. The gloomy squares, deserted, conquered and terrible, struggled formidably with death, for Ulm, Wagram, Jena, and Friedland were dying in it. When twilight set in at nine in the evening, one square still remained at the foot of the plateau of Mont St. Jean. In this mournful valley, at the foot of the slope scaled by the cuirassiers, now inundated by the English masses, beneath the converging fire of the hostile and victorious artillery, under a fearful hailstorm of projectiles, this square still resisted. It was commanded by an obscure officer of the name of Cambronne. At each volley the square still diminished, but continued to reply to the canister with musketry fire, and each moment contracted its four walls. Fugitives in the distance, stopping at moments to draw breath, listened in the darkness to this gloomy diminishing thunder. When this legion had become only a handful, when their colors were but a rag, when their ammunition was exhausted, and muskets were clubbed, and when the pile of corpses was greater than the living group, the victors felt a species of sacred awe, and the English artillery ceased firing. It was a sort of respite; these combatants had around them an army of spectres, outlines of mounted men, the black profile of guns, and the white sky visible through the wheels; the colossal death's head which heroes ever glimpse in the smoke of battle, advanced and looked at them. They could hear in the twilight gloom that the guns were being loaded; the lighted matches, resembling the eyes of a tiger in the night, formed a circle round their heads. The linstocks of the English batteries approached the guns, and at this moment an English general, Colville according to some, Maitland according to others, holding the supreme moment suspended over the heads of these men, shouted to them, 'Brave Frenchmen, surrender!' Cambronne answered, *'Merde.'* To Cambronne's exclamation, an English voice replied, "Fire!" The batteries flashed, the hillside trembled, from all these throats of brass came a last eruption of grape, a vast cloud of smoke vaguely whitened by the rising moon rolled up, and when the smoke had been dissipated, there was nothing. The dreaded remnant was annihilated, the guard was dead. The four walls of the living redoubt lay low, with here and there a scarcely perceptible quiver among the corpses. Thus the French legions, grander than those of Rome, expired on Mont St. Jean, on the earth sodden with rain and blood."

Hugo quite needlessly apologized for quoting the Frenchman's laconic reply to the summons to surrender. He was writing history, and no milk-and-water euphemism could have expressed Cambronne's defiance and contempt. Of course John Bull pitilessly shot to death that heroic fragment of the Old Guard, which forgot in its supreme hour that while fool-hardiness may be magnificent, it is not war. I would have put a cordon of soldiers about that pathetic remnant of Napoleon's greatness and held it there to this good day rather than have plowed it down as a farmer plows jimson weeds into a pile of compost; but John Bull is not built that way—is impregnated with the chivalry of Baylor. Cambronne's reply is the only objectionable word in the entire work, and certainly it might be pardoned in a scrap of history by people whose press and pulpit have apotheosized "Trilby," Du Maurier's supposititious prostitute. I presume that the Phila. school board is about on an intellectual and moral parity with the trustees of Baylor —haven't the remotest idea whether *merde* means maggots or moonshine. Victor Hugo was a lord in the aristocracy of intellect; his masterpiece is Nature's faithful mirror. *Ame de boue* should be branded with a hot iron on the hickory-nut head of every creature whom its perusal does not benefit. His description of the Battle of Waterloo is to "Ben-Hur's" chariot race what Mount Aetna in eruption is to a glow worm. It transcends the loftiest flights of Shakespeare. Before it even "The Wondrous Tales of Troy" pales its ineffectual fires. It casts the shadow of its genius upon Bulwer's "Pompeii" as the wing of the condor shades the crow. Byron's "sound of revelry by night" is the throbbing of a snare drum drowned in Hugo's thunders of Mont St. Jean. Danton's rage sinks to an inaudible whisper, and even Aeschylus shrivels before that cataclysm of Promethean fire; that celestial monsoon. It stirs the heart like the rustle of a silken gonfalon dipped in gore, like the whistle of rifle-balls, like the rhythmic dissonance of a battery slinging shrapnel from the heights of Gettysburg into the ragged legions of General Lee. I have counselled my contemporary to be calm; but by heaven! it does stir my soul into mutiny to see a lot of intellectual pismires who have secured positions of trust because of their political pull in the Tenderloin, hurling their petty scorn at Victor Hugo. It were like Carlyle's "critic fly" complacently rubbing its hinder legs and giving its opinion of the Parthenon, like Aesop's vindictive snail besliming the masterpiece of Phidias, like a Baylor professor lecturing on the poetry of Lord Byron. Every writer of eminence since the days of Moses has had to run the gauntlet of these slight people's impotent wrath. While slandering the prophets of progress and religion they have vented their foul rheum on all the gods of literature. Kansas, I am told, put a man in the penitentiary for sending through the mails biblical texts printed on postal cards. Speaking of Goethe's "Wilhelm Meister," Carlyle says:

"'Meister,' it appears is a vulgar work; no gentleman, we hear in certain circles, could have written it; few real gentlemen, it is insinuated, can like to read it; no real lady, unless possessed of considerable courage, should profess having read it at all!"

And yet "Wilhelm Meister" changed the whole current of European literature—the work was practically committed to memory by the noblest men and women of the world. We hear the venerated Queen of Prussia repeating from it in her cruel exile,

> "Wer nie sein Brod mit Thranen ass,
> Wer nicht die Kummervollen Nachte
> Auf Seinem Bette weinend sass,
> Der Kennt euch nicht, ihr himmlishen Machte."

Let the Phila. school board and the Baylorian managers construe it if they can.

> "Udi vura udorini udiri cicova cilti mora
> Udorini talti hollna u ede caimoni mora."

What? I guess "nit." The idea of keeping "Les Miserables" away from the ladies!—just as tho' there could be found in the whole country a 16-year-old maid with any pretensions to intelligence who hasn't wept over little Cosette, been in love with Enjolras and "doted on" Gavroche and Jean Valjean! So ultra nice has the world become that we must skip the Canticles. Shakespeare's plays must now be clapper-clawed to make them palatable. Alexander Pope's philosophic rhyme must be deleted with dashes. Walt Whitman's poetry is too strong for the average stomach. But we continue to fire into the bosoms of our families the daily press with its specialization of Hogan's Alley and the Yellow Kid, reeking with its burden of ads. of abortion recipes and syphilitic nostrums—even take our wives and daughters to the Tabernacle to be told by Sam Jones that if they don't think he has backbone he'll "pull up his shirt-tail and show 'em!" Byron was vigorously denounced by the vindictive Miss Nancy's of his day, but scornfully replied:

> "I have not loved the world, nor the world me;
> I have not flatter'd its rank breath nor bow'd
> To its idolatries a patient knee."

There seems to be nothing left that we may safely read except Watt's Hymns, Talmage's sermons and the pathetic story of Mary's Little Lamb—a promising diet truly, upon which to rear intellectual titans. The remarkable thing about this purist fad is that all the Podsnaps wear pants—the ladies are not on tenter-hooks all the time lest something be said or written that will "bring a blush to the cheek of a young person." It is the he-virgins, the bearded women who are ever on the watch lest young femininity become impregnated with an idea. This country's got a bad case of *mulus pudor*—and needs an heroic dose of double-action liver pills.

THE SCIENCE OF KISSING.

I note that a Britisher named Prof. Bridger has been infringing my copyright by proclaiming, as an original discovery, that kissing is an excellent tonic and will cure dyspepsia. When the o'er busy bacteriologists first announced that osculation was a dangerous pastime, that divers and sundry varieties of bacteria hopped blithely back and forth engendering disease and death, I undertook a series of experiments solely in the interest of science. Being a Baptist Preacher and making camp-meetings my specialty, I had unusual opportunity for investigation, for those of our faith are strict constructionists of the Biblical law to "greet one another with a kiss." I succeeded in demonstrating before the end of the tenting season that osculation, when practiced with reasonable discretion and unfaltering industry, is an infallible antidote for at least half the ills that human flesh is heir to. The reason the doctors arrived at different conclusions is that they kissed indiscriminately and reasoned inductively. They found on casting up the account that bad breath and face powder, the sour milk-bottle of youth and the chilling frost of age, comprised six-sevenths of the sum total. Under such conditions there was nothing to do but establish a quarantine. I pointed out, as Prof. Bridger has since done, that a health microbe as well as a disease bacillus nidificates on the osculatory apparatus, and added that failure to absorb a sufficient quantity of these hygiologic germs into the system causes old maids to look jaundiced and bachelors to die sooner than benedicts. Kisses, when selected with due care and taken on the installment plan, will not only restore a misplaced appetite, but are especially beneficial in cases of hay fever, as they banish that tired feeling, tone up the liver, invigorate the heart, and make the blood to sing thro' the system like a giant jewsharp. I found by patient experiment that the health microbe becomes active at 15, reaches maturity at 20, begins to lose its vigor at 40, and is quite useless as a tonic when, as some one has tersely expressed it, a woman's kisses begin to "taste of her teeth." Thin bluish lips produce very few health germs, and those scarce worth the harvesting; but a full red mouth with Cupid curves at the corners, will yield enormously if the crop be properly cultivated. I did not discover whether the blonde or brunette variety is entitled to precedence in medical science, but incline to the opinion that a judicious admixture is most advisable from a therapeutical standpoint. Great care should be taken when collecting the germs not to crush them by violent collision or blow them away with a loud explosion that sounds like hitting an empty sugar hogshead with a green hide. The practice still prevailing in many parts of this country of chasing a young woman over the furniture and around the barn like an amateur cowboy trying to rope a maverick, rounding her up in the presence of a dozen people, unscrewing her neck and planting almost any place a kiss that sounds like a muley cow pulling her hind foot out of a black-waxy mudhole, and which jars the putty off the window panes, possesses no more curative powers than hitting a flitch of bacon with the back of your hand. I prithee, avoid it; when a girl runs from a kiss you may take it for granted either that the germ crop is not ripe or you are poaching on somebody else's preserves. The best results can be obtained about the midnight hour, when the dew is on the rose, the jasmine bud drunken with its own perfume, and the mockbird trilling a last good-night to his drowsy mate. You entice your best girl into the garden to watch Venus' flaming orb hanging like the Kohinoor pendant from the crescent moon. You pause beneath the great gnarled live oak, its myriad leaves rustling softly as the wings of seraphs. Don't be in a hurry, and for God's sake, don't gab—in such a night silence is the acme of eloquence. "In such a night Troilus Grecian tents where Cressid lay." She watches the fireflies respiring in phosphorescent flame amid the clover blooms, while you watch her, and twine a spray of honeysuckle in her hair. Your clumsy fingers unloose the guards and her fragrant tresses, caught up by the cool night wind, float about your face. Somehow her hand gets tangled up with yours, and after a spasmodic flutter there remains a willing prisoner. The fireflies have failed to interest her and she is studying the stars. You move your shoulder forward to give her head a rest and get hold of her other hand. Be patient; when she wants you to kiss her she'll find means to make it manifest, and a maid worth kissing despises a forward man. She looks very beautiful with her face upturned in the moonlight; but don't say a word about it, for there's a little of the poseur about all the daughters of Eve. She withdraws her eyes from the stars, slowly turns them dreamily upon yours, and you note that they are filled with astral fire. They roam idly over the shadowy garden, then close as beneath a weight of weariness. Her head rests more heavily against your shoulder and her bosom trembles with a half-audible sigh. There is now really no occasion for further delay. Do not swoop down upon the healthgerms like a hungry hen-hawk on a green gosling, but incline your head gently until your carefully deodorized breath is upon her lips—there pause, for the essence of enjoyment is in anticipation. The man who gulps down a glass of old wine without first inhaling its oenanthic and feasting his eyes upon its ruddy splendors, is simply a sot. Wait until you have noted the dark lashes lying upon the cheek of sunflushed snow, "the charm of married brows," the throat of alabaster, the dimple in her chin, the wine-tint of her halfparted lips with their glint of pearl—wait until her eyes half open, look inquiringly into yours, and close again, then cincture her gently but firmly with one arm, support her chin with the other hand, and give the health germs ample time to change their home. A kiss to have any scientific value, should last one minute and seven seconds by Shrewsbury clock, and be repeated seven times, not in swift succession, but with the usual interval between wine at a symposiac. Byron did these things differently, but the author of "Don Juan" is not a safe example for young folks to follow. He pictures Mars lying with his head in the lap of Venus,

"Feeding on thy sweet cheek, while thy lips are
With lava-kisses melting while they burn,
Shower'd on his eyelids, brow and mouth as from an urn."

That may be eminently satisfactory to Mars, but scarce proper for Venus. It is exciting, but not scientific. It suggests charity children gorging themselves with plum pudding, rather than poetic natures drunken with beauty and fragrance, swooning 'neath the sweetness of a duet sung by their own chaste souls. The dyspeptic who cannot recover by following my prescription, deserves to die. The pessimist whom it doesn't make look at life thro' rose-tinted glasses, should be excluded from human society. The hypochondriac whom it doesn't help ought to be hanged. There is not a human ill—unless it be hypocrisy—for which Nature does not provide a remedy, and I recommend the health germ which builds its nest on lovely woman's lips as worth more than the whole bacteria medica. I don't know whether it will raise the dead, but I've always doubted the story that Egypt kissed the cold lips of her Roman Antony—have suspected it would have brought me back to life and love had I been dead a month. The unscientific catch-as-catch-can kiss has no more beneficial effect than slapping yourself in the face with a raw beef-steak. It is but a slight improvement on the civilization of Ashantee, where a man proposes marriage by knocking his Dulcina down with a club and dragging her through the backwoods' pasture by the hair of her head; but kisses properly taken—beneath the stars and among the roses—are the perennial fount of youth for which Ponce de Leon sailed far seas in a vain search for the blessed Bimini.

WANTED: ONE WORD.

I have just discovered the shameful exility of the English language, its poverty of expression, its inadequacy as a mental exchange medium, its utter inability to describe what it were a crime to leave uncatalogued. We have a great many vitriolic words, sesquipedalian words, even what the Germans are wont to call "thunder words;" but none of them, either singly or in combination, can by the grace of inflection or poetic license, be made to answer my purpose. I want a real nice word with which to signify something awfully nasty; but would, for this occasion only, dispense with euphemism were it sufficiently expressive. I must have a word woven or a warp of shame and woof of infamy by some foul Duessa plying her loom among the damned—a word that will signify a featherless two-legged animal who is neither man nor ape; whose soul is but the suspiration of a sick buzzard and his cerebral convolutions the writhing of malodorous maggots; who is a criminal and not confined, a lazar and not compelled to cry "unclean;" who is a suppurating sore on the body social, the guide philosopher and friend of nigger rape-fiends—a creature so foul that were Doll Tearsheet his mother, Falstaff his father and Perdition his birth-place, he would shame his shameless dam, disgrace his graceless sire and dishonor his honorless country. I have explored the English tongue from abc to xyz, examined the terminology of reptalia, attended political conventions and even heard Sam Jones preach; but find no word, printable or otherwise, in the vernacular of the polite or the *patois* of the vulgar covers the case, which may be thus described: A rather pretentious newspaper entitled the *Times* is published in Los Angeles, Cal., by an alleged white man, and has been having considerable to say in denunciation of the Southern people for lynching negro rape-fiends, and thus protecting to the extent of their power the honor of their homes. In addition to its own crass comments on a subject of which it is ignorant as a troglodyte of trigonometry, the *Times* opens its columns to the excrementitious bile of every cowardly blackguard who desires to befoul the Southern people and apotheosize the nigger rape-fiend. The copy before me was forwarded to this office by a Californian with the following comment: "You recently discovered, as you supposed, the world's meanest man in Massachusetts; you will learn from the marked articles that there are others." One of the marked articles is a communication to the *Times* from C. H. Sparks, who adds "University of Chicago" to his patronymic, perhaps for the same reason that we tie a tail to a kite—to "make it go." Whether he's a graduate of the institution backed by Jno. D. Rockefeller with the fruits of his buccaneering, a member of the faculty and paid with money obtained by fraud, or simply keeper of the cuspidores, or grand deodorizer of the vessels of dishonor, is not in evidence. I suppose, however, that he's a Ph. D., LL. D., X. Y. X., or other multititular he-tommy who has wandered down to Los Angeles to recover somewhat from the evil effects of toting so much text-book ignorance. Anyway, C. H. Sparks is not the blatherskite we're after; but as he has thrust himself upon our attention, we will drive a cowboy boot far enough under his coat-tails to tickle his gall-bag with our Mexican spur and then pass blithely on to a more resourceful liar, a more accomplished calumniator. Sparks—of the "University of Chicago," please remember—says he has made "a long and extended observation and looked very carefully into the condition of the negroes." He now affirms that "thousands of them are living higher, purer and nobler lives than their former masters!" What do our fathers and mothers think of that assertion by C. H. Sparks—"of the University of Chicago?" He continues as follows: "The American negro is not the most immoral being in existence; to-day, in the black belt of Alabama, there is not as great a percentage of illegitimacy as there is in the Kingdom of Bavaria, and a dozen other places which I might mention" (but he doesn't mention). From the general tone of his article it may be fairly inferred that Sparks considers that the darkey has come precious near cornering the world's stock of decency. If he be superior morally to his old masters, the inhabitants of Bavaria and the Caucasians of a dozen other countries, it is small wonder that Julian Hawthorne desires to improve the white breed by injecting into it a little Ethiopian blood! Sparks says that "it is commonly asserted than less than 40 years ago every negro in this country was either himself a bastard or was the child of illegitimate born parents." He does not question the correctness of this statement, which, in justice to the negro be it said, is only approximately true. From what Sparks "grants" was a state of universal bastardy or second-hand illegitimacy, to a moral status superior to that of the Caucasians of a dozen or more countries, "in less than 40 years," is what we might call unprecedented progress! If the Ethiop keeps up that tremendous gait for another 40 years, he will be entirely too good for this gross earth. If Sparks knew aught of anthropology, he would be aware that it requires many generations and favorable circumstances to transform a notoriously immoral race into one of honor and respectability; were he familiar with history he would know that whenever the negro has been excluded from frequent contact with the white man, or where the latter has failed to dominate, he has almost immediately reverted to savagery; did he possess an atom of information, tempered by ever so little sense, he would know that whatever progress the black has made since his release from bondage is due to the example and encouragement, the opportunity for education and financial betterment supplied by the Southern people—that despite his notorious *vis intertae* he has been carried forward somewhat by the tremendous *vis intalis* of Caucasian civilization. Sparks—"of the University of Chicago" —estimates the morals of the colored people by "statistics of illegitimacy," which demonstrates that, despite his "long and extended observation," he knows absolutely nothing about the negroes or the laws of various nations—that his "observations" were taken from the window of a Pullman car. Statistics of illegitimacy take cognizance only of people "born out of wedlock"—that is, of women known to be unmarried. In most European countries a child born out of wedlock remains a bastard tho' its parents intermarry; in most American states the intermarriage of the parents, tho' at the age of 100 years, legitimatizes all their children; hence Sparks' "statistics" are altogether useless. And there is another important feature with which this learned Theban is evidently unfamiliar: Practically all female negroes, in Alabama and elsewhere, who have reached the child-bearing age, are married—or supposed to be; and statisticians are not much addicted to chasing certificates of wedlock in colored settlements. A married woman may give birth to a dozen brats by as many different men without enhancing the "percentage of illegitimacy" in her neighborhood. I do not say there are no virtuous negro women—how could I know?—but I do say that with the average wench the possession of a husband, real or pretended, like the flowers that bloom in the spring, "has nothing to do with the case." She finds a husband first—if convenient—and then experiments with paramours of every race and complexion. It is frequently charged by trans-Ohio pseudo-philanthropists and negrophiles that I am "the black man's enemy." Such is far from being a fact. While these fellows are stuffing his head with rank folly, I tell him the truth. While they spill the scalding sob over "his pitiable condition," I find him employment. While they give him dangerous advice, I set before him good healthy grub. They encourage him to make criminal assaults on Caucasian women for which I have to help hang him. The gross immorality of the negro is a stubborn fact which every man of sense would know must be so, tho' he had never received any definite information on the subject. I do not censure him for it any more than I censure a dog for slaughtering sheep—I simply say that the sheep-killing dog must die, that the black man who criminally assaults a white woman must perish as quickly as we can get our hands on his goozle. The negroes are an inferior race; their intelligence is sadly circumscribed; their animalism is strong, while their moral concept is weak. But a few years ago they ceased to be degraded savages only to become abject slaves. During but one generation have they had opportunity to make real progress, and this opportunity they have improved as well as we could reasonably expect; but when Sparks assumes that in "less than forty years" they have attained to a moral and intellectual attitude which the white man has reached only after a struggle of more than 40 centuries, he simply advertises that the "University of Chicago" is responsible for the fact that a piebald ass is at large in Los Angeles. He is probably one of that numerous class who scribble for the press because they have a prurient itch to see their names in print—who uncork themselves on every occasion, and with their more than Boeotian ignorance and Gascon impudence beslime every subject. But, as I remember in the hitherto, he's not the huckleberry for my basket—I have but dallied with him to cool my blood before turning my attention to a creature who cannot be properly dealt with in language I would care to print. Besides, I have to be a trifle careful how I call a spade a spade, for every infernal rascal I expose, every liar I put in the public pillory, every dirty seducer of half-wit maids I denounce, every tradesman I find trying to defraud his creditors by a bogus failure, every arrant hypocrite whose "unctuous smile makes the widow lean" that I strip of the Lord's livery, at once advises the postal department that the Iconoclast is "indecent" and "should be suppressed." Which proves that

"Rogue ne'er felt the halter draw
With good opinion of the law."

If the Iconoclast were one-half so foul as the souls of those who denounce it for waging uncompromising war on "all that loveth and maketh a lie," it would indeed disgrace the cloacae of Rome, the sewers of Paris and add fresh horrors to a pestilential cess-pool. Sparks' stupid diatribe or pigeon English is quite o'ershadowed in the matter of deliberate villainy and imaginative mendacity by one "Geo. D. Taylor, M. D.," who gives his address 252 1-2 S. Main St., Los Angeles—which I imagine must be a Chinese opium den or nigger variety dive. I will quote a few lines from his fulmination, trusting that it will not provoke any Southerner to waste decent buckshot on the misbegotten brute, and thus prevent him stinking himself to death, which he seems in a fair way to do. Ladies are requested not to read the following paragraph, as filtering it through their pure minds were like soiling white samite with the belchings of buzzard that had crammed its craw with poison-infecting carrion. He inquires why the negro cannot be trusted among white women and children now as well as before the war—a question which I have frequently answered for the edification of the fools that ask it—and then proceeds to "spread himself" as follows:

> The negro is tempted more now than then, and led on by the white woman in the majority of cases, and everything goes well until they are caught. The Southern negro is no more lustful than the Southern white man. When the white man wants to commit his crime he seeks a black woman, and of course you never hear it, or should he seek a white woman he simply blacks his face, commits the deed, some poor negro is lynched, many times he helps to do it, and that ends it. We know of many instances of this kind. Ninety-nine per cent. of the negro men of the South are afraid to insult a white woman, if they were so inclined, and the women, knowing this, they make the first advances.

That's why I am advertising for a new word—one that will aptly describe "Geo. D. Taylor, M. D.," and at the same time burn no holes in Uncle Sam's asbestos mail sack. Of course it were easy to suggest that the mother of such a mental abnormality expends much time scratching fleas with her hind feet; but the dog is man's best friend, and to accredit Taylor with so decent an origin were fulsome flattery. I suspect that "Geo. D. Taylor, M. D.," is a saddle-colored coon, one of those yaller bipeds with which the bummers and beats who followed in the wake of Sherman's boys so liberally sprinkled the South, and whom we have expended so much good money transforming into impudent preachers who publicly clamor for white wives, quack doctors who become the silent partners of negro undertakers, and peanut politicians who sell votes in blocks-of-five, when they should have taken an ox goad and driven the whole caboodle into the cotton-patch. There are several of these creatures, begotten by thieving white bummers and black bawds, who, after feeding on our bounty and acquiring at our expense all the education that could be pumped into their beefy brains, have sneaked off a thousand miles or so, and, from such points of safety, foully insult their benefactors. We will not discuss such vermin; for if it be "a waste of lather to shave an ass," what must it be to criticise an impudent coon who cannot be conveniently reached with a club? The existence of such things upon the earth is strong presumptive evidence of the truth of the old dogma that "God ordained some to be damned for his greater glory." The appearance of the communication of "C. H. Sparks, University of Chicago," and "Geo. D. Taylor, M. D.," in the same column, was eminently appropriate, they being two of a kind. We may reasonably suppose that Taylor is Sparks' family physician and officiates at the birth of his babies, for the latter would quite naturally entrust such delicate duties to negroes, who are so eminently superior to their old masters. The two should be yoked together and scourged naked through the world, not with a thong of dry bull-hide, yet with a desiccated implement of torture supplied by that useful and interesting animal; but we would have to employ a Digger Indian to do it, as the malodor of such mangy simians would inoculate a decent white man with the black death. It is the editor of the *Times* who really needs attention for circulating such rotten slanders, not alone of Southern ladies, but of the whole Caucasian race. He knew when he admitted the Chicago idiot's article that it was a tissue of falsehood aimed at people who had never harmed him. He knew when he printed the insane drivel of Taylor—the cowardly spawn of a pole-cat—that it was a malicious calumny. He knew that in every case in which a black beast has criminally asaulted a white woman, his victim became the accuser, if he had not taken the precaution to kill her. He knew that many of the negroes lynched for rape in this section had forcibly debauched little girls in short dresses, some of them toddling babes, whilst others had victimized women past 80. He knew that during the past 200 years there has not been half a dozen well-authenticated cases of white men blacking their faces and committing such a crime. He knew that instead of Southern white women making advances to black bucks, they dread them worse than death by torture and eternal damnation; yet he cheerfully prints these infamous charges, preferred by a cowardly coyote who realizes that, being so distinct from those he defames, there is little danger that he will be hunted down and his lying tongue ripped out by the roots. But Taylor had best cork himself; when the Iconoclast has placed his calumny before half a million Southerners whose wives and daughters he has defamed, he may have callers anxious to examine his complexion through the sights of a six-shooter. I will not express my opinion of the *Times* man, not now—it wouldn't look well in print. If it should ever be convenient to tell him personally what I think of him, and there are no ladies present, perhaps I can find a word that will answer my purpose. If it be possible for a good tree to bring forth foul fruit—if Apples of Sodom will spring from a Ben-Davis stem—then perchance his father was a gentleman. His mother was probably a respectable woman, who, becoming frightened by some hideous nightmare, brought forth a monster. Hamlet might "unpack his heart with curses" leveled at the cowardly assassins of his sire; but it were useless to waste adjectives upon an editor who suffers a lousy nigger to puke through his columns into the fair faces of millions of noble women. I can but wonder what will become of the *Times* editor when the breath leaves his feculent body and death stops the rattling of his abortive brain, for he is unfit for heaven and too foul for hell. He cannot be buried in the earth lest he provoke a pestilence, nor in the sea lest he poison the fish, nor swung in space like Mahomet's coffin lest the circling worlds in trying to avoid contamination, crash together, wreck the universe and bring again the noisome reign of Chaos and old Night. The dam rascal seems to be a white elephant on the hands of Deity, and I have some curiosity to know what he will do with it.

"THE UNWRITTEN LAW."

The recent decision of Judge Falconer, of Lexington, Ky., to the effect that an "unwritten law," superior to penal statutes, authorizes a husband to kill an unfaithful wife's paramour, is provoking no end of comment, and appears to be generally approved by high-minded people. The decision was rendered in the case of the State vs. J. S. Harris, charged with the murder of Thos. H. Merritt, whom he surprised one evening in the act of industriously hugging his alleged better half and taking a psychic lunch off her ruby lips. Judge Falconer declared that "human law in its declared portions had decreed no adequate punishment for the violator of the home;" that "no wife yields herself to the despoiler till he has weaned away from her husband that love which is the foundation of the marriage relation," and that the unwritten law of human nature excuses the husband who avenges himself by homicide. There is no question but such is an "unwritten law" of the American people; but whether it should be so is a very perplexing problem. Dishon. W. C. P. Breckinridge declares emphatically that Judge Falconer's decision "is neither good law nor good morals"; but as he had the presumption to lecture on "Morals" while posing as a pillar of the Presbyterian church and breaking the laws of God and man by living in adultery with Madeline Pollard, his opinion is not apt to cut much ice with respectable people. It seems to me that had I been convicted of knocking the sawdust out of the Seventh Commandment while lecturing young people on morals and religion, I should have avoided a discussion of the "unwritten law" pertaining to adultery. Still it does not follow that a man convicted of law-breaking knows nothing about law, or that one adjudged guilty of adultery must be unfamiliar with the canons of decency. It must be confessed that the world's intellectual giants have seldom been Josephs—that if only men who have never transgressed be permitted to discuss Judge Falconer's decision, the ladies will have the conversation pretty much to themselves. Luther emphatically declares that

"The man who loves not wine, women and song, remains a fool all his life long,"

and if the wine be good, the woman pretty and the song well sung, I am prepared to agree with the alleged father of the Reformation. The one only thing that G. Gleveland ever did suggestive of a man of genius was to send a substitute to war, while he remained in Buffalo to fill beakers to the brim and tread "the primrose path of dalliance" with a buxom widow. The nation would have been a billion dollars better off had he remained with Widow Halpin and his wine instead of going to Washington. I could never understand why people who account themselves all-wise and eminently respectable, wash Cleveland's fat feet with their worshipful tears and dry them with the hairs of their heads, while pointing the loaded finger of scorn at Madeline Pollard's paramour. Breckinridge's argument cannot be answered with his own record, however bad that may be. His closed carriage episode no more proves Judge Falconer to be right than his hypocrisy proves the Christian religion to be wrong. The "unwritten law" is a subject that has several sides. I confess I do not see what else a man of spirit can do on finding his wife unfaithful except put a handful of buckshot under the cuticle of her paramour. While the effusion of blood does not eliminate the family disgrace, nor restore happiness to his home, it is some satisfaction to kill the man who made him a cuckold.

He may secure a divorce from the woman and learn to heartily hate or wholly despise her; but he cannot rest content while the violator of his home is a mile this side of hell. But if it be proper that one man should die for such an offense, then all should be slaughtered if they could be found, and I much fear that would prove more destructive than a second flood—that while the average "injured husband" was taking a pot-shot at some "foul seducer" a third party would be pumping lead in his direction. As remarked in the hitherto, Josephs are a rather seldom commodity in this country. Of course every man should be virtuous as Adonis, able to resist even the soft blandishments of Venus Pandemos; but—. It has been frequently said that the devil when fishing for he-saints baits his hook with a sunbonnet; which abundantly proves that he understands his business. Doubtless there are men, whom the doctors have not yet pronounced dead, who will not talk "soft sawder" to every pretty woman with a tooth for taffy; but they are almost as scarce as icebergs in Texas or preachers who can hear a "call" that means a 60 per cent. cut in salary. This is not as it should be, and I'm trying to effect a reformation by the force of good example —by positively refusing to flirt with any lady past the age of fifty. The average man protests against the single standard of morality for the sexes; allows to his own the larger liberty. He knows that he entrusts the keeping of his honor to the woman he weds, not to the men she may chance to meet. He knows that many if not most would gladly "lead her astray," but that they cannot do so unless she furnishes the string. He knows that if she be minded to remain pure, she will prevent by womanly tact or repel with scorn all improper advances—will give no man an opportunity to "wean away from her husband that love which is the foundation of the marriage relation." Yet despite all this, when the shadow of dishonor falls upon his home, he insists that his wife is the victim of a "designing villain," and that said designing villain must die. If the woman in the case be very young, or inexperienced, or weak-minded, or victimized by means of drugs or brute force, then let the husband use a shot-gun and see that there's a dozen buckshot in each barrel; but if she be a woman of average intelligence and mature years, the fault, in so far as family honor is concerned, is hers alone, and the "unwritten law" become violative of that very "human nature" on which Judge Falconer founds his decision. A man should never kill another for a crime which he has duplicated, or would be apt to commit under like conditions. There are many wives who never expect to be unfaithful, but who are so eager for admiration, so hungry for flattery, that they indulge in "little harmless flirtations" with the deliberate intent of entangling the affection of certain "poor fellows." It is a very pretty pastime, this of playing with human hearts, and not infrequently affords a foolish husband—who happens to be "almost damned in a fair wife"— much amusement. It flatters his vanity to see others "sighing like a furnace"—or pretending to—for the property in his possession. Madame's "conquests" are chuckled over, and she is tacitly encouraged to "mash." Such a woman, wedded to so weak a man, will not go far ere she finds a worthier master—is caught in a web of her own weaving; the liaison is discovered, and there is another appeal to the "unwritten law." Thousands of well-meaning women, yet with all the sexual ferocity of a Valeria Messalina beating in their blood, are married but not mated—and Judge Falconer himself informs us that "though human laws may regulate human nature, they cannot control nature's whirlwinds." What then? Has nature no whirlwinds but those of wrath? Is anger the one only thing capable of producing "a condition of mental irresponsibility" during which one cannot be held accountable by the courts. Many wives are so grossly neglected by their husbands that the holy flame that once burned so brightly on the altar of Love mounts no more—and the turnpike to perdition is paved with the ashes of loves that are dead. Doubtless this "unwritten law" will long continue operative, but I move that it be amended that the worthy wife will be required to shoot the bustle off the libidinous old heifer who wrecks her home. Judge Falconer assures us that "the relations of man and wife are warning to all the world that third parties interfere at their peril"; but he does not tell us what third party's interference caused the trouble adjudicated in his court. Mrs. Harris was the mother of two children, proof positive that she had reached the age of discretion. That she was employed as copyist by Mr. Merritt argues that she was not altogether an idiot. We will suppose that her employer was also married and the father of a family: Now did she attempt to "wean" his love away from his wife, or he attempt to "wean" her love away from her husband? Who inaugurated the flirtation which developed into amorous dalliance. If the man, the injured husband is avenged; if the woman, what about the injured wife? Her husband's affections were alienated, he was killed, her children were left fatherless and possibly unprovided for—all the work of a disreputable old drab. Harris can, if so disposed, forgive his erring wife—as has become the usual custom in our "best society"—and let Love's young dream flow smoothly on as in days of yore; Mrs. Merritt can also forgive her husband—but he's in his grave. Much as I dislike Breckinridge the hypocrite, I incline to his view that Judge Falconer's decision "is neither good law nor good morals"; and I would add that it is not good sense. It is not good law because it places the life of the average citizen at the mercy of any hoodlum who may be married to a harlot. If Mr. Quickly should slay Sir Walter Raleigh for any reason, he has only to plead that his victim was intimate with his wife, and the old dame would take pride in acknowledging the soft impeachment. It is not good morals, because it relieves woman of the responsibility of protecting her own purity. It is not good sense, because it assumes that the man who will follow where a voluptuous woman leads is an unnatural monster. I am no apologist for the libertine; but I do protest against placing women on the lower level occupied by man, sexually considered. To kill a man for dallying with his neighbor's wife is eminently satisfactory to the husband, but is no compliment either to the good sense or moral concept of womankind. Since the dawn of civilization virtue has constituted her chief charm, the one particular in which she has risen immensely superior to the sterner sex. Had all the harlots of the past sixty centuries been hanged in their swaddling clothes the world would have lost but little; had all the men who have loved women not wisely but too well been so served, history would be a white mark on a snow bank and you couldn't scrape up enough people on the great round globe to make a village as large as Waco. Ancient Israel would have been painfully shy of Kings, and the Lord been short several of his "well belowed." The Tribe of Judah would have been *non est,* we would not have the Proverbs of Solomon, and even the Psalms of David might have been abridged by Uriah's butcher-knife in the boudoir of Bathsheba. We would have no Shakespeare and no—but prithee, let's switch to politics.

GOING FORWARD BACKWARDS.

Reformers Who Can't Reform.

I sometimes suspect that we have hitched our mule to the subsequent end of our boasted Car of Progress, and that, with ears and tail erect, the animal is bearing us toward the abyss instead of some celestial abode; also that our busy reformers are striving desperately to lift themselves over a nine-rail fence by their own boot-straps. I take it upon myself to call a halt in order that we may get our bearings and learn for a surety whither we are bound. It seems to me that we have hypnotized ourselves with this universal cackle of progress, are mistaking shadow for substance and driving blithely to the devil. Conditions, according to trustworthy report, have already become desperate, our Car of Progress with its Salmoneus thunder rolling, not over a well-paved turnpike to some Beulahland, but along a pathway of human bones sodden with blood and tears. Desperate, I say; meaning thereby not only that it becomes ever more difficult for the workman to win his modicum of bread and butter, but that honor, religion, patriotism—all things our fathers esteemed as more precious than fine gold—are well-nigh departed; that the social heart is dead as a salt herring, pulsating only with galvanic power; that all has become brummagem and pinchbeck, leather and prunella; that the curse of sterility has fallen upon the womb of the world and it can no longer produce philosophers, poets, prophets—heaven inspired men—but only some pitiful simulacra thereof, some worthless succedanea for such, whose object is not to do their God-appointed task tho' the world reward them with a gibbet, but to win wages of gold and grub, to obtain idle praise by empty plausibility, to float like irisate bubbles or painted bladders on the highest wave, not of a tempestuous ocean that tries the heart of oak and the hand of iron, but of a pitiful sectarian mud-puddle or political goose-pond. The great men of this generation are not those who bring Promethean fire from beyond the stars, but rather the Vulpine-headed who devise more cunning ways to get fat geese. We have abandoned the Ark of the Covenant, with its Brotherhood of Man, its solemn duties and sacred responsibilities; and are striving to manage matters mundane on a basis of brute selfishness, without a soul of sentiment, a conscience or a creed—except the credo of the Golden Calf.

"Progress," cried the cheerful idiot, *alias* the optimist; "do look at our wonderful progress!" Aye, I see it—and smell it. Progress may be sure and swift down a soaped plank into wild ocean-depths with a ten-pound shot at the subsequent end of thee for ballast; or it may be with painful steps and slow toward the eternal mountain-tops where breaks the great white light of God, and there is on more of darkness and of death. Progress mechanical, the industrial unit multiplied by two, by ten; and with such improved weapons for waging war upon the grisly gorgon of want, nearly nine millions of the Industrial Army in India alone dead upon their shields, and other millions falling! Hosannahs mounting heavenwards (or sinking hellwards) in costly churches here, the starving babe tugging at the empty breast of its dead mother there—while a pious sovereign in her jubilee year contributes one-third of one day's salary for the relief of her suffering subjects and piously mumbles that giving to the poor is lending to the Lord! The earth and elements brought into subjection; all miracles hitherto outmiracled by our wondrous wealth-creating machinery; the very lightnings, that once flamed lawless through the sky, harnessed down by cunning hands and made to toil for man; yet millions even in America, the granary of the world, boasting itself the refuge of the poor and oppressed, unable to do victorious battle with the frost-jotuns and hunger-plants—to win, with all their high endeavor, the blessings of a home! We have actually made such progress in the science of production that half the population of this planet must go hungry. Yet Russell Sage and other multi-millionaires who are doing the dog-in-the-manger act, prate of "over-production!" Men are ragged because they have made too much cloth, hungry because they have produced too much hog and hominy, must live in mean huts because they have sawed too much lumber and made too many bricks—so says Russell Sage; and there be people who imagine that a man who accumulates great wealth must necessarily possess common sense. The fact is that the acquisitive faculty is seldom conjoined with a high order of intellect—it is simply an animal instinct which guides its possessor to fresh waters and fat pastures. Daniel Webster, whose colossal intellect might, "like the elements, furnish forth creation," could scarce make both ends meet; but Russell Sage, his senescent brain rattling in a hickory-nut head, is able to celebrate his 82nd birthday by running a robber "corner" on Manhattan. The "over-production" theory is about the measure of Sage's mind when he thinks of aught but the personal accumulation of hard cash. Half the world's population are hungry, ragged and wretched because they have been robbed—because the possessors of 5, 50 and 100 million dollar fortunes are impudent thieves who manage to prevent the workman enjoying the fruits of his toil, who steal the very nozzle off the nursing bottle in the mouth of his babes.

I picked up a copy of *Puck* the other day, one of those would-be humorous papers that give a fellow hay-fever. While I was glancing over its wooden wit and cartoons that had evidently slipped their trolley wire, and wondering if there was anybody outside the insane asylum who could be hired to read it regularly, I found two pages of cheap pictures illustrating the blessings which a generous plutocracy is conferring on the thankless poor. It seems that, thanks to the charity of the American millionaires, a poor devil may obtain almost anything without money and without price, whether it be a soup bone, a dose of pills, an installment of Saving Grace or a collegiate education. It is very easy to be generous with other people's money. It is not charity, but justice the American workingman wants. Give the toiler his own, and you may dispense with Rockefeller's magnificent monuments to his own sweet memory. Robin Hood, Jesse James and other marauders of that ilk, were somewhat noted for their generosity; but they never pretended that the giving away of a small percentage of their swag transformed them from disreputable footpads into seraphs feathered like a peacock. They didn't have quite so much hypocrisy as Brother Rockefeller and others who manage to appropriate the earnings of better people and steer clear of the catch-holes and penitentiary.

Progress in government, to where the greatest of nations cannot, with all its ballot-boxing, torch-light processioning and negro suffrage, so much as govern itself, but is led around by the nose like a foolish cow and systematically milked by foreign Shylocks. Progress in religion until there's no more a divine message from on high, no God in Israel; only fashionable pulpiteering to minister to languid minds, the cultivation of fads and the flaunting of fine feathers; else blatant blackguardism by so-called revivalists, who, with the ignorance of an ape united with the presumption of a peddler, set up as teachers of the people—all constituting an ethnic fore-court to Infidelity, and under the supervision of a devil quite up-to-date. Progress in science until we know that spring water is full of bacilli and switch to Prohibition bitters warranted to kill anything but a salamander in an asbestos overcoat; that even the rosebud lip of beauty is aswarm with microbes flourishing skull and crossbones, instead of beckoning the sons of men to a nectareous feast for the Olympian Gods. Progress from the heroics of Homer and the vates'-visions of Dante, to Alfred Austin's milk-sick doggerel, the raucous twitterings of grown men who are trying to do the bulbul act instead of harvesting hoop-poles, planting hogs and drawing a fat bacon-rind down the shining blade of a bucksaw; from the flame-sighs of Sappho that breed mutiny in the blood, to the pulseless maunderings of atrabilarious females whose prating of "passion" makes us seasick whenever we hear the swish of a petticoat. Progress from presidents like Andrew Jackson, with hearts of hickory, to boneless gran'dames who permit Cuba to be made a reeking slaughterhouse at our very doors because her sons like our own sires, love liberty; deny the divine right of crowned and sceptred vermin on the body politic to rule and rob, have declared that all men shall be equal before the law—permit this work infernal lest, forsooth, they offend certain royal fatheads across the sea who are ever poking their beefy proboscises into Uncle Sam's business. Yes, we have progressed backwards until this country, once the proud habitat of men with iron in their blood, is breeding mugwumps like Senator Palmer, preachers like Coochee-Coochee Parkhurst, Anglomaniacs like Willie Wally Astor, politicians like Boodle Hanna, presidents like McKinley, of the sawdust head, and miscegenationists like Julian Hawthorne. It is the general consensus of opinion that there's something radically wrong, and there's no lack of remedies. You will find these panaceas, each with the trademark of some particular school of therapeutics blown in the bottle, each provided with certificates to its curative powers. "You pays your money and you takes your choice" —homeopathic free-trade Democracy, allopathic high-tariff Republican, electric Populism, hydropathic Prohibition— and dodge regret as best you may. Strange that all these catholicons for earthly ills propose to inaugurate a new and greater Saturnian age by improving the pecuniary condition of certain people—as tho' the scarcity of money in this or the other pocket were the one only evil. Certainly a better distribution of wealth were desirable, but a distribution of God's Grace were far preferable. Given that, all other worthy reforms will follow; without it we simply chase this or the other *ignis-fatuus* to our fall. I do not mean that we shall solve the Sphinx-riddle by acquiring a case of the camp-meeting jerks, by seeking sanctuary from the minatory monster in the amen-corner. Not exactly; the average church is about the last thing to which we need look for relief. I have noticed that shouting hosannahs has no tendency to make one more truthful in a horse-trade—that when a man confesses himself the chief of sinners he may feel obligated to substantiate his testimony. I have never yet known a man to borrow any money at a bank on the unctuosity of his amen; but I am acquainted with people who weep real water because I refuse to come within their religious pen-fold, who can beat the devil himself at dodging an honest debt. There's Bro. W. O. Baker, of Burnett, Tex., for instance, whose holy zeal once led him to preach against the Iconoclast at Liberty Hill—and the echoes of his fine scorn had scarce faded out of the atmosphere before his past-due promissory note for something like a hundred dollars was offered to me for a year's subscription to the paper he had denounced. It is needless to say that the note is not in my possession—I'm playing no 100-to-1 shots on Baptist preachers. Were I in the habit of purchasing gold bricks and other such property, I might have in my ash-barrel a great deal of the past-due paper of people who are powerful in prayer. To save tedious correspondence, I will remark, *en passant,* that people who desire to make me a present of accounts against Rev. Sam Small will be required to prepay the postage. Some people may imagine that a preacher who doesn't pay his debts is worse than a footpad, as he adds lying and hypocrisy to despoliation; but, like Bobby Burns, my heart is so full of charity that I'm even inclined to apologize for the devil. It's possible that a majority of our ripsnortin' sensational revivalists are so busy trying to seduce halfwit "sisters" that they actually forget their commercial obligations. Many preachers make an honest effort to live faithfully up to their professions, and such are the salt of the earth, but I much fear that the church is a trifle short of chloride of sodium. If all professing Christians were Christlike, the millennium would hit the earth within four-and-twenty hours; but we have too many serving God solely for the long green. One atheistical Stephen Girard playing Good Samaritan in a plague-swept city; one deistical Tom Paine braving the guillotine for the rights of man; one Father Damien laying down his life for the lepers in Molokai; one Sister of Charity bravely battling with the reeking slums of a great city, were worth a billion sanctified windbags prating of "sacrificing all for Jesus," yet who never risk life or gold in the service of their God.

"Laborare est Orare, Work is our Worship," cried the old monks, those brave souls who carried the cross around the world as advance guard of civilization, despite all hardships in defiance of all dangers—men for whom life was no Parisian masquerade, but "a battle and a march." Work is worship. Aye, when a Pere Marquette or a Father Damien does it for other's sake, cheerfully accepting disease and death as worldly wages; but wind-jamming by a sleek jackassicus, with eye in fine frenzy rolling towards the fodder rack, is not calculated to make heaven rejoice. The old monks were real men, with a touch of the berserker in their blood, caring for naught but victory over the powers of darkness and the devil, standing at their posts like Roman sentinels tho' the earth rocked beneath their feet and the heavens rained fire. Real men, whatsoever their religion or race, their education, occupation or intellect; the men who glory in their work regardless of reward, are ever the world's heroes and its hope. Milton has almost made Satan respectable, has well-nigh hallowed his work of wickedness by endowing him with all infernal heroism, by making him altogether and irremediably bad instead of a moral mugwump—by picturing him with a heart of any fate instead of painting him as "willing to wound and yet afraid to strike." By God's grace I mean not the kind you catch at one of Sam Jones' minstrel shows—given as excuse for passing the contribution plate, with invitation extended the sons of Belial to "spit in it" if they can do no better; not the so-called "gifts of the Holy Ghost" that make a woman want to swing her sunbonnet, holler with her mouth open, hug all the brethren

and chew the nether lip of the preacher; but rather an end
everlasting to Brummagem and make-believe; a return to the
Ark of the Covenant; a recognition of the fact that the soul
is not the stomach—that man owes to his fellows debts which
cannot be cast up at the end of each month and fully discharged with a given number of dollars. You may preach
reform of this and teach reform of that until nightmares
plow corn and Senators earn their salaries; but we must
have reform of men before we can have any other reform
whatsoever worth the price of the parchment. You can no
more extract wisdom from folly or justice from knavery
than you can distill blood from turnips or God's grace from
amen groans. Our ideals are all wrong—we're going forward backwards and if somebody doesn't head us off we'll
soon find hades to pay and the bank broke. Palaces and
jewels and costly raiment and monies and lands—these by
thy gods, O Israel—mere fly-specked eidolons, false sera-
phim worthy no man's worship. They must be cast down
from their high places, and Faith, Hope and Charity—triune
transcendent—grace our altars ere man learns that

> "—— because right is right, to follow right
> Were wisdom in the scorn of consequence."

Diogenes was content with a tub, while Alexander sat
down by the ever-moaning sea and wept his red bandana full
of brine because Cristoforo Colombo has not yet come to
enlarge his knowledge of geography, to intimate that the
Christian Amazons of the City Book Store of Emporia,
Kan., still remained unconquered and unconquerable. And
now both Diogenes and Alexander are dead—"gone glimmering through the dream of things that were"—and little
it matters to them or to us whether they fed on honey of
Hymettus and wine of Falernus, or ate humble pie with a
knife and guzzled moonshine whisky out of a gourd—
whether they dined at Delmonico's or worked a farmer's
wife for a cold potato and absorbed it in the fence-corner.
The cynic who housed in a discarded soap-suds receptacle
and clothed himself with second-hand cotton-bagging is rich
today as he that reveled in the spoils of Persia's conquered
kings and kicked the bucket by trying to shoot out the bar-
room lights while carrying a "load." The mold of either
may stop a crack in a colored Republican's cabin to keep the

wind away; but the life, the soul, no longer chained to this paltry me, "uncumber'd wantons in the Force of All." King and cynic, tub and palace, lantern and sceptre, all have perished; he that butchered thousands to glut his greed for what fools call glory, shines no brighter through the murky shadow of the centuries than he that made a worthier conquest of himself. The haughty empires Alexander reared have long since crumbled into dust; the wild goat browses in their deserted capitals, the lizard sleeps upon the broken thrones and the jackal slinks about the forgotten altars and ruined fanes. Even the land that boasts his birth hath become an appendage of the barbarous Ottomite—stands, like "the Niobe of nations,"

"An empty urn within her withered hands,
Whose holy dust was scattered long ago,"

but the philosophy of the other lives on from age to age to point the folly of such mad violence as that of Philip's imperious son, who sought to make the world his monument, yet sleeps in a nameless sepulchre.

And you, who are neither Diogenes nor Alexander, what strive ye for? It is said that one eternity waited for you to be born, that another is watching to see what you will do now that you are here. And canst do naught better than burn incense at Mammon's shrine, attire thyself in purple and fine linen and fare sumptuously every day? Is that the work for which one eternity waited, for which another is watching? Know ye not that the poorest beggar, sleeping in hedges and living on "handouts" is an earth passenger also and thy brother, traveling his hundreds of millions of miles per annum—where think you? Among the stars—circumnavigating the sun! For him as for thee does Aurora gild the last and Apollo hang the western sky with banners of burnished gold; for him as for thee does Luna draw the limpid waters around a rolling world and "Bootes lead his hunting dogs afield in their leash of sidereal fire;" for him as for thee have heroes set their breasts against the bayonet and Christ given up the ghost on Calvary. If you do but accumulate and do not create, then you are an object more pitiable than the beggar, for the toilers must suffer the cost of both your keep, and he is content with crumbs and cast-off clothes, draws from the general fund only to consume and not to hoard—is only a pitiful nuisance while you are an insufferable curse. What would I have thee do? Even the work that lies next thy hand. Cast thy petty ambition and paltry pride to the dogs and do somewhat to honestly earn the grave in which thou shalt sleep so long, forgotten of men —something quite other than hoarding the treasure of others for thine own pusillanimous posterity, and, like the foolish peacock, displaying thy rich plumage on dress-parade, injecting notes of dissonance into the divine harmony through the opening in thy head. Wait not until a man be driven to crime by the iron law of necessity, a woman to dishonor, a child to beggary, then organize some fake relief expedition for thine own glory; but extend a helping hand in time to avert the sin and shame. True, there is more joy in heaven over one sinner saved than over ninety-and-nine who had not gone all the gaits; but you are not expected to push people into the sea that you may throw them a life-line and tickle a lot of hermaphroditical angels by exhibiting them as salvage. Your shoulders are broad and strong; let the weaker fall in behind thee and be shielded somewhat by thy strength. The soldier strikes not in his own defense but for the honor of his flag, in defense of those who cannot fight; strike thou, not for the promotion of thine own selfish purpose, but for the honor of thy race, in the name of those who falter and fall in the grim warfare against Want. The noblest success this world can boast is the man who creates wealth and uses it wisely and well—he is the hero of the industrial war, the leader of the host and champion of the helpless; the most pitiful of all failures is the man who succeeds only in making money, who bows himself to the dust before the work of his own hands. A thieving fox will fatten where an honest dog will starve to death, will live at ease where the other is scarred with wounds; and we have too many sleek Reynards nosing about the sheep-pens and dovecotes of the people, too faithful Gelerts doing stubborn battle with predaceous beasts.

When we have altered our ideals; when success is no longer a synonym for vain show; when the man of millions who toils and moils for more is considered mad; when we learn that all the precious metals of Plutus cannot equal the splendor of the sunset sky beneath which the poorest trudge, the astral fire that flames at night's high noon above the meanest hut; that wealth cannot recall one wasted hour, restore youthful strength, or bid the loved and lost return to regale us with the music of their laughter; that the "almighty dollar" is lord only of the brute in man, good only to protect him from the weather and fill his belly; when we have ceased chasing foolish bubbles through the Serbonian bogs of Make-Believe and become real men and women instead of simpering puppets wound up by stale custom to cut fantastic capers before high heaven, then may we throw our social drugshop with its panaceas to the dogs. We must learn that "it is not by money or money's worth that man has his being;" that "there is a God's universe within our head, whether there be a torn skull-cap or a king's diadem without." The chief trouble with this nation is not too much or too little tariff, but rather too much artificiality and plausibility—too much of that silver-spoon pseudo-respectability which felt itself degraded by association with Bobby Burns, tolerated Shakespeare and "patronized Providence." A thorough-paced rascal—Satan himself with his principles frankly declared and faithfully adhered to—were preferable to one of your good God good devil fellows, your moral mugwumps and intellectual hybrid who is neither cold nor hot. "Glorious, heroic, fruitful for all Times," says the philosopher, "is the constant speaker and doer of Truth. If no such is to be vouchsafed us, let us at least have the melancholy pleasure of beholding a decided Liar."

CREDIT AND PRICES.

I will have to mix it a little with A. J. Utely, who writes a very curious article for the July *Arena,* in which he attempts to demonstrate that the contraction or expansion of credit has no effect upon the level of prices. Mr. Utely is evidently a close student of economics, but has succeeded in arguing himself into some very glaring absurdities. As the questions with which he deals are important, I will state his premises and conclusions briefly and endeavor to steer him out of the logical labyrinth in which he has become lost.

Mr. Utely accepts the quantitative theory of money, approved by most economists since Adam Smith, and which assumes that, other things being equal, prices rise or fall in consonance with the expansion or contraction of the exchange media in circulation; he agrees with the standard authors that the value—the purchasing power—of money does not depend upon the intrinsic qualities of the materials of which it is made, but upon the effective supply relative to the money-work to be done; that whatever is generally recognized by the people as an exchange medium is money; he quotes with approval the view of John Stuart Mill that even inconvertible paper will act on prices; denies that gold and silver alone possess this power, and cites the period of the civil war when, with little coin in the country, prices ranged phenomenally high, then while admitting that bank checks, bills of exchange, etc., do money-work, declares that neither these nor any other class of credit can possibly have any effect on prices. He adds: "From the time a bill is drawn until finally paid, an amount of money equal to the demand of the bill must be held out of circulation for its payment. It adds nothing to the circulation, and in no sense does it constitute a part of the circulating medium." Further on he says. "The most conservative estimates place the national, municipal, corporate and individual debts in the United States at $30,000,000,000. The secretary of the treasury estimates the amount of money in circulation at $1,600,000,000. There is not in fact one-third the amount available for use."

This puts us face to face with a perplexing problem: With less than one-third of $1,600,000,000 available for use, how do we manage to hold out of circulation an amount equal to the bank checks, bills, etc., floating about? And how does it happen that more than 90 per cent. of all bank receipts are in checks and bills of exchange? According to Mr. Utely, America is holding out of circulation to meet its floating bank paper a good deal more money than any two nations in this world have got! Men who learn political economy altogether from books are quite apt to fall into ludicrous errors. It is not true that from the time a bill is drawn until it is paid a corresponding amount of money is withheld from circulation, any more than it is true that government keeps a gold dollar in the treasury for the redemption of every outstanding paper dollar. With his nose deep in the dust of his library, Mr. Utely is unable to see how we manage to make a check or bill of exchange good without locking up sufficient money to meet it on demand, and concludes that such is the practice of commerce; but it isn't. Thousands of others harbor the same hallucination—imagine that 70,000,000 people transact all their business with a currency which Utely estimates at less than $7 per capita. We have almost quit doing business with the dollar, have made the banks our exchange medium. "But," they cry, "you cannot check money out of a bank unless you put money in." Good sirs, we neither put money in the bank nor check it out except in trifling transactions; we simply loan our property to the bank in a specified amount, and it is transferred from one to another on our order by the banker's book-keeper. Let us see if Mr. Utely is correct in the assumption that checks, drafts, etc., add nothing to the volume of the effective exchange media: I sell 100 bales of cotton at $50 each and I am paid in a check as a matter of course; but instead of drawing the money and hiding it in a rusty stove-pipe, I have the cash value of the cotton passed to my credit. I owe Mr. Mann a $50 stallion fee and give him my check therefor. Instead of cashing it, Waco's *arbiter elegantiarium* places it on deposit. He owes Col. Parrott $50 for services rendered, gives him a check for same, and all the latter receives for it is a brace of crooked marks in his bank book. Col. Parrott owes Judge Clark $50 on account and gives him a check in that amount, which the latter transfers to Mr. Dupree to help establish a genealogical institute for the benefit of North Carolinians who aspire to shine in Waco society. The latter makes it payable to a St. Louis jewelry firm—perhaps—the latter deposits it, and it is passed to the account of the bank on which it is drawn. Not one of these checks has moved a dollar of money. None of us need money unless we are confronted by the contribution box, get into a two-bit poker game or want to buy the beer. I really placed 100 bales of cotton with my banker, and then transferred one bale to my creditor, who passed it on in the discharge of his obligation to another. And the other 99 bales: Does the banker keep them corded up, metaphorically speaking, awaiting my order? Certainly not. He knows about how much money, or rather how much wealth, he will be made custodian of each month, and about how much he will have to return, and the surplus is loaned—passed to the credit of others for a consideration. This system of exchange is practiced throughout the civilized world. Cities and states and nations effect their exchanges just as do individuals—employ the banks as a medium for the transfer of commodities. Mr. Utely says:

> Suppose that every dollar now claimed to be in circulation in the United States should be withdrawn from the channels of trade: Prices would fall; would, in fact, be completely annihilated.

It would certainly demoralize business, but could not annihilate prices. People would still require clothing and food and fuel; to secure them exchanges would have to be effected in some manner, even tho' by primitive barter, and where there is exchange there must be exchange value. The farmer would not give away his surplus pork and potatoes because there was no money in the country; he would trade them for sugar and soap. The withdrawal of all our governmental money would be very bad for business, because we require a universally recognized exchange medium for our smaller transactions, and because it would deprive us of our unit of value. It would be like taking the yard measure from the cloth merchant. It would indeed be an awkward predicament; but what would happen if, instead of abolishing our governmental money, we abolished all our banks, eliminated from circulation the non-governmental paper now doing 95 per cent. of our money-work, destroyed all credit and came squarely down to that chief *desideratum* of so many forks-of-the-creek economists, a "cash basis?" That would be a rather awkward situation also. Every dollar would have to do the work of twenty, and granting the correctness of the quantitative theory of money—would have twenty times the purchasing power it now possesses. In other words, prices would fall so enormously that a commodity that now sells for a dollar would bring a nickel. Our 75 billions of wealth would shrink to less than 4 billions, but our 30 billions of debt would show no decrease. That would look something like the "repudiation" we have heard about in the recent campaign—would, I opine, be more serious than being reduced to the necessity of barter. One of Mr. Utely's arguments against credit as a factor in price is unique enough to have been picked up at some country lyceum in Kansas. He says in substance:

> One of the most familiar illustrations given by those who contend that credit will raise the general level of prices is that of a man entering the market to buy cotton. They say that if he buys $5,000 worth for cash and $5,000 worth on credit, the second purchase will tend to advance the price in the same manner and to the same ex-

tent that the cash purchase did. Let us suppose that he purchased the second lot on 90 days' time: At the end of 90 days he must pay for it. If he draws the $5,000 with which to pay this debt from money invested in the cotton trade, such withdrawal will tend to depress the price of that staple to the extent that it was stimulated by the credit. The withdrawal of that sum from some other industry will tend to depress prices in the industry from which it is withdrawn, and the general level will remain unaltered.

Men buy cotton (real, not speculative,) for one of two purposes: to use or to sell. If the man in question bought for the former purpose we may expect him to pay for his purchase with the product of his mill; if for the latter, it is reasonable to suppose that he will sell in time to discharge his debt. In either case he pays for the cotton with the cotton itself, maintains his credit and his credit is a portion of his working capital. Let us say that I require two cars of book paper for this issue of the Iconoclast, and that I have only money with which to pay for one: If I have no credit I can use but one car-load, the effective demand for book paper is contracted that much and has a tendency to lower the price; but if I can secure the extra car on credit, I use it, sell it, pay for it and make a profit. It is true that this credit, while enhancing my effective capital, adds nothing to the general stock, for I but borrow from the general stock with which to conduct my business; but it makes capital more effective by providing a profitable market for two cars of paper where only one could have been otherwise used, increases the efficient demand for a product and thereby stiffens the price. Nor is this all: The extra car of paper which credit enables me to purchase must be made. It must be printed, mailed, and distributed by the postal department. This means more employment for labor, with a consequent tendency to a higher wage rate, and the wage rate is an important factor in determining "the level of prices." It means more people with purchasing power, greater consumption of general products, with a tendency to enhance prices. Of course it may be urged that in borrowing capital to use in my business I prevent the owner employing it in some other enterprise where it would have a similar effect on price—that my credit simply makes a hole to raise a hill, and the general level remains unaltered; but let us turn the plank around and look at it from the other end. Suppose instead of having too little capital, I have double what my business requires: Of course I could employ the surplus in new industries; but I find that to give them the personal attention necessary to make them profitable, I must relinquish my present business. Clearly I must either lock my surplus capital up or loan it. Naturally, I decide to do the latter, and the result is that my capital has double the effective power that it possessed before. Many prosperous farmers and professional men are so situated—most loan the surplus or allow it to remain idle. Men become wealthy and do not wish to be longer burdened with business—somebody must take their capital and employ it. There is something like 2 billions in the American savings banks, the property of 5 million depositors. The employment, the continued purchasing power of many of those people, their efficient demand for the products of others and its inevitable effect on prices, depends upon the loan of their capital; yet Mr. Utely writes a dozen pages to "prove" that credit has no effect upon prices!

Abolish credit and the country would go to the bow-wows. I do not mean by this that debt is a blessing by itself considered, or that every man who borrows a dollar is a public benefactor; but that without credit, with the counting and transfer of cash with every transaction, our exchanges could not be so expeditiously effected; that it makes it possible to employ all our capital, and that to its fullest capacity. If we transact but 5 per cent. of our business with two billions of governmental money, how much would it require to enable us to transact it all by that medium? Evidently twenty times as much, or some 40 billion dollars—a fact for the careful consideration of all who believe that our every dollar should be intrinsically worth 100 cents, else have such a coin behind it! Money, of whatsoever make, must be paid for by the people employing it, just as they pay for all other trade tools; hence one-half of the national wealth would not suffice to provide us with a gold and silver currency equal to our needs if we eliminate credit. But credit, like many other good things, is badly abused. Capital taxes production and exchange too heavily for its help, takes too large a toll. A very small fraction of the 30 billions of American indebtedness is in low interest-bearing bonds. Some of it costs 10 per cent. a month, while probably 7 per cent. per annum is not far from the general average. That means an interest charge of more than two billions a year, or about $150 for every actual wealth-producer, to which must be added the cost of an extravagant government, the maintenance of schools for both embryo philosophers and incipient idiots, pensions to men who ruptured their conscience dodging the draft, churches in which goose-headed gentry preach Prohibition and other brands of politics, rent to descendants of rat-catchers, whose holdings have become valuable through the industry of others, profits to middlemen and monopolists— every penny of which must, directly or indirectly, come from Labor's thin purse. Is it any wonder that the American workingman is poor! It has been urged that I am inconsistent in advocating the free coinage of silver, in urging an increase in the volume of governmental money, while pointing out that the bulk of the nation's business is done with a commercial currency having for basis, not a few buckets of gold and bushels of silver, but the wealth and credit of the people. It is quite true that our system of bank transfers is being steadily perfected, making governmental money of ever less importance as an exchange medium; but this does not reduce the currency question to a demagogical nonentity, and for the very simple reason that the governmental dollar remains our measure of value, 5 per cent. of our exchanges are still effected with it, and it is "the little leaven that leavens the whole lump." So long as the dollar remains our unit of value, through law or custom, and we are compelled to transact a portion of our business with it, the quantitative theory applies as forcibly as tho' we had no other exchange medium. So long as there remains an amount of work, be it large or small, which only the actual dollar can do, the currency question must remain one of very considerable importance. As wealth-creating machinery is perfected, the wages of labor affect less and less the cost of production; but so long as we must have men to manage our machines and there remains considerable work which can only be done by hand, it matters a great deal whether the *entrepreneur* can secure a full complement of help. The purchasing power of our generally accepted unit of value is governed by the supply relative to the demand, whether that demand be large or small, for a few millions or for many billions, and as it rises or falls all checks, drafts, etc., must of necessity do the same, just as when the value of gold rises or falls, all paper money based thereon must follow suit, hence it is important that we prevent undue appreciation of our "money of final payment" by an arbitrary reduction of its volume while its legitimate money-work is actually increasing, altho' it may be relatively decreasing.

THE COURAGE OF WOMANKIND.

A gentleman of wide experience as frontiersman, soldier and purist, recently remarked to me: "Women are more truthful than men; they exhibit more gratitude; they are the superiors of men in physical courage."

This testimony will doubtless appear not a little startling to many who have ever regarded women as "the weaker vessel"; but I believe it will be confirmed by every careful student of humankind. That women possess more moral courage than men is generally admitted; but that physical is the necessary correlative of moral courage does not appear to have occurred to the average individual. The two virtues—if they be indeed binary—are so interdependent that divorcement is practically impossible. Why does a child accused of a misdemeanor confess its fault and accept punishment, when, by a subterfuge, it could escape castigation? Because it fears the scourge of conscience more than the maternal slipper. It must choose between two evils, and it elects the least. Without moral courage it would lie, because having naught to fear from conscience; without physical courage it would lie, because unable to accept bodily suffering that could be avoided. When the soldier rushes upon shotted guns we call it physical courage; when a voluptuous woman denies the improper importunities of her lover, we call it moral courage; yet the efficient causes of these actions are identical. The soldier does not desire to be killed or crippled, but dreads the deserter's shame more than the guns of the enemy, and the woman considers self-denial preferable to dishonor; hence courage, call it by what name you will, is but the balancing of one ill against another, and the acceptance of what the world elects to call a lesser. It regards the instincts of the dog and the ferocity of the savage as great physical and little moral courage; but such objections are idle without some knowledge of the ethics of dogdom and the moral concept of the savage. You cannot measure the moral courage of man or beast until you have ascertained the moral code applicable to the civilization or intelligence of his kind. The different races of men and the various orders of animals diverge widely in their natures, some being mild, others murderous. We cannot measure the heart by the standard of the hound, nor the gentle-souled Bengalee by the ferocious Britisher who finds pleasure in useless effusion of blood.

A New York merchant chattering to a reporter recently, asserted that men are more honest than women—prompter in the discharge of their debts. He evidently overlooked two very important facts, viz.: that a woman can often obtain credit where her husband cannot, because it is a more delicate matter to refuse her, and that with men to whom credit is extended, a reputation for commercial integrity often constitutes an important part of their working capital. A woman who neglects to settle—especially if she possess tact and beauty—is not hounded so fiercely as the male malingerer. Good name in such matters is with woman merely a sentiment, while with the average man it is business; hence the male rascal will frequently pay, while the female rogue, having nothing tangible to gain by an affectation of honesty, laughs her tradesmen to scorn. Much of the shoplifting is done by women, they having better opportunity for that kind of knavery; but of the forgeries, burglaries and embezzlements a vast majority are the work of men.

Junius Henri Browne—angels and ministers of grace defend us! where did he find it?—has been telling the few old maids and anile Mugwumps who still worry through *Harper's Weekly,* what he doesn't know about "Woman's Courage." He assures us that women affect timidity they do not feel, because their supposed helplessness is considered a charm by the opposite sex. I trust that Junius Henri Browne will not topple his name over on me if I dissent from his very pretty but undigested dogma. It is neither cowardice nor affectation that makes so many ladies scream at sight of a bug or mouse, but sheer nervousness. You seldom see a healthy countrywoman clamber upon a table to avoid a harmless creeper. Our city-bred American women are neurotic; but this ill is being rapidly alleviated by the sensible outdoor exercise now coming generally into favor. A rightly constituted man glories in a courageous woman—a woman all womanly, without a suggestion of aggressive masculinity; but who could, if need be, go to the block as bravely as Marie Antoinette, strike as deadly as Hannah Dustin, or emulate the deeds of Saragossa's beautiful lioness when Spain's enemies were foiled by woman's hand before a battered wall.

Chappies like Junius Henri, whose sidewheel whiskers and trigeminous titles are giving them spinal curvature, may fancy hysterical maids; but a sure-enough American, competent to raise a crop of world-compellers all bearing his trade-mark, prefers a Grace Darling or a Molly Pitcher. He knows that, if mated with her equal, such a woman will never suckle worthless sons. Junius Henri next informs us that while woman may possess certain kinds of courage, she has not that which enables her to face physical danger with fortitude, to look on ghastly wounds or sustain great bodily suffering. I wonder who told him that? If I knew so little about women, I'd never undertake to manage one. Woman does not, as a rule, resent an insult with a blow or do the Amazon act, because forbidden by custom and weakness of body. She does not court danger for the sake of gaining a reputation for courage; but when confronted by it, will, in almost every instance, bear herself as royally as her big brother, and that without the powerful prop of pride upon which he leans—the fear of that curse which blasts the male coward. Woman encounters the perils of the frontier, of shipwreck, of conflagration, and the distress of famine, with heroic fortitude. In new countries she is not infrequently a daring rider and a splendid shot. When a cry of fire is raised in a crowded hall or theater, the men are usually first to drop the linchpin out of their *sauviter in modo* and start a stampede. Any experienced physician will testify that women bear pain and encounter death with greater fortitude than do men—that they become more readily accustomed to the sight of suffering and the ghastly scenes of surgery. Many of our most celebrated hospitals are under the immediate charge of women, notably the Charity Hospital at New Orleans, with its 10,000 patients per annum. Let a child be injured, and a woman who has never looked upon a wound will minister to it with a steady hand, while a man who has trod a dozen sanguinary battlefields, becomes faint, distracted, useless.

"Foiled by a woman's hand before a battered wall."

A woman is capable of grander heroism, greater self-sacrifice, nobler morality than man, and for the simple reason that her nature is, so to speak, of finer texture—because she is less a brute than her companion. Her courage differs from that of man much as the courage of a high-bred gentleman differs from that of a Bowery bouncer. The latter really enjoys a brutal fisticuff, but a thread of cold steel will stop him. To the gentleman a bruising-bout

is an abomination; but he will take his position before a
dead shot with apparent indifference. It is this higher
courage which woman possesses. If she starts more readily
at trifles she will go with a steadier step to the supreme
sacrifice. A finely constituted mind instinctively shrinks
from the brutal; but where honor, principle, or the well-
being of loved ones is concerned, it is ready to lead the forlorn hope. It faces inevitable death with a placid brow,
while the "nerve" of a coarser nature either breaks completely down or indulges in mock bravado. Man is incapable of that intensity of suffering, mental or physical, which
a delicate woman often uncomplainingly endures. If men
instead of women were required to suffer the pains of parturition there wouldn't be enough people left on earth in
two hundred years to organize a base-ball nine—and I'd
be the first laddie-buck to take the vow of celibacy under
such a dispensation. Courage! The sting of a hornet
while severe pain to a man is madness to a woman; yet
the former will dance the Highland fling and howl like
a defeated candidate, while the latter, after one startled
scream of surprise sets placidly about doctoring herself.
The fact of the matter is that man wouldn't have amounted
to much had not the Creator sent woman to steer the miserable savage against the tree of knowledge and shoulder
nine-tenths of his trouble, while he's snorting like a mad
bull over the remainder and imagining himself a hero. I'm
very fond of the ladies—but I wouldn't be one of them for
the world. In a moment of mental aberration I might
marry some J. Henri Browne.

A FRIEND OF THE FAMILY.

I learn from the *Chicago Drover's Journal* that "one roof
now shelters Millionaire John Bradbury and his pretty wife
who had deserted him, but pride still stands between them
and reconciliation"; also that "Bradbury says he is willing
to forgive his wife, but being the offended party he expects
the overtures to come from her." The *D-J* assures us that
they have a suite of rooms at the Hotel Wellington, but
"are still occupying separate apartments"; that "a few tears
and a husband's kind word will bring this romance to a
dramatic finale." The *D-J* slings in a great deal more soup

from the same putrid pot, calculated to raise the gorge of even *Town Topics'* readers. Who in the name of Balaam's talkative burro is Millionaire John Bradbury? So many "pretty wives" of millionaires—money covers multitudinous uglinosity as well as sexual sins—are having escapades, "romantic" and otherwise, and getting themselves forguv, that a scandal in high life is ancient history ere it is two weeks old. "Millionaire John Bradbury," eh? Isn't he the Californian with a pint of Injun blood surging about inside of him, whose wife run off with a crummy English tramp, whom she supported by peddling the Bradbury jewels among the pawnbrokers? Wasn't this interesting couple overhauled by the police in a 'Frisco hotel at the request of the injured husband? Didn't we hear considerable at the time about Mr. John Bradbury's murderous Injun blood and the sinister light in his ebon eye when he discussed the subject? Didn't the press make us shudder and groan by predicting that John would give his Injun blood a chance to hump itself, would wreak an awful r-r-revenge on the bloody Hinglishman who was strumpetizing the wife of his buzzum? And isn't the "fell destroyer" alive and enjoying three square meals per day—paid for with the Bradbury diamonds? I'm not sure that John is the heap big Injun who "never forgets or forgives," and who was expected to lay for the destroyer of his home with a two-edged tomahawk in each hand, even follow him across the tumultuous wave tho' he had to walk—to rest not until the scalp of his enemy dangled from the ridgepole of his palatial wigwam, yet who didn't so much as make a toy-pistol play when he had the opportunity; but I incline to the view that I'm on the right reservation. He is willing to overlook what the *D.-J.* euphemistically calls her "romance," to restore a debauched woman to her old place in his heart and home, if not in his confidence; but his terrible "pride" prevents him doing so until she suggests that it would be agreeable—until she intimates that she prefers a round million—with her husband to beggary with her paramour. John is hanging around her door with absolution ready, waiting to be "asked!" It seems to me that "pride" of that kind needs a carbolic acid bath and a coat of calsomine. The husband who receives back into his home a libidinous old heifer whom he knows has dishonored him, has no more idea of manly pride than has a hound pup, no more conception of gentlemanly self-respect than has a dunghill rooster. Men of some little respectability have married reformed Magdalens; but no man of honor ever received back a wife who had become a bawd. The man who does so, be he millionaire or mendicant, makes a mockery of marriage, insults every decent woman in the world by proclaiming that wifely purity is a thing of little worth, that the ruined honor of a family can be repaired as easily as a broken bike. But Bradbury is not the only animal of his kind on earth. We do not have to go as far as California and hunt up half-breed Injuns to find men equal to such infamy—men who boast of their family "pride" while hanging their hat on a cuckold's horns and keeping what Othello would call a "cistern" that had been befouled by lecherous toads. Even here in Waco, the hub of chivalry, the Camelot of King Arthur's court, where honor is supposed to be the all-in-all, it were not difficult to find a creature who can give Bradbury pointers in the science of shamelessness and double discount him in all that makes for human degradation. Suspecting, like Tolstoi's Poydynschew, that somebody was poaching on his preserves, he proceeded to investigate, and like the hero of the Kreutzer Sonata, he seems to have found that his prophetic soul had not played him false, whatever his wife had done. Producing a six-shooter as big as a sugar-barrel, he shut his eyes, blazed away—and killed a horse, which seems to have been the only respectable member of the informal picnic party. Having recovered his property, the Waco warrior hauled it in triumph home, and boasted, so it is said, that the escapade would soon blow over and she would be received into Waco's best society! The gay Lothario still lives, but the horse is dead—offered up to the immortal gods a sacrifice for sin. It seems that the male offender squared himself at home by pleading that it was a repetition of the Potiphar and Joseph episode, and that when laid hold of, his garment, unlike that of the pious Hebrew, was too tight to slip and too strong to tear. Anyway, I'm pleased to learn that husband, like the hero in the play, "arrived in the very nick of time." To this little melodrama, enacted in the suburbs of our eminently religious city, I shall offer no objection; for if the husband is content the world should be satisfied. Christ forgave Mary Magdalen. As he wasn't married to her at the time, it was unnecessary to satisfy the law regarding the wages of sin by boring a hole in an innocent horse. But while the Waco warrior was "vindicating his honor" and frightening a tender-foot with his noise, he was having a little "romance" of his own, the latter fact being my only excuse for defiling white paper with a recital of his rather interesting family affair, some knowledge of his equine sacrifice being necessary to a comprehension of his iniquity. There was a poor but eminently respectable widow living in the city with her young daughter and still younger son. It appears that this fellow had known them in another state, which fact he utilized to become the officious friend of the family. He watched over it like an old gander over a brood of goslings. The girl was about 18, one of those sweet, trusting maids who know nothing of the world and its ways. The friend of the family became very solicitous about the health of the mother. He gave her little son a situation. He paid surreptitious court to her daughter. It was Mephistopheles vs. Margaret, and with the usual result—lovely woman stooped to folly to find too late that men betray, as Mr. Goldsmith would remark. The maid became *enceinte* by this inhuman monster. The trusting mother was made to believe that she had some dropsical disease. The acquaintances of the friend of the family knew of the *liaison* and its unhappy consequences, and begged him to send the maid out of the city, to take some steps to conceal her shame; but he treated the suggestion with brutal contempt. The mother, becoming alarmed by her daughter's condition, called in a doctor. "*Enceinte*—seven months," said Aesculapius. The mother fell back in a dead faint. When she recovered consciousness she hurried with her family to the depot, not even pausing to take down her birds that were singing in the porch. She could not breathe during another day the atmosphere of a city infested by the unclean beast that had broken her heart. From a far northern city she wrote to a real estate agent to sell her little home at any sacrifice—she had shaken the dust of Waco from her feet forever. And this animal hasn't been tarred and feathered. He walks the streets of Waco and white men speak to him as tho' nothing had happened. There was some talk of making him the subject of a surgical operation; but "what is everybody's business is nobody's business," and he is still virile and vicious. The widow is crushed; the life of her young daughter is forever blighted; her little son will be shadowed so long as he lives, by his sister's shame. And the author of this infamy is the fellow who vindicated the honor of his own home—by shooting a horse. If "money is omnipotent," as the French say, he will never be punished, not in the eminently respectable and ultra-religious city of Waco. But perhaps when the girl's brother grows up he will know how to handle a shot-gun. "The years," we are told, "are seldom unjust."

BARONS VS. BARONS.

For many moons past a dozen or so letters a day from Republicans and Demmy-Reps., each bearing in its bosom a pale green postal order or velvety dollar bill and a vigorous protest couched in unmistakable English, have insinuated themselves into this sanctum. The pecuniary end of said epistles are carefully filed away for the benefit of the foreign mission fund, while the protests are deposited in the cast iron waste-basket, which is kept on the ice-box as a precautionary measure against spontaneous combustion. The complaints of these, my misguided brethren who have followed the Markhanna rainbow into the Serbonian bogs, are many and grievous, but the one that comes to the surface oftenest is that I allude to McKinley as the creature of the tariff barons, while the silver barons were sponsors for my own much beloved Billee Bryan of Nebraska—that it's a case of the pot calling the kettle black. Oh well, even little birds in their nests cannot always agree, every blessed birdlin', wants the worm and tries to spread its mouth widest. Prithee, good sirs, unbutton your collars and let us sit down a moment under the soothing influences of the electric fan and look into this baronial business, not with labored perscrutation and blood-heating partisanship, but with the passive interest that one views a last year's prize fight by means of the vitascope. Selfish old world isn't in it?—the purse such a powerful factor in shaping one's political opinions, what he calls patriotism, the *argumentum ad hominem* gets so near a fellow's heart! Yes, yes; "the smoke of battle has rolled away," as the Houston *Post,* Cypress Switch *Sentinel* and other great moulders of public opinion would say, and we can now see clearly that the tariff barons expected to profit by the election of McKinley, the silver barons by the election of Bryan—that each gave up more or less stuff "for the good of the cause," the salvation of the country. This much is frankly conceded by both sides; and honest confession is good for the soul—granting of course that a politician's got a soul, that he isn't a corporation, with Greed, Gall and Gab constituting the board of directors. But that, as Kunnel Kipling—one of Billy Reedy's poets—would remark in his charming hair-trigger way, is another story. That the tariff barons put up the most dust is doubtless due to the fact that they had most to gain by electing their man. Thus far the two parties of feudal gentry—the Red and White Roses of the late unpleasantness—are on a political and moral parity, each championing the cause which he expected to fill his purse, each doing the "educational" act to further his own interest. That's what we call "practical politics" in this country the *sauve qui peut* principle. Excuse my French; I have to take it out and look at it occasionally to assure myself that it's still there. But we were talking of the war of the barons, with "national honor," "good of the country," and soforth, as bone of contention. We will admit that each contingent of barons was a little worse than the other, just for the sake of argument; but this does not necessarily bring the respective candidates to the same intellectual and moral level. A great deal of money can be legitimately expended in a "campaign of education," in appealing to the reason of the people. To plead that a candidate is ignorant of the methods employed by his managers to secure his election, were to brand him a hopeless idiot. I have not heard of a single effort made by Chairman Jones or his representatives to corrupt the ballot, of one man who was offered money to vote for Bryan. On the other hand, Mark Hanna and his representatives bribed the very niggers of Texas, who don't know how to vote anything but the Republican ticket. The presidency was brazenly bought for McKinley, and with his full knowledge and consent, granting of course that he is not a miserable Toomtabard stuffed with straw; but no attempt was made to buy votes for Bryan; hence, whatever may be the respective merits or demerits of the silver and tariff barons, we must concede that in the matter of honor and patriotism the Buckeye suffers sorely by comparison with the Nebraskan—that the pot has good cause to animadvert upon the complexion of its culinary companion. Both the tariff and silver barons frankly admitted that the policy they advocated would redound to their pecuniary profit, but insisted that it would also benefit the whole people. We will not fight that merry war over again this hot weather. I freely concede that the silver barons supported Bryan, and contributed liberally to his campaign fund for no more patriotic reason than that they believed, despite the solemn asseveration of all Republicans and Demmy-Reps. to the contrary, that his election would put money in their purse. I say their asseveration to the contrary, for they insisted and still insist that free coinage would sink the silver dollar to its bullion value, that we would have a 40 or 50 cent dollar, that Uncle Sam is powerless to raise the value of the white metal; and if this be true, it follows as an illative consequence that the people would be despoiled by the miner, that the latter would make no more than his present profit. Of course when they discourse learnedly of the wily silver baron selling Uncle Sam 40 or 50 cents worth of bullion for a dollar, they mean a 40 or 50 cent dollar, as otherwise these economic wiseacres would hang themselves with their own halter—would sprain a kidney and rupture a surcingle leaping from premise to conclusion. But I am not willing to unite with the "sound money" men in thus clearing the silver barons of all suspicion of selfishness, in apotheosizing them as patriots who have only the good of the people at heart. I insist that free coinage would help them by enhancing the price of their product, by making the much-talked of "40-cent dollar" impossible; and that it was the realization of this fact which induced them to support Bryan of Nebraska. I think they had a dim suspicion that whatsoever increases demand has a tendency to enhance price, and *vice versa;* that they had figured out that the law of supply and demand being still unrepealed by any worthy Populist, free coinage of the white metal would mean dearer silver and cheaper gold, that if our $600,000,000 of "yellow boys" became frightened at their pale-faced brother and went abroad the effect would be to make the gold currency of other nations more redundant, and that a redundant currency means a smaller purchasing power for the unit of value, and approach of the two metals toward a parity. No, gentlemen, you can't convince me that the silver barons are not selfish—that they simply wanted to make a few tons of 40-cent dollars to enable the Democrats to "repudiate their debts."

KILLING OF CANOVAS.

Now that all the principalities and powers have condoled with Spain over the killing of Canovas; now that Golli has been sentenced to the garrote and our own "able editors" and oratorical wind-jammers have vigorously denounced him as a "cowardly assassin," suppose we make a reasonable effort to understand what this slaughter by an anarchist really signifies. *Ogni medaglia ha il suo riverso,* say the Italians, meaning thereby that what has a before must have a behind, that there are at least two sides to every subject—including even the killing of Canovas. Thanks to the pernicious activity of our "great public educators," alias the press, the American people have a very anamorphic idea of anarchy and anarchists. They suppose that anarchy is synonymous with violence and disorder, wrong and outrage; that such condition is desired by its devotees; that the latter are composed altogether of the idle, the vicious and the criminal. Their idea of an anarchist is a cross between a Bowery bum and a vampire bat—a low-browed brute, a filthy fellow who loafs about the subcellar boozing kens of great cities, drinks gallons of beer, builds gaspipe bombs and shrieks for oceans of blood—all of which they gather from the foolish scribblings of ignorant editors who mistake an abnormal imaginative faculty for an inexhaustible tank of valuable information. They will probably be a little surprised to learn that anarchism owes much to the teachings of Christ, that St. Paul is considered by many of its converts as the original high priest of the cult, that the utterances of some of the world's greatest philosophers are habitually quoted in its apologetics and that many of the best people of Europe subscribe to its principles. Strange as it may appear to those who rely upon the daily press for information, a man can be an enthusiastic anarchist without growing a crop of piratical whiskers, neglecting his bath and carrying an infernal machine in his hat, a bull-dog pistol in the hip-pocket of his "pants" and a dynamite bomb in each coat-tail pocket. The word "anarchy," according to the best authorities on the subject, "is employed to signify, not chaos, but an order of things that excludes the idea of external government, and depends on individual self-control and voluntary co-operation." Its avowed object is attainment of the fullest liberty, the highest possible development of individualism. Anarchists believe that all government is useless and oppressive; that without it there would be less crime, greater prosperity, more altruism, a happier life for the "common herd." Nihilism and anarchy are one and the same, practically considered. The nihilists are composed chiefly of the university students and the better educated people of the Russian empire. The reigning family, its immediate dependants, and the squalid peasantry, so recently serfs and still avatars of poverty and ignorance, are enthusiastic monarchists. Nihilism, or anarchism, reduced to its last analysis, means simply "nit," is a pure negation. That is also its significance in religion and science. Philosophic nihilism, so-called, would reduce even the super-abundant materiality of G. Cleveland to an equal status with his mentality—"mere appearances with no substratum of reality." Anarchism is the legitimate child of political oppression. Seeing that government was responsible for so much evil, men concluded that it was wholly bad, unnatural, an insufferable nuisance, and began agitating for its complete abolition. Such a campaign of education did not please the powers, and the result was a terrible persecution. Occasionally the worm turned and some active enemy in high place perished. Rome persecuted the early Christians, and, because there were some who did not turn the other cheek to the smiter, all were denounced as disreputable, dangerous, and many crimes of which they were innocent were laid at their door. The cross was once hated, despised and dreaded more than the red flag is to-day. What the anarchists are to Europe, the Catholics were to England in the time of Titus Oates, the Huguenots to France in the days of Catherine de Medici—a people regarded as enemies of the established government and capable of any crime. Just as an occasional Christian struck at the pagan oppressors, so an occasional anarchist strikes at their persecutors. Conspiracies, plots, desperate ventures by individuals, may be expected whenever a class of people, for religious, racial or political reasons, is cruelly maltreated and is not powerful enough to make open war upon its enemies. Oppression is the cause of which anarchy is the effect. Atheism is the natural correlative of social anarchy, the dogma of nihility, or nothingness, carried to its legitimate conclusion. But it is more than a revolt against the sceptre and the mitre; it is a protest against conditions, social and industrial, in which "the individual withers and the world is more and more."

Anarchism would make every man an independent entity instead of a molecule in a mighty organism, the unconsidered fraction of a great machine. In my humble opinion the thesis of anarchism reduced to practice could but result in endless confusion and the retrogression of the race; but while the dream is idle, it is beautiful, considered solely in its earthly aspect, in that it is of a perfect if an impossible ideal. When all men become just we will no longer have any use for law, and absence of law is political anarchy. In all Europe the anarchists had no more uncompromising enemy than Canovas. The tortures he inflicted upon many of them are too dreadful to be told—the soul of a Caliban would sicken at the recital. True, many of those he tortured had committed crimes; but the efficient cause thereof was his own tyranny—it was but an application of *lex talionis*—the law of retaliation. That Canovas was a statesman of considerable ability can not be gainsaid; but he was the incarnation of cruelty. What Jack the Ripper was to the slums of London, Canovas was to the world at large. The atrocities perpetrated in the Philippine Islands by the Spanish soldiery had his sanction; Weyler, the Cuban butcher, was simply his creature and executed his orders. Canovas seems to have "got drunk with blood to vomit crime"—and the worm turned once more. I do not approve the principles of anarchism, I do not sanction assassination; nor can I regret the fate of Canovas. "The wage of sin is death"; this latter-day "Spanish fury" but reaped as he had sown. Golli is guilty of a terrible crime, but not of a "cowardly" one, as the "able editors" would have us believe. Brutal and bloody it was, deserving the world's condemnation; but no coward deliberately does that for which he knows he must quickly die. Great Caesar fell by the hands of those who professed to be his friends, and who hoped to graps the reins of government as they fell from his dead hands; Canovas was slain by an enemy who expected no reward but the rope; yet we crown the bust of Brutus with laurel boughs and spit upon the grave of Golli. The one, accompanied by a patrician mob, struck down "the foremost man of all the world" because he was "ambitious"; the other murdered the servant of a petty queen because he was a monster.

PRAYERS FOR THE PAGAN.

The American press has been making merry at the expense of those pious people who prayed for the conversion of Colonel R. G. Ingersoll, the eloquent Agnostic. It had not occurred to me that the act contained any of the elements of humor; but a skilled chemist can get sugar out of an old shoe, and an editor whose sense of ridiculous is abnormally developed may find fun in a funeral. Whether the press disbelieves in the efficacy of prayer, considers the Colonel beyond redemption, or classes religious ceremonies under the head of "Amusements" I do not know; but it occurs to me that even a futile attempt to benefit our fellow man should be spoken of only with respect. This simple act of faith, this outward evidence of an inward grace marks an important change in the attitude of the church toward dissenters. It is another Star of the East, ushering in a new religious epoch; a glimmer of light in the darkness, heralding the coming day—

> "A poising eagle that burns
> Above the unrisen morrow."

It is a fragrant life-giving oasis in the dreary desert of profitless dogmatism, swept by the hot Harmattan winds of religious bigotry and sectarian hate. I wish that the whole Christian world would pray earnestly and often, not for Ingersoll alone, but for every one encompassed by the darkness of Doubt—for all those who say in their hearts "There is no God." If it would do so, the Kingdom of Heaven would be near at hand. It is much better to pray for a dissenter than to persecute him; better to win him with kindness than to pursue him with calumny. When the worst of criminals is shipwrecked upon a stormy sea we hasten to his aid. We plunge into the swirling breakers and brave the treacherous rocks, while above the storm rings the cheer which informs the fainting wretch that hearts of oak are hastening to his rescue. But when one of God's noblemen is cast away upon the dark sea of Infidelity; above him only the starless night, below him hopeless death, no boat puts forth from the shore to succor or to save, no prayers are uttered for his preservation—every voice that comes to him from that land he cannot reach is pregnant with a curse. After all these years the maledictions are for a moment hushed, and in their place there rises the fervent prayer. At last, from Christian lips there bursts the cry, "To the rescue—man the life-boat!" Had such ever been the practice of the church there would not be an Atheist today in all the earth. You cannot war upon kindness—all the logic of man cannot cope with the power of love. There may be spots on the sun; but while it fills the land with light and life all admit that it is good. The tree may be gnarled and misshapen, but if its flowers yield fragrance and its fruits strength, the axe will not be laid to its root. Revealed Religion may run counter to the laws of Science and regard not the rules of Reason; but while Faith, Hope and Charity be the sign on its forehead and all-embracing Love the transcript of its heart, Logic will bow at its altars and Philosophy worship at its fanes. The prayers for the great Agnostic, even tho' he dies in his doubts, have not been labor in vain. They proclaim once again, "Peace on earth and good-will to men." They were evidence that there still burns within the church a living spark of that all-embracing love which, more than the miracles, attested the divinity of Christ, and is destined, let us devoutly hope, to bind the great round earth everyway,

"With gold chains about the feet of God."

They will convert others even tho' they fail to bring Ingersoll into the fold. At last the church is marshaling its forces beneath a flag that can be carried in triumph around the world—the snowy gonfalon of the Prince of Peace. *In hoc signo vinces!* The brand of the bigot and the empoisoned arrows of those who persecute in the name of Christ have recoiled with ten-fold force upon the church. "Those who live by the sword shall perish by the sword." In attempting to destroy men like Ingersoll the church has well nigh destroyed itself. The well-informed know full well that, morally and mentally, Ingersoll has few equals and no superiors within or without the church; hence every attempt to belittle and belie him has added new recruits to the great army of Infidelity. Where his well-rounded periods caused one to doubt, the brutal attacks made upon him by ignorant zealots and ministerial mountebanks have made a thousand despair. Every cowardly lie told about him by professors of religion has but enhanced his power for evil; every effort to discredit his genius and cover him with contempt has but added fresh terrors to that iconoclastic hammer which like the weapon of Thor, rocks the world. Prayer may not alter the plans of the Infinite, but it disarms the enemies of the Christian faith. If it does not reach to the highest heaven it fills the earth with sweetest incense and covers the rocks with flowers. By praying for Infidels, the church will soon have them praying for themselves, and that "with faith believing."